Christian Doctrine

SCM CORE TEXT

Christian Doctrine

Mike Higton

scm press

British Library Cataloguing in Publication data

A catalogue record for this book is available
from the British Library

978 0 334 04019 4

First published in 2008 by SCM Press
13–17 Long Lane,
London EC1A 9PN

www.scm-canterburypress.co.uk

SCM Press is a division of
SCM-Canterbury Press Ltd

Typeset by Regent Typesetting
Printed and bound in Great Britain by
William Clowes Ltd, Beccles, Suffolk

Contents

List of Plates

Introduction

What is this book?

What is this book? It is an overview of Christian doctrine, aimed at under-graduates. It is not, however, a survey of all the major options in the interpretation of Christian doctrine, nor is it a detailed account of the history of those doctrines. It is, rather, my attempt to *make sense* of Christian doctrine – to provide one way of seeing how it all hangs together, and what it might mean. It is my extended suggestion for the sense that might be made of the life of Christian faith in the world.

So, what is this book? It is my attempt to help students, and other readers, *think through* Christian doctrine. Writing it has involved such a process of thinking through for me, and I have tried to write in such a way as to get my readers thinking too. I very much want my readers to see *why* it might make sense to say the things that Christian doctrine says, and to see *what it might mean* to say those things. It is a long book, I know, but that's because I have tried to put in as many as possible of the ideas, images and analogies that help me think these things through. I hope my way of thinking is not so eccentric as to make them useless for everybody else.

So, what is this book? It is an extended exploration of one way of telling the Christian story. I think Christians can make sense of themselves as creatures being drawn to share or participate in the life of their Creator. In Part 1, I focus on the life of God, and the way in which it is opened up for God's creatures. In Part 2, I focus on the life of the world, and the way in which it is drawn into participation in God's life. Part 1 looks at the life of God as Trinity, and at the incarnation of the Son and the sending of the Spirit. Part 2 looks at creation, providence and eschatology, at suffering and sin, and at the Church. Part 2 also finishes with two chapters that look at the Bible and at the sources for theology. I have put those chapters at the end deliberately, because my way of making sense of the nature and sources of theology is too tangled up with my way of making sense of Christian doctrine to be presented on its own at the beginning.

Where does this book come from?

Where does this book come from? I have for some years now been teaching one year of a two-year Certificate in Theology to evening class students in Exeter. I inherited a syllabus, and lots of advice, from others who had taught the class before me – most recently, Tim Gorringe and Jeremy Law – and have slowly tried to make that course my own. I also, a few years back, created an online version of that course, with the help of my colleagues Susan Graham, Jim Little and Stephen Dawes. It is that online version that has provided the basis of this book – though the job of turning it into a book has taken longer, and been more complicated, than I had imagined at the start. The online origins still show, I suspect, in the number of weblinks that I provide. I owe a great deal to the colleagues I have mentioned, who helped me learn how to teach the evening classes, or helped me learn how to put material together engagingly for the online course. Even more than to them, though, I owe a debt of gratitude to my students, who have been very good at letting me know when I'm talking rubbish, or when I am losing them in unnecessary complications, or when I am pushing one of my metaphors just a little bit too far. Some of those students, if they look carefully, might discover themselves, peering round corners in this book; all of them have shaped it for the better.

I should also say that I owe a lot to the American theologian Daniel Migliore. We have never met, and I don't suppose he's ever heard of me, but I've used his book *Faith Seeking Understanding: An Introduction to Christian Theology* (now in its second edition – Grand Rapids, MI: Eerdmans, 2004) as the main textbook in those evening classes for a few years now – so he has had quite an influence on the way that I present things, an influence that is probably acknowledged inadequately in my footnotes.

Where does this book come from? It comes in large part from the people who have taught me to do theology in the way that I do it. If you look carefully at these pages, you might be able to see the fingerprints of my parents, Tony and Patricia Higton, who always want to know *why* I as a theologian say the things that I do, and how those things relate to the Bible; of my teacher David Ford, who showed me what being a theologian involved, and who introduced me to the way that theological topics ramify and interconnect and spread in all sorts of unexpected ways; of the American theologian Hans Frei who was the subject of my doctoral work, and whose elusive but generative writings have coloured my whole theological vision; and of Rowan Williams, about whose theology I wrote a short book while teaching the course that became this book, and who therefore (as you will see) gets quoted rather a lot here. I should at this point confess to some self-plagiarism as well: anyone who has read my *Difficult Gospel: The Theology of Rowan Williams* (London: SCM Press, 2004) will find that several passages from it appear, reworked, in this book.

Where does this book come from? From conversations with friends – particularly late at night in the bar at Society for the Study of Theology conferences. I can remember, and am grateful for, conversations on topics that appear in this book with Nick Adams, Jon Cooley, Tim Gorringe, David Hewlett, Steve Holmes, David Horrell, Karen Kilby, Morwenna Ludlow, John McDowell, David Moss, Rachel Muers, Paul Murray, Chad Pecknold, Ben Quash, David Rhymer, Chris Southgate, Francesca Stavrakopoulou, Susannah Ticciati, Paul Wignall and Mark Wynn. On every topic that appears in this book, at least one of these friends knows much more than I do. To my way of thinking, that means that they are the ones who should be blamed for anything I've misunderstood or distorted, as well as thanked for anything I've got right.

Where does this book come from? From SCM Press, who commissioned it, and who have been very, very kind about the five deadlines that I missed, and the word limit that I trebled. Many thanks to Barbara Laing, Mary Matthews and Christine Smith for their patience and trust. They also let me publish a version of Chapter 10 on its own as *Deliver Us: Exploring the Problem of Evil*, Church Times Study Guides (London: SCM Press, 2007).

Where does this book come from? Above all, from an author who is surrounded and supported by his family. I am deeply thankful to my wife Hester – and only hope that I manage to support her in her work[1] even half as much as she supports me in mine – and to my two children, Bridget and Tom, currently aged 4 and 2, who have interrupted my work on this book, scribbled on it, dribbled on it, and kept me from thinking that it is the most important thing that I do. They have also, quite unintentionally, made me think differently about all sorts of theological topics, and so appear in unexpected places all over these pages. I dedicated *Difficult Gospel* to Bridget, so this book is dedicated to Tom – because I want to, and because life with him is great.

Notes

1 If you need a fantastic academic proof reader and copy editor, go to <http://www.academicedit.co.uk/>.

Part 1
Life in God

1

Making Sense

This first chapter is designed to steer you away from one set of expectations that you might have for this book as a whole, and towards another that I think might help you to make better sense of it. I want to distract you from the treacherous charms of the idea that theology is made up of abstract theories about God, and try to interest you instead in the suggestion that it has to do with individuals and communities making practical sense of their lives in relation to God.

I am going to

- note that the word 'theology' means something like 'rational discourse about God';
- acknowledge that 'rationality' may not be an obvious aim when the subject one is discussing is God;
- suggest nevertheless that, at its most basic, the word 'rationality' refers to the ways in which people make sense of their lives as they live them, and test the sense that they have made;
- argue that communities as well as individuals engage in these ways of making sense of themselves and testing that sense;
- suggest that the sense that Christian communities have made of themselves is dominated by the claim that they have been laid hold of by God in Jesus of Nazareth; and
- propose some ways in which the study of theology as an academic discipline might relate to this sort of ordinary Christian sense-making.

Preparation

- Ask yourself what you think 'rational' means. When, if at all, do you think you most clearly display 'rationality' in your life? Does such rationality have anything to do with faith?
- Ask yourself why you are studying theology, and what you hope the study will do to you or for you. Why are you reading this book in particular? If you have any kind of Christian faith yourself, how does this study relate to it? If you do not, what rationale do you have for studying specifically *Christian* doctrine?

Additional reading

If you want to accompany this chapter with some reading that will give you alternative vistas on similar subject matter, try:

Karl Barth, *Evangelical Theology: An Introduction* (Grand Rapids, MI: Eerdmans,

1979 (1st edn, 1963). An introduction not so much to the content of theology as to the attitude and attentiveness required of the theologian.

Ellen Charry (ed.), *Inquiring After God: Classic and Contemporary Readings*, Blackwell Readings in Modern Theology (Oxford: Blackwell, 2000). A collection of ancient and modern texts demonstrating the variety of contexts in which Christians have 'inquired about God'.

Daniel J. Treier, *Virtue and the Voice of God: Toward Theology as Wisdom* (Grand Rapids: Eerdmans, 2006). A detailed argument for seeing theology as a pilgrimage of personal and communal transformation.

Should theology exist?

In the 1980s, British Telecom commissioned a series of television adverts starring Maureen Lipman. In one, her grandson tells her on the phone that he has failed his exams, passing only Sociology. Lipman replies, 'An ology? He gets an ology and he says he's failed. You get an ology, you're a scientist!'[1]

She's right, in a way: the ending '-logy' comes from the Greek word *logos*, and in this kind of context (the context of academic study and exam results) it does mean something like 'ordered discussion' or 'rational discourse' – something like 'science', if one is speaking broadly.[2]

Combine that '-logy' ending with *theos*, the Greek word for 'God', however, and you get *'theology'* – that is, Godology. Theology is rational discourse about God or even the *science* of God – and even if one is prepared to accept sociology as a science, one might balk at this.[3] One might wonder whether 'God' and 'rational discourse' can appropriately be squeezed together in the confines of a single word. It is not a word, after all, that you will find in the Bible – or at least, not quite. It is true that some manuscripts of the book of Revelation have the heading *Apokalupsis ioannou tou theologou*, 'the Revelation of John the *theologian*', but John deserves no congratulations from Maureen Lipman, because the *-logos* ending in his case means something very different, as a sixth-century inscription from Asia Minor explains. It praises John as the beloved disciple who reclined on God's breast, and who was therefore given

the ineffable words through which he has shown us his divine and unfathomable inspiration, by reason of which he was fittingly called son of thunder – and *theologian*.[4]

John is a 'theologian' (and the word creeps into the very edges of the Bible) not because he has managed to master the divine subject matter and set it out in rational order, but because he has himself been mastered by God, overwhelmed and disordered, and entrusted with inspired utterances or oracles from God – with *logoi* from *theos*.[5] The writer of Revelation is about as far from the popular culture image of the scientist or the –ologist, as one could get: no Bunsen burner and test tube, no clipboard and questionnaire, no study desk and bookshelves. He is the seer on Patmos, caught up 'in the Spirit', hearing a voice like a trumpet, seeing a vision of God, and falling on his face as though dead (Revelation 1.9–10, 17).

Perhaps, then, the word 'theology' is an oxymoron, and the kind of studious activity it normally names is illegitimate? If knowing God is a matter of personal encounter, or of overwhelming involvement, or even of inspired utterances and visions, perhaps rational investigation is simply an irrelevance – a category mistake, like trying to measure the height of love? Or, worse, perhaps it is a way of trying to *avoid* encounter and involvement with God by holding God's utterance at arm's length, objectifying and analysing it so as not to have to listen to the challenge it issues?[6]

Those are serious questions, and I don't raise them simply in order to dismiss them. I *do* think that there is something uncomfortable about the word 'theology', almost as if two magnets were being pushed together the wrong way round, and I *do not* think one should quash too easily the rumour that intellectual mastery is an inappropriate goal to pursue if one's subject matter is God. My task in this chapter (and in the two that follow) is not to *solve* these questions, but to sidle around them, suggesting that there might be forms of 'rational discourse about God' that do not get quite so big for their boots.

Between Athens and Jerusalem

In the second century after Christ, the North African theologian Tertullian wrote:

> The Lord chose the foolish things of the earth (1 Corinthians 1.27) to confound philosophy. Philosophy is the stuff of worldly wisdom, which boldly asserts itself to be the interpreter of the nature and activity of God. But what is there in common between Athens and Jerusalem, between the Academy and the church? Our system of beliefs comes from the Porch of Solomon's Temple, who himself taught that it was necessary to seek God in the simplicity of our hearts. We have no need to be *curious* about Jesus Christ, or to be *inquisitive* about the Gospel; when we believe, we don't desire to believe anything more.[7]

Tertullian was worried that false teachers were corrupting the beliefs and practices of his church, and that their teachings were born from a surfeit of philosophy – the pagan philosophy that he associated first and foremost with Athens, the city of Plato and Aristotle. Christian faith, he said, has little to do with the ambitious attempts of the philosophers to sort the world out for themselves. It is based on a simple, humble acceptance of the faith delivered in God's city of Jerusalem – not in any academy of philosophers, but in the Temple. What has Athens of the philosophers got to do with Jerusalem of the simple faithful? Why, if one has received faith from God, would one need to corrupt it by attempting to sort it out according to one's intellectual curiosity?[8]

Discussion

Ask yourself, or debate with friends or fellow students: Should faithful believers heed this warning, and put this book down right now? If not, why not?

Key points

- 'Theology' means 'rational discourse about God'.
- It is questionable whether rationality is an appropriate aim when one's subject matter is God.

Novels and gossip

For some, the very term 'rationality' brings clammily to mind something cold and inhuman, something indifferent to human life and community. Some will ask what warm Christian faith can possibly have to do with such coldness.[9]

The meanings of rationality

When people ask whether theology is rational, it is often quite difficult to work out what they mean, because the word 'rational' can mean a whole variety of different things.

1 They might be asking whether theological claims have any place now that everyone (supposedly) knows that the natural world, structured by knowable laws of cause and effect, is all that there is.
2 They might be asking whether theological claims work in the same way as scientific claims – justified only insofar as they provide ways of accounting for the available empirical evidence.
3 They might even be asking whether theological claims can be deduced logically from indubitable starting points, rather like mathematical theorems.[10]
4 They might be asking whether theological claims fit in with the ideas of some philosophical movement that they take as their guide to thinking about reality – existentialism, perhaps, or Marxism, or post-structuralism.
5 They might be asking whether theological ideas fit together into a comprehensive and coherent worldview, forming an interlocking system of ideas that can order one's understanding of anything and everything.
6 They might simply be asking whether theological claims can be put forward in clear and consistent ways, avoiding ambiguity and contradiction.
7 They might be asking whether theologians develop their ideas honestly and responsibly, in ways that are genuinely responsive to criticism and attentive to detail.[11]

As you will see, when I talk about 'rationality' in this chapter, I will be hovering closer to the end of this list than to the beginning.

Exercise

Search online for reviews of Richard Dawkins's rationalist attack on religion, *The God Delusion* (London: Bantam, 2006) – and try teasing apart the different meanings of 'rational' employed by him, his supporters and his detractors.

I want to suggest two examples of rationality at work that might persuade
you that it need not be kept in the fridge. For both of them, 'rationality' has
something to do with an interplay between creative and critical impulses. On
the one hand, there is the creative impulse that, faced with an unruly mess
of experience or information, tries to develop some coherent way of talking
about it all, some way of *making sense* of it all. On the other hand, there is
the critical impulse that looks out for the ways in which the unruly mess of
experience or information wriggles out of one's grasp, and calls into question
the sense one has made. I think a good case can be made that this interplay
is crucial in those homes of rational enquiry, the scientific laboratory and the
academic library – but also that it can be found alive and well, living incog-
nito among ordinary people, in houses and bars and fish and chip shops.

Imagine, first, that you were reading a Jane Austen novel, one that was new
to you. And imagine that in the thirteenth chapter, after the arrival of a letter
in which the hero's intentions were unexpectedly clarified to the heroine, a
horde of pirates were to descend from the coast, kidnap her and whisk her
away to their sea-cave hideout. You would, I imagine, be surprised. And the
fact that you were surprised would indicate that the most important constituents of rationality were at work.

You would be surprised because the horde of pirates ran against your expectations about the book. You would be surprised, that is, because in reading
the book you had built up some kind of picture of what *goes* and what *does not*
go in the world in which the story was taking place. Your surprise would be
evidence that, as well as simply reading the events of the story as they happen,
one after the other, you had (with some part of your mind) been stepping back
and sketching in the broader landscape within which the story's events were
happening. That would have involved you developing at least rough expectations about the geographical setting (you would be surprised if an episode
involved visiting a glacier, or an asteroid crater); it would have involved rough
expectations about the temporal setting (you would be surprised if a rock star
moved into the area – even if he did turn out to be a single man in possession
of a good fortune); it would have involved more subtle expectations about the
genre and the limitations of this kind of story (you would be surprised by the
appearance of a ghost, or of the Spanish Inquisition).

This is rationality in one of its raw forms: the mostly unacknowledged
sketching in of expectations and predictions, which accompanies one's reading of a story and allows one to be surprised, or pleased, or upset, or confused
by the way the story goes. In fact, it is this kind of thinking that allows one
to experience a story as *having* a plot, as *having* characters and as *having* a
setting: if one had no such scaffolding of expectations and understandings,
one would experience the book simply as a tangled spaghetti of unconnected
sentences.

This process of making sense is ongoing and dynamic. As one carries on
reading, one's half-hidden theories and hypotheses are constantly being
revised. Even if nothing so out of place as a pirate posse turns up, one will
find plenty that upsets the pictures one has begun to sketch. One might, for
instance, have started to paint a mental portrait of a central character as an
arrogant and unfeeling boor, only to find the heroine receiving a letter that

places his behaviour in a new light – and so finding that one is forced to revise one's thinking (just as she is forced to revise hers). Part of the pleasure of reading the book is precisely that of having one's expectations confounded, and part of the skill of the writer is in helping one to build up the misleading expectations in the first place, before knocking them down. (Try reading Dorothy L. Sayers's *Five Red Herrings* if you want a classic and, as the title suggests, very deliberate example of such misdirection.[12]) Even when one comes back and reads the same book a second or third time, one is likely to find that some of one's picture of its story, its world and its characters is challenged, and that one sees things at least slightly differently. (Another good example is Charles Palliser's *The Quincunx* – a book whose very last sentence sends one back to reread the whole story again with new eyes.[13])

There is nothing really new going on when some people choose to put into words their expectations and predictions (or their sense of how the book challenges existing claims and theories) and to publish them in academic and literary journals.[14] Such academic attempts at the rational investigation of the novel are nothing but more formal and explicit versions of the raw, ordinary rationality that we all use all the time when we are reading.

Exercise

Try watching the first episode of a new television drama serial, and then discussing with friends how you have started sketching out the setting for this story. What have the clues been? What assumptions and expectations do you now have about the story's plot, characters and world? As you watch more, are any of those assumptions or expectations challenged?

As a second example, consider *gossip*. I don't mean here the kind that spreads maliciously embroidered stories about some unfortunate neighbour. I mean our ongoing, friendly and informal chatter about the lives and doings of family, friends and colleagues – the kind of chatter that constantly hazards *interpretations* of the people around us and plays around with those interpretations. 'Well, I think he shouts at her because he's a bit insecure', 'Oh, she goes for quiet men, haven't you noticed, they're all the same; it's all of a piece with the way she treats her secretary', or 'Do you know, I had him completely wrong; I thought he was rude, but all along he was just being shy' – and so on: constant attempts to find reasons for what people say and do; constant attempts to build up pictures of how people work; constant attempts to revise those pictures when people turn out not quite to fit into them. That too is raw rationality at work.

If you listen carefully to the kind of friendly gossip I'm talking about, you might be amazed at how supple and sophisticated it can be. Perfectly ordinary people turn out to be capable of deploying complex, multilayered, psychologically acute, detailed and responsive pictures of their friends, colleagues and relations. Perfectly ordinary people, we might say, turn out to be sophisticated *theorists* of their friends and colleagues.[15]

Now, I know this is a somewhat provocative example. One of the problems with gossip is that we are often better at the building up of initial pictures of how people work than at revising them when new facts come our way. Gossip can all too easily give prominence to one-dimensional caricatures of the people we don't like, caricatures that then 'stick', however the person concerned acts. And part of the problem is that gossip is often carried on in such a way that the person gossiped about is the last one to hear how he or she is being described, and so the last person who can directly and explicitly challenge any unfairness in the portrait.

But that problem simply highlights the fact that being rational can't simply mean being good at developing pictures of how people work, but must also mean being alive to the ways in which what is being talked about does not quite match those pictures. Rationality, if it is to be fully human, must be dynamic and ongoing; it involves both the building up of pictures *and* the willingness to have those pictures tested by what they purport to describe.

Rationality is sometimes presented as if it gets to work when one has shut the door on the mess and confusion of ordinary life, retreated into one's study and cleared the desk of all that might be distracting. It is presented as working best with abstract and pure ideas, and as working towards saying something about ordinary life only slowly, awkwardly and unconvincingly – as in the popular culture image of the absent-minded professor who knows everything about time machines or ancient hieroglyphics, but nothing about doing up shoelaces or undoing bras.[16] You might have begun this book with the assumption that academic theology was bound to involve that kind of rationality: dry, abstract, removed from ordinary life.

That is not the picture of rationality I have in mind, however. Both the examples I have given (of the rationality involved in reading a novel and of the rationality involved in benign gossip) are intended to suggest something very different. Where is rationality to be found? The answer I am suggesting is, 'All around us'. All around us we find two things combined. On the one hand, we find people *making sense* of their surroundings, of their friends, of the things that they read, seeing them not simply as collections of random characteristics, but as situations or people or stories that have some kind of consistency to them. On the other hand, we find people revising the sense that they have made, realizing that they have been mistaken, realizing that the picture they have built up doesn't allow them to make sense of some new episode or fact or encounter, and so realizing that some new sense is needed. All around us we find the *making*, the *breaking* and the *remaking* of sense.

This making, breaking and remaking of sense *is* rationality. And to be *more* rational, if this is what rationality is, is to be more attentive, more careful about this making, breaking and remaking. To be more rational is to make sense in ways that are alive to a broader gamut of experience; it is to become more sensitive to all that calls the sense one has already made into question. To be more rational is to be more alive, more fully engaged. When reading a novel, for instance, being more rational might mean allowing one's picture of the hero to become more alive to all the subtle signals that the story so far has given – to be, in one sense, more *impressionable*. And it will be to read with more readiness to have one's picture challenged and redrawn as the story goes on, to read with more sensitivity to any little signals that might begin to tell us that all is not as it has seemed.[17]

Exercise

Try Jane Austen's *Pride and Prejudice* (the book is best, but one of the television or film adaptations will do[18]) and watch how Elizabeth makes sense of Darcy – and look particularly for the role that careful reading of letters plays. In Elizabeth Bennet, Jane Austen provides a portrait of true, human rationality at work.[19]

Key point

- To be rational about something is to make good sense of it – and to be sensitive to those things that could upset the sense that you have made.

Communal sense

In the remainder of this chapter, I am going to suggest three related ways in which Christian theology involves 'making sense'. I am going to begin, in this section and the next two, by looking at some of the ways in which Christian *communities* have gone about making sense of themselves – and the place that 'Christian doctrine' has had in that sense-making. Then, in a section entitled 'The meaning of life' (pp. 21–24), I will turn to the ways in which an *individual* might go about making sense of his or her life, and the new possibilities for making such sense that are offered by Christian doctrine. And finally, in 'Watching the world' (pp. 24–26), I will turn to look briefly at the ways in which the whole *world* is powered by pervasive and persistent ways of making sense, and at various kinds of critique of the world therefore made possible by Christian doctrine.

We can begin thinking about the rationality, the sense-making, involved in the life of a community by comparing it to the sense-making involved in reading a novel. By participating in any community's life, members will begin to gain some sense of the kind of community it is, of what makes it tick, of how it works and why. They will begin to learn the *story so far*, and begin to make sense of it in ways not too dissimilar from what happens when they read a novel. Their ability to go on participating in this community appropriately (rather than sticking out like pirates in a Jane Austen novel) will depend on their having made good sense of that story.

Think of what it is like moving to a new workplace: the initial awkwardness and clumsiness slowly wearing off as you learn how the place works, not just in the obvious ways necessary for doing your job, but in all the subtle and invisible ways that distinguish an insider to this organization from an outsider.

In a religious community, much of the kind of sense-making involved might be pretty low level: *this* is the sort of thing we do every Sunday, whereas *this* is the sort of thing we only do at major festivals; *this* is the sort of way we treat newcomers; *this* is the kind of school we send our children to; *these* are the kinds of jokes you can tell in church.[20]

From time to time, however, members of this community might find themselves emerging into uncharted waters, unsure of how to go on. What happens when your community floats from being powerless to being powerful, or the other way round? What happens when the patterns of members' working lives change, and make regular attendance impossible? What happens when your leaders are involved in a scandal? What happens, in other words, when the story does not simply drift along in much the same channel as before, but reaches some more or less dramatic transition?

When this happens, members of a community may find themselves uncertain about how to proceed; their normal habits of action and imagination may not be enough to carry them through. They may be forced to think more explicitly than they normally do about what it is that they are doing – to find some new way of telling the story so far that will allow them to make sense of this new episode, and to write new chapters in the story in ways that don't betray what has gone before.

Imagine, for instance, a Christian community that devotes a great deal of time, money and energy to running a Sunday school for children. People coming into the community would slowly learn how much this meant to the church, what kinds of involvement in it were possible for them, what could and could not be suggested as appropriate activities. All this would show that newcomers were learning this bit of the community's story well enough to know how to go on. Much of the time, the reasons for all this activity won't be clear to people: this is simply what this community does, and it knows how to do it well.

Now imagine what happens when numbers attending the Sunday school slowly but inexorably decline, until the expenditure of time, energy and money becomes patently absurd. Painful though it might be, members of that community might need to pause and discuss *why* they were engaged in this activity in the first place. In a discussion in a church meeting, some might stress that this activity has been more than a way of amusing the children while their parents went about the serious business elsewhere, and more even than a way of training the children up so that they might go on to be good adult churchgoers at some point in the future. The Sunday school has been run because the children are *already* full members of the church, but need to have ways of participating in the life of the church that are appropriate to their age and that don't make it impossible for other age groups to experience forms of worship appropriate to *them*.

This attempt to explain why this community has a Sunday school might well be an invention, in one sense: it might well be that the Sunday school in its present form evolved without anyone saying or thinking anything quite like this. However, it might also be a matter if discovery: it might, that is, be a good way of bringing to the surface the kinds of instincts that various people in the community have had about how it should be run. It might be a good way of crystallizing into an explicit account a widespread but vague, mostly implicit sense of what this activity means, or of providing a banner under which people with all sorts of implicit account might rally.

Of course, the appropriateness of this way of making sense might be disputed. Others might suggest that children can't really be seen as full church members until they have undergone adult baptism or confirmation, or until they are old enough to understand what the Christian gospel means – and that 'preparation' for that transition *should* be the keynote of the Sunday school's life.

In the end, whichever of these ways of making sense of the Sunday school's existence wins enough hearts and minds will become the basis upon which this community revises its practice. The community can look for new ways in which it could use the time, energy and money that had previously been put into the Sunday school, while still pursuing the 'same' goals. Perhaps the community will set up regular 'all-age worship' services and a midweek evening youth club. Perhaps it will start examining what it is about their normal Sunday services that is inappropriate for children, and see where else in the church's life those things might be relocated. All sorts of futures are possible, but each will involve some stab at making sense of the present and the past.

Finishing *Edwin Drood*

I have mentioned the kinds of sense-making that might be involved in reading a novel. Think of the difference that there might be between the kinds of sense-making that would be involved in reading Dickens's *Great Expectations* for pleasure, and the kind that might be involved in reading his unfinished novel *Edwin Drood* with a view to writing your own ending to it (as many authors have).[21] The kinds of attentiveness you would need when reading *Edwin Drood* would not be fundamentally different in *kind*, but the need to write your own fully appropriate ending to the novel would force you to pay deeper, closer, more persistent attention.

You would have to come up with some way of grasping the plot, the meaning, of the parts that Dickens had completed: spotting a way of making sense of the hints and clues that he left behind. Your way of making sense would be your own invention, and it might be a controversial one, but it would have to be as responsible as you could make it to what Dickens had already written. Without such a way of making sense, there is no way that you could continue where Dickens left off – even if, in practice, your way of making sense of his words will only fully emerge as you write and revise your continuation.

You can think of Christian theology as the sense-making that is involved when churches want to know how to continue the story so far. A church is, after all, a community that has a whole set of deeply ingrained practices: worshipping; telling stories about Jesus and the early church; reading Jewish Scriptures; baptizing; celebrating the Eucharist; carrying out various forms of mission; and so on. Theology emerges wherever Christians seek to go on doing these things in new circumstances, or seek to deal with changes, challenges and conflicts to them, or seek to pass them on to new generations, or to communicate about them or propagate them beyond their existing cultural settings. Theology is not, or need not be, the imposition of some cold, rationalizing scheme on to the rich and breathing life of a community; it is an inevitable part of how this rich and breathing life is carried on, and passed on.[22]

Exercise

Can you think of any examples of churches, or other groups or communities, that have had to make new sense of themselves in the face of some crisis or change in circumstances? Did that making of sense follow the pattern I have described?

Key points

- To be rational about one's community's life is to make good enough sense of it to know how to go on.
- To be rational about one's community's life is also to be sensitive to those things that could question the sense that you have made.
- 'Making sense' of the community's life is a creative act, but one that tries to be responsible to the life of the community.
- 'Making sense' is a potentially controversial activity.

The place of doctrine

I have not quite said enough to explain the basic character of Christian theology. There are, after all, all sorts of different ways that a community might make sense of itself. In some religious communities, this kind of sense-making might be largely delegated to a charismatic leader or group of leaders – people who are seen so to embody all that is best in the community that they can be trusted to know at an intuitive level, or perhaps by divine inspiration, how the community should respond to a new challenge. No one way of telling the story of the community's ideas or principles is given absolute pride of place – rather, it is the ability of the leader to discern the appropriate account at the appropriate time that is central. (To the question, 'Who are we?', such communities might answer simply 'Ask our leader; we are his people!')

In other religious communities, the process by which members make enough sense to go on will be closer to the ways in which lawyers and judges interpret existing laws for new situations. They build on a secure knowledge of the existing history of cases, and therefore have a good grasp of how rulings that makes legal sense can be put together. When they make decisions in ambiguous or unusual cases, they hope to decide those cases in ways that follow existing precedent as far as possible, even when their new decisions themselves set new precedent. (To the question 'Who are we?', such a community might reply, 'We are the community held together by this law.')

Following the letter of the law

It can be tempting to think that all the ways in which communities will 'make sense' of themselves in times of change will have some kind of 'letter'/'spirit' structure. That is, it can be tempting to think that communities always have to look behind the 'letter' of current practice (the detailed present shape of what they do) to discern the 'spirit' (the deep principles or ideas or commitments or intentions behind that present shape). Faced with an unprecedented situation, the community alters the letter, but tries to express the same spirit.

However, not all communal rationality works in quite that way. For instance, Orthodox Jewish law does not allow people to work on the Sabbath, and the definition of 'work' given in some classical sources is very broad, so that, for instance, pushing wheelchairs, prams and pushchairs turns out not to be allowed. If someone concerned to alleviate these difficulties worked with a letter/spirit mentality, he might try to discern the deep *principles* at stake in this law – its 'spirit' or 'intention' – and then propose a reformation of the letter of the law that would protect that spirit. That is not, however, the way that certain Orthodox Jewish communities have operated. They do not see themselves as having the freedom to tinker with the letter in this way; instead, their solution is to look at the letter more closely. For instance, in the classical formulation of the Sabbath work laws there are various exemptions, including certain locations in which some kinds of work are allowed. In particular, although disallowed in public spaces, some work is allowed in *private* spaces – with 'private' being defined as spaces fully enclosed by a wall pierced by doors (such as a room or courtyard). Rabbis have looked at the words used in the law's precise definition of such private space, and tried to see ways in which other, larger kinds of space than were originally envisioned could be included under the same verbal definition. In this case, they realized that a large area – even a whole section of a town – could be turned into private space by the creation of an 'eruv', an area surrounded by fences or walls, broken only by 'doors' each of which consists of two posts and a lintel (in modern eruvim, most often telegraph poles linked by wire). There are many such eruvim around the world, and in 2002 a large area of North-West London around Golders Green was (somewhat controversially) turned into one – thus allowing a greater degree of freedom to orthodox Jews living within it on the Sabbath. Those who automatically think in terms of letter and spirit often find this sort of development bizarre; but the orthodox proponents of the eruv claim that they can find flexibility in the law precisely by keeping strict hold of the letter, and challenging assumptions about its spirit or intention.[23]

In Christianity, a large portion of the discussion of what is central and what is peripheral, of what can be changed and what must be kept the same, of how the same faith can be lived in different circumstances, has tended to cluster around certain *teachings* that are held to underlie and hold together the diverse practices and customs of Christian people. These teachings are held to spell out the basic plot of the story so far, and to provide resources for writing fresh chapters of the story to come, in any and every new situation. Discussion of how Christianity should respond to new situations, or to challenges, or to internal disagreements, has tended very often to circle around the ongoing exploration and restatement of these teachings, of their implications, and of the ways in which they relate to and support the whole rich and complex tapestry of Christian life. Such teachings are often called 'doctrines' (which is simply a word derived from the Latin for 'teachings', just as 'doctor' originally meant 'teacher').[24] The teachings in question normally have something to do with how Christian people understand themselves and their world as relating to the God who has laid hold of them in Jesus Christ.

'Who are we?' Part of the answer that Christians have traditionally given – the part on which discussions of Christian doctrine tends to focus – is, 'We are the people who believe and celebrate the story summarized in *these* teachings; we are the people who believe themselves to have been laid hold of by God in Jesus Christ.' 'We believe in God, the Father Almighty ...'[25] That does not mean that the life of Christian communities is a life *derived* from a set of teachings, as if the teachings came first and the life second; rather it means that the teachings have emerged as relatively stable points in the swirl of ways in which Christians have made sense of their life together.

The indispensable basis of Christian identity

When Adolf Hitler came to power in Germany in 1933, the German churches came under pressure to conform to Nazi ideology. Jewish Christians were compelled to leave the ordained ministry, and the churches were expected to accept the authority over their internal affairs of the German state (the 'Reich'), headed by Adolf Hitler. Many of the churches, the so-called 'German Christians', adopted these measures – some of them very willingly. Adolf Hitler was praised as a prophet come to purify the church.

Some Christians in Germany did, however, resist. At a meeting of theologians, church leaders and others at Barmen in 1934, the theologians Karl Barth and Hans Asmussen drafted a declaration (the 'Barmen Declaration') proclaiming that these measures ran against the deep commitments of the Christian Church – the deep sense made by Christian life. And they did so by drawing on certain central Christian *doctrines* that they believed were betrayed by these measures. Here are some extracts:

> In view of the errors of the 'German Christians' and of the present Reich Church Administration, which are ravaging the Church and at the same time also shattering the unity of the German Evangelical Church, we confess the following evangelical truths ...[26]
>
> The Christian Church is the community of brethren in which, in Word and Sacrament, through the Holy Spirit, Jesus Christ acts in the present as Lord. With both its faith and its obedience, with both its message and its order, [the Christian Church] has to testify in the midst of the sinful world, as the Church of pardoned sinners, that it belongs to [Jesus Christ] alone and lives and may live by his comfort and under his direction alone, in expectation of his appearing.

We reject the false doctrine that the Church could have permission to hand over the form of its message and of its order to whatever it itself might wish or to the vicissitudes of the prevailing ideological and political convictions of the day. ...

The Confessing Synod of the German Evangelical Church declares that it sees in the acknowledgment of these truths and in the rejection of these errors the indispensable theological basis of the German Evangelical Church as a confederation of Confessing Churches. It calls upon all who can stand in solidarity with its Declaration to be mindful of these theological findings in all their decisions concerning Church and State. It appeals to all concerned to return to unity in faith, hope and love.

Here we see one kind of Christian communal rationality at work: digging down in a time of crisis to discover what teachings provide the 'indispensable ... basis' of the Church's life, in order to see how those teachings can help members of the Church 'in all their decisions'. We see, in other words, a church community trying to make sense of itself in order to know how to go on. It is just such Christian ways of making sense that are going to be our main subject matter from now on.

Exercise

A translation of the whole Barmen Declaration can be found online at the United Church of Christ, http://www.ucc.org/faith/barmen.htm; it is adapted from the one in Robert McAfee Brown, *Kairos: Three Prophetic Challenges to the Church* (Grand Rapids. MI: Eerdmans, 1990). Read the whole Declaration now, and note what teachings (doctrines) are drawn on to support the resistance to Nazism.

Key points

- Explicit Christian ways of making sense have often tended to circle around certain key teachings.
- Teachings about how God has laid hold of the world in Jesus Christ have been particularly important among such teachings.

Rationality in Corinth

We can see the emergence of Christian sense-making, and get a stronger sense of how it works, in the earliest extant Christian literature: the epistles of Paul of Tarsus.

In the years after his conversion, Paul travelled around spreading the message about Jesus and founding Christian congregations. When it came to tending these churches, however, problems arose. The churches were so widespread that he could only stay in touch intermittently, from a distance, by

sending envoys and letters.[27] He sometimes relied simply upon his own personal authority and upon the loyalty that members of those churches felt for
him.[28] But such a strategy doesn't work at all well over a distance, especially
when there are other, more charismatic teachers rather closer at hand bidding
for your readers' loyalty. Instead, Paul tried to convince the churches that any
guidance he was now offering them was not in fact an attempted exertion
of his personal authority. Rather, he was simply clarifying the implications
of the faith they already knew and lived. He claimed that his teaching was
simply a continuation of the story they already believed. So Paul tried repeatedly to lead his various congregations to see that what they already knew and
believed concerning the Christian faith – the basic practices, experiences and
teachings with which they were familiar – contained in embryo all the guidance they now needed if they wanted to know 'how to go on' in a Christian
way in the complexities of their current situation.

In 1 Corinthians 8, we see Paul trying to answer a question posed by the congregations in Corinth: Was it acceptable for them to buy and eat meat from the
Corinthian markets, even though they knew that it would have been offered
to idols during the slaughtering and preparation process? After stating the
problem, Paul gives advice to the Corinthians that he presents as derived at
least in part from knowledge they already have – that there is no God but one
(v.4), that there is one Lord, Jesus Christ (v.6), that Christ died for each member
of the congregation (v.10), and so on. Later in the letter (ch. 10) he returns to the
same topic, and in order to refine his advice draws on further ideas already
known to them (for example, concerning the Eucharist in v.16, or creation in
v.26). There, he explicitly tells the Corinthians to 'judge for yourselves what I
say' (v.15). That is not a declaration that they should make their own minds up
independently, but a prompt to them to *recognize* what he was saying as an apt
description of their own faith.

This practical need to help distant churches know how to govern themselves meshed with his deepest Christian beliefs. He believed that the world
had been addressed by God in Jesus Christ. The kind of 'making sense' that
he pursued is therefore the attempt to know how to go on given that one has
been addressed in this way. ('Who are we?' 'We are the ones who have been
addressed by God in Christ.') This address was clearly not one that directly
told one everything one might possibly want to know; it did not, for instance,
tell Paul directly the answer he needed to give to Corinthian questions about
idol meat. Nevertheless, Paul clearly believed that God's address already tells
one all one needs to know in order to *work out* how to handle the question of
idol meat – whether to shun it or whether to accept it, or whether to leave that
up to the consciences of individual Christians. So instead of answering the
Corinthian queries by dragging out some extra bit of the original message that
he hadn't got round to telling them before ('Oh, by the way, here's what Jesus
said about meat'), he argues that what the Corinthians know about the gospel
already gives them the basic tools they need to work out how to answer their
own question, if only they would recognize it. He reasons on their behalf, giving them an answer by showing them how to make sense of themselves.

It would be possible to say, therefore, that Paul's message to the Corinthians,
as he responds to all the questions they have about how to live out their faith,

is contained in the verse I have already quoted: 'Judge for yourselves what I say!' He believes that they can find the answer to questions about how to go on by digging down into what they already believe – into the basic Christian teachings that have been passed on to them – and by discerning what implications those teachings have for their conduct in the current situation. Of course he thinks he is the best guide to their existing belief, the one able to offer the most convincing ways of telling their story so far, but this isn't quite the same as simply relying upon his personal, charismatic authority, or the authority of a clear instruction already delivered to them.

Neither is it simply a case of straightforwardly 'applying' the faith they already have, of course. The Corinthians are going to have to work, with his guidance, to understand that faith more deeply, to see more of how it might hang together, how it might make sense. But as they pursue that investigation of the basic teachings of their faith, they will find (Paul believes) that they are enabled to see more clearly how to go forward in the world. God in Christ has already said to them all that they can need to hear.[29]

Exercise

Try reading through the whole of 1 Corinthians with my description of it in mind. Have I made good sense of what Paul does in that letter?

Key point

- Some of Paul's letters suggest that the way in which Christian communities can know how to go on is by exploring and interpreting the basic Christian teachings to which they are committed, and discerning the implications of those teachings for their conduct in the world.

The message of the cross

[18]The message about the cross is foolishness to those who are perishing, but to us who are being saved it is the power of God. [19]For it is written,
   I will destroy the wisdom of the wise, and the discernment of the discerning I will thwart.
[20]Where is the one who is wise? Where is the scribe? Where is the debater of this age? Has not God made foolish the wisdom of the world? [21]For since, in the wisdom of God, the world did not know God through wisdom, God decided, through the foolishness of our proclamation, to save those who believe. [22]For Jews demand signs and Greeks desire wisdom, [23]but we proclaim Christ crucified, a stumbling block to Jews and foolishness to Gentiles, [24]but to those who are the called, both Jews and Greeks, Christ the power of God and the wisdom of God. [25]For God's foolishness is wiser than human wisdom, and God's weakness is stronger than human strength. ...

2 When I came to you, brothers and sisters, I did not come proclaiming the mystery of God to you in lofty words or wisdom. ²For I decided to know nothing among you except Jesus Christ, and him crucified. ³And I came to you in weakness and in fear and in much trembling. ⁴My speech and my proclamation were not with plausible words of wisdom, but with a demonstration of the Spirit and of power, ⁵so that your faith might rest not on human wisdom but on the power of God.

⁶Yet among the mature we do speak wisdom, though it is not a wisdom of this age or of the rulers of this age, who are doomed to perish. ⁷But we speak God's wisdom, secret and hidden, which God decreed before the ages for our glory. ...

¹²Now we have received not the spirit of the world, but the Spirit that is from God, so that we may understand the gifts bestowed on us by God. ¹³And we speak of these things in words not taught by human wisdom but taught by the Spirit, interpreting spiritual things to those who are spiritual.

1 Corinthians 1.18–25; 2.1–7, 12–13

Exercise

Read this passage carefully, and then, before you carry on to read my comments, try answering this question: Do you think that Paul's comments on 'wisdom' here rule out an academic theological exploration of Christian faith?

Despite all that I have said so far, careful readers are bound to ask whether we can take seriously Paul's insistence that the Corinthians should 'judge for themselves' – after all, it is the Greeks who desire wisdom, while Christians simply proclaim Christ crucified. The wisdom that Paul is talking about is, of course, primarily the wisdom of Athens, in Tertullian's terms, and so the kind of wisdom that emerges from the arguments of the Greeks (the 'debaters of this age', wise by human standards).[30] I don't think, however, that Paul's critique can be restricted simply to one or two specific brands of Greek philosophy; I think it makes sense to construe Paul's target as human wisdom or human judgement more broadly: 'the wisdom of the world', 'a wisdom of this age', a wisdom of 'lofty words' and 'plausible words'. It is the prevailing wisdom of the age; it is the normal way in which people were making sense of themselves and of their world in that time and place; it is the wisdom that enabled the man and woman on the Corinthian street to know how to go on as participants in their world.[31] Clearly 'judge for yourselves' can't really mean, 'judge according to human wisdom'. So what can it mean?

For Paul, the wisdom of the world is utterly foolish because it renders people incapable of making sense of what God was doing on the cross. It is wisdom that assumes that the world's spring is wound by the kind of power or strength conspicuously absent in the 'weakness' of the cross – a kind of power or strength that actually leads only to destruction. If you make sense of yourself and your world in these prevailing ways, Paul says, the idea that God was addressing the world in 'Jesus Christ, and him crucified' will be nonsense to you – sheer foolishness – and you will, presumably, be incapable of judging truly for yourself.

But the foolishness of the cross is the foolishness and weakness of God, tripping up the world's wisdom. And it is therefore, Paul says, the beginning of a new kind of wisdom. 'We have received ... so that we may understand ...' he says; God's foolishness is something the Corinthians can be 'taught'. Certainly, the spiritual wisdom to which Paul calls his readers is an understanding based on *faith* – but it is a form of understanding nonetheless, and so a way of making sense of oneself and one's world. Paul is calling for the Corinthians to develop ways of thinking about the world that will allow the story of the cross to make sense. What do they need to believe about themselves, about their world and about God for this story not to be foolish nonsense? How, if the cross has become a central focus of their lives, can they make the kind of sense that will allow them to go on living in its shadow?[32]

Finishing *Edwin Drood* again

I described earlier the kinds of sense-making that might be involved in trying to write a continuation for Dickens's unfinished novel, *Edwin Drood*. You can imagine an author beginning her continuation of the novel with a chapter in which some startling new incident cast the whole of the story so far in an unexpected new light, making the reader revise his opinion of nearly everything that had happened so far, including his estimate of the motives of various characters and of the relationships between them.

Something like that has happened for Paul. The advent of Jesus has cast a new light on to his story, the story of his people and the story of his world. His recognition of this new light has not involved him in tearing up the earlier chapters of the story, but it has made him see them in a whole new way. He will now read his life, Jewish Scripture and the whole world in this new, controversial way – but he will claim that this new way of reading allows him to make deeper, truer sense of what he is reading, and so to write a more compelling continuation.[33]

For the Corinthian community to go about making this new kind of sense involves them allowing some of their existing ways of making sense to be broken open. It involves them allowing themselves to be tripped up by the teaching that God has addressed the world in the life and death of Jesus Christ. Later in his correspondence with them, Paul speaks of 'destroying arguments and every proud obstacle raised up against the knowledge of God, and taking every thought captive to Christ' (2 Corinthians 10.4–5). The 'taking captive' of their every thought to Christ is the result of insistently taking all their ways of making sense to the cross, to ask whether they still make sense if God is indeed addressing them there. It is this *process* of breaking and remaking to which, according to Paul, Christians are called – and it is involvement in this process that underlies any ability they might have, in his eyes, to judge for themselves.

Key points

- For Paul, the way God has addressed the world in Jesus Christ upsets some of the sense that the Corinthian community has been making of itself.
- Paul also believes that the way God has addressed the world in Jesus Christ enables the Corinthians to make surprising new sense of themselves.

The meaning of life?

If we take our cue from Paul, we will see Christian theology as in the first place an activity of Christian communities – the activity in which such communities take stock of themselves in the light of the activity of God that they believe has called them into being, searching ever deeper into that core in order to see its implications in ever new situations. To study Christian doctrine is to study some of the key ways in which Christian communities have ended up making such sense of themselves and of their world over the past two millennia.

A lot of the people who study theology, however, do so less because they are part of Christian communities that are struggling to know how to go on, and more because they are enquiring individuals trying to make sense of their own lives and of their place in the world. Thankfully, much of what I said earlier about making sense also applies at this individual level. After all, as you live your life, you inevitably make sense of yourself as you go along: you make sense of the story that your own life tells and learn to hazard some guesses about what makes you tick.

Such sense-making is in the background much of the time, but a crisis or a change in circumstances can bring it to the fore. A couple of years ago, I was faced with the possibility of applying for a job at a different university. In the past, when something like that has happened, it has always been pretty obvious to me what I wanted; I have not had to think very hard about what I am applying for and why, only about what to do to avoid making a fool of myself. This time, however, I was genuinely unsure whether I wanted to move or stay. Thinking about it led me to ask uncomfortable questions about what I really wanted and why. I realized, for instance, that I had a rather fanciful vision of myself as becoming a somewhat old-fashioned kind of scholar, slowly working away in book-lined studies and dusty libraries on long, learned articles – and that one of the things driving my application for this job was the thought that the other University would allow me to do more of that. The more I thought about it, the more I realized that this picture of who I wanted to be didn't really do justice to the kinds of work I actually enjoyed most; it was a way of making sense of myself that was not in fact very convincing. I had to think hard about whether, if I acknowledged the more diverse things that I really wanted from an academic job, the proposed move still looked like the right one to make. In other words, this minor crisis provoked me to see that some of the stories I told myself about how I worked and what I wanted were actually untrue, and helped me come to some new, slightly more realistic understanding of how I ticked.

This is a fairly trivial example, and I am sure that even so I am over-dramatizing it. The bigger the crisis or disruption, however, the deeper one might have to dig in order to make liveable sense. One might get pushed beyond comfortable reliance upon habit and made to ask what one *really* cares about, what one's *deeper* commitments are. Who are you? Who do you want to be? Posed in the abstract, these can be deeply self-indulgent questions, redolent of teenage angst, sounding portentous while not actually getting hold of any real query. But when they arise in the disrupted course of a life, when a person is striving to make enough sense to go on, or enough sense to feel that he or she has not simply 'lost the plot', they can be urgent and unavoidable. Such a person looks for ways of making sense that do justice to what she knows of herself and of her situation. It is not that she simply discovers the right way of making sense, because the process of making sense is always a creative (and controversial) process. But she tries to come up with a way of making sense that does as much justice as possible to the situation and to what she knows of herself.

Espedair Street

Towards the end of Iain Banks's *Espedair Street*, the central character and narrator, Daniel, whose life has been falling apart, has a moment in which things quite suddenly make a certain kind of sense. He is walking down Espedair Street when, as he says,

> slowly a feeling of contentment, intensifying almost to elation, filled me. I couldn't say why; it felt like more than having gone through a period of mourning and come out the other side, and more than just having reassessed my own woes and decided they were slight compared to what some people had to bear; it felt like faith, like revelation: that things went on, that life ground on regardless, and mindless, and produced pain and pleasure and hope and fear and joy and despair, and you dodged some of it and you sought some of it and sometimes you were lucky and sometimes you weren't, and sometimes you could plan your way ahead and that would be the right thing to have done, but other times all you could do was forget about plans and just be ready to *react*, and sometimes the obvious was true and sometimes it wasn't, and sometimes experience helped but not always, and it was all luck, fate, in the end; you lived, and you waited to see what happened, and you would rarely ever be sure that what you had done was really the right thing or the wrong thing, because things can always be better, and things can always be worse.[34]

This is an example of the kind of rationality I have been talking about. Danny has taken the great mess of experience, of action and rebuff, success and failure, that the novel has described, and come – by whatever conscious and subconscious processes – to an understanding of the stage on which all that drama has been played out. It is not quite that he has made sense of his story, rather that he has made sense of the world in which his story took place, and in which lives can't be expected to make much sense.

Danny's vision is not a theological one: he makes no recourse to God, to any kind of providence, to any overarching plot. Nevertheless, the 'sense' at which he arrives is not simply the sketching in of assumptions about the social and geographical setting of a particular story; it is something deeper. Danny, we might say, has arrived at an apprehension of the total moral context within which he lives – the texture of the whole world in which his actions and interactions play out, for better or worse. One question that will be worth keeping in mind is how Danny's vision might relate to specifically Christian ways of thinking about the total moral context. When set alongside a vision like this, must Christian ways of making sense seem like too-easy consolations? Must Christian ways of making sense deny the sheer messy contingency of things that Danny sees?

Paul presents the message of the cross of Christ as a challenge to the Corinthian community's ways of making sense, but the same message can be as much of a challenge to the ways individuals make sense of themselves and their world. The gospel can, for Paul, be seen as the biggest crisis of them all: the irruption into one's life of the disruptive, disquieting message of the cross – forcing a re-evaluation of all the sense that had glued one's life together.

As well as being a communal discipline, therefore, theology can be a discipline that involves careful, sometimes painful attentiveness by an individual to the sense by which she lives her life – a process that involves teasing out some of the assumptions and images and dreams and prejudices that shape what she thinks of as normal or proper or acceptable, allowing those to be challenged by the different ways of making sense offered by the Christian gospel. Theology can be what you might call a *spiritual* discipline, encouraging deep, careful attentiveness to one's habits, one's relationships, one's assumptions – not simply for *in*formation's sake, but for *trans*formation.

In this light, I don't think that it is *only* members of Christian communities who can study Christian theology, or those who have (or will have) some responsibility for influencing the course that such Christian communities take. *Anyone* can explore and examine the ways of making sense that are explored by Christian communities. Of course, some who are not themselves members of Christian communities will study Christian ways of making sense simply in order to understand how one group in their society understands itself and the world, and that in itself is an important approach. But some others who would not identify themselves as Christian will study Christian theology in order to see whether Christian teachings challenge the sense they have made of themselves, and whether some of the pathways by which Christians go about making new sense of themselves are pathways that they themselves could follow, or whether thinking through their reasons for not following those pathways will itself bring them to a new sense of themselves.[35]

Some will perhaps feel themselves to be somewhere in the borderlands of a Christian community, and will study Christian theology in order to discern whether or not they really are members, and what coming down off the fence might mean.

And some who are already convinced Christians will see it as a means of exploring and deepening their own faith, of 'taking every thought captive', just as Paul suggested.

So although the study of Christian doctrine is certainly *tied* to Christian communities (because the ways of making sense that are being explored are ones that have grown in the soil of those communities), it is not *restricted* to members of those communities: it can be studied by all sorts of people for all sorts of reasons – sometimes simply because they are trying to understand how others live, but often as part of an individual's own journey of sense-making.

Exercise

Go back to the question that I asked you to consider in preparation for this chapter. Why are you studying theology? Where, if anywhere, do you fit among the categories I have just described?

Key points

- To be rational about one's life is to make good enough sense of it to know how to go on – while being sensitive to those things that could question the sense that one has made.
- The Christian gospel challenges the sense that people have made of their lives.
- Christian theology suggests new ways of going about making sense of one's life.
- Christian theology is first of all an activity of Christian communities, but it can also be studied by others for a variety of reasons.

Watching the world

The world around us takes the shape that it takes in large part because of the kinds of sense that the people in it make. People make deep, mostly unnoticed assumptions about what is natural, normal, appropriate, allowable – and the direction of their lives is in part shaped by those assumptions, in part by the interaction and conflict between their assumptions and those of others. This is true at the small scale, and you can see it played out, say, in a family where different assumptions are made by a mother and a daughter over what forms of dress count as acceptable, and over what 'acceptable' means in the first place. But it is also true at the larger scale, where the ways that a society or culture functions depend upon matted tangles of assumptions spread below the surface of its life – assumptions and disagreements about what kind of standards of living are sustainable, assumptions and disagreements about the roles of men and women, assumptions and disagreements about differences between races, and so on. The process I spoke of in the previous section, of careful, sometimes painful attentiveness, teasing out some of the assumptions and images and dreams and prejudices that shape what one thinks of as normal or proper or acceptable, and allowing those to be challenged by the different ways of making sense offered by the Christian gospel – that process can be applied on this broader scale as well: attending to and challenging the ways of making sense that power our world. The process of 'taking every thought captive' must eventually extend to this wider stage – the stage of culture and politics.[36]

And that means that to be theologically proficient is to become *critically attentive* to the world. To become theologically proficient is to start taking critical notice of the ideas and patterns of thought that make the world go round. To become theologically proficient is to learn what happens when you start examining and questioning all those ways of making sense in the light of the gospel, asking what difference might be made to those ways of making sense by the belief that God has addressed the world in Jesus Christ. This kind of intellectual activity has been said to involve having 'the Bible in one hand and the newspaper in the other'.[37] It is vital to learn all that you can about the Christian story, and the ways in which Christian teachings have been explored and examined over the years, but it is just as vital to read a newspaper, to read novels, to be interested in current affairs, to begin learning to read the whole world around you as carefully as you can. Real proficiency in Christian theology will only emerge as that careful reading of the world and the exploration of the Christian gospel meet and interact with each other – just as the Corinthians were sent deeper into their understanding of the gospel when they were forced to think through challenging situations in the world, and sent deeper into their understanding of that world when they were led by Paul to examine it in the light of the gospel.

In this chapter, I have asked some fairly broad, fairly abstract questions about what rationality is and how it works, and have started setting out some ideas about specifically Christian rationality. This kind of discussion is, I think, important – particularly for those who want to go further in academic theology where such questions about rationality are often debated at fearsome philosophical length. If you are studying theology in an academic context and get asked to write an essay on some title like 'What is theology?', this is likely to be the kind of discussion in which you are expected to get embroiled. Important though all this may be, however, its primary purpose is to clarify some of what is going on in the real heartland of theological enquiry: the attempt not simply to talk about the ways that Christians have of making sense of themselves and their world, but actually to get stuck in directly to the rather richer and more varied intellectual activity involved in exploring and critiquing, in the light of Christian teachings, the sense that all of us are always making of ourselves and of our world.

Key points

- The world around us – its culture and politics – is driven by deeply embedded ways of making sense.

- Christian theology calls those ways of making sense to account.
- To become proficient in theology it is not enough to get to know Christian doctrines well; one must also cultivate a critical curiosity about the way the world works.

Going further

Here are some directions in which you could pursue further the topics touched on in this chapter:

1 My discussion of 'rationality' has been what philosophers would call a 'non-foundationalist' one. That is, my picture of rationality has not involved finding some absolute and inviolable starting point ('foundation') against which all ways of making sense could be tested. Rather, I've suggested that rationality operates 'in the midst of things', as people take stock of where they've got to, using the mental tools available to them. If you want to take this further, you could look at Stanley J. Grenz and John R. Franke, *Beyond Foundationalism: Shaping Theology in a Postmodern Context* (Louis-ville: WJKP, 2000), D. Z. Phillips, *Faith after Foundationalism: Critiques and Alternatives*, new edn (Boulder: Westview, 1995), or Fergus Kerr, *Theology After Wittgenstein*, 2nd edn (London: SPCK, 1997).

2 Much of what I said about rationality assumed the priority of 'abductive' over 'deductive' or 'inductive' reasoning. That is, it gives priority to the development or employment of hypotheses that would make sense of the data in question, rather than the deduction of necessary consequences of the data or the proposal of rules on the basis of regularities in the data. For more on this, see Peter Lipton, *Inference to the Best Explanation*, International Library of Philosophy, 2nd edn (London: Routledge, 2004).

3 My description of the way that communities make sense of themselves needs to be probed further. It should not, for instance, be assumed that a viable communal life requires an identical way of making sense to be shared by each participant, or that learning one's way about in a community is therefore a matter of acquiring precisely the same understanding as others in that community. A community may work precisely by the interaction of differing ways of making sense that mutually reinforce one another. See Timothy Jenkins, 'The country church – the case of St. Mary's, Comberton' in *Religion in English Everyday Life: An Ethnographic Approach*, Methodology and History in Anthropology (Oxford: Berghahn Books), pp. 41–74. Jenkins also provides a useful account of 'apprenticeship' as the way in which both ordinary people and academic investigators learn their way about in such complex social settings. See 'Fieldwork and the perception of everyday life', *Man* 29.2 (1994), pp. 433–55.

4 My account of how individuals make sense of themselves similarly needs further probing. People never make clear, coherent and comprehensive sense of their own or other's lives, and attempts to make sense of a life are as much proposals of ways forward as descriptions of the past or present. See Rowan Williams, 'The Suspicion of Suspicion: Wittgenstein and Bonhoeffer' in Williams, *Wrestling with Angels: Conversations in Modern Theology*, ed. Mike Higton (London: SCM Press, 2007), pp. 186–202, esp. p. 190.

5 Lastly, there's a question that haunts this whole book. Do descriptions of Christian doctrine capture the ways in which any real Christian community makes sense of itself? Do descriptions of Christian doctrine really crystallize the inchoate sense that drives the lives of Christian individuals and communities? Or do those individuals and communities regulate themselves in quite different ways, and use Christian doctrine simply as window dressing?

Notes

1 See Wikipedia contributors, 'Beatrice Bellman', *Wikipedia: The Free Encyclopedia*, http://en.wikipedia.org/w/index.php?title=Beatrice_Bellman&oldid=114564754.

2 Maureen Lipman was not the first: *The Oxford English Dictionary*, 2nd edn (Oxford: Oxford University Press, 1989) has the following citation from 1811. 'She ... was therefore supposed to understand Chemistry, Geology, Philology, and a hundred other ologies' – Edward Nares, *Thinks I To Myself: A Serio-ludicro*, vol. 1, 5th edn (London: Sherwood et al., 1811), I.68.

3 The description of theology as a 'science' is more common in translations of German theology than in works natively in English. In English, 'science' tends now to be used exclusively for the pursuit of knowledge based on the systematic interrogation of the empirical data provided by observations and experiments, whereas the German equivalent (*Wissenschaft*) has a broader meaning, denoting an ordered investigation where the methods adopted and rigorously pursued are those known to be appropriate to the nature of the subject matter. See, for instance, Wikipedia-Autoren, 'Wissenschaft', *Wikipedia, die freie Enzyklopädie* http://de.wikipedia.org/w/index. php?title=Wissenschaft. For German theological usage, see Karl Barth, *Church Dogmatics*, vol. I: *The Doctrine of the Word of God*, Pt 1 (Edinburgh: T&T Clark, 1976), pp. 5–6; for an English usage, see Alister E. McGrath, *A Scientific Theology*, 3 vols (London: Continuum, 2001–2003).

4 Quoted in Allen Brent, 'John as theologos: the imperial mysteries and the Apocalypse', *Journal for the Study of the New Testament* 75 (1999), pp. 87–102: p. 88; I've reversed the order of the final epithets. The inscription assumes the traditional identification of the 'beloved disciple' who leant against Jesus' breast in John 13.23 with both the author of the Gospel and the author of the book of Revelation.

5 Note that *logos* is the nominative singular ('word'), *logou* the genitive ('of the word') and *logoi* the nominative plural ('words').

6 See Chapter 6, p. 151 for discussion of a passionate call to 'Be suspicious of all the "ologies" that try to explain everything – from astrology to psychology to theology.'

7 Tertullian, *De praescriptione haereticorum* 7, translation based on that in Alister E. McGrath, *The Christian Theology Reader* (Oxford: Blackwell, 1995), pp. 5–6. For a different translation, see A. Cleveland Coxe (ed.), *Ante-Nicene Fathers*, vol. 3 (New York: Christian Literature Company, 1885), pp. 243–65, available online at the Christian Classics Ethereal Library, http://www.ccel.org/ccel/schaff/anf03.v.iii.vii.html.

8 Typing the phrase 'Athens and Jerusalem' into an internet search engine like Google reveals how common a trope it has become for the uneasy relationship between faith and reason or church and academy. On 4 April 2007, there were more than 50,000 hits for such a search.

9 On 27 April 2007, I found the phrase 'cold reason' 21,800 times online via Google, 'coldly rational' 11,700 and 'cold rationality' 9,430. By contrast, the phrase 'warmly rational' appears 69 times, and the very first hit is for a page with the line 'Is warmly rational an oxymoron?' – in an Amazon.com customer review for Vincent Ruggiero, *Beyond Feelings: A Guide to Critical Thinking*, 7th edn (New York: McGraw Hill, 2004), http://www.amazon.com/Beyond-Feelings-Guide-Critical-Thinking/dp/customer-reviews/007282896X.

10 Anselm of Canterbury's argument for the existence of God is sometimes held to be an example of this: attempting to prove the existence of God from premises that do not depend upon experience. For a standard presentation of the argument that takes it in that way, see Gideon Rosen, 'Anselm's Ontological Argument' (no date), available online at Rosen's Princeton page, http://www.princeton.edu/~grosen/puc/phi203/ontological.html. For a rather different take on Anselm, see Karl Barth, *Fides Quaerens Intellectum: Anselm's Proof of the Existence of God in the Context of His Theological Scheme*, tr. Ian Robertson (London: SCM Press, 1960 [German original: 1931]) and John Overton, 'Arguing Anselm's Argument', *Modern Theology* 17.1 (2001), pp. 3–19.

11 This list is based on that provided by Tyron Inbody in *The Faith of the Christian Church: An Introduction to Theology* (Grand Rapids, MI: Eerdmans, 2005), pp. 43–7.

12 Dorothy L. Sayers, *Five Red Herrings* (London: Harper and Row, 1931).

13 Charles Palliser, *The Quincunx: The Inheritance of John Huffam*, 2nd edn (Harmondsworth: Penguin, 1995).

14 For a fictional (and humorous) portrait of an academic expert on Jane Austen, see Morris Zapp, a character in David Lodge's novel *Changing Places: A Tale of Two Campuses* (London: Secker and Warburg, 1975).

15 The sophistication of this ordinary human theorizing becomes very visible when one looks at those (such as some who suffer from Asperger's Syndrome) who find it difficult. Mark Haddon's novel, *The Curious Incident of the Dog in the Night-time* (London: Red Fox, 2004) provides a fictional example.

16 The last of these is often overcome by the end of the film.

17 For an account of how this kind of rationality is (or should be) present in academic work, see my *Vulnerable Learning: Thinking Theologically about Higher Education* (Cambridge: Grove Books, 2006).

18 See the Joe Wright film with Keira Knightley (Universal Pictures et al, 2005), full details on the Internet Movie Database at http://uk.imdb.com/title/tt0414387/; or the Simon Langton adaptation for television with Jennifer Ehle (BBC, 1995), http://uk.imdb.com/title/tt0112130/. The book is available online at Project Gutenberg: http://www.gutenberg.org/etext/1342.

19 See Duke Maskell and Ian Robinson, 'Jane Austen, leading authority on liberal education' in *The New idea of the University* (Thorverton: Imprint Academic, 2002), pp. 36–56.

20 There are some good descriptions of church communities by anthropologists that might help you see the sort of thing I mean. See, for example, James L. Peacock and Ruel M. Tyson, *Pilgrims of Paradox: Calvinism and Experience among the Primitive Baptists of the Blue Ridge*, Smithsonian Series in Ethnographic Enquiry (Washington: Smithsonian, 1989) or R. Stephen Warner, *New Wine in Old Wineskins: Evangelicals and Liberals in a Small-town Church* (Berkeley: University of California Press, 1988).

21 See Charles Dickens, *The Mystery of Edwin Drood* (London: Chapman and Hall, 1870). One attempted conclusion was by Leon Garfield (New York: Pantheon, 1980), another by Charles Forsyte, *The Decoding of Edwin Drood* (New York: Scribners, 1980), but there have been many more.

22 Some good histories of theological development manage to show the place of theological ideas in the lives of the individuals and communities involved. For bril-

liant examples, see Peter Brown, *The Rise of Western Christendom: Triumph and Diversity 200–1000 AD*, Making of Europe Series, 2nd edn (Oxford: Blackwell, 2002) and his earlier *Augustine of Hippo: A Biography* (London: Faber and Faber, 1967).

23 The NW London Eruv is described at www.nwlondoneruv.org/map.shtml; some details of the controversy surrounding its creation were reported (rather one-sidedly) by the BBC in August 2002 news.bbc.co.uk/1/hi/england/2182994.stm; Daniel Faigin provides a clear explanation of eruvim at the *Soc.Culture.Jewish Newsgroups'* Frequently Asked Questions page: www.scjfaq.org/faq/07–09.html.

24 'Doctor of medicine' is only the sixth sense of the word given by the *Oxford English Dictionary*, the previous five all having to do with general teaching or education. The secondary medical sense was, however, already in evidence by the fourteenth century, so it is not quite the upstart that we academic doctors sometimes suppose it to be.

25 The use of creeds as a staple element in the worship of many congregations witnesses to the centrality of teachings in Christianity. By saying 'We believe …', the congregation is not simply proclaiming what they believe; they are proclaiming who they are. Credal statements have been used in baptismal liturgies for as long as they have existed; they begin being used in eucharistic worship from at least the sixth century in the East, and the eleventh in the West. See Joseph A. Jungmann, *The Mass of the Roman Rite: Its Origins and Development*, tr. Francis A. Brunner and Chares K. Riepe (London: Burns and Oates, 1959 [German original, 1951]), pp. 295–8.

26 In this context 'evangelical' means simply 'based on the Christian gospel', rather than pointing to any party or theological movement within the Christian Church.

27 For good introductions to Paul of Tarsus, see David Horrell, *An Introduction to the Study of Paul*, 2nd edn (London: Continuum, 2006); Morna Hooker, *Paul: A Short Introduction* (Oxford: Oneworld, 2003) and James Dunn (ed.), *The Cambridge Companion to St Paul* (Cambridge: Cambridge University Press, 2003).

28 See Paul's ambivalent discussion of his authority in 2 Corinthians 10.

29 For more on the roots and methods of Paul's ethical teaching, see David Horrell, *Solidarity and Difference: A Contemporary Reading of Paul's Ethics* (London: Continuum, 2005), Richard Hays, *The Moral Vision of the New Testament: A Contemporary Introduction to New Testament Ethics* (London: Continuum, 1997), and Brian Rosner, *Understanding Paul's Ethics: Twentieth-Century Approaches* (Grand Rapids, MI: Eerdmans, 1995).

30 See above, p. 5.

31 The introductions to most good commentaries on 1 Corinthians contain a description of Corinthian life, sketching some of what it meant to be a participant in that world. See, for example, Anthony Thiselton, *The First Epistle to the Corinthians*, New International Greek Testament Commenatary (Grand Rapids, MI: Eerdmans, 2000), pp. 1–28; see also Edward Adams and David Horrell (eds), *Christianity at Corinth: The Quest for the Pauline Church* (Louisville: WJKP, 2004).

32 The phrase at the very beginning of the passage quoted, 'the message about the cross', translates the Greek phrase *ho logos tou staurou* – the *logos* of the cross. We would not be getting too far from Paul if we said that the -ology in theology is defined by this logos of the cross. Cross in Greek is *stauros*, so we might say that theology is staurology, 'crossology': the 'science' of making sense of oneself and one's world in the light of Christ's cross.

33 See Francis Watson, *Paul and the Hermeneutics of Faith* (London: Continuum, 2004).

34 Iain Banks, *Espedair Street* (London: Abacus, 1990), pp. 224–5. It is a little unfair to quote the relevant passage on its own because, in order for the 'revelation' not to sound cheap, you need to know the story that leads up to it and explains it. You need to see how all this could emerge as an answer for Danny within the context of the questioning forced upon him by his life.

35 I have tried to avoid, as much as possible, assuming that my readers will share my Christian faith. So rather than speaking about 'us', I have tried to remember to talk about 'Christians' or about 'me', or to the unspecific 'one' – even though that has sometimes led to a little awkwardness. I hope it leaves a little space for those who are simply interested onlookers.

36 See the discussion of ideology and ideology critique in Chapter 8, pp. 202–05.

37 The phrase can be found attributed to Martin Luther, Abraham Lincoln, Charles Spurgeon, D. L. Moody, Reinhold Niebuhr and Billy Graham – but the most common attribution is to Karl Barth, the Swiss theologian whose work on the Barmen Declaration I've already mentioned (above, pp. 15–16).

2

Knowing and Loving

In Chapter 1, I argued that theology was an exploration of the sense that Christian communities and individuals make of themselves. In this chapter, I will set out what I take to be the most encompassing aspect of that sense: Christians have made sense of themselves as those who have been addressed, or laid hold of, by *God*. For Christians, true knowledge of oneself and of the world is inextricably bound up with knowledge of God. But what does 'God' mean, and what is it to *know* God? In this chapter, I will argue that the nature of God is only properly known in the lives of those whom God has laid hold of – those whom God is addressing and drawing lovingly to Godself, and who share in God's life. And so I will introduce the main lines of a basic Christian narrative that I will be elaborating in chapters to come: Christians can make sense of themselves as those who are being drawn into the loving life of God, to participate in that life in their own way.

I am going to

- claim that the meaning of the word 'God' cannot, for Christian theology, be obvious, but has to be learnt by attending to God's address;
- suggest that to know God is to know oneself to be lovingly addressed and drawn into love by God;
- suggest that, in some ways, knowing God is more like knowing a piece of music than it is like knowing a fact; and
- argue that the knowledge of God is not found in ideas or theories, but in particular lives caught up into participation in God's life.

Preparation

- Ask yourself how you would respond if you were asked what the word 'God' means
- If you have internet access, type 'define:God' into Google, and see what definitions it turns up. Which of these seem helpful to you, and why? Which seem unhelpful? How close are they to the answer you have given?

Additional reading

I have taken my own way into the subject matter of this chapter, but if you want to read some alternative accounts that will throw a different light on it, try:

Nicholas Lash, *Holiness, Speech and Silence: Reflections on the Question of God* (Aldershot: Ashgate, 2004). A good, brief reflection on what it means to try to speak about God.

Mark McIntosh, *Mystical Theology: The Integrity of Spirituality and Theology*, Challenges in Contemporary Theology series (Oxford: Blackwell, 1998). A substantial introduction to a strand of Christian theology that has challenging things to say about what knowledge of God means.

Norman Russell, *The Doctrine of Deification in the Greek Patristic Tradition*, Oxford Early Christian Studies (Oxford: Oxford University Press, 2004). A detailed and weighty history of the idea of participation in God's life.

The God who addresses

According to Christian theology, people begin making true sense of themselves and of their world only when they see themselves in relation to God. To leave God out of account would be like making sense of a novel without paying any attention to the central character or to the crucial incidents in which that character makes his or her presence felt. Or – perhaps a better analogy – it would be like trying to make sense of the orbits of the planets without reference to the gravitational pull of the sun. Who a person thinks she is, what she thinks is possible, how she thinks she should act, what she things of the shape and texture of her world – all these look different if they are thought through in relation to God.

I am not going to start this discussion of God with the question, 'Does God exist?', for the simple reason that one cannot ask about the existence of something when one does not yet know what that something is supposed to be.[1] The question of the *meaning* of the word 'God' has to come before the question of the *existence* of any referent of that word – and the meaning of the word may not be as straightforward as one might think. Someone might say, 'It is obvious, isn't it. Everyone knows what "God" means, even if they disagree about whether God exists, or about some of the things God happens to have done? God is an omnipotent being—' but then Paul of Tarsus might interrupt, speaking about God's weakness, and the supposedly 'obvious' definition might start slipping from one's grasp.[2]

Rather than seeking out a definition of the word 'God' that comes from nowhere, because it is (supposedly) 'obvious', I am going to turn to a characteristic practice by which the meaning of the word 'God' has been explored within a specific religious tradition. I am going to examine a focal scriptural text that both Jews and Christians have turned to repeatedly when pondering the nature of God: the story of Moses' encounter with the burning bush in Exodus 3. I am not approaching this text as a historical critic might, trying to identify the precise context in which it was written or tease out its likely meanings in that context. Rather, I am approaching this text as a participant in a tradition of theological thinkers and writers who have found in it the germ of ideas that have proved resilient and generative for their thinking about God, and who have continued to use this text as a sounding board for their ongoing exploration of God's nature and identity.[3] So, rather than asking what this text meant in whatever Near Eastern context historical research can place it in, I will be asking what meanings it yields when read in the context of this ongoing theological tradition – a tradition that has assumed that the one talked about in this text is the God of the whole Bible, the God of Christian life, the God of the whole creation,[4] and so assumes that it is a text that can be mined for themes and ideas that can to some extent be abstracted from the particular story it tells and fed into a more generalized discussion of the meaning of 'God'.[5]

[13]Moses said to God, 'If I come to the Israelites and say to them, "The God of your ancestors has sent me to you," and they ask me, "What is his name?" what shall I say to them?'

[14]God said to Moses, 'I am who I am.'

He said further, 'Thus you shall say to the Israelites, "I am has sent me to you."'

[15]God also said to Moses, 'Thus you shall say to the Israelites, "The Lord, the God of your ancestors, the God of Abraham, the God of Isaac, and the God of Jacob, has sent me to you": This is my name forever, and this my title for all generations.

[16]'Go and assemble the elders of Israel, and say to them, "The Lord, the God of your ancestors, the God of Abraham, of Isaac, and of Jacob, has appeared to me, saying: I have given heed to you and to what has been done to you in Egypt. [17]I declare that I will bring you up out of the misery of Egypt, to the land of the Canaanites, the Hittites, the Amorites, the Perizzites, the Hivites, and the Jebusites, a land flowing with milk and honey."'

Exodus 3.13–17

Exercise

Before reading on, think about this passage from Exodus. What answer or answers do you think it gives to the question, 'Who is God?' or 'What does "God" mean?'

Moses stands shoeless in front of the burning bush, receiving a terrifying commission to speak to Pharaoh on behalf of the Israelites – and their God. He anticipates the Israelites asking, 'What is this god's name?' but he is not worrying that they will simply be asking after an extra bit of information about a god they otherwise understand quite well. Moses is expecting them to ask which god is behind this mission, whether this god is friend or foe, and what kind of face this god turns towards them. The God of the burning bush gives Moses three kinds of answer.

1 'I am who I am,' says God. Whatever else it might mean, this is surely in part a claim that this is a God who is not going to be defined, grasped or tied down: this is a God who is free. The Israelites will not gain power over this God by learning how to place and define him; this God will remain in charge and out of their grasp. Who is this God? That's for God to decide; God will be just who God wants to be.

It is, in other words, not simply the Israelites' uncertainty or ignorance that

forces the question, 'Which God?' It is a question raised by this God's freedom
to transcend and exceed any definitions that the people are capable of producing. The only way to know who or what this God is will be to wait upon the
ways in which this God will make Godself known.

No tame lion

'One day you'll see him, and another you won't. He doesn't like to be tied down
... It's quite all right. He'll often drop in. Only you mustn't press him. He's wild,
you know. Not like a *tame* lion.'

Mr Beaver describing Aslan, in C. S. Lewis's
The Lion, the Witch and the Wardrobe.[6]

A few verses earlier, on first hearing the voice from the burning bush say,
'I am the God of your father, the God of Abraham ...', Moses 'hid his face, for
he was afraid to *look* at God' (v.6) – but he did not stop his ears. The freedom
that God declares in the name 'I am who I am' is allied with this privileging of
hearing God over *seeing* God. If you think about seeing something, it is easy to
think of yourself as in control, surveying from a good vantage point, inspecting and assessing. After all, you can look at something that is lying in front
of you passive and prone. If you think instead about hearing something, it is
much less easy to think of yourself as fully in control. You *wait* until you are
addressed, straining your ears but hearing nothing until the silence is broken
by the one for whom you are listening. The reality for which you are listening
has to be active. One way of paraphrasing the answer that God gives in verse
14 of this passage would therefore be 'God said to Moses, "You want to see
who I am? Listen!"' This is, after all, the God who has chosen to *speak* to Moses
from the burning bush, interrupting the settled pattern of Moses' life. And,
looking more broadly within the Old Testament, this is the God who *speaks* to
call the world into being, and whose word interrupts the lives of those called
to be prophets. This is a God who *addresses*, and Moses and the Israelites are
not to think of themselves as those who can 'take God into account' – cast
their eyes over God and fit God into their big picture – but rather as those who
are addressed and called to account by this God.

2 A little later on, God repeats the name that God had given right at the
beginning of the encounter: 'The Lord, the God of your ancestors, the God of
Abraham, the God of Isaac, and the God of Jacob'. God points back, in other
words, to the stories of the patriarchs, the chiefs of the tribe of the Hebrews
before they moved into Egypt. The declaration of God's freedom is matched
with a declaration of God's faithfulness – a declaration that allows the Israelites to know who this God truly is by looking to the stories of what this God
has done.

Note, however, that readers of this text who turn back to the tales of the
patriarchs will not find stories there that provide a detailed biography or portrayal of God, or in which God appears directly as a walk-on character (except

in Genesis 3). They will find, rather, stories of ancestors who were themselves repeatedly interrupted and addressed by God – and who heard, followed, struggled with and rebelled against this calling God. Moses and the Israelites are pointed to stories in which God is portrayed most often as the invisible and mysterious source of captivating and demanding address, and in which the true character of that address is seen most clearly in the messy lives of those who obey and fail to obey it.

Moses and the Israelites are to understand God as the one who addresses them, and as the one whose address has become visible in the interrupted and transformed lives of their ancestors.

Power games

There is another way of reading this declaration, and it is one we should not ignore. The deity of one particular human group – the group of Abraham, Isaac and Jacob – is here being claimed as the master of a broader landscape. Look! This God's writ runs even out here in the wilderness, away from the shrines of the homeland; this is a God capable of making his own shrines! And as the power and reach of this God is stressed, so the power and reach of those associated with this God is strengthened. At the time when this was written there were some in Israel who did not associate themselves with the God of Abraham, Isaac and Jacob – and one can imagine them feeling distinctly nervous about this bid for power. You can also imagine some in other nations hearing in it a potential claim on their territory by the descendants of Abraham, Isaac and Jacob. Or you could imagine, coming right up to date, some readers made distinctly uncomfortable by a text in which God declares himself for a succession of exclusively male leaders, and a people defined in terms of its relation to those leaders. And so you might hear a tension between the ungraspability of the God who 'will be what God will be' – the God who is not at the Israelites beck and call – and the usefulness of a God who is on 'our side'.

This is a theme to which we will be returning. The declaration of faithfulness – the declaration that God can in some way be reliably identified – is always *particular*: it is always made in language that belongs more to one group than another, always made in terms that are tangled up in relations of power between communities and individuals. That entanglement is the inevitable price of any claim about God's identifiability. It is when we consider the Christian identification of God in and with Jesus of Nazareth, and its implications for a world of multiple religions, that we will address this question most directly.[7]

---

3 I have suggested that God identifies Godself by a declaration of freedom, and by a declaration of faithfulness. I have skipped over one part of God's answer to Moses, however. Moses is to say to the Israelites, 'I am has *sent me to you.*' Moses is not to tell the Israelites about an interesting encounter that he had one day with a God who has little to do with them. Moses is not even to tell the Israelites an interesting fact about their own back-story: the stories by which this God identifies Godself are not just stories of far away and long ago.

To explain who has sent him, Moses is to tell the Israelites of a drama that is set to engulf them and drag them forward to a transformed future. After all, the self-identification that God provides to the Israelites spills over into promises about their future: 'I declare that I will bring you up out of the misery of Egypt, to ... a land flowing with milk and honey.'

You might say that the identification God gives to the Israelites at this point is deliberately incomplete. The Israelites will learn the identity of God not simply by paying attention to the stories of what God has done in the past, but by being caught up in a story that is still going on in the present and will lead them on into the future, as God guides them to the Promised Land. This faithful God is free to draw this people on further, to teach them more about who God is and who they should be in response. Remember, after all, that the revelation of God and the giving of the law on Mount Sinai – a revelation that is to take the Israelites into decisively new territory in their understanding of God – is an episode that this story has not yet reached, but towards which it is unstoppably rolling.

Knowledge of this God is not neatly wrapped up and delivered complete via Moses to the Israelites; it is in part *promised* to them – held out in front of them to lure them to the future.

Moses and the Israelites are to understand themselves as addressed, and as descendants of others whose interrupted and transformed lives have displayed the address of God. And they are to understand themselves as those who are in turn addressed by one who promises and commands, calling them on a journey to the Promised Land.

Blood and soil

In the light of the questions I raised earlier, we should not forget the fact that the promise made to the Israelites is one of land, and that the story in which they will be engulfed and which will lead them to this land is one of violent conquest. I happen to be writing these words amidst news reports of a war between Israel and Lebanon, and know that this conflict has some of its roots in different ideas about whose promised land Israel/Palestine is. I can't avoid asking, in this context, whether passages like Exodus 3 reveal Jewish and Christian claims about the identity of God to be irretrievably tied up with the contested claims on territory: the assertion of 'our' definition over 'theirs'.

Key points

- Knowing God is not, for Christian theology, a matter of getting a clear overview of God. It is a matter of knowing oneself to be addressed by one who is free and so cannot be tied down or boxed in.
- Knowing God is a matter of knowing oneself to be addressed by a God whose address is displayed in the lives of those God has interrupted and transformed.[8]

- Knowing God is a matter of knowing oneself to be addressed by a God who will be known more truly as one responds and is transformed.

Called to love

[7]Beloved, let us love one another, because love is from God; everyone who loves is born of God and knows God. [8]Whoever does not love does not know God, for God is love. [9]God's love was revealed among us in this way: God sent his only Son into the world so that we might live through him. [10]In this is love, not that we loved God but that he loved us and sent his Son to be the atoning sacrifice for our sins. [11]Beloved, since God loved us so much, we also ought to love one another. [12]No one has ever seen God; if we love one another, God lives in us, and his love is perfected in us. [13]By this we know that we abide in him and he in us, because he has given us of his Spirit.

[14]And we have seen and do testify that the Father has sent his Son as the Saviour of the world. [15]God abides in those who confess that Jesus is the Son of God, and they abide in God. [16]So we have known and believe the love that God has for us.

God is love, and those who abide in love abide in God, and God abides in them.

[17]Love has been perfected among us in this: that we may have boldness on the day of judgement, because as he is, so are we in this world. [18]There is no fear in love, but perfect love casts out fear; for fear has to do with punishment, and whoever fears has not reached perfection in love. [19]We love because he first loved us. [20]Those who say, 'I love God', and hate their brothers or sisters, are liars; for those who do not love a brother or sister whom they have seen, cannot love God whom they have not seen. [21]The commandment we have from him is this: those who love God must love their brothers and sisters also.

1 John 4.7–21

Exercise

Before reading on, think about this passage from 1 John. What answer or answers do you think it gives to the question, 'Who is God?' (or 'What does "God" mean?') What difference should it make to the answer you were asked to come up with in preparation for this Chapter? Can you see any connections with the Exodus passage?

The whole of 1 John can be read as another attempt to answer the question 'Who is God?' – and the connected question, 'Who should God's people be in response?' After all, the epistle begins with a declaration of the identity of God ('God is light' – 1.5) and finishes by reaffirming God's true identity and repudiating misidentifications: 'He is the true God and eternal life. Little children, keep yourself from idols' (5.20–21). The present passage contains something

of the same interplay between 'freedom' and 'faithfulness' that we saw in
Exodus 3. On the one hand, John insists that 'No one has ever seen God', and
we once again hear that the knowledge of God that God has made available
is not the same sort of knowledge as one might get by inspecting and gaining
an overview of some finite object. On the other hand, this passage affirms that
knowledge of God is possible because God's address becomes visible in the
stories of those who have been shaped by it. Here, however, it is not the varied
responses of the patriarchs to God's address that are in view, but what John
believes is the perfect response of Jesus Christ. It is because of Jesus Christ
that 1 John can begin with a flush of confidence in the knowability of God; this
letter treats of a truth that has not only been 'heard', but 'looked at' and even
'touched'. The author has encountered God's address in the flesh. And, as the
letter proceeds, it becomes clear that what he has encountered has a very specific character. The true God, for John, the one whom he has encountered in
Jesus Christ, has become tangible as *love*.

Love and justice

One should beware drawing the definition of this love too narrowly. Jesus said
'You shall love the Lord your God with all your heart, and with all your soul, and
with all your mind' and 'You shall love your neighbour as yourself' (Matthew
22.37–39; Mark 12.29–31; cf. Luke 10.27), but he presented this dual command as a summary of 'all the law and the prophets', and was quoting Leviticus 19.18. That passage from Leviticus is itself the climax of a passage that
deals with defrauding one's neighbour, mistreatment of the blind, slander,
legal impartiality – all sorts of matters of *justice*. When we speak about love in
this kind of context, we are not simply referring to a certain kind of feeling, or
even to the kind of relationship you might have with those who are especially
close to you: it also has to do with how you treat *anyone*. That is why I will, from
now on, speak interchangeably about 'love' and about 'love and justice'; I am
trying to keep this broader definition of love in play.

We need to tread carefully at this point, however, in order not to oversimplify
1 John's complex claims. Consider the following steps.

1 Instead of thinking one could know God in the way one knows ordinary
   objects, one might first move on to thinking that one might know God simply by knowing *about* what God has done – in this case, by knowing about
   God's loving address to the world in Jesus of Nazareth.
2 Further reflection on this passage might suggest a second step, however.
   One might realize that, for John, one truly knows how God has addressed
   the world in Jesus Christ only when one knows *oneself* to be addressed –
   only, that is, when the knowledge becomes self-involving.[9]
3 Still more reflection on John's words might suggest a third step. It seems
   that, for John, to know God is not simply to know about God's loving
   address. And it is not simply to recognize oneself as addressed lovingly
   by God. For one to know God is for one to respond to that address and be

transformed by it. One truly knows God only when one has God's love for the world working through one. One knows God by becoming in this world what God is Godself (v.17).

In other words, the knowledge of God that John describes does not take the same form that knowing a fact or believing a theory take. Rather, John is talking about his readers being transformed until they become, as it were, conduits for the reality they are trying to know – until not just their minds, but their whole lives get won into correspondence with God. To 'know' God is to become a participant in the same love and justice that God has shown to the world in Christ. This is a reality that a person knows – *only* knows – when it meets her, captivates her and begins working in and through her.

Exclusive Love?

Lest we think that this New Testament passage poses none of the questions that we saw in the Old Testament passage discussed on page 35, we should note the strong sense of separation from the world that pervades John's letters. Does John speak of a God who is known by those who find an *exclusive* love working within them – a love restricted to this specific community, and kept from the wider world? This is, after all, a letter that says 'Do not love the world!' (1 John 2.15) and condemns as liars and antichrists those who have left the community.[10]

Key points

- For John, to know God is to know that the world is addressed lovingly by God in Jesus of Nazareth.
- To know God is to know *oneself* to be addressed in this way, and to know oneself to be called to share in this love.
- More than that, to know God is to respond to that call, and by becoming loving to become like God.

God's music

What does it mean to say that one can know a reality only by living in a way that responds to it, or by participating in it, or by having it working through one? We can mean all sorts of different things when we say 'I know x'. I know that the Battle of Hastings took place in 1066; I know I have a slight headache coming on; and I know some of my students quite well. Is knowledge of God like the first of these? Does it have at its heart one's ability to provide a correct account – a collection of true statements about God? Is it like the second? Does it have at its heart some kind of 'internal' awareness? Is it like the third? Does it have at its heart involvement in an ongoing story of interactions between oneself and God, and knowledge of God's similar stories with others in the past?

The Johannine ideas that I've been exploring suggest that it is not quite like any of these (even if it may include elements of all of them). It suggests another model of knowing – one that is rather like the kind of knowing that takes place when one knows a piece of music, if one sings or plays it. The piece of music is, after all, something objective: it has an existence beyond me; I have to learn it and it makes sense to say that I can get it wrong. As I learn it, however, the distance between me and the piece of music starts shrinking. I can work on the piece until performing it 'becomes second nature' (which means, if you take it literally, 'until it becomes a new definition of who I am'). And while performing the piece remains something that *I* am doing, I can become so caught up in the piece of music that there's almost a sense in which it is the music that plays me. I become an instrument on which this piece of music plays itself out. I might start finding it difficult to know how to relate claims about what I do to claims about what the piece of music does – how the power of the music works on me, shaping me to itself. In the end, I might say that I become one of the ways in which this piece of music is present and active in the world.

Becoming the music

'Every rehearsal of the Maggiore Quartet begins with a very plain, very slow three-octave scale on all four instruments in unison: sometimes major, as in our name, sometimes minor, depending on the key of the first piece we are to play. No matter how fraught our lives have been over the last couple of days, no matter how abrasive our disputes about people or politics, or how visceral our differences about what we are to play and how we are to play it, it reminds us that we are, when it comes to it, one. We try not to look at each other when we play this scale; no one appears to lead. Even the first upbeat is merely breathed by Piers, not indicated by any movement of his head. When I play this I release myself into the spirit of the quartet. I become the music of the scale. I mute my will, I free my self.'

Michael, in Vikram Seth's *An Equal Music*[11]

'As [God] is, so are we in this world' (1 John 4.17). If one follows John, then one might think of God as being like a melody playing eternally, and of knowledge of God as consisting in one's ability to play that melody oneself – or, rather, as the discovery that one can *be played by* that melody, becoming an aspect of that melody's presence in the world. To know the God who lovingly addresses the world is to become one who loves with a godly love – or, rather, it is to have God's love and justice become what is happening in and through one. To know God is to be won by God into a godly life.

This is a way of thinking about knowledge that blurs the distinction between *knowing how* and *knowing that*. I know *how* to ride a bike; I know *that* my desk is made from pine. If knowledge of God is as I have been suggesting, however, then to know *that* God is love (to know what God is like, what sort of reality God is) and to have been taught *how* to live a godly life are inseparable, almost identical. One has learnt something about the melody that is God only when one has learnt to have that something present in one's performance of the melody. Conversely, everything one learns about performing the melody more truly is a form of learning about the melody itself. One cannot separate learning how to live a godly life from learning the identity of God. To know God is to be caught up in the love and justice that are God's life – to 'become participants in the divine nature' (2 Peter 1.4).

Divinization

'The end of faith is the real revelation of what is believed. And the real revelation of what is believed is the ineffable embrace of it, which is brought about in proportion to the faith of each person. The embrace of what is believed is the return of the believer home to his origin, which is now his end. But the return of the believer home to his origin, as to his end, is the fulfilment of his longing. Now the fulfilment of his longing is the rest of the loving heart in eternal motion around the beloved. But the rest of the loving heart in eternal motion around the beloved is eternal, immediate delight, ... participation in the supernatural blessings of God. And this is the forming of those who participate, into the likeness of what they participate in; but such a likening consists in the actively realized identity of the participants with what they participate in, which comes to its fullness with the likeness itself. And this identity ... is divinization.'

Maximus the Confessor, *Quaestiones ad Thalassium*.[12]

'Here my exalted vision lost its power.
But now my will and my desire, like wheels revolving
with an even motion, were turning with
the Love that moves the sun and all the other stars.'

Dante, *Paradiso*[13]

Key points

- For Christian theology, one cannot separate learning the identity of God from the taking on of godly life.
- Knowledge of God is participation in the life of God.

God is love

Of course, my musical analogy can only be pushed so far. In particular, it is not very good at capturing the sense of God's freedom – the living and active independence of the one who says 'I am who I am.' Perhaps instead I should augment the metaphor somewhat and add the *composer* of the piece of music into the picture. That would enable me to speak of the music of God's life now as the free action of a divine composer, and I would be able to say not just that I know God when I 'become the music' that God has composed, but also that I know God by *acknowledging* that this music is a gift, coming to me with love from a free source – acknowledging that it has been addressed to me, and that I am therefore being caught up in a music that is *someone's*.

Thanksgiving

For Christian theology, knowledge of God involves both living the life of love into which God calls one and acknowledging the source of that life. That does not mean, however, that it has a thoroughly practical aspect (loving), coupled with a thoroughly theoretical aspect (acknowledgement), because the characteristic form that this acknowledgement takes is not some intellectual acceptance, but *thanksgiving*.

I recently had a conversation with a Christian friend who said that she was not yet praying with her three-year-old daughter because her daughter could not yet understand what 'God' meant. She thought that, given this inevitable lack of understanding, 'praying' wouldn't be real; it would all be a game, a pretence – not really prayer at all.

My wife and I explained that we *did* play the praying game with our two-year-old every night, using a standard prayer that begins 'Dear God, thank you for Bridget's day; thank you for x; thank you for y; thank you for z ...' – with the x, y and z being suggested by Bridget. (A typical list might include 'thank you for dinner, thank you for ice cream', and so on).

Yes, it is a game; and no, this two-year-old did not understand what 'God' meant in any sense that would have satisfied our friend. Our argument, however, was that this game was precisely *how* our daughter was learning what 'God' means. She understood 'thanking' pretty well, as an expression of some kind of delight at things that have happened during the day; she was beginning to understand the idea of thanking *someone*, so that 'God' was beginning to mean for her 'the one to whom we say thank you for anything and everything'. And that, it seems to us, is a very large part indeed of what is involved in understanding what 'God' means. By learning to thank, Bridget was learning the nature of God.

Exercise

What else could we have been doing with or saying to our toddler to help her learn what 'God' means?

In order to do justice to John's insights, however, I would need to say that God does not simply compose or perform this music; he *is* this music – and at this point the analogy begins to slip from my fingers. After all, John does not just say that God loves, but that God *is* love. In other words, the conviction of this text appears to be not simply that one does (or could) know lots about God already, and might then find out one extra thing, that this God who one already knows is *also* a God who loves. No, for this text the primary thing, the controlling thing, the first thing, in some ways the *only* thing one knows about God is this love and justice.

Suppose I were telling you about the spring of a mountain stream. I might tell you that this spring was located on a patch of moorland and emerged from a certain crack in the rock. If I were telling you how to find the spring, I might say, 'Look out for the rock that is heavy, limestone, cracked and shaped like a pulpit; *that's* the spring.' I would be saying that, in addition to having all those other properties (being heavy, made of limestone and so on) this rock is *also* the source of the water. Of course, you might respond (if you were a pedant) by saying, 'No, you don't mean that: the rock itself is not the spring; it is *the crack in the rock* that is the spring.' I, trying to be even more pedantic, might answer, 'Not even the crack; the rock and the crack in it are simply where we *find* the spring; the spring itself is the water bubbling up in that place.'[14] The spring, logically speaking, is simply the start of the stream; the spring is that-without-which-there-would-be-no-stream. The spring *is* (the beginning of) the stream, and the stream *is* (the continuation of) the spring. And, of course, if we are being this pedantic then the spring itself cannot be described as heavy, limestone, cracked, or shaped like a pulpit, because we can't say that the bubbling-up-of-the-water is heavy, or limestone, or any of those things. The only words we will properly use to describe the characteristics of the spring will be words that describe the emerging-of-the-water – the spring is 'fast', perhaps, or 'pure', or 'constant'.

John's usage seems to be a little like this. He is not telling us that (as we all know) the word 'God' means an all-powerful, all-knowing being – and that Christians believe that this powerful, knowing being is *also* the source of the love that they have encountered. He is telling us that the word 'God' refers to the emerging-of-this-love; God is that-without-which-there-would-be-no-love. God *is* this love, and this love *is* God. Any other qualities that can be predicated of this God will be qualities of the-emerging-of-this-love. This is, for John, simply what the word 'God' means – and at this stage it is still an open question as to whether it will be appropriate to say of this source any of the other things that people have wanted to say about 'God' – an open question whether we will want to go on and say that this emerging-of-love, this spring of love, is all-powerful, or all-knowing, or personal, or whatever. In the beginning, Christian theology knows only one thing about God: God *is* love.

To the question, 'Who is God', I am suggesting that the proper Christian answer is not, in the first place, 'God is an omnipotent, omniscient, omnipresent being' but 'Look at the love and justice that pours forth in Christ, and that are, however weakly and inadequately, welling up in our lives and in the world. Well, God is the source of that: that love and justice *is* God's life, pouring through us. And yes, that life is, we believe, invincible and it is present everywhere, so we might start using words like "omnipotent" and "omnipresent" – but only because the first thing that we say is "God is love."'

The two powers of God

There was, in late medieval theology, a popular way of explaining God's power that got dangerously close to denying this absolute priority of love. Theologians like the medieval English Franciscan William of Ockham spoke of God's free decision to enter into a covenant with the world, and distinguished between God's 'absolute power' (*potentia absoluta*), the ability of God to choose whether or not to enter into this covenant, and God's 'ordained power' (*potentia ordinata*), the freedom of action that God has left Godself within this chosen covenant. According to Ockham and others, while God is at heart absolutely free and absolutely powerful (*potentia absoluta*), God has used that freedom to decide for a course of action that now limits what options are available to God (*potentia ordinata*): God's freedom is restricted, but only by God's own free decision.

At first sight, this way of explaining matters, though somewhat technical, may sound like it is simply a spelling out of what is involved in the whole idea of God 'entering into a covenant': one must be able to speak of God both as free to enter into the covenant and (God's having done so) of God as bound by it.

While this is probably an unobjectionable distinction if, by it, one means that it is possible to imagine other ways in which God could have expressed God's love, it can be taken in another, more worrying way. It can instead suggest that love was a choice made by God, which God could have made otherwise, and that behind love there simply stands an absolutely unrestricted power of God – a power that could equally well have shown itself in hatred, had God chosen differently. God is a composer who has chosen to write a love melody, but God could equally well have chosen to compose a music of spite. To put it colloquially but appropriately, the danger of this 'two powers' theology is the suggestion that, deep down, God could have been whatever the hell God chose.[15]

Key points

- The word 'God' in Christian theology refers first and foremost to the source of the love that addresses the world in Jesus Christ.
- One cannot separate the identity of God from the stream of love into which one is drawn by this address.
- Praise and thanksgiving are the characteristic forms in which God is acknowledged as the source of that stream.

Learning to love

To know the Christian God is to know oneself to be addressed lovingly by God in Jesus Christ. More than that, to know the Christian God is to know oneself called by that address to become loving. And even more than that, to know the Christian God is to become loving, with this same love. One knows God by having the love and justice of God that poured forth in Christ welling up within one's life.

For Christian theology, then, God's loving address in Christ is the criterion for one's own love. John, after all, paints his readers as those who *should* love perfectly but who as yet love imperfectly, and who therefore need to learn to love better. And he believes that they can learn the character of true love, of godly love, in Christ – because the address that God made to the world in Christ was both a *call* to love and justice, and a revelation of the true *meaning* of love and justice.

Penitence

In the church in which I grew up, the liturgical introduction leading up to prayers of penitence included a quotation from 1 John 1.8:

> If we say we have no sin, we deceive ourselves, and the truth is not in us. If we confess our sins, God is faithful and just, and will forgive us our sins and cleanse us from all unrighteousness.[16]

This is no accident. If the kind of knowledge of God that John speaks of involves both loving with a Christlike love, and also recognizing the present inadequacy of one's love, then it will be marked by *penitence*. You might even say that prayers of penitence are one of the characteristic forms in which Christian knowledge of God is embodied.

The idea of 'learning to love' might seem an odd one. It is easy to think that one either loves someone or does not, and that there is not much one can do about it if one does not.[17] However, although that might be true of 'being in love', it is not true if one takes a broader and deeper definition of love. Consider, for instance, my love for my children. Of course, there is one sense in which that love is simply *there*: a matter beyond my will and control. There are all sorts of ways, however, in which I do need to *learn* to love them. I might need to learn, for instance, that some of what I think of as lovingly doing my best for them is actually my attempt to live my life again through them. I might need to learn that my supposedly loving refusal to say 'no' to them is actually damaging them, and at root a form of selfishness. I might need to learn that some of my ways of showing love to them are actually fed and distorted by my need to get certain kinds of responses from them, in order to feel valued. The list could go on: there are all sorts of ways in which I might need to learn that I have mistaken the nature of true love for them, and need to be taught it.

Exercise

Try reading Jane Austen's *Emma*,[18] and watch how Emma learns that what she takes to be her kind and thoughtful care – her love – for her friend Harriet is in fact a form of selfishness.

It is because love in this fuller sense needs to be learnt that this passage from 1 John – and, in general, the whole epistle from which it comes – insists on keeping together the knowledge of God that its readers will find by loving one another and the knowledge of God that they will find in the recognition of God's love in Christ. It keeps flitting from one to the other – saying, for instance, that we have God abiding in us if we abide in love, and that we abide in God if we confess that Jesus Christ is from God. To believe in Christ and to learn to love are not, for John's theology, two separate things. It therefore makes no sense to say, 'Why couldn't John have said all this wonderful stuff about love without harping on all the time about "belief in Christ" as well?' For John, commitment to love cannot be separated from discipleship to the Christ who teaches the world love's true nature.

God is, according to this theology, the reality that one knows – that one *only* knows – when one has God's love working on, in and through one. But the journey towards godly love is an endless one, and it is a journey on which Christians believe that they are led by Christ's constant tutelage.

I have been suggesting that Christian knowledge of God should not be thought of as being like simple knowledge of a fact, nor like knowledge of a theory, nor even like knowledge of an experience. The reality of God is not like other realities, and so the God is not known in the way that other realities are known. I have suggested instead that a person can be said to know God only if that person's whole life is being drawn into conformity to God – becoming loving as God is loving, and just as God is just. More precisely, I have suggested that knowledge of God does not simply consist in a static resemblance between God's love and the believer's love, but that it consists in the ongoing process by which the believer's love is actively shaped into ever deeper conformity to God. As (in one's own particular situation) one learns to love, as one learns justice, one is learning the nature of God.

Christian knowledge of God, I have argued, can therefore be thought of as an interplay between:

- the believer's grateful recognition of God as the one who loves her and as the one who is the ultimate source of her love;
- the believer's active living out of godly love and justice in the world;
- the believer's penitent recognition of God's loving address in Christ as the criterion for her love; and
- the believer's discovery that God's loving address in Jesus Christ is the spur to ever deeper love and justice.

One might say that in knowing God Christians know something *unplumbable* – a reality that they can never finish exploring, and so a reality of which there can be no final map, no finished representation. The only kind of representation that one can have of such a God is found in the moving image of lives exploring ever deeper, learning ever more of God's love and justice; God is known as the one to whom such lives are the appropriate response, and of whom such lives are the only true representation. God's life is the life into which these lives are drawn.

Key points

- To know God is to be caught up by God into the love and justice that are God's life, and to acknowledge the source of that love.
- Love needs to be learnt and, for Christian theology, Christ is the supreme teacher.
- Prayers of penitence will be one characteristic expression of the process by which love is learnt.

Knowing in particular

One only performs a piece of music by performing it in particular ways at particular times and places. Of course, there are plenty of generalities involved in such performances: one learns things about notes and scales and keys and rhythms that are the same anywhere and everywhere. But when it comes to an actual performance, the event in which it can truly be said that one knows the piece of music, all those generalities become subservient to the particular occasion, shaped by particular circumstances in ways that are unrepeatable. For most traditional forms of music, after all, it does not make sense to think that there could be a final performance of a piece, a performance so 'accurate' or complete that the piece would never need to be performed live again.

Similarly, if knowledge of God consists in living a godly life, a life of Christlike love and justice, then one only lives such a life by living it in particular ways at particular times and places. Of course, there might be all sorts of generalities involved, but in the end knowledge of God consists in the particular ways in which God's life is lived by particular people in their own place in the world.

What it means to learn Christlike love will look one way for a middle-class mother of two in Nairobi; it will look another for a Palestinian teenager in the West Bank; it will look another for an isolated single pensioner in Detroit, it will look another way for the abused daughter of a paedophile in São Paulo; it will look another for the English vicar of a large set of rural parishes; it will look another for the owner of a garment factory in Beijing. In each of those widely differing, infinitely complex lives, learning to love under the tutelage of Christ will be a long, costly and perhaps bewildering process; it will involve engagement with the realities and constraints of the context in ways that people outside will be in no position to understand fully. It will involve the reshaping of each person's particular individual history, and particular psychology; it will involve each of those people learning how to respond to and live with particular others who stand in specific relations to him or her; it will involve doing this in the context of a particular history, a particular culture, a particular political setting. Love and justice are learnt as particular people learn to love particular others in particular contexts.

Of course there will be all sorts of connections and commonalities between what love means for each of these people; of course there will be much that they can learn from each other, and much that they can learn from those who have thought about and explored love in the past. There is nevertheless no getting away from the need for each person to learn in his or her context, amongst the people close to him or her. Each person will learn in ways that will have a good deal to do with personal growth and development, with the task of building working friendships and family relationships, and with larger scale questions of social responsibility and political engagement.

In what does a piece of music's existence in the world consist? In a score, written down carefully and stored in a composer's archive? No: it consists in the multiple performances of the piece of music in thousands of different venues and times – performances that often feed off each other, as people learn to perform by hearing others perform and by reflecting on their own earlier performances, but performances that are nevertheless in the end all different. Just so, we might say that the kind of knowledge of God spoken of by John properly consists in the whole gamut of particular ways in which people live God's life in the world, and in their interconnection.

All this means that, if one wants to find experts in the knowledge of God, one shouldn't necessarily turn to academic theologians. Those who know God most profoundly are the 'saints' – those who have been so taken over by the music of God that their whole lives resonate to it; those who have been led deeper into the discovery of how to live the life of Christ in their own place and time. The expertise of academic theologians is an entirely secondary matter: it is a commentary upon such true 'expertise'.[19]

Filming performance

Imagine a television programme following a group of musicians as they prepared for a performance – a programme designed to provide insights into the nature of musical performance. It might mix interviews with players, clips from earlier performances, illustrated discussion of various basics about how performance works. Watching the programme, however, would not itself make you a performer; it would not even demonstrate that you wanted to become a performer. And similarly, to say that knowledge of God is inseparably bound up with the living of godly lives, and to say that this book is about knowledge of God, does not mean that you have to be committed to a godly life in order to read it and understand it, nor that your life will be made more godly if you do read and understand it. It does mean, however, that this book can't try to deal with the 'theoretical' aspects of the knowledge of God in abstraction from real godly lives, any more than the television programme could be about musical performance without ever looking at musical performers. If it is about the knowledge of God as understood in Christian theology, then it must be about godly lives.

Theology's proper currency, then, will not consist so much of theories as of *biographies*. Supremely, Christian theology looks to Jesus Christ as its holy book; but it also looks to the lives of all those individuals and communities who have heard the call of this God, who have begun to learn Christlike love and justice, and who therefore display the identity of God. Everything else is commentary.

Augustine of Hippo

Chad Pecknold writes this of Saint Augustine of Hippo (354–430):

There are few lives that have had as much attention as the life of Saint Augustine of Hippo. This is because he sought a vision of God that was inseparable from lived reality – including the reality of his own life. In his *Confessions*, Augustine recounts his childhood, his adolescence, his sexual life, his relationships with friends and family, and through all of this, he seeks to recognize and make known his relationship with God. His account in the *Confessions* of who God is is inseparable from his account of his own life.

A central point of Augustine's theology is that one's vision of God is inextricably united to a whole way of life in which human desire is well-ordered. To know God truly is to desire – to love – rightly, a matter not simply of correct ideas but of godly life, individually and corporately. It is not surprising, then, that Augustine's theological descriptions are infused with narrative: the narratives of his own life, the narratives of the Roman Empire – and pre-eminently, the narratives of Scripture.

Augustine learned to understand his own story not by being provided with lessons in abstract theology, but in the light of the scriptural story. From very early on, at the age of 18, he struggled to read the Latin Vulgate version of the Bible, and found it rhetorically vulgar and uncultured. His extraordinary intellectual abilities were more attracted to Cicero and Virgil, Plotinus and Porphyry. His intellectual journey was such that he advanced to become an ambitious professor of Rhetoric (the training ground for the best imperial politicians) through teaching posts in Carthage, Rome and finally, in Milan. It was in Milan, however, that Augustine came under the influence of Saint Ambrose, the bishop of that city, whose preaching of the scriptural narrative so impressed the 30-year-old that he began radically to question his life. In the summer of 386, Augustine wept in a Milanese garden with some friends, despairing of a life that seemed to him disordered. He heard a small child singing a nursery song, rhythmically chanting '*tolle lege, tolle lege*', which means 'take up and read, take up and read.' Augustine interpreted these words as a sign of God commanding him to 'take up and read' the Scriptures. And so he did. And he tells us that the key verse impressed upon him by God was 'put on the Lord Jesus Christ' (Romans 13.13–14) – a command, that is, to put on not a set of ideas but a life. Through this text, truth is revealed, and Augustine finds peace with God, finds that the darkness of his doubts, his anxieties, and his tears are relieved, and finds a scriptural 'light' infusing his heart and mind. Suddenly he could read the Scriptures in a new way, and effectively read his life in a new way too. What was this new way? What did 'putting on the Lord Jesus Christ' mean? It meant hearing God's word not as abstract philosophy inadequately couched in messy and vulgar stories, but as revolving around the life of Jesus Christ, who is God's Word made flesh, made life, for the sake of our salvation. Augustine came to believe that putting on this identity – being shaped into its likeness – transforms how we read, and enables us to participate in a therapy of desire which can teach us how to live lives (individual and communal) that perform God's love for the world.[20]

If we return to the question of the first chapter, then, and ask what sense Christians can and should make of their lives, a first approximation would be to say that Christians see themselves as being drawn, in all their particular locations in time and space, into the life of God – or, more fully, that they find themselves being drawn into that Christlike love and justice which are the life of God. That is, I am suggesting, in broadest outline the plot of the story that Christians can use to make sense of the messy data of their communal and individual lives: they are on a journey into the life of God.

Key point

- For Christian theology, knowledge of God is seen only in particular lives lived in particular contexts – the lives of those who have heard the call of God, and have begun to learn Christlike love.

Going further

1 The unknowability of God is a theme that has been explored most fully in mystical theology – that central strand of classic Christian theology that has concerned itself with precisely these questions of God's unknowability and the possibility of participation in God's life. I have already mentioned Mark McIntosh's *Mystical Theology* (Oxford: Blackwell, 1998), which is a good introduction; Denys Turner's *The Darkness of God: Negativity in Christian Mysticism* (Cambridge: Cambridge University Press, 1998) is a difficult but illuminating exploration if you want to go deeper.

2 The idea of participation in God's life – divinization or *theosis* – is an unfamiliar one to many modern Western Christians. It is, however, deeply embedded in the Christian tradition. The Russell book that I cited in the introduction to this chapter provides the best survey of the origins of this way of thinking – Jewish, biblical and patristic – but for some glimpses of *theosis* in other contexts, see Carl E. Braaten and Robert W. Jenson (eds), *Union with Christ: The New Finnish Interpretation of Luther* (Grand Rapids, MI: Eerdmans, 1998); A. M. Allchin, *Participation: A Forgotten Strand in Anglican Tradition* (London: DLT, 1988); and Michael J. Christensen, 'Theosis and Sanctification: John Wesley's Reformulation of a Patristic Doctrine', *Wesleyan Theological Journal* 31.2 (1996), available online at the Wesley Center Online, http://wesley.nnu.edu/wesleyan_theology/theojrnl/31–35/31-2-4.htm.

3 Is all this talk of 'God' *simply* a way in which Christians make sense of their lives and their world? Would answering 'yes' take us in the direction of theological non-realism, denying that there is any straightforward sense in which God is a reality prior to Christian sense-making, to which that sense-making must conform itself? Do I fall into the 'theological realist' camp if I say that Christians can't but make sense of their lives as not *just* their lives, and their world as not *just* their world, but have to make sense of them as given, held and loved? The issues here are complex ones, but a good introduction to the debate can be found in Colin Crowder (ed.), *God and Reality: Essays in Christian Non-Realism* (London: Mowbray, 1997) and

an impressive response in Andrew Moore, *Realism and Christian Faith: God, Grammar and Meaning* (Cambridge: Cambridge University Press, 2003).

4 If you want to take further my comments about theology's proper currency being biography, it is worth tracking down a copy of James W. McClendon's *Biography as Theology: How Life Stories Can Remake Today's Theology* (Nashville, TN: Abingdon, 1974). He not only presents four biographies, but reflects carefully on what theological use can be made of them. As David Burrell puts it in a review, 'McClendon's conceptual point is that religious affirmations take their meaning from the manner in which communities show they can be lived out, and that communities take heart and direction from those individuals who dare to embody what they proclaim.'[21]

Notes

1 For some interesting approaches to that question, see Denys Turner, *Faith, Reason and the Existence of God* (Cambridge: Cambridge University Press, 2004) and Michael J. Buckley, *At the Origins of Modern Atheism* (New Haven: Yale University Press, 1987) and its sequel, *Denying and Disclosing God: The Ambiguous Progress of Modern Atheism* (New Haven: Yale University Press, 2004).

2 This is why the appropriate reaction to, say, the attempts to disprove the existence of God of a prominent critic of theology like Richard Dawkins in *The God Delusion* (London: Bantam, 2006), is to ask, 'What *is* he talking about?' It is far from clear that he's talking about the God portrayed in Christian theology – and at very least that is a question that needs to be examined before the strength of his critique can be judged.

3 See, for example, the role that it plays in Thomas Aquinas, *Summa Theologiae*, I.13.11; available online in the 1920 translation by the Fathers of the English Dominican Province, at New Advent, http://www.newadvent.org/summa/1013.htm#11. For a similar Jewish approach, see Alexander Broadie, 'Maimonides on the Great Tautology: Exodus 3.14', *Scottish Journal of Theology* 47.4 (1994), pp. 473–88. See also Janet Martin Soskice, 'Athens and Jerusalem: Alexandria and Edessa: Is There a Metaphysics of Scripture', *International Journal of Systematic Theology* 8.3 (2006), pp. 149–62, esp. pp. 150–1.

4 This is not a trivial assumption. Whether the God of Moses and the rest of the Hebrew Bible was to be identified with the God of Jesus Christ and the New was a matter of acrimonious debate in the early centuries of Christianity. See my discussion of Gnosticism in Chapter 7, p. 178, and of Marcion in Chapter 16, p. 382.

5 This is such a familiar way of using scriptural texts, at least for anyone that has spent time listening to sermons or attending Bible study groups, that it is easy to lose sight of its being a specific hermeneutical practice, that makes sense on the basis of quite specific theological assumptions. To someone who does not share those assumptions – say, an atheist scholar of Near Eastern historical texts – it is bound to look highly dubious.

6 C. S. Lewis, *The Lion, the Witch and the Wardrobe*, (London: Lions, 1980), p. 166 (ch.17).

7 See Chapter 12, pp. 302–4 below.

8 Knowing oneself to be addressed is not a matter of each individual hearing a literal voice from God, or even having some mysterious personal experience that seems tantamount to hearing such a personal address. On the one hand, it has to do with living with, and learning to name God from, a lot of biblical and traditional stories

about God addressing individuals and communities (whatever one thinks about the literal truth behind those stories); on the other hand, it has to do with a sense, however ambiguous, uncertain and undramatic it might be, that one simply can't get away from taking the God of those stories seriously, as the God of one's own life.

9 See Donald Evans, *The Logic of Self-Involvement* (London: SCM Press, 1963) for a lengthy discussion of how doctrines or religious statements are not 'flat constatives' (i.e. abstract claims about what is true) but are self-involving (i.e. necessarily also claims about what is true *for me*).

10 For more on the Johannine community, see Raymond Brown, *The Community of the Beloved Disciple: The Lifes, Loves and Hates of an Individual Church in New Testament Times*, 2nd edn (Mahwah, NJ: Paulist Press, 1999).

11 Vikram Seth, *An Equal Music* (London: Orion, 1999), p. 12.

12 Maximus the Confessor, *Quaestiones ad Thalassium* 59, quoted in Hans Urs von Balthasar, *Cosmic Liturgy: The Universe According to Maximus the Confessor*, tr. Brian E. Daley (San Francisco: Ignatius, 2003 [from German 3rd edn, 1988]), pp. 170–1.

13 Dante Alighieri, *Paradiso* 33.142–5, tr. Robert and Jean Hollander, available at the Princeton Dante Project, http://etcweb.princeton.edu/dante/pdp/.

14 I do sometimes have conversations a little like this, strangely enough.

15 For a brief history of the distinction, see David Steinmetz, *Calvin in Context* (Oxford: Oxford University Press, 1995), pp. 42–5.

16 The Church of England *Alternative Service Book 1980* (Newgate: William Clowes, 1980), p. 48: Morning Prayer ¶3.

17 For a typical example, see Mike Newell's film, *Four Weddings and a Funeral* (Channel Four, Polygram and Working Title, 1994); for details, see the Internet Movie Database, http://uk.imdb.com/title/tt0109831/. Fiona (Kristin Scott-Thomas) nurses a hopeless passion for the central character, Charles (Hugh Grant). But she knows that he does not love her, and that there is nothing he or she can do about it. Any suggestion that he might *learn* to love her would be a transparently forlorn gambit on her part.

18 Jane Austen, *Emma* (London: A. Bertrand, 1815); available online at Project Gutenberg, http://www.gutenberg.org/etext/158. Alternatively, you could watch the film adaptation with Gwynneth Paltrow in the title role: Douglas McGrath, *Emma* (Miramax, 1996), see the Internet Movie Database http://uk.imdb.com/title/tt0116191/, or the television adaptation with Kate Beckinsale: Diarmuid Lawrence, *Emma* (A&E Television, 1996), see http://uk.imdb.com/title/tt0118308/.

19 It is therefore (somewhat uncomfortably) quite appropriate for you to ask whether I and other academic theologians are so unmusical as to be deaf guides to the music that the saints play.

20 Written for this book by C. C. Pecknold.

21 David Burrell, Review of James W. McClendon, *Biography as Theology, Journal of the American Academy of Religion* 43.3 (1975), p. 624.

3

Speaking of God

In Chapter 2, I argued that Christians can make sense of their lives, individually and corporately, as journeys on which they are being drawn deeper into the life of God, and in Chapter 4 I will explore some ways in which that basic claim can be expanded and enriched. This chapter, however, is a pause for clarification, and for the introduction of some distinctions and terminology that should make the way through the next chapter easier. I am going to look at different kinds of language that Christians use to speak about God and, in particular, examine the question of how Christians can speak about God at all without falling into idolatry.

I am going to

- suggest that, for Christian theology, God is in one sense strictly unknowable, but that in another sense God makes Godself known;
- claim that there are three broad types of Christian language about God: pragmatic, propositional and imaginative;
- introduce a fundamental distinction between God's immanent life and God's economy (or the economy of salvation); and
- explain the analogical nature of Christian talk about God.

Preparation

- Look through a Christian liturgy – you could try the 'Liturgy of St. Cyril', available online from the *Coptic Orthodox Church Network*, at http://www.copticchurch.net/topics/liturgy/liturgy_of_st_cyril.pdf – and note all the different ways in which God is named or described. Which of these ways of naming or describing or referring to God look to you to be metaphorical? Which look like they are direct or literal statements about God? Are there any that seem to you to be ambiguous?

Additional reading

If you want to accompany my chapter with other accounts of the nature of religious language, try:

Jeff Astley, *Exploring God-talk: Using Language in Religion*, Exploring Faith: Theology for Life series (London: DLT, 2004). A general introduction to theological language.

Dan R. Stiver, *The Philosophy of Religious Language: Sign, Symbol and Story* (Oxford: Blackwell, 1996). A somewhat more advanced account.

Nicholas Lash, *Holiness, Speech and Silence: Reflections on the Question of God* (Aldershot: Ashgate, 2004). Mentioned in the last chapter, but also very relevant here.

Freedom and Idolatry

[6]Thus says the Lord, the King of Israel and his Redeemer, the Lord of hosts: I am the first and I am the last; besides me there is no god. ... [8]Do not fear, or be afraid; have I not told you from of old and declared it? You are my witnesses! Is there any god besides me? There is no other rock; I know not one.

[9]All who make idols are nothing, and the things they delight in do not profit; their witnesses neither see nor know. And so they will be put to shame. [10]Who would fashion a god or cast an image that can do no good? [11]Look, all its devotees shall be put to shame; the artisans too are merely human. Let them all assemble, let them stand up; they shall be terrified, they shall all be put to shame. ...

[13]The carpenter stretches a line, marks it out with a stylus, fashions it with planes, and marks it with a compass; he makes it in human form, with human beauty, to be set up in a shrine. [14]He cuts down cedars or chooses a holm tree or an oak and lets it grow strong among the trees of the forest. He plants a cedar and the rain nourishes it. ... [16]Half of it he burns in the fire; over this half he roasts meat, eats it and is satisfied. He also warms himself and says, 'Ah, I am warm, I can feel the fire!' [17]The rest of it he makes into a god, his idol, bows down to it and worships it; he prays to it and says, 'Save me, for you are my god!'

[18]They do not know, nor do they comprehend; for their eyes are shut, so that they cannot see, and their minds as well, so that they cannot understand. ...

[21]Remember these things, O Jacob, and Israel, for you are my servant; I formed you, you are my servant; O Israel, you will not be forgotten by me. [22]I have swept away your transgressions like a cloud, and your sins like mist; return to me, for I have redeemed you.

Isaiah 44.6, 8–11, 13–14, 16–18, 21–22

Exercise

Before reading on, think about this passage from Isaiah. What does the author of this passage condemn, and what does he praise? What implications might this polemic have for Christian attempts to witness appropriately to God?

In the previous chapter, I argued that freedom and faithfulness – God's freedom to transcend any definitions arrived at by God's people, and God's faithfulness to the promises declared to those people in the past and in the present – are constitutive of God's self-identification. That continues to be true in this passage from Isaiah. At first sight, it presents us with two sets of people. On the one hand there are the people of Israel, directly addressed and declared to be God's witnesses; they know God as the rock upon which they stand and as their Lord, their King and their Redeemer. They know God's identity 'from of old', and may trust God to be true to it.

On the other hand stand the idolaters or false witnesses who are not addressed but described with biting sarcasm. They do not know God; they substitute for the true God things made with their own 'merely human' hands. They worship mundane realities that they can control and use for their own benefit; their gods are in their power.

In one corner, then, we have the true witnesses who rest in the hands of their God; in the other, the false witnesses who hold their god in their hands. There is a twist in Isaiah's oracle, however. God says to those who are being addressed directly and comfortingly as true witnesses, 'I have swept away your transgressions like a cloud, and your sins like mist; *return to me*, for I have redeemed you.' Having been addressed as those in the right, it becomes clear that they are no strangers to the wrong, and perhaps have not yet abandoned it. Tug on this thread and the passage, with its commendation of true witnesses and condemnation of false, unravels to reveal a plea to Israel to repent, to turn away from false witness and from idolatry, and to *become* the true witnesses that they are not. The problem of idolatry is not somebody else's problem – it is theirs.

This passage was, of course, written in a specific historical situation, and addressed to a people involved in various very specific forms of idolatry. Nevertheless, it is a tributary of one deep stream of Jewish thinking that was eventually to flow into a more radical interpretation of idolatry. Idols were eventually abjured not because they were representations of the wrong god, nor because they were the wrong kind of representation of the right God, but just because they were *representations*, and God was held to be beyond all representation. This God is held not to be the kind of God who can aptly be depicted 'in the likeness of anything that is in heaven above, or that is on the earth beneath, or that is in the water under the earth' (Exodus 20.4). No particular part of creation – visible or invisible, natural or artificial, animate or inanimate, human or animal – can be an adequate representation of the God who is the source of them all.[1]

Many theologians in both Judaism and Christianity have wrestled with the snares buried in any human description of God because they have been all too aware that human beings are perennially tempted to tame God, to remake God in their own image, or to slip God into their pockets. They have known that all descriptions that human beings might be capable of deploying are finite, because they are built from words whose everyday applicability is to finite things in the world, and because they are painted with imaginations all of whose colours come from life in the midst of that world. To use these descriptions of God is always to describe God in terms more normally applicable to things that are not God. Any talk about God – any picture, any image, any account, any story, any name, any description, any theory, any hypothesis – therefore presents believers with the temptation to absolutize something finite, something made with human hands (or human voices or human minds). That is, any talk about God presents a temptation to take a finite description not as a hand gesturing towards a God who is always more surprising than any description allows, but rather as a tool that enables the believer to grasp hold of God, to delimit God, to make God out as finite – to *define* God, and so to limit and define the demand that is made by knowing God.

Some Examples

Consider the following descriptions of God:

Rock: It is not difficult to see that this is a metaphor, describing God in terms appropriate to something that is not God. It is (or was, when the metaphor was fresh) a striking way of helping people to glimpse God's faithfulness and dependability, but the limit to how far one can take the metaphor is obvious; it is a limit that one would find oneself beyond were one to ask what God's mineral content was, for instance. Christians know that God is not a rock, so to describe God as one presents little temptation to idolatry.

Wise: What about this one, though? It too is a word whose meaning we learn first through ordinary human examples – from which we gather that it means something like 'able to judge appropriately, on the basis of long experience'. But what can one make of the idea of God having 'long experience', or even of God weighing up possible courses of action and judging appropriately?[2] There are clear limits to how far this description goes, too – even though, as we shall see below, descriptions of God as wise or good or loving don't work in quite the same way as the description of God as a rock.

Infinite: This might seem to be a good, abstract word, free from inappropriately material or human associations. But it, too, is a word whose meaning is learnt in particular contexts, as part of particular practices. It is possible, after all, to give a human (social, material) history of the contexts and practices and forms of imagination that have surrounded this word's emergence and development.[3] If one thinks that the word directly describes some characteristic of God (instead of being, say, a comment upon the inadequacy of all finite descriptions) one will eventually find that it too has smuggled in contraband assumptions or illegal connotations – material that properly belongs only on the creaturely side of the border.

Exercise

Return to the liturgy that you looked at in preparation for this chapter. Would you now assess differently any of the names or descriptions of God that you found in it?

God says 'I am who I am' and 'I am the God of your ancestors' to the same people, at the same time. It is not that one category of people, the idolaters, need to be reminded that God is beyond their false definitions, while another category of people, true witnesses, can be told to rest content with the proper definitions that have made it into their possession. This passage from Isaiah suggests, rather, that there might be an ongoing interplay between the two messages. On the one hand, the Israelites are told, 'Here is how God has defined Godself'; on the other, they are told, 'The God who has done this is, and remains, a God who is beyond all definition.' God makes Godself known – but God cannot be known.

This will seem like a direct contradiction until one realizes that the word 'know' has more than one meaning. If, by 'God can be known', we mean that God could be grasped and understood, defined and explained, or that human beings could gain intellectual mastery over this subject matter, then Christian theology denies that God can be known even by Christians, even by those to whom God has revealed Godself. God is, in that sense of the word 'know', radically and inherently unknowable.

For Christians, I said in the previous chapter, the word 'God' names the source of the life of the Christlike love and justice into which they believe they are being caught up. The relation in which they stand to that source will not be that of knowing subjects facing a known object, able to define it or to gain some kind of intellectual mastery over it. Rather, they will stand as those who are themselves in the process of being mastered by the one they face, and the forms of language appropriate to this will not be calm descriptions or abstract definitions, but expressions of praise, thanksgiving and penitence – language squeezed out of them as they find themselves grasped by God.

The unutterability of God

'For if a man cannot look upon the sun, though it be a very small heavenly body, on account of its exceeding heat and power, how shall not a mortal man be much more unable to face the glory of God, which is unutterable?'

Theophilus of Antioch, *To Autolycus*[4]

Consider someone illuminated by a bright light. The light shines on him and on everything around him, and enables him to see himself and his surroundings in new ways, and so to live in new ways in those surroundings. He can see the quality of the light by attending to how it shines on the different surfaces around him, and by paying attention to the way the shadows fall he can learn from where in the sky above him this light streams. In one sense, therefore, he can 'know' the source by seeing what and how it illuminates. But if he turns upwards, to face the source itself, the light will be blinding. He won't be able to see the source itself directly – not so as to see how it works, or how the light is generated in it. The light outstrips the capacity of his eyes, and they become useless, even though the searing blindness that he experiences is itself a sign that he is looking in the right direction. One ancient Christian writer described this as a 'brilliant darkness': a light so bright that it is tantamount to blackness.[5] Look directly at it and you can see no more than if you were left wholly in the dark.

This, too, is a metaphor that will only roll so far. Nevertheless, Christian theologians have often stressed that alongside the kind of knowing of God that I discussed in the previous chapter, a proper account of the knowledge of God must include this radical unknowing – this affirmation of the abiding unknowability of the source. 'No one has ever seen God' (1 John 4.12; John 1.18); 'no one shall see me and live' (Exodus 33.20). And this is no abstract conclusion forced upon Christians by speculative philosophers, denying something that Christians would otherwise have cheerfully affirmed; it is, rather, something that God is believed to have taught and to go on teaching. In the burning bush, in the prophecies of Isaiah, on the cross, God is weaning Christians from forms of knowing that have the nature of God all wrong.

Bridled minds

'God, indeed, from time to time showed the presence of his divine majesty by definite signs, so that he might be said to be looked upon face to face. But all the signs that he ever gave forth aptly conformed to his plan of teaching and at the same time clearly told men of his incomprehensible essence. For clouds and smoke and flame (Deuteronomy 4.11) although they were symbols of heavenly glory, restrained the minds of all, like a bridle placed on them, from attempting to penetrate too deeply.'

John Calvin, *Institutes of the Christian Religion*[6]

Yet, Christian theologians have affirmed, God does indeed make God-self known. God reveals Godself, and God's freedom does not trump God's faithfulness or promise. The knowledge in question is the kind of knowledge that I discussed in the last chapter: the knowing that is like knowing a piece of music; the knowing that consists in participation in what God is doing; the knowing that finds its object most clearly displayed not in an abstract definition but in an ensemble of lives being made holy. The negative declaration of God's unknowability is nothing more than the declaration that this kind of musical, living, participatory knowledge is the only kind of knowledge of God available. God makes Godself known, and in that very process makes known God's unknowability outside of this provision. God cannot be known in anything other than the ways in which God makes Godself known.

The question remains, however, whether this form of knowing leaves Christians any kind of speech *about* God? Does this kind of knowing allow Christians *any* direct description or definition of God's nature? Perhaps appropriately, in a discussion that focuses on forms of language other than direct, literal description, I am going to begin my answer to that question with an extended parable.

Key points

- All representations of God contain the possibility of idolatry.
- If by 'know' we mean 'grasp fully, define and explain', then God is unknowable.
- Christians nevertheless believe that God makes Godself known.

Acknowledging the sun

There was once a king who sought a counsellor who would understand the workings of the natural world. Many men and women applied for the post, but any appearance of knowledge or wisdom crumbled under his questioning, and he sent each of them away. One day, his servants told him that another applicant had arrived, that she was waiting in the Great Hall – and that she seemed promising. The king quickly made his way there from his chambers and, without any greeting, as soon as he had opened the door, he asked her: 'Tell me, madam, what is the sun'?

'It is a vast fire, sir, suspended in the emptiness of space.'

His face fell. 'Well then, tell me more. Is there air in space?'

'No, sir, I don't believe there is. Ah, I see your problem: fires need air to burn, so how can the sun be a fire in airless space?'

'Quite, quite. And what of fuel?'

'Fuel, sir?'

'Yes – fires need fuel. What fuel is burnt by the sun? Where does it come from?'

'A good question, sir. I answered hastily – the sun, I meant to say, is *like* a vast fire, and we may think of it imaginatively as being "suspended" in space.'

'So can you, then, tell me what the sun *really* is?'

The woman fell quiet for a while, and then looked up at him with a smile. 'No, sir, I do not know what the sun really is. At least, I cannot *tell* you what the sun really is, but—' she hesitated for a moment, and then continued, 'I can show you. Would you come with me, sir, over to the balcony?'

He was sufficiently intrigued to walk with her through the doors that opened on the East side of the room, onto the hall balcony. He glanced up at the morning sun, trying to glimpse something of its true nature – but as always the glance half-blinded him: he did not see the sun so much as the dancing spots that the glare left in his eyes. 'I can barely look at it, madam – and the same is true of you, I suspect.'

'Of course, sir, but that is not what I meant. Staring at the sun will not answer your questions about it. But you can feel its warmth, can't you?' He could, even through the breeze. 'And look out at your kingdom, sir: you may not be able to look at the sun, but the sun enables you to look at all this. That's what the sun is: the source of the warmth on your skin, and the light by which you see the world. You may not be able to know the nature of the sun directly, but you can know yourself and your world as bathed in its light.'

His grunt might have indicated approval, but after a moment he said, 'Very good, madam – but that is not enough. Anyone can feel that warmth and see in that light. I've been hoping to find an *expert*, someone who can tell me the sun's secrets. I was hoping you might be such an expert.'

'No, sir, not me.' She paused again, and then continued, 'but I do know where to find such experts. Look over there, and tell me what you see.' She pointed out at the landscape spread below them. He looked, and saw nothing but the spreading fields and his people at work on them. He frowned. 'Who out there is an expert on the sun, madam? Don't play games!'

'Over there, sir – those people in the fields. They work every day under the sun, and know what it feels like in every season. They work every day *with* the sun, and know when to plant and when to harvest, when to work in the fields, and when to stay in the shade, how to cover their heads to keep themselves cool, and how to treat themselves if they get burnt. If you want to know what the sun is, look at them. Or, better, go out there in the fields with them and start learning its ways. You won't necessarily find any new words for the sun in that way – you may still only be able to call it a vast fire hanging in space, knowing all the while that those words are inadequate – but you *will* know the sun, nonetheless.'

The king thought for a while, caught between a feeling that he was being cheated of a real answer to his question, and a building admiration for her response. After a minute or two staring down at the baked fields, he spoke again. 'But is there nothing you can say directly about the sun – no descrip-tion that you can offer me that is not pictorial and inadequate?'

'Well, yes, in a way. I have already done so, have I not, by describing what the sun is *not*. It may be *like* a fire, but as you demonstrated a moment ago we know quite firmly and clearly that it is not a fire in any sense we understand. More positively, though, I suppose we could also say quite firmly that the sun is the source of the heat and light that you feel and see with, and that those people are working with. That is a direct statement about the sun, even if we don't know *how* the sun is the source of these things.'

'Yes, yes – but the first is knowledge of what the sun is not, rather than knowledge of what the sun is.' He paused, and then continued, 'And the second does not really add anything to what you said before: it simply repeats your claim that the people in the field know the sun. Or rather, it gives the name "sun" to what the people in the field know. It is really a statement about their knowing of the sun, isn't it, not a statement that tells me directly what the sun is. Is there nothing else you can offer me?'

When she spoke again, it was with a half smile: 'Yes, sir, I have one more thing. Though I do not think it will satisfy you. The people down there in the fields tell all sorts of stories about the sun: that it is a golden apple thrown each morning by an imprisoned hero to his no-less imprisoned heroine; that it is a boat sailing across the sea with a burning sail; that it is – yes – a huge fire lit by the Gods to warm the earth, but that the demons sometimes steal the fuel and sometimes pile too much back on, trying to freeze or burn the earth. They don't seem to mind that the stories contradict one another. But those stories, sir, are important: they are part of the way in which those people *learn* how to live with the sun; they shape their imaginations, and so shape their actions. Because of those stories, people do know the sun not only in what they do, but in what they think and say, and their knowledge is true knowledge, sir, even if their words and stories are not ones that we could claim speak directly of the sun.

'Will that do, sir?'

The king paused before answering. He was still not satisfied: these were not the kinds of answers he had been hoping for. But he could not think of another way of asking his question, and in any case was now too distracted by the thought that he had no idea what salary it was appropriate to pay to this woman once he appointed her.

Pragmatic, propositional and imaginative

In this parable, the prospective counsellor offers the king three ways of speaking about the sun. Those three ways are analogous to three kinds of Christian talk about God.

The first kind of talk I call 'pragmatic' because it is focused on *activity*.[7] The prospective counsellor explains to the king that although she cannot tell him directly about the sun, the workers in the field do know about it – and their knowledge is shown in the patterns of their activity, the shape of their lives. She only gives the sketchiest possible outline of the sort of thing she means – they 'know when to plant and when to harvest, when to work in the fields, and when to stay in the shade' – but if she had wanted to tell the king in more detail what the workers know about the sun, she could have done so by describing their lives, their practices, in more detail. And that is what I mean by 'pragmatic' language: the kind of theological description that, as a way of speaking indirectly about God, speaks about the shape and texture of lives that *respond* to God. Christian theology can speak about the patterns of Christian life – of prayer, of worship, of mission, of reading, of relating – with the conviction that God is the reality to which that patterned life is a response. In the previous chapter, this was what I was suggesting: I was refusing to talk too directly and independently about God's love, and instead saying that one must attend to lives that have been and are lived in response to that love. Such lives, I said, are the best, the most direct language about God that Christians have: God is known in the lives of all those individuals and communities who have heard the call of God, who have begun to learn Christlike love and justice, and who therefore display the identity of God. Pragmatic *description* of such lives is therefore the best, most direct way that a theologian's words can speak about God. Everything else is commentary.

Cultural-linguistic theology

The American theologian George Lindbeck has suggested that Christians be thought of as analogous to a people who have a distinctive culture, and who speak a distinctive language. Think of an anthropologist visiting a remote island tribe whose language and culture are uncharted. The theologian's job, Lindbeck suggested, is like the job of this anthropologist: he must get to know this people's culture and language, trying to reach the point where he can understand both the language and the patterns and rules that govern the culture in which that language is embedded – discerning the cultural as well as the linguistic 'grammar' that shapes this people's life. Doctrines, for Lindbeck, are not primarily statements of theories about God's nature; they are ways of stating some of the rules by which this people governs its behaviour. It is only, he says, the lives that are governed by these doctrinal rules that should be thought of as making a claim about the nature of God.[8]

The second kind of language I am calling 'imaginative'. The prospective counsellor referred to the stories and metaphors that enable the workers in the field to pass on their understanding of life in the sun. This richly varied, extravagantly imaginative language is not mere decoration that could be abandoned without real loss to the substance of their understanding; it is a necessary part of how their understanding is shaped. In fact, the use of this imaginative language is one of the practices by which they relate to the sun: it is one of the practices that pragmatic language about them will describe. A pragmatic description will focus on *their saying* of these things, and the role taken by that saying in the overall shape of their lives. The imaginative language itself is the *content* of what they say: the stories and images and metaphors and parables that place in a communal store their wisdom about the sun.

The case with Christian language about God is similar. Christianity boasts a lush and extravagant growth of imaginative language about God. Such language is not dispensable; it is not mere decoration, or a sop for the hard of thinking. It shapes the imaginations of those who use it, and so shapes the lives that they live – and so it plays an indispensable role in sustaining and shaping the way that their lives respond to God.

Human beings are, after all, imaginative creatures, and inhabit the world by imagination. To be active in the world requires us to see the stuff around us not simply as a bewildering variety of pure sense-impressions, but to see it as a world of objects or circumstances with which we can interact. This 'seeing as' is a matter of imagination, and that imagination is shaped by metaphors and parables and stories more powerfully than by apparently direct, literal description. Staring in front of me now, I see a patch of grey with a strange, luminous patch of blue within it, and within the patch of blue a white rectangle speckled with black marks. Or rather, that's not what I see, unless I take my glasses off: I actually see a computer monitor, with a blue desktop pictured on it, and a white document on that desktop, covered with writing. I see it, in other words, as something I can understand and work with – as containing possibilities for action. My ability to see it in this way, and so my ability to engage with it, is shaped by my having learnt various metaphors, similes and stories: I see the blue desktop as being *like* a physical desktop, a space on which I can arrange my work; I see the white patch *as* a piece of paper on which I am typing – and so on.[9]

In just the same way, one could think, for instance, of Rowan Williams speaking of God loving 'the reflection of his love within creation; he cannot bear to be separated from it and goes eagerly in search of it, hungry to find in the created "other" the reality of his own life and bliss'.[10] Eagerness, hunger, inability to bear separation – these are words fit for finite human lives, words that are clearly inadequate when applied to God; and yet this inadequate, extravagant image is one that enables the reader to see the love of God in a new light, and so to respond to it and live with it in a new way. By making possible a richer lived response to God, it enables truer reference to God.[11]

The third kind of language I am calling propositional.[12] It is the kind of language that tries to set down in unambiguous language clear statements of fact about God. Its statements can then be subjected to careful logical analysis to see what does and what does not follow from them.

You will have noticed – and, after the last chapter probably not have been surprised – that the prospective counsellor is rather evasive about using this kind of language. There *are* direct statements in what she says, however, and they *are* direct statements that say something about the sun. What she says is, in fact, full of such statements.

On the one hand, she makes clear claims about what the sun is *not*, saying for example that 'it is not a fire in any sense we understand'. Yet she uses such language to ensure that the king will not be tempted to look for the wrong kind of statement about the sun. Her propositional statements both warn against thinking that there are direct, positive ways of speaking about the sun, and warn against taking imaginative language as if it were literal description. Nevertheless these statements do convey something, however indirectly, about the sun itself.

On the other hand, she spends a lot of time making the more positive claim that the king himself in minor ways, and the workers in the fields in richer and more complex ways, are genuinely responding to the sun. Her explanation of that is full of direct statements: she says things like, 'the sun *is* the source of the heat and light that you feel and see with, and that those people are working with'. As the king points out, however, what she says simply 'gives the name "sun" to what the people in the field know, and it is really a statement about their knowing of the sun … not a statement that tells me directly what the sun is'. Even though her propositional statements do make claims about the sun, and do so quite definitely and in one sense informatively, the claims are once again made indirectly.

You may recognize some of what I said in the last chapter and earlier in this as belonging squarely in this propositional camp. Most obviously, there was my claim that 'God' is the name of the source of the Christlike love and justice that flows through people's lives. That is a positive propositional claim, and it is definitely a claim about God, but it is not itself a direct description of God. It is a statement about *where one can find* something like a description of God: look to the lives of those caught up in God's life.

On the other hand, there is my negative propositional claim that God's own love is beyond human imagination and understanding, like the sun whose light we can see when it shines on the world around us, but which blinds us when we look towards it. That is equally clearly a kind of claim about God, but it is a negative one: it says who or what God is by denying that one's normal ways of naming and understanding realities in the world work in God's case.

In the kind of theology I am exploring in this book, propositional language is most at home in these indirect modes, talking about God by explaining why in God's case one should not look to one's normal ways of grasping and explaining reality but instead should look elsewhere – to the lives described in pragmatic language and to the imaginative language employed in those lives.

Propositionalism

Some theologians, of course, believe that propositional claims can do a great deal more than this. They hold that it is possible to speak much more directly and much more fully about the nature of God's life in a propositional idiom, setting down clear definitional statements about who and what God is. The philosophical theologian Richard Swinburne, for instance, at the start of his book on *The Existence of God*, states:

> I take the proposition 'God exists' (and the equivalent proposition 'There is a God') to be logically equivalent to 'there exists necessarily a person without a body (i.e., a spirit) who necessarily is eternal, perfectly free, omnipotent, omniscient, perfectly good, and the creator of all things.'[13]

Chapter 2 has already shown what I think of this. I believe it makes better Christian sense to see this kind of apparently direct, positive claim about God as in fact a commentary upon or summary of that deeper Christian knowledge of the love of God that is found in Christian lives.

Let me give an example. If Swinburne is asked to expand on what he means by 'omnipotent', he says:

> By God's being omnipotent, I understand that he is able to do whatever it is logically possible (i.e., coherent to suppose) that he can do.[14]

Later in this book (in Chapter 10), when I expand on what I think 'omnipotent' means, I say:

> If I say, for instance, that 'God is omnipotent', I won't understand what that means by trying to come up with an abstract definition, and then arguing about what God must be able to do. I will discover what those words mean as I learn what it means to live with the trust that there is no situation in which God's love fails, no reality or extremity in which God's love is extinguished or finally defeated.

That is, I take this sort of apparently direct, positive proposition 'God is omnipotent' as no more than a convenient shorthand for something more complex: a 'pragmatic' description of a pattern of Christian life and imagination, coupled with the propositional claim that this aspect of Christian life truly 'responds' to God. To treat it as a straightforward definitional claim as Swinburne does is, I believe, to mistake the kind of knowing of God that is available to human beings.

So, there are at least three different kinds of language at work in Christian theology: pragmatic, imaginative and propositional. Pragmatic language describes lives; imaginative describes the imaginations of the people living those lives; and propositional claims comment on the other two, making direct claims about what those lives and imaginations amount to.

Exercise

Try putting this threefold division to work. Either keep it in mind as you read through another chapter of this book, or read some other theology book, asking whether you can distinguish these three kinds of discourse – pragmatic, imaginative and propositional – and whether it helps to do so.

Key points

- Christian theology involves 'pragmatic' language: the description of the image of God in Christian lives.
- Christian theology involves 'propositional' language: statements that aim to speak clearly and directly about God.
- Christian theology involves 'imaginative' language: description of the stories and metaphors that help shape Christian imagination, and therefore Christian life.
- Propositional language, in the kind of theology I am exploring, is mostly used to lay out ground rules for other ways of referring to God.

Immanence and economy

One day, when the new counsellor was dining with the king, she reminded him of their conversation about the sun. 'Sir', she said, 'I have been thinking further about our knowledge of the sun. I wrote a letter to an astronomer I know – a man who spends all his time either observing the stars and planets, or developing mathematical models of how they move. He suggested a distinction that I had not thought of before.'

'What distinction is that?'

'Well, think about the workers in the field, and all the things they know about the sun.'

'Yes, yes: they know about its heat, its light, the patterns of its rising and falling, the changes in its strength throughout the year. We discussed all this.'

'Well, sir, my astronomer friend pointed out that not everything they know is of the same kind. The heat that they know, for instance, is truly the heat of the sun – even if they can have no idea of how the sun produces that heat, or what the heat of the sun itself is like all the way up at the sun itself. Even though the bearable heat that they feel, live with and respond to is very different from the unimaginable fire of the sun's own heat, they are right to think that the sun itself is, in some sense, hot – and to understand that hotness by analogy with the heat they themselves feel.'

'You do like making things complicated, don't you. I think I understand so far, though. Carry on!'

'He pointed out, sir, that many of the other things that the people know work rather differently. Take the rising and setting of the sun, for instance.

The sun itself does not rise and set; it is thanks to the turning of our world that we experience the sun as rising and setting. Or the strengthening and weakening of the sun over the seasons: that has, he says, to do both with the tilt of our world's axis, which means that the sun's path through our skies is at some times of the year more directly overhead than at other times; and it has to do with the path that our world takes around the sun, sometimes closer to the sun and sometimes further away.'

'I see your meaning. These things that the people know, they are facts about how we and our world relate to the sun, and not facts about the sun itself? Yes, yes, I see that. Sunset, sunrise, the seasons. Of course the sun itself does not move up and down; it does not grow hotter in summer and cooler in winter – it is constant. But, yes, the path that we take around it is so arranged that we experience it in these changing ways.'

'Yes, sir.'

'Ah, but has your astronomer friend noted that we take that path *because* of the sun, though? If I understand these matters aright, our world is held on its path around the sun *by* the sun. The movement we have that makes us experience the sun as rising and setting, strengthening and weakening, is a movement arranged by the sun, a movement the sun has given us?'

'Very good sir! I had not thought of that. I will write to him again at once.' She had learnt already that, even with this genial monarch, a little flattery now and then was a sensible precaution. After all, she did not want the sun to set any time soon on her position as counsellor.

This story can help us to make an important distinction, between claims about the sun as it is experienced in the lives of the people and claims about the sun as it is in itself. On the one hand, there are what we call 'economic' claims, not because they have anything to do with any financial arrangements, but because of an older sense of the word 'economy'. It comes from the Greek words *oikos*, meaning household, and *nomos*, meaning law, and could refer to the way someone puts their domestic affairs in order, the way that someone makes provision for his or her family. So 'economic' claims are, in this context, those that focus on the patterns into which the sun has arranged the lives of those who respond to it. How does the sun appear to those people, and how is the nature of the sun seen in the way that their lives are arranged?

On the other hand, there are 'immanent' claims. They are claims about what the sun itself is truly like, regardless of the position of the people making the claims. Immanent comes from the Latin *immanere*, to dwell or remain within, and can mean both 'indwelling' and 'inherent'. Here it is the latter that is in view: what properties are really *inherent* in the sun? What properties dwell not in the relationship between sun and observer, but in the sun itself?

The ambiguity of immanence

There are two different uses of the word 'immanent' in theology, and they should not be confused. On the one hand, there is the usage I am sketching at the moment: 'immanent' is used in contrast to 'economic' to speak about what is true of God in and for Godself. On the other hand, 'immanent' can also be used in contrast to 'transcendent' to talk about God's presence in and to God's creation – God's closeness or intimacy to the world. It is particularly important not to confuse these two meanings as they are almost direct opposites, one having to do with God considered in abstraction from any relationship to the world, the other having to do precisely with the intimate quality of that relationship.

In my story, claims about the heat of the sun are both economic and immanent. On the economic side the heat of the sun is something that the people experience, that they know and work with in their daily lives. Yet on the immanent side the astronomer claims that the people experience this heat from the sun because the sun *is itself hot*. The heat that the people experience and the heat that the sun has in itself might be of vastly different orders of magnitude, and the sun's inherent heat might be impossible to imagine properly (no one, after all, could ever experience it because to experience it would be to die); nevertheless, the two are intimately connected. The sun's immanent heat produces the economic heat that the people feel, and because of that connection, the economic claim that the sun *feels* hot can become the immanent claim that the sun *is* hot.

Claims about the sun rising and setting, however, are only economic. The people can rightly claim that the sun rises and sets – but what they are talking about is *only* the sun-as-seen-from-their-vantage-point, the sun-as-they-experience-it. The economic claim 'the sun rises and sets *for us*' cannot be turned into the immanent claim 'the sun itself inherently rises and sets'. Someone who lived not on a rotating planet but on a planet that always turned the same face towards the sun would not experience the sun as rising and setting: it would be a constant presence, always in the same quarter of their sky.

Alongside this talk about the sun that is only economic, and alongside the talk that is both economic and immanent, could one have talk that is only immanent? That is, could one have talk about what the sun is inherently like that was not at the same time talk about some aspect of how the sun appears in human lives? One might think, perhaps, of the theories of the astrophysicists, which declare that the sun has an inner core taking up about one fifth of its diameter, that this core has a density of some 150,000 kilograms per cubic metre, and that it is powered by a fusion reaction that converts hydrogen to helium. Even these, of course, are claims based on empirical data, and so claims that have their roots in some rather refined aspects of how the sun appears in our lives. The chains of analysis and disciplined speculation involved in developing these claims from that data are so long and tangled, however, that there remains very little direct sense in which claims about the size, density and nature of the sun's core are also claims about how we relate to and experience the sun. The economic base of these claims has been left so far behind that they have almost achieved pure immanence.

Of course, no one uses the words 'immanent' and 'economic' when talking about the sun: they are theological terms used when talking about God. 'Economic' refers to God's 'economy of salvation' – the arrangements that God has made for God's world, and the knowledge that God's people have in that economy of who God is *for them*: how God appears to them, from their vantage point (a position or vantage point that God has given them). 'Immanent', on the other hand, refers to what God is in Godself; God's inner or essential nature – what God is like not just when seen from one particular vantage point, but absolutely.

On page 58, I asked whether Christian theology allows any kind of direct description or definition of God's nature. I can now rephrase that question. Most of what I said in the last chapter was focused on the *economic* level, in that it had to do with who God appears to be in the lives of believers, or how the lives of believers constitute a kind of claim about who God is *for us*. I have also, in that chapter and this, been insisting on the unknowability of God – that is, the idea that direct, clear statements about God's nature are deeply problematic. In other words, I have been denying that God's *immanent* life is a reality that one can easily or straightforwardly talk about. So, the question that faces us now is, 'Does Christian theology allow one to say anything about who God is *immanently* – or does it abandon the attempt, and allow God's immanent life to remain wholly swathed in mystery?' I may say, economically, that to learn to know God is to learn to know oneself and one's world as bathed in God's love, and that to know God is to learn to recognize oneself and one's world as called to participate in that love. But can I go further, and say that God *is* love, immanently – that this love characterizes God's essential nature?

Key points

- In theology, 'economic' description of God refers to God as he is experienced, learnt and responded to by Christians caught up in the 'economy of salvation'.
- God's 'immanent' life is what God is in Godself.

Analogical language

Imagine that you have a CD player with one of those graphic displays on which there are several columns of coloured lights showing you the levels of sound being put out at different frequencies. Imagine that you have such a CD player in front of you, but that the speakers are disconnected, so that no sound is audible. Imagine that there is a CD in the player, and that you have pressed 'play'. No sound comes out, but the display is working, so you see the various columns of lights pulsating up and down, sometimes staying quite low and green, sometimes becoming taller and acquiring red tops.

In other words, you have a CD player equipped with visualization equipment, and what you see on that equipment has to do in general with that equipment's features, its connections and components. But what you see when this specific music CD is played is what happens when the connections and components of this equipment are taken up and used by this music: the music conforms this equipment to itself, and makes this utterly unmusical equipment (equipment that plays lights, not sounds) communicate something of the music.

You could describe the visual display that this equipment produces using words appropriate to the visual world: 'This bit of the music is very tall; this bit has lots of red; in this bit the column tops slope down to the right, in this bit they slope to the left; in this bit the whole thing is very jumbled up. ...' These are the spatial, visual words appropriate to the visual display, and they are not musical words as such; they don't tell us directly about the music (unlike words like 'loud' or 'quiet' or 'rumbling' or 'deep'). These visual words are adequate to the visual display, but they are decidedly inadequate as descriptions of the music: what would it mean to say that music was tall, red or sloped? Were you finally to connect the speakers, the music you would hear would utterly exceed this visual language that you have now developed for it.

And yet, because the graphical display is a faithful representation of the music, the description that you offer of it can, in a way, be *true* of the music. It is capable of getting hold of something real about the music; there is some feature of the music, some real feature, that corresponds to each of the words that you use to describe the display. When the columns are taller on the right than on the left, that does mean *something* about the music. When there is a lot of red on the screen, that does mean something too.

Something a little like that is going on in the move from description of the economy of salvation to claims about the immanent nature of God. A Christian can attend to and describe the patterns of the economy – the processes in history and in her life by which she believes God has addressed the world and begun to draw it into that love and justice which are God's life. She can speak and think about this economy using the pragmatic and imaginative language appropriate to it: language appropriate to a sequence of events and relationships lived out in time; language appropriate to human imaginations.

She can, however, believe that this economy is like the pulsating of the CD player's lights: it is a faithful transcription of the melody of God's immanent life, a transcription that is true to that life, even though it is a transcription for a medium utterly different from that life. This transcription does not make the immanent life of God fully knowable and graspable, any more than flashing lights let one hear a CD's music – but it does make possible some kind of true knowledge of that life. The full, unimaginable reality of the immanent life of God exceeds the economy just as surely as the music of Beethoven pouring out of the speakers would exceed the lines of green and red lights winking on and off on the front of a CD player – but she can claim that the immanent nature of God, while remaining utterly beyond her, is nevertheless truly given to her in the economy.

This picture of Christian speech about God suggests that one can arrive at a description that is in some sense true of God, even if the reality that one is describing so far exceeds one's ability to describe it that one cannot know *how* one's description is true. This is called 'analogical' speech: it works on the basis that there is an *analogy* or similarity between what one says using frail human words and God's immanent life, even though any such similarity is qualified by a still greater dissimilarity: the dissimilarity between God's life and the life of the world. The heat of the sun that I feel is analogous to the heat of the sun itself, even though the heat of the sun itself is not something I could possibly imagine: it exceeds the limits of what could be experienced by bodies like mine.

On reflection, this might seem a rather useless claim. Of what use is a true description of God if one cannot know what it means for it to be true – if the reality to which it points remains ungraspable? Christian theologians have replied that such description can be of use precisely because the primary purpose of one's talk about God is not the development of accurate description, nor the provision of explanatory theories or models of God. Christian talk *about* God is an ingredient in the processes by which Christian lives are conformed *to* God. The claim that Christian speech about God can, despite God's unknowability, be analogically true speech about God's immanent nature is simply one aspect of the broader claim that Christian *life* in response to God can, despite God's unknowability, be life that is truly being drawn to share in its own way in the immanent life of God.

The claim, as it were, is that the visual display is genuinely plugged into the music, such that someone whose attention and language is kept in conformity to that display is himself (in a sense) plugged into that music. Similarly, by the grace of God's action in the economy of salvation, Christian language can be genuinely plugged in to the music of God's immanent life, and so Christian life that is guided and shaped by this language can be genuinely plugged in to that divine music.

The kind of knowledge of God available to human beings, according to this theology, is not primarily a matter of accurate description or convincing explanation: it is primarily a matter of lives caught up to share in God's life. But within that kind of knowing-by-living there can, nevertheless, be a certain kind of theoretical knowing, a certain kind of ability to describe God, a certain kind of ability to speak the truth *about* God – a way of speaking that, even though it is limited and inadequate, can be meaningfully claimed to be true.

Key points

- Christian theologians have claimed that the economy of salvation is a transcription into creaturely terms of God's immanent life.
- They have claimed that to be caught up in this economy is therefore, in a sense, to participate in the immanent life of God.
- They have also claimed that the speech about God that the economy makes possible can be true speech about God's immanent nature.
- Such speech is true only analogically, however, and believers cannot know *how* what they say applies to God.

Love all the way

Why should it be important to make this claim? Once the distinction between 'economic' and 'immanent' has been made – the distinction between God as God is in Godself, and God as God appears to or engages with the world – why should anyone insist that Christian response to God, Christian life in relation to God, somehow connects with or shares in the *immanent* life of God?

As my parable about the sun suggests, to say that some claim about God is purely economic would be to suggest that what one sees of God from this vantage point might change were one to move to another vantage point. That is, to say that something is purely economic would be to say that, in principle, one could be in some time or place or situation or state from which that something would not be true of God – just as one could be on a planet from which the sun could be seen not to rise and set.

To insist that the claim that 'God is love' is not simply economic, but applies analogically to God's immanent life, is to claim that there is no imaginable vantage point from which God will not be seen to be love. There is no place that one could go to, no time at which one could arrive, no situation in which one could find oneself, in which God would be anything other than love. God is love all the way down.

That may sound like the kind of statement that nobody could disagree with. Yet if you think back to the previous chapter (or if you read on into the next), you will remember that, for Christian theology, the true meaning of love is found in Jesus of Nazareth. For a Christian theologian, to say that God is love all the way down is to say that God is *Christlike* all the way down. 'God is Christlike and in him there is no unChristlikeness at all', as the twentieth-century Anglican theologian Michael Ramsey said.[15] God, according to Christian theology, is *immanently* Christlike.

Against elitism

There is another reason for insisting on the link between an economic understanding of God and God's immanent life. It is that link that ensures that the understanding of God found among ordinary believers – the workers in the fields, who know how to live with and respond to God's love – is a knowledge that gets to the heart of who God is. There is not some different kind of knowledge available only to theological experts who have got beyond the economic level, a knowledge that leaves behind the naive level of ordinary believers and grapples with the *real* nature of God. The love of God that ordinary people know goes all the way down, and the only 'experts' are those who know most deeply that they are loved, and love most deeply themselves. Those are forms of knowledge that do not necessarily go with academic prowess or ecclesiastical preferment.

To insist that God is love, that God is Christlike, 'all the way down' – that to learn at Christ's hands the love of God is to learn the immanent heart of God – is to believe that one need have no hesitation about making a lifelong commitment to this way of learning God. This is a pathway, Christians trust, that goes all the way into the heart of God, and travellers along this path will never reach a time or a place where it peters out and leaves them stranded. To bind oneself to this pathway, to make the lifelong investment of time and energy and attention that is involved in taking it with utmost seriousness, is not to keep oneself to the economic shallows: it leads on, Christians believe, into the immanent depths.

Key point

• To claim that God makes God's immanent life known in the economy is to claim that what Christians learn about God in the economy can be trusted in all times and places.

The analogy of love

In the light of all this, I can say more precisely what is going on when Christians make the statement, 'God is love.'

1 In the first place, 'love' is a word that people learn in the midst of finitude – by being loved by parents or carers, by reading love stories, by falling in love, by loving their children, by living their lives. There is no one definition of 'love' that captures all of these; rather, people learn to use the word 'love' differently, but more or less appropriately, in each of a kaleidoscope of human activities, situations and relationships. The uses of the word 'love' that people learn are not simply 'univocal' (all meaning exactly the same thing); neither are they simply 'equivocal' (meaning several completely unconnected things). They are, rather, 'analogous': connected by various degrees of resemblance. 'Love' is already a stretchy word.

2 To say 'God is love' is to attempt to say something about God's immanent life. But to apply this word to God is to stretch it far beyond its ordinary limits – unless one starts imagining that God is simply a big version of a human being, with emotions and understanding and commitments that work in much the same way that ours do. Christians are certainly called by God's economy of salvation to imagine God as the one who loves the world passionately and consumingly, who is so given over to love that there is nothing in God that is not love. And yet they are also called to imagine one who loves purely – that is, one who loves without selfishness, without particular interests, without an ego that is fed or advanced by this love. So although Christians have certainly said that 'God is love', and have normally regarded themselves as saying something about God's immanent life when they do so, theologians have traditionally argued that Christians do not (and cannot) know quite *what* they are saying when they do so; they cannot imagine quite how love works in the case of God.

3 Nevertheless, Christians are committed to using this word of God because of what God has done – loving them in Jesus of Nazareth, and beginning to draw them into Christlike love. That is something that they can grasp; it happened and happens in the finite world of people and things, which is the very world for which their words are suited. So Christians say 'God

is love', not because they can imagine or define exactly how it is true – not because they can imagine or define exactly the God who is loving – but because they trust God as the ineffable source of the love that encounters them in Christ, and catches them up into itself.

4 Learning to say 'God is love' is therefore inseparable from the process by which Christians are taught what true love is by being loved truly. The love shown to them in Christ is not, they believe, simply one more example of love to set alongside all the others. It is *the* example of love – and learning to recognize oneself and the world around one as loved by this love begins to change one's understanding of (and so practice of) love. This is a love that one learns by learning to become loving.

5 Christian theologians have therefore affirmed that there is a sense in which 'love' is a word used *most* properly of God (even though they cannot know how love works in God's case). God is the source of perfect love, and God's love is the criterion for all human love. All a person's finite and imperfect loves are therefore given a standard outside themselves: they are called to account before God's love. To say 'God is love' is therefore inseparably bound up with the critique of all one's other ways of using the word 'love' – both the ways in which one has personally learnt (and sometimes mis-learnt) how to love, and the ways in which one's culture enshrines various ideas and confusions about love.

Love in culture

Learning the meaning of love involves a journey into the resources and problems of our culture. We are surrounded by images of love in books and films and television programmes and adverts and posters and songs. Some of them are good and some of them are dreadful; some of them are profound, and some of them have – to use a wonderful phrase from J. K. Rowling – 'the emotional range of a teaspoon'.[16] The journey on which Christians learn what 'love' means is a journey into discernment about all these images – a slow learning to differentiate between the help and the hindrance that each can offer. The field of 'theology and culture' (theological explorations of films and novels and television programmes and computer games) is not, as is sometimes suggested, a less-than-serious distraction from the real business of theology: it is an unavoidable part of learning the meaning of the word 'God'.

The statement 'God is love' certainly looks like a direct propositional statement about God. And to a certain extent, it does work like one: it conveys a kind of true information about God. But if my analysis of the nature of this analogical claim is right, it is not a statement that can be extricated from the Christian lives and imaginations that are its context. The claim 'God is love' cannot be separated from the kinds of reality spoken of in pragmatic and imaginative Christian language. This is a statement about God's immanent life only because it remains a commentary upon that economic reality.

Communicable and incommunicable

Traditionally, a distinction has been made between 'communicable' and 'incommunicable' attributes of God. Love is a classic communicable attribute: as I have been emphasizing, it is an attribute that can in some sense be shared by God's creatures. The same would be true for wisdom, justice, faithfulness and goodness, among many others; all of these work in the same way that I have been suggesting 'love' works. On the other hand, an incommunicable attribute would be something like 'omnipresence' – an attribute that can't be shared by God's creatures. That does not mean that to speak of God as omnipresent is somehow to capture God more directly. God's omnipresence is just as thoroughly unimaginable as God's love, and claims about that omnipresence are no less bound up with Christian lives and imagination. To say that 'God is omnipresent' is best thought of as a commentary upon Christian lives lived in the faith that there is nowhere one can go to evade God's presence, nowhere one can find oneself where God's love is not at work. There may be no meaningful sense in which Christians are called to become omnipresent themselves,[17] but even an incommunicable attribute like this is something that is best understood by looking to the patterns of Christian life.

Key points

- To say that 'God is love' is to use a stretchy human word.
- To say that 'God is love' is to stretch that word beyond its familiar limits.
- To say that 'God is love' is to comment upon the way that God appears in the economy of salvation.
- Saying that 'God is love' is inseparable from the process by which Christians learn the nature of love.
- God's love is the criterion for all human love.

Going further

1 You can find a clear introduction to the nature of analogy in theological language in Brian Davies, *An Introduction to the Philosophy of Religion*, 3rd edn (Oxford: Oxford University Press, 2003), ch. 7. David Burrell's *Analogy and Philosophical Language* (New Haven: Yale University Press, 1979) and his *Aquinas: God and Action* (Notre Dame: University of Notre Dame Press, 1979) are worth a look if you want a real mental workout.
2 I have not said very much about the use of metaphor to speak about God. A good place to start further exploration of this topic is with Janet Martin Soskice, *Metaphor and Religious Language* (Oxford: Clarendon Press, 1985) and Colin Gunton, *The Actuality of Atonement: A Study of Metaphor, Rationality and the Christian Tradition* (Edinburgh: T&T Clark, 1988), ch. 2: 'Metaphor and Theological Language'.

3 In discussions of the attributes of God, one in particular has caused a good deal of controversy: the *impassibility* of God – which can loosely be thought of as the idea that God cannot suffer. For a discussion of this attribute, see Thomas G. Weinandy, *Does God Suffer?*, new edn (Notre Dame: University of Notre Dame Press, 2000).

Notes

1 I will return to this in my discussion of the doctrine of creation, in Chapter 7.

2 For more on God weighing up courses of action, see Chapter 10.

3 See, for example, Paolo Zellini, *A Brief History of Infinity* (Harmondsworth: Penguin, 2005), Brian Clegg, *A Brief History of Infinity: The Quest to Think the Unthinkable* (London: Constable and Robinson, 2003) or Eli Maor, *To Infinity and Beyond: A Cultural History of the Infinite* (Princeton: Princeton University Press, 1987).

4 Theophilus of Antioch, *To Autolycus* 1.5, in A. Cleveland Coxe (ed.), *Ante-Nicene Fathers*, vol. 2 (New York: Christian Literature Company, 1885), p. 90, available online from the Christian Classics Ethereal Library, http://www.ccel.org/ccel/schaff/anf02. iv.ii.i.v.html.

5 Pseudo-Dionysius the Areopagite, *Mystical Theology*, 1 (997B) in *Pseudo-Dionysius: The Complete Works*, ed. Colm Luibheid (Mahwah, NJ: Paulist, 1987), p. 135. A different translation edited by Arthur Versluis, in which the relevant phrase is translated as 'dazzling obscurity', can be found in *Esoterica* 2 (2000), pp. 203–11, and is available online at http://www.esoteric.msu.edu/VolumeII/MysticalTheology.html.

6 John Calvin, *Institutes of the Christian Religion*, vol. 1, Library of Christian Classics 20, tr. Ford Lewis Battles (London: SCM Press, 1961 [from 1559 Latin text]), 1.11.3, p. 102. A different translation, by Henry Beveridge (Edinburgh: Calvin Translation Society, 1845–6), is available online at the Christian Classics Ethereal Library, http://www.ccel. org/ccel/calvin/institutes.iv.i.xii.html.

7 *Pragma* properly means a thing that has been done, a deed, an act – so 'pragmatic' means something like 'related to action'.

8 See George Lindbeck, *The Nature of Doctrine: Religion and Theology in a Postliberal Age* (Philadelphia: Westminster, 1984). For a good discussion, see Chad Pecknold, *Transforming Postliberal Theology: George Lindbeck, Pragmatism and Scripture* (London: Continuum, 2005).

9 Graphical User Interfaces for computers are regularly discussed in terms of the 'metaphors' they employ. See, for example, Steven Johnson, 'Is the computer desktop an antique: soon, Apple and Microsoft will need new metaphors for their operating systems', *Slate Magazine* (10 Dec 2002), available online at http://slate.msn. com//?id=2075219. See also Tim Rohrer, 'Metaphors we compute by: bringing magic to interface design', Online Center for the Cognitive Science of Metaphor, 1995; available online at http://philosophy.uoregon.edu/metaphor/gui4web.htm.

10 Rowan Williams, *Ponder These Things: Praying with Icons of the Virgin* (Norwich: Canterbury Press, 2002), p. 27.

11 If the 'pragmatic' category is my way of trying to do justice to the cultural–linguistic theology of George Lindbeck, the 'imaginative' is my way of trying to do justice to the work of some theologians normally considered his opponents – theologians like David Tracy, whom Lindbeck clumsily labelled 'experiential expressivists' (see Lindbeck, *The Nature of Doctrine*, pp. 31–2). See, for example, David Tracy, *The*

Analogical Imagination: Christian Theology and the Culture of Pluralism (New York: Cross-road, 1981).

12 I toyed with calling this form of language 'ontological' (i.e. 'relating to being'), because it is concerned with the making of direct claims about what (and whether) God *is* – but that sounded a little precious. It is my way of trying to do justice to at least some of those that Lindbeck would have labelled 'cognitivist' or 'propositional-ist' (Lindbeck, *The Nature of Doctrine*, pp. 16, 91).

13 Richard Swinburne, *The Existence of God*, 2nd edn (Oxford: Oxford University Press, 2004), p. 7.

14 Swinburne, *The Existence of God*, p. 7.

15 A. M. Ramsey, *God, Christ and the World: A Study in Contemporary Theology* (London: SCM Press, 1969), p. 99. This has implications for inter-religious dialogue, as we shall see: it means (if one takes it seriously) that such dialogue cannot operate by seek-ing a lowest-common-denominator understanding of God that takes the Christlike-ness of God simply as a Christian way of seeing a God who is not *inherently* Christlike. In Chapter 12, I will explore the implications that such a claim has for the relationship between Christianity and other religions – and argue that it need not mean a rigid Christian exclusivism.

16 J. K. Rowling, *Harry Potter and the Order of the Phoenix* (London: Bloomsbury, 2003), p. 406.

17 Although one could say that the call to proclaim the gospel everywhere is a call to a certain kind of omnipresence. For more on such proclamation, see Chapter 14, pp. 345–8 below.

4

The Threefold Way

In Chapter 2, I argued that Christians can make sense of their lives, individually and corporately, as journeys on which they are being drawn deeper into the life of God. In this chapter, drawing on some of the distinctions and vocabulary established in Chapter 3, I am going to fill in some more colour in this picture, and argue that this Christian journey must be thought of as a threefold journey into the triune life of God. In other words, my presentation has now reached one of the core doctrines of the Christian faith: the doctrine of the Trinity. Classical Christian theology claims that God should be understood as one God in three persons, Father, Son and Holy Spirit, and although that claim may seem a world away from the discussions of my earlier chapters, I will argue that all the main building blocks for the doctrine are already in place.

I am going to

- highlight two patterns in the Gospels – the first showing Jesus and the Spirit pointing to the Father, the second showing the Father and the Spirit pointing to Jesus;
- suggest that it is by knowing and sharing in the 'economy' made up of these patterns that Christians know God;
- argue that the God who is known in this way is not best thought of as an isolated individual;
- argue that the belief that God's immanent life is shared with the world in this economy makes it appropriate to say that God's life is a life of three persons in one substance.

Preparation

- Unless you have had no encounter at all with the doctrine of the Trinity, you might have at least a vague idea of what it is supposed to mean. Jot down for yourself now, very briefly, your current understanding of what the doctrine claims. It will be helpful later on to see whether and how your thinking has changed or developed.
- It is also worth glancing briefly at other people's definitions. Try typing 'define: trinity' into Google to see a wide range of short definitions. Are any of them helpful?

Additional reading

Books on the doctrine of the Trinity crowd the shelves these days, and it is difficult to choose between them. Nevertheless, if you are looking to accompany this chapter with some alternative accounts of the doctrine that steer clear of unnecessary technicalities, and remain grounded in Christian sense-making, I would recommend:

Christopher Cocksworth, *Holy, Holy, Holy: Worshipping the Trinitarian God*, Trinity and Truth series (London: DLT, 1997). An accessible account of the Trinity that, as the title suggests, keeps its eye firmly on Christian worship.

Nicholas Lash, *Believing Three Ways in One God: A Reading of the Apostle's Creed* (London: SCM Press, 1992). An astute and ruminative exploration of Trinitarian doctrine.

The kingdom of God

All that I have said so far about love and the knowledge of God must seem a world away from the teaching that Christians worship 'one God in three persons'. That doctrine might seem to require a journey away from attention to lives caught up in the life of God and toward something much more technical, abstract and speculative.

The first and most important step in the journey that leads to the doctrine of the Trinity is, however, a step *away* from abstraction. I am going to start from the rather general things I said in Chapters 2 and 3 about how the world has been addressed lovingly by God in Jesus of Nazareth, and push in the direction of the biblical stories and sayings that can give those claims more detailed content.

Jesus of Nazareth pointed to the God whom he called 'Father'. He is portrayed in the Gospels as one whose ministry was devoted to speaking about this Father to the people around him, and to calling those people to respond to this Father with trust, delight and obedience. He spoke in parables of the extravagant, questing mission of the Father to his people, calling them back to himself: the Father is the shepherd searching for his lost sheep (Matthew 18.12–14 and Luke 15.3–7), or the father eagerly awaiting his prodigal son (Luke 15.11–31), or the woman desperately hunting for a lost coin (Luke 15.8–10). And he spoke of the unlimited demand entailed by response to this Father: allegiance to the Father is, for instance, the pearl of great price, or the hidden treasure that will cost everything (Matthew 13.44–6); the way to the Father is the way of the cross, and to follow it is to lose one's life (Matthew 16.24; Mark 8.34; Luke 9.23).

The image around which Jesus arranged all this teaching was the 'kingdom of God' or 'kingdom of heaven'. That kingdom is both the great banquet to which all are invited (Matthew 22.2–14; Luke 14.16–24), and the imminent judgement of all that contradicts its rule (Matthew 24.45—25.13; Luke 12.35–48). Jesus acts out the invitation to this banquet by eating with tax collectors and sinners, and welcoming them to his table (Mark 2.15–17; Matthew

9.10–12; Luke 5.29–31; 15.1–2); he voices the kingdom's judgement against all that would close its doors in his condemnation of the hypocritical and the self-righteous (Matthew 23.1–36).

The establishment of this kingdom is not simply to be seen as an exercise of God's *power*. Jesus announces the kingdom of God as the regime of love and justice (Matthew 22.36–39; Luke 4.18–19), and his invitation to this kingdom is an invitation to a life that will live God's love in all circumstances: the command to love God and neighbour sounds the keynote of the kingdom (Matthew 22.37–40; Mark 12.29–31; Luke 10.27).

Jesus' life, as portrayed in the Gospels, is saturated with this proclamation: he simply *is* the one who points the world to the Father's kingdom, and so points the world to the Father.

Ignoring the kingdom?

Some writers have found in Jesus' proclamation of the kingdom of God or kingdom of heaven not a doorway into Trinitarian thought, as I will be suggesting, but a welcome escape from it, and from other ecclesiastical doctrines. H. G. Wells spoke for many when he wrote:

[I]t is a matter of fact that in the gospels all that body of theological assertion which constitutes Christianity finds little support. There is, as the reader may see for himself, no clear and emphatic assertion in these books of the doctrines which Christian teachers of all denominations find generally necessary to salvation. Except for one or two passages in St John's Gospel it is difficult to get any words actually ascribed to Jesus in which he claimed to be the Jewish Messiah (rendered in Greek by 'the Christ') and still more difficult is it to find any claim to be a part of the godhead, or any passage in which he explained the doctrine of the Atonement or urged any sacrifices or sacraments (that is to say, priestly offices) upon his followers. We shall see presently how later on all Christendom was torn by disputes about the Trinity. There is no evidence that the apostles of Jesus ever heard of the Trinity – at any rate from him ...

As remarkable is the enormous prominence given by Jesus to the teaching of what he called the Kingdom of Heaven, and its comparative insignificance in the procedure and teaching of most of the Christian churches.

This doctrine of the Kingdom of Heaven, which was the main teaching of Jesus, and which plays so small a part in the Christian creeds, is certainly one of the most revolutionary doctrines that ever stirred and changed human thought. ... For the doctrine of the Kingdom of Heaven, as Jesus seems to have preached it, was no less than a bold and uncompromising demand for a complete change and cleansing of the life of our struggling race, an utter cleansing, without and within.

H. G. Wells, *The Outline of History*[1]

One can add the Spirit of God to this picture. The Spirit is portrayed in the Gospels as that power of God that enables and impels Jesus' ministry, and as the power that is promised to Jesus' disciples to enable and impel them to respond to his proclamation of the Father's kingdom. The Spirit is the one who makes the kingdom of God, the kingdom of love and justice, real in Jesus' life and in the life of his followers. The Spirit is the Spirit *of* this kingdom (John 3.5–8).

For the Spirit as the one shaping Jesus' life and ministry, think of the claim that Mary's pregnancy was the work of the Spirit (Matthew 1.18–20; Luke 1.35); think of the Spirit pictured as a dove descending on Jesus at his baptism (Matthew 3.16; Mark 1.10; Luke 3.22; John 1.32–33) and as propelling him into the wilderness straight afterwards (Matthew 4.1; Mark 1.12; Luke 4.1); think of the description of Jesus as the one anointed by the Spirit to proclaim justice (Matthew 12.18; Luke 4.18–19), and the claim that his ministry in general is carried out by the power of the Spirit (Matthew 12.28; Luke 4.14; John 3.34).

For the Spirit as the one promised to the disciples, to enable and impel their discipleship, think of the claim that Jesus is the one who will 'baptize with the Holy Spirit' (Matthew 3.11; Mark 1.8; Luke 3.16), and of Jesus' followers as those who will receive the Spirit from him (Luke 11.13; John 7.39); think of the claim that this Spirit will enliven them (John 6.63) and speak through them (Matthew 10.20; Mark 13.11; Luke 12.12). In John's Gospel most clearly, the Spirit is the one who will continue the ministry of Jesus, drawing his followers into the love of God that he proclaimed and embodied (John 14.26, 15.26, 16.13). The Spirit impels and completes the work that defined Jesus' life and ministry: the mission to proclaim and extend the kingdom of the Father.

Exercise

Read through the Gospel of Mark – it is not very long. See whether you think the description I have just given captures adequately the relationship between Jesus, the Spirit and the Father in that Gospel. Are there aspects of that Gospel that do not fit the pattern I have sketched?

Key points

- Jesus is, in the Gospels, the one who points to the Father's kingdom of love and justice, and so points to the Father.
- The Spirit is portrayed as the one who enables and impels Jesus' proclamation of the kingdom.
- The Spirit is portrayed as the one who enables and impels others to become part of the kingdom.

The beloved Son

Jesus, empowered by God's Spirit, proclaims and extends the kingdom of the Father; the Spirit empowers and completes this work. Jesus and the Spirit draw the world to the Father.

Some readers will already be trying to join the dots and turn this summary into the doctrine of the Trinity. Others will be trying to rub out lines they think I am already drawing between these dots, if they suspect the doctrine of the Trinity is being smuggled in under their noses. At this stage, however, I mean no more than I say: that we find portrayed in the Gospels this pattern of relationship between God, Jesus of Nazareth (who calls God 'Father') and the Spirit.

In order to take a second step towards the doctrine of the Trinity, there is another pattern that we must attend to in the Gospel narratives: that by which the Father directs our attention to Jesus of Nazareth, and by so doing defines himself *as* the Father of this Son.

The crucial instance of this pattern comes with the resurrection. Jesus, the one who points to the Father, does not in the climax of the story step aside so that our gaze can pass from him and on to the Father. Rather, in the climax of the story, the Father places Jesus centre-stage: having handed everything over to the Father ('Father, into your hands I commend my spirit', Luke 23.46; 'it is finished', John 19.30) Jesus is resurrected and our eyes are drawn firmly back to him.[2] The most persistent theme of the resurrection stories is recognition of Jesus (Matthew 28.7, 10, 17–18; Mark 16.7; Luke 24.27, 31, 39; John 20.16, 18, 20, 26–31; 21.7), and in those stories, the proclaimer (the one who devoted himself to pointing away from himself and towards the kingdom) becomes the proclaimed (the one on whose face our eyes become fixed).[3]

This pattern can also be found in a crystallized form in two Gospel narratives in which the Father makes his only direct appearances in the narrative – or rather, when he has his only direct speaking role. The Father speaks in order to commend Jesus as his son at his baptism: 'You are my son, the beloved, with you I am well pleased' (Mark 1.11; Luke 3.22; cf. Matthew 3.17), and more fully at the transfiguration: 'This is my son, the beloved; listen to him!' (Mark 9.7; cf. Luke 9.35 and Matthew 17.5).

One can find more direct reflection on this theme in the Gospels as well. There is Matthew 11.27:

All things have been handed over to me by my Father; and no one knows the Son except the Father, and no one knows the Father except the Son and anyone to whom the Son chooses to reveal him.

But the theme is most ruminatively and expansively explored in John's Gospel, which insists that to know Jesus *is* to know the Father. See, for instance, John 14.8–9:

Philip said to him, 'Lord, show us the Father, and we will be satisfied.' Jesus said to him, 'Have I been with you all this time, Philip, and you still do not know me? Whoever has seen me has seen the Father.'

The Father has given Jesus to the world to allow the world to know the Father, and the world will know the Father not simply by looking where Jesus is pointing, but by looking at Jesus himself. John 3.16, that most famous of all biblical verses, proclaims the same message: 'For God so loved the world that he gave his only son, so that everyone who believes in him may not perish but may have eternal life.'[4]

Jesus is certainly, in the Gospels, one who predominantly points away from himself to the Father. He is clearly portrayed as one who depends on the Father, who is obedient to the Father, whose source and goal is the Father, who is subordinate to the Father. Yet in the same Gospels the Father also points away from himself towards Jesus. If one looks to the Father, seeking to know him and him alone, one finds him pointing to Jesus, and telling us to listen to this his son.

This rhythm in the Gospel portrayals resonates with one of the most striking facts about early Christianity: the role that Jesus played in Christian devotion. In the words of the New Testament scholar Larry Hurtado, 'a noteworthy devotion to Jesus emerge[d] phenomenally early in circles of his followers' and it 'was exhibited in an unparalleled intensity and diversity of expression, for which we have no true analogy in the religious environment of the time'.[5] We simply don't have evidence for a time in early Christianity when Jesus was not already the focus of devotion. The pattern in the gospel that shows us God, the focus of all worship, directing our attention to Jesus matches what did in fact happen among early Christians. Jesus was not simply seen as one who had communicated the proper form of devotion and discipleship, nor simply as one whose ministry had made proper devotion and discipleship possible: continued devout attention to Jesus himself was taken to be essential to proper devotion and discipleship. A focus on Jesus was at the core of Christian life, as the means by which a proper relation to God was shaped and upheld. As Jesus says in John 17.3, 'This is eternal life, that they may know you, the only true God, *and* Jesus Christ whom you have sent.'

Glory and self-giving

Recognizing this pattern makes an important difference to one's understanding of the nature of the relationship between Jesus and the Father, and specifically of the link between the Father's glory and Jesus' humility. After all, the high glory of an earthly king might properly be shown by the deep bowing of his subjects. Those subjects show the nature of their monarch by providing, as it were, a *negative* image of the king's glory: they abase themselves to show their lowliness, and so implicitly demonstrate the king's exalted majesty. However, even in his humility, even as he points away from himself, Jesus *positively* mirrors the Father, because the Father is also one who points away from himself, allowing Jesus to speak and act for him. The Son's self-giving picks up, repeats and returns the Father's self-giving. Each points to the other in order to provide his own self-definition.

In John 12, Jesus says '"The hour has come for *the Son of Man to be glorified.* ... Now my soul is troubled. And what should I say – 'Father, save me from this hour'? No, it is for this reason that I have come to this hour. Father, *glorify your name.*" Then a voice came from heaven, "I have glorified it, and

I will glorify it again." ... [Jesus said], "I, when I am lifted up from the earth, will draw all people to myself." He said this to indicate the kind of death he was to die' (vv.23, 27–28, 32–33). In John 17, Jesus says, 'Father, the hour has come; *glorify your Son so that the Son may glorify you.* ... I glorified you on earth by finishing the work that you gave me to do. So now, Father, glorify me in your own presence with the glory that I had in your presence before the world existed.' For John, the glorification of the Father's name (that is the manifestation of God's nature in the world), and the glorification of Jesus (the full manifestation of his proper place in God's work in the world) happen at the same time, and at the same place: when Jesus is raised up on the cross.

Exercise

Try reading through the Gospel of John, chapters 13—17. Pay attention to what is said or implied about the relationships between Jesus, the Father, the Spirit, the disciples and the world. See whether you think my descriptions of the patterns in the Gospels capture what is going on in that text.

It is in line with all this that the Spirit can be portrayed in the Gospels not simply as one who turns the world toward the Father, awakening the world to the Father's kingdom, but as one who brings the world *to Jesus*. In John 16.13–15, Jesus says,

But when he, the Spirit of truth, comes, he will guide you into all truth. He will not speak on his own. ... He will bring glory to me by taking from what is mine and making it known to you. All that belongs to the Father is mine. That is why I said the Spirit will take from what is mine and make it known to you.

Instead of simply being the one who inducts men and women into the kingdom of God that Jesus announces, the Spirit can also be seen as the one who draws men and women into knowledge of the Son as the one who points us to the Father and makes the Father known, and so the one who draws men and women into knowledge of the Father *as* the Father of this Son: the Spirit is not simply the Spirit of the kingdom of the Father, but is the Spirit of the Father and the Son.

Once again, do not think that I mean more than I say, here. I am not trying to argue that the obvious conclusion from what I have just said is that Jesus is divine, or that the Father, Son and Spirit are equal persons in the divine Godhead. I do not think my discussion so far allows us even to know what those claims *mean*, let alone know whether they are true. All I am doing is drawing attention to another pattern in the Gospels that complements the first: a pattern in which the Father and Jesus are related in mutual deference, and the Spirit draws believers into recognition of that relationship.

Gnadenstuhl

There is a form of artistic depiction of the Trinity called the 'Gnadenstuhl' or 'Throne of Grace', which seems to have been developed in Northern Europe in the twelfth century, and became popular as the Middle Ages wore on. The Father sits on the throne of grace – the 'mercy seat' of Exodus 25.17 – and holds out for our attention the cross on which the Son is hanging, with the Spirit hovering above him. If you look at the Father, you cannot but see the Son whom he holds out for your attention.

Key points

- In the Gospels, the Father is portrayed as pointing away from himself to Jesus.
- Jesus became a focus for devotion in early Christianity.
- The Spirit is portrayed in the New Testament as drawing people towards Jesus.

Reordered language

The second pattern I have been describing is one in which the believer's attention is not allowed to settle on the Father alone, but is shifted to the Son. This accords with one of the strange but persistent facts about the writers of the New Testament: instead of simply talking about God, and instead of simply referring to God as Father in the way that Jesus encouraged, we find that at least some of them started talking about God as 'the Father of our Lord Jesus Christ', defining the Father in relation to Jesus, and that, even more striking, alongside reference to God the Father *of* Jesus, formulae concerning God the Father *and* Jesus began to become natural, and sometimes even God the Father *and* Jesus *and* the Holy Spirit. Talk about God, in other words, began to get tangled up in the web of relationships between the Father, Jesus and the Spirit. Even if 'God' and 'Father' are synonymous in much of the New Testament, this is a God who can't be talked about truly, or fully, or appropriately, unless at the same time one also talks about Jesus and the Spirit.

Good examples of the twofold pattern can be found at the start of every letter in the Pauline corpus. For example:

- Romans 1.7; 1 Corinthians 1.3; 2 Corinthians 1.2; Philippians 1.2: 'Grace and peace to you from God our Father and from the Lord Jesus Christ.'
- Galatians 1.1, 3: 'Paul, an apostle, sent by ... Jesus Christ and God the Father, who raised him from the dead. ... Grace and peace to you from God our Father and from the Lord Jesus Christ.'

- 2 Thessalonians 1.1–2: 'To the church of the Thessalonians in God our Father and the Lord Jesus Christ. Grace and peace to you from God the Father and the Lord Jesus Christ.'
- 1 Timothy 1.1–2: 'Paul, an apostle of Christ Jesus by the command of God our Saviour and of Christ Jesus our hope. ... Grace, mercy and peace to you from God the Father and Christ Jesus our Lord.'

Threefold patterns can be found in other passages, such as these:

- Matthew 28.19: 'Go therefore and make disciples of all nations, baptizing them in the name of the Father and of the Son and of the Holy Spirit.'
- 2 Corinthians 13.13: 'The grace of the Lord Jesus Christ, the love of God, and the communion of the Holy Spirit be with all of you.'
- Galatians 4.6: 'And because you are children, God has sent the Spirit of his Son into our hearts, crying, "Abba! Father!"'
- Ephesians 5.18–20: 'Be filled with the Spirit ... giving thanks to God the Father at all times and for everything in the name of our Lord Jesus Christ.'
- 1 Peter 1.1–2: 'To the exiles of the Dispersion ... who have been chosen and destined by God the Father and sanctified by the Spirit to be obedient to Jesus Christ and to be sprinkled with his blood.'
- Jude 1.20–21: 'But you, beloved, build yourselves up on your most holy faith; pray in the Holy Spirit; keep yourselves in the love of God; look forward to the mercy of our Lord Jesus Christ that leads to eternal life.'

I am not making any claims about the *nature* of Jesus, the *nature* of the Spirit, or the *nature* of the Father (beyond the claim that they are all characters in a set of explicit and implicit biblical narratives). I am simply noting that the Father did not remain alone at the focal point of Christian devotion, or remain alone in Christian ways of speaking about God. Quite what that says about God's nature is a question I have yet to broach.

Key points

- In early Christianity, talk about God became talk about God as the Father of the Lord Jesus Christ.
- Talk about God regularly became talk about God *and* Jesus.
- Talk about God sometimes became talk about God *and* Jesus *and* the Spirit.

The threefold way

Any simple description of Christian life as involving a relationship to the Father is not enough on its own. Christian life is also life in the Spirit. Christian life is also life following Jesus. It is life captivated by, upset by, embraced by Jesus – life alongside Jesus, relationship to whom is constitutive for life in the

Father's kingdom. And this same Christian life is life that has been invaded by, transformed by, overwhelmed by, the Spirit – the Spirit who draws people to Christ, and impels and enables participation in that kingdom. It is only this Christian life, which is life in the Spirit and life shaped alongside Jesus, that is really life lived on the way to the Father by the road along which this Father has made himself known. Christian life is life that is created by, and in constant movement towards, the Father who is Father of the Son and sender of the Spirit.

One way of grasping these affirmations is by thinking of their negative counterparts:

- Christians are never so filled with the Spirit that they can dispense with being disrupted by Jesus; never so spiritual that they do not need to be judged by his self-giving on the cross: there is no getting beyond Jesus by means of the Spirit. To think otherwise is to speak of a different Spirit from that spoken of in the New Testament.
- Christians can have no relationship to Jesus that is not already some kind of living in the Spirit; without the Spirit making him present Jesus will recede into the past or be absent in heaven, and the believer can have nothing to do with him: there is no going to Jesus except by the Spirit. To think otherwise is to speak of a Jesus different from the risen, present Christ spoken of in the New Testament.
- Christians never approach so close to the Father that they can forget about the life, death and resurrection of Jesus; they can never find a place in the heart of the Father where there is no presence of the crucified and risen one: there is no leaving Jesus behind on the way to God. To think otherwise is to speak of a Father other than the 'Father of our Lord Jesus Christ' spoken of in the New Testament.
- Christians cannot rest content with looking at Jesus as a historical figure whose influence and importance is limited to one sphere; they cannot face Jesus without being faced with the question of how he reveals to us the one who is always and everywhere present and relevant, the one he called Father: there is no following Jesus without attending to the Father. To think otherwise is to think of a Jesus who is not the beloved Son spoken of in the New Testament.
- Christians can never so rely on the Spirit within them that they ignore the Spirit's relation to the creation, sustaining and redeeming of the whole world; there is no keeping the Spirit to a private 'religious' realm; there is no Spirit without that love and justice that are the Father's life: there is no Spirit without the Father. To think otherwise is to speak of a Spirit other than the Spirit of the kingdom of the Father spoken of in the New Testament.
- Christians cannot relate to the Father simply as the distant clockmaker behind the Universe, the deists' God who has no impact upon life except in a rarefied intellectual worship; to relate to the Father is to be caught up by his Spirit into intimate, revolutionary relationship with him: there is no relating to the Father without the Spirit. To think otherwise is to speak of a Father who is not the sender of the Spirit spoken of in the New Testament.

Grasping the chain

'He who has conceived of the Father, and has conceived of him by himself, has also received the Son into his mind; and having received the Son, he does not divide the Spirit from the Son, but ... forms an image in himself that ... is a mixing of the three in the same manner. And if someone mentions the Spirit alone, he has by this very confession received him of whom the Spirit is. And since the Spirit is of Christ and of God, as Paul says, just as he who grasps onto one end of a chain draws along with it the other end as well, so he who draws the Spirit, as the prophet says, through him also drags along together the Son and the Father. And if anyone truly grasps hold of the Son, he shall hold him on two sides: the one where he draws together his Father to himself, and the other where he draws his own Spirit.'

Gregory of Nyssa, *Ad Petrum*[6]

These are not meant to be restrictions by which one must abide in order to remain a member in good standing of the Christian club. They are, rather, ways of spelling out who Trinitarian theologians think they are speaking about when they speak about God. They are simply more explicit ways of stating the claims I have been exploring: that the Father points to the Son, and the Son to the Father, and the Father and the Son send the Spirit to lead people back to the Father and the Son – and that is simply who the Father, Son and Spirit *are*. For those who seek to follow the God of the Bible, the God of Jesus Christ, there is no getting away from this complex interplay.

Ecclesial and personal

There are two complementary ways of understanding these rules. In the first place, they could be thought of as a kind of Trinitarian grammar for church life, a way of checking that a church that is committed to the doctrine of the Trinity has not begun to live in misshapen ways. So, for instance, if a charismatic church becomes caught up in what it believes is a new wave of the Spirit's work, this Trinitarian grammar yields some appropriate questions: Is this movement taking the church deeper into its devotion to Christ crucified and risen?, and is it taking it deeper in its concern for the coming of the Father's kingdom of love and justice for the whole world? Those questions can be asked, and the church kept faithful to its Trinitarian creeds, even if there are few or none who have any technical theological expertise, or any precise knowledge of what the doctrine of the Trinity means.

In the second place, however, these rules can also be thought of on a more individual level as the grammar of a spiritual discipline, which asks the believer if she is willing to throw herself into learning the nature of God down this strange threefold path, remaining open to the call of the other two persons whenever her contemplation or practice is focused on one, and letting go of any apparently more secure grasp of God that she might have had outside of this venture.

> **Exercise**
>
> Taking either the ecclesial or the personal sense of these rules, can you think of or imagine any specific practices that would run counter to them? Try to think of three or four examples.

Key points

- According to Christian theology, to know the Spirit truly is to know Jesus, and to know Jesus truly is to know the Spirit.
- According to Christian theology, to know the Father truly is to know Jesus, and to know Jesus truly is to know the Father,
- According to Christian theology, to know the Spirit truly is to know the Father, and to know the Father truly is to know the Spirit.

Divine drama

If we were to put all this material together into a single story, it might look something like this:

Act 1 The Father sends Jesus, forming and empowering him by the Spirit; this is the Father's way of loving the world, as John 3.16 explains.

Act 2 The Spirit works within those to whom Jesus is sent, helping them to recognize in him the Father's love for them.

Act 3 The Spirit works within those who recognize this love, to draw them into conformity to Jesus, so that they may face Jesus' Father in Christlike love and obedience.

Act 4 They find that the Father to whom they look in Christlike love and obedience sends them into the world alongside Christ, as the body of Christ united and empowered by the Spirit, to love the world with Christlike love. They become themselves part of the Father's way of loving the world.[7]

There is a strange choreography here: a criss-crossing of movements by which believers are drawn into the pattern of relationships that holds together the Father, the Son and the Spirit. In Chapter 2 I argued that, in Christian theology, knowledge of God was not primarily a matter of having a set of correct concepts that succeeded in defining God, but was a matter of living in response to God's call – becoming part of the movement of God's life in the world. I argued in more detail that it was a matter of growth in love and justice, penitent recognition of Jesus of Nazareth as the guide who takes one deeper into this love and justice, and grateful acknowledgement of the *source* of the love and justice into which one was being incorporated. In this chapter, I have tried to make this a little more concrete by paying attention to some of the patterns in the New Testament. I have suggested that, for the Gospels, the journey into love and justice (into the kingdom of God) cannot simply be described as a journey undertaken with the help of Jesus and the Spirit, headed towards the Father: the 'movement of God's life in the world' is more to-and-fro, more circulating and criss-crossing than that. It is a movement that involves the believer being caught up by the Spirit in the Son's love of the Father, and in the Father's sending of the Son. It is a dance in which each partner in turn defers to the other and brings that partner forward. Jesus hands his followers over to the Father, The Father hands them over to the Jesus, and each is involved in giving them the Spirit who draws them back towards both. It is participation in this movement that constitutes knowledge of God, according to Christian theology.

I have not presented any of these comments and arguments because I believe that they somehow prove that the Spirit and the Son are divine, or that they somehow prove the appropriateness of talk of 'one God in three persons'. All I have been trying to do is to display some basic patterns in the economy of salvation as it is portrayed in the Gospels and elsewhere. I have talked about broad narrative patterns that can be found in the Gospels, about particular narrative incidents in which those patterns receive a crystallized form, about discursive passages in which aspects of those patterns are directly described, and about what one could call the distinctive twofold and threefold grammar for talk about God that began to emerge in the early decades of the Christian Church. I have tried to draw all these strands together in the image of a drama in which Father, Son and Spirit are *dramatis personae*, or in the image of a dance in which they are partners. And all that I am claiming at this point is that, for Christian theology, to know God is to know the God who is caught up in relationship with Jesus and the Spirit, and to know God is to get caught up in those relationships oneself – becoming a participant in the drama.

Rublev

Probably the most famous artistic representation of the Trinity is an icon painted in around 1410 by Andrei Rublev, depicting the incident from Genesis 18 in which three men or angels come to visit Abraham at a place called Mamre. Abraham addresses the three men in the singular, as if they were one person, and then as the story goes on a strange ambiguity arises about whether Abraham is speaking with them, or with God. Medieval Christian writers, eager to find Christian doctrines secreted already in the pages of the Old Testament, often took this strange story as a hint pointing towards the doctrine of the Trinity – and the icon-painter Rublev uses it as an indirect portrait of a three-personned God. He portrays the three angels sitting at the table at which Abraham is entertaining them, and sets the direction of their gazes, and the inclination of their bodies, so as to indicate a pattern of relationships and of deference between the three. As a result, the viewer's eye is not allowed to rest on any one of the figures, but is moved from figure to figure, following the image's subtle choreography.[8]

Key points

- The Father so loves the world that he sends the Son in the power of the Spirit; the Spirit draws people into recognition of the Father's love in the Son.
- The Spirit draws the believer into conformity to the Son, to face the Father in love and obedience; the Father, by the Spirit, sends the believer into the world with Christlike love.
- For Christian theology, to know God is to participate in this drama.

The heart of the doctrine

We have already reached the heart of the doctrine of the Trinity. The doctrine is nothing more nor less than the claim that true knowledge of God, true sharing of God's life *is* participation in this drama – the threefold drama of the economy of salvation. The word 'God' simply refers to the reality that Christians come to know, and whose life they come to share, as they find themselves, in the Spirit, caught up in the Son's love of the Father and the Father's sending of the Son.

To know God is to be drawn into that love and justice that has its fount and origin in the Father. It is to be drawn into that love in which one is formed by being conformed to the Son, who plays out that love again in a form that one can take on. And it is to be drawn into that Christlike love that is formed within one by the working of the Spirit, who conforms one to the love that unites the Son and the Father. God's life *is* this love, and this love *is* God's life. God is that reality that Christians know by participating in this threefold economy of love.

Trinitarian Christians claim that to know God in this way – by relating to Father, Son and Spirit; by participating in this drama – is to know God truly. That is, this is not a stage to get beyond. It is not a preliminary introduction. This threefold economy is a pathway that leads to the immanent depths of God. These are not simply the kindergarten slopes, to be abandoned in favour of something starker and purer once Christians have reached maturity: this is, according to Trinitarian theology, the one endless threefold path by which God is truly known. God is that reality that Christians come to know truly as they find themselves caught up in the threefold economy of Father, Son and Spirit.

Everything that remains in this chapter is simply icing on this cake, and even if there should not be another word in this chapter that makes the slightest sense to you, you have, if you have kept up so far, understood the heart of the doctrine of the Trinity.

Threefold prayer

'An ordinary simple Christian kneels down to say his prayers. He is trying to get into touch with God. But if he is a Christian, he knows that what is prompting him to pray is also God: God, so to speak, inside him. But he also knows that all his real knowledge of God comes through Christ, the Man who was God – that Christ is standing beside him, helping him to pray, praying for him. You see what is happening. God is the thing to which he is praying – the goal he is trying to reach. God is also the thing inside him which is pushing him on – the motive power. And God is also the road or bridge along which he is being pushed to that goal. So that the whole threefold life of the three-personal Being is actually going on in that ordinary little bedroom, where an ordinary man is saying his prayers.'

C. S. Lewis, *Mere Christianity*[9]

Exercise

Following the same pattern that C.S. Lewis uses for prayer, can you see how to redescribe Christian worship in Trinitarian terms?

Key point

• God is the one whom Christians know as they find themselves, in the Spirit, caught up in the Son's love of the Father and the Father's sending of the Son.

Imagining God

This chapter so far has been focused on a pragmatic description of the economy of salvation, setting out the patterns of dramatic action portrayed in the Gospels, the patterns of Christian speaking displayed in the New Testament more generally, and the patterns of Christian living that respond to Jesus and the Scriptures. All of these are the kind of historical, graspable, human realities to which pragmatic language is suited.[10] And to all this pragmatic material, I have now added one big claim in propositional mode: God is the reality that Christians know by participating in this threefold economy.

All that remains is to ask whether and how one may speak directly of or describe the God who is known in this way. What ways of speaking or thinking about God's immanent life, if any, are appropriate to this threefold path along which Trinitarian Christians believe one must tread?

This is a secondary question. After all, the primary reality of Trinitarian Christianity is not the words or images that Christians manage to deploy in order to describe God, but the ways in which their whole lives are caught up in the threefold economy of God, and so into God's own life of love and justice. Nevertheless, this secondary question is in its own way unavoidable and necessary: if Christians do not ask what ways of thinking about God are appropriate to this economy, they are all too likely to find themselves left with ways of thinking that are *in*appropriate – ways of thinking that subtly leech support from wholehearted participation in the economy.

A non-Trinitarian theologian might, for instance, suggest that Jesus and the Spirit should be thought of as purely economic realities. That is, she might suggest that Jesus and the Spirit are simply aspects of what God has done in history in order to draw people to Godself. She would suggest that they are like the rising and setting of the sun in the story I told in the previous chapter: aspects of how God relates to us, rather than aspects of who God is in Godself. In this view, it would only be the Father who is *true* God, only the Father who represents God's immanent life. Jesus would best be thought of, she might say, as something like a prophet, one called to proclaim God's truth; the 'Spirit' would perhaps simply be a name for God's activity working within individuals and communities. Attending to Jesus directly would not, for her, be an *essential* part of attending to God; it would simply be a stage on our way to attending to God, a rung that Jesus himself would urge us to leave behind in the end.[11] The Father, according to this non-Trinitarian, *is* God; the Son and the Spirit are simply what God *does*. God would *economically* be the Father of the Son and the sender of the Spirit, but there would be an immanent reality to God's life behind this sending, a reality not shaped or constituted by relationship to the Son or to the Spirit. If she wanted to speak compellingly of the immanent depths of God, she might do worse than turn to the words of *Green grow the rushes, O*: 'One is one and all alone and ever more shall be so.'

This non-Trinitarian theologian might suggest that the believer's true relationship to God is best seen as one in which the believer faces the Father as an 'I' facing a 'Thou'.[12] All other parts of the economy fall away: they lead to this relationship, but they are not essential to it. They are the scaffolding that God has provided to enable the believer to be lifted into this position.

It is to this picture that the Trinitarian Christian says 'No!', because it is a form of imagination of God that relegates the threefold drama of the economy to a secondary, subordinate place. It imagines a form of knowledge of God *beyond* the economy. It does not allow one to say, as I did a moment ago, that 'true knowledge of God, true sharing of God's life *is* participation in this drama – the threefold drama of the economy of salvation'.

It is certainly an attractively simple, easily graspable picture of God – it is a picture that 'comes naturally', perhaps – but Christians are faced with a choice between holding to it, and holding to the threefold economy. For the Trinitarian, this is no contest: one must give priority to the means by which God has made Godself known, and subordinate to it one's ability to imagine the unimaginable reality of God. Faithfulness to God's economy requires one to break and remake one's imagination of God.

Instead, Trinitarian Christianity says that it is the whole drama of the economy – the Father pointing to the Son, the Son to the Father, and the Spirit communicating between them – that is the revelation of God's immanent life. God has revealed Godself in a drama, an economy, a dance of reciprocity and deference between a Father, a Son and a Spirit. That is the way in which God has given God's life to the world, the model God has made of Godself, and even though the immanent life of God so far exceeds our imaginations that one cannot know *how* this model is true of it, Trinitarian Christians believe that it *is*, nevertheless, a true image of God.[13]

The Fatherhood of God

Some theologians in the early centuries of the Christian church drew attention to the fact that 'Father' is a relational term, because a person can only be a Father if he has children. They therefore insisted, in effect, that 'Father' must be an *economic* name for God, naming God by the relationships into which God has entered. 'Father' is a term applicable only to the arrangements God has made for the salvation of the world; it can't be used to speak of the immanent depths of God's nature. This view, however, was eventually rejected by the wider church as heretical. Theologians like Athanasius of Alexandria replied, in effect, that Christians who believed this would have to admit that Jesus did not, by revealing God as Father, reveal the inmost heart of God. Christians would have to say that Jesus had led them only to the outer courts of God's nature, and left them there. The immanent nature of God, God as God is in God's Holy of Holies, would be something fundamentally different from the face that God has turned towards the world in Christ.

Athanasius and others argued that, on the contrary, if Jesus reveals God as Father, and if Jesus really is revealing God to the world, then God must be *immanently* Father, not just *economically* Father. And yet they agreed that 'Father' is a relational term; it does not simply name a set of characteristics that an individual might bear on his or her own, but refers to someone who is related to another someone. So the immanent life of God can't be thought of as being like the life of an isolated individual. It must be thought of as the life of one-who-is-always-a-Father, and so of one-who-is-always-with-another; it must be thought of as the life of a Father-and-a-Son.[14]

The Trinitarian Christian will not, therefore, imagine herself as a believer facing the Father alone, with the rest of the economy left behind. She will make sense of herself as one being drawn ever more deeply into the choreography of the relationships between the Father, the Son and the Holy Spirit. She would relate to the Father as the Father of the Son, to the Son as the Son of the Father, and to the Spirit as the one who binds them into this community – and that will be her participation in the life of God.

To put it more simply, if God is the reality that one comes to know by participating in this threefold economy, then knowing God is more like joining a party than it is like facing an individual.

Key points

- If one is faithful to the threefold economy of salvation, God's immanent life cannot be imagined as represented by the Father only.
- The whole threefold economy is, according to Trinitarian theology, the self-revelation of God.

Three-personned God

The threefold economy is not, according to Trinitarian theology, simply a useful metaphor for God's life. It is not like saying, 'Consider the three-leafed clover: three leaves, but one plant. God is a bit like that.' Trinitarian theology does not simply say, 'Consider the relationships between Father, Son and Spirit in the Bible: three characters, but one economy. God is a bit like that.' It is not a matter of an accidental or fortuitous resemblance. This threefold economy is like the pattern of lights on the CD player's graphical display: it is a representation in our time-taking, finite, historical world of the immanent life of God – and it is so *because* it is the way in which the immanent life of God is showing itself to the world. The whole threefold economy is, according to Trinitarian theology, what God is doing in order to draw the world into God's immanent life, and so it is what God is doing in order to draw the world into the only kind of knowledge of God available. The threefold economy is God's self-revelation, God's revelation of God's immanent life. Trinitarian Christians do not simply say that God has a threefold economy, but that God *is* threefold – God *is* triune.

The threefold economy – a drama whose *dramatis personae* can only be properly identified in relation to one another – is, Trinitarian Christian theologians claim, the transcription of the music of God's immanent life into a form that can be played on economic instruments. The Son, the Spirit and the Father as we encounter them in the economy (in history, in forms that we can grasp, imagine and learn) are like the lights on the CD player's graphical display. In that analogy, I argued that there was some aspect of the music represented by each feature of those lights, even though the music itself utterly exceeded the visual display. In just the same way, Trinitarian theology argues that there is some unimaginable aspect of God's life that is represented by the Father who Christians know in the economy, some unimaginable aspect of God's life that is represented by the Jesus who Christians know in the economy, and some unimaginable aspect of God's life that is represented by the Spirit who Christians know in the economy.

That does not mean that Christians know what those unimaginable aspects of God's life look like, or how they work; it does not mean one can come up with a theory of how the immanent life of God is constructed, any more than the lights on the CD player enable one to grasp the realities of the music that they represent. Nevertheless, this economy represents God's immanent life.

The incarnation of the Trinity

If the whole threefold economy is God's self-revelation in history, then there is a sense in which we can say that the whole threefold economy is the incarnation of the Trinity. We will be looking in the next chapter at the language of 'incarnation' as it relates specifically to the Son, but in a looser sense it is not just the Son who becomes incarnate. Christians know the Son of God by knowing Jesus, a particular human being living in history. They also know the Spirit by means of the Spirit's effects in history – seeing not the wind, but the leaves that the wind shakes and the trees that it bends. And they know the Father by means of a set of stories, names, metaphors and practices that are told or used or lived in history. Christians know each of the persons economically: in history, in a way that is graspable by time-bound creatures like themselves. Indeed, 'economically' is the only way Christians *could* know the persons. This economic Trinity is, they believe, what the immanent Trinity is doing; it is, as it were, the immanent Trinity made flesh and living in the world, so that human beings might behold its glory.[15]

The traditional term used for what I have been calling an 'unimaginable aspect' of God's immanent life is 'person'. One must tread carefully at this point, however, because it is easy to assume that 'person' must mean 'a being a bit like us': a centre of consciousness, a being with some kind of will and understanding, a being endowed with *personality*. Yet the Greek word eventually used in the early Church's debates about all this, the word for which our word 'person' is supposed to be an equivalent, was *hypostasis* – a word that in this context implies a lot less than our 'person'. It means something more like 'a distinguishable reality'; one might even say 'a something'. Instead of saying 'there is some unimaginable aspect of God's life that is represented by the Father who we know in the economy', I could have said, 'There is an unimaginable *something* about God's life – an unimaginable *hypostasis* – that is represented by the Father who we know in the economy.'[16] To say that God's immanent life is a life of three persons is, therefore, to say no more than I have said already: that God's immanent life is faithfully given to us in this triune economy. The threefold economy is what God is doing to make God's life visible, knowable and shareable.

Person?

'When St. Augustine came to consider the use of the word *persona* in the theology of the Trinity – a word which after all was no more Scriptural than *homoousios* – he frankly admitted that to speak of God as *una persona* would have been no less appropriate than to speak of him as *tres personae*. But some word we must have wherewith to answer the question *Quid tres? –* "What are these three?"

And because of the poverty of our human language we say that the three are Persons – *non ut illud deiceretur, sed ne taceretur*, "not because that was what we wanted to say, but so as not to be reduced to silence". We cannot now substitute a better word, even if one were certainly available. We must continue to pray, "O holy, blessed, and glorious Trinity, three Persons and one God, have mercy upon us." And perhaps it is more important that we should think of the Holy Spirit dwelling within us as a "person" – a person who can be "grieved" (Ephesians 4.30; Isaiah 63.10) by our faithlessness – than that we should be over-careful to insist that the language we use does not mean what it says.'

John Burnaby, *The Belief of Christendom*[17]

Our word 'person' is not, however, wholly misleading. After all, we are referring to a 'something' in the immanent life of God that is aptly and faithfully represented by one of the *dramatis personae* in the economy – by one of the three essential, mutually-defining characters in the economic drama. So the 'person of the Father', for instance, is that ineffable something in the life of God that comes to the world, gives itself to the world, becomes visible and graspable and thinkable to the world, in this character in the economic drama – a character whose identity is inseparably bound up with the other two characters. To speak of that 'ineffable something' as a person is to say that it is a reality that is aptly given to the world in this 'personal' way – where 'person' now has the fuller meaning of 'character in a drama' or 'one whose identity is defined by his or her relations to others'.

A social Trinity?

Some theologians – proponents of a 'social Trinity' – suggest that it is appropriate to say directly that the immanent life of God consists of three persons in communion, using a much fuller sense of the word 'person'. That is, they think it appropriate to imagine the immanent life of God as three thinking and acting individuals, three centres of consciousness, eternally interrelating in patterns of deference and reciprocity. I am not so sure. I cannot see how to go further than I have gone above: the persons-in-relation of the economy are, I believe, the way that the immanent life of God comes to us, is given to us, is made visible for us, and knowing those persons-in-relation in the economy is the only way of knowing God. So although I believe *that* this economic reality is the faithful and true and adequate transcription of the immanent life of God, I do not know *how* it is such a transcription. The economy is the way in which the immanent life of God is given to my thought, my imagination, my life; and so each person is the way in which *something* of the immanent life of God is given to me – but of *what* it is that is given to me, I can only say that it is the unimaginable reality that truly shares itself with me in this way. So when I say that the immanent life of God consists of three persons in relation, I am using 'person' in the more austere sense: three 'somethings' in the one divine life of God.

Key points

- The whole threefold economy is, according to Trinitarian theology, what God is doing in order to draw people in to God's immanent life.
- The threefold economy leads Christians to speak of three 'hypostases' or 'persons' in God's immanent life.
- To speak of a 'hypostasis' in God's life is to speak of a 'distinguishable reality', a 'something'.

Divine substance

Alongside 'person' the other key term used in classical statements of Trinitarian doctrine is 'substance'. It sounds to modern ears as if it refers to 'stuff', the material out of which a thing is made. It is a translation of a Greek term (*ousia*), though, and (at least in this context) has a far less material meaning. The 'substance' of a thing is, to put it clumsily, 'what it is about a thing that makes it the kind of thing it is'. So, my substance is that about me that makes me human, rather than some other kind of reality.[18]

Trinitarian theologians wanted a way of saying that each person of the Trinity is fully God, and they used this word *ousia* to do so: God is three persons of one substance. 'Substance' refers, if you like, to what the three persons share.

This is difficult to state appropriately. That is, it is difficult to talk about this without subtly undermining the basic points that I have been making about the doctrine. One can end up, for instance, suggesting that God's life consists of three examples of the same kind of thing, three realities that share the same defining characteristics. And that in turn suggests that one could talk about the reality of God's life – this substance – in abstraction from the particular distinguishing characteristics of the three examples in which one finds it embodied. If my table and my chair and my ruler are three examples of the same kind of thing (wooden things) then I can talk about woodenness (consisting of hard, organic material derived from trees) without having to talk about the particular shape of any of the examples. If I and my wife and my two children are all examples of the same kind of thing (human things) then in the same way I can talk about humanness in abstraction from the features that distinguish us four. Is that how it is with the divinity of Father, Son and Holy Spirit?

Someone might say that *divine* substance – the defining characteristics of divinity – consists, say, in being omnipresent, omniscient, omnipotent and loving. And then they might say that the three persons, the three somethings in the immanent life of God who come to the world as Father, Son and Spirit in the economy, are each distinct examples of this divine kind of thing: each is an omnipresent, omniscient, omnipotent and loving reality. This essential, shared nature of God – omnipresence, omniscience, omnipotence and love – could therefore be discussed and understood in abstraction from the particular identities of the Father, the Son and the Spirit.

That, of course, would in turn mean that one had a way of thinking about, talking about, or imagining God that got behind the economy – a way of talking or thinking that was, at least in one sense, *deeper*, more basic, than ways of thinking about God that have been formed by attention to the three particular persons and their particular relations.

If, instead, one tries to talk about divine substance in a way that is true to the basic structure of Trinitarian belief, then one will have to say that the substance of God is the *life* that the three persons share – the life that is constituted by their interrelation. So if one talks about a characteristic of the divine life like omnipotence, one will not straightforwardly say that each person is omnipotent, but rather will say that God's way of being omnipotent is by being these three persons in relation. That is, any power that God has is always a power that has its origin in the Father, is focused in the Son and is brought to completion by the Spirit. It does not make sense to say that *each* of these is omnipotent, rather it is the power that the three have together, or that God has by being all three, that is omnipotent.

To put this in terms that sound less like a speculative explanation of the inner workings of God's action, one might say that the only way in which Christians fully experience the power of God in the economy is by experiencing it as a power that comes from the Father, as a power that draws the world into conformity to Jesus, and as a power that is brought to completion in them by the Spirit. It is only as a power that has this threefold economic shape that Christians know the one power of God.

The power of God

'Every operation which extends from God to the Creation ... has its origin from the Father, and proceeds through the Son, and is perfected in the Holy Spirit ... [T]he action of each concerning anything is not separate and peculiar, but whatever comes to pass, in reference either to the acts of [God's] providence for us, or to the government and constitution of the universe, comes to pass by the action of the three, yet what does come to pass is not three things. We may understand the meaning of this from one single instance. From him, I say, who is the chief source of gifts, all things which have shared in this grace have obtained their life. When we inquire, then, whence this good gift came to us, we find by the guidance of the Scriptures that it was from the Father, Son, and Holy Spirit. Yet although we set forth three persons and three names, we do not consider that we have had bestowed upon us three lives, one from each Person separately; but the same life is wrought in us by the Father, and prepared by the Son, and depends on the will of the Holy Spirit.'

Gregory of Nyssa, *To Ablabius (On Not Three Gods)*[19]

Exercise

The technical vocabulary of 'person' and 'substance' can be very confusing at first. Without rereading the last two sections, see if you can write down a brief paragraph defining each term *as I have used it* in Trinitarian theology – and then reread the two sections to see how well your words capture what

I have said. Incidentally, if I had asked you to write down a brief paragraph defining each term as *you* would use it in Trinitarian theology, would you have written anything different?

Key points

- The 'substance' of God is what the three persons share.
- This substance should not be thought of as a kind of being of which the three persons are examples.
- The substance is, rather, the life that the three share – the life that is constituted by them in relationship to one another.

One-in-three, three-in-one

Discussions of the doctrine of the Trinity sometimes get all tangled up in analogies that try to explain *how* something can be both three and one. You may well have heard some of them: God is like a triangle (three sides, one triangle), or a clover (three leaves, one plant), or water (ice, water, steam), or river (source, stream, estuary) – and so on. I have to admit that I do not find most of these remotely helpful, because they make the doctrine sound like it is some kind of mathematical paradox. Imagining how the immanent life of God functions is not our business.

There is, nevertheless, an important point behind these analogies: Trinitarian doctrine does involve holding together the threeness and the oneness of the dance of God's life. One of the temptations that Christian theologians have identified in Trinitarian theology is the temptation to focus on the one common life that the Father, Son and Spirit share, and to neglect the specificity of the three persons involved. Even some theologians who are apparently resolutely Trinitarian fall into this trap. One of the most prominent forms of it in contemporary theology is the temptation to take the doctrine of the Trinity as the claim that God's nature is the supreme instance of the general category 'community' or 'relationship'. The doctrine of the Trinity might be thought to tell us first and foremost that God is not an isolated individual but a community, a set of persons in relationship – and, so the argument goes, we need to be just as relational, just as much a community. The doctrine of the Trinity is held to have direct and obvious consequences for combating Western individualism, or for levelling church hierarchy, or for pushing us quite clearly towards a more egalitarian and community-minded understanding of human flourishing – and all the work in these claims is done by the *general* idea of community and relationality.

There is a lot of truth in such claims, and they should certainly not be dismissed out of hand. They are not, however, fully Trinitarian claims as they stand: they dwell on the general idea of God's life as communal and relational without making it clear that this can always and only mean the community specifically of these three: the Father, the Son and the Spirit. That is, these claims sometimes lose sight (at least temporarily) of the particular persons about whom the doctrine of the Trinity speaks. If Trinitarian theologians are to speak about the nature of community, or the importance of a relational understanding of life, they must eventually do so by grounding it not in a general account of personhood and relationality, but in reflection on the life specifically of the Father, Jesus and the Spirit. To put it another way: talk about the Trinity should not ever be something different from the Bible's talk about the grace of the Lord Jesus Christ, the love of God and the fellowship of the Holy Spirit.

The second temptation is so to focus on the specificity of each of the persons, Father, Son and Spirit, that one ignores the one life that they share. So, for instance, one might find a Christian devotional programme that assumes that one can and should have clearly distinct experiences of the Father, of the Son, and of the Spirit – turning to each in turn for a different kind of relationship. Or one might find theology that assumes that when discussing some doctrine – say, the doctrine of salvation – one can treat the 'work of Christ' fully and completely before moving on to the distinct 'work of the Spirit': the two 'works' might be co-ordinated in some way, but they are presented as separate activities, perhaps relating to different stages of a person's salvation.

Once again, this is less than fully Trinitarian. Trinitarian theology knows the three persons only as they take their places in a life together. The Father appears in the Gospels simply as one who sends the Son and the Spirit; the Son as one who points back to Father and hands over to the Spirit; the Spirit as one who teaches about the Son and leads to the Father. These three are who they are only in relation to one another, and so to know the Son one has to know the Son-as-related-to-the-Father-and-the-Spirit, to know the Spirit one has to know the Spirit-as-related-to-the-Son-and-the-Father, and to know the Father one has to know the Father-as-related-to-the-Spirit-and-the-Son. In Christian devotion, any experience of the Son that one might have is always experience *in* the Spirit, and experience directed *towards* the Father; if it is not those things then it is not experience of this Son – and so on. Or in the doctrine of salvation, the work of the Spirit is the work that the Spirit does in drawing people *to* the Father and the Son, involving them in the life between these two. If it does not do that, then it is not the work of this Spirit. For fully Trinitarian theology, one simply cannot pull any of the three persons out of their shared life for separate scrutiny – except as a temporary and obviously artificial aid to understanding.

Perichoresis and appropriation

The Greek word 'perichoresis' is used to speak of the kind of unity that the three persons in the economy share, and (analogously and unimaginably) the kind of unity that the three persons of the immanent life of God share. Perichoresis is graspable in the economy: it names the way in which one cannot ultimately extract any one of the *dramatis personae* from the other two; each is what it is only in relation to the other two. The word originally meant something like 'giving place to one another in turn', and came to mean something like 'being what you are in and through another' – the Latin equivalent is *circumincessio*; English translations use words like 'coinherence' or 'interpenetration'. We can see what 'perichoresis' means in the economy – it is displayed in the patterns I described in the early sections of this chapter – but once again we have no grasp on what it means in God's immanent life, except by saying that that immanent life aptly gives itself to us in an economy of three perichoretically related persons.

'Appropriation' is the word used to name the way in which consideration of the Trinity can start from any one of the persons. So you can start thinking about the Father, only to find yourself needing to refer to Son and Spirit in order to do justice to the Father; you can start thinking about the Son, only to find yourself thinking about the Father and the Spirit, and so on. Some doctrines have traditionally been linked to such ways of starting with one of the three. Consideration of the doctrine of creation, for instance, often involves starting with consideration of the Father as Creator. The doctrine is said to be 'appropriated' to the Father. If this is to be adequate Trinitarian reflection, however, such consideration will go on to include the involvement of the Son and the Spirit in creation too: creation will only be fully understood once it is understood as the one work of God, Father, Son and Holy Spirit.

Key points

- The community of the Trinity is always the community of Father, Son and Holy Spirit, and one should not become so enamoured of the general idea of 'community' as to turn away from the specific identities and relationships of these three.
- The three persons of the Trinity are, for Trinitarian theologians, so defined by their relations to one another that there can be no experiences of, or claims about, or relationship to one person that does not involve the other two.

It's the economy, stupid[20]

The doctrine of the Trinity as traditionally formulated does involve speaking of the triunity of God's immanent life (or of 'the immanent trinity', to use the traditional phrase), and it does involve speaking of the eternal persons of the Godhead – the eternal Father, the eternal Son and the eternal Spirit. But to speak this way is not to propose some other object for one's attention, separable from the economy – as if one might turn away, say, from Jesus and concentrate *instead* on the eternal person of the Trinity that lies behind him, or turn away from the movements of the Spirit in history and concentrate *instead* on the eternal Spirit that lies behind them. Rather, to learn to speak appropriately about God's immanent life is to learn to see the human being Jesus – a graspable, knowable, historical, economic reality – *as* the coming to the world of the ineffable, eternal Son; it is to learn to see the Father who appears in one's economic imaginations and words *as* the coming to the world of the eternal, ineffable Father; it is to learn to see the shakings and stirrings of the Spirit's historical, economic work *as* the coming to the world of the ineffable, eternal Spirit. It is to learn to see the whole patterned drama of the economy, into which Christians believe all are called, *as* the opening up to the world of God's own immanent life.

All this talk of 'economic' and 'immanent' should not, therefore, involve any scorn being poured on those who only know the economy, as if the Trinitarian theologian might ridicule their immaturity and point to the more abstract heights of knowledge available to the real experts. Instead, it insists that *the economy is enough*. Of course, one cannot (for traditional Trinitarian theology, at least) simply declare that the economy is God, full stop. That would be to reduce God to a graspable set of historical realities. Nevertheless, the doctrine of the Trinity declares that this graspable, knowable, effable set of historical realities *is* the ineffable God's way of making Godself known. This *is* the opening up for us, Trinitarian Christianity says, of the ineffable life of God – a life that is itself something like a drama, something like a dance, something like a community. This *is* the arrival in history of the immanent life of God that one can therefore know to be an eternal circulation of three hypostases in relation – even though one does not know what 'hypostasis' means in this case, or 'relation', or even 'three'. Never mind: whatever this immanent life is, it meets one here, and it is not *less* than what meets one here.

Rahner on the Trinity

The German Catholic theologian Karl Rahner famously insisted that 'The "economic" Trinity is the "immanent" Trinity, and the "immanent" Trinity is the "economic" Trinity.'[21] That is, to meet the economic Trinity *is* to meet the immanent Trinity; the immanent Trinity is not a separate object for Christian contemplation. God's immanent life is not simply *like* the economic face that God shows to the world; that economic face *is* the opening up for the world of God's own life.[22]

Key points

- All this talk of the immanent Trinity is not meant to distract attention from the economy, but to give one a way of seeing that economy.
- Trinitarian theology involves learning to see the persons of the economy *as* the coming to the world of the eternal persons of the immanent Trinity.

Imagining salvation

How then are Christians to grasp the doctrine of the Trinity? It tells them that God has both transcribed God's own life into terms that human beings can see, learn and grasp – and that God has done so not simply to *show* them that life, not simply to communicate to them, but to open that life up for their participation. It tells them that they have been invited to share the life that the Father, the Son and the Spirit share, and that when they share that community's life they are sharing in God's own life. It tells them not to think of a lonely god who made them to meet his need for company, but a loving community whose love overflows, and seeks others to join its delight. It suggests that the life of God is and always has been a feast, but that now it is a feast that they are invited to join: the banquet of the kingdom. And it tells them that their lives are inextricably interwoven with the Father, with the Son and with the Holy Spirit: that the same God is above them, beside them and within them; that the same God is the goal, the road and the motive force that drives them.

Of course, these are metaphors, parables and analogies rather than straightforward descriptions, but it is probably in such imaginative language, rather than in the austerities of propositional claims or even pragmatic description, that Christians best learn to grasp the nature of the economy of salvation in which they are being caught up. It is through such imaginative language that Christians might learn to glimpse, in a glass darkly, the triune face of God.

Key point

- Christians can make sense of their lives as lives on their way into the triune life of God: lives on the way to the Father, alongside the Son, in the power of the Spirit.

Going further

1 For a fuller understanding of the Trinity, you need to know more about the contexts in which the doctrine arose, the questions its framers were asking, the practices it fitted in to. As well as the books in note 14, see Ralph del Colle 'The Triune God' in Colin Gunton (ed.), *The Cambridge Companion to Christian Doctrine* (Cambridge: Cambridge University Press, 1997), which includes an overview of the history, and Basil Studer, *Trinity and Incarnation* (Edinburgh: T&T Clark, 1994), which tells the early history well.

2 There has been a revival of Trinitarian theology in recent decades, and discussion of the doctrine takes many forms. It is well worth sampling some of that variety: you can look among many others at a liberation theology perspective in Leonardo Boff, 'Trinity' in Jon Sobrino and Ignacio Ellacuría (eds), *Systematic Theology* (London: SCM Press, 1996), pp. 75–89; an Orthodox perspective in Vladimir Lossky, *The Mystical Theology of the Eastern Church* (London: James Clarke & Co., 1957), especially chapter 3, 'God in Trinity'; an Anglican perspective in Christopher Cocksworth, *Holy, Holy, Holy: Worshipping the Trinitarian God* (London: DLT, 1997); or a Baptist perspective in James W. McClendon, *Systematic Theology 2: Doctrine* (Nashville, TN: Abingdon, 1994), chapter 7, 'The identity of God'.

> 3 Karen Kilby's paper 'Perichoresis and projection: problems with social doctrines of the Trinity', New Blackfriars 81 (2000), pp. 432–45, available online at http://www.theologyphilosophycentre.co.uk/papers/Kilby_TrinNBnew.doc, is worth a look for its clear criticisms of theologies that take the general idea of 'perichoresis' as the real meaning of the doctrine of the Trinity, or that use the analogy of three persons too easily and directly to model the immanent nature of God. It would be a good exercise to read her paper and ask whether my presentation in this chapter oversteps the boundaries that she sets.

Notes

1 H. G. Wells, *The Outline of History* (Garden City, NY: Garden City Publishing Co., 1920): §29.2; available online at ibiblio: http://www.ibiblio.org/pub/docs/books/sherwood/Wells-Outline/Outline_of_History.htm.

2 I learnt this point above all from Hans Frei, *The Identity of Jesus Christ: The Hermeneutical Bases of Dogmatic Theology* (Philadelphia: Fortress Press, 1975).

3 The phrase 'the proclaimer became the proclaimed' is from Rudolf Bultmann, *Theology of the New Testament* (New York: Charles Scribner's Sons, 1951), p. 33.

4 The 'him' in 'believes in him' is clearly the Son rather than the Father. The passage is drawing a parallel between the Father's raising up of the Son and Moses' raising up of the serpent in the wilderness: those who looked on the serpent were saved, as will those be who look on the Son (John 3.14–16, referring to Numbers 21.5–9).

5 Larry W. Hurtado, *Lord Jesus Christ: Devotion to Jesus in Earliest Christianity* (Grand Rapids, MI: Eerdmans, 2003), p. 2.

6 This text was traditionally ascribed to Basil of Caesarea, as *Epistle 38: On the distinction between* ousia *and* hypostasis; it is now regularly ascribed to Gregory. This translation is from 'St Basil – Epistle 38', tr. M. C. Steenberg, published online in 2002 at http://www.monachos.net/downloads/epistle38.pdf, p. 4 (Loeb Vol. 190, pp. 209–10).

7 Acts 3 and 4 of this drama follow the two halves of the love command: love of God and love of neighbour. They also recall H. Richard Niebuhr's saying about Christ: 'Because he loves the Father with the perfection of human eros, therefore he loves men with the perfection of divine agape, since God is agape.' *Christ and Culture* (New York: Harper and Row, 1951), p. 28.

8 A high-resolution reproduction of the icon is available online at *Christian Art*, http://www.icon-art.info/masterpiece.php?lng=en&mst_id=161; for discussion of the icon's significance, see Paul Evdokimov, *The Art of the Icon: A Theology of Beauty*, tr. Stephen Bigham, 4th edn (Knob Hill, CA: Oakwood, 1996 [French original 1970]), pp. 243–57; reproduced online at eSnips: http://www.esnips.com/doc/ebo86f5c–6b5c–4364–932d–1294e16aeg9c/Evdokimov-on-Rublev-Trinitatis-icon. For more on Rublev himself, you could watch Tarkovsky's film, *Andrey Rublyov* (Mosfilm, 1969); see details on the Internet Movie Database at http://uk.imdb.com/title/tt0060107/.

9 C. S. Lewis, *Mere Christianity* (New York: HarperCollins, 2001 [original edn: 1952]), p. 163.

10 Those of you who know the work of Karl Barth may recognize here an echo of his 'threefold Word of God': the address of God meets us in Christ, in Scripture and in the Church's witness. See Karl Barth, *Church Dogmatics I/1. The Doctrine of the Word of God*, revised edn (Edinburgh: T&T Clark, 1975), pp. 88–124.

11 Recall 1 Corinthians 15.28: 'When all things are subjected to him, then the Son himself will also be subjected to the one who put all things in subjection under him, so that God may be all in all.'

12 See Martin Buber, *I and Thou* (London: Continuum, 2004 [German original, 1923]).

13 Note that the unimaginable mystery of God, God's unknowability, is not a sticking-plaster invented to cover up the difficulties in the doctrine of the Trinity – as it were, a matter of hand-waving dismissal in response to questions about how one God can be three. Rather the doctrine of the Trinity is a way of thinking about and relating to the unknowable mystery of God.

14 This is a simplified version of one of the strands of debate involved in the condemnation of Arius at the Council of Nicaea, and the debates of later decades that Athanasius of Alexandria managed to present as a contest between Arian and Nicene theology. See Rowan Williams, *Arius: Heresy and Tradition* (London: SCM Press, 2001); Lewis Ayres, *Nicaea and its Legacy: An Approach to Fourth-Century Trinitarian Theology* (Oxford: Oxford University Press, 2004); and John Behr, *Formation of Christian Theology*, vol. 1, *The Way to Nicaea*, and vol. 2, *The Nicene Faith* (Crestwood, NY: St Vladimir's Seminary Press, 2001 and 2004).

15 Cf. John 1.14.

16 Traditional formulations of the doctrine also talk about the relations between the hypostases in the immanent life of God – but again, they make it clear that we don't really know what we are talking about when we do this. *That* there is something in the divine life that corresponds to the economic relationship between Father and Son is clear; *what* that something is is beyond our grasp. Traditionally, the word 'generation' is used for the utterly mysterious relation between Father and Son, and 'procession' for the utterly mysterious relation between Father and Spirit.

17 John Burnaby, *The Belief of Christendom: A Commentary on the Nicene Creed* (London: SPCK, 1963), p. 203, quoting Augustine, *De Trinitate* 7.11. The prayer, 'O holy, blessed, and glorious Trinity' is from the Litany in the Church of England's 1662 *Book of Common Prayer*. For a strident critique of Augustine's understanding of 'person' in Trinitarian theology, see Colin Gunton, *The Promise of Trinitarian Theology*, 2nd edn (Edinburgh: T&T Clark, 1997), ch.3.

18 For a detailed history of the theological use of the word 'substance', see G. C. Stead, *Divine Substance* (Oxford: Oxford University Press, 1977).

19 In Philip Schaff and Henry Wace (eds), *Nicene and Post-Nicene Fathers*, Second Series, vol. 5 (New York: Christian Literature Publishing Co., 1892), p. 334; available online at the Christian Classics Ethereal Library, http://www.ccel.org/ccel/schaff/npnf205.viii.v.html.

20 The phrase 'It's the economy, stupid' was an electioneering slogan coined by James Carville during Bill Clinton's campaign for the American presidency in 1992. It seems likely that he did not have in mind God's economy of salvation.

21 Karl Rahner, *The Trinity*, tr. Joseph Donceel (Tunbridge Wells: Burns & Oates, 1970), p. 22.

22 Rahner's rule can be interpreted in other ways. See, for a critical account, Randal Rauser, 'Rahner's Rule: An Emperor without Clothes', *International Journal of Systematic Theology* 7.1 (2005), pp. 81–94.

5

God's Human Life

In this chapter, I am going to approach the same territory that I explored in Chapter 4, but from a different direction, and with my focus firmly and constantly on Jesus. What kind of centrality does Jesus have in Christian faith? Does he have the kind of centrality in Christianity that one would expect simply of a founder of an influential movement? Does he have the centrality that one would expect of a great hero, or one endowed with remarkable powers? Does he have the centrality of an abiding exemplar? I will use some artistic depictions of Jesus to guide my exploration of various different models of Jesus' centrality, and approach by degrees the classical doctrinal claim that Jesus is one person, fully divine and fully human – that is, the claim that Jesus is central to Christianity because he is God's own human life. In other words, the subject matter of this chapter is *Christology*: the doctrine of Christ.

I am going to

- argue that any centrality Jesus has in Christianity he has as an entirely human being;
- suggest that Jesus can be seen as an exemplar of human life in all its fullness;
- argue that by itself this is not enough, and could in fact have debilitating consequences for those who follow Jesus; and
- suggest that Jesus must also be seen as God's action on the world's behalf, or God's way of loving the world.

Preparation

- Classical Christian doctrine claims that Jesus is, at one and the same time, both 'fully human' and 'fully divine' – but what do these two claims mean? Jot down two brief paragraphs, clarifying for yourself what you think. What are the most important things being said, and what are the most important things being denied, when these two classical claims are made?
- In this chapter, I will be showing you some famous pictures of Jesus, and presenting you with interpretations of those pictures. Spend some time now looking at pictures of Jesus without the clutter of my interpretations. There are plenty of places to look, especially online. For instance you could look on *Wikimedia Commons* http://commons.wikimedia.org/wiki/Category:Jesus_Christ, or Google Image Search http://images.google.co.uk/images?q=jesus, or Stephen Cook's *Images of Jesus through Two Millennia* site, http://www.beliefnet.com/story/22/story_2283_1.html. Do some exploring. What images stand out? Which ones do you like? Which do you hate? Why?

Additional reading

As accompaniments to this chapter, all of which approach Christology from unexpected directions, I recommend:

Rowan Williams, *The Dwelling of the Light: Praying with Icons of Christ* (Norwich: Canterbury Press, 2003) and *Ponder These Things: Praying with Icons of the Virgin* (Norwich: Canterbury Press, 2002). Two short devotional books, that nevertheless include clear explanations of Christological doctrine.

James Allison's book, *Knowing Jesus*, 2nd edn (London: SPCK, 1998). An enigmatic but enlightening account of what it means to *know* Jesus.

David Ford and Mike Higton (eds), *Jesus*, Oxford Readers series (Oxford: Oxford University Press, 2002). A collection of hundreds of extracts from texts in which writers from across the last two millennia have discussed Jesus.

The face of Christ

Deep in the Vatican, peering out from an elaborate seventeenth-century housing, there is an ancient, scarcely visible full-face portrait of a bearded man (see Plate 2). It was probably painted some time after the third century AD, but there is a legend attached to it that claims an older, stranger origin. This legend claims that there was an exchange of letters between Jesus and the ruler of the city of Edessa, a man called Abgar. The ruler is supposed to have sent his servant Hannan to Jesus with a letter saying,

> Your deeds have come to my notice, and your healings performed without either medicine or herbs. Having heard all these deeds of yours, I have thought of two possible explanations: either that you are God and have come down from heaven and do these things, or that you are the Son of God. For this reason I have written to ask you to take the trouble to come to me and cure me of my disease.[1]

Jesus was unable to go to Edessa because of all that he had to do in Israel, but he sent a reply saying,

> Happy are you, having believed in me without having seen me, for it is written of me that those who shall see me shall not believe in me, and that those who shall not see me shall believe in me

and he allowed Hannan to take a portrait of him back to Abgar. In some versions of the legend it was Hannan (who turned out, conveniently, to be Abgar's court painter) who painted the portrait; in other, more popular versions of the legend it was Jesus himself who provided the portrait, by miraculous means.

The legend is only one of several that circulated in the medieval Church attached to icons or statues intensely venerated as 'true likenesses' of Christ. There is the legend of St Veronica, who was said to have wiped Jesus' face with a cloth when he was on the way to the cross, only to find that the cloth had become imprinted with an image of his face.[2] There is the legend that St Luke himself painted a portrait of the infant Jesus in the arms of his mother.[3] There is the legend that Nicodemus the Pharisee exhausted himself attempting to sculpt an image of Christ on the cross, only to have it completed one night by an angel.[4] And, of course, there is also the much-debated Turin shroud – supposedly the burial cloth in which Jesus' body was wrapped, miraculously preserving an imprint of his body.

Pen portrait

There is a once-famous medieval text that purports to be a letter written by a Roman official in Palestine at the time of Jesus' ministry:

In these days there appeared, and there still is, a man of great power named Jesus Christ, who is called by the Gentiles the prophet of truth, whom his disciples call the Son of God, raising the dead and healing diseases: a man in stature middling tall, and comely, having a reverend countenance, which those who look upon may love and fear; having hair of the hue of an unripe hazelnut and smooth almost down to his ears, but from the ears in curling locks somewhat darker and more shining, flowing over his shoulders; having a parting at the middle of the head according to the fashion of the Nazareans; a brow smooth and very calm, with a face without wrinkle or any blemish, which a moderate red colour makes beautiful; with the nose and mouth no fault at all can be found; having a full beard of the colour of his hair, not long, but a little forked at the chin; having an expression simple and mature, the eyes grey, flashing, and clear; in rebuke terrible, in admonition kind and loveable, cheerful yet keeping gravity; sometimes he has wept, but never laughed; in stature of body tall and straight, with hands and arms fair to look upon; in talk grave, reserved and modest, fairer than the children of men.

Anonymous, *Letter of Lentulus*[5]

None of these (nor any of the other similar medieval legends) has any basis in fact, although some would except the Turin shroud, which still causes bitter debates between adherents and sceptics. But even if they don't display Jesus' features, they expose one of the connecting threads of Christian devotion: they witness to a fascination with Jesus Christ as a particular human being running through Christian life. They witness, that is, to the fact that Christianity has been animated not so much by commitment to a moral or spiritual *principle* as by captivation by a human *person*.

Of course, there are no known images of Jesus that can make any claim to be portraits painted in Jesus' lifetime – nor any reason to think that such a portrait was every painted. Nor is there in the Gospels or in any other of the earliest written records of Christianity any attempt to describe Jesus' physical appearance in words. For written descriptions one has to wait until the second century, and for actual attempts to draw, paint or sculpt something intended to be a *portrait* of Jesus one has to wait even longer.[6] There does not, in other words, seem to be in very early Christianity the kind of fascination with images of Jesus that was to flourish in the medieval period, and that might seem to our image-saturated society to be a necessary expression of any real interest in the person himself.

We do find, however, right from the very earliest forms of Christianity for which we have direct evidence, that the particular human being Jesus of Nazareth was a focus of Christian devotion, addressed in hymns and prayers and liturgical formulae. And we also find that one of the persistent shapes taken by that devotion was a fascination with passing on the *story* of Jesus. The early church was fascinated not so much by Jesus' appearance, as by what he did and by what happened to him.

What kind of centrality does Jesus have in Christian faith? These images of Christ clearly mean more than the portraits of the founder to be found on the boardroom wall of a modern business, and these stories about him are clearly more than interesting anecdotes. Jesus was not simply remembered because he was the founder of Christianity, nor because he was the one who first preached the Christian message. Jesus himself stands at the focus of Christian attention. Why is that?

Jesus in church

If you find yourself in a church service some time soon, pay attention to all the ways in which Jesus is referred to or mentioned or depicted – in songs or prayers or sermons or stained glass or posters or inscriptions. ... Is Jesus given some kind of central place? In what ways? What role or roles does Jesus seem to play in the life of this church, according to what you see and hear in this service?

Key point

- Captivation by a particular human being, rather than a set of principles or proceeses, lies at the heart of Christianity.

Fully human: Finitude and bodiliness

Georges de la Tour's painting of a newborn child (see Plate 3) may or may not be a picture of the infant Jesus. It was first flatly catalogued as 'representing a woman carrying a swaddled infant in her arms, and another woman holding a lit candle which illuminates the tableau',[7] and it may have been conceived simply as a touching domestic scene, a scene of great ordinariness. A mother cradles her newborn baby, wrapped tightly in swaddling cloths; baby and adoring mother are lit only by a single candle, shielded by the hand of another woman – the grandmother, perhaps, or a nurse. All needs met for the moment, the baby sleeps, wrapped and held, dependent and frail. The baby, the mother, the nurse – they could be anyone. Yet it is no surprise that a modern art historian describes it unhesitatingly as a picture of 'St Anne and [the] Virgin to whom a child has been miraculously born'[8]: it would not be too far out of place among a thousand other such images about which there is no question.

This possible confusion between domestic and religious subject matter is not insignificant. After all, much Christian devotion has anchored itself on the claim that the Jesus who stands at the centre of their devotion was once a tiny defenceless baby, frail and dependent, swaddled and nursed by his mother, in *just the same way* that other babies are.

Yet it was no foregone conclusion that Christian devotion should end up taking this form. There was a strong tendency in the ancient world for heroes to be seen as elevated above the ordinary constraints of humanity, and for a long time it looked as if Christianity was going to be no exception. One of the ways in which Jesus was claimed to be central to Christian faith and life was precisely as some kind of superhero, someone over whom the mess, dirt, pain and suffering of ordinary human life had no power, and from whom it ran like water off a duck's back. A superhero like that would have the strength to carry his followers away from pain, suffering and confusion – or perhaps he would pass on to them his amazing powers?

There are plenty of texts from the first few centuries of Christianity in which the *ordinariness* of Jesus' humanity, its frailty and dependence, were vigorously denied. Jesus' job, said some, was not to save us *as* human beings, but to save us *from* our humanity – to lift us out of finitude, bodiliness and diversity to some other sphere where we need not be troubled by them. How could he himself, if he was to save us from these things, have been mired in their fleshy mess? It is possible to find texts from the first centuries of the Church that state this quite blatantly. There are texts that claim that Jesus' body had no ordinary bodily functions; there are texts that deny that he truly suffered; and there are texts that portray him as the enemy of the material world.[9] Even some quite mainstream texts show a good deal of the same embarrassment with the constraints of human nature. Eusebius of Caesarea, whose theology was in his day considered extremely respectable, wrote in his 'Demonstration of the Gospel' early in the fourth century after Christ that 'There is no need to be disturbed in mind on hearing of the birth, human body, sufferings and death of the immaterial and unembodied Word of God' – a claim that, of course, can't but make one wonder whether his readers *were* likely to be disturbed by these things – and he goes on to speak of the divine Word taking on a human body and playing it like a lyre, a metaphor that could make Jesus' body seem like a dispensable puppet for a divine puppeteer who will not himself be sullied by the sufferings and limitations that he allows the puppet to experience.[10]

An ordinary baby

The African theologian Tertullian, who we met in Chapter 1, wrote a treatise *On the Flesh of Christ* in which he attacked the views of Marcion, a theologian who seems to have been embarrassed by the idea that Jesus might ever have been an ordinary baby.[11] Tertullian addresses Marcion with heavy sarcasm:

Beginning then with that nativity you so strongly object to, orate, attack now, the nastiness of genital elements in the womb, the filthy curdling of moisture and blood, and of the flesh to be for nine months nourished on that same mire. Draw a picture of the womb getting daily more unmanageable, heavy, self-concerned, safe not even in sleep, uncertain in the whims of dislikes and appetites. ... You shudder, of course, at the child passed out along with his afterbirth, and of course bedaubed with it. You think it shameful that he is straightened out with bandages, that he is licked into shape with applications of oil, that he is beguiled by coddling. This natural object of reverence you, Marcion, be-spittle: *yet how were you born?*

Tertullian, *On the Flesh of Christ*[12]

Despite this tendency, it was in the end the affirmation that Jesus' body, mind and soul were fully human that became definitive of Christian orthodoxy, if not always of Christian sensibility. When, in AD 451, the Council of Chalcedon issued an authoritative statement on Christology, a statement that was held to be binding by a large part of the Christian Church at the time, and has been since, it included the claims that Jesus was 'perfect [i.e. complete] in manhood', and that he had been made 'in all things like unto us, sin only excepted'.[13] Such orthodox Christian faith asserts that Jesus is fully, unreservedly human: that he grew in Mary's womb, that he was born bedaubed with afterbirth, and that he was 'straightened out with bandages', 'licked into shape with applications of oil', and 'beguiled by coddling', as Tertullian put it.

We must reckon, orthodox Christian theology says, with a Jesus who has a human body, a human mind, human strengths and all those human weaknesses that are not themselves sinful, who thinks and acts in the way that human beings think and act – not only when an infant in his mother's arms, but through his whole life, his passion and his death. Jesus of Nazareth is presented in the Gospels as a finite creature, one actor amongst many in a social scene. Like us, he lives in an environment he can't fully control; like us he is hedged about by limits he can't overcome. Like us he faces frustration; like us he is jostled in a confined space by the plans and actions of others. Like us, he can only act in limited ways, and he can only make a limited difference – and like us he has only a limited degree of control over the difference that he makes. Like us, he is dependent upon others. Like us, he can be injured; like us he can be killed.

And, like us, he was shaped by his context. He grew up at a particular time and in a particular place, enmeshed in a particular set of relationships; his identity was shaped by his environment, just as we are shaped by ours. He would have been shaped profoundly by his relationship with the mother who swaddled him, nursed him and raised him. To claim that Mary's identity was irrelevant to Jesus' identity would be to deny Jesus his full humanity – even if that doesn't allow us easily to read anything of Mary's character from that of the son whom she must have influenced so strongly. He was also shaped by growing up as a Jew in a Jewish world: his identity is a thoroughly and ineradicably Jewish identity, formed by Jewish practices, Jewish Scriptures, Jewish ideas, Jewish people, albeit at a time and in a place where Judaism was in complex interaction with the Hellenistic culture of the eastern Roman world. To deny the Jewishness of Jesus, to deny that it is constitutive of his identity, is to deny his full humanity: Judaism provided the womb from which the baby Jesus emerged, the swaddling bands that surrounded him from the moment that he appeared, and the nurture that allowed him to grow towards maturity.

All of this is part of what it means to be truly bodily, truly creaturely, truly particular. Jesus of Nazareth was fully, entirely, human; he was a finite creature. Whatever centrality in Christianity is claimed for Jesus, it must not – if it is to be consistent with this central affirmation – involve any claim that Jesus was somehow insulated from his context, so as to receive his identity direct and fully formed from above; it must not involve any claim that Jesus had some extra faculty or capacity bolted on to this human nature like the superpower of a hero;[14] and it must not involve any claim that some aspect or part of this humanity was tinkered with so as to be immune from finitude. Jesus of Nazareth is, in orthodox Christian theology, unreservedly and unadulteratedly human. What place, then, does he have at the focus of Christian life?

Not quite human

In the centuries since AD 451, when the question was supposedly settled, Christians have often remained reluctant to accept Jesus' full humanity, and have developed all sorts of ways, some of them more blatant, some of them more subtle, of holding up a picture of Jesus that is not *quite* human. As an example of the more subtle versions of such thinking, consider the quite unscriptural idea that Jesus somehow suffered in a way that was quantitatively and qualitatively different from ordinary human suffering – taking him into realms of suffering that no other human being has or could have experienced, and making him more to be pitied than any other human being before or since. In such thinking, Jesus' suffering is turned into something other than human suffering, and so Jesus himself becomes something other than fully human. This is one accusation that has been levelled against Mel Gibson's film, *The Passion of the Christ*[15] – that it pushes the depiction of Christ's suffering to such an extreme, beyond even that brutality needed for an accurate portrayal of the state-sponsored torture that killed him, until it becomes impossible to believe that someone who was 'only human' could have remained alive and conscious throughout. The film seems to suggest that Jesus' endurance was in some sense *super*human, and so denies him full humanity.

Exercise

Try watching some other films that portray Jesus. Are their ways in which their portrayals fail to show him as fully human?[16]

Key points

- According to orthodox Christian theology, Jesus is fully human.
- This means he is a finite and embodied creature.
- To claim that Mary's identity was irrelevant to Jesus' identity would be to deny his full humanity.
- To deny the Jewishness of Jesus is to deny his full humanity.

Fully human: The fullness of human life

Jesus is, for Christian devotion, not simply the founder of Christianity, nor simply the proclaimer of its central message, and nor is he a hero who is worthy of Christian devotion because of his superhuman ability to avoid the trials and tribulations of human life. How are Christians to think of him?

In the 1440s, Piero della Francesca painted a serenely calm image of Christ's baptism for the priory of San Giovanni in San Sepolcro, Tuscany. Like other pictures of Jesus' baptism, this picture would have helped those who saw it to put their own baptism into a wider context: Jesus was baptized in his time and place, and now I am baptized; I in my time and place am baptized after him, thanks to him, into him.[17]

This specific picture, however, portrayed Jesus with striking realism, using all the techniques of Renaissance art to create the illusion of a solid, realistically physical human being. And it portrayed him as a beautiful participant in a harmonious order.[18] Piero arranged the whole picture with mathematical precision, giving it a careful geometrical structure that held the main elements of his composition in balance (see Plate 4).[19] Although the edges were later obscured, the painting's overall shape originally consisted of a perfect circle centred on the dove of the Spirit, half overlapping with a perfect square that has Christ standing on its central vertical. Piero placed important vertical and horizontal elements on the lines of an evenly spaced grid, lending the whole a sense of spacious order, but superimposing over that grid diagonals that direct one's attention and give the picture focus. A whole set of diagonals seem to converge on Christ's hands, and the picture is cut by another line joining the only moving elements in the scene: the Baptist's outstretched arm and the back of the man undressing ready for baptism in the background. This is a Jesus poised and balanced, standing at the harmonious centre of a beautiful order.

Aldous Huxley once wrote of Piero that 'Even his technically religious pictures are paeans in praise of human dignity',[20] and in similar vein one might say that this painting is as much a picture of Renaissance humanism – that is, of the new confidence and delight in human beauty and capacity that flourished in the European Renaissance – as it is a picture of the gospel. The central figure is both Jesus Christ at one moment in the gospel story and a Renaissance everyman: a representation of an ideal, a fully fleshly yet perfectly balanced human being. It is a picture that can be set alongside other great Renaissance portrayals of human poise and possibility like Michelangelo's famous marble sculpture of David, or the equally famous sketch by Leonardo da Vinci

('Vitruvian Man') of a human being set symmetrically within a square and a circle.

Piero's painting hints at one deep current of Christian thinking about Jesus: the idea that Jesus shows us human life without the distortions and accretions that prevent it from being beautiful. The painting shows us a Jesus whose purity does not make him less than, more than, or other than human, but rather makes him *fully* human. Piero paints a physically beautiful Jesus to represent metaphorically the beauty of *life* to which all human life can and should attain.[21]

In Christian devotion, Jesus has not simply been seen as fully human in the sense of being unreservedly embodied and unreservedly historical; he has been seen as fully human in the sense of living human life to the full, living it as it should be lived. His life has been seen as human life lifted by God to its proper height, blazing an upward trail along which all other human beings are called: humanity lifted up towards God.

Without sin

Jesus is traditionally understood to have been utterly sinless – yet though that conviction has been firm, there has been less consensus on *how* Jesus remained sinless. Some have simply said that God arranged for it to be so, and that God was free to do so: God brought it about that there was this life in the world that was without sin. Others have said that Jesus was a 'God-intoxicated man',[22] who had a vision of God's love so clearly in front of him that he simply could not desire to sin. Others have said that one can only point to the work of God's Spirit, who leads and impels and shapes Jesus' life. The crucial point in each case, however, is that sin is *not* understood as a proper part of being human. It may be a disease endemic in the human population, but it is not (as it were) genetic: to be human and to be sinless is not a contradiction in terms. For God to keep Jesus sinless is not to prevent him from being human; it is to free him to be *fully* human.

Gabriel Fackre writes:

The intention of the traditional concept of the perfect humanity and 'sinlessness' of Jesus can be expressed with the help of the imagery of vision and light. Jesus' true and fulfilled humanity was constituted by his clear-sighted perception of, and unswerving obedience to, the vision [i.e. of God]. He saw the light and lived and moved and had his being in it. Because the light drew near to him, it so captured his gaze and orientation that it possessed him. He followed its path to the end. The tales of temptation at the opening and close of his ministry portray the persisting invitation of the powers of darkness to turn aside from the direction of light. But his commitment was undeviating, the 'set' of his will and behaviour arrow-straight.[23]

One of the ways in which Jesus has been central in Christian life has therefore been as *exemplar*: as the pattern to which Christians believe their lives should be conformed. Here is a man stripped of the vices that confine human life in destructive patterns, and filled instead with all the virtues that free and truly beautify human life. As Jesus says in John's Gospel, 'You call me Teacher and Lord – and you are right, for that is what I am. So if I, your Lord and Teacher, have washed your feet, you also ought to wash one another's feet. *For I have set you an example*, that you also should do as I have done to you' (John 13.13–15).

Imitation of Christ

Imitation of Christ has been a recurrent motif in Christian devotion down the centuries. Perhaps most famously, it was one of the keynotes of a late medieval movement known as the *Devotio Moderna*, and found expression in that movement's most celebrated literary work: Thomas à Kempis's *The Imitation of Christ*[24] – a book of astonishing popularity that has been reprinted some three thousand times since it was first written. The fascinated reaction to the book of Maggie Tulliver, the heroine of George Eliot's novel *The Mill on the Floss*,[25] gives some indication of how influential à Kempis's book could still be even in the mid-nineteenth century.

With all this, one could compare a much more recent form of devotion which, though it draws on some of the same theological ideas as the *Devotio Moderna*'s version of imitation, has grown in very different air: the late twentieth-century popularizing on bracelets, T-shirts, jewellery, bumper stickers and posters of the mnemonic *WWJD* – 'What would Jesus do?

Is this, then, the answer to our question? Is Jesus' centrality to Christian faith primarily the centrality of an exemplar? That is, is Jesus central to Christianity simply as the perfect embodiment of the virtues to which human beings are called, or is there more to it than that?

Key points

- Jesus can be understood as the one who is 'fully human' in the sense of showing us human life perfected and unrestricted.
- As such Jesus can be understood as an exemplar for human life.

Too high a bar to jump?

Look again at Piero's painting. Although I have been describing Piero's Jesus as beautiful, it is a kind of beauty that leaves many viewers today cold. In the first place, this Jesus perhaps suffers from Piero's attempts to make him an idealized figure, despite his solidity and particularity. Even though it was almost certainly painted from a particular human model, who had all the specificity and particularity that every human body has, is this is a figure who has had some of the marks of a particular history and character brushed out of his face and body in order to be made into an everyman?

In the second place, we are in our society perhaps too used to being presented with images of idealized human bodies, perfectly poised and balanced, not to be suspicious of the effects of an image like Piero's. Does this representation of a beautiful body not simply set an impossibly high bar for us to leap over, condemning us either to disgust at our own less perfect bodies or to unrelenting anxiety as we pursue the ideal?

In the third place, there is the simple fact that what looked beautiful to a Tuscan painter in the middle of the fifteenth century does not necessarily look beautiful now. By painting a real, physical human being, has Piero inevitably painted someone who belongs to a specific time and place – someone who, perhaps despite Piero's intentions, and despite what I said a moment ago, remains too solid, too located, too context-bound to be an everyman?

The three questions that Piero's painting raises suggest questions that one might put to the current of Christian thinking that sees Christ *primarily* as exemplar, *primarily* as the model of human life lifted to God. In the first place, to claim that Jesus' significance lies in his perfect embodiment of universal virtues comes perilously close to denying his real, full-blooded humanity. To focus our attention on the facets of Jesus' character that could and should be emulated by anybody else is to turn away from his individual specificity – his unsubstitutable story. It is to deny, in effect, that Jesus is thoroughly particular, thoroughly embedded in his particular time and place, thoroughly shaped by his specific context, as he lives in ways appropriate to the peculiar complexes of events and opportunities among which he found himself – or at least it is to deny that any of that finally matters. To take Jesus' significance to lie in his role as universal exemplar is to get close to enshrining a set of principles rather than a real person at the heart of Christianity.

In the second place, it is easy to see how Piero's picture could fail to be a message of good news. If Jesus is simply seen as marking the height to which one must jump, or the ideal shape to which one must reduce oneself, the message about him is likely to produce as much anxiety and despair as any impossibly thin supermodel can produce in those of us who are more amply constructed, and find dieting difficult. If Jesus is an exemplar showing the perfection of human life, he is just as likely to be heard as a word of condemnation, showing up just how far everyone else falls, and know they will go on falling, from the heights that he occupies.

Shallow Hal

The film Shallow Hal[26] asks where true human beauty lies. The eponymous hero, played by Jack Black, is too shallow to care about the character or virtue of the women he tries to date; he cares only about idealized surface beauty. Then he meets a man who hypnotizes him, putting him into a state where he will no longer see women's actual appearance, but will instead see as physically beautiful only those women who have beautiful personalities. Hal meets Rosemary, a vastly obese women who is ridiculed for her ugliness wherever she goes. Hal does not see this obesity, however: he sees her as beautiful

– and she is played by Gwyneth Paltrow, without a fat suit on whenever we see her through Hal's eyes, with it whenever we see her normally.

It is a fairly inconsequential film, although it does make a decent attempt to dramatize a familiar but regularly ignored piece of wisdom: you should not judge a book by its cover. The only real problem with it from a theological perspective is that the standard it sets up for *true* human beauty, while laudable in itself, could be just as disheartening, just as debilitating, as the standards of physical beauty set by supermodels and Hollywood starlets. Rosemary, and the other characters who appear beautiful to Hal, are frighteningly saintly: they are characters who have devoted themselves in extraordinary ways to the welfare of others. To live up to their worthy standard will require moral dieting every bit as impossible as the physical variety.

In the third place, the virtues displayed in the life of the young, Jewish male protagonist of the Gospels, itinerant and unmarried, are not obviously or immediately appropriate for any and every person in any and every time and place. It is simply not clear that Christian life can or should consist in 'reading off' from Jesus patterns of behaviour to be adopted by every one in every circumstance, from powerful rulers and police officers to battered wives and sweatshop workers. It is simply not true that he faced every situation that believers will face, and however helpful it might be to ask, 'What would Jesus do?', there are times when there is no obvious answer to that question, and even times when asking the question can be a way of avoiding the messy complexities and unavoidable compromises of one's situation. If the exemplarist approach comes perilously close to ignoring Jesus' full humanity, it also comes equally close to ignoring the full humanity – the particularity, the difference – of his Christian followers.

Key points

- To claim that Jesus' significance lies in his perfect embodiment of universal virtues comes close to denying his full humanity.
- If Jesus is simply seen as marking the height to which his followers need to jump, the message about him is likely to produce anxiety and despair.
- The virtues displayed in Jesus' life are not obviously or immediately appropriate for any and every person in any and every situation.

Imitation and obedience

These questions about the exemplarist tradition – that strand of Christian devotion that finds Jesus significant primarily as an example to be followed – can be sharpened if we turn to another image of Jesus, one very different from Piero's. The Jesus Piero paints is entirely poised and balanced, entirely serene and untroubled. He displays no signs of tension, no signs of struggle or suffering; his skin is like marble, and he stands as straight as a statue. Yet

the Gospels portray a Jesus who spends little time in those moments of exaltation when the story is filled with light and peace; they portray a Jesus who
lives meshed in conflict, and who soon goes his way into humiliation, torture
and death. We can find an image that admits more of this suffering than did
Piero's if we turn to a painting by the Sicilian painter Antonello da Messina,
who in around 1475 painted a picture of Christ enduring his flogging.

One of the first Italian painters to work with oil glazes, Antonello was able
to use the new medium to give his pictures great depth and realism.[27] Christ's
skin glows with warm light, his hair falls in drooping ringlets, tears glint on
his cheek. The painting breathes sadness, and everything about it is intended
to awaken the viewer's pity. It is in that sense a deeply sentimental painting
– and it is a painting in which all narrative context has been stripped away:
we see no Pilate, no crowd, no soldiers. We are simply directed to gaze on this
sorrowful face.

Antonello's painting is simply one example from a vast quantity of works,
produced particularly from the fourteenth century onwards, that focus their
attention relentlessly on the suffering of Christ the man of sorrows. By awakening the viewer's pity, these images were supposed to awaken a sense of the
awful fate that Christ had willingly suffered on one's behalf, to nurture a desire
to live so as to cause Christ no more pain, and to provide an image of the quiet
resignation and sober fortitude that were to be the pattern of such life.

Christ suffered uncomplainingly, the message runs, and his followers too
must be willing to suffer uncomplainingly, accepting without question the
fate that God throws their way. Such a strand of thinking could draw on biblical passages like Philippians 2.5–8, where Paul says, 'Let the same mind be
in you that was in Christ Jesus, who … emptied himself, taking the form of a
slave … humbled himself, and became obedient to the point of death'. Even
more strikingly, it could draw on 1 Peter 2.18–21:

> [18]Slaves, accept the authority of your masters with all deference, not only
> those who are kind and gentle but also those who are harsh. [19]For it is to
> your credit if, being aware of God, you endure pain while suffering un-
> justly. [20]If you endure when you are beaten for doing wrong, where is the
> credit in that? But if you endure when you do right and suffer for it, you
> have God's approval. [21]For to this you have been called, because Christ also
> suffered for you, leaving you an example, so that you should follow in his
> steps.

The dangers inherent in this approach can be seen in a nineteenth-century
text that takes the argument of 1 Peter a few steps further. Christ's suffering,
it says,

> is the motive which removes the love of sin: it mortifies sin by showing its
> turpitude to be indelible except by such an awful expiation … it excites to
> obedience; it purchases strength for obedience; it makes obedience prac-
> ticable; it makes it acceptable; it makes it in a manner unavoidable, for it
> constrains to it; it is, finally, not only the motive to obedience, *but the pattern
> of it*.[28]

This may not seem too objectionable, until one realizes that it comes from an 1835 book called *The Philosophy of Manufactures*, by a man called Andrew Ure, and that he is discussing the role that Christianity can play in producing a compliant workforce suitable for factory work – part of his larger argument in praise of the factory system. In Ure's hands, Christ as exemplar has, in effect, become Christ as taskmaster, inculcating docility and resignation among the poor, making sure that they will produce profit for their rich masters. Yet although Ure sets this out with stark clarity, he is only stating explicitly the worst implications of this wide stripe of Christian piety stretching back through Antonello da Messina and beyond, a piety that can even claim some support from 1 Peter and Philippians. Christ as exemplar, as the image of human life pleasing to God, can all too easily become a taskmaster showing believers how impossibly high they must jump – or, in this case, how impossibly low they must bow.

Key point

- Christ as exemplar can become Christ as taskmaster, inculcating docility and resignation.

True obedience

One can't get away from the kind of picture painted by Ure simply by downplaying Jesus' obedience – at least, not without downplaying the Gospels at the same time. After all, obedience even more than love is given as Jesus' leading characteristic in the Gospels. Two aspects of that obedience, however, take us far away from Ure's picture of a generalized, docile obedience imposed upon believers in all circumstances.

In the first place, the obedience of Christ portrayed in the Gospels is very specific – a specificity still present in Philippians and (just) in 1 Peter, but stripped away by the time we get to Antonello, and positively rejected by the time we reach Ure. What do I mean by the specificity of Christ's obedience? Well, one needs to ask both *to whom* Jesus was obedient, and *to what purpose*. In other words, the most important thing to notice is that it is not obedience as a generic virtue, but obedience specifically and only *to the Father, for the sake of the kingdom*. Jesus is portrayed again and again as the one who does what the Father desires, and not as the exemplar of an obedience that his followers should offer to anybody and everybody, in any circumstance. Instead, one should see Jesus' obedience as his unstinting involvement in the divine mission to which he dedicated his life – the mission of the kingdom. Jesus obediently lives out God's love for the world.

After all, the extract I have taken from Philippians does not simply describe Jesus as humble in the abstract; its description of Jesus' humility is part of a larger description of Jesus' journey from the Father and to the Father. Similarly, the advice I quoted from 1 Peter is not given simply as abstract advice on how to live in any and all circumstances (though it does admittedly get close to that); it is given precisely as guidance on how to proclaim the news of God's mission in Christ and win people to that mission when living under the conditions of the Roman Empire. And obedience to God does not automatically and unproblematically fit one for dependence on or obedience to worldly authority, whatever Andrew Ure (or 1 Peter) might say. After all, Jesus displays this obedience most clearly when he is in the process of being tortured and executed as a dissident by the authorities running his country. If Jesus' obedience is obedience to the Father, by the same token it is obedience directed towards the Father's kingdom of love and justice. Jesus' self-giving is not self-giving for self-giving's sake – self-giving in order to meet some generic ideal of humility and resignation. It is, rather, self-giving for the sake of the Kingdom: self-giving with a mission. It is the kind of self-giving that comes from being wholly caught up in a mission in the world, rather than the kind of self-giving that comes from meekly letting the world roll over you. Jesus, we might say, did not suffer torture and death because he quietly stayed at home, waiting for his society to crumble under the feet of the occupying Romans. He suffered torture and death because his ministry, his pursuit of the kingdom, challenged those in power and threatened their control.

In the second place, one can note that, for Christian theology, obedience to God is not like other forms of dependence, because God is not like others. Dependence upon God is – as I will be discussing further when we come to the doctrine of creation – dependence upon one who selflessly and truly wills one's flourishing and one's integrity, and one who selflessly and truly wills the flourishing of the whole world of which one is a part. It is, after all, dependence upon a God who *is* love-and-justice. This God, it is claimed, does not stand over against us as another ego competing with ours, but is rather the context in which one can grow towards full life and true relationships.

In this view, dependence upon God is more like dependence upon the air one breathes than it is like dependence upon one's driving instructor. It makes sense to say that, ideally, a person will one day become mature enough to go driving without his instructor's help; it doesn't make so much sense to say that, ideally, he will become mature enough to breath without oxygen's help. There can be no sense here that obedience to God involves getting subordinated to someone else's schemes and plans, schemes and plans (like those of the factory owner) that are all too likely to be an imposition on one's individuality and integrity.

Jesus, Christians believe, was wholly caught up in the service of the Father's kingdom of love and justice, agitating for that kingdom in the midst of the world. It is not that he is seen as squashing his own individuality and integrity so as to make way for God's mission, quietly accepting God's command as an imposition upon his life. Rather, he is portrayed as one whose whole life is caught up in and saturated by the Father's mission; he lives it and breathes it, such that it has become his own mission. This mission is no imposition upon him: he *is* this mission.

Exercise

Read the different versions of the Gethsemane story (Matthew 26.36–46; Mark 14.32–42; Luke 22.39–46). What kind of relationship between Jesus and the Father is suggested there? Think about your own answer before reading the following discussion by Karl Barth. Do you agree with him?

Karl Barth writes: 'Jesus prays that this hour, this cup of wrath, might pass from him, might be spared him. He prays therefore that the good will and the sacred work and the true word of God should not coincide with the evil will and the corrupt work and the deceitful word of the tempter and of the world controlled by him. ... He prays that God should not give him up to the power the temptation of which he had resisted and willed to resist in all circumstances. ... Surely this is something which God cannot will and allow. Such is the prayer of Jesus as prayed once in Luke, twice in Mark, and as many as three times in Matthew. ... But he only prays. He does not demand. He does not advance any claims. He does not lay upon God any conditions. He does not reserve his future obedience. ... He prays only as a child to the Father knowing that he can and should pray, that his need is known to the Father, is on the heart of the Father, but knowing also that the Father disposes what is possible and will therefore be, and that what he allows to be will be the only thing that is possible and right. If we understand the beginning of Jesus' prayer to God in this way – and how else can we understand it in view of what the texts say and in the context of the Gospels – then the meaning of what follows is clear: "But, or nevertheless, not what I will, but what thou wilt." (Mark 14.36; Matthew 26.39) Or more explicitly: "Nevertheless, not my will, but thine, be done." (Luke 22.42) Or even more explicitly: "O my Father, if this cup may not pass away from me except I drink it, thy will be done." (Matthew 26.42) ... This is not a kind of return of willingness to obey, which was finally forced upon Jesus and fulfilled by him in the last hour; it is rather a readiness for the act of obedience which he had never compromised in his prayer. The proviso "if it be possible" which was an integral part of the prayer now comes into force. The prayer reckoned on the possibility of quite a different answer. This is what had made it a genuine prayer to God. But now this possibility fades from view. Jesus does not change his mind when he says, "Thy will be done." After pausing with very good reason, he now proceeds all the more determinedly along the way which he had never left. ... He faces the reality the avoidance of which he had so earnestly desired. Because it is the reality of the will of God he grasps it as that which is better, which alone is good. He does not do so in sad resignation, therefore, but because he will and can affirm this reality and this alone. ... This is not a withdrawal on the part of Jesus, but a great and irresistible advance. It is not a resignation before God. It is an expression of the supreme and only praise which God expects of man and which is rendered to him only by this one man in place of all, the praise which comes from the knowledge that he does not make any mistakes, that his way, the way which he whose thoughts are higher than our thoughts actually treads himself, is holy and just and gracious.'

Karl Barth, *Church Dogmatics*[29]

We are now very close to the doctrine of the incarnation. In Christian theology, Jesus' activity is seen as, as it were, *transparent* to the Father's will. He was, his followers claimed, so open to the will of the Father, so captivated by it, so saturated by devotion to the kingdom, that it made sense for them to speak of his acts as being the acts of God working through him. In the terms of the musical metaphor used in Chapter 2, Jesus' commitment to the music was such that the music was playing him as much as he played it; he was so attuned to the melody that the Father was playing that he could be understood as the transcription of that divine melody for playing on a human instrument. Jesus' obedience matters in Christian theology not because by it he shows Christians the virtue of going quietly, but because he is the Father's kingdom of love and justice made audible; he is God's captivating music made flesh.

Key points

- Jesus' obedience is always obedience for the sake of the Father's kingdom of love and justice.
- It is therefore sometimes an obedience that requires disobedience to worldly authority.
- Jesus' obedience is always obedience to the Father.
- It is therefore an obedience that is no imposition upon him.
- Jesus is, for Christian theology, the one wholly transparent to God's mission.

God's gift

We have moved from the claim that Jesus is a perfect example of godly life to the claim that Jesus enacts God's life in the world. We are close to the heart of the doctrine of the incarnation already, but a few more steps in the argument are necessary.

In 1510, Matthias Grünewald painted a crucifixion scene for a monastic hospital (see Plate 5). Where Piero della Francesca's baptism picture was built from converging symmetrical lines, this picture was built from dislocated curves; where the former has a Jesus whose white skin looks like marble, this Jesus looks as if his body is already starting to decompose. Grünewald has done everything he can to heighten the horror: Jesus' extremities already seem to be gripped by rigor mortis; his skin is covered with bleeding wounds; his lips are grey; the cloth that wraps him is smeared and tattered; his limbs are twisted and his bones stand out, and the agony of his death is reflected in the stricken faces of the figures on the left: the two Marys and John the beloved disciple.

Although far less sentimental than Antonello da Messina's painting, less blatantly designed to tug at the heart-strings, the focus on Christ's passion is no less strong. There are, however, two crucial differences. Where Antonello's painting was quite possibly designed for private contemplation, this painting was created for a very specific public context; and where Antonello's painting stands on its own as an object of devotion, Grünewald's is but one part of a larger sequence.

This painting was produced for the church of the Isenheim monastery at Colmar, a hospital particularly dedicated to the care of those suffering from 'St Anthony's fire'. An earlier writer described it:

> The intestines eaten up by the force of St. Anthony's Fire, with ravaged limbs, blackened like charcoal; either they die miserably, or they live more miserably seeing their feet and hands develop gangrene and separate from the rest of the body; and they suffer muscular spasms that deform them.[30]

Those suffering from this disease would, at climactic moments in the year's liturgical round, see this image of Christ, his limbs blackened, twisted and covered in sores. This is, in other words, a picture of a Jesus who has come unreservedly to share the situation of the sufferers who see it. This is Jesus being *in* the world the demonstration of God's costly love *for* the world – a love that is utterly selfless, utterly self-giving; a love that seeks nothing for itself, but only seeks to be with the one loved, whatever the cost might be. The hospital patients could see on the cross the extreme point of the giving that Jesus had consistently demonstrated during his life. He had stepped over ritual and legal and social barriers, and the barriers created by wrongdoing and deceit, in order to eat and drink with sinners, and touch the sick and leprous. He made himself available, and allowed himself to become socially and ritually unclean, and to be tainted with the reputation of the sinners with whom he ate. The cross is of a piece with all this: Christ now stands fully on the side of broken, sinful, dying humanity, refusing in any degree to keep himself aloof. He is giving himself totally – even to the point of standing with them in separation from the Father. And in this extremity of self-giving, the suffering believer sees the self-giving of God; he sees God to be a God whose desire is for the broken world, and in whom nothing is held back from that desire. He sees a God who will step over any barriers and boundaries in order to be with the world.

There is more to the Isenheim altarpiece than this, however. This crucifixion scene was painted on the outermost panel of an altarpiece that could open up to display other images. On certain feast days, the doors could be opened to reveal scenes of celebration and light, including a startling resurrection scene (see Plate 6) in which a white-limbed Christ glowing with golden light soars free and healed from the grave. When combined, the two pictures, crucifixion and resurrection, glow with *promise* – a promise from the Father, who is the one who raises from the dead. The self-giving of the cross is not the end in itself: it is directed towards resurrection, the raising to new, perfected life of the diseased and broken body of Jesus, and the diseased and broken body of the sufferers for whom he died. This Jesus has come to share their life so that they might share his – a 'sweet exchange', as the anonymous second-century *Epistle to Diognetus* puts it.[31]

Note something else about this picture of the resurrection, though. In most of what I said in the previous section, the focus fell firmly on what Christ *did*

– his intentions, his activity, his deliberate carrying into effect of the Father's mission. In painting the resurrection, however, Grünewald is painting a Jesus who is alive and active, but not as the consequence of his own action. Jesus is raised from the dead by the Father, not by his own will or ability. The action portrayed in this picture is the Father's, even though the Father does not directly appear. And that fact might send us back to the crucifixion image with a new thought. This is a picture of Jesus' self-giving, certainly, but it is also a picture of Jesus as himself a gift, given to the suffering patients by God. Recall, after all, that this is an altarpiece, and would have been seen during celebrations of the Eucharist: the patients in this hospital would have seen a Jesus who had come to share their condition just at the moment that they received his body and blood as a gift from the hands of the priest.

The claim of orthodox Christian theology is not simply that Jesus' action was so obedient to the Father as to be transparent to the Father's will. The claim of orthodox Christian theology is not simply that by his obedient action Jesus shows the world the heart of the Father. Rather, the claim of orthodox Christian theology is that the entirety of Jesus' fully human life, lived out from birth to resurrection in a specific time and place, is a gift from God. This life *is* God's activity on the world's behalf, it *is* a creative word spoken by God to the world, bringing about the world's salvation. Jesus is, Christians say, the hand of God reached down into the midst of history, into the world of human beings and their plight, grasping hold not just of the Isenheim lepers in the midst of their suffering, but all of humanity, in order to raise them up with Christ to new life – the life of the resurrection, the life of glory, the life of perfected love and justice that is the life of God. Jesus is, in Christian theology, God's way of loving the world.

No achievement

The stories of Jesus in the Gospels are not stories of his *achievements*. They do not show the process by which he became virtuous, or show him fighting to overcome all that might have held him back. He is faced with temptations, certainly – but there is no hint that he must struggle to overcome them. Only in Gethsemane do we see a brief glimpse of such struggle. In the Gospels, Jesus is already the man (or baby) of God when he first appears. He does not so much show believers how to reach God, as show how God has reached them.

Contrast this with Nikos Kazantzakis's novel *The Last Temptation of Christ*, and Martin Scorsese's film adaptation. The film opens with a quotation from the prologue to the novel scrolling up the screen:

The dual substance of Christ – the yearning, so human, so superhuman, of man to attain to God or, more exactly, to return to God and identify himself with him – has always been a deep inscrutable mystery to me. This nostalgia for God, at once so mysterious and so real, has opened in me large wounds and also large flowing springs.

My principal anguish and source of all my joys and sorrows from my youth onward has been the incessant, merciless battle between the spirit and the flesh ... and my soul is the arena where these two armies have clashed and met.[32]

Kazantzakis carries on, later in the Prologue,

Struggle between the flesh and the spirit, rebellion and resistance, reconciliation and submission, and finally – the supreme purpose of the struggle – union with God: this was the ascent taken by Christ, the ascent which he invites us to take as well, following his bloody tracks. ...

If we are to be able to follow him we must have a profound knowledge of his conflict, we must relive his anguish: his victory over the blossoming snares of the earth, his sacrifice of the great and small joys of men and his ascent from sacrifice to sacrifice, exploit to exploit, to martyrdom's summit, the Cross.[33]

This is captivating and compelling – but it is not the gospel.[34]

Key points

- Jesus, by sharing the lot of suffering humanity, is held to demonstrate the Father's love for the world.
- Jesus shares this mortal life so that they might share his risen life.
- Christians believe that Jesus is God's way of loving the world.

The heart of the doctrine

It is time to take stock of the claims about Jesus that I have been exploring in this chapter (and to some extent in the previous chapter as well). I began with the claim that Jesus of Nazareth is unreservedly and unadulteratedly human. That is, he is not human with some inhuman powers or faculties added on, nor human but with some ordinary feature or limitation of human life missing. He lived an utterly finite, utterly creaturely life, a biological and cultural existence as a human being defined by nature and by nurture, utterly embroiled in a particular history, desiring, learning and suffering.

Yet, Christians claim, to encounter this human being is to encounter the love of God. In the first place, Jesus is portrayed in the Gospels as the *proclaimer* of God's love: he gives himself over to the proclamation of the Father's kingdom of love and justice. In the second place, he does not simply proclaim this love, he *shows* it. He puts his money where his mouth is. In the third place, however, Jesus' commitment to the kingdom is such that it has taken over his life: *it* acts through *him*. As I put it earlier, his obedience is such that we may say of his acts that they are the Father's acts, acting through him. The Father's kingdom flows in his veins; he is himself an outpost of that kingdom.

It is this captivation by the kingdom that enables Christians to say that Jesus was fully human in a second sense: he shows them human life as it should be, united to God, caught up in God's life. He shows that although sin may be endemic among human beings, it is not a necessary part of being human. Human beings properly belong in the stream of this divine life, and to be sinners is to live like fish out of water. Where we flounder, Jesus swims.

There is even more to Jesus' relationship to the kingdom than this, however. Christian theology claims that Jesus is *the Father's way of loving the world*. That is, he is not simply an example (or *the* example) of kingdom life; he is not simply an ambassador for the kingdom. He is what the Father is doing to establish the kingdom: he is the kingdom's foundation. Whilst it might make sense to say that all human beings are called to full humanity, and so to be where Christ is, fully immersed in the flow of God's life, this further claim about Jesus is one that is made about him alone. Jesus is the lynchpin of the economy of salvation.

God gives this human life to the world: bringing this life into being, and by the Holy Spirit impelling, animating and driving it, from conception on, to take the shape that it does. And God does so because this human life is God's way of setting the world on fire, of rekindling it to glory. God gives this fully human life to the world, in order to give God's own life to the world. This is the central claim of the Christian doctrine of incarnation.

Person and work

In many traditional discussions of Christology, you will find a distinction between the doctrine of Christ's *person* and the doctrine of Christ's *work*. The doctrine of Christ's person treats of his humanity and divinity. The doctrine of Christ's work treats of his achievement of humanity's salvation. Yet to speak of incarnation – the doctrine of Christ's person – is to speak of what God is doing by means of this human life – the doctrine of Christ's work, and the distinction should never be allowed to become a separation.

Key points

- Jesus proclaims God's love.
- Jesus shows God's love.
- God's love acts through Jesus.
- Jesus is God's way of loving the world.

A place in the Son

In Chapter 4, I argued that for Trinitarian theology knowing God is a matter of participation in the threefold economy. God is what Christians know, the life in which they participate, the life that makes itself at home in them, as they are drawn into this economy. I argued that it made sense to say that the immanent life of God that is known in this economy is, in some sense, one substance in three hypostases, and that the threefold economy is the opening up for creatures of this triune immanent life. Within that Trinitarian scheme, Jesus is seen specifically as the coming to the world, the self-revelation, of the second hypostasis of God's triune life, the hypostasis we name (for Jesus' sake) as the eternal Son.

This may sound like it says something rather different from what I have been saying in this chapter so far. After all, in this chapter I have been claiming that Jesus shows us the *Father*, and that Jesus is what the *Father* is doing. Yet in the last chapter, I said that Jesus shows us the *Son*, and that Jesus is what the *Son* is doing.

The difference is only apparent, however. These are really different ways of saying the same thing. After all, in a Trinitarian perspective, to know God is to be drawn into that love and justice that has its fount and origin in the Father; it is to be drawn into that love and justice that is formed within one in the power of the Spirit; and it is to be drawn into that love and justice that one recognizes in Jesus and is conformed to by being conformed to him.

The specific role Jesus plays in the whole drama of the threefold economy is therefore that of the one who makes the love of God, the love that comes from the Father, visible and shareable – the one in whom it is put in terms in which it can be imprinted upon a human life. The Spirit may press me into the mould, and the shape I take on may be one that responds to the Father – but the mould is Jesus. Jesus is the one in whom the life of God, the life that flows from the Father, becomes visible.

So while I used the word 'incarnation' loosely of the process by which the whole immanent Trinity shows itself in the threefold economy, it is a word that is more properly used of Jesus alone. Jesus is, by the Spirit, the *visibility* of the love that unites the Trinity; Jesus is that triune love made *flesh*.

In order to make the connection between Trinity and Incarnation more graspable, we have to risk a journey into more deeply imaginative language about the immanent life of God.[35] The eternal Father, we might say, lives a life of eternal self-giving love. That is, we can imagine the Father always and eternally being a source-giving-rise-to-an-other. Early Christian theologians compared this to a spring of water. You can't have a spring that at some later point produces a stream; rather, as soon as you have a spring you have a stream. The stream depends on the spring, certainly, but the spring never exists without the stream – the stream does not come 'after' the spring in any temporal sense. So it is with the Father. The Father eternally pours himself out, and never exists without the one who is poured out: the Son.[36]

The Father's life of self-giving love is played again in the Son. The Son is a repetition of the Father's life, but the Son's life is, as it were, a variation on the Father's theme, because that life of self-giving love does not, in the Son, take the form of absolute source, but of a response. In the Son, the life of eternal self-giving love is a giving-*back*; the Son eternally pours himself out in obedience and delight in the Father who gives him his being.

Fountain and stream

'When we speak of God the Father and God the Son, we do not speak of them as different, nor do we separate each: because the Father cannot exist without the Son, nor can the Son be separated from the Father, since the name of Father cannot be given without the Son, nor can the Son be begotten without the Father. Since, therefore, the Father makes the Son, and the Son the Father, they both have one mind, one spirit, one substance; but the former is as it were an overflowing fountain, the latter as a stream flowing forth from it: the former as the sun, the latter as it were a ray extended from the sun. And since he is both faithful to the most high Father, and beloved by him, he is not separated from him; just as the stream is not separated from the fountain, nor the ray from the sun: for the water of the fountain is in the stream, and the light of the sun is in the ray.'

Lactantius, *Divine Institutes*[37]

Now, it is this second form of the life of God, this eternal Son, playing the Father's life back to him, that comes to the world in Jesus of Nazareth. And that is not accidental: this is the form of God's life that is apt for incarnation, for being shown in the life of a creature, because creaturely life is itself necessarily dependent and responsive; to be a creature is not to be an absolute source. The Son's responsive, dependent form of the one life of God is apt for incarnation in a way that the Father's life on its own could not be.

So Trinitarian theologians have said that it is only *because* God's eternal, immanent life already contains this second, responsive form, that the incarnation of God is possible. God is free to become incarnate because, and only because, God is triune. In fact, Trinitarian theologians have gone further. It is only *because* God is Triune, only *because* God's immanent life also involves this second, responsive form, that the idea of any creaturely participation in the life of God makes sense. And so it is only because God is Triune that we can think that God created the world for participation in God's life. And since (as we will be discussing in Chapter 7) that is what creation *is*, for Trinitarian theology, the existence of the eternal Son in the life of God is a necessary condition for God creating the world. It is only because God is Triune, only because God's eternal life contains this second, responsive form, that God is free to create, free *for* creation.

In other words, Trinitarian theologians say, the Son's place in the eternal life of God is the place that is held open for the world. It is the space in the life of God marked out for the participation of God's creatures: it is God's freedom for the world. And, speculative and imaginative though this discussion has been, one must say something like it if one wants to say that human beings conformed to Jesus by the Spirit, facing the Father and facing the world with the Father's love, are being drawn into the life of God, and made participants in the circulation of God's life.

Key points

- Jesus is the visibility of God's life in the world.
- The Son repeats the Father's self-giving love, but in a responsive, dependent way.
- The being of the Son is the condition for the possibility of incarnation.
- The being of the Son is the condition for the possibility of creation.

The hypostatic union

According to Trinitarian theology, the eternal Son is one hypostasis, one 'something' of the eternal life of God: the Son is part of what it is and always has been to be God. This Son is and always has been fully divine, possessing a fully divine nature; the Son is and always has been an essential dimension of the divine substance. The eternal Son is, as the Nicene Creed says, 'of one substance' (Greek: *homoousios*) with the Father.

Jesus is the *dramatis persona* in the economy in and by which this aspect of God, the eternal Son, becomes visible and tangible in the world. We might say, imaginatively, that the eternal Son, while remaining everything that he has eternally been, has taken on in Jesus a new way of acting and appearing. God has created in the world a fully human life that will display in the world the life of the Son – the self-giving love and justice of God in its responsive form. To use the classical terminology, we can say that the Son has 'assumed' a fully human nature.

What the Son has assumed is a full human nature, not just some human qualities. That is, what God has created in the world is a complete human being – with a human body, a human mind, a human soul, a human spirit, a human will, human consciousness, human memory, finite and frail, bodily and limited. But this human life is *the Son's* human life. Precisely because of the nature of the Son – as the one in whom the one life of God is played in responsive, dependent form – this human being is an instrument on which the eternal Son's life can be played.

The claim is not that the infinite, unlimited and eternal Son 'turned into' the finite, limited and creaturely human person Jesus. What would that mean? Nor is the claim that the eternal Son and the human Jesus share a mind, or a will, or a soul, or anything, so as to make up one composite personality. Nor is the claim that Jesus is a human personality made up from some human parts and some divine parts. What would any of that mean? If we said anything like that, we'd start calling into question the real, ordinary humanity of Jesus pretty quickly.

Miraculous signs

The incarnation is sometimes discussed as if the virgin birth were a necessary mechanism for ensuring that Jesus ended up both human and divine – as if Mary provided human DNA and God provided something divine to mix in with it. This is to misunderstand both incarnation and the virgin birth. The virgin birth depicted in the New Testament, and any historical reality to which those texts refer, is a *sign*: it communicates something about Jesus (that his whole life is a gift from God) rather than being the mechanism by which that something is ensured. The same is true with other miracles associated with Jesus. They are not *proofs* of his divinity, because his divinity does not consist in him having some extra, superhuman, miracle-working power; they are signs that God is, through Jesus (as through his disciples) working for the salvation of the world.

To say that this human life is the *Son's* human life is to say that this Jesus shows one the life of the Son, and so the whole life of God – opening that life for one's participation. This is the way that the eternal Son gives himself, unreservedly and completely: transcribing for a creaturely instrument the whole life of God in Sonly form. And to say that this human life is the Son's human life is to say that Jesus, as it were, has no existence outside this showing: this is what he was brought into being for. This utterly defines who and what he is. To know Jesus *is* to know the Son, and to know the Son *is* to know the life of God.

So Jesus is the eternal Son's humanity: his life, his sufferings, his death, his resurrection are the eternal Son's life, sufferings, death and resurrection. And the eternal Son's life, love and justice are Jesus' life, love and justice. In a sense, the Son *is* Jesus; Jesus *is* the Son. This human being or human nature, Jesus of Nazareth, and the eternal Son who has a divine nature, are not two, they are one: they are united in one *hypostasis*.

Think of a portrait painted in oils. The painting is entirely made of canvas and paint. There is absolutely nothing there other than canvas and paint: one could scrutinize every millimetre of the painting, use any instrument one liked, and one would find only canvas and paint. And yet the painting is a painting *of* someone; it is a portrait. What is this? Paint and canvas? Yes, but look again: what is this? It is a smiling face. *Who* is it? It is the artist, because this is a self-portrait.

The 'what' questions are nature questions, and (rather clumsily) my answers could be rephrased to say that this portrait has a painty nature and a facey nature. The 'who' question is the hypostasis question: Who do you see? Who meets you here? Who acts upon you here? The artist–sitter, who gives herself to me in this way.

So it is with Jesus of Nazareth. There is nothing there other than a human life: he is utterly human, unreservedly and unadulteratedly human. No amount of scraping away at his surface will uncover anything other than a human being. And yet according to incarnational Christianity this human being is a portrait of the eternal Son, and in it we see the divine life. What is this? It is a human being: a fully human nature. Yes, but look again: what is this? It is the divine life of love and justice – it is the divine nature. So *who* is it? It is God, the eternal Son; it is his self-portrait, and he gives himself to the world in this way.

The Definition of Chalcedon

'Following the holy Fathers we teach with one voice that the Son and our Lord Jesus Christ is to be confessed as one and the same, that he is perfect in Godhead and perfect in manhood, very God and very man, of a reasonable soul and body consisting, consubstantial with the Father as touching his Godhead and consubstantial with us as touching his manhood; made in all things like unto us sin only excepted; begotten of his Father before the worlds according to his Godhead but in these last days for us men and for our salvation born of the Virgin Mary the Mother of God according to his manhood. This one and the same Jesus Christ, the only-begotten Son, must be confessed to be in two natures, unconfusedly, immutably, indivisibly, distinctly, inseparably, and that without the distinction of natures being taken away by such union, but rather the peculiar property of each nature being preserved and being united in one person and subsistence, not separated or divided into two persons, but one and the same Son and only-begotten, God the Word, our Lord Jesus Christ, as the prophets of old time have spoken concerning him, and as the Lord Jesus Christ, hath taught us, and as the Creed of the Fathers hath delivered to us.'[38]

Exercise

Read through this definition carefully, in the light of my discussion in this chapter. Is there any of it that still does not make sense? Is there any of it that you think I have not explained or done justice to? Is there any of it you think I have contradicted or reinterpreted out of all recognition?

Key points

- The Son assumes a human life in Jesus of Nazareth.
- The Son does not cease in the process to be the eternal Son, fully divine.
- Jesus is the human life of the Son.
- The Son is who encounters us in Jesus.
- The Son is two natures in one *hypostasis*.

Believing in the incarnation

What is it to believe in the incarnation? It is not a matter of being adept at mental gymnastics, juggling natures while balancing on hypostases. All of that is *commentary* upon belief in the incarnation. Belief in the incarnation itself is the belief that the human life of Jesus of Nazareth is God's gift to the whole world, God's word to the whole world – and to oneself. It is the belief that in the life Jesus lived in his specific time and place, the heart of God, the creator and fulfiller of the whole world was exposed. And so, at its simplest, belief in the incarnation is the determination to 'take every thought captive to Christ' (2 Corinthians 10.5), because belief in the incarnation is the belief that this particular human reality is of universal significance. To believe in the incarnation is to live the conviction that it is in relation to this man that any and all things will become who they were made to be. To believe in the incarnation is to allow constantly renewed attention to Jesus to rearrange and transform every and any area of one's life, and every and any aspect of one's world.

Jesus of Nazareth is a human being, not a set of ideas or principles. One cannot summarize a human being. Any attempt to state in general terms *what* the implications are of following Jesus can only be a secondary commentary, sketching the barest outline of a reality that will inevitably be much more thoroughly particular. Nevertheless, to give an indication of the kind of re-arrangement and transformation that Jesus brings, we may say that to believe in the incarnation is to learn to recognize oneself as the object of the same unsettling love that this man showed to his disciples, to the sinners in Israel, to the lepers in Isenheim – and to recognize oneself as called to the same love. And it is to learn to recognize the world as loved by the same love, and called to the same love. Belief in the incarnation therefore means learning to recognize all those around one as people for whom God has given God's life; it means learning to recognize that there is no context in which the call to Christlike love and justice is inappropriate or irrelevant. To use Jesus' own summary, we may say that to believe in the incarnation is to declare one's allegiance to the kingdom of love and justice, and to live as its subject.

Key points

- Belief in the incarnation is the belief that the particular human life of Jesus of Nazareth is of universal significance.
- To believe in the incarnation is to allow constantly renewed attention to Jesus to rearrange and transform every area of one's life.
- Belief in the incarnation is allegiance to the kingdom of love and justice.

Going further:

1. There are so many critical questions surrounding the doctrine of the Incarnation that it is hard to know where to begin. One idea that generated a lot
   of heat during the late 1970s and 1980s, and still spits and fizzes today, is
   the question of 'myth'. What kind of language is the doctrine of the incarnation meant to be? Is it, perhaps, best thought of as 'myth': not in the popular
   sense of the word, simply meaning 'false', but in the sense that important
   truths are being conveyed in a pictorial guise? The papers in John Hick

(ed.), *The Myth of God Incarnate* (London: SCM Press, 1977) discuss all this at some length. You can also look at some of the replies: Michael Green (ed.), *The Truth of God Incarnate* (London: Hodder and Stoughton, 1977); Michael Goulder (ed.), *Incarnation and Myth* (London: SCM Press, 1979); and A. E. Harvey (ed.), *God Incarnate* (London: SPCK, 1981). I particularly like Herbert McCabe's responses, printed in *God Matters* (London: Continuum, 2005), pp. 54–74.

2 Another question that has been raised is about the maleness of Jesus. If this male human being shows us God's life, doesn't that directly or subliminally lead us to think of God in male terms? The question is posed forcefully by Rosemary Radford Ruether, *Sexism and God-Talk: Toward A Feminist Theology* (Boston: Beacon, 1983), chapter 5. You can find interesting answers in Sandra Schneiders, *Women and the Word: The Gender of God in the New Testament and the Spirituality of Women* (Mahwah, NJ: Paulist, 1986); and Richard Bauckham and Rowan Williams, 'Jesus: God with us' in Christina Baxter (ed.), *Stepping Stones: Joint Essays on Anglican, Catholic and Evangelical Unity* (London: Hodder and Stoughton, 1987): pp. 21–41.

3 The presentation of the doctrine of the incarnation often proceeds by way of an enumeration of *heresies* – views of Christ that were excluded as erroneous as the orthodox view developed. Find a good theological dictionary or encyclopaedia, and look up the following: *docetism*, *ebionitism*, *adoptionism*, *Arianism*, *Nestorianism*, *Apollinarianism*, *Eutychianism*, *monophysitism* and *monothelitism* – and see if you can work out how they relate to the Christology I have been explaining. For some of these, see Ben Quash and Michael Ward (eds), *Heresies and How to Avoid Them: Why it Matters What Christians Believe* (London: SPCK, 2007); for heresy more generally, see G. R. Evans, *A Brief History of Heresy*, Blackwell Brief Histories of Religion (Oxford: Blackwell, 2003).

Notes

1 Moses of Chorene, *History of Armenia* 6, in A. Cleveland Coxe (ed.), *Ante-Nicene Fathers*, vol. 8 (New York: Christian Literature Company, 1886), p. 152; available online at the Christian Classics Ethereal Library, http://www.ccel.org/ccel/schaff/anf08.ix.xiii.vi.html, translation modernized.

2 In early legends (see *The Death of Pilate* in A. Cleveland Coxe (ed.), *Ante-Nicene Fathers*, vol. 8 (New York: Christian Literature Company, 1886), p. 466; available online at the Christian Classics Ethereal Library, http://www.ccel.org/ccel/schaff/anf08.vii.xxii.html) Veronica is the woman Jesus healed of a flow of blood in Mark 5.25–34, and her picture is a painting; it is not until the late medieval period that the story about her wiping Jesus' face appears. See Ioannes Bollandus et al. (eds), *Acta Sanctorum: Februarii*, vol. 1 (Antwerp: Ioannem Meursium, 1658), pp. 449–57, available online at the Bibliothèque Nationale de France, http://gallica.bnf.fr/ark:/12148/bpt6k6027x/f1.chemindefer). The legend associating her with an image of Christ perhaps arose because a connection was made between her name (which is actually a Latinized form of *Berenike*, Berenice) and the words *vera icon*, 'true image'.

3 Orthodox icons of Mary 'Odigitria' (the one who shows the way – she is shown

pointing to the infant Jesus on her lap) are said to be derived from this Lukan portrait – see Wikipedia contributors, 'Icon', Wikipedia, *The Free Encyclopedia*, http://en.wikipedia.org/wiki/Icon. An internet search on Google Images (http://images.google.com/) for 'Odigitria' will provide you with numerous examples.

4 One sculpture that is claimed to be by Nicodemus is the Volto Santo (Holy Face) held at the Cathedral of San Martino in Lucca, Tuscany; see 'The Volto Santo in Lucca' at *Waytuscany* (no date), http://www.waytuscany.net/rooten/tradizioni_religiose_630.htm and Francesco Carrara, 'Il Volto Santo', Lucca Citta d'Arte, http://www.itclucca.lu.it/interessanti/luccacittadarte/2id/VOLSAN/IL%20%20VOLTO%20%20SANTO.html.

5 From J. K. Elliott (ed.), *The Apocryphal New Testament: A Collection of Apocryphal Christian Literature in an English Translation* (Oxford: Clarendon Press, 1993), p. 543; also reproduced as text 132 in the book cited in n.9.

6 For an account of one early set of Christian paintings, see Alastair Logan's account of the Hypogeum of the Aurelii in Rome, in *The Gnostics: Identifying an Ancient Christian Cult* (London: Continuum, 2006), chapter 7.

7 Benedict Nicolson and Christopher Wright, *Georges de la Tour* (New York: Phaidon, 1974), 160.

8 Nicolson and Wright, *Georges de la Tour*, p. 48.

9 A sample of relevant texts can be found in David Ford and Mike Higton (eds), *Jesus*, Oxford Readers series (Oxford: Oxford University Press, 2002); see texts 68 and 69, pp. 78–9.

10 Eusebius of Caesarea, *The Proof of the Gospel, Being the Demonstratio Evangelica of Eusebius of Caesaria, I*, Translations of Christian Literature, Series I: Greek Texts, tr. W. J. Ferrar (London: SPCK, 1920), 4.13, p. 188 – reproduced in Ford and Higton, *Jesus*, pp. 82–4, as text 71, and available online at Early Christian Writings, http://www.earlychristianwritings.com/fathers/eusebius_de_06_book4.htm.

11 For more on Marcion, see Chapter 16, p. 382 below.

12 Quintus Septimius Florens Tertullian, *On the Flesh of Christ*, 4, in *Tertullian's Treatise on the Incarnation*, tr. Ernest Evans (London: SPCK, 1956), p. 13; this extract reproduced in Ford and Higton, *Jesus*, text 70, pp. 80–2; available online at The Tertullian Project, http://www.tertullian.org/articles/evans_carn/evans_carn_04eng.htm.

13 Council of Chalcedon, 'Definition of Faith'; see the portion of the text reproduced on p. 131, and the bibliographical details in note 38 below.

14 The life of Jesus has not, in classical Christian theology, been thought to be like that of David Dunn (Bruce Willis) in M. Night Shyamalan's *Unbreakable* (Touchstone Pictures, etc., 2000), Internet Movie Database http://uk.imdb.com/title/tt0217869/: the slow discovery of special powers hidden in his humanity.

15 Mel Gibson, *The Passion of the Christ* (Icon Productions, 2004); for more details, see the Internet Movie Database, http://uk.imdb.com/title/tt0335345/.

16 If you are able to get hold of them, try (for the sake of variety) Cecil B. DeMille, *The King of Kings* (DeMille Pictures, 1927), see the Internet Movie Database, http://uk.imdb.com/title/tt0018054/; Nicholas Ray, *King of Kings* (MGM, 1961), http://uk.imdb.com/title/tt0055047/; Pasolini, *Il Vangelo secondo Matteo* (Arco Film, 1964), http://uk.imdb.com/title/tt0058715/; George Stevens, *The Greatest Story Ever Told* (George Stevens Productions, 1965), http://uk.imdb.com/title/tt0059245/; and Martin Scorsese, *The Last Temptation of Christ* (Cineplex–Odeon/Universal, 1988), http://uk.imdb.com/title/tt0095497/.

17 A very good reproduction can be found online at the National Gallery's website, http://www.nationalgallery.org.uk/cgi-bin/WebObjects.dll/CollectionPublisher.woa/wa/work?workNumber=NG665. For a discussion of the baptized viewer to the painting, see Marilyn Aronberg Lavin, *Piero Della Francesca's Baptism of Christ* (New Haven: Yale University Press, 1981), pp. 109–13.

18 Harmony is taken as the main theme of the painting in M. Tanner, 'Concordia in Piero della Francesca's "Baptism of Christ"', *Art Quarterly* 35 (1972), 1–20; see also Carlo Ginzburg, *The Enigma of Piero*, 2nd edn (London: Verso, 2000) but also Creighton Gilbert's review of an earlier edition of Ginzburg's book in *The Journal of Modern History* 55.4 (1983), pp. 754–6.

19 A somewhat different analysis is given by B. A. R. Carter, 'A Mathematical Interpretation of Piero della Francesca's Baptism of Christ', in Lavin, *Piero Della Francesca's Baptism of Christ*, pp. 149–63.

20 Aldous Huxley, 'The Best Picture' in John Pope-Hennessy, *The Piero della Francesca Trail* (New York: Little Bookroom, 2002), p. 7.

21 In choosing this particular incident, Piero perhaps suggests that it is in baptism that the believer's journey towards this beauty is begun.

22 The phrase 'ein Gottbetrunkener Mensch' is attributed to the German author and thinker Novalis (Georg Philipp Friedrich Freiherr von Hardenberg), according to *The Oxford Dictionary of Quotations*. He was speaking about the philosopher Baruch Spinoza.

23 Gabriel Fackre, 'Christ in Chiaroscuro', *Theology Today* 33.1 (1976), pp. 40–9: p. 48; available online at http://theologytoday.ptsem.edu/apr1976/v33–1-article8.htm.

24 An American edition (Milwaukee: Bruce, 1940) is available online at the Christian Classics Ethereal Library, http://www.ccel.org/ccel/kempis/imitation.i.html. For background, see John H. Van Engen (ed.), *Devotio Moderna: Basic Writings* (New York: Paulist, 1988).

25 George Eliot, *The Mill on the Floss* (London: William Blackwood and Sons, 1860); available online at Project Gutenberg, http://www.gutenberg.org/dirs/etext04/mlfls10h.htm. See especially Book IV, Chapter 3.

26 The Farrelly Brothers, *Shallow Hal* (20th Century Fox et al., 2001); see the Internet Movie Database, http://uk.imdb.com/title/tt0256380/.

27 Antonello da Messina, *Christ at the Column*, c. 1475–8; reproduced online at the Louvre's website, http://cartelen.louvre.fr/cartelen/visite?sru=car_not_frame. Note that some have claimed that the picture is a copy by another painter of a lost original by Antonello – see, for example, Giorgio Vigni, *All the Paintings of Antonello da Messina* (New York: Hawthorn, 1963), 33, cat. no. 78.

28 Andrew Ure, *The Philosophy of Manufactures* (London: Charles Knight, 1835), pp. 423–5, cited in E. P. Thompson, *The Making of the English Working Class* (Harmondsworth: Penguin, 1980), p. 398. I am grateful to my colleague Tim Gorringe for drawing my attention to this passage.

29 Karl Barth, *Church Dogmatics IV: The Doctrine of Reconciliation*, Pt 1 (Edinburgh: T&T Clark, 1956), pp. 267, 269–72.

30 From Siegebert of Gembloux's twelfth-century *Chronicon*, extract translated in Andrée Hayum, *The Isenheim Altarpiece: God's Medicine and the Painter's Vision* (Princeton: Princeton University Press, 1980), p. 21.

31 *The Epistle to Diognetus*, 9, in A. Cleveland Coxe (ed.), Ante-Nicene Fathers, vol. 1 (New York: Christian Literature Company, 1885), p. 28; available online at the Christian Classics Ethereal Library, http://www.ccel.org/ccel/schaff/anf01.iii.ii.ix.html.

32 Nikos Kazantzakis, *The Last Temptation of Christ* (New York: Scribner, 1998), p. 1 – as quoted in Martin Scorsese, *The Last Temptation of Christ* (Cineplex-Odeon/Universal, 1988), http://uk.imdb.com/title/tt0095497/.

33 Kazantzakis, *The Last Temptation*, p. 2.

34 As Cyril of Jerusalem says in his *Catechetical Lectures* 4.7: 'For the throne at God's right hand he received not, as some have thought, because of his patient endurance, being crowned as it were by God after his Passion; but through his *being*'. In Philip Schaff and Henry Wace (eds), *Nicene and Post-Nicene Fathers*, Second Series, vol. 7 (New

York: Christian Literature Company, 1894), p. 20, available online at the Christian Classics Ethereal Library http://www.ccel.org/ccel/schaff/npnf207.ii.viii.html.

35 'Imaginative' in the sense discussed in Chapter 3. As always, this journey into imaginative discussion of God's immanent life is undertaken for the sake of a deeper grasp of the economy.

36 Note that early Christian theologians ended up using the word 'beget' for this kind of relationship: the Father 'begets' the Son, or eternally gives rise to the Son, rather than giving birth to or making the Son at a particular point in time. The eternal Son, they said is 'begotten, not made'.

37 Lactantius, *Divine Institutes* 4.29, in A. Cleveland Coxe (ed.), *Ante-Nicene Fathers*, vol. 7 (New York: Christian Literature Company, 1886), p. 132; available online at the Christian Classics Ethereal Library, http://www.ccel.org/ccel/schaff/anf07.iii.ii.iv.xxix.html.

38 Council of Chalcedon, 'Definition of Faith' in Philip Schaff and Henry Wace (eds), *Nicene and Post-Nicene Fathers*, Second Series, vol. 14 (New York: Christian Literature Company, 1900), pp. 264–5; reproduced in Ford and Higton, *Jesus*, pp. 100–01, as text 86, and available online at the Christian Classics Ethereal Library, http://www.ccel.org/ccel/schaff/npnf214.xi.xiii.html.

6

The Enlivening Spirit

In Chapters 2 and 4, I argued that Christians can make sense of their lives, individually and corporately, as journeys into the life of God – or, more specifically, as threefold journeys into the triune life of God. By participating in the economy of Father, Son and Holy Spirit, Trinitarian Christians believe that they are drawn into the immanent heart of God. In Chapter 5, I dwelt on the place of Jesus in this economy; in this chapter, I turn to the role of the Spirit. I have already said a fair amount about the Spirit. I introduced the Spirit as the power of God that enabled and impelled Jesus' ministry, and as the power promised to the disciples to enable and impel their discipleship. I spoke of the Spirit drawing people into the kingdom of God, making that kingdom a reality in history, and I spoke of the Spirit drawing people to Jesus. In this chapter, I will look more directly and exclusively at the nature and work of the Spirit, taking into account a wider range of biblical materials, as well as taking a glance at some of the claims made for the Spirit in more recent times. The technical term for this chapter's subject matter, then, is *Pneumatology*: the doctrine of the Holy Spirit.

I am going to

- show that in the Old Testament the Spirit is one name given to the life-giving, community-shaping, justice-building power of God;
- argue that in the New Testament the Spirit is the Spirit of Christ, and the Spirit of the life of God, which is love and justice;
- claim that there can be, for Christian theology, no sphere of 'spirituality' separable from the practices and processes by which common life is formed and by which the powers of injustice are challenged;
- suggest that the Spirit's work is to shape people until they become gifts to one another, giving more of Christ to one another.

Preparation

- Classical Christian doctrine claims that the Holy Spirit of God is living and active, working in the world and among God's people in mysterious, invisible ways. But who or what is the Spirit, according to Christianity? What does the Spirit do, and how? Jot down now a paragraph for yourself in which you try to answer those questions.
- 'Spirit' is a word that is used in many ways. If you have internet access, you can see Google's list of online definitions at http://www.google.com/search?q=define: spirit; other online definitions are available at http://dictionary.reference.com/ search?q=spirit. Look at some of these definitions now. How many of them do you think are relevant or appropriate when our topic is the Holy Spirit? Are any

of the relevant definitions that you have found particularly helpful, or particularly unhelpful?

Additional reading

Less has been written about the Spirit than about the Trinity or about Christology, but as an accompaniment to this chapter, I would recommend:

Eugene F. Rogers, Jr, *After the Spirit: A Constructive Pneumatology from Resources Outside the Modern West* (Grand Rapids, MI: Eerdmans, 2005). Skip straight to Part II for a wonderful description of the Spirit's roles in the economy of salvation.

The Spirit in the Old Testament

In Chapter 4, I introduced the Spirit with the following words:

> The Spirit is portrayed in the Gospels as that power of God that enables and impels Jesus' ministry, and as the power that is promised to Jesus' disciples to enable and impel them to respond to Jesus' proclamation of the Father's kingdom. The Spirit is the one who makes the kingdom of God, the kingdom of love and justice, real in Jesus' life and in the life of Jesus' followers; we might think of the Spirit as the Spirit *of* this kingdom.

This may have reinforced the common but quite false idea that reference to the Spirit is fundamentally a *New Testament* phenomenon – one of those additions that early Christians made to the idea of God they inherited from Judaism. It is fitting, then, to begin our more detailed discussion of the Spirit with a careful look at resources from the Old Testament.

Exercise

Look up the following texts: Genesis 1.2; 6.3; 41.38; Exodus 31.3; 35.31; Numbers 11.17, 25–29; 16.22; 24.2; 27.18; Deuteronomy 34.9; Judges 3.10; 6.34; 11.29; 13.25; 14.6, 19; 15.14; 1 Samuel 10.6, 10; 11.6; 16.13–14; 19.20, 23; 2 Samuel 23.2; 1 Kings 18.12; 22.24; 1 Chronicles 12.18; 2 Chronicles 15.1–7; 18.23; 20.14, 20; Nehemiah 9.20, 30; Job 27.5; 32.8, 18; 33.4; 34.14; Psalms 51.11; 104.30; 139.7; 143.10; Isaiah 4.4; 11.2; 32.15; 34.16; 42.1; 44.3; 61.1; 63.10–11, 14; Ezekiel 1.12, 20, 21; 2.2; 3.12, 14, 24; 8.3; 11.1, 5, 19, 24; 36.27; 37.1, 5, 6, 9, 14; 39.29; 43.5; Daniel 4.8–9, 18; 5.11–12, 14; 6.3; Hosea 9.7; Joel 2.28–29; Micah 3.8; Haggai 2.5; Zechariah 4.6; 7.12. Do you see any common themes emerging? Could you begin to sketch what the main uses of 'spirit' language are in these texts?

If you have worked your way through the list suggested in the Exercise, you will have looked up very nearly all the references to the Spirit of God or Holy

Spirit in the Old Testament. The word 'spirit' gets used in a variety of ways, and I have only listed those where talk about the Spirit seems to be a way of talking about God's activity or involvement in the world.[1]

Very roughly, the texts divide up into three broad categories:

- there are texts that deal with the whole of creation, or all living things;
- there are texts that deal with God's relationship to particular individuals; and
- there are texts that deal with God's relationship with the people of Israel.

That is over-neat – there are plenty of texts that do not quite fit into that way of dividing things up – but it is a start, at least.

The Spirit and creation

The Spirit of God hovers over the waters of creation in Genesis 1.2; we are told that if God were to remove his Spirit, life would cease (in Genesis 6.3, frequently in Job, in Psalm 104.30 and elsewhere in the Psalter, and so on). God *breathes* life and vitality into creation, and the breath God gives, the Spirit God breathes into creatures, becomes their life, their breath. When it departs, they return to dust. The Spirit is God's sustaining presence, holding creation in being, but more particularly the Spirit is God's *life*-giving activity, working to animate creation from within, giving creation its own life and dynamism.

The Spirit and individuals

I have divided these texts into seven very rough categories.

- Bezalel son of Uri in Exodus 31.3 is filled with the Spirit and given various kinds of practical skill, with the Spirit seen perhaps as the source of his excellence, his dexterity – at least insofar as his skill becomes available for adorning the Tabernacle.
- The Spirit enables people to interpret dreams (as in Genesis 41.38 and throughout Daniel), and there is perhaps a little of the previous idea here, of the Spirit providing and enhancing a skill, but also a sense of being given extraordinary piercing insight: seeing truly, in a way that human beings cannot normally do.
- The Spirit catches individuals up into ecstatic fervour, removing them from the ordinary run of life and sense, and placing them on the edge of things as living markers of God's strangeness and power. See, for instance, several of the texts in 1 Samuel.
- The Spirit is portrayed as one who 'catches people up' in a rather different sense: there are several texts in 1 Kings and in Ezekiel where the Spirit seems to be Elijah's or Ezekiel's personal teleport system, albeit one over which they have little control. The Spirit breaks in to the ordinary continuities, the ordinary predictability of life, in service of a more mysterious, less containable purpose.

- The Spirit raises individuals up as powerful leaders, fighting for the liberation of the people of Israel, as repeatedly in Judges. The Spirit erupts in an individual in order for them to overthrow the oppressors.
- The Spirit equips individuals to be leaders in a more peaceful sense, giving them the wisdom and the discernment that is needed, particularly for judging (for ensuring justice, for ruling justly); see, for instance, Deuteronomy 34.9, Daniel 6.3. That is linked to the sense of 'anointing', where an individual is given as it were the right to rule, but only insofar as he rules in obedience to God's just law (not as the kings of the Gentiles rule, who think they are their own masters).
- Lastly, the Spirit enables individuals to speak the word of God in a given situation: the word that will pierce the veils of convention and half-truth, and will show right as right, and wrong as wrong; the word that will bait unjust rulers, and condemn idolaters.

It seems to me that there are two sides to what the Spirit is said to do here. On the one hand, there is the Spirit as God's upholding of just and proper order: the Spirit who enables individuals to contribute to the building of well-ordered life, whether it be in the quite literal sense in which Bezalel builds, or in the more metaphorical sense in which a wise ruler builds. The Spirit, we might say, is a Spirit of Wisdom.

Set alongside that, however, is a picture of the Spirit as God's disruptive interference, who takes the sensible and throws them into prophetic frenzy; who raises up angular prophets to bellow from the sidelines and judges to wage wars of liberation; who challenges the unjust order of things, and names idols for what they are. This is the Spirit, we might say, of Judgement.

By this Spirit, men and women of God *become* men and women of God both by learning (being built up in wisdom, being shaped into a just ordering of life) and unlearning (repeatedly having their idolatries exposed and challenged, their distortions and betrayals of the truth named and condemned). The Spirit is the agency of God animating and directing this process – nurturing justice and wisdom among the people, coaxing it from their existing resources, but also bringing the people up against what is beyond their resources, what exceeds and judges them, and calls them to new life.

The Spirit and Israel

Alongside references to the Spirit that focus on creation, and references that focus on individuals, there are also references that focus on the people of Israel as a whole. I find three rough categories here.

- There are a few texts (such as Isaiah 63.11) where just as an individual creature is understood to be alive only so long as it has God's Spirit within it, so Israel is understood to have God's Spirit within her, to be animated by that Spirit – and to be in mortal danger when she loses that Spirit. The Spirit sustains, animates and enlivens the people as a whole.
- Then there are texts in which the Spirit is spoken of as the leader and teacher of the people (Nehemiah 9.20 and 30, for instance) – and even if that leading

and teaching is carried out by means of individual prophets, it is the people who are the true object of the Spirit's action.

- And then there are also texts that focus on the future: on the Spirit as the one who will enliven the people, and who will lead them, on the Day of the Lord, into true flourishing (as in Isaiah 44.3 and elsewhere). This hope appears to be, on the one hand, for the people to become a people who are themselves filled with the Spirit – as, perhaps most famously, in Joel 2.28, where there is the vision of everyone becoming a prophet. On the other hand, it is a hope for God to raise up a great spirit-anointed leader (as in Isaiah 11.2): someone who will be the completion and perfection of the spirit-enabled wise rulers and builders of the past.

Here again, in other words, we see the Spirit spoken of both as the source of what well-ordered life the people do now have – as their sustainer, guide and teacher – and as the one who will bring them the life that they do not yet have, indeed a life which is simply not in their power to create for themselves, but which will come to them as the gracious gift of God.

We may perhaps summarize all of this – the references that have to do with creation, those that have to do with individuals, and those that have to do with Israel as a whole – by saying that the Spirit is the power of God for life. The Spirit is God animating all life and leading creatures towards well-ordered, just and flourishing life – by drawing out and nurturing natural skills and sense, certainly, but also by erupting against idolatry and oppression, raising up individuals and forming communities that will name and resist distortions of true life. The Spirit animates life from within, not in a static way (not simply flicking a switch which turns the whole animated display of life on) but rather in a dynamic and purposeful way, leading life on and pointing it to the perfection it has not yet reached, and which it so frequently denies.

In the Old Testament, then, God is sometimes described as acting by means of God's 'Spirit': an enlivening force at work in creation, in individuals, and in Israel. Little or nothing is said about what kind of reality the Spirit is – little or nothing, for instance, about how distinct the Spirit is from God – but a great deal is said about what the Spirit *does*. The Spirit is simply the name that Old Testament authors find for that power of God invisible and active among them, drawing them back to God from idolatry and oppression, and on into God's just future.

Key points

- In the Old Testament, God is sometimes described as acting by means of God's 'Spirit'.
- The Spirit is the power that sustains, animates and enlivens all life.
- The Spirit is the power that draws out and nurtures skills, wisdom and justice.
- The Spirit is the power that erupts against idolatry, injustice and oppression.

The Spirit in Acts

I have already in Chapter 4, pages 79–80, discussed the Spirit's appearances in the Gospels and in some other parts of the New Testament, and I don't plan on repeating that material here. However, I did not cover any of the appearances of the Spirit in the Book of Acts, despite the fact that the Spirit is one of that book's central characters.

When the Spirit is spoken of in Acts, some at least of the Old Testament portrayal that we have been exploring lies in the background, perhaps most often the hope that on the Day of the Lord the Spirit will enliven and lead the people into true flourishing life, and the hope that the Spirit will anoint a leader who will be the completion and perfection of the spirit-enabled wise rulers and builders of the past.

In Acts 2, for instance, Peter is portrayed explaining to the astonished crowds just what has happened to the disciples upon whom the ecstasy of the Spirit has fallen. He draws on a prophecy from Joel concerning the pouring out of the Spirit on the day of the Lord (Acts 2.16–21), and goes on, with the help of a quotation from Psalm 16 (Acts 2.25–28) to claim that this Spirit has been poured out upon them at the hands of Jesus, the anointed one, the Messiah or Christ. Ideas about God's Spirit drawn from the Old Testament are refocused by being referred to Jesus.

We have already seen that Jesus is portrayed in the Gospels as shaped and directed by the Spirit, that is, as one on whom the Spirit rests; but Peter's explanation that the Spirit has been poured out at the hands of Jesus points back to the claim made by John the Baptist at the start of each of the Gospels that Jesus will 'baptize you with the Holy Spirit' (Matthew 3.11; Mark 1.8; Luke 3.16; John 1.33) – that the one on whom the Spirit rests will pour out this Spirit onto others. In Acts, the Church is presented as the community of those on whom the Spirit has been poured out at Jesus' hand, and initiation into that community is presented as a matter of receiving this Holy Spirit in Jesus' name.

The community of Christ's followers is understood in Acts to be the community of the Spirit – the community drawn together by, filled with and impelled by the Spirit. And that Spirit is the same Spirit who rested upon Jesus, and the same Spirit of life, truth and justice who animated and guided the people of Israel.

Key points

- In Acts, Jesus is the one who pours out or baptizes with the Spirit, as well as being the one on whom the Spirit rests.
- This claim has for its background Jewish hope for the outpouring of the Spirit on the Day of the Lord.

The Spirit in Paul and John

There are two main locations of discussion of the Spirit in the New Testament that we still have to consider: the Pauline Epistles and the Gospel of John. However, rather than trying to cover them in a quick survey, like the one I have been pursuing so far, I am going to examine three texts in detail.

[11]If the Spirit of him who raised Jesus from the dead dwells in you, he who raised Christ from the dead will give life to your mortal bodies also through his Spirit that dwells in you.

[12]So then, brothers and sisters, we are debtors, not to the flesh, to live according to the flesh – [13]for if you live according to the flesh, you will die; but if by the Spirit you put to death the deeds of the body, you will live. [14]For all who are led by the Spirit of God are children of God. [15]For you did not receive a spirit of slavery to fall back into fear, but you have received a spirit of adoption. When we cry, 'Abba! Father!' [16]it is that very Spirit bearing witness with our spirit that we are children of God, [17]and if children, then heirs, heirs of God and joint heirs with Christ – if, in fact, we suffer with him so that we may also be glorified with him.

[18]I consider that the sufferings of this present time are not worth comparing with the glory about to be revealed to us. [19]For the creation waits with eager longing for the revealing of the children of God; [20]for the creation was subjected to futility, not of its own will but by the will of the one who subjected it, in hope [21]that the creation itself will be set free from its bondage to decay and will obtain the freedom of the glory of the children of God. [22]We know that the whole creation has been groaning in labour pains until now; [23]and not only the creation, but we ourselves, who have the first fruits of the Spirit, groan inwardly while we wait for adoption, the redemption of our bodies. [24]For in hope we were saved. Now hope that is seen is not hope. For who hopes for what is seen? [25]But if we hope for what we do not see, we wait for it with patience.

[26]Likewise the Spirit helps us in our weakness; for we do not know how to pray as we ought, but that very Spirit intercedes with sighs too deep for words. [27]And God, who searches the heart, knows what is the mind of the Spirit, because the Spirit intercedes for the saints according to the will of God.

[28]We know that all things work together for good for those who love God, who are called according to his purpose.

Romans 8.11–28

Exercise

Read this text carefully and then, before you carry on to read my commentary, ask yourself who or what the Spirit is in this passage, and what the Spirit does.

The resurrected Christ is, in this passage, the forerunner, the trailblazer – one who has been raised to life in God by God's Spirit, and who therefore shows Christians the way that they are going to follow. In him they see where they are headed: not to the abandonment of their bodies, but to full bodily life, real life, life in God. The power of the Spirit is the power that draws them towards that future, and makes it real to them now. The Spirit is the power of that future already living in them, holding in its hands the transformed people that they will one day be. The Spirit worked this transformation in Jesus and so can be seen as a pledge of the same transformation for others. Believers can now, if they choose, live according to the flesh, ignoring this pledge of the future, ignoring the directedness of their lives towards their future in God. Or they can live 'according to the Spirit'. That is, they can live in anticipation of this future, living here and now in the light of what they will one day become.

And what the Spirit tells them they will become is heirs of God: full, grown-up children, sharing unrestrictedly in the life of God's family, adopted alongside Christ as God's children, and so having the future alongside Christ and with the Father to look forward to. When Christians call upon God as Father, they are living according to their adoption, and living according to the future they have as full heirs in this family. So, whenever Christians acknowledge God as Father, whenever they grasp what God is doing with them and for them, drawing them to himself as his children, that simply *is* the work of the Spirit.

At the moment, however, that reality is hidden. It is hidden in believers' weakness, and in a world like ours it takes the form of suffering, just as it did with Jesus: dying to distorted and broken ways of living, living against the grain of a world committed to selfishness and violence. Believers groan under this, but wait with patience for the time when God by God's Spirit will make the true order of things visible. They can live in the sure knowledge that the Spirit now holds up to God the image of what they shall be in that future, so that God looks at them and sees what they will become, not simply what they currently are.

This salvation for which Christians wait is, however, also the salvation of creation. Paul's picture seems to be something like this: creation is, in its current state, futile: it is missing its proper fulfilment; it is a knife with an unsharpened blade. But it will receive its fulfilment alongside, or in, or through, the revelation in its midst of children of God. It is as if God had not yet finished creating the world, because between the penultimate stage of his creating work (the creation of human beings to tend the garden) and the end (full communion between God and creatures), creation has had to travel by a long detour, awaiting the completion and perfection of human beings. Only with human beings' completion and perfection will the work of creation receive its proper orientation and order, and be completed in the Sabbath rest. As it stands, the creation, forced to wait for its completion until humanity has been won back to its proper course, groans, waiting for that completion, just as Christians groan who have the pledge of the Spirit but do not yet experience the full reality of their relationship to the Father. The Spirit is the pledge of the completion of creation, the agency of God to draw creation to that completion which is full and unimpeded relationship with the Father. The Spirit is the power of God working for the perfection of creation; the Spirit is the power of the future.

14¹'Do not let your hearts be troubled. Believe in God, believe also in me. ²In my Father's house there are many dwelling places. If it were not so, would I have told you that I go to prepare a place for you? ³And if I go and prepare a place for you, I will come again and will take you to myself, so that where I am, there you may be also. ⁴And you know the way to the place where I am going.' ⁵Thomas said to him, 'Lord, we do not know where you are going. How can we know the way?' ⁶Jesus said to him, 'I am the way, and the truth, and the life. No one comes to the Father except through me. ⁷If you know me, you will know my Father also. From now on you do know him and have seen him. ...

¹⁵'If you love me, you will keep my commandments. ¹⁶And I will ask the Father, and he will give you another Advocate, to be with you forever. ¹⁷This is the Spirit of truth, whom the world cannot receive, because it neither sees him nor knows him. You know him, because he abides with you, and he will be in you. ...

²⁵'I have said these things to you while I am still with you. ²⁶But the Advocate, the Holy Spirit, whom the Father will send in my name, will teach you everything, and remind you of all that I have said to you. ²⁷Peace I leave with you; my peace I give to you. I do not give to you as the world gives. Do not let your hearts be troubled, and do not let them be afraid. ...

15²⁶'When the Advocate comes, whom I will send to you from the Father, the Spirit of truth who comes from the Father, he will testify on my behalf. ...

16¹³'When the Spirit of truth comes, he will guide you into all the truth; for he will not speak on his own, but will speak whatever he hears, and he will declare to you the things that are to come. ¹⁴He will glorify me, because he will take what is mine and declare it to you.'

John 14.1–7, 15–17, 25–7; 15.26; 16.13–14

Exercise

As before, read this text carefully and ask yourself who or what the Spirit is in this passage, and what the Spirit does.

Jesus is going to prepare a place for the disciples in his Father's house, and he will lead them there. They can rest assured; they do not need to be troubled. There is not some extra stage on the journey, hidden from them: they know the way, they can see it clearly (if they would only realize the fact). The way home – the way to their true home with God – is open to them. And that is because Jesus is the way. Not in the sense that he has been made into an arbitrary gatekeeper, such that they have to please him in order to be let into the space he guards, but because the place where they are headed, the life with God which he goes to prepare, is Christ-shaped. To get into this space, you must become Christ-shaped; if you take on a different shape, you arrive somewhere else. And the space that Christ prepares for us is Christ-shaped because God is Christ-shaped: if you have seen Jesus, then you have seen his Father. Jesus is the means by which God has declared to the world the nature of God's life; Jesus is the means by which God has, as it were, thrown open the doors of God's life and invited the world to share it.

But where does the Spirit fit in? In verses 15–17 of chapter 14, it becomes clear that Jesus – who goes on ahead to prepare the way, and whose death and resurrection, we might say, complete his demonstration of the shape of God's life in the midst of the world – does not leave believers simply to trudge along behind him by their own resources, shaping themselves so as to conform to the pattern he has shown them. They yearn to be shaped like Christ, to follow him, to be with him, and that means yearning to obey Christ's commands (the commands by which he crystallizes for them what it means to live a life shaped like his). But he does not leave them alone in the midst of a world that operates according to thoroughly different criteria, a world that does not recognize this shape of life, a world in which life lived in this fashion is liable to lead to execution. Rather, they are left with the Spirit. The Spirit bears the truth; the Spirit knows the life of God in which all things have their source and end. And in loving Christ, and seeking to follow in Christ's footsteps, believers already know the Spirit. The Spirit is not something extra, a second lesson after the first lesson that Jesus taught them. The Spirit is, as it were, the power of what Christ has already shown them, the power of Christ's life, the power of God's Christ-shaped life, living in the world's midst – or, rather, the spirit is an agent endowed with that power. The Spirit's role is fundamentally therefore one of teaching or instructing: of leading believers deeper into the shape of God's life that Christ has opened up to them. Whenever someone is being led deeper into conformity to Christ, whenever someone is being formed alongside Christ for life with the Father, that simply *is* the Spirit at work: that is the power of God's life, drawing that person to God. The Spirit, for John, is the power of God's Christ-shaped life, drawing believers ever deeper into that life.

> 12¹Now concerning spiritual gifts, brothers and sisters, I do not want you to be uninformed. ²You know that when you were pagans, you were enticed and led astray to idols that could not speak. ³Therefore I want you to understand that no one speaking by the Spirit of God ever says 'Jesus be cursed!' and no one can say 'Jesus is Lord' except by the Holy Spirit. ⁴Now there are varieties of gifts, but the same Spirit; ⁵and there are varieties of service, but the same Lord; ⁶and there are varieties of working, but it is the same God who inspires them all in every one. ⁷To each is given the manifestation of the Spirit for the common good. ⁸To one is given through the Spirit the utterance of wisdom, and to another the utterance of knowledge according to the same Spirit, ⁹to another faith by the same Spirit, to another gifts of healing by the one Spirit, ¹⁰to another the working of miracles, to another prophecy, to another the ability to distinguish between spirits, to another various kinds of tongues, to another the interpretation of tongues.

[11]All these are inspired by one and the same Spirit, who apportions to each one individually as he wills.

[12]For just as the body is one and has many members, and all the members of the body, though many, are one body, so it is with Christ. [13]For in the one Spirit we were all baptized into one body – Jews or Greeks, slaves or free – and all were made to drink of one Spirit. ...

[27]Now you are the body of Christ and individually members of it. [28]And God has appointed in the church first apostles, second prophets, third teachers, then workers of miracles, then healers, helpers, administrators, speakers in various kinds of tongues. [29]Are all apostles? Are all prophets? Are all teachers? Do all work miracles? [30]Do all possess gifts of healing? Do all speak with tongues? Do all interpret? [31]But strive for the greater gifts.

And I will show you a still more excellent way. 13[1]If I speak in the tongues of men and of angels, but have not love, I am a noisy gong or a clanging cymbal. [2]And if I have prophetic powers, and understand all mysteries and all knowledge, and if I have all faith, so as to remove mountains, but have not love, I am nothing. [3]If I give away all my possessions, and if I hand over my body so that I may boast, but do not have love, I gain nothing.

1 Corinthians 12.1–13, 12.27—13.3.

Exercise

Once again, read this text carefully and ask yourself who or what the Spirit is in this passage, and what the Spirit does.

Paul seems to be writing to a community that threatens to be torn apart by the claims to inspiration made by various individuals within it. It sounds as though different people feel that they are being led or impelled by the Spirit in different directions, and there is conflict brewing between them. There are even (perhaps) some who feel that the Spirit is leading them to new areas not obviously connected with what they have learnt of Jesus. This is a community (or a group of individuals) which is concentrating on the power of God they experience working within them, determined to be led by that power wherever it leads, and trusting to that power within them as their authority. And Paul, while not wanting to deny that the Spirit does work within them in powerful ways, explains that they have missed the point: if they think like that, they do not yet know who the Spirit is.

Paul tells them that they should not be so sure of their instincts, of their experience: after all, didn't they feel powerfully attracted to idols before they were Christians? Didn't their experience mislead them then? To say that they have received the Spirit is not simply to give a name to the strong or powerful feelings within them, or to their extraordinary experiences – it is to say that they have received the Spirit *of Jesus*. The Spirit is the power who leads them to the true God seen in Jesus (rather than idols); they therefore know the power of the Spirit whenever they are being drawn closer to Jesus, and deny it whenever they are being drawn further away. The Spirit simply is the power who leads them more deeply under the Lordship of Christ.

Think back to the exegesis of text from earlier in this same letter in Chapter 1. I noted Paul's stress upon the unexpected nature of God that is discovered in Christ: God's folly and weakness, God's Christlikeness. The Spirit is the power of God leading the Corinthians more deeply into that knowledge, and anything that does not lead them more deeply into that knowledge is not the Spirit of God, however marvellous, convincing or powerful it may seem to be.

All the different experiences of empowerment, all the separate gifts that individuals in this community believe themselves to be given, only make sense to the extent that they can be understood as gifts of this one Spirit, gifts of this one Lord. They are gifts that will lead the Corinthians deeper into the knowledge of the one God of Jesus Christ into whose life they have been baptized.

Paul explains further that the individual gifts people receive must not be thought of as gifts that separate some into an elite realm of power and ecstatic experience. They must instead be gifts that feed the whole body, that build it up, bind it together and take the whole body of believers deeper into knowledge of this God. There is, it seems, something about being drawn under the lordship of Christ, something about being drawn deeper into the knowledge of the God of Jesus Christ, that inherently involves being drawn into that knowledge *together*. But there is also something about being drawn together in this way that doesn't involve becoming identical: it doesn't involve becoming clones of Jesus. Each is empowered in a different way for the sake of the whole body; each is given a different contribution to make. And what matters is not how dramatic or exciting or exotic others find the gift that some individual has, but the extent to which it helps to build up the body. What matters is the extent to which it helps form the people deeper in knowledge and love of the God of Jesus Christ. Some of the most important ways in which that will happen will be by way of inconspicuous service, humble and unobtrusive: if it builds up the body, it is the work of the Spirit no less than the working of miracles or the delivery of prophecies.

It becomes clear later on in 1 Corinthians, by the way, that Paul is particularly fond of prophecy. Prophecy is the speaking of the truth, or the making clear in a particular time and place of what it means to follow Christ and to live according to the Spirit. Prophecy is the naming and exposing of the tempting alternatives that would actually, in this situation, be idolatry. It is the kind of speaking that brings conviction and transformation. But even prophecy is not in itself the point. All these gifts are real gifts, real work of the Spirit, only if they lead people together deeper into the life of God. And that means that they are gifts, are the work of the Spirit only if they lead people deeper into love and justice. If someone does something that works against Christlike love and justice, it is *not* the work of the Spirit. If someone does something that leads into Christlike love and justice then it *is* the work of the Spirit. That is all that one needs to know. That simply is, for Paul, who the Spirit is, and there is no independent way of identifying the Spirit. The Spirit is the power of God's Christ-shaped life, drawing Christians together into that life; the Spirit is the power of love drawing them into love.

These three texts seem to me to complement each other well. They each involve a picture of the Spirit as the power of God drawing people deeper into the life of God; they all involve a picture of the Spirit doing so by conforming people to Christ, who is the image of God's life. But each passage concentrates on different aspects of this. The Romans 8 passage concentrates on the Spirit's role in drawing people to God as children of God; the John 14 passage concentrates on the Spirit's role in leading people deeper into Christ, who is the image of God; and the 1 Corinthians 12 passage concentrates on the Spirit's role in leading people deeper into love for one another, which is the shape that people's lives should take if they are being conformed to Christ and so drawn to the Father.

I have also suggested that, in these passages, although the Spirit's power is contrasted with the way of the world – with forms of life and thought that work against love, or that deny the kind of self-giving that Christ displayed – the Spirit is not opposed to matter, or to bodies, or to community. The Spirit is the power of God working to complete and perfect God's creation, the power of God seeking to unlock and liberate the whole created order. The Spirit is the power of Christ's bodily resurrection, leading not away from the human body, but to that body's completion and perfection. The Spirit is the power of God leading people deeper into corporate life, deeper into love for one another – not pulling individuals out into their own private ascent towards God, but sending individuals more deeply into contact with one another. For these biblical authors, the Spirit is the Spirit of Christ, and the Spirit of the life of God, which is love and justice.

Is the Spirit a 'person'?

Should one call the Holy Spirit a 'person'? There are various reasons for saying 'Yes'. In the first place, you may remember that 'person' in classical Trinitarian theology is used as an equivalent to the Greek word *hypostasis*, and means something like 'distinguishable reality'. To say that the Spirit is a person is, in the first place, simply to say that one can distinguish the Spirit from the Father and the Son when one talks about God. Even that much might seem questionable, however: it is not clear in the Old Testament texts that we looked at, for instance, that talk of 'God's Spirit' is anything other than a roundabout way of saying 'God'. Are the Father and the Spirit truly distinguishable? To answer that, we can turn to the second sense of 'person' that I used in Chapter 4, and recall that the drama played out in the Gospels and described in the rest of the New Testament is a drama of three *dramatis personae*. However mysterious and tenuous the grip of the term *dramatis persona* might be on the Spirit, to speak of the Spirit as a person is to assert that talk of the Spirit can't be completely reduced to talk of the other two *personae*.

To call the Spirit a 'person' means more than this, though. Christians believe they encounter the Spirit working in and through creaturely realities, communicating God's love – and we don't really know how to talk about love without our talk being talk about *persons* who love. Love is not an impersonal force, and we do not know how to talk about it without using the language of will, of intention, of attitude. Even if Christians know that such language must fall short of the ungraspable reality of God's immanent life, and so fall short of the ungraspable reality of the Spirit, it would be a mistake to think that one could do better by saying any *less*. Another way of putting this is to say that to speak of the Spirit as a person is a good corrective to any talk of the Spirit that makes her sound like a thing or a force – say, a thing that you have inside of you, or something like a magnetic field, impersonally reorienting everything that comes into its vicinity.

Of course, like all human attempts to speak about God, this stretches language to its limits, and just because Christians might have good reason to call the Spirit a 'person' does not mean that they can think of the Spirit as a person *just like them*, only invisible and with some amazing powers. It should be no surprise that there will be places where this language breaks down, and that some of the things that the Bible and the Christian tradition find it important to say about the Spirit (that the Spirit is a gift, for example, or that the Spirit is the love that the Father and Son have in common[2]) don't sound very personal.[3]

Key points

- The Spirit is the power of God drawing people deeper into the life of God by conforming them to Christ.
- The Spirit is the power of God drawing believers deeper into Christlike love.
- The Spirit is the power of God active in the resurrection.
- The Spirit is the power of God working to complete and perfect creation.

Spirituality

In the next two sections of this chapter, I want to look at two different suggestions that have been made about how Christian life relates to the Spirit. In each case, it seems to me both that there is much of value, and yet that there has been a mistaken attempt to rope off one part or aspect of life and to declare that this in particular is the special preserve of the Spirit. In both cases, even if a Christian's connection with the Spirit flows out into all the areas of his or her life, it is in this roped-off area specifically that the true home of the Spirit in Christian life is seen. On the one hand, we have some versions of 'spirituality', on the other, some tendencies within the charismatic and Pentecostal movements. At least some proponents of each claim that there is a special realm of properly spiritual experience and practice hidden in the heart of Christians' and others' lives with God, elevated some distance above ordinary, prosaic life.

The word 'spirituality' is a popular one these days. A search on the internet for occurrences of the word in April 2007[4] yielded about 60,000,000 results, from all sorts of sources; I'm afraid I didn't manage to check all of them. Some

are affiliated with particular religious organizations (so the first result from
the web search was from www.spirituality.com, which is actually a website
for the Christian Science movement); others declare their allegiance to broader
movements or traditions (e.g. a page from www.greenspirit.org.uk on Native
American spirituality); others are not tied so closely to any one organization
or tradition (e.g. www.spiritualityandpractice.com).

According to the 'Spirituality and Practice' website:

> To be spiritual is to have an abiding respect for the great mysteries of life
> – the profound distinctiveness of other souls, the strange beauty of nature
> and the animal world, the ineffable complexity of our inner selves, the un-
> fathomable depths of the Inexplicable One. The first step in the practice of
> mystery is to cherish the baffling, curious, hidden, and inscrutable dimen-
> sions of your existence and the world around you. Live with paradoxes.
> Give up the idea that you can always 'get it'. Be suspicious of all the 'ologies'
> that try to explain everything – from astrology to psychology to theology.[5]

The 'Spirituality and Health' site says,

> we're talking about experience, not doctrine. Though spirituality is a part
> of all religions, no religion can own it, and those who aren't comfortable
> with organized religion are no less involved in the journey. This approach
> honors questions, mysteries, and journeys of discovery over dogmatic
> answers, closed systems, and now-you've-made-it destinations. Respecting
> and drawing upon the world's great wisdom traditions (religions) as well
> as the latest insights from medicine, psychology, sociology, ecology, and the
> natural sciences, we speak to people from various religious traditions or no
> religious tradition at all.[6]

Between them, the two sites capture much of the meaning of 'spirituality' in
popular culture.

Although the language is different, there is much here that resonates with
themes touched on already in this book: the idea of a journey of discovery into
'the unfathomable depths of the Inexplicable One', of exploring mystery, of
honouring questions; the rejection of the idea that one can finally 'get it', and
of attempts to explain everything, a resistance to 'now-you've-made-it desti-
nations'. And looking more broadly at these sites and at others with a similar ethos, there is a strong sense that spirituality is not concerned so much
with getting the right ideas, as with developing the right practices – practices
that will help shape one's life into a journey of healing exploration. And even
though both sites illustrate an anti-doctrinal or anti-theological cast widespread in contemporary spiritual writing, it is hard not to feel that there too
they have a point. There are all too many examples of theological writing and
doctrinal proclamation that clearly do tie everything up too neatly, and make
God (and human beings' journey into God) an explicable object of exactly the
wrong sort. You may feel that this book itself has fallen into that trap in the
last three chapters.

Exercise

Using either an internet search engine, or the 'mind, body, spirit' section in a bookshop, browse through other examples of 'spirituality'. Is my characterization here fair?

In one sense, then, I have been talking about 'spirituality' all along, even though this is a book of theology and of Christian doctrine. And that should not be a surprise. After all, one definition that Christian theology could offer of 'spirituality' would simply be 'life in the Spirit': life as it is guided by, filled by, impelled by, uplifted by the Spirit; life given over to the Spirit; life exploring the things of the Spirit. Spirituality has to do, a Christian might say, with the Spirit welling up within us, and with all the practices or dispositions that might clear the channel for that upwelling, or stimulate it. To focus on 'spirituality' is, in Christianity, simply to take one way of talking about the whole journey of learning and unlearning by which the Spirit leads people deeper into the life of God. In other words, for Christian theology 'spirituality' is really just another name for Christian life, because Christian life simply *is* life in the Spirit.

If this is right, however, then there are various consequences. In the first place, it makes no sense to think that 'spirituality' could be a distinct *part* of Christian life, something one might be engaged in only some of the time. It doesn't make sense to think of spirituality even as a constant accompaniment to the other, more mundane aspects of one's life. It doesn't make sense to think of spirituality as the bit of Christian life that happens when one is on one's own, or a bit of Christian life that happens when one turns from action to contemplation, or a bit of Christian life that involves one escaping for a while from one's responsibilities and relationships, or the bits of Christian life that take place when one is calm, centred and breathing slowly. We might even say that it doesn't make sense – despite the impression given by popular accounts – to think that spirituality could be separated from institutions, traditions and doctrines. If life uplifted by the Spirit, life exploring the things of the Spirit, the life of learning and unlearning on the way to God, is the whole of Christian life, then it is just as much what Christians do together, what they do when they are organised, what they do when they are fulfilling their obligations, what they do when they talk and eat and work and relax and argue and calculate and decide. For Christian theology, spirituality covers the whole of Christian life.

In the second place, if the analysis I have been giving in this chapter so far is right, the work of the Spirit is to lead people before the Father, by shaping them after the Son. The Spirit is, for Christian theology, that power of God that lures and woos and impels and drives and enables and drags and excites people on journeys deeper into the God of Jesus Christ. 'Spirituality' can't, in a Trinitarian context, be a name Christians give to some aspect of their lives that is related to the Spirit, as distinct from aspects that have to do with the Father and the Son. Things simply don't divide up that way. And that means that Christians cannot separate a sphere of spirituality from the pursuit of the Father's kingdom, opened up to them by the Son. Christians cannot separate a sphere of spirituality from the pursuit of love and justice in the world. There is, for Christian theology, no sphere of 'spirituality' separable from the involvements, the compromises, the negotiations, the politics by which common life is formed, and by which the powers of injustice are challenged.

Key points

- 'Spirituality' concerns the shaping of lives, individually and corporately, by the Spirit, in conformity to Christ, on the way to the Father;
- 'Spirituality' is therefore simply another name, in Christian theology, for the whole life of faith – including its institutional and its political aspects.

The Spirit-filled life

We can't talk about 'life filled by the Spirit', and read passages like 1 Corinthians 12, without thinking about the Pentecostal and charismatic movements, which have had such a sweeping influence on the church over the last century. There is no way that I can hope to give an adequate overview of the variety of theologies and practices associated with this diverse family of movements. Rather than attempting that, therefore, I am going to approach this topic a little differently. I am going to introduce each of a series of subtopics by describing some relevant experience from my own past, and then describe how I now assess that experience as an academic theologian, in the light of the kind of theology I have been presenting. By doing this I hope to make it clear that I am simply reflecting on one person's experience of one variety of charismatic theology and practice, at one period in its development, hazarding criticisms whose applicability to other varieties of charismatic or Pentecostal life is questionable. My aim, after all, is not to provide a comprehensive appreciation or critique of these movements, but by thinking through this one example to clarify some aspects of the doctrine of the Spirit and the ways in which it might relate to Christian life.

Baptism in the Holy Spirit

I was brought up in a charismatic evangelical Anglican church, and until my mid twenties would unhesitatingly have described myself as a 'charismatic', and regarded that movement as one of the only hopes for the renewal and purification of the contemporary Church.

What did that mean? Well – to use the categories that I would have used at the time, which I think were normal in that particular context even if they might not now be so characteristic of the movement – one of the crucial aspects was that I had had an experience that I called 'baptism in the Spirit'. If you had asked me back when I was in my late teens, I would have described it something like this: I had been a Christian for several years, but was aware at some level that I was paddling in the shallows. I was, that is, aware that there were others around me who had a seriousness of commitment and intensity of devotion which, to be frank, I envied, even though it frightened me and even though I found plenty of excuses not yet to travel too far down that path.

However, the sense that there was more to Christian life than I was experiencing, and that I was holding out against that 'more', grew, until one particular Sunday evening, in a context of prayer and worship, I had an experience in which I felt that this logjam had suddenly been released. That evening, I experienced an intensity of devotion and joy that (I would have said then) was greater than anything I had known – but, more significantly, I felt able to make a deeper commitment to living the Christian faith, to swimming out from the shallows, than I had done before. Although the particular intensity of that evening faded, it did lead to genuine changes in my life: to new patterns of worship, to what seemed like access to new levels of devotional feeling and a new emotional involvement in worship, and to a greater level of commitment to living out the consequences of my faith in the various parts of my life.

At that time, following the normal categories used in my church, I would have described this as 'baptism in the Holy Spirit', and seen it as a sort of personal Pentecost.[7] It was not, in the thinking of that church, or in many charismatic and Pentecostal circles, the same as conversion: the two were distinct (though they could in some individuals occur at the same time). Both were normally peak experiences of sudden release and transformation, but while conversion was about initially coming to faith, and 'being saved', and was complete and effective in itself, baptism in the Holy Spirit was about being oriented and equipped for the long haul of the life of faith.

As I say, I am trying to describe this using the categories I would have used at the time. Many involved in charismatic renewal or in the Pentecostal movement would describe things in very different ways, or expect very different patterns of experience – but I don't think that my particular experience and way of understanding it would have been that uncommon at the time.

What are we to make of it? We can begin with a twofold warning. On the one hand, if any of this is taken as a suggestion that the Spirit is only present in some Christians, it is heading in a dangerous direction. Recall what I said back in Chapter 4: 'Christian life is ... life in the Spirit. It is life that has been invaded by, transformed by, overwhelmed by, the Spirit. ... And this same Christian life is life following Jesus.' If talk of 'baptism in the Spirit' as something separate from 'conversion to Christ' drives any kind of wedge between 'life following Jesus' and 'life in the Spirit', then it is a step away from Trinitarian theology, and a step away from the theology of Paul and John that we examined in the last section. On the other hand, the same *theological* worry has a direct *practical* application. If this talk of baptism in the Spirit is taken to suggest that there are fundamentally two ranks of Christians, then it is a theology that divides the body of Christ. And, looking at the way in which Paul in 1 Corinthians 12 describes the work of the Spirit, and gives us criteria for identifying the Spirit, we could say quite straightforwardly that if talk of baptism in the Spirit is used to stake out a fundamental division in the body of Christ, then it has nothing to do with the Spirit of Jesus. (And that means that if we feel able easily and as a matter of course to divide Christians or churches up into the 'live' and the 'dead', as I know I used to when I was a charismatic teenager, we are speaking against the Spirit of God.)

Having issued these warnings, however, I can say something more positive. The theology I have been presenting in this chapter would certainly agree that the Spirit leads people ever deeper into the life of God, on that journey of learning and unlearning that has been my subject matter through so much of this book so far. And it is certainly plausible to suggest that some moments of learning-and-unlearning – moments when one finds one's implicit idols shattered, and oneself reoriented to Christ – could be quite intense emotional and devotional experiences, even 'crisis' experiences. So we could certainly agree that the Christian life could for some involve a series of crisis experiences appropriately judged to be the work of the Spirit. We might even, in a particular situation, believe that whole communities stand in need of some 'wake-up call' of this form – although the danger is very high in such talk of falling into some kind of arrogant supposition that *they* need revival, while *we* have arrived. On the other hand, I don't see any way of saying that the Spirit's work *must* take the form of crisis experiences, and certainly do not see how one could argue that there must be any fixed number or sequence to them. Nevertheless, if we were to speak in terms of the possibility of baptisms in the Spirit, repeated events in which people are drawn ever deeper into Christ, we might not be too wide of the mark, at least for some people, some of the time.

Speaking in tongues

Having been, as I saw it, 'baptized in the Spirit' I also (some time later) 'spoke in tongues': that is, I experienced a sort of stream of freewheeling unintelligible babbling which allowed an outlet for (and, later on, a form of always-available doorway into) intense devotional feelings of various kinds that seemed to exceed my normal capacities of verbal expression.

At the time, I believed that this was – or at least was supposed to be – some kind of actual language, perhaps a heavenly language. I relished stories (many of which did the rounds) about people speaking in tongues and discovering that they were (like the apostles at Pentecost in Acts 2.4–6) speaking without understanding it themselves the language of some nearby foreigner. Or there were stories about scientific studies of tongues that had supposedly shown it to have the structure of real language, but no language known on earth. For myself, as far back as I can remember I was fighting a fairly deep-seated suspicion that in my case at least tongues was simply nonsense babbling, but I know I was at the sceptical end of the spectrum in that context.

Having once started, I continued to use tongues in private devotional prayer, at least sporadically. There were also contexts in services where everyone would pray out loud in tongues together, in a sort of strange half-singing tone that could sometimes be eerily beautiful. Sometimes, when in small groups praying about something specific, I or someone else would pray for a while in tongues. And occasionally, during times of open prayer in a service, someone would stand up and deliver what we used to call a 'word in tongues':

an example of speech in tongues felt to be a message for the community as a whole – unintelligible until the speaker or someone else in the room was 'given the interpretation'.

The church I was in thought baptism in the Spirit and speaking in tongues of very differing importance. Baptism in the Spirit was for everyone, although some new converts might experience it at the same time as conversion. Speaking in tongues was simply one possible 'gift' that some people who had been baptized in the Spirit might receive – and, however much it enabled the personal devotion of the person who received it, it was seen as one of the less important gifts (something which I realize is not the case in all corners of the charismatic and Pentecostal movement).

This time, let me start with the positive. One of the ways in which one might be taken deeper on the journey into knowledge of God is precisely by learning one's limitations, and so it makes sense to think that part of what one needs is some witness to the inadequacy of one's words and ideas: some kind of witness to the fact that God is always greater, always exceeds one's grasp. Traditionally, the most important form of such witness is silence: falling into silence when one's words run out, when one realizes that however much they point one in the right direction, however much they are, so far as they go, true (by the grace of God) they are nevertheless deeply inadequate. Speaking in tongues can, at its best, function in a similar way, and can perhaps be a salutary witness when reverent silence itself has become something one thinks one can understand and grasp – a witness to the breakdown of one's words of praise and prayer. God is greater than one's words, and one's words need to be broken and remade if they are to point to God – and even then, God will exceed them. Prayer dissolving into a kind of verbal noise can be a powerful witness to the reality of God.

Of course, here too we need to step gingerly. We have to guard against the kind of elitism that might come with saying that 'real Christians' speak in tongues, or that it is some mark of holiness or power. But I don't think that was much of a temptation in the context in which I grew up, and that suggests pretty strongly that it is not an *inherent* part of the package. We also, perhaps more seriously, need to ask whether and how speaking in tongues does genuinely build up faith. I have outlined one way in which it might, but Paul's rather ambivalent explanations of tongues in 1 Corinthians 14 should at least give us some pause. Only if it builds up the body of Christ, only if it takes one deeper on the journey into knowledge of God, can one think of it as a gift of God.

Beside those questions (Does it build up the people of God? Does it take one deeper into God?), all other questions about tongues pale into insignificance, at least for a theologian. Certainly questions about whether it is 'miraculous' or 'supernatural' are all but irrelevant. One doesn't find out whether something is from God by working out whether it is miraculous or supernatural: one finds out by asking whether it leads one back to God.

Nevertheless, as an aside, I should perhaps say that I am now personally convinced that speaking in tongues is not 'miraculous' or 'supernatural' – at least, not in the sense I would have believed when I was younger. That does not make me think it is not still valuable – though I think it helps me to ask precisely *what* its value is a little more calmly, without thinking it has to be all good or all bad, absolutely angelic or absolutely demonic. Speaking in tongues in various forms is a well-known religious phenomenon, one that normally occurs in heightened emotional and devotional states (at least initially), and which does so in all sorts of different religious contexts, Christian and non-Christian. It is precisely what it seems to be: a process in which the speech-making centres in the brain are excited, but without as it were going through the normal channels, the constraints of vocabulary and syntax. It doesn't make sense; it is not a language. And it is precisely because of that that it can speak to me of a God who is beyond my language, and beyond any language.

However, as I say, I do not think the debate about whether tongues is supernatural or natural is theologically very interesting – and the same would go for other gifts, like 'healing' and 'words of knowledge', things which we do not have space to go into here. To repeat: the general rule, which seems to me to be what Paul teaches us in 1 Corinthians 12 to 14, is that one doesn't check whether something is from God by working out whether it is miraculous or supernatural: one checks by asking whether it leads one deeper into the life of God.

Worship and ministry

I want to finish on a positive note, having been negative or ambivalent so far. There are two major effects that the charismatic movement has had, which are more straightforwardly positive. The first is in worship. The idea that worship should be lively and involving, and that it should make space for real emotional engagement, while by no means the exclusive possession of the charismatic movement, has certainly been an idea that has spread with renewed vigour with that movement's help. There are excesses of course, and anyone who has had any experience of them at all can point to some absolutely atrocious worship songs, or to worrying wider trends in worship-song lyrics – but then, that is as true of the older hymn-writing tradition, or indeed of any widespread and popular tradition of worship in the Church. It may not be a form of worship that engages everyone. (Perhaps as a reaction against my upbringing, I personally would not be unhappy if I never heard another worship song as long as I lived, and find that the kind of emotional intensity I once experienced in charismatic services I am now most likely to experience in something like an English cathedral evensong, if there is a very good choir.) Nevertheless, I think that when people look back on this period of Church history from some time in the future, they will see one of those explosions of intensity and excitement about worship that shake the Church periodically, and one that, however much it has (like all other such explosions) produced immense amounts of forgettable dross, and had its ambiguous aspects, has nevertheless contributed something powerful and lasting to the overall heritage of the Christian tradition.

But to take this from the level of personal opinion and pontification, and set us back on a more explicitly theological track: if the theology of the Spirit that I have been presenting is on the right lines, then it is indeed something we would expect from the work of the Spirit to take the Church deeper into the worship of God, and to open God's people up so that the whole of their lives, without reserve (their emotions, their minds, their bodies) are brought to God in worship, and overwhelmed by God there. If the charismatic movement has served as one reminder of this, then it will have done something of great importance.

Second, and with even less ambivalence, I would point to the explosion of interest in charismatic circles in what one might call 'every member ministry': the idea that every member of the body of Christ has something to contribute, some gift they have been given, some ministry to perform. If I had to pick one thing to keep from the form of the charismatic movement in which I grew up, it would be this. It seems to be an important renewal of the kind of message about the Spirit's work that we saw Paul giving in 1 Corinthians 12: the idea that life in the Spirit is life together, and life in which each of us has gifts to offer the body, and gifts to receive from the other members of the body. Life in the Spirit – life conformed to Christ, life directed to the Father – is life in an economy of giving and receiving in which every member is called to play a full role. If the charismatic movement has served as one reminder of this, then it will have done something else of great importance.

Exercise

Compare my story with those of other people. You may have had comparable experience yourself, or be studying theology in a class with others who have. There are also numerous books in which the story of charismatic renewal in particular individuals and particular churches is told.[8]

This has been a very hasty survey, and has only touched on a few themes from my own experience of the charismatic and Pentecostal movements. As with the earlier discussion of spirituality, however, I hope it is clear that – from the point of view of the kind of theology that I have been exploring – what is valuable in the movement is not some new access to a realm in which the Spirit is *really* present, nor any kind of 'rediscovery' of the Spirit, nor even some shift back to emphasis on the Spirit after a period of too much emphasis on the Son or the Father, nor any re-injection of the Spirit into churches from which the Spirit had somehow been lacking. Christian lives, whether they are marked by charismatic or Pentecostal experiences or practices or not, are always, without exception, lives lived in the Spirit, alongside the Son, on the way to the Father. Nevertheless, the charismatic and Pentecostal movements, just like other movements of renewal or transformation in the Church, do have their own distinct flavour. To the extent that this flavour becomes a gift for the building up of the whole body of Christ, it will be appropriate to judge these movements as in that degree a work of God's Spirit.

Key points

- Christian life is life baptized in the Spirit.
- That life is a journey that might include moments or periods of sudden deepening and discovery.
- Speaking in tongues can be a witness to the failure of human speech to do justice to God.
- The Spirit's role is to open a person up so that the whole of his or her life, without reserve (emotions, minds, bodies) is brought to God in worship.
- Life in the Spirit is life in which each person is given gifts for the building up of the whole people of God.

The symphony of the Spirit

The face of the Spirit

'The face of the Spirit is ... the assembly of redeemed human faces in their infinite diversity. Human persons grow to the fullness of *their* particular identities, but sharing in the common divine gift of reconciled life in faith, these are the *Spirit's* manifestation. The Son is manifest in a single, paradigmatic figure, the Spirit is manifest in the "translatability" of that into the contingent diversity of history.'

Rowan Williams, *On Christian Theology*[9]

The Spirit is the power of God drawing people deeper into the life of God by conforming them to Christ. Yet it does not make theological sense to think of that 'becoming Christlike' as involving people losing their differences, their particularities, so as to become *clones* of Christ. To say otherwise would be to assume that Christlikeness was something that could be borne identically by individuals in very different situations (the 'contingent diversity of history' in the quote from Rowan Williams above), however different their backgrounds, however different their positions. That in turn would mean that Christlikeness was something that could float above the messy involvements and relationships and histories in which believers are involved. Yet if Christlikeness were that kind of characteristic, it would have to be a characteristic that floated above Jesus' messy involvements and relationships and history too; it would have to be a characteristic that was only *illustrated* by Jesus, but that could have been carried equally well by somebody else. And, finally, to say that would mean that, once one had grasped the point, once one had understood that free-floating characteristic, reference to the actual complex stuff of Jesus' humanity would become superfluous, even a distraction. He would remain useful as a sermon illustration, perhaps, but the detachable message that he brought would be the real heart of the Gospel, the real focus of Christian faith.

To say all this would be to deny the doctrine of the incarnation. That doctrine claims, after all, that it is Jesus in his particularity – Jesus as the particular human being he is – who is God's Word to the world. He is not that Word *despite* being Jewish, *despite* being male, *despite* being from Nazareth, *despite* living in a particular time and place. He is God's Word precisely *as* that particular human being. He does not show the world how life is lived fully for God in general, in a way that could simply be repeated identically by anyone; he shows how life is lived fully for God by living his own particular life, in his own particular time and place.

Christians believe themselves called to be Christlike, to share in Christ's movement towards the Father and his movement towards the world that the Father loves, but this is a call that they can only fulfil by looking different from Christ. Just as it was the work of the Spirit to shape Jesus' life in his own time and place, so the work of the Spirit now is to make each person reflect Christ in his or her own particular way – the way appropriate to his or her circumstances, history, particular gifts, skills and opportunities.

The Spirit's work is to make each person an *exegesis* or commentary on Christ: one who shows what Christ's call can lead to in one particular time and place. Each person, with the Spirit's guidance, sees Christ from his or her own particular vantage point, and the Spirit's work is to make that person's life *show* what they *see*.

Think of what happens when a biblical text has commentaries written on it. In the first place, no commentary can substitute for the biblical text itself; in the second place, no single commentary could ever be a definitive and final commentary; every commentary is particular. So commentaries are secondary and particular. On the other hand, however, each commentary, if it is a good commentary, can – precisely in its secondariness and particularity – reveal more of the biblical text on which it comments; it can make the biblical text more fully legible.

If each person is made by the Spirit into a commentary on Christ, then while each such reflection is secondary (it is only a reflection, and could never substitute for the face of Christ himself) and particular (it is a commentary from only one particular vantage point), nevertheless each such commentary can make Christ more fully visible. In fact, rather than 'reflection', perhaps the appropriate image is 'refraction': the Spirit's work is to split the white light of Christ into a rainbow of particular colours, each of which shows something of what that white light contains.

The only way in which one can learn fully what Christlikeness means is by seeing these particular lives – the life of Christ, and diverse other lives which comment on his – beside each other, mutually interpreting one another. One might see a Francis of Assisi alongside Jesus, and be helped to see more of Jesus by the light one sees in Francis's face, and more of Francis by seeing him as a refraction of Jesus' light. And then one turns to a different face – a Dietrich Bonhoeffer, or a Julian of Norwich, or a Thomas Merton, or a Teresa of Avila – and sees Jesus differently again. And then one turns to one's neighbour and tries to see him or her in the light of the Jesus one has learnt to see in all these other faces, and one tries to discover what particular light this neighbour might himself throw upon Jesus.

As Rowan Williams has put it, in drawing us into conformity to Christ,

God wants particulars, not generalities. God does not, you might say, create clichés. What is bestowed on each of us is particularity, one utterly distinctive way of being Christlike. If that one distinctive way of being Christlike is frustrated or denied, then something in God's communication to the world is frustrated and denied. There is a sort of smudge across the revealed face of God.[10]

Christians *only* know Jesus fully – the Jesus of the Gospels, the Jesus who lived, died and rose again in a particular time and place – in the whole body of Christ interpreting and refracting him down the centuries. Jesus is not a principle; he is not the sort of general lesson that could be repeated identically anywhere and everywhere. Jesus is a person, and so the sort of reality that is explored fully only in the endless variety of particular relationships into which he enters. The body of Christ, in the sense Paul explores in 1 Corinthians 12, is the form that the Spirit's work must take, if the Spirit's role is to interpret the light of Christ. There is no tension between the *diversifying work* by which the Spirit fulfils each person in his or her particularity, making each person to be more, not less, himself or herself, and the *unifying work* by which the Spirit draws all people into Christ.

The Spirit is, in Christian theology, the transformer of the created world who moulds and kneads human beings in order to shape them for their future, 'perfecting' them, fitting them for their share in unfragmented communion. It is the Spirit's work to save them from isolation and separation, and break them into openness and responsiveness to one another's differences. It is the Spirit's work to draw what might otherwise be a cacophonic disunity into symphony. The Spirit worked to transcribe God's music for playing on the human instrument of Jesus of Nazareth; the Spirit now works to orchestrate that theme for an ensemble of billions.

Key points

- The Spirit's work is to make each person Christlike in his or her own place and time.
- The Spirit's work is to make each person a particular commentary upon Christ.
- To know Christ fully is to know him as he is commented upon in this way – and so to know the body of Christ.
- The Spirit's work is therefore to create difference-in-harmony, not sameness.

Giving and receiving

The Spirit's work is the work of *redemption*: a work in which each person's difference, each person's individuality, is made into a gift to all. This, I think, is the deeper reality of the 'gifts of the Spirit' described in 1 Corinthians 12. The gift that each person gives is not, finally, simply something that they *do*. The gift is what they *become*. The whole person – with all his or her particularity – becomes by the Spirit's work a gift to the whole body of Christ.

But if each person is made by the Spirit into a gift, then one must also ask about the ways in which these gifts are received. The Christian is called to become one who can recognize and receive the gifts that other people are becoming. The Christian is called to be attentive to those who do not fit neatly into their schemes and priorities: who show them something *different*, something they could not have seen or said themselves. Rowan Williams again:

> The stranger … is neither the failed or stupid native speaker, nor someone so terrifyingly alien that I cannot even entertain thought of learning from them. They represent the fact that I have growing to do, not necessarily into anything like an identity with them, but at least into a world where there may be more of a sense of its being a world we *share*.[11]

According to this vision, when faced with someone who does not simply replay to me the same old Christ I have already heard – who does not reflect to me Christ's light in precisely the colour I expect – I am called neither to condemn that difference as failure, nor to assume that that person is reflecting a different Christ, but rather to explore patiently how it might be that the Jesus who I know but who is not exhausted by my knowledge could be reflected from such different angles, in such different colours. I am called to look for the Christ that we share. Any challenges that we might make to one another, challenges to those aspects of each of our refractions of Christ that the other simply can't recognize as Christlike, must emerge from such serious, generous and hopeful paying of attention.

Key points

- The Spirit's work is a work in which each person's difference is made into a gift to all.
- The whole person – with all his or her particularity – becomes by the Spirit's work a gift.
- To be receptive to this gift is to look to see how the Jesus one knows is presented to one differently in the other person.

The Spirit in the world

On the one hand, the Spirit is the Spirit of Jesus, and so the work of the Spirit has a definite particularity to it: Christians who look to discern where the Spirit is present and active are looking to discover where they are shown more of this particular human life. On the other hand, the Holy Spirit is the Spirit of the God of the whole earth, and is present and active in all creation, and so there can be, in principle, no boundaries to where Christians look for this gift.

Wherever they find Christlike love and justice emerging in the midst of the world, or love and justice that make them understand more about Christlikeness, that simply is the work of the Spirit.

This is not a matter of searching for inexplicable occurrences of love and justice, sorting through the known causes of events and speaking of the Spirit only where some unknown, mysterious cause seems to be at work. Identifying the presence and activity of the Spirit is not a matter of causal explanation. The Spirit, as we saw very early on in the chapter, is at work in all creation, sustaining and upholding, so the ordinary causal connections of events are the realm of the Spirit just as much as their interruption or deflection.[12]

Rather, discerning the presence and activity of the Spirit is a matter of learning to recognize *who* is at work. What is the world? A great mess of events and circumstances, of causes and chances, interactions and ramifications. Yes, but look again: what is this? It is an arena in which, in fits and starts, in chances and changes, the life of God, Christlike life, can be seen. The life of God is here. So *who* do you see? It is God the eternal Spirit; it is the Spirit's self-portrait in countless faces, and the Spirit gives itself to the world in this way.[13]

According to Christian theology, the Spirit is, as I have said, at work in the whole of creation, upholding it, and animating it. And the Spirit is at work wherever human beings are being freed to become fully human, in the sense displayed in Christ. So the Spirit is at work not by simply neutrally holding creation in existence, but by labouring in creation to finish it, to complete it, to fulfil and perfect it, freeing it to be itself, drawing it to the end for which it was created. It is to this work of creation – a work that has its origin in the Father, its shape and exemplar in the Son, and its fulfilment in the Spirit – that we now turn.

On the Holy Spirit

In the late fourth century, there were long debates about the nature of the Holy Spirit, and specifically about whether the Spirit was truly divine, or was rather one of God's creatures. Basil of Caesarea was one of the theologians who argued most strongly that, as the Spirit is one person in the threefold economy by which the world is drawn into the life of God, so (as the revision of the Nicene Creed at Constantintople in 381 was to put it) the Spirit is truly 'the Lord, the giver of life', who 'with the Father and the Son is worshipped and glorified.'[14]
Basil wrote that the Spirit

is called 'Spirit of God' (Matthew 12.28), 'Spirit of truth which proceeds from the Father' (John 15.26), 'right Spirit' (Psalm 51.10), 'a leading Spirit' (Psalm 51.12). Its proper and peculiar title is 'Holy Spirit', which is a name specially appropriate to everything that is incorporeal, purely immaterial, and indivisible. So our Lord, when teaching the woman who thought God to be an object of local worship that the incorporeal is incomprehensible, said 'God is a spirit' (John 4.24). On our hearing, then, of a spirit, it is impossible to form the idea of a nature circumscribed, subject to change and variation, or at all like the creature. We are compelled to advance in our conceptions to the highest, and to think of an intelligent essence, in power infinite, in magnitude unlimited, unmeasured by times or ages, generous of its good gifts, to whom turn all things needing sanctification, after whom reach all things that live in virtue, as being watered by its inspiration and helped on toward their natural and proper end; perfecting all other things, but itself in nothing lacking; living not as needing restoration, but as supplier of life; not growing by additions, but straightway full, self-established, omnipresent; origin of sanctification; light perceptible to the mind, supplying, as it were, through itself, illumination to every faculty in the search for truth; by nature unapproachable, apprehended by reason of goodness, filling all things with its power. ... It sends forth grace sufficient and full for all mankind, and is enjoyed by all who share it, according to the capacity, not of its power, but of their nature.

Basil of Caesarea, *On the Holy Spirit*[15]

Key points

- The Holy Spirit is the Spirit of the God of the whole earth, and is present and active in all creation.
- Identifying the presence and activity of the Spirit is not a matter of causal explanation.
- Discerning the presence and activity of the Spirit is a matter of learning to recognize *who* is at work in the world.
- The Spirit works in creation to finish it, freeing it to be itself, and drawing it to the end for which it was created.

Going further

1 The theological implications of the Pentecostal and charismatic movements are worth exploring further. A good place to start is with Walter Hollenweger's *The Pentecostals* (London: SCM Press, 1972) – a classic description of the origins and early decades of the Pentecostal movement. Then see Amos Yong, 'Discerning the Spirit', *The Christian Century* (7 March 2006), pp. 31–3, available online at http://religion-online.org/showarticle. asp?title=3345; Paul W. Lewis, 'Reflections of a Hundred Years of Pentecostal Theology', *Cyberjournal for Pentecostal charismatic Research* 12 (2007); available online at http://pctii.org/cyberj/cyberj12/lewis.html – the latter useful in itself, but also for its extensive bibliography. Assessments of the charismatic movement can be found in David Middlemiss, *Interpreting Charismatic Experience* (London: SCM Press, 1996) and the General Synod of the Church of England's report, *We believe in the Holy Spirit* (London: Church House, 1991) – a report on the doctrine of the Spirit by various Anglican authors, dealing with the charismatic movement among other topics. For speaking in tongues specifically, see Cyril G. Williams,

Tongues of the Spirit (Cardiff: University of Wales Press, 1981). Online, UbuWeb's *Ethnopoetics: Soundings* project provides you with a chance to listen to what 'Glossolalia: speaking in tongues' actually sounds like at http://www.ubu.com/ethno/soundings/gloss.html, if you have never heard it. The clip they provide is made up of several extracts from an American worship service, where singing in English eventually gives way to singing in tongues.

2 When running through Old Testament references, there were various texts I left out (as explained in note 1 below). That omission made it easier to treat the Old Testament material as a collection of texts that made clear reference to a single, distinguishable reality: the Holy Spirit of God. Our task was then simply that of summarizing what those texts said about this reality. If the disallowed texts are allowed into the picture as well, however, it might become clearer that there are varieties of uses of 'spirit' language in the Old Testament, without clear-cut edges between them, and that while some of them sound like they are referring to the 'Spirit of God' in a sense something like the New Testament sense, others of them are clearly not – and there is a wide grey area between the two categories. This raises two connected critical questions. On the one hand, there is a question about the kind of interpretation I was engaged in. What authorizes the decision to look for texts that seem to describe the 'Spirit of God', and to divide them from those texts that use 'spirit' in other ways, but which are unsystematic-ally mixed in with them? And what authorizes the assumption that these very various Old Testament texts all describe the same distinguishable reality? On the other hand, what is the connection between the Spirit of God, the human spirit, the various kinds of spirit that God can be said to send or that can be said to comfort or afflict people, and so on? If the Old Testament can slip from talking about one of these to talking about another without apparent distinction, what does that imply?

Notes

1 I have excluded texts from three rather grey areas. There are places where it is said that God has given or will give someone a such-and-such spirit. 'I'll give you a languishing spirit', for instance, in Deuteronomy 28.65 – that seems to be a fairly obvious circumlocution for 'I'll make *your* spirit languish; I'll make *you* languish.' Then there are texts that, like Joshua 5.1, speak of someone simply 'having spirit'; those *could* be about having *the* Spirit, or God's Spirit, but to my mind they seem more likely to be a more metaphorical usage: a way of saying someone has vitality, energy, resilience. Lastly, I've left out texts like 1 Samuel 16.14 about God sending an evil spirit to trouble someone. In that passage from 1 Samuel, the evil spirit is explicitly contrasted with God's Spirit, and I've taken my cue from that passage, and excluded these 'evil spirit' passages from my list.

2 For the Spirit as gift, see Acts 2.38; for this and the Spirit as the love common to Father and Son, see Augustine, *De Trinitate* 19.37, in Philip Schaff (ed.), *Nicene and Post-Nicene Fathers*, First Series, vol. 3 (New York: Christian Literature Company, 1887), pp.

219–20; available online at the Christian Classics Ethereal Library, http://www.ccel.org/ccel/schaff/npnf103.iv.i.xvii.xix.html.

3 I am grateful to my colleague Rachel Muers for her help with this section.

4 Try http://www.google.com/search?q=spirituality.

5 Frederic and Mary Ann Bussat, 'Spiritual Practices – X: The Mystery' (no date) in their *Alphabet of Spiritual Literacy* at Spirituality and Practice, http://www.spiritualityandpractice.com/practices/practices.php?id=34.

6 'Frequently Asked Questions' (no date), Spirituality and Health, http://www.spiritualityhealth.com/newsh/items/blank/item_226.html.

7 Acts 2.1–13.

8 For a pair of older examples, see Dennis J. Bennett, *Nine O'Clock in the Morning* (Gainesville, FL: Bridge, 1970), and Tony Higton, *That the World May Believe: A Parish Church Moves from Renewal to Restoration* (London: Marshall–Pickering, 1985).

9 Rowan Williams, *On Christian Theology* (Oxford: Blackwell, 2000), pp. 125–6.

10 Rowan Williams, 'Catholic persons: images of holiness: a dialogue', in Jeffrey John (ed.), *Living the Mystery: Affirming Catholicism and the Future of Anglicanism*, (London: DLT, 1994), pp. 84–5.

11 Rowan Williams, *Christ on Trial* (London: DLT, 1993), p. 63.

12 We will explore the question of how God's action relates to the causal connections of creation in Chapter 8.

13 I am deliberately echoing what I said on p. 130. The reader might like to ask whether an equivalent passage could be written about the eternal Father.

14 The 'Nicene' Creed, English Language Liturgical Commission 1988 texts, available online at http://www.englishtexts.org/survey.html#thenicenecreed.

15 Basil of Caesarea, *On the Holy Spirit* 9.22, in Philip Schaff and Henry Wace (eds) *Nicene and Post-Nicene Fathers*, Second Series, vol. 8 (New York: Christian Literature Company, 1895), p. 15; available online at http://www.ccel.org/ccel/schaff/npnf208.vii.x.html; translation slightly altered.

Part 2
Life in the World

7

The Good Creation

In the first part of this book, I argued that Christians can make sense of their lives, corporately and individually, as threefold journeys into the triune life of God. I described how Christians saw Jesus of Nazareth as the visibility of God, God's way of loving the world and sharing God's life with the world; I described the Spirit as the power of God's Christlike love at work in the world, drawing it in conformity to Christ in love for Christ's Father and the world that the Father loves. In the second part of the book, my emphasis will shift slightly. I will be asking what the life of the world looks like once one sees it as caught up in this divine drama. In this chapter, we will explore the doctrine of creation, and I will try to show that it is not so much a claim about the process by which the universe, life, and human life in particular came into being, and more a claim about how the whole of the world and the whole of life depends at every moment utterly upon the same God who, by Word and Spirit, is drawing the world into fullness of life. The chapter begins an arc that will sweep on into a discussion of the doctrine of providence in the next chapter and culminate in a discussion of the end times ('eschatology') in Chapter 9.

I am going to

- show that biblical claims about creation are closely tied to claims about the covenant and the gospel;
- argue that the Christian doctrine of creation presents God as the context in which the world grows;
- explain why these ideas lead to the claim that God created the world 'from nothing';
- explain why these ideas also lead to claims about God's ungraspable, unknowable nature; and
- suggest that belief in the doctrine of creation has implications for how we think of ourselves as bodies and as participants in a wider natural environment.

Preparation

- What do you think are the most important claims which Christians have to make about God's creation of the world? Why do you think those claims are important? Do you think they are claims which are likely to conflict with what mainstream modern science says about the origins of the world in which we live? Jot down your thoughts before launching into the chapter.
- Have a look at the first few pages that turn up when you type 'doctrine of creation' into a web search engine.[1] What do those sites seem to suggest are the main reasons for caring about the doctrine – its main implications or lessons? What impact, if any, do these sites suggest that holding to the doctrine of creation will have on somebody's life?

Additional reading

For additional perspectives on the doctrine of creation to set along mine, try:

Colin Gunton, *The Triune Creator: An Historical and Systematic Study*, Edinburgh
Studies in Constructive Theology (Edinburgh: Edinburgh University Press, 1998).
A detailed history of the doctrine, coupled with Gunton's own restatement.

Jürgen Moltmann, *God in Creation: An Ecological Doctrine of Creation*, tr. Margaret
Kohl (London: SCM Press, 1985). A lengthy argument that a renewed understanding of God's relation to creation can help repair some of the damage
human beings have done to the world.

Creation and covenant

[1]I will sing of your steadfast love, O Lord, forever; with my mouth I will
proclaim your faithfulness to all generations. [2]I declare that your steadfast
love is established forever; your faithfulness is as firm as the heavens. [3]You
said, 'I have made a covenant with my chosen one, I have sworn to my
servant David: [4]"I will establish your descendants forever, and build your
throne for all generations."' *Selah*.

[5]Let the heavens praise your wonders, O Lord, your faithfulness in the assembly of the holy ones. [6]For who in the skies can be compared to the Lord?
Who among the heavenly beings is like the Lord, [7]a God feared in the council
of the holy ones, great and awesome above all that are around him? [8]O Lord
God of hosts, who is as mighty as you, O Lord? Your faithfulness surrounds
you. [9]You rule the raging of the sea; when its waves rise, you still them. [10]You
crushed Rahab like a carcass; you scattered your enemies with your mighty
arm. [11]The heavens are yours, the earth also is yours; the world and all that is
in it – you have founded them. ... [14]Righteousness and justice are the foundation of your throne; steadfast love and faithfulness go before you. ... [18][O]ur
shield belongs to the Lord, our king to the Holy One of Israel. ...

[38]But now you have spurned and rejected him; you are full of wrath
against your anointed. [39]You have renounced the covenant with your servant; you have defiled his crown in the dust. [40]You have broken through all
his walls; you have laid his strongholds in ruins. [41]All who pass by plunder
him; he has become the scorn of his neighbours. [42]You have exalted the right
hand of his foes; you have made all his enemies rejoice. ...

[46]How long, O Lord? Will you hide yourself forever? How long will your
wrath burn like fire? ... [49]Lord, where is your steadfast love of old, which by
your faithfulness you swore to David? [50]Remember, O Lord. ...

Psalm 89.1–14, 18, 38–42, 46, 49–50

Exercise

Read this Psalm carefully. Before reading my comments, ask yourself what
role the Psalmist's references to God's work of creation play in the Psalm as
a whole.

The whole of Psalm 89 is about David and about those who saw themselves as his descendants, the Davidic line of kings. The first part is a song about the steadfast love and faithfulness that God has shown to this Davidic line, which is seen as mirroring the stability of God's dealings with creation. 'I will sing of your steadfast love', says the Psalmist; it is 'as firm as the heavens'. But the stability of the natural world is not simply a useful metaphor for God's faithfulness to him: the stability of the natural world displays to the Psalmist the steadfastness and faithfulness of its creator, and it is the very same steadfastness and faithfulness which he sees played out again in God's covenant towards David and his line. The nature of the God in whom the Davidic line can have faith is displayed to them on the broad canvas of God's creative work.

In other words, there is an intimate link between the Psalmist's understanding of *creation*, and his understanding of God's *covenant* – God's promises, God's faithful compact – with Israel and Israel's king. One might say that the Psalm only speaks about creation because it wants to speak in a certain way about covenant: God's creation faithfulness functions as a backdrop, a back-projection from God's covenant faithfulness.

And that means that God's creative work is seen in highly charged terms. It is not simply the creation of a neutral space *within* which the drama of good and evil, of truth and falsehood, of faithfulness and unfaithfulness, will be played out. It is itself an act in the drama. God's creation of the world is not here presented simply as the calm speaking of a word that instantly brings a world into being; rather, it is presented in more mythological terms as the defeat of the monster Rahab, and the forcing back of the primal sea. The monster and the sea are symbols in Israel – in fact, more widely in the ancient Near East – for chaos, for dissolution, for dissipation, for disorder, for the unpredictable erosion of all stability. So God's creation of a faithful, reliable world is here being presented as the crushing defeat of unreliability, a campaign of shock and awe against unfaithfulness.

The world is held in being by God's constancy, by God's holding to God's promises; it is preserved from an existence entirely erratic, entirely arbitrary, entirely chaotic. Just so, the Psalm carries on, God's divine goodness gives the people a stable line of kings as a shield against the sea of political chaos, against the monsters of invasion and disintegration. God is faithful, the world is good, and the people are happy.

Except that they are not. The second part of the Psalm begins in verse 38 with the words, 'But now you have spurned and rejected him.' God has spurned the covenant, has allowed the walls of the kingdom to crumble into ruins, and has allowed David's line to be cut short. The supposed bulwark against chaos has vanished, and the sea has come flooding back. The goodness, the faithfulness, the reliability of God has been hidden behind death and Sheol, behind Rahab and the sea.

So the Psalm is not simply a calm and cheerful description of a perfect world. It is a call on God to *remember* faithfulness. This Psalm proclaims the goodness of creation as a way of proclaiming faith in and hope for redemption – as a way of proclaiming the belief that the chaos that has engulfed David's line is not the final word, that God's faithfulness is still there, hidden behind it all, and that God can bring it to the surface again.[2]

This Psalm's proclamation of the goodness of creation is made in a world that is quite clearly not good; it is made *despite* the evil of the world. In fact, it would be truer to say that this proclamation is made *because* of the evil of the world. The goodness of creation is proclaimed as a way of interpreting the evil of the world – a way of denying it ultimacy. It does not, this Psalm says, go all the way down, and it will not have the last word. To rest content with evil, as if it were simply part of how things have to be, is to forget God's covenant.

This Psalm shows us where the heart of the doctrine of creation stands. That doctrine does not have as its central question, 'How did God create the world?' We will see more clearly later on that a concern with *mechanism*, with the 'how' of creation, is a peripheral matter. The doctrine is more about the claim *that* God created the world than about *how*. Further, Psalm 89 suggests the doctrine does not trade in curiosity about an event deep in the past, over and done with; it is about the holding in being of a stable world now. We might say that the central topic is not simply that God *created* the world, but that God *creates* the world. Most importantly, however, God's holding of the world in being is portrayed in the doctrine as a matter of God's generosity, patience and goodness: the central affirmation is not simply that God creates the world, but that God creates the world *good*.

Not: **How** God **created** the world.
Not: **That** God **created** the world.
Not: **That** God **creates** the world.
But: **That** God **creates** the world **good**.

Creation for covenant

Each section in Karl Barth's massive *Church Dogmatics* begins with a short summary statement of the doctrine he is about to expound. When he reaches the doctrine of creation, his summary statement runs like this:

Creation comes first in the series of works of the triune God, and is thus the beginning of all the things distinct from God Himself ... But according to [the biblical witness] the purpose and therefore the meaning of creation is to make possible the history of God's covenant with human beings which has its beginning, its centre and its culmination in Jesus Christ. The history of this covenant is as much the goal of creation as creation itself is the beginning of this history.[3]

Key points

- Psalm 89 speaks of God's creative work as a backdrop to God's covenantal work.
- The goodness of creation is proclaimed as a way of interpreting the evil of the world, denying that it is ultimate or invincible.
- The core claim of the doctrine is therefore about creation's goodness.

Creation and gospel

[13][God] has rescued us from the power of darkness and transferred us into the kingdom of his beloved Son, [14]in whom we have redemption, the forgiveness of sins, [15]who is the image of the invisible God, the firstborn of all creation; [16]for in him all things in heaven and on earth were created, things visible and invisible, whether thrones or dominions or rulers or powers – all things have been created through him and for him. [17]He himself is before all things, and in him all things hold together. [18]He is the head of the body, the church; he is the beginning, the firstborn from the dead, so that he might come to have first place in everything. [19]For in him all the fullness of God was pleased to dwell, [20]and through him God was pleased to reconcile to himself all things, whether on earth or in heaven, by making peace through the blood of his cross. [21]And you who were once estranged and hostile in mind, doing evil deeds, [22]he has now reconciled in his fleshly body through death, so as to present you holy and blameless and irreproachable before him – [23]provided that you continue securely established and steadfast in the faith, without shifting from the hope promised by the gospel that you heard, which has been proclaimed to every creature under heaven.

Colossians 1.13–23

Exercise

Read this passage carefully and, before you read my commentary, ask yourself what the connection is between Christ and God's creative work.

Just as with Psalm 89, the context for this New Testament reference to creation is talk about salvation, about God's rescuing of his people from the power of darkness, God's making his people to be holy, blameless and irreproachable. The author's trust in God's redemptive, sanctifying purpose is strengthened by the affirmation that nothing in heaven or earth, visible or invisible, is out of the hands of the one who saves. But there is nothing here like Psalm 89's depiction of God defeating the monster Rahab; God is not portrayed as one who happens to be strong enough to struggle with chaos and defeat it, however easily. Rather, God is the world's context. God is the one in whom the whole of creation lives and moves and has its being: 'in him all things hold together'.[4]

Specifically, it is in *Christ* – the one who shed blood on the cross and was then raised, firstborn from the dead – that all things hold together. The salvation by which Christians believe God has caught them up in Christ, their reconciliation to the Father in the Son by the Spirit, is not a process that will take them away from the world, nor is it the bringing into creation of a foreign element (even if humanity was, before Christ, 'estranged' from God), and nor is it an extra to creation, something new and unexpected added to it. No, salvation in Christ is *proper* to the world, because the world is Christ's. In turning to Christ and being grafted by the Spirit into his body, the world is simply becoming what it was created to be. The rule of Christ is not a curb on the world's freedom, training it into shapes that are not its own – Christ's work is not like the tending of a bonsai tree, training it into bizarre shapes utterly unlike those that it would take in the wild. Rather, it is the freeing of the world from the darkness and estrangement that have distorted the unity and shape it was given in creation; it is the freeing of the world to be itself.

This text's affirmations about creation all circle around a central claim: that when Christians find salvation in Christ, they are at the same time discovering the deepest truth about themselves and their world. This is a salvation that does not take them away from the world, but sends them deeper into it. And that in turn means that these affirmations about creation are a way of saying something about sin and evil – about everything that stands in the way of love, reconciliation and holiness. It is sin and evil that are the foreign elements; *they* are the intruders that do not belong. To be human, to be a creature, is not the same thing as being a sinner, and is not the same thing as being caught up in evil: sin and evil are *distortions* of true creatureliness and of full humanity.[5]

This is why the gospel can be 'preached to every creature under heaven'. In Christ, believers find not salvation *from* the world, but the salvation for which the whole world was made. No part of the world is beyond salvation's reach. In this context, to say 'God created the world' is another way of saying 'Jesus is Lord'.

The only creator

'If ... the Creator made all things freely, and by his own power, and arranged and finished them, and his will is the substance of all things, then he is discovered to be the one only God who created all things, who alone is omnipotent, and who is the only Father rounding and forming all things, visible and invisible, such as may be perceived by our senses and such as cannot, heavenly and earthly, "by the word of his power" (Hebrews 1.3) and he has fitted and arranged all things by his wisdom, while he contains all things, but he himself can be contained by no one: he is the former, he the builder, he the discoverer, he the creator, he the Lord of all; and there is no one besides him, or above him. ... But there is one only God, the Creator – he who is above every principality, and power, and dominion, and virtue: he is Father, he is God, he the founder, he the maker, he the creator, who made those things by himself, that is, through his Word and his Wisdom – heaven and earth, and the seas, and all things that are in them: he is just; he is good; he it is who formed man, who planted paradise, who made the world, who gave rise to the flood, who saved Noah; He is the God of Abraham, and the God of Isaac, and the God of Jacob, the God of the living: he it is whom the law proclaims, whom the prophets preach, whom Christ reveals, whom the apostles make known to us, and in whom the Church believes.'

Irenaeus of Lyons, *Against Heresies*[6]

Key points

- In Colossians 1, God is the one in whom the whole of creation lives and moves and has its being.
- According to Christian theology, salvation in Christ is proper to the world, because the world is Christ's.
- Salvation frees the world to be itself.
- Salvation is not salvation *from* the world, but salvation *of* the world.

God's intimate presence

[1]O Lord, you have searched me and known me. [2]You know when I sit down and when I rise up; you discern my thoughts from far away. [3]You search out my path and my lying down, and are acquainted with all my ways. [4]Even before a word is on my tongue, O Lord, you know it completely. [5]You hem me in, behind and before, and lay your hand upon me. [6]Such knowledge is too wonderful for me; it is so high that I cannot attain it.

[7]Where can I go from your spirit? Or where can I flee from your presence? [8]If I ascend to heaven, you are there; if I make my bed in Sheol, you are there. [9]If I take the wings of the morning and settle at the farthest limits of the sea, [10]even there your hand shall lead me, and your right hand shall hold me fast. [11]If I say, 'Surely the darkness shall cover me, and the light around me become night', [12]even the darkness is not dark to you; the night is as bright as the day, for darkness is as light to you.

[13]For it was you who formed my inward parts; you knit me together in my mother's womb. [14]I praise you, for I am fearfully and wonderfully made. Wonderful are your works; that I know very well. [15]My frame was not hidden from you, when I was being made in secret, intricately woven in the depths of the earth. [16]Your eyes beheld my unformed substance. In your book were written all the days that were formed for me, when none of them as yet existed. [17]How weighty to me are your thoughts, O God! How vast is the sum of them! [18]I try to count them – they are more than the sand; I come to the end – I am still with you.

[19]O that you would kill the wicked, O God, and that the bloodthirsty would depart from me – [20]those who speak of you maliciously, and lift themselves up against you for evil! [21]Do I not hate those who hate you, O Lord? And do I not loathe those who rise up against you? [22]I hate them with perfect hatred; I count them my enemies. [23]Search me, O God, and know my heart; test me and know my thoughts. [24]See if there is any wicked way in me, and lead me in the way everlasting.

Psalm 139

Exercise

Read this Psalm carefully. Before continuing, ask yourself how the final paragraph fits in with the rest of the Psalm.

It is common, when Psalm 139 is quoted, for people to call a halt before they reach that final paragraph, put off by the sudden change in tone. What has been reverent and uplifting suddenly becomes harsh and vindictive. To omit those verses, however, is to disguise the fact that this Psalm is not a piece of speculative reflection on the nature of God's presence to human beings, nor a pious and comforting meditation on the intimacy of God's relation to the believer. It is a plea for help. It is a cry sent up from within a disordered world where the wicked thrive, those who deny God prosper, and where the situation of the righteous is parlous. It is a cry sent up from within a world where righteousness and wickedness are invisible, hidden behind a surface of unjust prosperity and indiscriminate suffering.

It is in this context that the Psalmist makes his declaration of faith in a God who sees truly, who can see past appearances (prosperity, adversity) to what lies beneath (wickedness, righteousness). It is a declaration of faith in a God who not only sees that hidden righteousness and wickedness, but has the power to make it visible to all: to vindicate the righteous, and to bring the wicked to nothing. It is a declaration of faith in the one who has the power to restore the deeper, truer order of things, to clean away the grime that has accumulated on the surface of creation until the true colours shine out again, and to re-establish love and justice.

There is, for the Psalmist, simply no possibility that these deep truths could be hidden from God. Despite that phrase about 'searching out', God sees these things not because God is very good at seeing through disguises, such that it would be very difficult, perhaps even impossible, to fool God, but because the very idea of hiding righteousness or wickedness from God is a nonsense. God knows the heart of the Psalmist, for instance, not because God has some kind of spiritual endoscope, but because God *made* that heart.

In other words, God does not 'enter into' a relationship with a ready-formed Psalmist; God does not 'get to know him', however successfully. God does not start from the Psalmist's outside and work inwards. No; everything about the Psalmist – his thoughts, his words, his inmost constitution – is already seen by God, already held by God, because it was made by God, written in God's book. To think of there being any aspect of the Psalmist beyond God's knowledge or control is, according to this Psalm, simply nonsensical.

The Psalmist also says that there is nowhere he can go in the world that would take him beyond God's reach. Although the world is a realm in which contradiction to God appears to thrive, it is not a realm any part of which is distant from God. If the wicked manage to deny God, they do not do so by backing away from the reach of God's hands, so that God must lunge if God wants to grab hold of them again. There simply isn't any direction that they can take that would count as a step away from God. Although it is possible to live for God or against God, there is, in reality, no going further away from or closer to God. God is not at some one location in the world, with some parts of the world more nearly in God's reach than others: God is everywhere – or perhaps it might be better to say, everywhere is in God.[7]

The doctrine of creation does not, then, attempt to describe a distant initiating event that set this world unrolling like a carpet away from the throne of its maker. Rather, it declares an obstinate faith that in all times and places, however dark and disordered they might be, the world is in the hands of the one who made it and who knows it and who cannot and will not abandon it. Rowan Williams has put it well.

> If God is faithfully present in the glory and the beauty of creation, what is going on when I don't sense that? Well, the answer is, the same thing is going on. God is going on. And how can I believe that? 'With face and hands clinging unto thy breast. Clinging and crying, crying without cease.'[8]

Key points

- The doctrine of creation is a declaration of faith in a God who has the power to vindicate righteousness.
- The doctrine claims that no part of the universe, and no part of the self, is beyond God's knowledge and control.
- The doctrine claims that God is the context in which the world grows.
- The doctrine claims that there is no place, time or circumstance in which God is not actively present.

Creation from nothing

Psalm 139 begins to expose one of the sinews of the Christian doctrine of creation. That doctrine in its classic form involves a rejection of one simple but misleading way of thinking about the relationship between God and the world, in which God on the one hand struggles with the world on the other, succeeding in knowing the world only because the divine gaze is so penetrating, and shaping it only because the divine strength is so great. Any such picture of struggle between God and the world in effect makes God and the world two realities within a context that contains both of them – a context that is bigger than the world, and also bigger than God: an arena in which they compete for space and control. This is not the picture that the classic Christian doctrine paints.

That doctrine does not express a hope that the world will be subdued by the force of a God who is outside it; it does not hope for an imposition of order from outside the world (an enemy army come to impose democracy, say). It is, rather, expressive of a hope for the world's true flourishing in God. God is the context in which the world grows: God is not an outsider to the world, because God is the space in which the world lives and moves and has its being.

Rather than thinking of God as an artisan, tinkering with the world on his workbench, one might think instead of God as the world's mother, and of the world growing in God's womb. The world, like a foetus, is not the same reality as the mother, but it is wholly dependent upon the mother; everything that sustains and nourishes it comes from the mother. It grows only because the mother has opened up a space within herself for something that is not her, and given herself over to the support of this something. The doctrine of creation speaks of this kind of absolute and ongoing dependence of the creation upon its creator, and of this kind of intimacy.

This means, incidentally, that talk of God's transcendence (that is, of God's difference from creation and Lordship over it) and talk of God's immanence (of God's presence in and to creation) go hand in hand. Transcendence and immanence are not qualities that need balancing off against one another, as if they pulled in different directions. God's transcendence *is* God's intimacy. That is, God's transcendence consists in the fact that God is not an element *in* the world, with a specific location, but that context upon which every creaturely thing utterly depends, resting upon God directly and entirely for its existence.

Against Gnosticism

A debate about creation was one of the first major Christian theological controversies. In the second century, there were various Christian groups that have been labelled 'gnostic'. At least some of those groups taught that creation was not an act of divine will, the deliberate and loving bringing into being of a reality distinct from God that God could love, but that it involved rather a process of 'emanation'. From the reality of God there emerged spiritual realities distinct from God, and from those spiritual realities there emerged further realities, somewhat less spiritual – and so on through numerous ranks of less and less spiritual creatures until eventually there emerged the gritty stuff of the material world. That world was not the direct creation of God, but the product of beings much lower in the hierarchy – even, perhaps, of beings so removed from God that they could be thought of as malevolent. The material world was seen as distant from the purely spiritual reality of God from whom it had ultimately descended, but it was connected to it by this great chain of emanations, and there were within it – within at least some human beings – sparks of more spiritual reality that could in principle return back up the hierarchies, from less to more spiritual, and so return to God.

In response to this kind of theology, theologians like Irenaues of Lyons insisted that creation was a direct act of God's loving will, bringing the whole world into being and holding it in being, and that even though that meant one must operate with an absolute distinction between the Maker and the made, rather than with a graded hierarchy of more and less spiritual, one could not properly think of creation as lying at any *distance* from God. God is immediately present to all that God has made.[9]

I argued in earlier chapters for the propriety of imagining God's life as a community of persons, united in love. In that context, the act of creation can be understood as that community making space within itself for the participation of others. That Triune life, which was complete in itself, is opened up in an act not of necessity but of delighted generosity – of the kind of joy that desires to share a pleasure with others. I spoke of 'perichoresis' as meaning, literally, something like 'giving place to one another in turn'. The doctrine of creation is the claim that the persons of the Trinity also make way for the world.

This is the point of the traditional Christian claim that God created the world *ex nihilo* – 'from nothing'. There is, Christians have said, no medium, no resistant stuff, from which God wrests creation: all that we can picture God as working on is, as it were, God's own life, so as to make space or give nourishment to creation. And if God's life is wholly generous, wholly giving, wholly caught up in delighted sharing (as the doctrine of the Trinity declares) then the act of creation is entirely proper to God's life.

Creation is not really to be thought of, in Christian theology, as an act of divine strength, or as a divine achievement. It is an act of love, and God is love. And the affirmation of the doctrine of creation by Christians is therefore the affirmation, in any and all circumstances, that the only source and ground of their lives and their circumstances is the loving generosity of God, and that their lives and their world grow in the medium of this loving generosity, nourished and upheld by it.

How on earth this affirmation can be made in a world of sin and suffering is a topic to which we will be returning.

Children of a lesser God

One corollary of all this, which has been rather unevenly realized in the history of Christianity, is that there can be no 'children of a lesser God'.[10] That is, there is a universalism built into Christianity: *all* people are created by God; all people owe their existence to the generosity of God. There are no groups of people who, simply by virtue of *what they are*, are more distant from God, or whose lives are not to the same extent gifts of God's generosity. Of course, all people live to one extent or another against the grain of this connection to God – but for all people that is a distortion of their true reality. Salvation, participation in the life of God, is (according to the doctrine of creation) equally proper to everyone, regardless of their sex, their race, their orientation, and their background.

Key points

- Christian theology does not picture creation as the outcome of God's struggle with some material.
- According to Christian theology, the only source and ground of our lives and our circumstances is the loving generosity of God.

Creation and incomprehensiblity

The claim that God has made all things from nothing provides the deepest ground of classical Christian theology's insistence that God is incomprehensible. Think, for instance, about the distinction between male and female. If God made them both, and if both are equally called to share the life of God, then one must think of God's life as being 'beyond' the difference between male and female. And so although one might use gendered language and images to speak of God – indeed, although one might find it impossible not to – one will know that ultimately such language must fail to grasp hold of a God who cannot be characterized as either male or female. God's difference from me, a male human being, is not like the difference from me of my wife, a female human being. It is a different kind of difference: God is *more* different than that.

But the doctrine of creation affirms not just that God made both men and women, but that God made all things – male and female, physical and mental, animate and inanimate, visible and invisible, material and immaterial, and so on – and made all things to share in the life of God. God is, therefore, *beyond* the distinction between physical and mental, *beyond* the distinction between animate and inanimate, *beyond* the distinction between visible and invisible, *beyond* the distinction between material and immaterial. God is beyond all distinctions between kinds and types of God's creatures, because God is creator of all. God's difference from the world is not like the difference of one creature from another creature, however great that difference might be. God is more different from me than my wife is; more different from me than a rock is; more different from me than a feeling of nostalgia is; more different from me than the colour blue is; more different from me than the number three is; more different from me than the idea of unity is. And that does not mean that God is very, very distant from me – because God is beyond the difference between proximity and distance; language about distance or closeness fails in the end to do justice to God no less than does language about male and female.

God is, according to the doctrine of creation, beyond all creaturely distinctions, and so although one may and must use all sorts of creaturely language and imagery to speak about God, God is not grasped and held by that language. And as we have no ways of speaking that do not trade in the coinage of creaturely distinctions, we have no language that is adequate to God.

No thing

The late medieval German theologian and philosopher, Nicholas of Cusa, was fascinated by the unknowability of God. He wrote a book, *De li non aliud* – *On God as Not Other*, in which he argued, in effect, that God was not a 'thing', not some particular object (of whatever kind) that could, like all things, be defined by means of some set of distinctions (a thing is always *this* not *that*). Although the details of Cusa's own presentation are – to say the least – somewhat abstruse, his general point holds: God is *never* one more thing in any list of things. God is no thing.[11]

That human beings can speak about God at all, Christian theology says, is not because human language inherently has the capacity to speak about God. It is only possible because God has grasped hold of human beings – of these language-using, distinction-making, creaturely and particular beings.

And although God remains God in the process, and so incomprehensible, un-knowable and unutterable, God is named on the basis of the way in which human beings see themselves being grabbed hold of, in Christ and the Spirit. Christians, in other words, can only speak directly and properly about God's *economy* – about God's work within creation for creation's salvation. And they can only trust that in speaking about and knowing this economy they are knowing the one whose economy it is, and that their speaking is part of the process by which they are being drawn into creaturely conformity to God's immanent life. They must, however, acknowledge that that immanent life re-mains utterly beyond them. This is what it means to worship the creator of all things.

This prohibition paradoxically extends to talk about creation itself. As the first three sections of this chapter should have made clear, Christian theology names God as creator on the basis of the economy of salvation – that is, on the basis of the ways in which they believe God relates to them in history. And that economy gives them all sorts of imaginative ways of gesturing towards God's creative act: talk of mothers' wombs, or of the extending of the commu-nity of the Trinity, and so on. But Christians can no more directly and finally grasp what it is for God to create than they can directly and finally grasp any-thing about God. Christians know that, on the basis of God's dealings with them, they cannot but imagine God as creator, but they also know that they cannot literally and fully know what it is for God to create.

Father or Mother?

I have used the name 'Father' to speak of the first person of the Trinity in order to keep a strong connection between what I say about the immanent life of God and what I say about the patterns, the drama, of the gospel story – in which the person in question is named by Jesus as his Father. The word 'Father' when used of God is therefore always shorthand for 'the one whom Jesus called Father' or 'the Father of our Lord Jesus Christ'.

This 'Father', however, is one whose life consists in a kind of self-giving which eternally gives birth to a Son; he is one whose generativity is more like a womb in which another is born and grows than like one who at some point makes a decision to create something external to himself. In any culture remotely like mine, that puts a cat among the pigeons that are kept by the male name 'Father'. In order to do justice to that disruption, one may need to turn for help in this to texts like Isaiah 66.12–13, which speaks of God as a mother, comforting Jerusalem by breastfeeding her, carrying her around, dand-ling her on her knees; or to Deuteronomy 32.18, Psalm 90.2 and Numbers 11.12, which speak of God giving birth to Israel. And one may need both kinds of imagery – paternal and maternal – to do justice to the image of God speak-ing creation into being, and providing the space within which creation grows and kicks. It may be only by the unstable, imagination-foxing mixture of these different patterns of imagery, male and female, that one can both speak aptly of God, and yet be reminded that God's immanent life is beyond one's imagin-ation, and cannot be pinned down on any of our gender maps.[12]

Key points

- God is, according to classical Christian theology, beyond the distinction between male and female.
- God is also beyond all other creaturely distinctions.
- All language, which inevitably works with those distinctions, fails when it tries to speak directly of God.
- Christians nevertheless claim that they are enabled to speak of God by God's economy of salvation.

Being creatures

The doctrine of creation in Christian theology is a two-edged sword. On the one hand, it calls human beings to acknowledge and celebrate God as God – as the ungraspable Creator and sustainer of all that is. On the other hand, it calls human beings to acknowledge that they are not gods but creatures, and to celebrate that fact.

If God is the creator, and so beyond any distinctions between mental and physical, material and immaterial, visible and invisible, flesh and spirit, then there is no greater bar to physical, material, visible, fleshy creatures like us human beings participating in the life of God than if we were somehow purely mental, immaterial, invisible and spiritual. Christians can therefore proclaim that the whole of creation, in all its parts, was made for participation in the divine life, which is not reserved simply for their spiritual part or aspect, some detachable soul or spirit that is understood somehow to relate more closely to God.

The central confirmation and ground of this affirmation is, for Christians, the incarnation. I explained in Chapter 5 that, for classical incarnational doctrine, Jesus' whole bodily, creaturely, finite life – material, visible and particular, caught up in a web of relationships and language, located at a particular point in space and time – was a life utterly caught up in and transparent to the life of God. The difference between God's life and creaturely life is not in Christian theology the kind of difference that would mean that creatures could only share that life or mirror that life to the extent that they ceased to be creatures. It is a different kind of difference, and the incarnation shows us that it makes sense to say that creaturely life can, in its own way, genuinely conform to and display the life of God without ceasing to be fully and entirely creaturely. Christians believe that the world is called to the fulfilment of its creatureliness, not the abandonment of it.

This means, however, that Christians are called to recognize that their creatureliness is not an impediment to, but is the material for, godly life. And since to be our kind of creature is (among other things) to be finite, to be bodily and to be dependent upon the environment and one another, Christians are called to see their finitude, their bodiliness, their dependence and their relationships as the material in which their participation in God's life will be displayed. God is making sculptures, and this is the kind of clay God is using

– and, like a good sculptor, God will work with the properties of the material, rather than fighting against it.

I will focus on just two aspects of this now. In the first place, we are bodies. We don't just *have* bodies, as if they were possessions that we could discard. We *are* bodies, and bodies are all that we are. The Christian hope is hope for resurrection, bodily resurrection like that of Jesus, and whatever mysterious fulfilment and completion of bodily life Christians hope for, belief in the resurrection of the body rather than the immortality of the soul means that Christian hope remains bodily. Now, it is often said that Christians in the past seemed to hate their bodies, and to live in denial of this claim – and there is altogether too much truth in that. Nevertheless, the adoption of ascetic practices, of self-denial, of various kinds of abstinence, can be seen in a much more positive light. It is not the rejection of bodily life as irrelevant or simply as a burden, but an attempt to shape and train it, to find ways in which bodily life with all its needs and appetites could itself be made to display a person's godliness: the shifting of the focus of their desires away from themselves and onto God and their neighbours. It need be no more antagonistic to bodily life as such than is an athlete who trains for hours a day in preparation for a big race, regulating diet, posture and activity according to some careful plan. Of course, in practice, this kind of ascetic training could all too easily slip over into disgust for the body and its needs, or into a dangerous denial of the physical necessities and pleasures of human life. But the basic idea beneath those distortions is correct, and is indeed essential to a Christianity that holds to the doctrine of creation: bodily life, precisely as bodily, is the material of salvation. As those who hold to the doctrine of creation, Christians are bound to ask how their bodily habits and actions contribute to or detract from the growth of love and justice. Should one buy fair-trade coffee? How do feasting and fasting both build up the church's common life? What is a Christian responsibility in a world that so pervasively turns bodies – particularly female bodies – into commodities in advertising and on fashion catwalks as much as in brothels and pornography? How can Christians model a loving acceptance of the frailty, mortality and laughable clumsiness of human bodies? How can Christians practise acceptance of all, whatever their body shape, size or colour? These are the sorts of questions that a doctrine of creation makes unavoidable.

Exercise

If you find yourself in a church service some time soon, look and listen and ask yourself whether this is a context in which the full bodiliness of all participants is recognized, and whether the bodiliness of salvation is affirmed.

In the second place, we human beings are entirely dependent upon our environment. Creation is a complex of interdependent parts, and we are inescapably part of it. Our existence, let alone our flourishing, is dependent upon an intricate web of connections and influences. The doctrine of creation calls upon Christians to recognize and celebrate that, rather than live in denial of it. To pursue love and justice, and the proper flourishing of human life, is inevitably also to care about the ways in which human beings fit into their wider natural environment. It is natural for Christians who have a doctrine of creation to care about farming, about rain forests, about urban planning, about the built environment, about climate change, about pollution, about the distance travelled by food to our supermarkets, about fish stocks, about energy production. Not to care at all about these things would be a denial that we are creatures. The doctrine of creation tells Christians that this whole interconnected world – the fragility and complexity of whose interconnectedness have become much more frighteningly visible in recent decades – is the world in which God is saving humanity, and the world that God made to share in God's own life.

This is not the place for a detailed examination of environmental theology. Nevertheless, we have already unearthed some of the bones of such a theology. In the first place, as I have been stressing, the earth is a whole – an interconnected web of dependences. In the second place, that this interconnected whole exists is, the doctrine of creation *ex nihilo* says, a result of God's love – it is a product of God's generosity, giving space to the existence of something other than God not out of need but out of delighted joy. In the third place, this interconnected whole that exists as an expression of God's delight can therefore be thought of as itself one vast symphony of praise to God. By being themselves, all creatures praise God: they reflect God's joy back to God. The mountains and the hills burst into song, and all the trees of the field clap their hands.[13] Rather than seeing themselves as separate from 'nature', and seeing nature as subordinate to their needs and projects, the doctrine of creation can suggest that human beings might be better thinking of themselves as players in an orchestra, to whom has been given the melodic line that weaves all the other instrumental parts into a whole and offers it back to the listening composer.

As this suggests, the doctrine of creation is a resource for the shaping of Christian imagination. It pushes Christians to re-imagine the world and their place in it, and so to begin to live in it differently. The world is not simply a warehouse of brute facts, nor an indifferent vastness: it is the creation of a creator, and love is 'creation's final law'.[14]

Key points

- Christian theology proclaims that the whole of creation, in all its parts, was made for participation in the divine life.
- Christians believe that they are called to the fulfilment of their creatureliness, not the abandonment of it.
- Bodily life, precisely as bodily, is the material of salvation.
- The doctrine of creation calls upon Christians to recognize and celebrate their dependence upon the natural environment, rather than living in denial of it.

Addendum: Creation and creationism

I would have liked to finish the chapter at this point, and move on to the next chapter's discussion of providence, which is really nothing but an extension of the discussion of creation. There is, however, one topic that it is sadly necessary to touch on, however briefly – if only because it is the topic that most people think of first when they hear the doctrine of creation mentioned, and to which many have devoted a titanic expenditure of energy. This is the topic of creation*ism* – that is, the claim that the Christian doctrine of creation involves a direct challenge to standard scientific explanations of the origins of the universe, or at least of life on earth, and that the upholding of this challenge is a vital duty for Christians in today's world.

It should have become clear by now that I do not believe that the role played by the doctrine of creation in Christianity has a great deal to do with *explanation*. That is, it does not have a great deal to do with accounts of *how* life originated on earth, or of *how* human beings appeared among the other life forms. I hope I have done enough to call into question the idea that belief in God as creator originally grew from any impetus towards explaining the way the world worked. From the evidence I have presented, the idea of God as creator seems to have more to do with God's people learning how to face evil, injustice and suffering than with their attempts to explain where we all came from. I contend therefore that it is a mistake to think of the doctrine of creation as a pre-scientific way of explaining the existence of the world – whether one then goes on to defend that pre-scientific way, or to attack it. That is not what the doctrine is about.

Of course, the doctrine does provide a kind of answer to the question, 'Why is there something rather than nothing?' – though it is a strange kind of answer. The answer that the doctrine gives is 'God', and that is not really a claim that could count as an *explanation*, God is that which we cannot grasp, and about whose act of creation we can only speak in language that we admit to be inadequate. What kind of explanation is that?

Again, the doctrine does claim that there is a purpose to creation: the extension of God's life for the inclusion of creation. But it is no obvious matter to see how to turn that claim into a claim about the processes or mechanisms by which the world ended up taking the shape that it now does. Even if one thinks that this claim tells one that God's purpose was to ensure that there would be conscious beings capable of love (and given some of the things Christians have wanted to say about the whole of creation praising God, it may be that even that is a step too far), it is not easy to see how to turn that into a claim about the processes or mechanisms by which such life arose. Even when speaking of the purpose for which the world was created, the doctrine of creation has little if anything to do with causal explanation.

The end of why

One way that Christians have sometimes thought about God as creator is by thinking of God as the place where the asking of 'Why?' stops. Faced with any thing or event in the world, we can always ask 'Why?' Why did that happen? Why is it there? And, given any answer to those questions, one can always (as my three-year-old daughter knows) ask 'Why?' again. Why do I feel warm? Because my radiator is warm. But why is my radiator warm? Because there is hot water in it. But why is the water hot? Because it has been heated by the boiler. But why? But why? But why? I can keep on asking the question, and if I keep on long enough I will either find myself asking about where human beings and their desires and needs come from, or where the material stuff that consti-tutes the world around me comes from, or where the laws of physics that keep the whole thing ticking over come from. Eventually, my questions will become unanswerable: Why is there anything at all? Why should it have any particular character? Medieval theologians suggested that God is where the asking of 'Why?' stops, because God is a reality that could not not be, a reality that is in no way contingent, a reality that it makes no sense to imagine not existing or not being precisely as it is – and so a reality for which the Why question finds no purchase. That is the difference, they said, between creator and creation: creation is the realm of 'Why?'; the creator is the only unquestionable answer. This is a claim that is absolutely independent of what there actually is in the world and how it works, and so a claim that is absolutely independent of any explanation of the world that works at the level of mechanisms and processes – it is not a response to the question, 'Why this particular thing?' but to the question, 'Why anything whatsoever?'[15]

When one looks at the vast majority of what gets said and written about the doctrine of creation these days, it is hard to avoid the sense that there are many who have taken a wrong turning, and have substituted vigorous defence of a set of quasi-scientific explanatory claims for adherence to the Christian doctrine of creation. In so doing, they have, with the best of inten-tions, helped to bury the real claims of that doctrine (which, as we have seen, are claims about covenant and gospel, claims about the good news of salva-tion). What proponents of creationism or intelligent design defend has little inherent connection to the heart of the Christian gospel, and the God to whom they refer in those defences does not seem to be clearly identifiable as the God of Jesus Christ – even if in the rest of their lives these creationists might be devoted Christians who follow that God wholeheartedly. If it is Christianity and the Christian gospel that they are wanting to defend, they have picked the wrong battle lines, and to the extent that they make the manning of those battle lines central to the public presentation of Christianity, they have con-tributed much to the contemporary discrediting and misunderstanding of the Christian faith.

Exercise

Whether you agree with me or not, see if you can mount a counter-argument in terms that you think might convince me. Why should debate about the timing or processes by which God created the world be of theological importance? What core Christian beliefs or practices might such debate be seen as safe-guarding or promoting?

Key points

- The doctrine of creation is not an effort at explanation of the world's origins.
- The doctrine does claim that God is the reason there is something rather than nothing.
- Creationism is in danger of substituting vigorous defence of a set of quasi-scientific explanatory claims for adherence to the Christian doctrine of creation.

Going further

1 There is much more that could be said about Christian attitudes to environ-mentalism. A famous article by Lynn White, 'On the historical roots of our ecological crisis', *Science* 155 (10 March 1967), pp. 1203–07, laid a good deal of the blame at the door of Christian theology; an extract from the article and some responses were printed in the *Journal of the American Scientific Affiliation* 21 (1969), pp. 42–7, and are available online at http://www.asa3.org/ASA/PSCF/1969/JASA6–69White.html. Positive theological responses to the environmental crisis can be found in, among many others, Michael Nothcott, *The Environment and Christian Ethics* (Cambridge: Cam-bridge University Press, 1996); John Cobb Jr, *Is it Too Late? A Theology of Ecology* (New York: Macmillan, 1971); Leonardo Boff, *Ecology and Libera-tion* (Maryknoll: Orbis, 1995); Celia Deane-Drummond, *The Ethics of Nature* (Oxford: Blackwell, 2003); and Rosemary Radford Ruether, *Gaia and God* (San Francisco: Harper, 1994).

2 What I have said briefly about the importance of bodies could be explored much more fully. Various questions about bodiliness are covered by Nancey Murphy, *Bodies and Souls, or Spirited Bodies?* (Cambridge: Cambridge University Press, 2006) and Elisabeth Moltmann–Wendel, *I Am My Body* (London: Continuum, 1995). One specific question that properly comes up is how Christians should live with disabled bodies. Nancy Eisland's *The Disabled God* (Nashville: Abingdon, 1994) is a key resource; as is Frances Young's *Face to Face*, 2nd edn (Edinburgh: T&T Clark, 1990).

3 To my mind, the real challenge which evolutionary theory poses to Christian theology is over the goodness of creation. The natural world, as pictured by evolution, is a battleground: the motor that drives evolutionary diversification is bloody competition; the long history of evolution is littered not just with slaughtered individuals, but with whole exterminated species – many more than are alive today. The picture is a bloody and violent one. Can one really call such a creation 'good'? We will be discussing the question of suffering and the goodness of God at length in a later chapter, but this particular issue will not be our focus. For those who want to pursue this question further, I recommend Christopher Southgate, 'God and evolutionary evil: Theodicy in the light of Darwinism', *Zygon* 37.4 (December 2002), pp. 803–24.

4 I have deliberately avoided, for reasons I explained, the kind of discussion of the doctrine of creation that gets mired in 'science versus religion'. I am not going to reverse that decision in this brief note, but simply suggest that the best preparation for discovering what positive contact there might be between theological and scientific ways of talking about the world around us is to inform oneself about the history and present state of science, and to try to capture the sense of wonder and delight that can accompany scientific exploration. Start with Bill Bryson's, *A Short History of Nearly Everything*, (London: Black Swan, 2004) and Oliver Sacks, *Uncle Tungsten* (London: Picador, 2002), and then take a look at the wide-ranging discussions in Christopher Southgate (ed.), *God, Humanity and the Cosmos*, 2nd edn (London: Continuum, 2005).

Notes

1 For example, the Google search http://www.google.com/search?q=%22doctrine+of+creation%22 delivered 117,000 hits on 23 April 2007.

2 Leonard Cohen's psalmist sings 'And even though / It all went wrong / I'll stand before the Lord of Song / With nothing on my tongue but Hallelujah' – from 'Hallelujah' on his *Various Positions* (Columbia, 1985).

3 Karl Barth, *Church Dogmatics III: The Doctrine of Creation*, Pt 1 (Edinburgh: T&T Clark, 1958), p. 41.

4 See Acts 17.28, quoting lines attributed to the sixth-century BC Cretan seer Epimenides (*Cretica*, line 4).

5 You may recall from the last chapter my discussion of Paul's comments on creation in Romans 8: sin is what prevents creation from being itself, from fulfilling its purpose. Sin subjects creation to futility, and it is the work of the Spirit to draw it back into its proper function.

6 Irenaeus of Lyons, *Against Heresies* 2.30.9, in A. Cleveland Coxe (ed.) *Ante-Nicene Fathers*, vol. 1 (New York: Christian Literature Company, 1885), p. 406; available online at the Christian Classics Ethereal Library, http://www.ccel.org/ccel/schaff/anf01.ix.iii.xxxi.html. There is a good, clear discussion of Irenaeus' doctrine of creation in Julie Canlis, 'Being made human: The significance of creation for Irenaeus' doctrine of participation', *Scottish Journal of Theology* 58.4 (2005), pp. 434–54.

7 See the quotation from Irenaeus given above: 'while he contains all things, but he himself can be contained by no one'.

8 Rowan Williams, '"From William Temple to George Herbert": Anglican Origins: Prayer and Holiness Part Two' (Melbourne: Institute for Spiritual Studies, 2002); available online at http://www.stpeters.org.au/iss/reports/RWjun02pt2.shtml. Williams quotes George Herbert's poem, 'Perseverance' the final stanza of which runs: 'Onely my soule hangs on thy promises / With face and hands clinging vnto thy brest, / Clinging and crying, crying without cease. / Thou art my rock, thou art my rest.' See F. E. Hutchinson (ed.), *The Works of George Herbert* (Oxford: Clarendon, 1941), p. 204.

9 For more on the Gnostics, see Alastair Logan, *The Gnostics: Identifying an Ancient Christian Cult* (London: Continuum, 2006) and *Gnostic Truth and Christian Heresy: A Study in the History of Gnosticism* (Edinburgh: T&T Clark, 1996); for more on Irenaeus, see Robert M. Grant, *Irenaeus of Lyons*, Early Church Fathers series (London: Routledge, 1997); Eric Osborne, *Irenaeus of Lyons* (Cambridge: Cambridge University Press, 2001); and the Canlis article listed in note 6 above.

10 The phrase was used as the title of a 1980 play by Mark Medoff, made into a film directed by Randa Haines (Paramount, 1986); see http://www.imdb.com/title/tt0090830/. It is derived from Alfred Lord Tennyson's *Idylls of the King: The Passing of Arthur*, in which the dying Arthur says, 'I found Him in the shining of the stars, / I marked Him in the flowering of His fields, / But in His ways with men I find Him not. / I waged His wars, and now I pass and die. / O me! for why is all around us here / As if some lesser god had made the world, / But had not force to shape it as he would, / Till the High God behold it from beyond, / And enter it, and make it beautiful?' (lines 9–17).

11 See *Nicholas of Cusa on God as Not-Other: A Translation and Appraisal of De Li Non Aliud*, 3rd edn, tr. Jasper Hopkins (Minneapolis: Arthur J. Banning, 1987); available online at http://cla.umn.edu/sites/jhopkins/NA12-2000.pdf.

12 That is not because God is best thought of as androgynous, either, for that is also an image that fixes God in place on our gender maps.

13 Cf. Isaiah 55.12.

14 Tennyson again (see note 10): this time, *In Memoriam A.H.H.* (London: E. Moxon, 1850), §§56; available online at Poet's Corner, http://www.theotherpages.org/poems/books/tennyson/tennyson04.html#56. But see below, Chapter 10, p. 238.

15 The most famous example is Anselm of Canterbury, who in his *Proslogion* 3 states that God 'cannot be conceived not to exist'; see Sidney Norton Deane (ed.), *St. Anselm: Proslogium etc.* (Chicago: Open Court, 1928), p. 8; available online at the Christian Classics Ethereal Library http://www.ccel.org/ccel/anselm/basic_works.iv.iv.1.html), and see also Anselm's reply to an objection by Gaunilo in the same volume, pp. 151–68; available online at http://www.ccel.org/ccel/anselm/basic_works.vi.ii.html.

8

Providence and Freedom

This chapter is a continuation of the previous chapter, on creation. I continue to ask what it means for Christians to see the world in which they live as a world caught up in the threefold economy of salvation, being drawn into participation in God's life. Elaborating themes already introduced in Chapter 7, I will be exploring God's ongoing care for creation: God's sustaining, animating and guiding work. I will also be exploring the nature of human freedom in this world – and taking a glance at what a lack of freedom looks like. Note, however, that I am not yet going to treat in full the question of suffering and evil, and how they can exist in a world that God creates and guides – that is a topic that will get a chapter of its own later on.

I'm going to

- introduce the traditional threefold division of providence into *conservatio*, *concursus* and *gubernatio*;
- argue that God's providential care for creation is a necessary condition for human freedom;
- argue that true human freedom depends upon God's guiding of the world into truth and love; and
- look at different ideas about whether and how God steers or shapes the course of events.

Preparation

- Is it possible to believe that God is present and active in everything that happens? If so, how does that presence and activity show itself? To put it another way, is God in *control* of the day-by-day course of events? If so, how does that control show itself? What difference would it make to live life with a firm conviction of that presence or control? Jot down some brief notes on your answer to these questions.
- When I checked just now, 'doctrine of creation' brought up 115,000 hits on an internet search engine; 'doctrine of providence' just 14,000.[1] And while a large number of the sites in the creation search were impassioned popular defences of the doctrine, the sites in the providence search are rather different. Have a glance through a few now. There is no need to go into great detail; just get a flavour.

Additional reading

To accompany this chapter, and provide alternative views of the landscape I am exploring, you could try:

Timothy Gorringe, *God's Theatre: A Theology of Providence* (London: SCM Press, 1991). An accessible exploration of different models of providence.
Paul Helm, *The Providence of God*, Contours of Christian Theology (Leicester: IVP, 1993). A traditional and philosophical approach, rather different from my own.

The one who sustains

The *Oxford English Dictionary*[2] defines providence as 'The action of providing; provision, preparation, arrangement', 'anticipation of and preparation for the future; "timely care"; ... prudent or wise arrangement, management, government, or guidance', and hence in theological contexts as 'The foreknowing and beneficent care and government of God ...; divine direction, control, or guidance.' The doctrine of providence is the doctrine of God's ongoing care for creation.

It might be tempting to think that the doctrine of *creation* describes God's initial action in setting the world going, while the doctrine of *providence* treats God's subsequent actions in tending (directing, controlling, guiding) what God has made. However, I have already argued that the doctrine of creation cannot be confined to beginnings, but speaks of God's intimate *ongoing* presence to the whole created order, so the distinction between creation and providence cannot be quite as clear cut as that. It is more accurate to say that discussion of providence will involve us looking at the subject matter of the last chapter again, but from a slightly different angle. We will be asking, in effect, 'What difference does the divine presence to the whole of creation make?' In particular, can one meaningfully say that events in the world are guided or shaped or directed by this presence?

The doctrine of providence is often discussed under three Latin headings: *conservatio, concursus* and *gubernatio* – God's conservation or sustaining of creation, God's concurrence with or accompanying of creation, and God's governance or steering of creation.[3] These three topics, taken in order, lead one step by step away from the questions and perspectives of the last chapter, with *conservatio*, the first, adding least to material I have already covered, *gubernatio* most.

Christian theology does not claim that God lit the blue touchpaper that started everything going, and then retired to a safe distance to watch (perhaps having read the warning in the Firework Code: Never go back to a lit firework[4]). Rather, the doctrine of creation affirms that the world continues in existence only because God actively and constantly upholds and sustains it – only because God *conserves* it in being. (You may recall that I also touched on this theme back in the chapter on the Spirit's work, when I looked at those Old Testament passages that speak of possession of God's spirit as a prerequisite for the continued life of all creatures.) This conserving, sustaining work of God can sometimes be imagined in dramatic, mythological terms as God holding back the forces of dissolution and nothingness, preserving a space in which ordered existence is possible by holding back the sea of chaos.[5] More often it has simply been pictured as God holding the whole world in the palm of God's hand.[6] In somewhat less pictorial and metaphorical mood, it can be thought of as the expression of God's constancy and faithfulness, giving continued and reliable existence to the world. However it is expressed, though, the central thought remains the same, and is simply a repetition of the idea at the heart of the doctrine of creation *ex nihilo*: the whole world, at every moment, depends utterly and only upon God for its existence.

This discussion of *conservatio* begins to tip towards the next heading, *concursus*, as soon as one asks what it means for God faithfully to hold in being something that is *not* God. One can only speak of there being things that are not God if those things have some kind of continuity and integrity of their own. After all, if one were to imagine God bringing into being nothing but a constant flicker of instantaneous and unconnected tableaux, one might speak of God's self-expression, or of God's generativity and creativity, but it is hard to see how one would justify talk of God creating something *other* than God-self. Conversely, as soon as one talks about God creating something other than Godself – as soon, in other words, as one talks about creation *ex nihilo* or *conservatio* – one is saying that God gives creaturely realities some kind of connectedness, some kind of extension, some kind of *nature* of their own. And that brings us to *concursus*.

The Elohim

In *The One Tree*, one of Stephen Donaldson's fantasy novel sequence *The Second Chronicles of Thomas Covenant*, the protagonists visit the land of the Elohim, beings whose creative work is just such a flicker of instantaneous and unconnected tableaux: 'Birds flew overhead, warbling incarnate. Cavorting in circles, they swept against each other, merged to form an abrupt pillar of fire in the air. A moment later, the fire leaped into sparks, and the sparks became gems – ruby and morganite, sapphire and porphyry, like a trail of stars – and the gems wafted away, turning to butterflies as they floated.'[7]

This is not creation, it is self-expression; it does not bring into being any reality with sufficient continuity to count as a being *other* than the creator.

Key points

- The doctrine of providence speaks of God's continual care for and involvement in creation.
- It is traditionally discussed under three headings: *conservatio*, *concursus* and *gubernatio*.
- *Conservatio* has to do with God's holding creation in being, sustaining its existence.

The one who accompanies

The world that God holds in being is not a static sculpture, and for God to hold the world in being means more than that God ensures that the same things exist from moment to moment. The world is a dynamic system, and the elements within it are active: they act upon other elements and are acted upon in turn. This is the form that the interdependence of creation, its connectedness and structure, takes. If God holds this kind of world in being, then God does not simply sustain each element in being, but sustains them as active.

Imagine that the world were an intricate orrery – one of those mechanical models of the solar system in which the planets rotate on their axes and move sedately around the sun, and the moons move around the planets. The planets and moons only turn and move when the whole model is connected to its power supply. The power from this supply enables each part of the model to do its own thing, and all the parts to mesh together into a working whole. To speak of God's *concursus* is to shift from thinking from God simply as the maker of this orrery, or as the owner of the room in which it is kept; it is to think of God as the power supply: the one who ensures that each of the parts is able to 'do its thing'. God is the one who energizes and impels all the parts of the model, and so animates the model as a whole.

Concursus literally means 'coming together, concurrence', but one can translate it in this context as 'accompaniment': God's providential action accompanies the activity of God's creatures, energizing it and empowering it; God underwrites the activity of God's creatures. Without God's concurrent activity, there could be no creaturely activity; with it, creatures can do what they do. God acts in all the acts of God's creatures.

Primary and secondary causation

The traditional terms used at this point are 'primary causation' and 'secondary causation'.[8] The words appearing in front of me on my computer screen do so thanks to a complex combination of causes: the tapping of my fingers on the keyboard, the operations of the computer, the workings of the screen. Yet this whole process only works, according to Christian theology, because God holds each part of it in being and sustains the proper activity of each part. God sustains my fingers in being, and sustains them *as* fingers, doing their fingery thing. God sustains the keyboard in being, and sustains it *as* a keyboard, doing its keyboardy thing. At a deeper level, all the countless electrons and neutrons and protons whose dance sustains the activity of fingers, computer and screen are held in being *as* electrons and neutrons and protons, and their proper activity is simply the way that God consistently and faithfully holds them in being *as* active. All that I might say about the activity of fingers, computers and screen, or about the electrons, neutrons and protons that are their constituents, comes under the heading 'secondary causation'; all that I say about God's activity as the enabling context for all this comes under the heading 'primary causation'.

When an electron does its electron thing, when a tree does its tree thing, when a sun does its sun thing – when any creaturely reality acts or moves in the way that is proper to it, that is (according to Christian theology) thanks to God's concurring activity. God enables and animates all creaturely activity: that is part of what it means to say that the world depends, entirely and at every moment of its existence, upon God. God is active in all creaturely activity as its sustaining and enabling context.

This idea becomes more complex, however, once one starts thinking about *human* action. What does it mean to say that my activity is a result of God's concurring or accompanying activity, or that God is acting in my acts? Consider the relationship that a novelist has to her characters. Clearly, anything that those characters do is something that the novelist *writes* them as doing; if she doesn't write it, they don't do it. But it will only be a good novel if she writes in such a way that the characters' actions are really *theirs*: if they fit with and flow from the characters' history and dispositions, and the circumstances in which they find themselves. If the novelist has shown us in detail the inner life of her characters, the actions they perform should emerge from that inner life; they should *belong* to the characters. So the actions in the novel are, in one sense, the characters' actions; in another sense they are of course the novelist's action: she acts in their acts. These two kinds of activity are not in competition because they are not on the same level – rather, the novelist's action is the context for and the sustaining of the characters' actions.[9]

The two Fernand Mondegos

In Alexandre Dumas' sprawling nineteenth-century novel, *The Count of Monte Cristo*, there is a character called Fernand Mondego. Or rather, the name 'Fernand Mondego' is bandied about *as if* it applied to a single character. The hero, Edmond Dantès, is betrayed by his rival in love, a man called Fernand Mondego. But when Edmond returns as the Count of Monte Cristo to exact his revenge, the man called Fernand Mondego against whom he directs his schemes is all but unrecognizable as his earlier betrayer. Robin Buss, the translator of the recent Penguin edition, notes that Fernand has changed 'from the brave and honest Spaniard with a sharp sense of humour, whom we meet in the early chapters, to the Parisian aristocrat whose life seems to have been dedicated to a series of betrayals. Fernand … seems to confirm a criticism of Dumas and of popular novels in general, namely that *they tend to sacrifice character to plot*.'[10]

Dumas knew the roles that he needed Fernand to play, and did not trouble himself to make those roles emerge convincingly from the interaction between Fernand's history, disposition and circumstances. He did not succeeded in this case in creating an independent character, because the actions attributed to 'Fernand' are too much driven by Dumas' own needs – his plot needs. For Dumas to have created and sustained a consistent character would have meant his accepting that he could not simply impose whatever plot he wanted; it would have involved a kind of self-imposed constraint upon Dumas' own action, a willingness to act only through the action *appropriate* to his character.

The doctrine of divine *concursus* is the claim that, in sustaining the world in being, in giving it its own integrity and continuity, God writes human activity like a novelist writing a novel. This doesn't mean that God curbs and controls human activity, constraining it to fit God's plan regardless of what human beings themselves want, any more than a good novelist curbs and constrains the activity of her characters. Rather, God's providential activity writes the world in such a way that people's acts can emerge from the interaction between their history, disposition and circumstances. God acts, and his act gives the world the kind of continuity and integrity that allows us to speak of real characters and their action. God acts in all human acts.

Exercise

Before carrying on, ask yourself whether you can see any problems with this way of talking about providence – and, specifically, whether it raises any questions about human freedom.

Key points

- To speak of God's *concursus* with creation is to speak of God as active in the acts of God's creatures – enabling, empowering and supporting creatures as active.
- Classic Christian theology claims that God is active in all human acts – enabling, empowering and supporting human beings as active.
- God is seen as giving the world the kind of continuity and integrity that allows us to think of human beings *as* acting.

Concursus and freedom

This way of talking about the relationship between divine and human activity always raises questions about human freedom. Does this affirmation of divine *concursus* imply that human beings are simply puppets in God's play? If we are characters written by a divine novelist, does that mean that we are not really free to do as we choose?

These worries are often given focus by the question, 'Could I have done otherwise?' If God has written the novel of my life, and has written the present (rather dull) chapter in which I got up this morning and started typing this chapter after breakfast, did I really have the freedom that I thought I had – freedom to do something different? Could I not have decided to take the morning off? Could I, perhaps more realistically, have decided to carry on tinkering with the previous chapter, rather than starting on this one? I certainly believed that I had such freedom, and I went through a process (albeit a brief one) of deliberating about what I should do. But if this is all a story that God is writing, was I constrained to do what God had planned?

It is worth noting that the question, 'Could I have done otherwise?' is an odd one, even if I don't bring God's providence into the picture at all. If I am thinking about possible external constraints upon my action, I certainly want to be able to say, 'Yes, I could have done otherwise', and simply mean that nobody and nothing forced me. I did not receive a letter threatening me with bodily harm should I not start work on this chapter. Not was I suddenly aware that, despite a decision to waste time playing *Luxor 2*,[11] some mysterious force impelled my fingers to start typing this chapter instead; there did not seem to me to be anything forcing my hand.

If I think about *internal* constraints, however, the picture is rather less clear – and the purchase of the question 'Could I have done otherwise?' is much weaker. I don't really think, for instance, that I could have decided to take the morning off – I would have felt too guilty. If I take all my habits and dispositions into account, I do not think it makes sense to say 'I could have taken the morning off.' Only if I were somebody different, with different ideas and priorities and feelings, could I have done that.

But what about a less drastic example? What about my decision not to spend time polishing the previous chapter and instead move on to this one? I could have made the opposite decision without it being out of character. I made the decision I did, however, because of the particular state of mind I was in this morning, the particular things I was thinking about, the ideas and feelings and preferences that happened to be floating through my brain at the time. If I ignore all those, then of course I could have chosen to do something different. Given all those, however, this is what I chose. And that is, of course, what I mean by saying that the decision was *mine*: it emerged from my thoughts, impressions, feelings, and preferences at the particular moment when I took it. If I could be put into *exactly* the same frame of mind, down to the very last detail of unconscious leaning or conscious distraction, I certainly hope that I would decide the same thing. If I did not, it would show that the decision wasn't really something that emerged from my deliberation, from *me*, at all. It would show that it was something that *happened* to me, out of the blue, entirely beyond my control. If I want to claim that I acted freely, I have to claim that I could *not* have done otherwise, all things considered.

In other words, if I am to see my actions as mine, I certainly need to be able to believe in an absence of external constraints, pressing on me from outside so as to 'force my hand'. I also, however, need to be able to believe that I determine my actions – that my actions emerge reliably from who I am at the relevant moment, and what I am thinking about, and all the detail of the state I am currently in. I need to be able to believe in the continuity between me and my action. When the doctrine of *concursus* says that God writes my action like a good novelist, it is precisely this latter that is being affirmed: God writes the world such that characters' actions can emerge properly from who they are and the circumstances in which they find themselves. Far from being a denial of human freedom, the doctrine of *concursus* declares that it is only God's providence that ensures that humans *can* act freely. It is only because God gives continuity and integrity to creatures by acting in all that they do that it makes sense to talk about free creaturely action at all.

Exercise

Are you convinced? Does this answer the questions you came up with at the end of the last section?

Key points

- Freedom is only in part an absence of external constraint.
- To be free implies that a person's actions are genuinely his or her own.
- The doctrine of *concursus* suggests that the continuity between a person and his or her action is in God's hands.
- God is, in this view, the guarantor that a person's actions can be his or her own, and therefore the guarantor of freedom.

The one who steers

When one shifts attention from *conservatio* and *concursus* to *gubernatio*, even more questions arise. The word originally referred to the steering of a ship by a helmsman, and it is used to talk about the ways in which God is steering or guiding the world towards a goal. One might be tempted to say that it is only with the discussion of *gubernatio* that one finally reaches providence proper.

One should be cautious, however, about how one approaches this topic. In the first place, one should recall discussion from the very first chapter about the 'foolishness' of God. If one starts thinking of God as some kind of despotic ruler, who either now or in the future will start violently whipping the world into shape, one has ceased to think about the God of Jesus Christ. Christians believe that Christ has shown the world what God's action looks like when it is made flesh; they believe that in Christ one may see that God is not a God of violent imposition, but of love. Whatever Christians say about God's *gubernatio* must be consistent with this: God will be no less Christlike in God's steering of all things towards their ultimate goal than God was in the incarnation.

Hollywood endings

We are deeply conditioned to reject the Christlikeness of God's *gubernatio* – and one of the agents that has conditioned us is the Hollywood film. In film after film, the goodies (however meek, reluctant and pacific they may have been) are finally pushed to the point where they must unleash some storm of violence in order to overcome the baddies, and restore good order. Think of *High Noon*.[12] Gary Cooper's Will Kane, now married to Grace Kelly's pacifist Quaker, Amy, plans to resign from his post as marshal, until he hears that the notorious criminal Frank Miller is returning to town with his men. Alone and unsupported by any of the good people of the town, Kane shoots two of Miller's men, and later kills Miller himself – but the third of Miller's men is killed by Amy, who has swapped her principles for a gun in order to save her husband. It is hard to see how she could have done otherwise; in the end, only violence will serve.

Imaginations formed in this tradition have trouble holding to the Christlikeness of God's *gubernatio*. In the end, we suspect, only violence will serve – and sin and suffering must go down in a hail of bullets.

One should also not forget what has been said about *conservatio* and *concursus* the moment one turns to *gubernatio*. Christian theology cannot think of God's steering work by picturing God on one side struggling with recalcitrant creation on the other. The continuity and integrity of creation – its resistance to arbitrary imposition – is also the act of God. To put it another way, the world's lack of constant and complete transparency to God is itself God's act, because God creates and sustains a world with its own continuity and momentum, not a glove puppet that would simply be an extension of God's own being.

Lastly, one should recall some of what I have already said about the end that God has for the world. In the chapter on the Spirit, and in the last chapter on creation, I described that end as 'creation being itself' – as creation becoming a symphony of praise to God, given a share in God's life by becoming what God made it to be. When I discussed incarnation, I argued that Jesus' transparency to the will of God was identical to his being fully human. But if the end that God has for creation, its sharing fully and unimpededly in the life of God, is like this, then one can't think of God's *gubernatio* as an *imposition* upon creatures or creation as a whole: a squashing of creation into a shape that is not naturally its own. Rather, the divine *gubernatio* in which Christians trust will better be thought of as God's freeing of creation to be itself.

Key points

- *Gubernatio* is God's steering of the world towards the end that God has for it.
- In Christian theology, that steering should not be seen as violent imposition.
- The continuity of the world – its resistance to steering – is also God's act.
- The end that God has for the world is its being itself.

Freedom, truth and love

The understanding of freedom that I need in order to take this idea further is a stronger one than I was using on pages 195–6, where people would count as free when they were free from external constraints, and able to act in accordance with their present states of mind.

The easiest way to understand the stronger meaning of freedom is by considering how someone who was free from external constraint, and able to act in accordance with his or her present state of mind, might nevertheless be anything but free. In John Fowles's strange novel, *The Magus*, the central character, Nicholas Urfe, encounters the reclusive millionaire Maurice Conchis and finds himself caught in a lengthy and bizarre psychological game that Conchis is playing.[13] Most of the time, Urfe is able to act in a way that would count as free according to the definition I used above: he is left free to do what his deliberations and inclinations suggest to him that he should do in the circumstances. At each stage, however, he finds that Conchis has elaborately set him up: that his deliberations and inclinations have been so shaped by the half-truths and lies that have been told to him, and that the circumstances in which he makes his decisions have been so stage-managed, that his apparently free actions simply follow a bizarre script invented by Conchis.

The unfreedom of Nicholas Urfe is only an extreme case of a much more general kind of constraint. For all of us, the ways in which we see the choices available to us, and the ways in which we find ourselves leaning towards one or another, are deeply and irrevocably shaped by what we have received from others. I am the person that my parents have made me, my schooling, my friendships, my marriage, my children, my reading, my conversations, the films and television programmes and plays that I have seen. Some of that I will be able to track explicitly; much more of it will be a matter of undetected subterranean influence, subtly tilting me towards paths I might not otherwise have taken. The basic building blocks of this are pretty easy to see: it would not take Hercule Poirot to detect by looking at the path I take through life that I am recognizably English, recognizably someone born in the second half of the twentieth century, recognizably middle class, recognizably educated. A keener eye might spot that I am not just English but a southerner; not just born in the second half of the twentieth century but in the 1970s; not just middle class but some kind of upper middle; not just educated but university-educated. Those things will show themselves subtly and unavoidably in the things I say, the ways I dress, the company I keep, the possessions I own, the jokes I tell, the books I write. And those are simply the bluntest and broadest of the ways in which I have recognizably been influenced by my upbringing and situation.

What I think of as my free action turns out to be no less scripted than Nicholas Urfe's supposedly free action – scripted in my case not by reclusive millionaires but by my parents, my teachers and my peers. I may, much of the time, be free to do as I desire – but my desires themselves are not chosen but inherited, and shaped by all the circumstances of my life.

Fashion and freedom

When I go shopping for clothes, I am supposedly exercising real freedom – the kind of freedom that, in our world, is held up as a paradigm of all freedom. I am presented with multiple possibilities, and nobody forces me to choose any particular one: I buy this pair of black trousers, but I could equally well have done otherwise. We can imagine various forms of constraint that might affect me – a lack of money, perhaps, or a work culture that dictated closely what I must wear, or a need to impress people by choosing clothes that I think they would like rather than the clothes I would choose if left to my own devices. As it happens, I think of myself as fairly free from those sorts of constraints. I am genuinely free in the clothing choices that I make.

Or so it seems. When I go into the shop and pick out what looks good to me, what seems desirable to me, I will choose something different from what I would have chosen ten years ago. My tastes have changed, and I am attracted by different things now. That in itself is not a problem, except that I find that the way in which my tastes have changed is roughly parallel to the ways in which millions of other people's tastes have changed. I am not a person very concerned with fashion (just ask my family, friends and colleagues) but I find that the clothes I like now are recognizably clothes of the noughties, just as the clothes I liked ten years ago were recognizably clothes of the nineties. Without any desire to be fashionable, and so without any sense that fashion is an external constraint pushing me in directions I do not want to go, I find that by some means changes in fashion have subtly changed my desires. As the fashion magazine editor Miranda Priestly (Meryl Streep) says to her dowdy and cynical assistant Andy Sachs (Anne Hathaway) in *The Devil Wears Prada* – and might say to me, 'It's sort of comical how you think that you've made a choice that exempts you from the fashion industry when, in fact, you're wearing the sweater that was selected for you by the people in this room.'[14]

In my clothes purchases, when I am supposedly a free consumer, I am in part playing out a script written for me by the changing fashions of my world. Advertisers and trendsetters have (at least in part) scripted my supposed freedom for me – and that is only the beginning of the lack of freedom that is hidden within my apparently free choices of clothes.[15]

Exercise

Why are you reading this book? Try to think through some of the different factors that led to your decision to do so, or that made you the sort of person for whom doing so made sense. Do you think there was, in your decision to read it, any freedom *beyond* all those factors?

All this is, of course, part of what it means to be a creature. Nothing about me is my own creation *ex nihilo*. And if I only count as free that which is undetermined, uninherited, unshaped by circumstance, unscripted by other people, then, yes, freedom will turn out to be an illusion, and my search for *that* kind of freedom will in fact turn out to be an impossible attempt to escape creatureliness.

That is not, however, the only way of thinking about freedom. I might accept that I am inevitably and irrevocably dependent, and that my ability to see what is possible and what is desirable in any situation is not something I invent for myself. But it might still be possible to distinguish between inherited ways of seeing what is possible and desirable that are false, and inherited ways of seeing that are true – or at least between ways of seeing that are fals*er* and tru*er*. And it might also be possible to distinguish between inherited ways of seeing what is possible and desirable that turn me into a puppet for someone else's interests, making me a means to their ends, and those that do not – or at least between ways of seeing that are more and less subordinating.

Once one has abandoned the idea that *real* freedom can be captured with the question, 'Could I have done otherwise?', or with the model of the consumer self standing in front of a range of affordable supermarket choices, it turns out that the only real kinds of freedom available to me as a creature are being freed from delusion, and being freed from subordination to another's interests – freedom from distorting, destructive and demeaning forms of dependency, not freedom from dependency *per se*.

This is what I am hoping for if I speak of God's *gubernatio* as the freeing of creatures to be themselves. Insofar as it is directed towards creatures like me, God's *gubernatio* is the process by which God teaches me the truth, or disillusions me, stripping me of the delusions that bind me to falsehood – and is the process by which God makes real in my life God's pure love for me, a love that does not subordinate me to anybody's interests, because God has no interests. That is true freedom, and the only kind of freedom available to creatures.

The point about the purity of God's love is a crucial one – and repeats a claim I made in the last chapter. The Christian doctrine of creation claims that God did not *need* to create: creation should not be seen as serving God's interests, scratching God's itches or meeting God's needs. It is not a stage in God's self-realization. Rather, Christian theology understands creation as a gratuitous and free act of a God whose Trinitarian life is already complete in itself. God creates out of delighted joy: bringing creation into existence for it to be itself. God's love for the world is therefore seen as a completely pure love: a love without interests, a love without ego or selfishness. And it is because God has this kind of love for the world that God can be the source of real freedom in the world. Only dependence upon one who unselfishly desires one's flourishing can be a *freeing* dependence.

No agenda

'[W]e can trust the maker of heaven and earth precisely because he *is* the maker of heaven and earth. ...

'God is the unique source of everything. Therefore, there is nothing God is forced to do. There is nothing alongside God, nothing by nature extra to God or beyond God. God is never one thing among others. So there can be no question of God having to do anything at all that he doesn't want to do. And because he cannot need anything, because he contains all reality eternally and by nature, the only thing that can "motivate" his action is simply what he is, the kind of God he is. What he *does* shows us what he *is*.

'Put slightly differently, this means that God can't have a selfish agenda, because he can't want anything for himself except to be the way he is. So if the world exists because of his action, the only motivation for this that we can even begin to think of is sheer unselfish love. He wants to give what he is to what isn't him; he wants difference to appear, he wants an Other to receive his joy and delight. He isn't bored and in need of company. He isn't frustrated and in need of help. ...

'The love that God shows in making the world, like the love he shows towards the world once it is created, has no shadow or shred of self-directed purpose in it; it is entirely and unreservedly given for our sake.'

Rowan Williams, *Tokens of Trust*[16]

Key points

- Our understanding and our desires are deeply shaped by our history and circumstances.
- That deep shaping means that simply having the freedom to do as our understanding and desires dictate is not real freedom.
- The only kinds of freedom available to us as creatures are freedom from illusion, and …
- … freedom from subordination to the interests of others.
- In Christian theology, God is the ultimate source of these kinds of freedom.

Providence, eschatology and discernment

To learn to see the world as the theatre of providence is to learn to trace hints and signs of real freedom, truth and love – but also to learn to see where apparent freedom is really a disguise for constriction and distortion. Look at the babble of language and image amidst which we live. What is being said in all that about who we are and what we are for? What stories are being told about the world and human life? Which stories seep into us and shape our perceptions, our desires and our actions? What are the scripts by which our lives run?

Consider the following exchange, which takes place in Dodie Smith's *I Capture the Castle*, chapter 7:

'You can only be a gentleman if you're born one, Miss Cassandra.'

'Stephen, that's old-fashioned nonsense,' I said. 'Really, it is. And by the way, will you stop calling me "Miss" Cassandra?'

He looked astonished. Then he said: 'Yes, I see. It should be "Miss Mortmain" now you're grown up enough for dinner parties.'

'It certainly shouldn't,' I said. 'I mean you must call me Cassandra, without the "Miss". You're one of the family – it's absurd you should ever have called me "Miss". Who told you to?'

'My mother – she set a lot of store by it,' he said. 'I remember the first day we came here. You and Miss Rose were throwing a ball in the garden and I ran to the kitchen door thinking I'd play, too. Mother called me back and told me how you were young ladies, and I was never to play with you unless I was invited. And to call you "Miss", and never to presume. She had a hard job explaining what "presume" meant.'

'Oh, Stephen, how awful! And you'd be – how old?'

'Seven, I think. You'd be six and Miss Rose nine. Thomas was only four, but she told me to call him "Master Thomas". Only he asked me not to, years ago.'

'And I ought to have asked you years ago.' I'd never given it a thought.[17]

In this extract, the relationship between Stephen and Cassandra is deeply shaped by class. A little later, she says of her sister Rose, 'I know that she thinks of him as – well, as a boy of a different class from ours' and adds 'Do I think it, too? If so, I am ashamed of such snobbishness!'[18] But whether she is embarrassed by it or not, the fact is that class *does* have a role in their relationship, and does affect the way in which she sees him and he sees her. Before this incident, she has never really questioned that.

Cassandra lives in a world where 'class' is like a part of the landscape. Everyone acknowledges it, and few people question it. Stephen himself believes that it is an *inherent*, natural feature of the world: you are either born a gentleman or not, and there is nothing you can do about it. He thinks it quite natural and proper that it should shape the way one relates to other human beings, and this belief that it is natural and proper is deeply ingrained in him. He has been being taught it at least since he was seven, and it is a view of the world held in place by such small but pervasive things as the fact that he always calls Cassandra 'Miss' and Thomas 'Master'.

So, here we have a deep-seated way of seeing the world, which most of the time is simply not questioned, and is assumed to be natural and quite unalterable. It is passed on in part by means of various customs and practices, and it deeply shapes the relationships between people, affecting the way in which power and status are distributed in relationships.

We also have, on Cassandra's part, someone who has been taught to believe in egalitarian ideals, but who is slowly realizing that the way in which she sees the world and other people is not as free from this deep-seated sense of class as she might have believed. She becomes determined no longer to let it shape the way she sees and feels: she determines to attack the specific customs that hold it in place (Stephen's calling her 'Miss'), and she worries away at the ingrained 'snobbishness' that she now, for the first time, sees in herself.

This is a perfect example of 'ideology' and 'ideology-critique'. An ideology is any way of seeing, thinking about and talking about the world that is pervasive in a particular society or community. It is any such pervasive way of seeing the world that deeply shapes the relationships between people, particularly relationships of power and status, and that the people concerned mostly see as being inevitable, unalterable and natural – or fail to 'see' at all. 'Ideology' can also refer not just to the pervasive way of seeing the world, but to the various customs and practices by which that way of seeing is inculcated and passed on – the whole educational apparatus that gets people seeing the world in that way in the first place, and the practices that keep it in place once it is there.

'Ideology' is sometimes used in a neutral way, when it simply refers to any deep-seated pervasive way of seeing the world shared by a particular community or society, whether they are good and truthful ways of seeing the world or distorting and destructive. More often, though, the word has negative connotations. On the one hand, 'ideology' has a negative ring to it if the focus falls on the fact that a pervasive way of seeing the world is wrongly being assumed to be natural and unavoidable and unquestionable; there's at least a whiff of deception and falsehood about that. On the other hand 'ideology' is used particularly for those pervasive ways of seeing the world that help keep social inequalities in place – like the class difference between Cassandra and Stephen, or like racism, or sexism, and so on.

Practising ideology critique

When faced with a text or a film or a television programme, you can ask questions like the following.[19]

1 What assumptions are being made about what is natural, just and right?
2 Who do these assumptions disadvantage?
3 What arrangements of power and status are assumed between the various individuals and groups mentioned in the text?
4 How are those arrangements made to appear as if they were normal?
5 Is anything about those arrangements 'airbrushed out'?
6 What 'binary oppositions' shape this text: for example, good/evil, natural/unnatural, tame/wild, young/old. Which side of each opposition is valued, and which side devalued? How are people or groups represented as falling on one side or another of these oppositions?
7 What people, classes, areas of life, experiences, are conspicuously absent from this text?
8 What and how does this text 'mystify': in other words, how does it surround particular things, people, groups or arrangement with general, powerful auras?
9 Most broadly, what vision of human possibility appears to lie at the heart of this text?

So, in the extract from *I Capture the Castle*, Cassandra

1 questions Stephen's assumption that it is *natural* for him not to be a 'gentleman', and she does so
2 because this assumption disadvantages him, and
3 because it places him as in a subordinate class, with inferior power and rights, yet this assumption
4 is made to appear normal by pervasive habits of speech and behaviour; and it
5 obscures the fact that Cassandra and her family are utterly dependent upon Stephen for their welfare – he is, at this stage, their only breadwinner.
6 Elsewhere in the book, Cassandra's musing on Stephen brings in other oppositions than just that between 'middle class' and 'lower class': 'cultured' versus 'uncultured', 'good with words' versus 'clumsy with words', 'artificial' versus 'natural' and so on.
7 Cassandra realizes at various points that she has never really thought about where Stephen sleeps, or whether he is as hungry as she is – she has conveniently airbrushed out various aspects of his life.
8 Her temptation is to 'mystify' Stephen by representing him to herself as primarily physical or natural rather than intellectual and cultured – a mystification that means that she doesn't have to face up to what she really feels about him.
9 All in all the vision that Cassandra rejects when she critiques this ideology is that of a class-structured rural idyll: the rich man in his castle, the poor man at his gate, God made them, high or lowly, and ordered their estate.[20]

Exercise

This weekend, buy a newspaper that comes with a glossy lifestyle magazine. Read a selection of articles, and see if you can hazard an ideology critique along the lines I have suggested.

When it comes to more subtle examples than the one I've been working with so far, ideology critique can be a far more complex and difficult process. Imagine beginning to tease out what is going on in our society's ways of advertising, for instance, or in Australian soap operas. What do they train us to see as natural, inevitable and right? In what ways do they imprison us? What stories do they tell us about ourselves and our world – and how do those stories differ from what the Christian gospel tells us? After all, if God's *gubernatio* is understood as God's freeing work, this is one of the arenas in which it will operate: bringing to judgement the distorting scripts that shape our lives.

Key points

- To understand God's providential work, which is the source of freedom, it is important to understand our lack of freedom.
- Ideology critique is one way of unmasking the constricting scripts by which one's life is run.

Providence in the world

If God's *gubernatio* is God's freeing work, then it is identical to the economy of salvation. 'Gubernatio' is simply another word for the work of Christ and the Spirit by which the triune God draws the world to Godself, freeing it to be itself. In other words, the subject matter of the doctrine of providence turns out to be nothing other than the same subject matter that I have been presenting all along, especially in the chapters on God, on the Trinity, on incarnation and the Spirit; all that has changed is the particular direction from which I am questioning that same subject matter.

The question now is this: When Christians say that God draws the world to Godself by Word and Spirit, what are they saying about the way in which God's action appears in the world and shapes the world? How does talking about God doing this to and for the world relate to the regular patterns of activity and relationship – the chains of cause and effect, the uniformity of natural processes – that Christians can see in the world around them, which they understand as upheld by God's sustaining and accompanying work, and which are their normal means for explaining how and why things happen?

I argued, in my discussions of *conservatio* and *concursus* that the continuity and integrity of creation, its power of self-determination, should be seen as God's act. Nevertheless, God has clearly been seen in Christianity as 'steering' creation towards an end, even if that steering is seen as the overcoming of all that distorts and constricts creation, and even if the end is imagined to be creation freed to be itself. How does this goal-directed steering mesh with the continuity and integrity of creation? If the world proceeds entirely according to the orderly causal patterns, the laws, that are proper to it, what room is there for saying that God guides or steers or impels or draws it to some particular goal?

There are various models that one might turn to – ways of thinking about the continuity and integrity of creation that might help one think how it could be open to God's steering work. The simplest is the idea that, from time to time, God's purpose for the world leads God to suspend the normal rules by which it works. This is what, in recent centuries, people have tended to mean by 'miracle': some break in the chains of cause and effect that normally bind the world together, when something happens that would not or could not otherwise have happened: divine discontinuities in the creaturely order.[21]

There are some ways of talking about this possibility that seem to run counter to the involvement of God in creation's normal ordering. That is, God is sometimes portrayed as a divine tinkerer, who has set this great machine of the world going, but who now sees that it is not quite running on course, and so reaches in to make adjustments. At very least, God's gubernatorial work seems in such a picture to be opposed to, or discontinuous with, God's conserving and concurring work. At worst, this seems to be a God who is absent whenever the world is running as normal.

There are, however, ways of taking this rule-suspension possibility that don't fall into the same trap. Consider a political constitution. It might have rules about how the ordinary regularities of political life are to be suspended at times of particular crisis, in order to preserve the most basic structures and activities of the society whose constitution it is. It may be that at such times of particular crisis one will be able to see at work the deepest commitments that underpin the constitution, commitments that are normally tacit. Just so, some would say, if there are times when the ordinary regularities and continuities of creaturely life are suspended, that is only because the deeper patterns of God's creation are running in those moments counter to the surface regularities that we normally think of as creation's unbreakable laws. These breaks or discontinuities do not, as it were, represent God suspending the rule of law and reverting to arbitrary diktat; rather they represent the unexpected and temporary visibility of the *deepest* regularities that God has, in God's patience and faithfulness, given to creation. It is in such miracles, some might argue, that the real nature of creation's continuity and integrity is most clear, because those deep continuities have to do precisely with creation being ordered towards its fulfilment in God's life. Creation's constant and pervasive orientation to that end sometimes cracks the surface web of efficient causality that we think of as the laws of nature.[23]

Efficient and final causes

The philosopher Aristotle identified four different kinds of 'cause' – although his use of that term was rather broader than ours tends to be.[22] Roughly speaking, he was identifying four different ways of answering the question 'Why is that thing what it is?' Consider a chair. The 'material cause', according to Aristotle, is the stuff out of which it was made, the stuff that has been worked on and changed in order to make the chair: the wood. The 'formal cause' is the shape or definition that has been give to the wood: it has been made into a thing with a back, a seat, and legs or a pedestal – all the elements of something chair-shaped. The 'efficient cause' is the power that has produced the change in the wood – in this case a carpenter with the knowledge of how to work wood, and the tools with which to shape it. The 'final cause' is the end or goal for which the chair was made: it is a thing for sitting on.

In modern science, the focus has been squarely on efficient causality: a change occurs in a system because some force acts upon that system. A planet's trajectory is pulled into a curve by gravity; the water boils because heat is applied; I move my fingers because electrical impulses are sent down nerves to trigger contractions in my muscles.

The claim that I am exploring is that the laws of efficient causality that govern the universe rest upon deeper laws of *final* causality that specify what this universe is for – and while those deeper laws require that the laws of efficient casualty reign undisturbed most of the time, it is possible that from time to time those deeper laws require the suspension of efficiency.

Some theologians, however, would argue that we don't need to assume any such suspension of the laws of nature in order to claim that God is drawing the world towards a particular goal. They note that, on present understanding, the natural laws or regularities that structure the universe appear to have some 'give' in them. Quantum mechanics has shown us that events do not follow one another in chains of rigidly determined causation, but are probabilistic: that is, there is a probability that the current state of a system can give rise to a given future state, a probability that it will give rise to different future states, and no way of predicting absolutely which will happen. The appearance of apparently rigid determination in the natural world is due to the unimaginably small scales at which these probabilistic processes operate. Any event that is large enough for us to take notice of in the normal course of things is therefore composed from vast numbers of these probabilistic events. Throw a die once, and you are quite likely to get a 1 or a 6; throw it a thousand times and your average score is going to be pretty close to 3.5. Throw it many billions of billions of times, and your average score will be overwhelmingly likely to be so close to 3.5 as to be identical, for all practical purposes. It is, therefore, no paradox to note that quantum mechanical theories, far from making accuracy and precision impossible, can actually give rise to astoundingly accurate and precise predictions. Nevertheless, quantum mechanics does appear to describe a world in which, at some level, the same initial conditions can give rise to multiple different futures, and – as some theologians have eagerly suggested – it might therefore be possible for God to influence outcomes without disturbing the laws by which creation runs. And the level of freedom allowed to God for such influencing is much larger than one might expect: God can, as it were, make all the countless billions of dice in a given game turn up 6, so that something utterly unheard of happens at the scales of time and space with which we are familiar, even though nothing extraordinary, nothing rule-breaking, is happening with any of the tiny quantum components of that event.

Once again, this suggestion can be taken in a variety of ways, with at one end of the spectrum images of God choosing at particular times and places to intervene in the otherwise normal running of things in order to push the outcome in a particular direction, and at the other end of the spectrum the suggestion that the quantum mechanical laws that govern the universe rest upon a deeper set of consistent and faithful divine intentions and commitments that actually shape *all* quantum mechanical events, normally very subtly, sometimes quite blatantly.

As well as the idea that God suspends the laws of nature from time to time, and the idea that those laws have enough 'give' in them to allow God to shape their outcomes without breaking them, there is another idea, a little more difficult to convey. This is the idea that, even if the laws were rigidly deterministic, and even if God did not break them at any point, God might nevertheless have the freedom to shape the outcome to which those laws point. Consider someone doing a Sudoku puzzle. He or she fills in the 9×9 grid of numbers so that each of the digits from 1 to 9 appears exactly once in each row and in each column of the grid, and in each of the nine 3×3 sub-grids of which the larger grid is composed. Working with the grid, with these rules about how it must be filled in, and with the scattering of digits already filled in by the setter, the successful puzzler works out the unique way in which the rest of the grid *must* be completed. The grid, the laws and the initial conditions absolutely determine the final outcome. Suppose, however, that one of the initial digits filled in by the setter were to be erased. The confused puzzler might now find that there were several different ways in which the grid could be filled in, each of which fully obeyed the laws of Sudoku, and each of which abided by the other initial digits placed by the setter. The fixed initial conditions and the rigid laws would no longer completely determine the final grid, and the puzzler would be free to choose which outcome she wanted, according to her own whim – choosing, say, the grid in which her favourite number appeared in the top left corner. The constraints of the laws and the initial digits would leave enough freedom for the puzzler to set her own extra constraint.

A theologian might claim that God's decision to create the world was something like the setting and solving of such a Sudoku puzzle. God, it might be claimed, chose to create a rigidly law-governed world, and set Godself various constraints upon the world that was to be created (it must give rise to living beings capable of love, say; it must contain one human life that fully displays the life of God in creaturely form – and so on). And God might have discovered that there were multiple possible worlds that met all these constraints, just as there are multiple solutions to a Sudoku puzzle with one initial digit erased. And so this God would have the freedom to set extra constraints, choosing to bring into being one of these worlds that was in some other respect desirable – choosing the one that led to the goal that God had in mind, say, or choosing a world in which more faithful prayers happen to be followed by chains of events that look like answers than in any of the others. The world thus brought into being would be completely, deterministically law-governed, but God would nevertheless have chosen its shape in some detail.

This is, of course, a deeply anthropomorphic and mythological analogy. Nevertheless, the central idea is that a creator who in some sense has the freedom to choose the laws by which the universe will run, and to set the initial conditions upon which those laws will operate, might consistently be said to have the freedom to shape the world that is the outcomes of those laws, even if those laws are rigidly deterministic. It is not necessary to think in anthropomorphic fashion of God examining a set of possible worlds, deliberating about them, and then choosing – solving the Sudoku puzzle of creation, as it were (and in the chapter on evil and suffering, we will see some reasons for rejecting such a picture). Nevertheless, this analogy does perhaps show us that it is a mistake to think that God's creative bringing into being of even a completely law-governed world necessarily prevents us from talking about God's shaping, steering work: God's *gubernatio*.

Miracles

'Miracles' are normally taken to be events that cannot be explained by natural means, or whose natural explanation is so overwhelmingly unlikely that other explanations must be sought.[24] Debates about such miracles have tended in modern times to focus on whether miracles are possible, whether sufficient evidence can be gathered to justify belief that a particular event was a miracle, and on whether miracles count as good evidence for the existence of God.

The discourse of explanation and evidence that is the main context for modern discussions of miracle was not nearly so central before the seventeenth century or so. Of course, miracles were understood to be 'wonders' – to be astonishing, unexpected and amazing. But they were also understood to be 'signs', and the emphasis often fell not on how they could be explained, or upon their evidential value, but upon what they communicated or showed: the power and glory and love of God for God's creatures.

If one wanted to retrieve these pre-modern discussions of miracle, one might say that a miracle is any event that dramatically and forcefully anticipates the kingdom of heaven, any event that dramatically and forcefully shows Christlike life being formed in the present, whether or not the event has a natural explanation, however likely or unlikely. Such events will not necessarily do anything to provide evidence for sceptics of the existence of God, even if for Christian believers they are doorways to deeper knowledge of God.

Having set out these possibilities (and without any claim that my list is exhaustive), I should lay my cards on the table. I must admit that I am an agnostic about this particular question. I can see some of the fascination that comes from exploring these theories – but I do not see that I have any place to stand from which I could make an informed judgement about whether and how God's *gubernatio* works. As a Christian, I believe I am called to place my trust in God and in the future that God has for the world; I believe (as I shall elaborate in a short while) that I am called to pray in faith in all situations, calling upon God's aid; and I know that I stand in a tradition that has frequently and unashamedly talked about God responding to such prayer, God shaping the course of specific events and the course of the world in general, a God of intervention and interaction. I do not, however, have a clear sense of what all this amounts to, or of what sense to make of it all. The one exception that I would make is that (for reasons that I touched on briefly, and that I will explore more fully in Chapter 10) I think I am pushed much more to those accounts that speak of a constant, faithful underlying pattern to God's action in and towards the world, lying beneath the regularities that science investigates, rather than towards a more anthropomorphic picture of God considering what to do, how to respond, whether to act, in each and every situation. That in itself, however, does not help me choose between these three models, or even to say if any of them are anywhere near the right lines.

On the one hand, I am aware that I live in a world of closely meshed interdependences, chains of efficient cause and effect. I am aware that I rely upon the world having this kind of structure every time I think or act, and expect the world either to make reliable sense, or expect my action to make a predictable kind of difference. I switch on a light switch, and place my trust in the regularities of the electrical world as investigated and tied down by generations of scientists and engineers.[25] When the light fails, I change the bulb, or check the fuse, or call in an electrician, and show at each step that in practice I believe that at least this bit of the universe runs according to well-understood laws. At another level, I acknowledge the multiple ways in which I am formed and shaped by the world around me, and can only think and act because of what I have inherited from others. I am aware that even at those times when I think I am acting independently and freely, I am doing so in ways that are incontrovertibly dependent upon ideas and habits and skills that I have learnt, and that I am simply playing out again deluding stories about freedom and independence that are passed around in my culture. I believe myself to be, in other words, wholly part of creation, and so wholly and unreservedly wrapped in chains of finite dependency upon all the other creaturely realities that have formed my context since the moment of my conception.

And yet, despite acknowledging this lack of freedom, I trust that God has this whole interconnected web of creation, of which I am simply a part, in hand – and that God is drawing it to Godself, and freeing it for fulfilled, godly life. I trust, in other words, that the whole web of creaturely interdependence is itself dependent upon God, and that this deeper, infinite dependence somehow shows itself in and through the course that all those finite dependences take. I trust in particular that the future that God has for the world already appears in glimpses and hints in the midst of the world, and I trust that I am being given eyes to recognize those glimpses and hints, to recognize and share in Christlike love, and so to begin to be free.

Yet I do not know how this works, nor expect to know, even though I do think I can understand enough to see that I am not simply believing the impossible when I believe all this. Instead of explaining the mechanisms by which finite and infinite dependency relate, all I can do is to look for, learn to recognize, and try to point to, Christlike love and godly freedom wherever they appear, and live in such a way as to trust that this love and freedom are not simply one more variety of random froth churned from the chaotic waters of the world, but are the fingerprints of God's saving *gubernatio*.

Key points

- God's governance might involve the breaking of the natural laws that govern the universe – or their suspension in favour of deeper laws.
- It might involve the exploitation of 'give' in those laws.
- It might involve something akin to the freedom to choose the constraints that order the world.
- Trust in God's providence does not, however, require a firm answer to these questions.

Asking for God's help

The nature of this trusting agnosticism might become clearer if I examine a central example: intercessory and petitionary prayer. Although the terms are frequently used interchangeably for any kind of prayer in which one asks for God's help, 'petitionary' is sometimes reserved for prayers in which one asks for God's help for oneself (or perhaps one's closest family and friends), 'intercessory' for prayer in which one asks for God's help for some other person or people. The crucial question in our context is whether and how God *answers* such prayers. Are Christians to think of God hearing their requests, and then (sometimes) intervening in the world in order to bring about something that would not otherwise have happened?

Liturgical intercession

Formal liturgies often contain some kind of intercession. One of the most famous is the following from the Book of Common Prayer.[26]

O Lord, shew thy mercy upon us.
And grant us thy salvation.
O Lord, save the Queen.
And mercifully hear us when we call upon thee.
Endue thy ministers with righteousness.
And make thy chosen people joyful.
O Lord, save thy people.
And bless thine inheritance.
Give peace in our time, O Lord.
Because there is none other that fighteth for us, but only thou, O God.

O God, make clean our hearts within us
And take not thy Holy Spirit from us.

What does a prayer like this assume about the way that God relates to the world, and the way that God works in the world? What would one have to believe in order to say this prayer with integrity? After all, it includes petitions for 'salvation', for 'joy', for 'righteousness', for 'clean hearts' and for the presence of the Holy Spirit; it describes God's action as 'hearing', 'blessing', 'giving', 'saving' and 'fighting'; and it involves prayer specifically for one person ('the Queen'), for a distinct group ('ministers'), for the church ('thy chosen people'), and for the world more generally ('peace in our time'). What kind of answer must one believe possible in order to pray this prayer with trust and hope?

Exercise

If you find yourself in a church service any time soon, spend some time listening to all that is said or sung, and identifying ways in which God's aid is called on. What kind of picture of God's ability to govern or steer the world is painted in the service as a whole?

The easiest answer to give is that the prayer obviously changes something, because it changes the person praying, and is (or can be) part of the process in which that person is drawn deeper into the life of God. The prayer can be seen as a process in which the person praying learns to stand towards situations in the world as God stands towards them: to be called out of preoccupation and self-centredness, to learn to see the situation against the backdrop of God's love and so to learn to see what is wrong as a constriction or distortion of the flourishing that God desires for the world, and to learn to share the divine desire for that flourishing to be unimpeded. Such prayer can be an apt expression of protest against all in the world that stands in the way of love, and it can be an embodiment of the trust that no place or situation or person has finally escaped from the hand of God, and that God has the power to redeem even the darkest tragedy. If one pictures God's love as a stream pouring over the world, then intercessory prayer might be seen as a matter of aligning oneself with the flow of this stream, being turned by it to face the world that God loves.

Does such prayer change the situation for which one is praying, however? Of course, if it is a situation over which the person praying has some influence, the changes in him might lead to changes in the situation. But what happens when the situation is beyond such influence or control?

In one sense, Christian theology has consistently declared that prayer does *not* directly change the world. It is not effective *in and of itself*; it is not a technique for getting things done, or a form of productive effort by which human beings can achieve things. All prayer is directed to God, and petitionary and intercessory prayers are calls upon God to act, to save, to help. If such prayer 'works', it does so because the God upon whom it calls works, not because the prayer itself is a tool in the hands of the person praying.

1 'Cross', Photo by Szczepan1990.

2 Anonymous, *Mandylion of Edessa*, tempura on linen, stretched over wood; (?3rd–5th Century); now held in the Papal chapel in the Vatican; photograph by M. Wolfgang.

3 Georges de la Tour, *Le Nouveau-Né (The Newborn Child)*, oil on canvas (c.1645); Rennes Musée des Beaux-Arts.

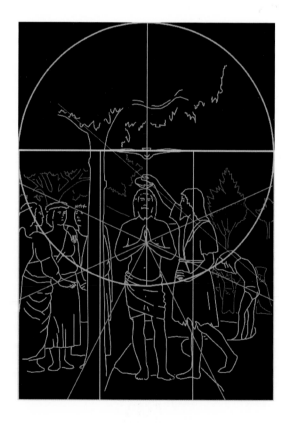

4 A mathematical analysis of Piero's *Baptism*, by Mike Higton.

5 Matthias Grünewald, *Crucifixion* (Eisenheim Altarpiece), oil on wood (1510); Colmar, Musée d'Unterlinden.

6 Matthias Grünewald, *Resurrection* (Eisenheim Altarpiece), oil on wood (1510); Colmar, Musée d'Unterlinden.

7 Diego Rivera, *Jacques Lipchitz (Portrait of a Young Man)*, oil on
canvas (1914); Museum of Modern Art, New York.

If I ask whether such prayer changes the situation for which I am praying, I am really asking whether such prayer modifies the way in which God's action meets and changes that situation. I am asking whether God's action can be thought to *respond* to the prayer in some way, such that the prayer becomes the *occasion* for a change in the world.

All my earlier discussion about God's agency in the world comes into play here: whether I am to think of God 'breaking' the normal laws of nature, or of God exploiting the give in those laws, or of God using the freedom that God has in creating the world to bring about a world in which God's purposes are fulfilled. But there is now an added kick to the question: even if I grant that in some such way God does steer the world towards an end, am I to think that God does so *in response* to the prayers of God's creatures?

In all of the models that I outlined, it is possible to think that God has so arranged matters that God's activity becomes more directly evident at some times and places in the world – producing hints and signs of the flourishing that God has for the world. And it is possible to think that, by God's grace, where and when this happens depends in part upon the prayers of God's creatures. I heard once of an office building in which, if the right combination of windows happened to be open, a strong breeze would blow through the building and slam the doors, even on an apparently windless day. A secretary on the fourth floor, say, unaware that the relevant pattern of windows open around the building was nearly complete, might open his own window only to hear doors slamming immediately all over the building. So it might be with prayer: prayer opens a window, and it might be that the opening of that window somehow completes a set of circumstances that lets the wind of God's action blow through the world in a particular way, shaping events half a world away. It may be that the world that God has made, as well as having all the visible interdependences and links of cause and effect that science rightly investigates, is by God's grace webbed together in this other way as well, such that my prayer can be the occasion for changes that have little or nothing to do with the influence or agency I normally think of myself as having.

As with the more general topic of the previous section, I find myself an agnostic here too. It may be that something like this does indeed hold. It may be, on the other hand, that prayer has more to do with the person praying becoming aligned to the love of God as it pours upon the world, and trusting that this unfailing love is present and active, however hidden it might be, in the situation about which he is praying. I do not know which of these is true, but neither do I think that I need to know. As a Christian, I believe myself called to pray in all things and to trust in all things – and that ought to be enough for me. The doctrine of providence has little to do with explanation, and much to do with trust.

Key points

- Intercessory prayer changes the person praying, aligning him or her with God's love.

- Prayer is not in and of itself effective; it is a call upon God to effect something.
- Some Christian theologians argue that God's action in the world is shaped by human prayers.
- Others argue that prayer has more to do with trusting that God's unfailing love is present and active in all situations, however hidden it might be.

Going further

1 Traditionally, the doctrine of providence has been closely related to the practice of 'figural reading' of the Bible – the kind of reading that claims that characters or incidents from the Old Testament, for instance, are 'fulfilled' in Christ – are 'types' or 'figures' of Christ. This connection is worth exploring further for the illumination it casts on what providence means. I have written about this in chapters 6 and 7 of *Christ, Providence and History: Hans W. Frei's Public Theology* (London: T&T Clark, 2004).

2 The nature of human freedom is, of course, a perplexing and bewildering one, and the line I have taken in this one skirts some deep quagmires. To explore the question further, try Richard Bauckham, *God and the Crisis of Freedom: Biblical and Contemporary Perspectives* (Louisville: WJKP, 2002); David Burrell, *Faith and Freedom: An Interfaith Perspective*, Challenges in Contemporary Theology series (Oxford: Blackwell, 2004); Thomas Pink, *Free Will: A Very Short Introduction* (Oxford: Oxford University Press, 2004); Daniel C. Dennett, *Freedom Evolves*, new edn (Harmondsworth: Penguin, 2004); John Searle, *Freedom and Neurobiology: Reflections on Free Will, Language, and Political Power* (New York: Columbia University Press, 2006); Ian Carter, Matthew Cramer and Hillel Steiner (eds), *Freedom: A Philosophical Anthology* (Oxford: Blackwell, 2006); and Gary Watson (ed.), *Free Will*, Oxford Readings in Philosophy, 2nd edn (Oxford: Oxford University Press, 2003).

Notes

1 On http://www.google.com/, 25 April 2007.

2 *The Oxford English Dictionary*, 2nd edn (Oxford: Oxford University Press, 1989).

3 The threefold division is standard in Lutheran and Reformed dogmatics; for summaries see Heinrich Schmid, *The Doctrinal Theology of the Evangelical Lutheran Church* (Minneapolis: Augsburg, 1961), pp. 170–4, available online at the Christian Classics Ethereal Library http://www.ccel.org/ccel/schmid/theology.iv.iv.i.html, and Heinrich Heppe, *Reformed Dogmatics* (London: George, Allen and Unwin, 1950), pp. 256–80.

4 See http://www.welephant.co.uk/Bonfirestory020.htm – the Fireworks Code at The National Fire Safety Charity for Children's *Welephant* site.

5 See Karl Barth's discussion of creation and the exclusion of chaos in *Church Dogmatics III: The Doctrine of Creation*, Pt 1 (Edinburgh: T&T Clark, 1958), pp. 101–10.

6 Think of the song 'He's got the whole world in his hands' (origins unknown); the words are available online at http://ingeb.org/spiritua/hesgotth.html.

7 Stephen Donaldson, *The One Tree*, The Second Chronicles of Thomas Covenant, vol. 2 (Glasgow: Fontana/Collins, 1982), p. 122.

8 The distinction goes back to Plato, *Timaeus* 14: 'All these are to be reckoned among the second and co-operative causes which God, carrying into execution the idea of the best as far as possible, uses as his ministers.' Translation from Benjamin Jowett (ed.), *The Dialogues of Plato*, vol. 3, 3rd edn (Oxford: Oxford University Press, 1892), p. 466; available online at Project Gutenberg http://www.gutenberg. org/catalog/world/readfile?fk_files=38758&pageno=76.

9 Dorothy L. Sayers (who knew a thing or two about being a novelist) discusses these matters in *The Mind of the Maker* (London: Methuen, 1941), ch. 5; available online at *World Invisible*, http://www.worldinvisible.com/library/dlsayers/mindofmaker/ mind.c.htm.

10 Robin Buss, 'Introduction' in Alexandre Dumas (Père), *The Count of Monte Cristo* (Harmondsworth: Penguin, 2003 [French original: 1844–5]), pp. xi–xxi: p. xx; my emphasis.

11 *Luxor* 2 (MumboJumbo, 2007), available at http://www.mumbojumbo.com/ game/game/44; it is a procrastinator's dream.

12 Fred Zinnemann, *High Noon* (Stanley Kramer Productions, 1952); see http:// uk.imdb.com/title/tt0044706/.

13 John Fowles, *The Magus* (London: Jonathan Cape, 1966).

14 David Frankel, *The Devil Wears Prada* (20th Century Fox, 2006); see the Internet Movie Database, http://uk.imdb.com/title/tt0458352/.

15 If you think you are free from such scripting yourself, try reading the chapter on dress codes in Kate Fox's *Watching the English: The Hidden Rules of English Behaviour* (London: Hodder, 2005): pp. 267–94.

16 Rowan Williams, *Tokens of Trust* (London: SCM Press, 2007), pp. 11–13.

17 Dodie Smith, *I Capture the Castle* (London: Virago, 1996 [original edn: 1949]), pp. 104–5.

18 Smith, *I Capture the Castle*, p. 110.

19 Closely based on 'Ideology: A Brief Guide', an exceptionally clear guide to ideology critique produced by John Lye in 1997, at Brock University in Canada: http:// www.brocku.ca/english/jlye/ideology.html.

20 I am quoting the now often-dropped second verse of Cecil Frances Alexander's hymn, 'All things bright and beautiful', first printed in her *Hymns for Little Children* (London: Joseph Masters, 1848); available online at Cyberhymnal, http://www. cyberhymnal.org/htm/a/l/allthing.htm.

21 Heppe, in *Refomed Dogmatics* (see note 3 above) states that one form of providence is 'The form of divine gubernatio in which God is active without second causes or uses them in a manner deviating from their orderly appointment and activity is God's performance of miracle' (p. 263).

22 See Aristotle, *Physics* 2.3, tr. R. P. Hardie and R. K. Gaye and *Metaphysics* 5.2, tr. W. D. Ross (Adelaide: University of Adelaide Library, 2000); available online at http:// etext.library.adelaide.edu.au/a/aristotle.

23 Augustine writes that 'God, the Author and Creator of all natures, does nothing contrary to nature; for whatever is done by him who appoints all natural order and measure and proportion must be natural in every case.' He continues, 'There is, however, no impropriety in saying that God does a thing contrary to nature, [if we mean that] it is contrary to *what we know* of nature. For we give the name nature to the usual common course of nature; and whatever God does contrary to this, we call a prodigy, or a miracle. But against the supreme law of nature, which is beyond the knowledge both of the ungodly and of weak believers, God never acts, any more than He acts against himself.' Augustine of Hippo, *Reply to Faustus the Manichaean*, 26.3, in Philip

Schaff (ed.), *Nicene and Post-Nicene Fathers*, First Series, vol. 4 (New York: Christian Literature Company, 1887), pp. 321–2; available online at the Christian Classics Ethereal Library, http://www.ccel.org/ccel/schaff/npnf104.iv.ix.xxviii.html. See also Rowan Williams's discussion in *Wrestling with Angels* (London: SCM Press, 2007), pp. 268–70.

24 The Scottish philosopher David Hume provided a classic definition: 'A miracle may accurately be defined, a transgression of a law of nature by a particular volition of the deity, or by the interposition of some invisible agent', *Enquiries Concerning the Human Understanding*, ed. L. A. Selby-Bigge, 2nd edn (Oxford: Clarendon Press, 1902 [original edn: 1777]), p. 115, n.1; available online at The Online Library of Liberty, http://oll.libertyfund.org/Texts/Hume0129/Enquiries/0222_Bk.html. Thomas Aquinas had already defined miracles as, 'Things that are done occasionally by divine power outside of the usual established [or observed] order of events.' *Summa Contra Gentiles*, 3.101, tr. Joseph Rickaby (London: Burns and Oates, 1905); available online at the Jacques Maritain Center http://www2.nd.edu/Departments/Maritain/etext/gc3_101.htm.

25 The German theologian and biblical critic Rudolf Bultmann went rather further, and argued that 'It is *impossible* to use electric light and the wireless and to avail ourselves of modern medical and surgical discoveries, and at the same time to believe in the New Testament world of spirits and miracles.' From 'The New Testament and Mythology' in *Kerygma and Myth*, vol. 1, ed. Hans Werner Bartsch (London: SPCK, 1953), pp. 1–44: p. 5, emphasis mine.

26 Available online at the Church of England, http://www.cofe.anglican.org/worship/liturgy/bcp/texts/mpep/morning.html.

9

Facing the End

Once again, I continue to ask what it means for Christians to see the world in which they live as a world caught up in the threefold economy of salvation, being drawn into participation in God's life. This chapter completes an arc that began in Chapter 7. To that chapter's discussion of creation, and Chapter 8's discussion of providence, I now add a discussion of 'eschatology': God's bringing of creation to its appointed end, the completion or fulfilment of the work of creation.

I am going to

- introduce the idea of the end as a 'horizon';
- argue that an eschatological vision can be a recipe for political discernment and activism; and
- discuss the 'four last things': death, judgement, heaven and hell.

Preparation

- What end awaits the world? What end awaits individual human beings? Do you think there will be a 'second coming'? A 'hell'? A 'heaven'? Briefly jot down some of your thoughts before starting the chapter.
- The topic of 'the end times' receives a great deal of fervent attention. Typing 'end times' into an internet search engine turns up all sorts of material,[1] some of it very strange, some of it rather disturbing. Have an explore, and ask yourself whether anything that you see connects with the kind of theological vision I have been exploring in this book.

Additional reading

For alternative viewpoints to accompany this chapter, try:

James Alison, *Raising Abel: The Recovery of the Eschatological Imagination* (New York: Crossroad, 1996), published in the UK as *Living in the End Times: The Last Things Re-imagined* (London: SPCK, 1997). A book that makes strong links between eschatology and devotion to Christ.

Gerhard Sauter, *What Dare We Hope: Reconsidering Eschatology*, Theology for the Twenty-first Century (London: Continuum, 1999). A careful survey of different approaches to eschatology, together with his own constructive proposal.

Facing the end

In the whole of this book so far, and especially in Chapter 8, the idea that God has an end for the world, or that the world has its future in God, has been a recurring motif. The world was created, Christian theologians have said, for life in God, and God is drawing all things towards that life by means of the threefold economy. In other words, everything I have said so far has had an *eschatological* cast – where 'eschatology' is the doctrine of 'the last things' (the *eschata*, in Greek) or 'the end time' (the *eschaton*).

Christians live in a world that has a *horizon* to it, a horizon towards which they see the world heading. Wherever or whenever Christians find themselves, whatever present arrangement they inhabit, their faith interrupts them and prompts them to gaze ahead, and glimpse something of the country towards which they are journeying. This horizon lies beyond any present view Christians have of the world, and colours all their responses to it. Each situation, each event, each reality can be seen as happening against the backdrop provided by God's future, and is in part *defined* by its relationship to that future. The world is not simply 'one damn thing after another', for Christians; it is a world on its way to God.[2]

Christians have differed, however, in how they have understood the connection between their present environs and this looming horizon. On the one hand, Christians have sometimes thought about this horizon as a future towards which God is working steadily in the present. That is, they have understood God to be steering the world incrementally in the direction of the end, accumulating now all the resources that will eventually be spent to establish the kingdom. On the other hand, Christians have sometimes thought about this horizon as a future for which they can only wait: an end that will come 'like a thief in the night' (1 Thessalonians 5.2) decisively and suddenly setting to rights a broken world.

On the whole the emphasis in Christian theology has fallen on the latter way of thinking. However much the world might be oriented towards God's future, however much there may be by God's providence signs, tendencies and movements in the present that hint at it and point towards it, however much the world might be made for this end and bear the signs of that making, that future will eventually arrive as a reversal to the world's flight from God – a challenge to and a transformation of all the present ways of the world. As such, the future horizon remains beyond any future that human beings can now project on the basis of the current state and direction of the world. Christian hope is a form of trust, not a form of optimism; it waits upon God's faithfulness to God's promises, rather than cheerfully estimating the likely outcome of present tendencies.

All this means that one must be very careful to distinguish the hope for God's future that Christians profess from something that sounds superficially similar. This Christian orientation towards the future is not about *progress*; it is not a matter of the world slowly accumulating godly practices and understanding, growing generation by generation away from violence, ignorance and confusion towards the sunny uplands of the future.[3] It is not a matter of processes and mechanisms that one can explain and predict. In fact, when Christians have tried to give descriptions of how the world might go between now and the end, they have tended to say that it may well get worse and worse, until God steps in to set it all to rights.[4]

Yet the other branch of Christian eschatological conviction has been important too: the conviction that even though God's future will come as a gift, it is a gift that Christians are already receiving, in provisional, partial forms.[5] Or (to put the same thing the other way around) Christians wait upon a gift that will not require them to empty their cupboards once they receive it, but will itself be capacious enough to gather up and hold all that God is doing in their midst in the present. After all, the gift for which Christians wait, the future for which they hope, is God's own capacious life – life that is not absent from the world in the present.

Resurrection

Jesus' resurrection has provided a primary model for Christian eschatological thinking. Although the very fact that Christian theology speaks in terms of 'bodily' resurrection means that Christians have placed a good deal of emphasis on the *continuity* between Jesus' pre-resurrection life and the life which comes after the resurrection, the fact that they also take seriously Christ's death means that there is a strong element of discontinuity as well. The resurrection is not seen as the natural continuance of Jesus' life, or its evolution to a higher level. Jesus is raised by God, as a gift from God, and what God gives in the resurrection is a *transformative* continuation (a fulfilment, a perfection) of who Jesus was. The resurrection is God's gift: a gift of the future life of the world now.[6]

Christian authors have sometimes spoken of three comings or advents of Jesus. There was the first advent, when he was born as a baby in first-century Palestine. That advent was the coming of God's life into the present: a portion of creaturely life was caught up and shaped so as to be utterly transparent to God. That first advent was the establishment of an outpost in the present of the future that God has for the world.

There is also an 'intermediate advent'.[7] By the power of the Spirit, Christ's life is made present in the world in the lives of his disciples. Their Christ-formed lives become signs and foretastes of the future, of which the Spirit is their 'pledge' or 'deposit' (Ephesians 1.14). The future of the body of Christ pledged by the Spirit is a future in which each person becomes a gift to the whole body, and in which each person becomes the recipient of the gifts that each other member is, receiving more of Christ from them. As the seventh-century Byzantine theologian Maximus the Confessor puts it, 'each of us will bring to completion that Body that itself brings all things to completion in each of us, filling everything and itself brought to fullness by all things'.[8]

To shift the metaphor somewhat, one could think of each person as a text about Christ that at present is garbled and corrupted, and can only be read in snatches and with caution, but which in the eschaton will be edited into full legibility. And just as Christ is known more fully in the commentary upon him provided by the life of each one of his followers, so one might think of each person in the eschaton not simply as a text that says one thing about Christ – a simple propositional statement about him, say – but as a poem that each member of the body will read and understand differently.

This intermediate advent never ends. Rather than thinking of the eschaton as the *end* of giving and receiving (because all will have been given, all received) one can think of it instead as the transition to unrestricted giving and receiving – the continual and unlimited arrival of Christ. Wherever Christians receive Christ in the present, and so experience little advents, they can think of them both as the coming to them of more of the Christ of the first advent, and as the breaking through into the present of anticipations of this future life of unrestricted advent.[9]

As well as speaking about this ongoing 'intermediate advent', however, Christians have also spoken of a *final* advent of Christ. In the words of the Nicene Creed, 'He will come again in glory to judge the living and the dead, and his kingdom will have no end.'[10] That is, as well as imagining their journey towards the end as a journey on which they become Christlike, a journey on which *his* life becomes visible in *theirs*, Christians have also imagined the fulfilment of that journey not simply as *their arrival* at Christlikeness, but as *Christ's return*. Christians have traditionally hoped for Christ's return in glory to gather to himself all those in whom his life has taken root.

The fulfilled life to which the Spirit draws the body of Christ only reaches fulfilment when it is brought into circulation around the living presence of the one who is its referent. The body of Christ is also the Bride of Christ, and the final advent has been thought of as the wedding of this Bride to Christ, the intimate union between all the images and reflections of Jesus that are found in Christian life and their original.

> They will see his face, and his name will be on their foreheads. And there will be no more night; they need no light of lamp or sun, for the Lord God will be their light, and they will reign for ever and ever. (Revelation 22.4–5)

After all, if it is by journeying into the threefold economy that human beings participate in the life of God, then the only apt way of imagining the consummation of that economy is as unrestricted, unstinting fellowship with Jesus, in the power of the Spirit, in the presence of the Father. Without knowing quite what it is that their imagination refers to, therefore, the Trinitarian logic of

Christian theology compels Christians to imagine the end to which God is drawing them as an end in which Jesus is wholly present and alive to them – a future in which Jesus has 'come again'. It is no accident that one of the oldest Christian prayers known to us is *Maranatha!*, which means, *Come, O Lord!* (1 Corinthians 16.22 – cf. Revelation 22.20).

The primary question for Christian eschatology is not 'When?', nor 'How?', nor even 'In what form?' The primary question is 'Who?' And the answer that Christians have given is simply that it is Christ, the visibility of God's life, who stands at the end. Christ is the eschatological horizon: the direction and movement that the world has when seen against that horizon is a direction and movement towards him.

Exercise

If you should find yourself in a church service any time soon, spend some time carefully watching and listening – and ask yourself whether any eschatological expectation, hope or desire is expressed anywhere in the service.[11]

'Without knowing quite what it is that their imagination refers to', though. One should be wary of any attempt to tie down precisely material that in the biblical witness and in Christian reflection is only confusingly and variously set out. As the American theologian Hans Frei said,

> Either to affirm that it is simply Jesus Christ as he was in past history, or to affirm that it is simply God manifest in Jesus rather than Jesus Christ himself, who will stand at the latter end, is an unwarranted short-cut of the New Testament's complexity and therefore an illegitimate dissolution of its mysteriousness.[12]

What the final advent will be, and how it will sum up and fulfil the first advent and the intermediate advent, is not something that Christians know, or need to know.

Three advents

'We know that there are three comings of the Lord. The third lies between the other two. It is invisible, while the other two are visible. In the first coming he was seen on earth, dwelling among men; he himself testifies that they saw him and hated him (John 15.24). In the final coming all flesh will see the salvation of our God (Luke 3.6), and they will look on him whom they pierced (Zechariah 12.10 and John 19.37). The intermediate coming is a hidden one; in it only the elect see the Lord within their own selves, and they are saved. In his first coming our Lord came in our flesh and in our weakness; in this middle coming he comes in spirit and in power; in the final coming he will be seen in glory and majesty. ...

'Because this coming lies between the other two, it is like a road on which we travel from the first coming to the last. In the first, Christ was our redemption; in the last, he will appear as our life; in this middle coming, he is our rest and consolation.

'In case someone should think that what we say about this middle coming is sheer invention, listen to what our Lord himself ways: "If anyone loves me, he will keep my word, and my Father will love him, and we will come to him" (John 19.23).'

Bernard of Clairvaux, *On the Advent of the Lord*[13]

Key points

• Christian hope is a form of trust, not optimism.
• Christian orientation towards the future is not about progress.
• Christians have imagined the fulfilment of their journey into God not simply as their arrival at Christlikeness, but as Christ's return.
• The world's future in Christ provides a horizon that colours all understanding of the present.

Setting the world to rights

Visions of the great and terrible 'Day of the Lord', on which God will come to exercise judgement on the earth, punctuate the prophetic texts of the Old Testament (for example, Isaiah 13.6; Ezekiel 30.3; Joel 2.1 and so on) and are re-echoed in the New (1 Thessalonians 5.2; 2 Peter 3.10). It is not so much an end of time that is envisaged, as an end to the present order of things – an end to the time when distortion and destruction cloud the face of creation, when the wicked flourish and the righteous perish.[14] The biblical authors see on the horizon God's invincible establishment of the divine reign on earth, a gift and a judgement that will come like a thief in the night, but reign like a king forever.

Most Christian theologians have taken this kind of vision to refer to an event that will take place on some future date in history: there will one day be a reckoning, a final setting to rights of the world. This final event was anticipated in the first coming of Christ, who inaugurated the kingdom of God in the midst of a dark and distorted world; it is anticipated in the intermediate coming of Christ, in the lives of those in whom the Spirit works; but this work awaits completion on the Day of the Lord, when Christ will return to the earth in glory.[15]

Some other theologians have thought instead that the 'judgement' spoken of is that which, by Christ and the Spirit, comes to each person in her own time and place, rather than being an event that will take place at some one point in history. They hold that imagining an approaching literal end to the present order of things is a way of dramatizing the sense that each individual, each society, faces the unavoidable Christ-shaped judgement of God. The horizon is and will remain just that: the limit at the edge of what one can now see. Just like tomorrow, the horizon never comes.[16]

Still others are content to leave their answer to these questions ambiguous – to talk about and hope for the coming of the end, without knowing quite what their talk refers to. Nevertheless, whichever different ways all these theologians jump, they have a common commitment to the idea that Christianity's eschatological vision is a vision that places all present life, corporate and individual, under the impending judgement of God. This vision provides a horizon that decisively reshapes Christians' view of life in the present.

Exercise

Pause for a moment to think which (if any) of these interpretations comes most naturally to you.

For some, such a vision has been a passport to quietism – that is, to the idea that because God will sort all things out in the end the believer's job is simply to watch and pray, waiting patiently for the end. There is no point in their agitating for change now, for none of their activities can bring the kingdom one inch nearer.

For others, however, a Christian eschatological imagination has led them in quite the opposite direction. Many of the most radical movements for change in Christian history have also been the most radical in the strength of their eschatological commitments. It seems to have been the case that a strong eschatological imagination regularly consorts with deep *restlessness* with the current state of the world.[17]

On the one hand, because current realities are seen against the horizon of God's future, they are themselves seen not to be final, not to be ultimate, not to be inevitable, not to be unquestionable. Whatever shape the world is in right now, the eschatological imagination says that *there is more than this* – and that this present reality stands under the judgement of the reality to come.

On the other hand, the eschatological vision also provides a glimpse of a different ordering of the world. It may only be a vision 'through a glass darkly',[18] and it may be a vision of an order that human beings could not possibly bring about by themselves, but it can be a light sufficient to show believers that some aspects of their world's current order witness to God's future, making room for it – and that other aspects deny that future and shut the doors to it.

This combination is a recipe for social and political action: a belief that the shape of the world is not absolutely fixed, coupled with some glimpse of what the shape of the world *should* be.

Reconciliation

Imagine a society split into two feuding groups, each with its own distinct culture. Imagine this society blighted by the hatred and violence between these two groups. The Christian eschatological vision might, quite simply, be of both groups living harmoniously together, of each group having the best things about its culture fulfilled and completed, and of the differences between them becoming a matter of celebration rather than of exclusion, each contributing something distinctive to their common life. In the current state of things, this vision may sound like 'pie in the sky' – a ridiculously naive and fluffy picture with no relationship to reality. It may even be impossible to see how groups so different could ever coexist peacefully (let alone celebrate their diversity) without one or other of them having to be defeated and assimilated by the other. And because the vision Christians have is of a future that *God* has for the world, rather than of a future that they can directly bring about, Christians will not necessarily have any access to a straightforward and clear Christian political programme that would only need to be implemented for the problems of this divided society to fall away.

Yet holding on to their eschatological vision, however dimly grasped it is, however hard to imagine concretely, may mean that Christians oppose any moves that simply *assume* that there could be no common future for these two groups, or no way forward without one side being defeated. And this vision, however dimly grasped, may mean that Christians support and get involved in those plans – however risky they might seem – that try to keep open at least the *possibility* of reconciliation.

In fact, it is quite important that Christians on either side do *not* begin with the assumption that they know clearly in advance the shape that reconciled life will take in the future, if the process of reconciliation is not to take the form of them squeezing the other group into their own vision. It is in the process of getting involved, in the process of working for peace, in the process of holding on to and working with those faint signs and promises of the future that they can detect in the mire of the present, that Christians will discover a fuller content for their eschatological vision.[19]

The kind of political engagement that goes with eschatological vision is best thought of as exploratory – not out of any desire to keep everything vague and unobjectionable, but because what Christians believe the future holds is the life of God, which is always greater than any of their limited imaginings of it. Christians glimpse a vision of the future, and that vision enables them to give a critique of the present and to work to change it. But it *is* only a glimpse of the future that they get, and as they explore further, as they actually involve themselves in shaping the present, their vision itself gets changed and deepened. Their journey of action in the world in the present is at the same time a journey of exploration deeper into the eschatological vision that drives them – and they will find that their ideas and practices are challenged and remade in the process.[20] As yet, they see that future only 'through a glass darkly', and their attempt to live towards it is bound to be tentative and fallible, carried out not in confidence that the future is within their grasp and that they are capable of constructing it, but that they are within *its* grasp, and may trust themselves to it.

Key points

- Some theologians see the 'Day of the Lord' as an event that will happen once and for all at some particular point in history.
- Some see it as an event that happens again and again, as each individual and community faces the judgement of Christ.
- An eschatological imagination can stimulate restlessness with the present state of the world, and provide a glimpse of how things should be, and so be a driver of social and political activism.

Eschatology and discernment

The exploratory political engagement to which the Christian eschatological vision lends itself is of necessity a matter of learning discernment. Consider the following two texts:

> [1]Let every person be subject to the governing authorities; for there is no authority except from God, and those authorities that exist have been instituted by God. [2]Therefore whoever resists authority resists what God has appointed, and those who resist will incur judgement. [3]For rulers are not a terror to good conduct, but to bad. Do you wish to have no fear of the authority? Then do what is good, and you will receive its approval; [4]for it is God's servant for your good. But if you do what is wrong, you should be afraid, for the authority does not bear the sword in vain! It is the servant of God to execute wrath on the wrongdoer. [5]Therefore one must be subject, not only because of wrath but also because of conscience. [6]For the same reason you also pay taxes, for the authorities are God's servants, busy with this very thing. [7]Pay to all what is due them – taxes to whom taxes are due, revenue to whom revenue is due, respect to whom respect is due, honour to whom honour is due.
>
> Romans 13.1–7

> [5]The beast was given a mouth uttering haughty and blasphemous words, and it was allowed to exercise authority for forty-two months. [6]It opened its mouth to utter blasphemies against God, blaspheming his name and his dwelling, that is, those who dwell in heaven. [7]Also it was allowed to make war on the saints and to conquer them. It was given authority over every tribe and people and language and nation, [8]and all the inhabitants of the earth will worship it, everyone whose name has not been written from the foundation of the world in the book of life of the Lamb that was slaughtered. [9]Let anyone who has an ear listen: [10]If you are to be taken captive,

into captivity you go; if you kill with the sword, with the sword you must be killed. Here is a call for the endurance and faith of the saints.

Revelation 13.5–10

Exercise

Carefully read both passages. What does each suggest about the nature of worldly authority? How might one's responses to secular authority differ if one took one of these passages rather than the other as one's guide?

In both these passages, the authority of worldly rulers is presented as given by God – but that is where the similarity stops. In Romans 13, authority is given to worldly rulers by God, and those rulers are represented as God's servants: they carry out God's will; they punish the evil and reward the good. Here, worldly authority is fundamentally godly, and to resist worldly rulers is to resist God.[21] In Revelation 13, however, authority is given to a worldly ruler by God – but now only in the sense that God in God's patience *allows* that ruler authority for a time. The ruler is presented as God's enemy: one who blasphemes against God, who is adored by the evil and punishes the good. Here, worldly authority is fundamentally demonic, and to resist this ruler is to show faithful endurance.[22]

The tension with which I began (between God's future as a kingdom being built already in the present and God's future as a sudden transformation ready to break in on a godless world) is played out again between these two passages. On the one hand there is a vision of the present political order as a preparation for and servant of God's future, holding open space in the present for godly life that anticipates that future. On the other there is a vision of the present political order as a denial of God's future, inimical to godly life – the final sclerotic hardening of hearts before God breaks in. In the former, witness to and anticipation of God's future is found not just among the coterie of believers, but (at least in part) in the large-scale social and political order of their world. In the latter, this witness is found among martyrs, flickers of protest and resistance who witness not by building something secure and lasting, a solid and visible foretaste of the kingdom, but by refusing to make calculations of efficacy and practicality, and allowing themselves to be conquered rather than worshipping the beast.

That Christianity can give rise to both Romans 13 and Revelation 13 – and to the broader tensions in eschatological thinking that they represent – calls into question any easy answer, whether it be wholesale affirmation of the present social order, or wholesale rejection. It questions grand gestures of either acceptance or denial, and instead calls believers to *discernment*: to careful attention to the present against the backdrop of the future. There is no substitute for looking, interpreting, assessing and risking fallible political judgements, no shortcut to purity and moral safety. Christians can only look at the world and ask where it is open to God's future and where closed – and then look again, and again, and again.

A Christian might ask, for instance whether the political regime under which she lives allows that differences between individuals and groups could be not insuperable problems but *gifts*, contributions to a common good that no group can imagine or construct on its own. That kind of eschatological vision obviously stands against various forms of exclusion, in which difference is simply understood as deviance or failure. It also obviously stands against various forms of violence in which one individual or group would seek to deny another a voice, or would seek wholly to define what the other may and may not say. It also stands, however, against the kind of laissez-faire tolerance that lets different groups flourish in their own enclaves, and provides no spaces within which the mutual interaction and cross-fertilization of those groups becomes possible. This kind of eschatological vision might push her towards seeing society as an ongoing conversation, not simply a collection of individual voices.[23] Where in the present can she see such conversation emerging? What are the forces that undermine it? What may she affirm, and what must she deny?

By such questions, eschatological thinking tips believers into politics, forcing them to take responsibility for the present shape of their world.

Exercise

Can you think of any aspects of your present political context that call for a Revelation 13 response rather than a Romans 13 response? If so, why? What aspect of a positive Christian theological vision is being denied or undermined?

Key points

- The application of eschatological imagination to present social and political realities requires discernment.
- Eschatological imagination provides important questions to ask of present social and political realities, rather than easy answers.

The four last things

In many traditional discussions, eschatology is broken down into four topics – the 'four last things', death, judgement, heaven and hell.[24] The focus in such discussions tends to be on eschatology as it affects the individual, rather than the more corporate vision that I have just been discussing.

Death

Death can be thought of in several different ways in relation to eschatology. First, the fact that I will die means that I am not granted unlimited time, and so not granted unlimited opportunity to mould my impact on the world, or unlimited chances to reshape who I am. My acts now have weight. In this sense, I already experience something of this dying during my lifetime: the death of others, and the metaphorical death of relationships, the movement of people beyond the places and times in which I can interact with them, re-inforces the sense that I only get one go at life, and can't waste what oppor-tunities I am given. Words spoken in haste cannot be taken back, lost friends cannot be confessed to. Death can be seen simply as finitude writ large: it is a final turn of the screw on one aspect of what it is to be a creature.

Second, the fact that I will die, and die before very long at that, means that the eschatological horizon is not, for me personally, a distant vista that simply decorates the far, far limits of my vision. In combination with the other 'last things', the fact of death has been taken in Christian theology to mean that the future that God has for the world is a future that stands close to each one of us. Life is short, and then the end comes.

Third, however, death is seen in Christianity as a path that has been taken before us, and therefore as a path that can be followed without fear, because someone familiar is waiting for us. And that brings us to the second of the 'four last things'.

Judgement

Christians have traditionally claimed that the beginning of the future that God has for the world can be pictured as an act of divine judgement. I have explained already in my discussion of Psalm 139 the idea that, however ob-scure and confused the world seems to us, Christians believe that the truth of things is clear to God. God is the one who sees all distortions, delusions and dishonesty for what they are, and who recognizes and traces back all the dis-torted scripts that we follow in our supposed freedom. But God is also the one who sees what this obscure and confused mess can become, how it already contains hints and suggestions of the future that God has for the world. In the language of earlier chapters, God sees what it is about each person, each community, that could become a unique contribution to the life of the body of Christ. Christians have imagined God's judgement as just such a two-fold making clear: the exposure of all that distorts and betrays the life that God has for the world, and the uncovering and drawing out of all that, however partially, already hints at it or embodies it.

When I said, a moment ago, that 'My acts now have weight', this expected judgement was the context: I will soon die and (so Christians have tradition-ally claimed) face this twofold judgement upon all that I am, all that I have, all that I have done. The horizon towards which I am oriented in the present is a horizon of judgement – the combined promise and threat that all things will be made clear: all victims remembered, all unsung heroes sung, all things done in darkness brought to light, all pretence blown away.

It is important, however, not to get the tenor of this claim wrong. It can be easy to forget that the judge in question is the God of Jesus Christ, the God who is love, and that this judgement is traditionally pictured as judgement at the hands of Jesus himself. The source and context for this judgement is therefore God's unfailing, invincible, unfathomable love for the one judged. The condemnation of all in a person that resists or denies Christ is seen not as the bringing of that person up against a purely external standard, but a freeing of that person to be truly himself or herself: the freeing of that person to become the gift that he or she is. 'Judgement', in this view, is nothing other than a final welcome into the life of God, which is a welcome *home*. To put it another way, if a horizon of eschatological judgement looms over my world, it is not the surveillance of some impersonal thought-police, checking my conduct against an abstract rulebook; it is a horizon beyond which stands my true self, which is my self in Christ.

Hell

This is the name that Christians have given to the future that God has for all that distorts and betrays God's life. Traditionally, hell has been seen as a place of eternal punishment, of torment for those who have set themselves deliberately against the life of God. It is perhaps becoming more common now for it to be seen as a matter of annihilation or destruction – the end of all that contradicts and distorts the life of creation, necessary if that creation is to be fulfilled. *If* this is all that one means by 'hell' (and I don't claim to have established that it should be) then it is simply a consequence of what I have said about heaven. To speak of creation freed from all that constricts and distorts it is to think of creation with the constrictions and distortions identified, exposed and consigned to destruction: it is to think of those constrictions and distortions judged and consigned to the wastebasket. Some such destruction is an inherent part of the picture I have been painting, and any Christian hope for the future of what is true, real and free in their own lives and the life of the world around them automatically brings with it a desire for the stripping away of all that is false, fake and constricting.[25]

Heaven

This is the name that Christians have given to the fulfilment or completion of all that now points to or participates in God's life – all, as it were, that meets with the positive judgement of God. The kingdom of heaven is the realm of creation freed fully and finally to be itself, and so to share without impediment in the life of God.

It should not, if it is to be consonant with the kind of theology we have been exploring, be thought of as involving being whisked off to another world: it is the fulfilment of *this* world. It should not be thought of as the abandonment of creatureliness: it is the fulfilment *of* creaturely life. It should not be thought of as the end of bodily life: it is the fulfilment *of* bodily life. It is that end for which God created the world.

Souls and bodies

Traditional Christian theology evolved quite an elaborate scheme for talking about the eschatological place of bodies. It was claimed that, on death, the disembodied soul went immediately to the place that God's judgement assigned to it, but that this soul had only a partial existence; only with the resurrection of the body and the reuniting of body and soul would judgement be complete, and the full experience of salvation or damnation be possible.[26]

Although this scheme both seems to be overly speculative, and to rely upon a metaphysics of body and soul that many will find off-putting, it does point to two aspects of Christian hope. That hope is for a resurrection of each person to full, bodily life – the only life that can be imagined for creatures like us. And yet that hope is not dented or distracted by the dissolution of bodies in the grave (or the crematorium). Christians who hold to a belief in bodily resurrection have to believe that in some sense the strings of their bodily identity are held by God until they are reconstituted at the resurrection. If one is prepared to give the name 'soul' to what I have just called 'the strings of ... bodily identity', then this is not that far from the traditional picture.[27]

Many ways of picturing or imagining heaven are deeply off-putting, and one of the main reasons for this is their tendency to deny the creatureliness of the citizens of this kingdom: denying that they are finite, that they are temporal, and so on. Some of the richer imaginings of heaven in the Christian tradition, however, celebrate this – and see heaven not as a static and all-but-disembodied state, but as a journey together ever deeper into the still-ungraspable reality of God, albeit a journey not cumbered with the constrictions and distortions that now hold it back.

Nevertheless, inadequate though it may be, imagination is all that believers have. Christians believe they have been shown something of what is true, real and free in their own lives and the life of the world around them. They believe that they have been shown that those things do have a future. But all Christian imaginings of heaven are simply an attempt to place those dimly grasped hints and suggestions into a story or a picture of their own invention, which they can grasp, but which cannot do more than gesture in the direction of the unimaginable fulfilment of Christian hope. They are like attempts to draw a map of a far country based simply on the glimpses one has of its peaks on the distant horizon of one's own land. And what they dramatize, above all, is the sense pervasive in Christianity that believers' lives, and the life of the whole world, have to do with God – that God not only upholds them but sees them, guides them, judges them, and has a future for them. All in life that participates in the Christlike life of God, all that witnesses to Christ, has a future; everything else – all that constricts and distorts and drags down that life – does not. And it is to those distorting, constricting realities, and to their lack of future, that we now turn: to evil (Chapter 10) and to sin (Chapter 11).

Imagining Heaven

'When humanity has laid aside everything that is of the earth and noiseless and silent, it joins the sound of its own strings and the loudness of its drums in the heavenly choirs. ... A combination of angels and humans ... will produce that sweet sound of thanksgiving through their meeting with one another. And through one another and with one another they will sing a song of thanksgiving to God for his love for humanity which will be heard throughout the universe.'

Gregory of Nyssa, *Treatise on the Inscriptions of the Psalms*[28]

'It is as hard to explain how this sunlit land was different from the old Narnia as it would be to tell you how the fruits of that country taste. Perhaps you will get some idea of it if you think like this. You may have been in a room in which there was a window that looked out on a lovely bay of the sea or a green valley that wound away among mountains. And in the wall of that room opposite to the window there may have been a looking-glass. And as you turned away from the window you suddenly caught sight of that sea or that valley, all over again, in the looking glass. And the sea in the mirror, or the valley in the mirror, were in one sense just the same as the real ones: yet at the same time they were somehow different – deeper, more wonderful, more like places in a story: in a story you have never heard but very much want to know. The difference between the old Narnia and the new Narnia was like that. The new one was a deeper country: every rock and flower and blade of grass looked as if it meant more. I can't describe it any better than that: if you ever get there you will know what I mean.'

C.S. Lewis, *The Last Battle*[29]

'So long as heaven is conceived as a compensation for the failures and the ills of earth, the picture of it we frame is bound to be ... painted ... in the colours of *happiness*, relief from the "miseries of this sinful world". Heaven, we say, will be a state of bliss; and everyone will think of it in terms of those experiences of his own earthly life which have come nearest to giving him complete satisfaction. Such pictures, of course, will vary indefinitely: they may take their key from moments of rest, of activity, of thought, of contemplation; but always we shall be constructing for ourselves our own heaven. ... And so long as we are – no doubt unconsciously – prescribing to God the kind of heaven he must provide for us if we are to welcome the prospect of it, we are betraying our unfitness for the only possible heaven, which is a life of which God and not ourselves will be the centre.'

John Burnaby, *The Belief of Christendom*[30]

Key points

- All people face death, and so eschatology is of direct and imminent relevance to everyone.
- Christian theology pictures what follows death as a judgement – but a judgement at the hands of Christ.

- All that constricts and restricts God's life, and so prevents creatures from being themselves, is destined for destruction.
- 'Heaven' is the name Christian theology gives to the future God has for all that participates in God's life.

Going further

1 The connections between eschatology and politics are complex ones. Alongside the more historical works cited in note 17, it is worth exploring the connections in contemporary politics. A good place to start is Michael Northcott's controversial book, *An Angel Directs the Storm: Apocalyptic Religion and American Empire*, new edition (London: SCM Press, 2007).
2 In this chapter, I have dealt with hell rather sketchily. There has been, in recent years, a vigorous debate among evangelical theologians about the reality of hell. See Christopher Morgan and Robert Peterson (eds), *Hell Under Fire: Modern Scholarship Reinvents Eternal Punishment* (Grand Rapids, MI: Zondervan, 2004) and John Walvoord, Zachary Hayes, Clark Pinnock, *Four Views on Hell*, Counterpoints Series (Grand Rapids, MI: Zondervan, 1997). For more historical reflections, see Alan Bernstein, *The Formation of Hell: Death and Retribution in the Ancient and Early Christian Worlds* (Ithaca, NY: Cornell University Press, 1993); Philip Almond, *Heaven and Hell in Enlightenment England* (Cambridge: Cambridge University Press, 1994); and Geoffrey Rowell, *Hell and the Victorians* (Oxford: Oxford University Press, 1974).
3 I have discussed hell and heaven – but not purgatory, which in some branches of Christianity is believed to be a state that those who are being saved pass through, in order to be purified, on their way to heaven. For a fascinating account of the emergence of the doctrine of purgatory, see Jacques le Goff, *The Birth of Purgatory*, tr. Arthur Goldhammer (Chicago: University of Chicago Press, 1984 [French original, 1981]).

Notes

1 'End times' brought up 857,000 hits on Google on 30 April 2007, for instance.

2 The description of some history writing as adopting 'that one damn thing after another approach' has been attributed to the English historian Arnold Toynbee and to Winston Churchill. The American writer Elbert Hubbard said 'Life is just one damned thing after another' in *The Philistine: A Periodical of Protest* (December, 1909), p. 32; the American poet Edna St. Vincent Millay wrote in a letter of 24 October 1930: 'It's not true that life is one damn thing after another – it's one damned thing over and over.' In *Letters of Edna St. Vincent Millay*, ed. Allen R. MacDougall (London: Greenwood Press, 1973).

3 See Nicholas Lash, *A Matter of Hope: A Theologian's Reflections on the Thought of Karl Marx* (Notre Dame: University of Notre Dame Press, 1982), especially ch. 18.

4 See the whole of Mark 13.

5 This idea provided the title and one of the key themes of a recent book: David Fergusson and Marcel Sarot (eds), *The Future as God's Gift: Explorations in Christian Eschatology* (London: Continuum, 2000).

6 The German theologian Wolfhart Pannenberg speaks of 'the prolepsis of the *eschaton* ... the end of everything that happens' as 'having already happened in Jesus' in *Jesus – God and Man*, 2nd edn, tr. Lewis Wilkins and Duane Priebe (Philadelphia: Westminster, 1977 [from 5th German edn 1976]), p. 157.

7 To call it 'second advent' would lead to confusion with 'the second coming'. 'Intermediate' is clumsy, but will have to do.

8 Maximus the Confessor, *Ambigua* in *Patrologia Graeca* 91 (Halle, 1857), 1281A, translated by Brian Daley in his translation of Hans Urs von Balthasar's *Cosmic Liturgy: The Universe according to Maximus the Confessor* (San Francisco: Ignatius, 2003 [German original, 3rd edn, 1988]), p. 358.

9 For an attempt to speak about the perfection of Christian corporate life in the eschaton, see Miroslav Volf, 'The Final Reconciliation: Reflections on a Social Dimension of the Eschatological Transition', *Modern Theology* 16 (2000), pp. 91–113, reprinted in James Buckley and L. Gregory Jones (eds), *Theology and Eschatology at the Turn of the Millennium* (Oxford: Blackwell, 2001), pp. 89–111.

10 This wording is from the English Language Liturgical Commission's 1988 text; it is available online at http://www.englishtexts.org/survey.html#thenicenecreed.

11 If you go to an Anglican church that uses the Book of Common Prayer, you may find you have a copy that includes a table for calculating the date of Easter until the year AD 8500 (see, for instance, the facsimile copy at the Internet Archive, http://ia331311.us.archive.org/1/items/bookofcommonprayoochuriala/bookofcommon prayoochuriala.pdf, p. 28). Does this suggest a triumph of anal retentiveness over eschatological imagination?

12 Hans Frei, *The Identity of Jesus Christ: The Hermeneutical Bases of Dogmatic Theology* (Philadelphia: Fortress, 1975), p. 164.

13 Bernard of Clairvaux, 'Sermo 5: De medio adventu, et triplici innovatione' *In Adventu Domini*, in *Patrologia Latina* 183 (Paris, 1854), 50D–51D; this translation available online at The Crossroads Initiative, http://www.crossroadsinitiative.com/library_ article/321/Three_Comings_of_the_Lord__St._Bernard.html.

14 But see A. Joseph Everson, 'The Days of Yahweh', *Journal of Biblical Literature* 93.3 (1974), pp. 329–37: 'the Day of Yahweh was not viewed in the pre-exilic and exilic eras of Israel's history as a singular, universal, or exclusively future event of world judgement. Rather, the Day of Yahweh was a powerful concept available to the prophets for their use in interpreting various momentous events – past, future or imminent', even though 'In the late post-exilic era the portrayals of the Day of Yahweh tend to become more and more cataclysmic and universal in character under the influence of apocalyptic thought' (pp. 335–6).

15 This, or something like it, is the pervasive traditional view. See, for instance, Heinrich Heppe's summary of Reformed orthodoxy on this point: 'Christ will one day retun to earth in a real, visible and local manner'; he also cites Amandus Polanus, *Syntagma Theologiae Christianae* (Hanover, 1625), 6.65: 'This arrival of Christ will be true, visible and local, not phantastic or imaginary or invisible or placeless.' In Heppe, *Reformed Dogmatics*, tr. G. T. Thomson (London: Allen and Unwin, 1950 [German original 1861]), p. 696.

16 See Rudolf Bultmann, *History and Eschatology: The Presence of Eternity. The Gifford Lectures 1955* (Edinburgh: The University Press, 1957).

17 For the relationship between eschatological beliefs and social or political activism (a relationship which has many more varieties and possibilities than I have suggested), see Norman Cohn, *The Pursuit of the Millennium: Revolutionary Millenarians and Mystical Anarchists of the Middle Ages*, revised edn (Oxford: Oxford University Press, 1975); Theodore Olson, *Millennialism, Utopianism, and Progress* (Toronto: University of Toronto Press, 1982); for the dangers of quietism, specifically, see Robert Anderson,

Vision of the Disinherited: The Making of American Pentecostalism (New York: Oxford University Press, 1979), p. 129.

18 1 Corinthians 13.12, King James Version.

19 For more on reconciliation, see John de Gruchy, *Reconciliation: Restoring Justice* (London: SCM Press, 2002).

20 I give a detailed example of this spiral of changing practice and understanding in Chapter 16, pp. 396–7.

21 To see the kind of use that has been made of this passage in political theology, follow up the page references provided in the Scripture index to Oliver O'Donovan and Joan Lockwood O'Donovan (eds), *From Irenaeus to Grotius: A Sourcebook in Christian Political Thought* (Grand Rapids, MI: Eerdmans, 1999), p. 836; see also several of the texts in Andrew Bradstock and Christopher Rowland (eds), *Radical Christian Writings: A Reader* (Oxford: Blackwell, 2002): John Milton, *The Tenure of Kings and Magistrates* (1649), pp. 115–19; James Nayler, *Behold You Rulers* (1658), pp. 148–61; *The Kairos Document* (1985), pp. 286–304; see also the pages cited under 'Romans 13.1–8' in the index of Harro Höpfl, *Luther and Calvin on Secular Authority*, Cambridge Texts in the History of Political Thought (Cambridge: Cambridge University Press, 1991), p. 94.

22 See Christopher Rowland, 'Unmasking Ideology', *The Bible in TransMission*, Autumn 2003; available online at the Bible Society, http://www.biblesociety.org.uk/exploratory/articles/rowland03.pdf; see also Judith Kovacs and Christopher Rowland, *Revelation*, Blackwell Bible Commentaries (Oxford: Blackwell, 2004), pp. 147–59.

23 To pursue some of these ideas further, see the discussion surrounding Jeffrey Stout's book, *Democracy and Tradition* (Princeton: Princeton University Press, 2003). See David Fergusson, 'Beyond Theologies of Resentment: An Appreciation of Jeffrey Stout's Democracy and Tradition', Chad Pecknold's 'Democracy and the Politics of the Word: Stout and Hauerwas on Democracy and Scripture', and Jeffrey Stout, 'Survivors of the Nations: a Response to Fergusson and Pecknold', *Scottish Journal of Theology* 59.2 (2006), pp. 183–234.

24 See, for example, 'Formulas of Catholic Doctrine' in the *Compendium of the Catechism of the Catholic Church* (Vatican: Libreria Editrice Vaticana, 2005); available online at http://www.vatican.va/archive/compendium_ccc/documents/archive_2005_compendium-ccc_en.html. For theological and devotional reflections based around the four last things, see Thomas More, *The Four Last Things* (1522), available online at the Center for Thomas More Studies, http://www.thomasmorestudies.org/library_1.html.

25 I am not at this point going to discuss the question of whether under this heading 'all that contradicts and distorts the life of creation' one will find any *people*, according to Christian theology – i.e. the question about who, if anyone, will 'go to hell'. That's a topic that can wait until Chapter 11, where I will have more to say about other aspects of this topic as well.

26 For a Protestant version, see Heppe, *Reformed Dogmatics*, ch. 28, §§3–6, pp. 695–7; for a Catholic version, see the *Catechism of the Catholic Church* (Vatican: Libreria Editrice Vaticana, 1993), Part I, Section 2, Ch. 3, Article 11, ¶997: 'In death, the separation of the soul from the body, the human body decays and the soul goes to meet God, while awaiting its reunion with its glorified body. God, in his almighty power, will definitively grant incorruptible life to our bodies by reuniting them with our souls, through the power of Jesus' Resurrection.' Available online at the Vatican Archive, http://www.vatican.va/archive/catechism/p123a11.htm.

27 Aquinas's definition of 'soul' as the 'form' of the body lies in the background here. See, for a brief introductory analysis, Joseph M. Magee's discussion of 'Body and Soul' at the Thomistic Philosophy website: http://www.aquinasonline.com/Topics/soul.html.

28 Gregory of Nyssa, *Treatise on the Inscriptions of the Psalms*, tr. R. Heine, (Oxford:

Clarendon Press, 1995), pp. 120–1. I am grateful to my colleague Morwenna Ludlow for directing me to this quote.

29 C. S. Lewis, *The Last Battle* (London: Lions, 1980 [first edn, 1956]), p. 160 (ch. 15).

30 John Burnaby, *The Belief of Christendom: A Commentary on the Nicene Creed* (London: SPCK, 1963), p. 194.

10

Suffering and Love

In Part 2 of the book, I have been examining ways in which Christians can make sense of the world and of their own lives within it if they believe that God is, by God's threefold economy, drawing all things into participation in God's own life. Chapters 7, 8 and 9 sketched the overarching framework for such an understanding, describing the world as coming from, being held in and moving towards the life of God. The present chapter and Chapter 11 take a somewhat different approach to the same subject matter, and look at all in the world (and in Christians' lives) that stands against God's life, and how God responds to it.

In this chapter I am going to explore the challenge to Christian claims about God posed by the existence and prevalence of suffering in the world. I will argue that seeking an answer to this challenge consistent with the kind of theology I have been exploring requires a re-examination of what it means for Christians to talk about God's love and power, and what it means for them to live in response to them.

I am going to

- explain the standard form taken by the challenge to Christian faith posed by suffering;
- examine a range of standard answers to the challenge;
- look at some of the criticisms that have been levelled against those standard answers; and
- set out an answer to the challenge consistent with the theology explored so far in this book.

Preparation

- The most common reason that people give if asked why they don't believe in God is that they cannot see how God could allow all the suffering and misery that there is in the world. See now if you can do two things as preparation for this chapter. First, try jotting down for yourself as clearly as possible the nature of the problem. Why might the existence of suffering and misery count against Christian claims about the existence and nature of God? Second, jot down some notes on the kinds of response you think Christian theology might be able to give to this problem.
- Rather than looking on the web for discussions of the 'problem of evil', it might be better preparation for this chapter to remind yourself of some of the real evils – the real examples of suffering – that prompt the question we will be exploring. Wikipedia is a useful resource here, and you could try the following pages: Holocaust; Beslan school hostage crisis; 2004 Indian Ocean earthquake; 1755 Lisbon Earthquake.[1]

Additional reading

As an accompaniment to this chapter, I recommend:

- D. Z. Phillips, *The Problem of Evil and the Problem of God* (London: SCM Press, 2004). A clear, angry and incisive critique of many responses to the problem of evil, from an astute philosopher of religion.
- Kenneth Surin, *Theology and the Problem of Evil* (Oxford: Blackwell, 1986). Another serious critique of many theological answers to the problem of evil.
- N. T. Wright, *Evil and the Justice of God* (London: SPCK, 2006). A New Testament scholar provides an accessible exploration of relevant biblical resources.

Suffering

Most students of theology in the first half of the nineteenth century would at some point have found themselves with William Paley's 1802 *Natural Theology* in their hands, reading an account of how the natural world in all its parts demonstrated the existence of a benevolent God:

> In every nature, and in every portion of nature, which we can descry, we find attention bestowed upon even the minutest parts. The hinges in the wings of an *earwig*, and the joints of its antennae, are as highly wrought, as if the Creator had nothing else to finish. We see no signs of diminution of care by multiplicity of objects, or of distraction of thought by variety. We have no reason to fear, therefore, our being forgotten, or overlooked, or neglected.[2]

This marvellous world, so carefully and lovingly designed and built, does admittedly contain some suffering – some 'privation' and 'disappointment' – but if we see this from a religious perspective we will admit that even these are well-designed contrivances, 'not without the most salutary tendencies',[3] and that

> Health and sickness, enjoyment and suffering, riches and poverty, knowledge and ignorance, power and subjection, liberty and bondage, civilisation and barbarity, have all their offices and duties, all serve for the *formation* of character.[4]

After all,

> Of all views under which human life has ever been considered, the most reasonable, in my judgement, is that which regards it as a state of *probation*. ... It is not a state of unmixed happiness, or of happiness simply; it is not a state of designed misery, or of misery simply; it is not a state of retribution; it is not a state of punishment. ... It accords much better with the idea of its being a condition calculated for the production, exercise, and improvement of moral qualities.[5]

The world was, according to Paley, the work of a creator whose intentions were transparently good, and whose power and ability were unlimited; and none of the vicissitudes of life or nature did anything but confirm his existence, power and benevolence.

It is perhaps an understatement to say that not everyone has been convinced by visions like Paley's, and specifically by the ease with which visions like his take human suffering and the suffering of the natural world to be fitting pieces of a beautiful jigsaw. One representative of the dissatisfaction felt by many was a nineteenth-century gentleman who had read and enjoyed Paley's books while a theology student at University. He was a keen amateur naturalist, and instead of heading from his theological studies into a position in the church, as he and his family had intended, he found himself embarking on an impromptu career as an explorer, geologist, botanist and zoologist. Yet, fascinated and delighted though he was by the variety and intricacy of the natural world, he found that the more he saw of it the more it appeared to him as a world of 'cruelty ... incalculable waste ... death, famine, rapine'.[6] The number of species that had gone their way to extinction, the fierce and bloody competition of those that survived, the ever-presence of predators and parasites – how could these be the elements of a well-ordered and harmonious whole? The poet Tennyson was to put some of these same doubts into words in 1850. We have, he said, trusted 'that somehow good / Will be the final goal of ill ... That nothing walks with aimless feet'; we have trusted that 'God was love indeed / And love Creation's final law', but 'Nature, red in tooth and claw / With ravine, shriek'd against [t]his creed.'[7]

All this, however, was not what finally caused our theology student turned naturalist to break decisively with Paley's creed. After all, in the same notes in which he wrote about the cruelty and incalculable waste of nature, he could still argue that 'from ... the concealed war of nature ... the highest good which we can conceive, the creation of the higher animals, has directly come'. That so much waste and loss has eventually produced such creatures as ourselves should, he said, 'exalt our notion of the power of the omniscient Creator'.[8]

No; the decisive blow against Paley's vision fell some years later, in 1851, when after a short but distressing illness, and even more distressing attempts at treatment, the naturalist's ten-year-old daughter died at a sanatorium in Malvern. Her name was Annie. It was a very ordinary tragedy, and the ripples of loss and grief spread no further than they normally do, and dissipated just as quickly as they normally do, leaving lasting pain only for her family. But for her father the event crushed what remained of his Christian faith. The death of his beloved daughter finally made real and personal for him the blank, impartial cruelty of nature that his botanical and zoological researches had uncovered.[9] What finally made a benevolent deity impossible for him to believe was not some overview of suffering's quantity, pervasiveness or persistence in the natural world, nor his glimpses of similar suffering in humanity at large, but a close-up of one dying child who for him was of inestimable value. The man's name was Charles Darwin, and the reasons for his loss of faith – both his general acknowledgement of the preponderance of suffering in the world at large, and the personal loss that drove that acknowledgement into his heart – are what we call 'the problem of evil'.

Annie

'[L]ooking back, always the spirit of joyousness rises before me as her emblem and characteristic: she seemed formed to live a life of happiness. ... We have lost the joy of the Household, and the solace of our old age:– she must have known how we loved her; oh that she could know how deeply, how tenderly we do still & shall ever love her dear joyous face.'

Charles Darwin, 'The death of Anne Elizabeth Darwin'[10]

Key points

- The phrase 'the problem of evil' can refer to the sheer quantity, pervasiveness and persistence of suffering in the world.
- The phrase 'the problem of evil' can also refer to the intensity of the suffering undergone by particular individuals in specific circumstances.

The problem of evil

When theologians and philosophers of religion refer to 'the problem of evil' they often have in mind not the challenge to faith that erupts from direct involvement in suffering, but the intellectual difficulty posed by the bare fact of suffering's widespread existence. How is it possible to sustain belief in a good God, they ask, when we can all see in front of us a world marred by pervasive and persistent suffering? This is the kind of problem that did not trouble Paley, and that Darwin at first found himself able to overcome; it found its most famous formulation in the work of the Scottish philosopher David Hume:

> Is [God] willing to prevent evil, but not able? then is he impotent. Is he able, but not willing? then is he malevolent. Is he both able and willing? whence then is evil?[11]

More recently, the argument has been spelt out somewhat differently – as the apparent mutual incompatibility of the following four claims:

1 Evil exists;
2 God is good;
3 God is omnipotent;
4 A good being will always eliminate evil as far as it is able.[12]

Exercise

Pause for a moment at this point and, before reading about various proposed solutions to this problem, make sure you see the force of this argument against the existence of a good and all-powerful God. Can you think of any responses to it? Do you think it captures Darwin's eventual reason for losing his faith?

The philosophers and theologians who discuss this problem often distinguish between two kinds of evil: moral and natural. For instance, the *Internet Encyclopedia of Philosophy*, in one of its articles on the problem of evil, provides the following definitions:

> **Moral evil**. This is evil that results from the misuse of free will on the part of some moral agent in such a way that the agent thereby becomes morally blameworthy for the resultant evil. Moral evil therefore includes specific acts of intentional wrongdoing such as lying and murdering, as well as defects in character such as dishonesty and greed.
> **Natural evil**. In contrast to moral evil, natural evil is evil that results from the operation of natural processes, in which case no human being can be held morally accountable for the resultant evil. Classic examples of natural evil are natural disasters such as cyclones and earthquakes that result in enormous suffering and loss of life, illnesses such as leukaemia and Alzheimer's, and disabilities such as blindness and deafness.[13]

The example most frequently cited when discussing *moral* evil – an example that is used to show up the glibness or inadequacy of at least some attempts to provide a resolution to the problem of evil – is the Holocaust: the calculated debasement, torture and murder of six million Jews, millions of Poles and Serbs, half a million Bosniaks, hundreds of thousands of Roma and people with disabilities, tens of thousands of homosexuals, and many thousands more by the Nazi regime in Germany.

For *natural* evil, there is no single example that provides the same intensity of focus, but older discussions often cite the 1755 Lisbon earthquake, which killed between 60,000 and 100,000 people and shook the confidence of Enlightenment Europe, and more recent discussions often cite the 2004 Indian Ocean tsunami, in which a quarter of a million people died.

All is well?

'Come, ye philosophers, who cry, "All's well",
And contemplate this ruin of a world.
Behold these shreds and cinders of your race,
This child and mother heaped in common wreck,
These scattered limbs beneath the marble shafts –
A hundred thousand whom the earth devours,
Who, torn and bloody, palpitating yet,
Entombed beneath their hospitable roofs,
In racking torment end their stricken lives.
To those expiring murmurs of distress,
To that appalling spectacle of woe,
Will ye reply: "You do but illustrate
The iron laws that chain the will of God"?'

Voltaire, *Poem on the Lisbon Disaster – or, an examination of the axiom, 'All is well'* [14]

Key points

- Many believe that the existence and prevalence of evil in the world contradicts the claim that the world is in the hands of a benevolent God.
- Moral evil is that evil that flows from human misdeeds.
- Natural evil is that evil that flows from natural processes.

The standard conversation

'Theodicy' is the name given to the attempts made by theologians and philosophers of religion to justify continued belief in a good God despite the existence of all the suffering that results from such moral and natural evil. More bluntly translated, theodicy is the 'justification of God' – the attempt to argue that God deserves to be called good despite all the evil that exists in God's world.

Over the years there has been no shortage of attempts to provide a theodicy, and the arguments come in many flavours. The most prevalent theodicies, however, tend to have the same basic structure: they claim, as did Paley, that there is some greater good that God could only achieve by creating a world in which moral and natural evil is possible or unavoidable. The evil is there, and it is genuinely evil in itself, but (so the argument goes) it is there *for a reason*, and if and when that reason is fully known, we will accept that God was *justified* in allowing it. We will accept that evil's existence and prevalence is consistent with God's perfect goodness.

There are two versions of this kind of 'greater good' argument that are by far the most prevalent. The first is the 'free will defence', which says that the greater good desired by God is the existence of beings capable of free response to God and to one another in love. This freedom that God desires for us, however, is precisely the same freedom that allows us to *refuse* love, and to turn to various forms of hatred and harm. God could not have preserved us from all such harm, so the argument goes, without depriving us of freedom, and depriving creation of its good goal.[15]

The second defence, which sometimes goes by the name 'soul-making theodicy', is related. It argues (in a similar vein to Paley) that personal suffering is a necessary part of the process by which we learn to become fully moral persons. The argument is not now that by making us the kind of beings capable of free response, God has also made suffering possible, but the other way around: God has permitted us to suffer, because it is the endurance of such suffering that allows us to become beings capable of free and loving response to one another and to God. This world is a 'vale of soul-making' – a place of preparation for a future with God.[16]

There are also two further versions of this kind of 'greater good' argument that, though rather less common now than the free-will and soul-making defences, have been prominent at other times. On the one hand there is what one might call the 'aesthetic defence', which says that God's desire is for us to recognize and delight in what is good, but that such recognition and delight is only possible if we have something with which to contrast the good: only if we can compare the good with, and prefer it to, suffering and evil can we truly delight in it.

The Mosaic

An example of the aesthetic defence can be found in Jill Paton Walsh's novel, *Knowledge of Angels*, when the monk Beneditx takes the sceptic Palinor to see a mosaic portraying the beauty of heaven. 'Do you see that even to make such a scene of brightness as this, the master artificer needed tessarae of dark glass as well as of bright glass? ... dullness is in the service of light here; dark pieces are in the service of the whole.' Palinor's response is typical of responses to such theodicies: 'No glass is dark enough to stand for the suffering of a tortured and dying child.'[17]

On the other hand there are what one might call 'secret plan' defences that, instead of proposing a large-scale and general description of how evil is connected to a 'greater good', suggest that God allows each specific evil as a particular inscrutable step of an unimaginably complex plan, the end point of which is the great good of salvation. So the eleventh-century theologian Abelard says

> Who could be unaware that God's highest goodness, which permits nothing to happen without a cause, arranges even evil things so well, and also uses them in the best way, so that it is true that it is good that these evil things happen, although the evil itself is in no way good?[18]

Abelard's prime example is the evil of Judas' betrayal of Jesus: an evil act, which caused great harm – but which God arranged for good.

I have run through these descriptions pretty quickly, and have not paused to unpack any of the nuances or complexities that their defenders and critics have explored.[19] This is simply a sketch of what seems to me to be the 'standard conversation' about the problem of evil. It is a conversation that involves giving general answers to a general question: it does not rely upon detailed reference to the stories of particular evils (except as illustrative examples); it does not rely upon detailed reference to the Christian gospel. Faced with an argument that appears to disprove the existence of a good, omnipotent being by reference to the simple facts of evil's existence, persistence and prevalence, these defences show that the two sides of this abstract equation can in fact be reconciled – answering the challenge in the same generalized terms in which it was posed. But is that enough?

Exercise

Pause again, and ask yourself the following questions. Which, if any, of these responses from the standard conversation do you find most convincing, and which least? Why?

Key points

- Standard theodicies argue that God allows evil for the sake of some greater good.
- Some argue that the greater good in question is the existence of human freedom.
- Some argue that it is the formation of human moral agents.
- Some argue that it is the possibility of recognizing goodness *as* good.
- Some argue that evil plays unknown roles in God's inscrutable plan for the world's good.

Changing the subject

This 'standard conversation' – the whole tradition of 'greater good' theodicy, working at a fairly abstract level – has come in for a good deal of serious criticism. Sometimes the criticisms have come from people who want to reform and improve the defences, and tie them a little more closely to the resources of the Christian gospel, or to the details of actual evils. Sometimes, and particularly in recent years, the criticisms have come from people who reject the whole project of 'theodicy'.

There is not space enough here, even if I had the skill, for me to spend time exploring all the relevant arguments and making an informed judgement about whether the standard conversation has received a knock-out blow from its opponents, or whether it can be rescued by one means or another. What I do hope to be able to do in the space available, however, is to indicate the *kind* of criticisms that have been levelled and suggest how they might lead us to 'change the subject' – to rethink what the problem of evil is, and what kind of response it calls for.

Theodicy as anaesthetic?

The first criticism focuses on the fact that standard theodicies appear, implicitly or explicitly, to be aimed at allowing believers in God to *come to terms* with evil: to find a proper place for it in their thinking. Is it possible that one effect of such theodicy is to *anaesthetize* us to evil? Do such theodicies whisper in our ear, whenever we are faced with some situation of great suffering, 'It isn't as bad as all that; don't worry – it's quite proper that this sort of thing should happen, and in any case God will make it up to the victims in the end'? Might theodicy, by reconciling the existence of a good God with the existence of evil, reconcile *us* to evil?[20]

Even if the logic of the theodicists' arguments is flawless, if those arguments lead us to make our peace with evil then they are themselves evil. For a believer to construct a theodicy would, in this case, be like standing idly beside a stream in which someone is drowning, spending the last seconds of the drowner's life working out how you can live with the tragedy and still keep your faith.

When we turn on the television to see a news report of a young girl kidnapped and subjected to hours of horrendous torture and repeated rape before being killed and dumped in a ditch, is there not something disturbing about the attempt to see how this event might be a piece in a beautiful jigsaw – or about any attempt to 'make sense' of this that might lessen one's revulsion and outrage, one's sense that this event does not belong, that it stands as an offence against all goodness, and that it *should not be*?

The thinking and arguing that one does on this as on any other topic are not isolated activities taking place in some abstract mental sphere: they are the activities of men and women living life in the world, and it is as necessary to take responsibility for the effects of this activity as it is to take responsibility for the way one drives one's car or relates to one's neighbours or invests one's money or speaks to one's relatives. If theodicy blinds one to the evil of evil, one should not indulge in it.

Who, in any case, is theodicy for? This criticism suggests that it speaks primarily to *spectators*, not to victims, and not to those who share a world with victims and are bound to them by ties of love and responsibility. If we are to 'change the subject', then, it will have to be in the direction of some conversation about the problem of evil that treats us as *participants* – and one that does not make it easier for us to bear the torments of others.

Exercise

Imagine that you are a defender of the standard conversation. How would you respond to this criticism?

Letting God off the hook

The second criticism is related, in that it too attacks these theodicies for brushing the true burden of suffering under the carpet. But rather than asking what this might do to believers, the second criticism focuses on what it says about *God*.

The easiest way in to this criticism is to turn away from the abstract fact of evil, and focus on particular evils. Think, for instance, about the painful death of Darwin's daughter Annie, or of that girl who was raped, tortured and murdered. Does it make moral sense to say that the sufferings of either of them were *justified* because of some 'greater good'? That is, can one look at the suffering and death of either as a 'price worth paying' in order to secure the existence of a greater good – say, the existence of beings capable of responding in loving freedom to God?

Almost everyone who discusses this question mentions at this point Fyodor Dostoevsky's nineteenth-century novel *The Brothers Karamazov*, in which Ivan Karamazov makes an impassioned protest against the idea that any good future could be worth the price of one abused child's suffering. Ivan tells the story of a five-year-old child who had been tortured by her parents.

They beat her, thrashed her, kicked her for no reason till her body was one bruise. Then, they went to greater refinements of cruelty – shut her up all night in the cold and frost in a privy, and ... smeared her face and filled her mouth with excrement, and it was her mother, her mother did this. And that mother could sleep, hearing the poor child's groans! Can you understand why a little creature, who can't even understand what's done to her, should beat her little aching heart with her tiny fist in the dark and the cold, and weep her meek unresentful tears to dear, kind God to protect her?

For what greater good, Ivan asks, could this possibly be a price worth paying? What greater good is

worth the tears of that one tortured child. ... If the sufferings of children go to swell the sum of sufferings which was necessary to pay for truth, then I protest that the truth is not worth such a price. ... [T]oo high a price is asked for harmony; it's beyond our means to pay so much to enter on it. And so I hasten to give back my entrance ticket, and if I am an honest man I am bound to give it back as soon as possible. And that I am doing. It's not God that I don't accept, Alyosha, only I most respectfully return him the ticket.[21]

Perhaps Ivan should not 'accept' this God, however. Surely any version of 'greater good' theodicy that simply involves God writing off Annie Darwin, or the raped and murdered girl, or the tortured child in the outhouse, in order to secure some greater good, has ceased to speak about a God worthy of worship?

What, however, if the greater good secured is not one that involves writing off the dead child? What if the greater good is one in which those children themselves will be tended and healed after death – so that it is not a matter of them being sacrificed to the greater good of others? Well, there are some conceptual difficulties about saying so, which we would need to explore if we were treating this topic in more detail. For instance, if the dead child can be taken to a 'better place' without in the end having been robbed of anything irreplaceable, why couldn't she have been taken there in the first place? Why couldn't we all? What happens to the idea that this world of suffering is *necessary* to the good that God has for us if it is possible to be hoisted out of this world and taken straight to that good? But even if we ignore such questions and accept that this consolation or healing is possible, and will constitute a greater good *for the suffering child herself*, that good stored up in the future does not make the present evil any less evil. The path that God has chosen, in this picture of things, is a path along which real evil happens, even if it is evil that is followed by consolation or healing.

One might compare this to what happens when a human being is faced with a choice between two evils and can at best choose the lesser. The lesser of two evils is still evil, and while she might be justified, in the sense that no one could properly condemn her, she does not remain *innocent*: she can't avoid becoming the person who has done this evil thing, even if she could not have done anything different.[22] Similarly, if we imagine God choosing this path that leads through evil to greater good, we are still imagining God choosing a path that leads through evil. Even if done for the sake of good, evil is still evil.

Suppose that I were faced, like Charles Darwin, with the prolonged and painful death of my own daughter. Whatever thoughts I might have about the consolation that God will have for her in future can and should do nothing to prevent what is happening now from being horrifying, from crushing my heart. Even if I were to grant everything to the theodicists' arguments, and agree that nothing about this terrible situation can tell me that God is not good, that would not prevent the situation being terrible; it would not prevent it being an abomination – something to which I can only properly react with horror. The philosopher D. Z. Phillips, drawing on a larger scale example, puts it this way:

> [W]hen evil is necessitated in terrible circumstances, the evil in the means is as objective as the good in what has to be done. … If God can allow [the Holocaust] *without a second thought*, then, like Dostoevsky's Ivan Karamazov, we respectfully return him the ticket. If he allows it *after a second thought* [i.e. giving full weight to the objectivity of the evil and taking responsibility for it], God is involved in sorrows in such a way that he cannot emerge morally unscathed.[23]

If we imagine a God who deliberately chooses the way of evil for the sake of a greater good, then we might perhaps, be able to hold on to a belief in a good God, but it will now be a God who has reluctantly been forced to do evil, a God who has in one sense lost God's innocence.

Neither I nor D. Z. Phillips is saying that this *is* the proper way to think about God's relation to the evil that happens. It is simply that this God who has lost God's innocence is all that seems to be on offer at the end of a standard 'greater good' theodicy. We might, with that approach, get to the point where we can get God off the hook, and show that God could not have done otherwise. But we will still be left with a God who is, however unavoidably, involved in evil – who has been forced to *do* evil. If we are to 'change the subject', it will have to be in the direction of some conversation about the problem of evil that does not focus on getting God off the hook or demonstrating God's freedom from blame, but rather asks what God's goodness means if it has to do with God's passionate care for and loving involvement in every aspect of the world that God has made, however dark.

Exercise

Imagine again that you are a defender of the standard conversation. How would you respond to this criticism?

Is this the God of Jesus Christ?

This brings us to the threshold of the third main criticism of the standard conversation about theodicy. What God does this theodicy speak about? It speaks about a God who is good – although we have just seen that the kind of goodness it talks about might be suspect. But it also talks about a God who is powerful, indeed who is all-powerful, omnipotent. And it is perhaps here that the standard conversation most obviously fails, in that it describes a kind of power that has little to do with the God of the Christian gospel.

You will find a discussion of omnipotence in many of the texts in which the standard conversation about the problem of evil is carried on. The authors analyse God's nature as all-powerful, often in amazingly abstract terms. God, we are told, must have the power to do anything that is not logically contradictory; God is a being of absolutely unfettered freedom, who may do whatever God chooses.[24]

This is not the God of the Christian gospel, because the understanding of power involved is one that is rejected by the gospel. The power of God that the gospel teaches us about is the power of love, and only the power of love. It is not that God is power, and has chosen love, but that God is love – and any power of God is and can only be the power of that love. We can't talk about what God can and cannot do by considering in the abstract what 'omnipotent' must mean, but can only talk about what God can and cannot do by asking what the love revealed in the gospel can and cannot do. And while, yes, we will not be being faithful to a Christian understanding of God's power unless we say that it is not constrained by anything that is *not* God, we must still say that God *is* constrained by who God is, and that God is love.

What power does God have? It is that power that is called weakness and foolishness in 1 Corinthians 1.25. More precisely, it is the power to become incarnate, and the power to die. That is, it is the power that we see clearly in Jesus of Nazareth, and most clearly on the cross – which is where, as John's Gospel tells us, God's glory is most visible. And, yes, Christianity has traditionally claimed that this power of divine love is at work in everything that happens, that it is the power that sustains, accompanies and guides the whole of creation in every moment of its existence, that it is invincible and indestructible, ever-present and ever trustworthy – but it is all those things only as the power of love.

The standard conversation sometimes seems to miss this completely. D. Z. Phillips says of one of the proponents of the standard conversation that his arguments

> suggest that God's essential nature is sheer power, but that, now and again, at rather crucial moments, he decides not to exercise it. … [T]he 'humbling' [i.e. the incarnation] seems to be a decision to do what he would not normally do. Orthodox Christian teaching, however, teaches that the 'humbling' teaches us something essential about God. That he took 'the form of a servant' is not meant to imply that normally his form is quite different. … Rather, it implies that if God wanted to reveal something essential about himself on earth, 'the form of a servant' was itself essential to doing so.[25]

If we are to 'change the subject', then, it will have to be in the direction of some conversation about the problem of evil that speaks about how a God with *this* kind of power relates to the evil in the world.

Exercise

Once again, imagine that you are a defender of the standard conversation.
How would you respond to this criticism?

Do we know what we're talking about?

There is one more criticism that I want to explore. It is levelled against the
implicit picture painted in the standard conversation of God choosing what
kind of world to create by weighing up the costs and benefits. The criticism
arises because it is not at all clear that Christians know what they are talking
about when they talk about God like that. It is a way of talking about God that
has lost its moorings in faith, and become idle and abstract speculation about
God's means and methods.

I am not trying to rule out all talk about the nature of God's creation of the
world. The claim that the world we live in depends entirely upon God's loving
will is properly a central one in Christian faith – as is the claim that this world
rests *only* upon that loving will. Christians have expressed that latter claim
by saying that God was not in any way *constrained* to create by something
external to God.

I can also see the importance of saying that the divine will that underlies
the world cannot be thought of as a selfish will. It is not to be thought of as the
will of one who stands to gain something from creation, and so it is appropriate to express this by saying that God was not constrained to create *even by
God's own nature*.

If we consider these deep-seated claims about the world's relationship to the
love of God, we will be able to see the soil in which Christian talk about God's
'free decision' to create the world is rooted. The image of God freely choosing is a graphic way of trying to grasp and express these deep convictions
that Christians have about the divine will that sustains and guides them, and
that they trust sustains and guides all things. But this remains a way of trying to capture in a graspable image a reality that is, ultimately, ungraspable.
Christians must acknowledge the inadequacy of words like freedom and constraint, internal and external, selfishness and love, decision and action, when
they are speaking about the unfathomable reality of God's life. This image
is given what content and mooring it has because it is rooted in the ways
Christians have been taught by the gospel to see themselves and their world
as faithfully and lovingly addressed and held by the God who is beyond their
words. But, even though this image may be the best way of capturing this
aspect of the Christian vision, it doesn't amount to a clear explanatory theory
that tells them that God is in fact something more-or-less like a human agent,
and that creation was in fact something more-or-less like a human action,
consequent upon something more-or-less like a human decision.

To think that one can speak meaningfully of the 'options' available to God,
to think that one can speak of God engaged in a process of 'choosing', and to

think that one can talk about this process involving God's 'weighing up' of prices that God is or is not willing to pay: that seems to me to assume that we do have just such a clear explanatory theory. It is to pull the language of God's creative freedom from its moorings and leave it bobbing about in our minds with nothing to hold on to.

It is not that I think one can say *nothing* about God's creation of this world. It is simply that I do not think one can say enough to launch a theodicy. Suppose one ran with the ideas about God's power that I sketched at the end of the last section, for instance. One could quite appropriately say that the God known in Jesus Christ cannot be thought to have the power to create a world over which God would rule as a despot – not because there is some external constraint preventing him from doing so, but because it makes no sense to say that *the God known in Jesus Christ* would do this. And one could similarly say that the only kind of creation that can be attributed to the Christian God is creation as an act of selflessness – which one might *picture* as God desiring not to be all that there is, God making space for an 'other' who is not simply an extension of God's own desires, God making something that is given its own way of being. 'Desiring', 'selflessness', 'making space' – all these are, of course, words that we know to be inadequate to the reality of God, and we know that we cannot begin to imagine the reality to which they point. Yet these claims are given some content and mooring because they are rooted in the ways Christians have been taught by the gospel to see themselves and their world as addressed and held by God. They are given *just enough* content and mooring for Christians to go on speaking like this, and to know that their words are not simply empty. God's creative work is like this – in some respects. It resembles this – in part. Those resemblances, however, stand within a much greater dissimilarity: God is *not* more-or-less the same as a very powerful human being.

So on the one hand it does seem to makes deep sense to speak of the Christian God creating a world that has its own integrity, structure and continuity – which has its own way of being that God upholds. It *is* deeply appropriate to speak of God giving time and space to creatures who can act not as the puppets of God's whims, but according to the structure, the nature, that God has given them – and who are, in that sense, made for freedom. And one might even say, when one sees that the world's freedom and one's own give rise to evil, that one cannot imagine how that could have been wholly avoided in this kind of free world.

On the other hand, I do not think that one has anywhere to stand if one tries to turn all that into an *explanation* of the origin of the world, or of the evil in it, declaring that from what we know of the choices available, God 'had' to choose this one.

If one is to 'change the subject', then, it will have to be in the direction of some conversation about the problem of evil that tries to do justice to the ways in which one's language about God is learnt, and to the faith in which it is anchored. And it will also have to be in the direction of some conversation about evil that does not rely too much upon one's ability to explain *why* God had to make this kind of world.

Exercise

One last time, imagine that you are a defender of the standard conversation. How would you respond to this criticism?

Key points

- Standard theodicies have been criticized as being sops for spectators, reconciling them to the evil in the world.
- Standard theodicies have been criticized for getting God off the hook, while leaving God compromised by unavoidable involvement in evil.
- Standard theodicies have been criticized for working with an idea of 'omnipotence' that bears little relation to the Christian gospel.
- Standard theodicies have been criticized for presuming too much upon one's ability to grasp and describe the process by which God created the world.

A different approach

God is not any kind of object that one can scrutinize and explain. One cannot have a theory of God, or an explanation of God. All one's words fail one and one's imagination falters if one tries to pin God down, not because one is not clever enough but because one is a *creature* and one's words and one's imagination are only fitted for grasping hold of creaturely realities. The creator who is one's source, sustainer and goal is beyond all understanding.

In Chapters 2 and 3 I argued that knowing God is a matter of learning to see oneself and one's world in a certain way, a matter of learning to *live* in a certain way, and of becoming in one's place and time a reflection of the love that God pours out upon the world. So, the heart of the question of theodicy is not 'How do I construct a theory that explains how God can be loving and good, and still be the creator and sustainer of a world like this?' The question is rather, 'Can I see myself as loved, see the world around me as loved, and live in echoing response to that love, in such a world as this?' Can I go on saying 'God is love' in these ways in a world of suffering and destruction?

Of course, seeing myself as loved, and seeing the world around me as loved, and living in echoing response to that love in the world, can't but involve me in *some* kind of thinking about and imagining of the one who is the source of this love, even if those thoughts and imaginings are attempts to picture the unpicturable, describe the indescribable, and so bound to be inadequate to the ungraspable reality of God. But putting it this way round shows us that my ways of thinking about and imagining God are, in a sense, secondary: they rest upon, and draw life from, my recognition of and participation in the love that God pours out upon me. If I say, for instance, that 'God is omnipotent', I won't understand what that means by trying to come up with an abstract definition and then arguing about what God must be able to do. I will discover what those words mean as I learn what it means to live with the trust that there is no situation in which God's love fails, no reality or extremity in which God's love is extinguished or finally defeated. And that is not something I am going to understand in any depth by sitting here typing at my computer, or that you are going to understand in any depth by reading this book. It is not a matter of ideas and arguments, or definitions and defences: it is a matter of living, or of *learning* to live a certain way in the world. And it is tested not primarily by checking a set of arguments for validity, or a set of definitions for accuracy; it is tested by asking whether this way of living is possible in our world without delusion, escapism and insensitivity.

If one is to speak truly about God, then, and to speak truly about God's relationship to evil, the only way one can get going is by resisting the temptation to speak about God in the abstract, and instead to attend to the ways in which one is met by God's love, called by God to love, and enabled to live the love of God in the world.

The God of the covenant

Can Christians see themselves and their world as loved by God, without turning a blind eye to the suffering and destruction that pervade the world? Well, Christian (and Jewish) talk about God's love is rooted in God's covenant with Israel. Talk of a God of loving-kindness is not a deduction made by early theologians, based upon the harmony that they saw in the world around them; it is not an explanation for the world's order and habitability, proposed by philosophers or the ancient equivalent of scientists. Talk of God's loving-kindness is not originally the province of those who saw the world around them as Paley did, as a harmonious whole unbroken by any discordant note.

Talk of the loving-kindness of God is first found on the lips of those who recognize that they have been caught up in a *covenant* with God in history. And it is very often the province of those who trust in this covenant and call upon God to honour it at times of disaster, and in exile. God's loving-kindness is spoken of most clearly when the integrity and continuity of Israel is threatened and disrupted; we could say that talk of God's loving-kindness *has its home* in such times and places: it is above all the language of those who trust that the covenant is still there, deeper than their present trials.

Among the most characteristic forms taken by talk of God's loving-kindness, therefore, we find *protest*: calls upon God to fulfil the covenant promises; calls upon God to demonstrate what the worshipper trusts is true – that slavery, disaster, exile and death cannot break God's covenant. Remember my discussion of Psalm 89 in Chapter 7, for instance. It opens 'I will sing of the Lord's great love for ever!' and runs on for 37 verses of high praise for this God who 'founded the world and all that is in it' (v.11). Yet later in the same Psalm we find the questions: 'How long, O Lord? Will you hide yourself for ever … Lord, where is your steadfast love of old, which by your faithfulness you swore to David?' (vv.46, 49).

If this is where we find language about God's loving-kindness, then there are three things we can say about the problem of evil and the project of theodicy.

1 It is simply wrongheaded to say that the existence of slavery, disaster, exile and death *contradicts* talk of God's loving-kindness. Language about God's loving-kindness does not emerge as a theory about God that might then be challenged by the arrival of suffering and disorder. It emerges as a call upon God in the midst of suffering and disorder; it is, from the beginning, part of a way of life that responds to evil, and lives in the midst of evil.

2 Equally, to think that talk of God's loving-kindness should somehow *reconcile* one to slavery, disaster, exile and death is just as wrongheaded. Talk of God's loving-kindness is in part an expression of distress and incomprehension in the face of evil. In fact, it *sharpens* the worshippers' recognition and hatred of evil: it gives her a backdrop against which to see evil *as* evil – to see it as an intrusion, an abomination, something that should not be.

3 And, finally, talk of God's loving-kindness has nothing to do with letting God off the hook, or helping God to wash God's hands of responsibility. Characteristically, talk of God's loving-kindness is an element in expressions of yearning and sometimes angry calls upon God in the midst of trials. God's people protest to God in the name of God's own promises, not because they think God answerable to *them*, but because they think God answerable to Godself: God's own promises are their court of appeal.

The God of Jesus Christ

Christian talk about God is rooted even more deeply in what God has done in Jesus of Nazareth. Saying 'God is love' is, again, not a way of proposing an abstract theory about God's nature. It is a form of words that has its home in lives shaped by the recognition that God has loved the world in the life, death and resurrection of Jesus of Nazareth. The claim that 'God is love' has its home among those who are discovering how to live in a way that will affirm and proclaim that Jesus' love for the world was not simply a passing, accidental moment in the world's history, but a word spoken for the whole world's salvation.

Just as with the talk of God's covenantal loving-kindness, talk of God's love that has its roots in encounter with Jesus is not a theory about God concocted when things were going well, which might then be tested when things go badly. The source of language about the love of God is, for Christians, a story in which violence, torture and execution, the denial and attempted destruction of love, are centre stage – and, from the start, Christians have affirmed both that the world to which Jesus came is 'his own' (John 1.11) (that is, that he belongs there, and that what he shows us is the deep truth of this world) *and* that this world crucified him. Christian talk of God's love is, from the beginning, part of a way of responding to and living in the midst of evil.

Of course, the story of Jesus is also a story of redemption and of resurrection: of God refusing to allow evil to have the last word. To go on saying 'God is love' in the face of evil is to trust in this God of redemption and resurrection, trusting in the power of love that worked in and through Jesus, rather than in some more abstract omnipotence or benevolence. But that means that the power in which Christians trust, the power to which they refer when they say 'God is love' is *not* the kind of power that steps in to prevent crucifixion.

To trust in, or hope for, *that* kind of power is to trust in a different God from the one who is known here. The power in which Christians trust when the say 'God is love' is not a power that crashes in, all guns blazing, like the saviour in a Hollywood blockbuster. It is a power that works by 'weakness and foolishness': by becoming incarnate, and by dying.

It is also a power that works by resurrection. In the words of David Bentley Hart:

> As for comfort, when we seek it, I can imagine none greater than the happy knowledge that when I see the death of a child I do not see the face of God, but the face of His enemy. It is not a faith that would necessarily satisfy Ivan Karamazov, but neither is it one that his arguments can defeat: for it has set us free from optimism, and taught us hope instead. We can rejoice that we are saved not through the immanent mechanisms of history and nature, but by grace; that God will not unite all of history's many strands in one great synthesis, but will judge much of history false and damnable; that He will not simply reveal the sublime logic of fallen nature, but will strike off the fetters in which creation languishes; and that, rather than showing us how the tears of a small girl suffering in the dark were necessary for the building of the Kingdom, He will instead raise her up and wipe away all tears from her eyes – and there shall be no more death, nor sorrow, nor crying, nor any more pain, for the former things will have passed away, and He that sits upon the throne will say, 'Behold, I make all things new.'[26]

And in the words of Rowan Williams:

> If theologians speak at this point of the significance of post-mortem existence, it is not to justify or explain suffering, but to try and imagine a context ample enough for the subject of profound injury to grow into a different kind of self-perception. Such contexts exist in our ordinary experience, in therapeutic relationships, new kinds of communal life, and the sheer unpredictable range of stimulus that might or might not effect a transformation. For those whose death cuts them off from any such possibilities, theology can only point to its fundamental belief in a God who is faithful and eternal, and say, 'if there is hope, it lies there'. If it knows its business, it will not want to go much further.[27]

Key points

- The question of theodicy can be reformulated as a question about the possibility of living a certain way in a world of suffering.
- Christian talk about God as love is not an abstract theory, but part of a lived response to a world of suffering.
- For Christian theology, God's response to evil is one that works by 'weakness and foolishness': by incarnation and by crucifixion.
- Christian theology hopes for the future with God of those who suffer.

The God of those who suffer

I have argued that saying 'God is love' or 'God is good' is not a way of proposing an explanatory theory that brings with it claims about the choices available when God created the world. Instead, they are statements whose natural
home is in the midst of suffering: they are statements of faith in a God who
still holds believers tight, even when all around is dark.

The question of evil is, therefore, not 'Can one reconcile the claim that God
is good with the claim that there is evil?' Rather, the question is, 'Is it really
possible for people to go on trusting in the covenant promises of God, and living in response to those promises, in the face of extremities of suffering?' and
'Is it possible for them to do so without evasion and delusion?'

Those are not questions that can be asked in the abstract, or answered in a
short chapter in a book. They are questions that are asked and answered in
the lives of those who face actual evils, and particularly those who are taken
to the extremities of suffering. To hold fast to God in lament and worship in
the face of evil, and to carry on living out godly love in defiance of evil: *that* is
what it means to say 'God is love'; that is what it means to affirm the goodness
of God in defiance of evil. And, in the end, *only* the lives of those who face the
extremities of evil in the name of God, with the love of God, provide the kind
of answer to the problem of evil appropriate to Christianity.

Of course, we need to be very careful about how we make any claim like
this. For every person who has faced the extremities of suffering in the name
of God, with the love of God, there are others whose faith and love have all
too understandably been destroyed. I am not recommending that we tally up
the scores; this is not about constructing arguments that will prove to sceptics that the Christian vision is true. And it is not (heaven forbid!) about saying that suffering is *justified* because in some cases it produces people who
respond so nobly. And it is certainly not about saying that those whom suffering crushes are to be blamed, or silenced, or passed over quickly for the sake
of my faith. If faith and love persist in the face of the extremities of suffering,
Christians cannot think of it as an *achievement* – a heroic effort on the part
of the sufferer. It is a *gift*, a gift of God's grace, which they and we can only
receive with thankfulness.

I am, rather, claiming that the lives of those who face the extremities of
suffering open-eyed, but with faith and love, show me that faith in God's love
is possible in a world like this. They show me that faith in God's love does
not *have* to be destroyed in the extremity of suffering, and does not *have* to
be a form of delusion or evasion in such extremity – but that it can be a way
of living with and responding to such suffering: it can be a way of winning
a kind of victory over such suffering even while being crucified by it. They
perhaps show believers who have not been pushed to such extremity that
they can hold to their own faith with integrity, without denying the existence
of extreme suffering, or betraying those who do suffer such extremity. And
so those who suffer in this way become for Christians, like Christ in the passion, signs that teach what faith and love mean when they are stripped of all
consolations and comforts – and so signs that teach what true faith and love
are like everywhere. Such lives are the only theodicy worth having.

There are, of course, two huge gaps in my argument – gaps that mean that, if you have understood it and if you agree with it, you might well put this book away with dissatisfaction and go out and so something more useful instead.[28]

In the first place, there is the fact that in this section I have told no actual stories, either of those who have faced the extremities of suffering in faith and love, or of those who have been crushed. I skipped from talking about the need to attend to such witnesses to talking about the implications once one has done so. I am afraid I could not see a way in which, in the space available, I could include such stories without so squashing them down that they became glib anecdotes, devoid of all the texture and depth that would make them worthwhile – all the honesty and directness which would *show* you what happens to faith and love when they are squeezed of all easy consolations, and which would allow you with fear and trembling to ask whether what you read was a product of evasion and delusion, or of open-eyed realism.

Of course, Christians will know where to look for one such story: there are four versions of it bound into the Bible, at the start of the New Testament. But if you want to pursue this further, you will need to fill the gap I have left, and look to and learn from those whose lives follow the pattern of Jesus' own, through their own Gethsemanes and Golgothas.

There is another gap, though. What I have just said could still sound as if it is a message for spectators, looking to the witness of those who suffer so as to bolster and justify Christian faith: seeing their lives, fates and faith as proofs that this faith is secure. Christians are *not* spectators, however. They suffer themselves, and they share the same world as all who suffer, and the question is not whether their faith is intellectually justifiable in such a world, but whether they can learn to respond to that world in a way consistent with the claim that God is love. The point is not to get to the end of this chapter and breathe a sigh of relief because a problem has been solved; this chapter contains no *answer* to the problem of evil. No argument responds adequately to evil, not even an argument properly supplemented with the stories of those who have suffered. The only response that means anything is found in lives shaped by protest, by lament and by Christlike love. If Christians do not have those things, then no theodicy will help them; if they do, then they are – however feebly, however falteringly – participants in the only answer that the problem of evil needs.

Exercise

Is this an adequate response? If possible, discuss this with others who have read this chapter.

Key point

- The only theodicy worth having is provided by those who, without delusion, hold on to the love of God in the midst of extreme suffering.

Going further

1 As well as investigating further the 'standard conversation' about theodicy, using the resources pointed to in note 19 on p. 257, it is well worth looking at some of the authors who have criticized that conversation in much more detail than I have. I recommend particularly, Karen Kilby 'Evil and the limits of theology', *New Blackfriars* 84 (2003), pp. 13–29, available online at the Centre of Theology and Philosphy http://theologyphilosophy centre.co.uk/papers/Kilby_EvilandLimits.doc, Terrence W. Tilley, *The Evils of Theodicy* (Washington, DC: Georgetown University Press, 1991), and the books by Phillips and Surin listed in the introduction to this chapter. See also Marilyn McCord Adams, *Horrendous Evils and the Goodness of God* (Ithaca and London: Cornell University Press, 1999), and Brian Davies, *The Reality of God and the Problem of Evil* (London: Continuum, 2006).
2 To start filling the gaps I left in my argument, and look at particular stories of suffering and faith, see Stanley Hauerwas, *Naming the Silences: God, Medicine and the Problem of Suffering* (Edinburgh: T&T Clark, 1993), Margaret Spufford, *Celebration* (London: Fount, 1989) and 'A revelation of divine love' in Ann Loades (ed.), *Spiritual Classics from the Late Twentieth Century* (London: The National Society / Church House Publishing, 1995) and Elie Wiesel, *Night* (London: MacGibbon and Key, 1960).

Notes

1 Wikipedia contributors, 'The Holocaust', 'Beslan school hostage crisis', '2004 Indian Ocean earthquake' and '1755 Libson earthquake', *Wikipedia: The Free Encyclopedia*, http://en.wikipedia.org/.

2 William Paley, *The Works of William Paley*, vol. 4: *Natural Theology* (London: Davison, 1830), p. 376.

3 Paley, *Natural Theology*, p. 372.

4 Paley, *Natural Theology*, p. 367.

5 Paley, *Natural Theology*, p. 366.

6 Charles Darwin, *The Foundations of the Origin of Species: Two Essays Written in 1842 and 1844*, ed. Francis Darwin (Cambridge: Cambridge University Press, 1909), pp. 51–2; available online at The Complete Works of Charles Darwin Online http://darwin-online.org.uk/EditorialIntroductions/Freeman_Sketchesof1842and1844.html.

7 Alfred Lord Tennyson, *In Memoriam A.H.H.* (London: E. Moxon, 1850), §§54, 56, emphasis mine; available online at the Other Pages, http://www.theotherpages.org/poems/books/tennyson/tennyson01.html.

8 Darwin, *Foundations*, p. 52.

9 Adrian Desmond and James Moore, *Darwin* (London: Michael Jospeh, 1991), p. 387. See also Randal Keynes, *Annie's Box: Charles Darwin, His Daughter, and Human Evolution* (London: Fourth Estate, 2001). A dramatization of Darwin's reaction can be found in a novel by Harry Thompson, *This Thing of Darkness* (London: Review, 2005), p. 529.

10 This is Darwin's own brief memorial to his daughter, written a week after her death. It can be found in *The Correspondence of Charles Darwin*, vol. 5, ed. Frederick Burkhardt (Cambridge: Cambridge University Press, 1990): Appendix II, pp. 540–2; this extract is from p. 542.

11 David Hume, *Dialogues Concerning Natural Religion*, ed. Norman Kemp Smith (London: Nelson, 1947), Pt. X, p. 198 (available online at The Gutenberg Project, http://www.gutenberg.org/etext/4583); he is paraphrasing an argument of Epicurus, cited in Lactantius, *De Ira Dei* XIII, in A. Cleveland Coxe (ed.), *Ante-Nicene Fathers*, vol. 7 (New York: Christian Literature Company, 1886), p. 271, available online at the Christian Classics Ethereal Library, http://www.ccel.org/ccel/schaff/anf07.iii.iii.xiii.html.

12 This is the *'logical* problem of evil' (for which the existence of evil contradicts the existence of a good God), as opposed to the *'evidential* problem of evil' for which the quantity, prevalence and persistence of evil constitutes evidence that the existence of a good God is improbable. I have taken my formulation of the logical problem from Christopher Southgate and Andrew Robinson, 'Varieties of Theodicy: An Exploration of Responses to the Problem of Evil Based on a Typology of Good–Harm Analyses' in Robert J. Russell, Nancey Murphy and William Stoeger (eds), *Physics and Cosmology: Scientific Perspectives on the Problem of Evil in Nature* (Berkeley, CA and Vatican City: CTNS and Vatican Observatory, 2007).

13 Nick Trakakis, 'The Evidential Problem of Evil', *The Internet Encyclopedia of Philosophy* http://www.iep.utm.edu/e/evil-evi.htm.

14 From Voltaire, *Toleration and other Essays*, ed. Joseph McCabe (New York and London: G. P. Putnam's, 1912), pp. 255–63; available online at the Online Library of Liberty, http://oll.libertyfund.org/Texts/Voltaire0265/OnToleration/HTMLs/0029_Pt05_Lisbon.html.

15 See, for instance, Alvin Plantinga, *God, Freedom, and Evil* (Grand Rapids, MI: Eerdmans, 1977).

16 The phrase is from John Keats, 'Letter to George and Georgiana Keats, 21 April 1819' in H. E. Rollins (ed.) *Letters of John Keats 1814–1821*, vol. 2 (Cambridge: Cambridge University Press, 1958). It is put to this use by John Hick, *Evil and the God of Love* (London: Macmillan, 1966), pp. 207–76.

17 Jill Paton Walsh, *Knowledge of Angels* (London: Black Swan, 1994), pp. 176–7.

18 Abelard, *Collationes*, ed. John Marenbon and Giovanni Orlandi (Oxford: Clarendon, 2001): II.210, p. 211, translation modified.

19 The literature on the standard conversation is vast. Two good places to start are James R. Beebe, 'The logical problem of evil' in *The Internet Encyclopedia of Philosophy*, 2006, http://www.iep.utm.edu/e/evil-log.htm and Michael Tooley, 'The problem of evil' in *The Stanford Encyclopedia of Philosophy*, 2002, http://plato.stanford.edu/entries/evil/. Each article has a good bibliography.

20 This is the argument of Terrence W. Tilley, *The Evils of Theodicy* (Washington, DC: Georgetown University Press, 1991); see especially his call for the abandonment of what I have been calling the standard conversation, on p. 219.

21 Fyodor Dostoevsky, *The Brothers Karamazov*, tr. Constance Garnett (London: Heinemann, 1912 [Russian original: 1879]), ch. 35; available online at Pennsylvania State University, http://www2.hn.psu.edu/faculty/jmanis/dostoevs/karamazo.pdf.

22 D. Z. Phillips, *The Problem of Evil and the Problem of God* (London: SCM Press, 2004), pp. 41–2, uses William Styron's *Sophie's Choice: A Novel* (New York: Random House, 1979) as a powerful example to illustrate this point.

23 Phillips, *The Problem of Evil and the Problem of God*, p. 46.

24 For a sample discussion, see Joshua Hoffman and Gary Rosenkrantz, 'Omnipotence' in the *Stanford Encyclopedia of Philosophy*, 2006, http://plato.stanford.edu/entries/omnipotence/.

25 Phillips, *The Problem of Evil and the Problem of God*, pp. 178–9

26 'Tsunami and Theodicy', *First Things* 151 (March 2005): pp. 6–9: p. 6; available online at http://www.firstthings.com/ftissues/ft0503/opinion/hart.html – quoting Revelation 21.

27 Rowan Williams, 'Redeeming Sorrows: Marilyn McCord Adams and the Defeat of Evil' in *Wrestling with Angels: Conversations in Modern Theology* (London: SCM Press, 2007), pp. 255–74: p. 263.

28 I'm alluding to a children's television programme called *Why Don't You?* (BBC, 1973–1995) the opening titles of which asked the question, 'Why don't you just switch off your television set and go and do something less boring instead?' before giving way to a magazine-style programme full of ideas for things you *could* have been doing if you weren't watching it.

11

Sin and Salvation

All through this book I have been discussing the ways in which Christians can make sense of their lives and of their world as being drawn on a journey into the life of God, to share the life of God. In other words, the central topic of the whole book has been *reconciliation* – the (re)uniting of the world with God. To put it another way, the central topic of the whole book has been soteriology: the doctrine of *salvation*.

In this chapter I am going to place salvation centre stage, and examine two facets of it that have so far only been implicit: the idea that Christians are saved specifically from sin, and the idea that Christ's death and resurrection are the cause of their salvation.

I am going to

- show that 'salvation' can mean many things;
- define 'sin' and 'grace';
- explore different metaphors for Christ's role in salvation; and
- examine the 'penal substitution' metaphor and some alternatives to it.

Preparation

- What do you think of when you think of 'salvation'? What are human beings saved *from*? What are they saved *for*? *How* are they saved? Briefly jot down your thoughts on these questions.
- If you have internet access, type 'define:salvation' into Google and look at the definitions that appear. Are any of these helpful? Are any unexpected?

Additional reading

Salvation is a huge topic, and it has been approached from countless directions. As accompaniments to this chapter, you might like to try:

Paul Fiddes, *Past Event and Present Salvation: The Christian Idea of Atonement* (London: DLT, 1989). Provides both an historical survey and a constructive proposal.

John McIntyre, *The Shape of Soteriology* (Edinburgh: T&T Clark, 1992). A good introduction to various biblical models of salvation.

Rowan Williams, *Resurrection: Interpreting the Easter Gospel* (London: DLT, 1982). A thought-provoking analysis of how the risen Christ enacts reconciliation.

What for, what from and how?

To save something is to move it from peril to safety. I'm typing this chapter on a computer, and were the computer to crash these words would be lost. To 'save' the document is to put it beyond that peril by storing it in a form that can't be touched by ordinary computer crashes. When I was at school, I don't think I ever managed to 'save' a goal at football (which is probably why I've ended up as an academic) but had I done so it would have been by seeing off the peril of a particular goal being scored against my team. With both those examples, the simplest way to explain what 'save' means is by specifying what we are being saved *from* – loss of data, or the loss of the game. Those descriptions, however, can only make sense because we make some prior assumptions about what this saving is *for*: for the writing of this book, or for the winning of the game. Only because we have some idea of the good outcome that we would like to achieve, or the good state in which we would like to remain, can we make sense of the idea of something imperilling that good. Ideas about what we are saved *from* go hand in hand with ideas about what we are saved *for*. And those ideas are tied together by some idea of *how* the saving takes place: I get the computer to make a copy of my document in non-volatile memory, or on a storage device; I prevent the ball from crossing into the area where, by the rules of the game, it constitutes a point against my team. The *how* is tied to the *what from* and the *what for*.

It is the same when we consider salvation in Christian theology. Ideas about what people are saved *from*, about what people are saved *for*, and about *how* people are saved are inseparable: a different vision of what people are saved for will suggest different ways of understanding the peril and the process by which it is avoided; a different understanding of the danger people are in will suggest different ways of seeing the kind of saving that is needed, and the good that will result when this danger is seen off.

The nature of the discussion earlier in this book makes it easiest to begin by asking what we are saved *for*. 'Salvation' comes originally from the Latin *salvare* which itself is connected to *salus*, 'health'. Etymology is no guide to usage, and *salvare* soon came to mean 'to rescue' as much as to 'heal', but thinking about salvation in terms of health is no bad place to start. As David Ford writes in *Self and Salvation*, 'Health can be physical, social, political, economic, environmental, mental, spiritual, moral and so on.' Salvation, if it is salvation of human beings in all their multifaceted existence, and 'If it is understood to have to do with a God of creation', will involve all these dimensions.[1]

The architecture of salvation

Some idea of the variety of Christian visions of the saved life can be gleaned from the different ways in which Christians have designed and built churches. To enter many Byzantine churches is to be drawn into a golden cave, filled with the light of candles illuminating icons of the saints and apostles; to be saved here is to enter the communion of saints as a novice initiated into mysteries.

To enter a gothic cathedral is to find oneself in a garden of pillars, a stone Eden where every line draws one's eyes upwards to the canopy of heaven; to be saved here is to participate with proper humility in a creaturely life in harmony with these heavenly heights. To enter a baroque church is to be confronted with a glorious vision, an explosion of light and ornament in which everything is caught and set in motion by the light streaming from God's throne and from God's eucharistic presence on earth; to be saved here is to share this rapturous vision, and reflect its light. To enter a neo-classical chapel is to find oneself in a space for preaching and sober reflection, a place of calm order and decorum; to be saved here is to become a pure hearer of the Word, and to live in untainted orderly obedience to it. To enter many modern churches is to come into a space designed for fellowship and families – chairs in the round and a coffee bar, perhaps; to be saved here is to be drawn into friendly fellowship with God and neighbour, away from pretension and obscurity.

It should be no surprise, then, that in the Bible and the Christian tradition, there have been endless ways of speaking about and imagining the end that God has for the world: it is the possession of the pearl of great price; it is the homecoming; it is the great harvest; it is the return to Eden; it is the vision of God. It has been imagined as true peace – *shalom* – the kind of peace that is not simply the absence of strife, but the good order of a thriving community, at ease with itself and the world. It has been imagined as abundant feasting, a time of communal celebration and enjoyment. It has been imagined as initiation into true knowledge. It has been imagined as the arrival of a child at maturity, as the harmony of a symphony, as the coming of dawn. It is understood as the world's inheritance of the life for which God intended it – a share in God's own triune life. And it is understood as the triumph of goodness, truth and beauty: the triumph of the goodness of unimpeded fellowship between people, between people and their environment, between people and God; the triumph of that true knowledge of Creator and creatures which is the heart of human freedom; and the triumph of that beauty in which the light of Christ is visible in everyone and everything.

Feasting

I would like to have the men of Heaven
in my own house;
with vats of good cheer
laid out for them.

I would like to have the three Marys,
their fame is so great.
I would like people
from every corner of Heaven.

I would like them to be cheerful
in their drinking.
I would like to have Jesus, too,
here among them.

I would like a great lake of beer
for the King of Kings.
I would like to be watching Heaven's family
drinking it through all eternity.

The Heavenly Banquet, ascribed to St Bridget.[2]

What human beings are saved *from* is anything that militates against this life, this goodness, truth and beauty; anything that hinders its growth, anything that pulls people away from it, anything that makes it seem impossible: the breakdown of relationships between people, between people and their environment, between people and God; that ignorance which is not simply the absence of knowledge of particular facts, but illusion and delusion, distorted knowledge or misunderstanding; the failure to show the light of Christ in one's life, or to see it in oneself or in others. Fear, imprisonment, distortion, incompleteness, futility, violence – all are forms of the breakdown or failure of godly life. Just as no one image captures all the dimensions of health, so no single, simple definition captures the peril from which Christian theology proclaims that human beings are saved: the problem is as multifaceted as the life that it undercuts.

As well as picturing what they are saved *from* and what they are saved *for*, Christians have pictured the *process* of salvation in any number of ways. They have used such images as reconciliation (re-creation of relationships where they have broken down), healing (putting right some disease or distortion, some virus corrupting the world's software), liberation (setting free from hostile powers), sanctification (making holy; the nurturing of godly life), justification (no longer being counted as an outlaw or exile, but being reinstated as a member in good standing of the people), revelation (the communicating or uncovering of the truth), victory (the defeat of the forces that hold people back from salvation), ransom or redemption (the paying of some cost to free those who hold people captive),[3] propitiation (the appeasing of the wrath of God) or expiation (the expunging of impurity, dishonour or guilt by means of sacrifice).[4] As David Ford notes in the book cited above, language about this process can be drawn

from the religious cult (sacrifice), the law court (guilt, judgement and justification), warfare (victory), the marketplace (exchange, redeeming slaves or prisoners), the family (parent–child relationships, adoption), medicine (healing), history (exodus, exile), politics (satisfaction in relation to the honour of a superior, liberation from oppression), friendship (laying down life), and nature (light and darkness, seeds dying and bearing fruit). Many of these have been followed through with great intensity in imagination, thought, feeling and practice.[5]

Salvation is not one simple, graspable topic in Christian theology: it is as unruly as life.

Key points

- Christians have had many different ways of talking about what they are saved *for*.
- They have had many different ways of talking about what they are saved *from*.
- They have had many different ways of talking about *how* they are saved.
- The how, the what from, and the what for are inseparable.

Sin

When we are thinking about human beings as those who are the *victims* of all this peril, we call it 'suffering' – and the discussion of God's response to suffering in the previous chapter was therefore already a discussion of salvation. However, if we are thinking about the ways in which this peril is the *result* of human activity (in the broadest sense) we consider it under the heading 'sin' – and Christian theological discussions have tended to use the word 'salvation' most of all when discussing this side of the world's plight.

In the earlier chapters of this book I spoke at length about the positive Christian vision of life in God. All we need to do to start defining sin is to ask how human beings obstruct and impede that life. In the light of the doctrine of God that I explored in Chapter 2, one could think of sin as the failure or refusal of love: failure or refusal to recognize oneself as loved, failure or refusal to learn to love, failure or refusal to love. Sin is anything in human action that cuts off the circulation of love. In the light of the doctrine of creation that I discussed in Chapter 7, one could also think of sin as the failure or refusal to acknowledge creatureliness: the failure or refusal to recognize one's utter dependency upon others, upon the wider environment and upon God, or the refusal or failure to recognize that the world in turn depends in part upon one – that one does have one's own sphere of action and responsibility. In the light of the doctrine of the Spirit that I outlined in Chapter 6, one could think of sin as the failure or refusal to be or to recognize oneself as a gift to the body of Christ, or to receive others in the body of Christ as gifts. In the light of the doctrine of providence that I outlined in Chapter 8, one could think of sin as failure or refusal to attend and respond to the signs of God's presence and activity in the world. In other words, one could take each of the positive doctrines that are explored elsewhere in this book, and ask how it is that human beings might fail or refuse to live according to this vision. 'Sin' is the name Christian theology gives to all that.

Pride

Feminist theologians have long criticized that resilient strand of the Christian tradition that claims that pride is the root form of sin. Valerie Saiving Goldstein, in a famous 1960 article, described the traditional picture, as she found it refracted in the work of contemporary theologians, in these terms:

> Man's freedom ... brings with it a pervasive fear for the survival of the self and its values. Sin is the self's attempt to overcome that anxiety by magnifying its own power, righteousness, or knowledge. Man knows that he is part of the whole, but he tries to convince himself and others that he *is* the whole. ... Sin is the unjustified concern of the self for its own power and prestige; it is the imperialistic drive to close the gap between the individual, separate self and others by reducing the others to mere objects which can be treated as appendages of the self and manipulated accordingly.[6]

She argues that this is a plausible and powerful account of sin, but that it is one written primarily by men, for men. Describing the effects of the traditional nurturing roles that have dominated women's lives, Saiving suggests that the paradigmatic problems for women in a patriarchal society are different:

> A mother who rejoices in her maternal role ... knows the profound experience of self-transcending love. But she knows, too, that it is not the whole meaning of life. ... The moments, hours, and days of self-giving must be balanced by moments, hours, days of withdrawal into, and enrichment of, her individual selfhood if she is to remain a whole person. She learns ... that a woman can give too much of herself, so that nothing remains of her uniqueness; she can become merely an emptiness, almost a zero without value to herself, to her fellow men, or, perhaps, even to God.[7]

The root form of sin in this situation is not pride, it is 'underdevelopment or negation of the self'.[8]

Of course, 'sin' has tended to be the name given by Christians most of all to deliberate acts of transgression or omission – blameworthy acts by individuals who knew, or should have known, better. Theological discussion, however, takes a somewhat broader view. As well as the disordered action, theologians attend to the disordered motivations and desires that inspired or were expressed in the action, and the disordered vision or understanding that lies behind those desires. And that means that questions of blameworthiness or culpability get more complex. I know what it means to be responsible for my actions – but am I responsible in the same way for my desires and motivations? And am I responsible in the same way for my understanding or vision? My discussion of freedom in Chapter 8 should already have alerted you to ways in which these questions can be very difficult to answer, and so to ways in which even that initial affirmation about being responsible for my actions might be rather difficult to make without qualification. That is why the definition I originally gave of sin did not put blameworthiness or culpability centre stage: I spoke of 'human activity (in the broadest sense)' that denied or worked against the good that God has for the world. It should be clear that unconscious or well-meaning or coerced or accidental human action might fall into this category just as easily as the deliberate actions of some individual who knows he is doing wrong.

One of the biblical passages that has become central in Christian thinking about sin is the story of Adam, Eve, and the serpent.

[1]Now the serpent was more crafty than any other wild animal that the Lord God had made. He said to the woman, 'Did God say, "You shall not eat from any tree in the garden"?' [2]The woman said to the serpent, 'We may eat of the fruit of the trees in the garden; [3]but God said, "You shall not eat of the fruit of the tree that is in the middle of the garden, nor shall you touch it, or you shall die."' [4]But the serpent said to the woman, 'You will not die; [5]for God knows that when you eat of it your eyes will be opened, and you will be like God, knowing good and evil.'

[6]So when the woman saw that the tree was good for food, and that it was a delight to the eyes, and that the tree was to be desired to make one wise, she took of its fruit and ate; and she also gave some to her husband, who was with her, and he ate. [7]Then the eyes of both were opened, and they knew that they were naked; and they sewed fig leaves together and made loincloths for themselves.

[8]They heard the sound of the Lord God walking in the garden at the time of the evening breeze, and the man and his wife hid themselves from the presence of the Lord God among the trees of the garden. [9]But the Lord God called to the man, and said to him, 'Where are you?' [10]He said, 'I heard the sound of you in the garden, and I was afraid, because I was naked; and I hid myself.' [11]He said, 'Who told you that you were naked? Have you eaten from the tree of which I commanded you not to eat?' [12]The man said, 'The woman whom you gave to be with me, she gave me fruit from the tree, and I ate.' [13]Then the Lord God said to the woman, 'What is this that you have done?' The woman said, 'The serpent tricked me, and I ate.' ...

[22]Then the Lord God said, 'See, the man has become like one of us, knowing good and evil; and now, he might reach out his hand and take also from the tree of life, and eat, and live forever' – [23]therefore the Lord God sent him forth from the garden of Eden, to till the ground from which he was taken. [24]He drove out the man; and at the east of the garden of Eden he placed the cherubim, and a sword flaming and turning to guard the way to the tree of life.

Genesis 3.1–13, 22–24

Exercise

Read this passage carefully, and then pause before reading my commentary. What is sin?

This is a story of things going wrong in Eden. Eden is portrayed as a land of flourishing relationships: flourishing relationships between people (Adam and Eve, made for each other as partners, who, as the end of chapter 2 tells us, live together in unashamed nudity), flourishing relationships between humans and the natural world (the picture is a pastoral one: they work the garden, living off its produce, naming and living alongside the animals), and flourishing relationships between humans and God (God walks among them in the garden planted for them). It is a land in which Adam and Eve are provided with an abundance (Adam works but he does not toil, and his and Eve's needs are met in the garden). It is, finally, a land in which human beings have a vocation that makes them participants in God's creative action (God plants the garden, but Adam is set to till it, working with what God provides to further its flourishing).

It is when we ask how this idyll is destroyed that things get more confusing. This is, after all, a deeply perplexing text. No matter how many times I read it, and how many commentaries and expositions I read by other people, there remain knots in it that I don't know how to untie. It is one of those texts that reminds me that the Bible does not simply make easy and effortless sense, and that even texts that have become crucial episodes in Christian tellings of the story of salvation can at times fit rather awkwardly into that story.

Reading this text as a Christian, who has inherited a tradition of reading that takes it as a foundational exposé of the nature of sin and punishment, I find myself faced with a host of interconnected questions.[9] What is the tree of the knowledge of good and evil? Why is it there? What kind of knowledge does it give? What is wrong with gaining that kind of knowledge? What, exactly, is the sin that Adam and Eve commit? Is the problem for Adam and Eve simply their breaking of an arbitrary restriction that has been set for them as some kind of test? Or is there something inherently dangerous with eating from the tree, so that God's command is more warning that ban?

And what is the nature of the temptation to which Eve and Adam fall? One moment, it is represented as a temptation to 'be like God', the next (more mysteriously) as a temptation to gain knowledge and wisdom, and the next (rather prosaically) as the lure of fruit that looks good to eat.

Then there are the unexpected consequences. The serpent, speaking against God, has claimed that Adam and Eve will not die, and that their eyes will be opened; sure enough they do *not* die and their eyes *are* opened. But although the tree is called 'the tree of the knowledge of good and evil' the knowledge it conveys is clearly not knowledge of what is banned and what is allowed – Eve demonstrates in conversation with the serpent that she knows that much already. What she and Adam gain from the opening of their eyes is knowledge of their own nakedness, and an attending shame and fear: they gain shame when they see their nakedness, and fear when they realize that God is in the garden and will see their nakedness. Adam does not say to God, 'I was afraid because I had disobeyed you,' but 'I was afraid *because I was naked*.' What has happened? What has the fruit of this tree done to them?

This shame, it seems to me, is a clue to a reading of this text that follows the Christian tradition in seeing this as a paradigmatic tale of sin and its punishment. What, after all, is shame? It has something to do with seeing yourself as you imagine others see you – an internalized version of the external scrutiny you imagine yourself to be under. And so it is indeed a form of knowledge, of self-knowledge ('this is what I look like') but it is knowledge without love. Shame involves a form of knowledge that sees accurately but judges harshly, a knowledge that consists in unforgiving scrutiny. Adam and Eve have their eyes opened, but apparently only to become aware for the first time of their naked precariousness – whether the emphasis is supposed to fall on the frailty that they discover in themselves, or whether it has more to do with their discovery of the uncontrollable nature of their desires. They see themselves accurately as finite, weak, needy or unreliable.

The fruit of the tree, we might say, makes them *judges* – and this is what, in this reading of the story, 'knowledge of good and evil' means. They do not gain information about what is right and wrong; they gain the stance of a judge who metes out sentences, condemning and accepting – the position that (as the story itself shows) belongs properly to God. Adam and Eve seek to stand in the place of God and then condemn themselves for not being gods. And in this, of course, they do see accurately (they *are* finite creatures, they are not gods) but they do not see *truly*: they do not see the proper dignity (rather than shame) of their position. In the light of the theology that I have been presenting in this book so far, we might say that Adam and Eve do not see the vocation for which they were created, to glorify God as creatures, to participate in the life of God as creatures. They do not see the love that binds the creator to his creatures and creatures to their creator. All they see is that they are creatures, and that there is a gulf fixed between them and their creator.

Thin sin

In the light of Genesis 3, what should one say about a society in which people – and particularly young women – are taught to despise their bodies by being bombarded with images of impossibly thin models and celebrities, and in which salvation is offered through a variety of regimes designed not to heal this distorted vision, but to force one's body into compliance with it, and in which people are held in a constant state of calorie-counting guilt about their failures to comply? A society that thinks beauty fits into 'size 0' is a society that has eaten fruit from the same tree as Eve.

Knowledge that is accurate but untrue seems to be the hallmark of the serpent. After all, everything the serpent says is accurate, but it is only ever a partial picture. The serpent does not see or does not convey the whole picture, the context in which the things that it sees move. So, for instance, it accurately sees that Adam and Eve will not immediately die when they eat the fruit of the tree; it accurately sees that when they eat it their eyes will be opened and they will (as God later confirms) gain a kind of knowledge that belongs to God; it fails to see (or fails to tell) what the knowledge they gain will do to them. It will tip them into shame, into a cycle of blaming and accusing, into rivalry, into distorted relationships with each other, with God and with the world. They will begin to die.

Before ever any punishment has been imposed, the consequences of their action are seen in a disruption of their relationship with each other (shame, and a little later, blame), and a disruption of their relationship with God (fear). It would be possible (though perhaps a little too smooth) to see the explicit punishment that God later imposes as nothing more than a spelling out, a making concrete, of the damage that they have already done to themselves.

What, then, does 'sin' look like in this passage? There is, of course, that first sinful action, which is a deliberate decision to do something that has been forbidden. The later actions of Adam and Eve, however – their hiding, their blaming – are no less actions that distort and destroy the harmony of Eden, and so no less sin. Yet they are more the outworking of now diseased understanding and loveless imagination than the deliberate transgression of commands. However simple sin may have been to start with, it has begun to metastasize.

Key points

- Sin is anything in human activity that stands in the way of salvation.
- Sin includes, but is not restricted to, deliberate acts of transgression.
- Sin is also found in the outworking of distorted vision and disordered desires.

The power of sin

Sin is any human activity (in the broadest sense) that gets in the way of salvation: anything that gets in the way of fullness of life; anything that gets in the way of one's being drawn deeper into the life of God. Imagine the life of God as a dance, with more and more people being drawn into the dance. To jab out your elbows, or to trip up your neighbours, disrupts the dance; it makes it impossible for you or for them to join in fully with the dance. That's not because there is some stickler of a dance master who has unrealistic standards of perfection that he imposes on all the dancers, a master who sends you off if he doesn't happen to like the way you move. Rather, it is inherent: if you behave like this, you break the dance. Similarly, 'sin' should not be thought of as the transgressing of any one of a long list of arbitrary rules set up by God to please Godself, but is simply anything that breaks the dance of participation in God's life.

Certainly, deliberate transgressions of commands would disrupt things ('I don't care what the caller says, I'm going to step to the right now. Oops, sorry!'). But the dance could also be disrupted in more subtle ways. If you had been taught to dance in ways completely unsuited to this dance then, however much you were conscientious and willing, you might find that you could not help but disrupt the dance at first. On other occasions, you might simply find yourself caught up in the ripples of clumsiness and collision set off by somebody else's mismove, unable to do anything but choose which of three people you're going to collide with, or exactly where you are going to fall over. Or you might – to strain the metaphor a bit further – find that the environment you were dancing in had been erected by people who simply did not understand the dance (a room that was too narrow, or with a floor that was too slippery), and that try as you might you and those around you weren't going to be able to dance properly until something had been done about the room.

We can make all this more real if we think about racism as an example. Using our dance metaphor, racism would be the refusal or inability to dance properly with those of another race, even though they share the same dance floor with you. There are, of course, all too many deliberate racist acts committed knowingly by individuals. But what about someone who has been brought up in a culture saturated with negative images of those of other races? He might try to overcome that inheritance, but be all too aware even at the times when he is struggling to be most fair that it *is* a struggle for him: he cannot but *notice* people's race, and only keeps above the racist assumptions he grew up with by an explicit act of will. He knows he can't relax his vigilance, and so knows that that he simply is not 'colour blind': he simply is not able to behave entirely naturally with people of another race because he is too self-conscious about his need to do so.

Or what about someone working in an organization that relies very strongly upon personal recommendation by existing members when recruiting new members and when promoting people within the organization? She might find that however open she and her colleagues are to welcoming ethnic minorities into the organization, very few from those minorities actually make it in, and even fewer get promoted – because networks of interracial friendship are not yet pervasive enough in the surrounding society, and most people from ethnic minorities do not know existing members of the organization well enough to get their recommendations. And what if, in turn, one of the things preventing the growth of interracial friendships in their society is precisely the fact that people don't meet many from ethnic minorities in the organizations of which they are a part?

In other words, racism can be a matter of deliberate individual transgressions, but it can also be more complicated: it can also be part of the way we are shaped by our upbringing and environment, and it can also be deeply embedded in the ways in which our society is organized – in ways which go well beyond any ideas of personal transgression and responsibility. We can speak of corporate racism, a racist culture, maybe even institutional or systemic racism – and in each case we are still talking about something that issues in patterns of human action that hold salvation at bay, and keep human beings from true flourishing together.

Christians have long said that the sin from which human beings need saving is not simply to be found in deliberate individual acts of transgression, but rather is something deeper and wider – something that human beings inherit, and can't avoid. Racism, for instance, is not simply my individual racist acts, but is the racist culture I grow up in (which beds down in me however much I try to avoid it) and the racist structures of the society I live in (which make eradicating racism at times almost impossibly difficult, even with immense good will and widespread good intentions). I need saving not just from the consequences of the particular sins I commit, but from the sinful air I breathe and the sinfulness of the world I inhabit.

It is not therefore the product of some bizarre metaphysical speculation, or of the mistranslation of a verse in Romans 5, that Christian theologians have spoken of sin being inherited,[10] of it infecting people prior to any responsible or irresponsible action of their own. It is the product of tracing back the circuits of sinful action and finding that they do not simply terminate in the sovereign wills of responsible individuals, but in this mess of influence and context in which those individuals are all embedded. Beyond the individual, culpably sinful act, there is the power of sin from which it takes its strength and direction – and Christian theology has called this power 'original sin'.

Christian theology has at this point notoriously spoken about even tiny babies as infected with sin. A baby is born needing a loving environment in which to grow, so as to grow up herself to be loving. It does not happen automatically, and it does not happen all at once. There is nothing wrong with being a baby, nothing wrong with babies being as self-centred as they always and inevitably are, nothing wrong with them needing to grow into maturity, needing to grow into life and love. None of that is 'sin'. But no baby born in our world is born into the wholly loving environment she would need in order to grow properly.

It is not that the baby has somehow *done* something wrong – and the proponents of original sin do not say any different. The baby does, however, lack something: she lacks the environment she needs because she is part of the distorted, sinful human race. She stands in need of the salvation of that human race just as much as its older, less innocent members do, if she is to grow into the life that God has for her. The baby is born into a world with polluted air, and is bound to grow up with some degree or other of distortion, and to become part of the system that recycles this air. It is not her fault, but it is becoming part of who she is from the moment she is born – and it is most certainly something from which she needs to be saved. 'Original sin', if this is what we mean by it, is not so much a crime that deserves to be punished as a wound that needs to be healed.

We saw that, in Genesis 3, the result of Adam and Eve's sin is a kind of death: the rise of rivalry and evasion, of shame and fear, in the place of the relationships that constitute real life. That 'death' becomes the arena in which Adam and Eve's children grow up, it beds itself down in them and shapes their perception of themselves, each other and their world; they breathe in this death and exhale it again themselves.[11] And so on down the line. Adam's sin, the traditional doctrine says, becomes the sin of all of us. Human beings would all still stand in need of salvation, even if the only particular act of sin (the only deliberate, individual transgression) ever committed was Eve's – because even then this lack of sin would only be achieved by people pinching their noses and struggling not to live according to the death they are inevitably breathing in, the death that flows from that sin. Human beings stand in need of a change of air, and that's not something they can produce themselves.

Exercise

Pause for a moment. Are you convinced? Can the definition of 'sin' be broadened in this way beyond the realm of individual acts of deliberate transgression?

Key points

- The power of sin is found in the way people are shaped by a sin-ridden environment.
- The power of sin is found in the way in which people's freedom to act rightly is curbed by circumstances.
- The power of sin is found in the way institutions perpetuate patterns of sinful action.

Grace

If the problem faced by humanity were simply the existence of culpable bad choices made by free individuals, it might make sense to think that human beings could simply pull their moral socks up and exercise their freedom more responsibly. They might need a wake-up call; they might need something to stiffen their resolve; they might need reminding of the standards of good and evil – but freedom from sin would ultimately rest in their own hands, and the biggest need would simply be for them to get on with acting well.

If, on the other hand, we see sin in the disordered desires and distorted vision from which human actions emerge, then freedom from sin will be a more difficult goal to reach. Human beings will need to be *worked on* in order to be freed to do the good: they will need to have their vision corrected and their desires reoriented. Any talk of human beings as actively responsible for doing good will have to go hand in hand with (indeed, be carried by) talk of human beings as *recipients*, and of freedom from sin not as something achieved, but as something *given* – as 'grace', to use the traditional theological term.

Pelagius and Augustine

For the Western Church, the debate between Augustine of Hippo and Pelagius (a theologian from Britain) in the early fifth century put the question of grace at the top of the theological agenda. The historian Peter Brown describes the clash.

> Like many reformers, the Pelagians placed the terrifying weight of complete freedom on the individual: he was responsible for his every action; every sin, therefore, could only be a deliberate act of contempt for God. Augustine was less sure that a fallen human nature could bear so great a weight: 'Many sins are committed through pride, but not all happen proudly ... they happen so often by ignorance, by human weakness; many are committed by men weeping and groaning in their distress. ...' The Catholic church existed to redeem a helpless humanity; and once the essential grace was given, he could accept with ease in his congregation the slow and erratic process of healing.[12]

> The basic difference between the two men, however, is to be found in two radically different views on the relation between man and God. It is summed

up succinctly in their choice of language. Augustine had long been fascinated by babies: the extent of their helplessness had grown upon him ...
[and] he had had no hesitation in likening his relation to God to that of a
baby to its mother's breast, utterly dependent, intimately involved in all the
good and evil that might come from this, the only source of life.

The Pelagian, by contrast, was contemptuous of babies. 'There is no
more pressing admonition than this, that we should be called *sons* of God.'
To be a 'son' was to become an entirely separate person, no longer dependent on one's father, but capable of following out by one's own power the
good deeds that he had commanded. The Pelagian was *emancipatus a deo*;
it is a brilliant image taken from the language of Roman law: freed from the
all-embracing and claustrophobic rights of the father of a great family over
his children, these sons had 'come of age'. They had been 'released', as
in Roman Law, from dependence on the *pater familias* and could at last go
into the world as mature, free individuals, able to uphold in heroic deeds the
good name of their illustrious ancestry: 'Be ye perfect, even as your Father
in Heaven is perfect.'[13]

Exercise

Pause for a moment to decide where you stand. Are you more with Pelagius or
more with Augustine? Wholeheartedly or with caveats and qualifications? Do
you see any dangers in the side for which you have opted?

If one is to grasp these points, it is important not to fall back into inadequate
ways of thinking about human action and divine action, or human freedom
and divine freedom. You will remember from my discussion of providence
and freedom that it is a mistake to think of human and divine action as competing with one another, so that human beings would be active only where
God is not, and God active only where they are not. I spoke of human freedom
not as a freedom from God's control, a freedom consisting entirely in the absence of constraint, but of freedom as a matter of dependence upon truth and
love. The only kind of freedom available to human beings is being dependent
in ways that are not mired in delusion, and in ways that do not subordinate
them to the interests of another.

Being passive, being recipients, being dependent – these are not states in
which human beings find themselves only when they are not acting. They
are present *in* all human action. All human action emerges from desires,
understanding and circumstances that the actors did not ultimately choose
for themselves. And all human action starts chains of consequences going in
the world over which the actors will have little or no control. To speak about
freedom from sin as a gift, as something human beings receive, is not to say
that human beings are normally active and in control, but in this context must
become passive and dependent. Human beings are always dependent, even
when they are active – and the only question that matters is dependence *upon
what*, or *upon whom*.

Trent

Some Protestant polemics would make you think that this is a point on which Protestants and Catholics differ, and that only Protestants insist on the priority of divine action or on absolute human dependence. A quick glance at the Council of Trent, the sixteenth-century Council in which the Roman Catholic Church stated its case against the Reformation, should be enough to puncture this myth.

Canons concerning justification:
1. If anyone says that a person can be justified before God by his own works, done either by the resources of human nature or by the teaching of the law, apart from divine grace through Jesus Christ: let him be anathema.
2. If anyone says that divine grace through Jesus Christ is given solely to enable a person to live justly and to merit eternal life *more easily*, as if each could be done through free will without grace, even though with a struggle and with difficulty: let him be anathema.
3. If anyone says that, without preceding inspiration of the holy Spirit and without his help, a person can believe, hope, love and repent, as he ought, so that the grace of justification may be granted to him: let him be anathema.

Council of Trent, *Decree on Justification*

The disagreement between the Protestant Reformers and the Roman Catholic teaching of Trent is not about whether God's grace has absolute priority: it is about what happens next. The next canon is one that the Reformers could not have accepted:

4. If anyone says that a person's free will when moved and roused by God gives no co-operation by responding to God's summons and invitation to dispose and prepare itself to obtain the grace of justification; and that it cannot, if it so wishes, dissent but, like something inanimate, can do nothing at all and remains merely passive: let him be anathema.'[14]

In the Tridentine position, God's prevenient grace, working purely according to God's good pleasure and not in reponse to any merit or openness on the part of the human subject, as it were repairs and switches on the broken free will of that subject. Once that has happened, however, the subject can use that awakened freedom either to co-operate with, or to reject, the ongoing work of God's grace that leads the person to salvation. It is this that Protestants have traditionally rejected.

Christian theology claims that God is at work to save human beings from sin, to free people from destructive and distorting dependencies. As I said in the chapter on the Spirit,

whenever Christians acknowledge God as Father, whenever they grasp what God is doing with them and for them, drawing them to himself as his children, that simply *is* the work of the Spirit.

and

> Whenever someone is being led deeper into conformity to Christ, when-
> ever someone is being formed alongside Christ for life with the Father, that
> simply *is* the Spirit at work: that is the power of God's life, drawing that
> person to God.

Growth into godly life or 'sanctification' as it is known, even when it is a
change in the patterns of human *action*, a change in which human beings are
active participants, is seen by Christians as entirely the gift of God's Spirit,
drawing them deeper into the life of God. Sanctification is God giving God's
own life to God's creatures.

Of course, being creatures, the only ways they have of receiving that gift
are creaturely. Changes in the patterns of human vision, desire and action find
their way into human lives along the connections that embed each human life
in its context. Grace works its way into human beings through what they see,
hear, taste, touch and smell: that's what it means to be a creature. Theologians
have expressed this by saying that God's grace is always 'mediated' to human
beings, that there are always 'means' of God's grace – means by which that
grace finds its way into human lives. Even if we were to imagine God stepping in and acting upon someone directly, without mediation, that action
could only become real in the person's life once it had become a pattern of
change in the embodied life in the world which that person is – and so, in that
way at least, become 'mediated' again.

Nevertheless, to say that these creaturely influences and triggers are 'means
of grace'[15] is to say that they are tools in the hands of God, and that ultimately,
whatever means God uses, the healing of human beings from sin is received
from the hands of God. It is God, Christians say, who is at work to overcome
the sin that has sabotaged God's creatures' sharing of God's life. It is God who
steps over the barriers that human beings have individually and collectively
created to participation in God's life. God takes the initiative, and whatever
movement there might be of human beings back to God depends utterly upon
a prior movement of God towards human beings. 'We love because he first
loved us', as 1 John 4.19 puts it. The world is enabled to share in the life of God
only because God has first shared God's life with the world. For Christian
theology, the root and source of any and all salvation is God giving God's
own life to the world, making it real and active in a world that is resistant and
antagonistic towards it.

Key points

- According to Christian theology, human beings are recipients of salvation,
  not its creators.
- Freedom from sin is understood as a gift of God.
- 'Grace' is the name Christian theology gives to the activity of God freely
  giving salvation to human beings.

Salvation in Christ

And so we return to the core theme of this book: the root and source of any and all salvation that is God's gift of God's life to the world, by Christ and the Spirit. In the next three sections of this chapter I will focus on one question about this that has been central in Christian thinking about salvation. What exactly is the role of Jesus in salvation – and, specifically, what is the role of Jesus' *death*?

The Protestant theologians Martin Bucer (1491–1551) and Andreas Osiander (1498–1552) developed a framework for thinking about this question that has become very influential. They drew on a bit of medieval and patristic biblical exegesis, which noted the different categories of people who are portrayed as 'anointed' in the Old Testament, and who can therefore be seen as forerunners of the Messiah (that is, the 'anointed one'). Jesus, they said, can be thought of as *prophet*, as *priest*, and as *king*. Bucer wrote:

> Just as they used to anoint kings, priests and prophets to institute them in their offices, so now Christ is king of kings, highest priest, and chief of the prophets. He does not rule in the manner of an external empire; he does not sacrifice with brute beasts; he does not teach and admonish only with an external voice. Rather, by the Holy Spirit he directs minds and wills in the way of eternal salvation; by the Spirit he offered himself as an expiatory sacrifice for us, so that we too might become an acceptable offering to God; and by the same Spirit he teaches and admonishes, in order that those destined for his kingdom may be made righteous, holy and blessed in all things.[16]

Jesus, we might say, is a prophet to the extent that his life, death and resurrection cure people's distorted vision. His life, death and resurrection can be thought of as *showing* them God, and showing them their true nature – showing them true divinity and true humanity. Within the whole narrative of his life, death and resurrection, the cross is a focal point of this showing: it is there that they see the 'foolishness' of God; it is there that they see that God's life, and true human life, consists not in self-assertion but in self-giving. By showing them true godly life, Christ's life, death and resurrection awaken and reorient their desires: however slow they are to learn, his life teaches them to love love. This is not simply the presentation of a moral example that shows them how to live, nor a demonstration that allows them to understand what God is like – it is a therapy for broken eyes and hearts.

Jesus is king to the extent that he is understood to be the living lord of one's life, and to the extent that one's life is thought of as discipleship to this master. Christians believe that it is in ongoing, constantly renewed following of Jesus that true flourishing is to be found. Christian life is thought of as life under the lordship of Jesus, or life under Jesus' reign, which is the kingdom of God. Jesus' life, death and resurrection can be thought of as establishing a colony of God's kingdom in the midst of the realm of the enemy. The cross, in this light, can be thought of as a victory over that enemy kingdom – as long as one recognizes that it is a strange kind of victory. Jesus refused to obey the laws of rivalry, violence and self-protection by which this enemy's world runs; he lived *in* this world, but he lived as a citizen of a different country. The cross is what happens to those who refuse the ways of this world: they are crushed and discarded. Jesus' victory, however, did not consist in violent overthrow. It consisted in remaining faithful to the kingdom of God, even to the point of death. The cross is an act of supreme resistance, and the resurrection is God's refusal to allow this resistance to vanish: in the resurrection, God takes Jesus' resistance on the cross and makes it the beachhead of God's kingdom on earth – giving it the future that Jesus' persecutors thought they had cut off.

It is when we come to consider Christ as priest that matters become more contentious.

Key points

- Jesus can be seen as a prophet to the extent that his life, death and resurrection heal distorted vision and understanding.
- For the prophetic understanding of Jesus, salvation is a matter of revelation.
- Jesus can be seen as a king to the extent that his life, death and resurrection establish the kingdom of God in the midst of the world.
- For the kingly understanding of Jesus, salvation is a matter of resistance and victory.

Sacrifice and substitution

Jesus is priest to the extent that his life and particularly his death are seen as a sacrifice on the world's behalf. Sacrifices could mean many things in the ancient Jewish and Roman worlds, but the most relevant idea seems to be of sacrifice as a response to impurity, dishonour and transgression. The person who transgressed or who became impure or dishonoured needed to be expelled from the people and the presence of God. The appropriate sacrifice could prevent their expulsion or allow their reinstatement: it either placated God, so that he turned away his wrath, or it took away the impurity. That is, a clean animal would be sacrificed as a substitute – either giving God a life to placate his wrath, or having the impurity transferred to it and destroyed or expelled with it. For the earliest Christians, brought up in a world where sacrifices like this were a pervasive reality, sacrifice would have needed no explanation: it would simply have been obvious, one of the ways that the world works – and it would have been an easily available metaphor for speaking of what had happened with Christ. And it is worth noting that such sacrifice is not a judicial process; it is not about legal condemnation, sentencing and acquittal; it does not work by what we would recognize as a logic of guilt and punishment – it has a cultic logic of its own, not a logic borrowed from the law courts.

The metaphor allowed early Christians to capture in a graphic image the idea that Jesus was pure, and that his life and death had become the source of new life with God for those who had been estranged from God. At the heart of this image were ideas of substitution or exchange. He had shared his life with sinners so that sinners could share his life with God. He, the pure one, had suffered and died, and now they, the impure ones, had been made alive. He had become the victim of sin and sin's consequences, so that they might be given a life freed from the power of sin.

Of course, if one presses this metaphor then questions start to arise about quite *how* this substitution works. Is it that God's anger is placated by this offering? Is it that sinners' impurities are somehow transferred to Jesus? The use of the metaphor by early Christians did not require that they had any clear or plausible answer to either of those questions: the metaphor enabled them to grasp and convey the basic *shape* of what had happened, rather than necessarily providing an explanation of *how or why* it happened.

It is important to remember that this talk of Jesus as priest, or of his life and death as a sacrifice, is metaphorical – just as is the description of his life and death as the victorious founding of a beachhead in enemy territory, or the description of them as a therapy for distorted vision and disordered desire. As I stressed at the beginning of this chapter, Christians have employed a bewildering variety of metaphors or analogies to make sense of salvation, and in particular to make sense of Jesus' role in salvation. If Jesus' life, death and resurrection are the life of God come into the world, then we might expect them to be ungraspable and inexhaustible, capturable only in the clash and cacophony of a thousand inadequate images. Sacrifice imagery would have been particularly strong in the New Testament period – to observe or be involved in animal sacrifices must have been a powerfully visceral experience (if you will pardon the pun) – but that does not mean that Christ's death simply is, literally and straightforwardly, a sacrifice or that the logic of sacrifice explains exactly how and why Jesus had to die.

As the centuries went by, Christianity moved from a world dominated by cultic sacrifices (whether Jewish, Graeco-Roman, or those of the peoples beyond the Roman Empire to which Christianity spread) to one in which real sacrifices were rare or absent. Sacrifice ceased to be a living, meaningful reality in most Christian's lives, and so the language of sacrifice stopped making immediate, visceral sense. Christians began looking for other metaphors or analogies that would help them *explain* the Bible's sacrificial imagery – help them bring it alive again. And the key source to which they turned was the world of the law court: the judicial, forensic or penal world.

The basic storyline of sacrificial substitution began to become one of *penal* substitution – substitution of the one punished. We have been judged guilty, this new story says, and have been sentenced to death. Christ, however, though innocent, is willingly killed in our place, taking the punishment that should have been ours. The sentence has been executed, judicial wrath is satisfied, and we the guilty may go free.

Calvin on substitution

In the sixteenth century, when the great Reformer John Calvin wrote his long exposition of the Christian faith, *The Institutes of the Christian Religion*, he gave a powerful and influential summary of the problem of sin, and of the solution provided by penal substitution. '[C]ondemned, dead, and lost in ourselves,' he said, we 'seek righteousness, liberation, life and salvation in Christ' (II.xvi.1) – but we must 'earnestly ponder how he accomplishes salvation'.

> No one can descend into himself and seriously consider what he is without feeling God's wrath and hostility toward him. Accordingly he must anxiously seek ways and means to appease God, and this demands a satisfaction ... God's wrath and curse always lie upon sinners until they are absolved of guilt. Since he is a righteous Judge, he does not allow his law to be broken without punishment, but is equipped to avenge it. (II.xvi.1)

> All of us ... have in ourselves something deserving of God's hatred. ... But because the Lord wills not to lose what is his in us, out of his own kindness he still finds something to love. However much we may be sinners by our own fault, we nevertheless remain his creatures. (II.xvi.3)

> This is our acquittal: the guilt that held us liable for punishment has been transferred to the head of the Son of God. We must, above all, remember this substitution, lest we tremble and remain anxious throughout life – as if God's righteous vengeance, which the Son of God has taken upon himself, still hung over us. (II.xvi.5)[17]

Exercise

Before reading on, decide what you think of this. Do you think it is a coherent and plausible account of Christ's atoning work? Can you see any problems with it?

This has become probably the most pervasive way of telling the story of Jesus' place in salvation in the modern world – and also one of the most controversial. Several serious and interlocking questions have been posed to it, some of which would also apply to the sacrificial substitution which penal substitution is intended to interpret, some of which are specific to the penal model.

In some crude versions of the substitutionary story, the wrathful Father demands punishment or sacrifice, and the merciful Son placates the Father by meekly providing it. This has, famously, been called 'cosmic child abuse',[18] and it is not difficult to see why. More thoughtful versions of the penal substitution story, however, stress that the Father and the Son act in concert, providing in their shared mercy the substitute that their shared justice demands. As John Stott, a staunch defender of penal substitution, put it, 'it is the Judge himself who in holy love assumed the role of the innocent victim, for in and through the person of his Son he himself bore the penalty which he himself inflicted'.[19]

Nevertheless, there is a more serious charge here. It appears that God's justice and God's mercy are pitted against one another. On the one hand God is merciful and loving and wants to forgive, and on the other God is holy and righteous and has to condemn. In some presentations of penal substitution, these are presented as two sides of God's character that are equal, opposed and balanced, such that whatever God does must equally express both sides. The righteous God, justly wrathful against human sin, must punish it, and will not forgo this punishment because to do so would be to abandon justice – and yet this same God is merciful, and desires the salvation of sinners, and so takes the punishment upon himself.

It has been argued that it is thanks in part to the effect on our imaginations of centuries of reflection on the gospel presented in these terms that we now naturally assume that justice and mercy are opposed in other areas of our life – in penal policy, for instance, where we assume that the demands of forgiveness and mercy pull in one rather unrealistic direction, but the implacable demands of righteous punishment pull in quite another. It has been suggested, in particular, that the prevalence of this kind of theology – its pervasiveness in hymns and sermons and prayers and books – has fed our society's belief that punishment is fundamentally *retribution*: the automatic and necessary paying back in punishment of the wrong that someone has done, with any other effects of the punishment – deterrence of others, reformation of the guilty party, restoration of the relationships broken by the crime – strictly secondary.[20]

There is, however, no need to see justice and mercy opposed in this kind of way. More careful discussions of penal substitution certainly talk both of God's wrath and of God's love – but they are not presented as equal and opposite forces, which God somehow has to balance. Rather, God's love is absolutely and completely primary: God is love – and 'wrath' (or righteous anger) is simply an expression of God's love. If God is drawing the world to Godself in love, then God must work against all that keeps the world from being drawn together in love – God *must* work against sin, seeking to destroy it; God must *hate* it. God hates what destroys the world, because God loves the world; God's wrath is directed against what constricts and reduces our life, because God's desire is for the fullness of our life. God's 'wrath' is not the flaring of God's tetchy temper at things that happen to irritate God, but rather is the name we give to the inevitable fact that, for God to be loving, God's will must be set against all that prevents love. 'Love' and 'Wrath', 'Mercy' and 'Justice' are not opposed forces in God; they are not even opposite sides of the same coin: 'wrath' is simply and only one of the ways in which God's love works itself out, 'justice' simply and only one of the ways in which God's mercy works itself out.

In order to understand where that leaves penal substitution, we need to examine another criticism that has been made. And we can best approach that criticism by looking at this passage from a fairly typical popular presentation of penal substitution, culled from an American evangelistic website:

If you and I were in prison and on death row (looking to be executed soon), and you felt compassion on me and would like to be my substitute and take my place at the electric chair, do you think the chief officer of the prison would let you take my place so I could go free? No, he would not! Why? Who then would take your place, for you deserve to be punished in the same way? The only way anyone could be considered to take another's place in prison on death row is if he is not guilty of a crime and is not on death row.[21]

As it stands, and stated as bluntly as this, this is clearly nonsense. What do *you* think would happen if an innocent party offered to take the place of a convict on death row?

One can certainly imagine a *fine* being paid by somebody other than the person fined – at least, if the fine were imposed primarily in order to ensure that the cost created by the crime should be met.[22] When one turns away from fines to the death penalty, however, I find it impossible to see how the logic is supposed to work. What kind of system of justice would be satisfied if it got a death, any death, regardless of whether it was the guilty person who died? What kind of system of justice would be *more* satisfied with the death of an innocent person than with the death of the mass murderer it has condemned?

There may be some system in which this makes sense, but it will not be a system of *justice*: the penal metaphor will need to be abandoned. The crucial phrase in Calvin's presentation is 'the guilt that held us liable for punishment has been transferred to the head of the Son of God'. 'Transference of guilt' is not an idea that makes sense in a law court: it is an idea from the realm of sacrifice, describing one of the mysterious transactions that were believed to lie at the heart of sacrifice. The change from sacrificial to penal metaphors has not actually taken us any further forward.

Exercise

Whether or not you agree with me, can you see any ways of defending the penal substitution theory from my criticisms? Try to come up with the outline of a defence.

There is, however, another way forward. We can, I think, imagine a situation in which a severe punishment is imposed not as a way of enacting retribution – not as a way simply of giving a criminal 'what he deserves', full stop – but rather as a way of working towards the healing of all those who have been harmed by the criminal's actions. We can imagine a rationale for a severe punishment which says that, sadly, there is no other way in which the harm done can be contained, its effects limited and to a certain extent undone, and the criminal himself prevented from further harming himself, his victims, and the surrounding society, than by this severe punishment being carried out.

I think that we can, in that case, imagine a stranger turning up who says: 'Hang on, there *is* another way. There is another way in which we can achieve the same containment and healing of the harm done – in fact, a way in which we can achieve an even greater healing, a deeper healing. It will meet the needs of the victims, of the criminal, of the surrounding society, at least as deeply as the severe punishment you were contemplating. It will do all that you were hoping the punishment would do: it will bring the criminal face to face with the enormity of what he has done; it will comfort and reassure his victims; it will uphold a proper sense of what is right and wrong in the surrounding society ... everything. And yet the criminal will not need to be severely punished for this to happen. Of course, this comes with a cost, but I'm entirely willing to pay that cost ...'

For the moment, let me bracket out the obvious question as to *how* this stranger's miracle cure might be supposed to work and *what* the cost is. Let me simply concentrate on the logic of the claim itself. I think we can make sense of what is being said here. That is, I do not think it is obvious nonsense in the same way that the 'death row' example appears to be.

Note that this argument *only* makes sense, however if one has a particular view of punishment – one which, I suspect, is not the most widespread or most deeply embedded view of punishment in our society. More explicitly than most versions of penal substitution that I have come across, it requires one to think about punishment in a more liberal rather than a more conservative direction, seeing punishment as directed towards the healing of all concerned, rather than punishment having an intrinsic, obvious retributive logic and needing no further justification.

Anselm and satisfaction

It is worth noting that one of the key figures in the rise of the penal substitution model for salvation, Anselm of Canterbury, did not really teach substitutionary *punishment* at all. For Anselm, a person who sinned against another owed that person 'satisfaction': the restoration of whatever had been taken from the victim (including a restoration of the honour of the victim that had been impugned). Only if this 'satisfaction' (as it was called) could not be paid would the criminal need to be punished. For Anselm, it is not that Jesus is *punished* in our place, but rather that Jesus voluntarily pays the *satisfaction* that we are incapable of paying, so that *no one* needs to be punished.[23]

Note that, although the story that I have told involves a kind of substitution, it is not quite as straightforward a substitution as the classical doctrine suggests. It is, in the reconstruction I have given, not so obvious that the cost the stranger is willing to pay must be exactly the same as the severe punishment the criminal will be avoiding: it is a lot less obvious that it is appropriate to describe the stranger's solution straightforwardly and directly as a simple transference of the punishment from the criminal to the stranger – or rather more obvious that to describe it as involving such a transference is no more than a metaphor.

However, all this will only make sense if one has some plausible content to give to the stranger's claim. It will make sense only if one has some way of understanding how what the stranger proposes will have the effects that he claims, and will involve the cost that he sets out. In other words, even if the reconstruction of penal substitution that I have given works, there is a big gap at the middle of it. If the reconstruction I have given is going to work, then we are going to need to fill in that gap somehow, by turning to other metaphors and stories and analogies and explanations.

Classic penal substitution is normally taken to be a basic way of explaining how human beings are saved: it may not say everything that needs to be said, its proponents aver, but it does make sense in its own terms; you can proclaim penal substitution to somebody and expect them to be able to make sense of it without needing to be introduced immediately to any other models of salvation. The penal substitution model is, it is claimed, a plausible way of making sense of the substitutionary shape of the gospel story to audiences for whom sacrifice is no longer a living reality.

Yet it has this hole at its centre that cannot be filled in penal terms. The penal story is good on stressing the seriousness of sin, God's hatred of it and the inevitable cost of dealing with it. It is good on insisting that Jesus (or at least his death) is not simply illustrative of salvation, but necessary to it, so that in some sense the world's salvation has already been achieved by Christ on the cross – points to which we shall be returning. But it does not actually provide any model or analogy – in fact, the model it tries to provide obviously breaks down – when it tries to suggest *how* this particular cost is necessary, or how Christ's death is a relevant price to pay.[24]

We need to look elsewhere if we are to plug this gap. In the previous section, under the headings 'King' and 'Prophet', I suggested some directions in which one might look for such models or analogies; in the next section, I have tried to fill out those hints a little more fully.

Three views

It has become commonplace to speak of there being three main theories of the atonement:

1 the 'Latin', 'objective', 'Anselmian', 'satisfaction' or 'substitution' theory;
2 the 'subjective', 'Abelardian', 'moral influence' or 'exemplarist' theory; and
3 the 'Orthodox', 'classical', 'ransom' or 'Christus Victor' theory.[25]

Roughly speaking, the first of these is the theory that I examined in this section, relating to Christ as priest; the second relates to what I said in the previous section in relation to Christ as prophet, and the third to what I have said in that section in relation to Christ as king.

The commonplace presentation suggests that the 'Christus Victor' theory dominated for the first thousand years of Christianity, until (in the West) changes in intellectual and social culture prompted two new, but opposed theories: the Anselmian (which became the Western orthodoxy) and the Abelardian (which was regarded as defective or heretical until the modern period, when it became the standard liberal theological approach).

Widespread though this narrative is, it is deeply misleading, not least because Anselm, Abelard and their Patristic forebears had a good deal more in common than this narrative supposes. For Abelard and Anselm, Caroline Walker Bynum writes:

Both Anselm and Bernard [of Clairvaux] in fact agree with Abelard that empathetic participation in Christ's suffering arouses humankind to a love that is the first step towards return and reconciliation. Moreover, Abelard himself ... speaks ... of Christ's love providing justification – that is, offering something objective that repairs the chasm opened in the universe by sin. Like Bernard and Anselm, Abelard sees both the cross and the mass as sacrifice and satisfaction. In other words, there are subjective and objective elements in the theories of both Anselm and Abelard. Indeed, to all twelfth-century thinkers, Christ's suffering on the cross both induces response and effects ontological repair; it wrenches the hearts of humans towards empathy and healing, and it provides a totally undeserved and God-given bridge across the breach torn in the cosmos by Adam's disobedience in the garden of Eden. ... There are not two redemption theories (Abelardian and Anselmian) in the Middle Ages but one.[26]

For Anselm and the Patristic tradition, David Bentley Hart writes:

the closer the attention one pays Anselm's argument, the harder it becomes to locate the exact point at which he supposedly breaks from patristic orthodoxy. The divine action follows the same course as in the 'classic' model: human sin having disrupted the order of God's good creation, and humanity having been handed over to death and the devil's rule, God enters into a condition of estrangement and slavery to set humanity free. ... Formidable linguistic shifts aside, Anselm's is not a new narrative of salvation.[27]

Key points

- The penal model of substitution arose as a way of trying to explain the Bible's sacrificial language.
- The model does not explain how guilt can be transferred to Jesus.
- The model can be salvaged if the 'punishment' is understood as the paying of the costs inherent in the restoration of sinners and victims to flourishing life.

Transfiguring acceptance

Because God loves the world and desires to draw it into love, Christians believe that God must hate all that keeps the world from love. When faced with people who have grown up in polluted air, so twisted and distorted by sin as to be incapable, to one degree or another, of the love to which they are called, the God in whom Christians believe cannot simply be indifferent to their plight. God yearns and strives for the healing and remaking of these lives.

Christians have sometimes put this quite starkly. God, they have said, desires to kill my 'old self', my distorted and self-centred or self-hating self; and God desires to create for me a 'new self': a self open to others, a self resting in the knowledge that it is loved and unrestricted in its capacity to love. God desires my crucifixion and my resurrection.

The incarnation is, according to Christian theology, God's way of doing this. God saves the world by living in its midst a fully reconciled life: a life that is unrestricted in its capacity for love, wholly aware that it is loved, wholly caught up in love for God and wholly caught up in love for the world that God loves: a life that refuses to defend a safe location for itself in the world and also refuses to declare itself irrelevant and let itself disappear; a life that is lived for others, and which takes the inevitable shape that such selflessness takes in a world like ours: the journey to the cross.

Human beings encounter true humanity in Jesus, and that encounter both judges them (showing how their lives should look but do not) and calls them (showing them the true form that their lives can take, by God's grace). Believers respond by accepting Jesus as their judge and as their saviour – that is, by saying in response to the judgement that they encounter in him: 'Yes, kill my old self!'; and by saying, in response to the full life they see in him: 'Yes, bring me alive with you!' They commit themselves to the way of the cross and the way of resurrection: going down with Christ into the grave, and leaving their old selves there, and rising with Christ to new life, learning to be loved and to love. The processes by which these things happen are not abstruse metaphysical transactions or mystical infusions; they are the encounters and relationships that one can see portrayed in the Gospels. They are what happen when people meet Jesus, and are transformed.

Jesus is, in this understanding, God's way of loving the world because he is God's way of killing people and God's way of bringing them back to life. Looking at those whom he is saving, God sees not so much what they are, as what they will be – God sees their unChristlikeness condemned and destroyed, and their Christlikeness fulfilled. To put it in more traditional language, God sees Christ's righteousness, not their sinfulness, not because that righteousness is already complete in them, but because this is what God has declared in Christ that God will do in them, and what God has begun by the Spirit to do in them already – and what they have accepted, in accepting Christ, that God should do. For Christians, their lives no longer make sense on their own. They are lives that have Christ's name stamped on them, and so lives that are marked for destruction and reconstruction, crucifixion and resurrection.

There is indeed a substitutionary logic in this understanding: Christ has stood in the place of sinners so that they might stand in his. He has lived unselfishly among them and suffered the consequences of their animosity and hatred, in order to destroy that animosity and hatred and to make it possible for them to live beyond its shadow. But he did not suffer and die so that they would not have to, but in order that they might die *with* him, and so be raised to life with him.

Let me put all this a different way, using a story from the Old Testament as a parable.

³Jacob sent messengers before him to his brother Esau in the land of Seir, the country of Edom, ⁴instructing them, 'Thus you shall say to my lord Esau: Thus says your servant Jacob, "I have lived with Laban as an alien, and stayed until now; ⁵and I have oxen, donkeys, flocks, male and female slaves; and I have sent to tell my lord, in order that I may find favor in your sight."' ⁶The messengers returned to Jacob, saying, 'We came to your brother Esau, and he is coming to meet you, and four hundred men are with him.' ⁷Then Jacob was greatly afraid and distressed. ...

¹³From what he had with him he took a present for his brother Esau, ¹⁴two hundred female goats and twenty male goats, two hundred ewes and twenty rams, ¹⁵thirty milch camels and their colts, forty cows and ten bulls, twenty female donkeys and ten male donkeys. ¹⁶These he delivered into the hand of his servants, every drove by itself, and said to his servants, 'Pass on ahead of me, and put a space between drove and drove'. ... ²⁰For he thought, 'I may appease him with the present that goes ahead of me, and afterwards I shall see his face; perhaps he will accept me'. ...

33¹Now Jacob looked up and saw Esau coming, and four hundred men with him. So he divided the children among Leah and Rachel and the two maids. ²He put the maids with their children in front, then Leah with her children, and Rachel and Joseph last of all. ³He himself went on ahead of them, bowing himself to the ground seven times, until he came near his brother. ⁴But Esau ran to meet him, and embraced him, and fell on his neck and kissed him, and they wept.

⁵When Esau looked up and saw the women and children, he said, 'Who are these with you?' Jacob said, 'The children whom God has graciously given your servant'. ... ⁸Esau said, 'What do you mean by all this company that I met?' Jacob answered, 'To find favour with my lord.' ⁹But Esau said, 'I have enough, my brother; keep what you have for yourself.' ¹⁰Jacob said, 'No, please; if I find favour with you, then accept my present from my hand; for truly to see your face is like seeing the face of God – since you have received me with such favour.'

Genesis 32.3–7, 13–16, 20; 33.1–5, 8–10

Jacob made a habit of running away. When he had stolen the blessing due to Esau, he fled to the land of his uncle Laban. Years later, once he had taken from Laban more than Laban intended to give, he fled back again. This second flight, however, brings him back towards Esau, and as soon as his brother looms on the horizon Jacob begins to panic. He makes elaborate defensive preparations – spending all the substance he has acquired in order to turn away Esau's anger.

But Esau runs to meet him, embraces him, falls on his neck and kisses him; he steps past all his brother's defensive preparations and unexpectedly accepts him. Jacob, all his elaborate preparations undone, weeps in his brother's arms – and becomes a theologian. He says to his brother, 'Truly, to see your face is like seeing the face of God, since you have received me with such favour.' In

Esau's disarming acceptance – this gratuitous, undeserved, unearned acceptance, acceptance that sweeps away all the attempts that Jacob has made to
secure it, acceptance that makes a new future possible despite the tangled
history that lies behind them – Jacob recognizes the likeness of God.

Jacob's entire self is built from deceits, strategies, negotiations and defensiveness. He has practised it in all his encounters: snatching what he can from
life, and running from the consequences. That is simply who he now is, and
we have seen no hint of any buried resources that might help him become a
different kind of person; even in the midst of their encounter, Jacob tries to win
Esau over by offering him further gifts and by calling him 'my lord'. But Esau
responds, 'I have enough, *my brother.*' Esau reminds him that not everything
can be negotiated, that he loves him because of the givenness of the blood
relationship between them, rather than because of anything Jacob has managed to earn or coerce. And this reminder of a relationship deeper than negotiation, deeper than defence and coercion, acts as a judgement upon the self that
Jacob has built, the self that he has become. It marks that self out as unnecessary, as destructive, as an obstacle to the recognition of this true relation.

Yet Jacob, it seems, could not fully accept Esau's sincerity. He weeps; he recognizes the face of God in Esau's face – but if you read on you will see that he
does not stop negotiating. Apparently still worrying that Esau is acting only
to further his own advantage, Jacob refuses to call him 'brother', and keeps up
his strategic use of the language of 'lord' and 'servant'; he urges his gifts upon
Esau again and makes his excuses so that they need not travel too far together.
No common future is built upon the moment of clarity and recognition that
Esau's generosity has allowed, and the last that we hear is that the land has
proved insufficient to support both of them, and that Esau with all his wives
and children and livestock and property has moved to a place 'some distance
from his brother'. The two men continued to relate as rivals, as competitors,
unable to find a common good in a land of limited resources; they do not find
a way of living together as brothers, held together by a bond deeper than
competition. Esau's disarming acceptance of his brother, which undermines
and judges the defensive stratagems from which Jacob had built his life, is not
allowed to do its transformative work.

The Christian gospel tells of something like the glimpse of God's face that
Jacob saw in the face of his brother Esau. It is a message of disarming acceptance – the news that one is held by a gratuitous love that undermines and
overthrows the self one has built from defensiveness and calculation, or lost
in self-hatred and distintegration. One is met by a love that steps over all the
boundaries one has scratched around the territory one calls one's own, all
the ways one has of deploying one's substance to negotiate a position in the
world, all the subtle stratagems one uses to protect oneself against rejection,
or all one's ways of making oneself invisible, all one's ways of vanishing behind other people's substance and stratagems. One is, Christians say, accepted
by a love that is non-negotiable, as unavoidable as a blood relationship, and
so by a love that one can neither secure nor avoid: a love in the face of which
one's manoeuvring and bargaining or disappearing and self-deprecation are
irrelevances. It is a love that exposes and condemns the acquisitive, defensive,
strategic 'self' or the dissipated, fretted, untended 'self' that one has created.

So this Christian gospel is good news that crucifies. It eats away at the diseased roots of one's self-understanding, one's understanding of others and one's understanding of the world. The gospel is, Christians say, the message that, because one is held in a loving regard that one can neither coerce nor fight off and that has no shadow of selfishness about it – no shadow of one's being co-opted into somebody else's strategies or fantasies – one is set free to see and to love one's own finitude, one's own limitation, one's own mortality, and to surrender that finite, limited, mortality to the love that upholds the world. Because the gospel assures one that one is held by a love that invites one truly to be oneself, one discovers that one does not need to carve out, fence round and defend any other kind of space in the world; one does not need to throw up walls to keep out the barbarians; and one does not need to hide behind the faces of others.

To believe in this loving acceptance is to know that one's old self is judged and overturned; to hear this 'Yes' is to hear a 'No' to the current shape of one's life. And so the gospel comes, according to Christianity, as a completely free, utterly gratuitous, totally unearned gift – but nevertheless as a gift that one has to learn to accept, if one is not like Jacob to walk away from it, carrying one's possessions with one. In older Christian language, the gospel is an inextricable mix of 'justification' (the news that one is accepted, despite one's unworthiness) and 'sanctification' (the total reshaping of one's broken, defensive life to make it a reflection of this gratuitous love, which is one's learning of what this free acceptance means).

In the view I am expounding, justification precedes sanctification: it is both the condition for and the driver of sanctification. It is not that God accepts human beings once they have become holy or in view of the fact that they will become holy; God accepts them *so* that they will become holy.

God's sending of Jesus *is* God's way of accepting the world – or, more fully, the sending of Jesus and the Spirit is God's way of accepting the world. *That* Jesus and the Spirit are sent is God's justifying, accepting work; wherever they are received, wherever God's accepting work becomes real in people's lives, that is sanctification.

Having said so much about crucifixion and resurrection, and so emphasized the extent to which the Christian gospel speaks about a discontinuity between one's 'old' self and one's 'new' self, it is important to balance this with a picture of salvation that stresses continuity more. We can, perhaps, use the image of 'transfiguration'.

The Christian gospel assures me that my whole self – the self that I have become, that includes all the grit and moss that I have picked up – is the arena in which God is at work, to transform me and ready me for life lived ever deeper in God's love. God wants to make my whole life, everything that I am, shine with the light of Christ.

It is true, of course, that there is in Christian understanding no way towards God which does not involve what I have been calling crucifixion: the putting to death of one's 'old self'. But the process in which that takes place does not have to be seen as a process in which one ceases to be oneself, or as a process in which one is severed from one's history. It can be seen, rather, as a process in which one's whole self, with its history, is *redeemed*. The forgiveness, the acceptance, that meets one in the gospel is a forgiveness that takes hold of all this mess that one is, and uses it as the material of one's salvation.

Rowan Williams, in his book *Resurrection*, uses Simon Peter's encounter with the risen Jesus in Galilee as an example of this. Having betrayed Jesus three times, Simon Peter is deliberately reminded by Jesus of his betrayal.

> Simon has to recognize himself as betrayer: that is part of the past that makes him who he is. If he is to be called again, if he can again become a true apostle, the 'Peter' that he is in the purpose of Jesus rather than the Simon who runs back into the cosy obscurity of 'ordinary' life, his failure must be assimilated, lived through again and brought to good and not to destructive issue.[28]

Jesus invites Peter to discover that his betrayal has not broken the call that God has for him. He is invited to discover that Jesus 'accepts, forgives, bears and absolves the hurt done',[29] and that he can take Peter the betrayer and make him the feeder of his sheep. What Peter receives is not 'innocence' – the pretence that his betrayal did not happen – but transfiguring grace.

Grace, then – God's gift in the gospel – need not be understood as the gift of forgetfulness; it does not enable a Christian to pretend that her past has never happened. It is not the gift of a wholly new identity unrelated to what she has so far been. Like Jesus on the lakeshore, it reminds her of her history, takes her through it again, but invites her to see how the person who did all this, who is broken in all these ways, can become an icon of God's life in the world.[30]

This learning is a process in which one's self continues to be *made*. It is not the unlocking of an innocent self locked away behind this history, essentially unaffected by it; it is the transformation of the self that *is* this history. But the process of crucifixion and resurrection that I have been talking about is also a process in which one's self is *found*: it is a process in which one uncovers the self that one is in the purposes of God, the self that God who sees one truly knows one to be, the self that is 'hid with Christ in God' (Colossians 3.3). One is called to the process of 'becoming who one is'.

God is, in this view, a bit like a conversation partner with whom one can discuss oneself, who constantly prompts one to think again, when one has settled into forgetfulness, or into smug or despairing attitudes towards one's past actions and present options. God constantly needles one towards knowledge of one's deepest truth; and the crucifixion and resurrection of one's self that God brings about is not an imposition, but one's awakening to true freedom. In calling human beings deeper into Godself, God is at the same time calling them deeper into an undistorted self-knowledge, self-knowledge *without shame*.

Exercise

Do the accounts that I have presented in this section do the job I required them for? That is, do they plug the gap in the middle of the penal substitution theory?

Key points

- To be saved is, according to Christian theology, to be crucified and raised with Christ.
- God's loving acceptance of people (justification) precedes God's making them holy (sanctificaton).
- Justification rests on nothing other than God's gratuitous love.
- Sanctification involves God's loving redemption of a person's whole history.

Going further:

1 In this chapter I have swept past more detailed discussion of the nature of justification and its relationship to sanctification, even though this is still a complex issue with big implications for ecumenical debate. It is worth looking at the recent remarkable Lutheran–Catholic *Joint Declaration on the Doctrine of Justification*, available online at the Evangelical Lutheran Church in America, http://www.elca.org/ecumenical/ecumenicaldialogue/roman catholic/jddj/index.html. Other good resources include Gerhard Forde, *Justification by Faith* (Mifflintown, PA: Sigler, 1991); Hans Küng, *Justification: The Doctrine of Karl Barth and a Catholic Reflection* (London: Burns and Oates, 1966); Veli-Matti Karkkainen, *One With God: Salvation As Deification And Justification* (Collegeville, MN: Liturgical Press, 2005); and Alister McGrath, *Iustitia Dei: A History of the Christian Doctrine of Justification* (Cambridge: Cambridge University Press, 1986).

2 The debate about penal substitution is also a hot one. In fact, it seems to be one of the fault-lines of contemporary theology. On one side of the divide stand those who dispensed with the penal substitution model long ago, and barely give it a thought except to find fault with it again; on the other side stand those for whom it is the pith and kernel of the Christian gospel. To my eye, there does not seem to be a great deal of middle ground. Good accounts include Steve Holmes, 'Can Punishment Bring Peace? A Reconsideration of Penal Substitution' *Scottish Journal of Theology* 58.1 (2005), pp. 104–23; Kim Fabricius, 'Ten Propositions on Penal Substitution', Faith and Theology blog, 1 August 2006, http://faith-theology.blogspot.com/2006/08/ten-propositions-on-penal-substitution.html; and Steve Jeffrey, Mike Ovey and Andrew Sach, *Pierced for Our Transgressions: Rediscovering the Glory of Penal Substitution* (London: IVP, 2007) together with a response by N. T. Wright, 'The Cross and the Caricatures', *Fulcrum* 23/04/2007, http://www.fulcrum-anglican.org.uk/page.cfm?ID=205.

Notes

1 David Ford, *Self and Salvation: Being Transformed*, (Cambridge: Cambridge University Press, 1999), p. 1.

2 Poem attributed to St Bridget, reproduced in Eugene O'Curry, *Lectures on the Manuscript Materials of Ancient Irish History* (Dublin: James Duffey, 1861), Appendix

124, p. 616, translating a poem found in vol. 17 of the Librairie des Ducs de Bourgogne at the Bibliothèque Royale de Belgique. This version re-edited by Sean O'Faoláin (who missed out a verse about 'flails of penance' among other things) and reproduced by Mary Jones on the Celtic Literature Collective, http://www.maryjones.us/ctexts/brigitbanquet.html.

3 'Ransom' tends to be used if it is the devil that is paid, 'redemption' if the cost is paid more abstractly to the power of sin and death.

4 My list is drawn in part from John McIntyre, *The Shape of Soteriology* (Edinburgh: T&T Clark, 1996).

5 Ford, *Self and Salvation*, p. 3.

6 Valerie Saiving Goldstein, 'The Human Situation: A Feminine View', *The Journal of Religion* 40.2 (1960), pp. 100–12: p. 100.

7 Goldstein, 'The Human Situation', p. 108.

8 Goldstein, 'The Human Situation', p. 109.

9 I am not suggesting that this is what this story would have meant to its original authors or its original audiences. This is a Christian reading: a reading that starts by putting this story in the position that Christian tradition has given it (as the story of the first sin and its punishment, the paradigm of all sin and punishment) and then reads it again to see ways in which it might not quite fit into the traditional story as normally told, and ways in which it might be reread so as to make us reconceive the topics to which, in Christian tradition, it is tied.

10 The Greek text of Romans 5.12 speaks of death spreading to all people *'eph'ho* all have sinned' – probably best translated as 'inasmuch as all have sinned'. The Latin text that Augustine used translates *eph'ho* as *in quo*, and Augustine read it as *'in whom* all have sinned' – i.e. in Adam. See, for example, Augustine, *A Treatise Against Two Letters of the Pelagians* 4.7, in Philip Schaff (ed.) *Nicene and Post-Nicene Fathers*, First Series, vol. 5 (New York: Christian Literature Company, 1887), pp. 419–20; available online at the Christian Classics Ethereal Library http://www.ccel.org/ccel/schaff/npnf105.xviii.vi.vii.html.

11 Cain and Abel might well have sympathized with Philip Larkin's claim that your mum and dad 'fill you with the faults they had / And add some extra, just for you.' 'This Be the Verse' (1971) from *High Windows* (London: Faber and Faber, 1974); available online at Art of Europe http://www.artofeurope.com/larkin/lar2.htm.

12 Peter Brown, *Augustine of Hippo* (London: Faber and Faber, 1967), p. 350 quoting Augustine *De natura et gratia* 29.33.

13 Brown, *Augustine*, pp. 351–2, quoting Pelagius, *ad Demetrius* 17, and Matthew 5.48.

14 'Council of Trent, Session 6, 13 January 1547: Decree on Justification' in Norman P. Tanner (ed.), *Decrees of the Ecumenical Councils*, vol. 2 (London: Sheed and Ward, 1990), pp. 671–81: p. 679. Another translation, tr. J. Waterworth (London: Dolman, 1848) is available online at the Hanover Historical Texts Project, http://history.hanover.edu/texts/trent.html.

15 I will have more to say about 'means of grace' when we turn in Chapter 13 to discussion of the Church and the sacraments.

16 Martin Bucer, quoted in Geoffrey Wainwright, *For Our Salvation* (Grand Rapids, MI: Eerdmans, 1997), p. 104.

17 John Calvin, *Institutes of the Christian Religion*, tr. Ford Lewis Battles (London: SCM Press, 1961), pp. 503–6, 509–10; a different edition, tr. Henry Beveridge (Edinburgh: Calvin Translation Society, 1845) is available online at the Christian Classics Ethereal Library, http://www.ccel.org/ccel/calvin/institutes.iv.ii.xvii.html.

18 Rita Nakashima Brock, *Journeys by Heart: A Christology of Erotic Power* (New York: Crossroad, 1988), p. 56. The phrase was used by evangelical leader Steve Chalke in *The*

Lost Message of Jesus (written with Alan Mann) (Grand Rapids, MI: Zondervan, 2003), p. 182, and set off an avalanche of controversy. Type 'cosmic child abuse chalke' into an internet search engine to see what I mean.

19 John R. W. Stott, *The Cross of Christ* (Leicester: IVP, 1986), p. 159.

20 This is, broadly speaking, the argument of Timothy Gorringe, *God's Just Vengeance* (Cambridge: Cambridge University Press, 1996); see especially pp. 85–103.

21 Steve Sullivan, 'Substitution' in the *Ankerberg Theological Research Institute Theological Dictionary* http://www.johnankerberg.org/Articles/_PDFArchives/theological-dictionary/TD4W1199.pdf, p. 3.

22 If the fine were primarily punitive, I don't think even this would make sense. Imagine a large fine imposed on a major corporation because it had polluted a river – a fine that went beyond the costs of cleaning the river, and that was described by the judge as punitive. Would it be acceptable if some completely unconnected body, completely innocent of pollution, stepped in to pay the fine instead?

23 See Anselm of Canterbury, *Cur Deus Homo?*, I.12–15, 19–25 in Sidney Norton Deane (ed.), *St. Anselm: Proslogium etc.* (Chicago: Open Court, 1928), pp. 200–7, 219–36; available online at the Christian Classics Ethereal Library http://www.ccel.org/ccel/anselm/basic_works.html.

24 It is here that we see a drawback of seeing different ways of talking about the atonement as a series of independent models, each of which is consistent in its own way and each of which can be set alongside other similarly consistent models, capturing different aspects of the multifaceted truth. That turns out to be too neat, and this model at least turns out to be incomplete even on its own terms, and to require other models even to make sense.

25 The great proponent of this threefold division was Gustaf Aulén, *Christus Victor: An Historical Study of the Three Main Types of the Idea of Atonement*, tr. A. G. Hebert (London: SPCK, 1931 [Swedish original: 1930]).

26 Caroline Walker Bynum, 'The Power in the Blood: Sacrifice, Satisfaction, and Substitution in Late Medieval Soteriology', in Stephen T. Davis, Daniel Kendall and Gerald O'Collins (eds), *The Redemption: An Interdisciplinary Symposium on Christ as Redeemer* (Oxford: Oxford University Press, 2004), pp. 180–1.

27 David Bentley Hart, *The Beauty of the Infinite: The Aesthetics of Christian Truth* (Grand Rapids: Eerdmans, 2003), p. 366.

28 Rowan Williams, *Resurrection: Interpreting the Easter Gospel*, (London: DLT, 2002 [1982]), pp. 28–9.

29 Williams, *Resurrection*, p. 30.

30 Rowan Williams, *Lost Icons: Reflections on Cultural Bereavement* (London: Continuum, 2000), p. 112.

12

Election and Rejection

I have repeated many times the claim that Christians can understand themselves *and their world* as being drawn into the life of God. That way of putting things – as well as many of the specific points I have made along the way, particularly in Chapter 11 – raises the question of the *scope* of salvation. So this chapter will continue the discussion of the last, but asks whether there is anyone who will *not* be saved. There is the general version of that question – *Will God save everyone?* – but there is also the more specific version – *What about other religions?* What place can other religions have in this Trinitarian and Incarnational theological vision?

I am going to

- examine Paul's argument in Romans 9–11, and ask how close he comes to saying that God will save everyone;
- ask who, if anyone, the Christian tradition places in hell; and
- ask whether a Trinitarian Christian can believe that followers of other religions will be saved.

Preparation

- Will everyone be saved? Are other religions ways of salvation? Is Jesus the only doorway to salvation? Is adherence to Trinitarian and Incarnational doctrine inherently imperialistic? Jot down your answers to these questions before starting on the chapter.
- To get a glimpse of the passions raised by one of the topics I will be considering, type 'universalism' into a search engine like Google, and take a look at the first few relevant entries.

Additional reading

As accompaniments to this chapter, I recommend:

Morwenna Ludlow, *Universal Salvation: Eschatology in the Thought of Gregory of Nyssa and Karl Rahner*, Oxford Theological Monographs (Oxford: Oxford University Press, 2000). An examination of an ancient and a modern proponent of universal salvation.

Michael Barnes, *Theology and the Dialogue of Religions*, Cambridge Studies in Christian Doctrine (Cambridge: Cambridge University Press, 2002). A wide-ranging reflection on Christian hospitality to, and learning from, other religions.

Who will be saved?

There has been a universalizing flavour to much of what I have been saying in this book as a whole and in the last chapter in particular: I have spoken of God drawing the world to Godself, of God accepting the world, and so on. Does this mean that all people are being, and will be, saved? In order to explore this question, I am going to spend some time examining a long passage in Paul's letter to the Romans in which he argues about matters that touch on these questions.

Exercise

The passage is too long to reproduce here in full, but you should find a Bible and read Romans 9–11 through carefully before continuing. Who, according to Paul, will be saved? How? Why?

Paul begins chapter 9 filled with 'great sorrow and unceasing anguish' (9.2) at the thought that his people (the Jews) will not be saved. If he could trade his salvation for theirs, being condemned so that they could be acquitted, he would. 'I could wish that I myself were accursed and cut off from Christ for the sake of my own people' (9.3).

Part of his anguish stems from his knowledge that the Jews are the chosen people, the recipients of God's promises (9.4). How can they now not be saved? Has God given up on his promises? Has he abandoned his people, de-selected his chosen ones? Is God unfaithful? (9.6)

The whole of Romans 9 to 11 is an extended attempt to answer this question. And it is a fascinating and extraordinarily complex biblical text. It is one of those texts that forces one to abandon forms of exegesis that take verses in isolation, out of context: it is a complex argument that only really makes sense – quite surprising sense – when one reaches the end. Rather than being the calm laying out of a settled clutch of opinions, presented in bullet-point form to his audience, in the first-century equivalent of a PowerPoint presentation, it bears all the hallmarks of being a struggle: ideas worked out on the go, conclusions established and then challenged, set up and then undermined, as Paul works towards a conclusion that is greater than the sum of its parts.

He begins with a simple argument. We cannot accuse God of abandoning Israel, if we understand the definition of Israel properly. 'Israel' has always meant those whom God calls and keeps, not those who happen to be descendants of Abraham (9.8). Look, Paul says (9.7–13): both Ishmael and Isaac were descendants of Abraham, both Jacob and Esau, yet God chose to favour Isaac and Jacob (younger sons in both cases). Israel has always been, right from the time of the patriarchs, whoever God chose it to be – and God has always felt free to ignore the most obvious descendants (the eldest sons) in favour of strange and wayward protégés. So if God chooses for true Israel now not to coincide exactly with the Jewish people, so be it. It is entirely in line with what God has done before. And we cannot accuse God of breaking God's promises – unless we accuse God of breaking them right back at the beginning, in those very first generations of Abraham's descendants who show us what these promises *mean*.

Paul appears to have got God off the hook, but only by catching him on another one. Isn't the picture of God that Paul has painted deeply unfair? (9.14) Yes, we cannot strictly accuse God of breaking his promises – but doesn't God deal with people in an intolerably arbitrary way? God is faced with two equally deserving sons of Abraham or two equally deserving sons of Isaac – equal claimants standing before God's throne – and God chooses to be nice to one brother and nasty to the other, irrespective of what they are like. That, surely, is unfair. But Paul suggests – if I understand him rightly – that to put the objection like this is to get the question the wrong way round. It is not that we start with equally deserving sons, and then one gets condemned and another saved. Rather, God chooses to bring into being an elected son and a reprobate son, and God shapes the reprobate son so as to display hardness of heart and rejection by God, and shapes the elect son so as to display obedience and acceptance by God (9.17–18). The decision that God makes (to elect or reject) matches exactly the overall shape of each son's life, because each son's life is shaped toward the decision that God has made. It cannot be said to be treating two equal claimants unequally: one son *is* undeserving (because he is reprobate), the other *is* deserving (because he is elect).

In line with my earlier discussions of providence, one might think of God as a novelist writing a novel in which there is a bad character who eventually gets condemned and a good character who eventually gets saved. It does not make sense to think of the novelist as faced, before she puts pen to paper, with two equally deserving cases and deciding unfairly to condemn one and to save the other. That is simply not an intelligible way to talk about what is going on. The condemnation and the salvation are deeply appropriate to the respective natures of the characters that the novelist has brought into existence for this very purpose.

Paul then has to deal with another difficulty that this argument has thrown up (9.19). If one thinks of those who are not saved, those with hard hearts, simply as characters who were written that way by God – characters who never in any meaningful sense had a chance to be anything different, can one really hold them responsible for what they do? (The reprobate son will, as Paul says, ask 'Why have you made me like this? – 9.20). Isn't God still being unfair in writing bad characters in the first place?

Paul's response at this point in his argument seems simply to be: 'Look, God can do what he wants. He's God. Full stop; end of debate.' But actually his argument is a little more subtle than that. Certainly he says, in effect, 'Who are you to question God's methods?' (9.21–22) But he goes on to begin explaining what he thinks God has achieved – what God's *ends* were. So his argument is something more like: 'Who are you to question God's methods: what overview have you got of other ways in which God could have achieved God's purposes? What insight have you got into what is possible and what is impossible?' Paul then directs attention to what God has, in fact, achieved: God has made known God's forbearance, in God's patient handling of those destined for destruction, and God has made known God's glorious mercy, in allowing some to share God's life (9.22–23). Going back to our novelist example, it is as if Paul is arguing that the novelist has brought her good character and her bad character into existence, and given them their respective fates, precisely so as to show us the nature of just and measured condemnation and merciful, gratuitous salvation.

At this point, Paul's argument seems to be complete. The remainder of chapter 9 is spent restating the fact that it is perfectly in line with God's activity depicted in the Old Testament that God should have chosen to save a remnant of Israel and some of the Gentiles, rather than simply saving Israel – and hinting at the fact that the distinction between who is elected and who is rejected is displayed in how people react to Jesus the stumbling block.

You may not, however, be satisfied that Paul has given a completely adequate answer. More to the point, I don't think *Paul* is satisfied with where he has got to by this point. He started with a cry of anguish about the apparent loss of salvation by his people. He has ended up by saying that God has brought some people into existence purely in order to reject them, and that God has done this in order to reveal God's nature. If we ask, *to whom* is this revelation made, then the answer must surely be that it is primarily to the elect (they are, after all, the ones who recognize what God is doing) – so Paul's argument is tantamount to the claim that some people are rejected in order to complete and perfect the salvation of those who are elected. The reprobate are there to ice the elect's cake. Paul began by saying that he would willingly be condemned if it could only mean the salvation of his rejected people – and yet he has ended up by saying, in effect, that it's okay really because those people have been unwillingly rejected so that he could be saved. The answer doesn't quite scratch where Paul is itching.

So, at the beginning of chapter 10, Paul returns to the anguish with which he began: his 'heart's desire and prayer … that they might be saved' (10.1). He tries to understand how it is that they could be condemned – not now in terms of God's overarching providential schemes, but in terms of how election and rejection play themselves out in people's lives. It is not to do with a lack of zeal on the part of the Jews: God has not hardened their hearts by dulling their desire (10.2). Rather, it is a lack of understanding, a lack of enlightenment, a lack of recognition – a lack of that flash of insight into what is going on in Jesus which leads some to confess and believe (10.6–13). Just as the novelist writes about a bad character who is condemned, and a good character who is saved, God brings into being the un-elect who hear about Jesus but do not see what is going on in him, do not confess and believe, and so are condemned, and the elect who hear about Jesus and do recognize what is going on in him, do confess and believe, and so are saved. And the ones who are chosen for salvation in this way, Paul stresses again, can be Gentiles just as easily as they can be Jews (10.19–21).

Having restated in these more detailed terms the basic problem with which he started (the desperately sad fact that the majority of his fellow Jews have not turned to Christ) Paul at the beginning of chapter 11 returns to the question that he had apparently solved in chapter 9: 'Has God rejected his people?' (11.1). Has God broken God's promises?

Paul reiterates in slightly different words the answer he has already given:

no, God has not rejected his people – he has simply chosen to save a remnant of them (as was often the case in the Old Testament). Verses 1 to 10 add little to the argument he has already given, leaving one to wonder what unfinished business Paul felt he had with this topic to make him re-cover the ground so quickly.

But then, in verses 11 and 12 of chapter 11, he makes a breakthrough into a new way of putting things, which sets all that he has said so far in a new context:

> [11]So I ask, have they stumbled so as to fall? By no means! But through their stumbling salvation has come to the Gentiles, so as to make Israel jealous. [12]Now if their stumbling means riches for the world, and if their defeat means riches for Gentiles, how much more will their full inclusion mean!

What if, he says, the condemnation is not final? He has argued, in effect, that some are condemned for the sake of those who are chosen – to complete and perfect the gifts given to those who are chosen. What if condemnation is not the final word for those who suffer it? What if the stumbling to which God has condemned them is not the final word? What if God also intends to save them? How much greater is the gift given to the elect if, instead simply of seeing that some are condemned in order to make way for their election, they see that those they thought condemned are also rescued alongside them. How much more glorious is that? (11.12)

At first, Paul describes this as if it were simply a case that the saving of some Gentiles might provoke some Jews to jealousy – so increasing the size of the remnant of Israel who will be saved. He presents it, in other words, as a partial amelioration of the condemnation of most of Israel (11.14).

But by verse 25, Paul has taken a further step. 'I want you to understand this mystery' he says. That is, 'I want you to listen to a secret – something you could not simply have deduced from what you already know, something that is a fresh insight into the ways of God – you might even call it a revelation.' 'A hardening has come upon part of Israel, until the full number of the Gentiles has come in. And so all Israel will be saved.' (11.25) We are no longer dealing with a slight blurring at the edges of the harsh and sharp picture that Paul had painted in chapter 9. We are dealing with a claim that puts that picture in an utterly different light.

God is not a novelist who has written a novel with a bad character who gets condemned and a good character who gets saved. The plot is far more complex than that. Yes, God has made it so that the majority of Israel fail to recognize Jesus. And yes God has done that for the sake of the salvation of the Gentiles, so that they can be grafted in. But in turn God has arranged for the salvation of the Gentiles in order to win the stumbling Jews back as well. His intention all along has been to save both Jew and Gentile, and the condemnation that he has inflicted has only ever been a temporary measure, designed to further and deepen salvation. God has not abandoned the Jewish people – historical Israel, genetic Israel. They are beloved (11.28). God's promises – Paul is finally able to say this cleanly and truly, with no qualifications or get-out clauses – are irrevocable (11.29).

Paul's argument finishes with that ringing statement: 'For God has imprisoned all in disobedience so that he may be merciful to all' (11.32). It is not
simply that Israel has been condemned for the sake of the salvation of the
Gentiles. It is not that Paul would need to be condemned for the sake of the
salvation of his people. It is rather that God has all along desired to save all,
and has simply used condemnation – stumbling, turning away, hardening of
heart – as part of the strange means by which to work towards that goal. 'For
from him and through him and to him are all things. To him be the glory for
ever. Amen.' (11.36)

This whole text is complex, and even when one has come up with an interpretation that seems to make sense of it, it is hard not to suspect that one might
be missing important parts of what is going on. Nevertheless, it does seem
clear that Paul, having started with a picture in which God chooses some and
rejects others, ends up with a picture in which even though condemnation
and election are the results of God's prior choices, condemnation is a strategic
device, a temporary measure, intended for the sake of salvation – and that includes the salvation of the very people who are for now living under condemnation. Having started with a picture in which God is contented to save some
small portion of humankind, and God's dealings with all are directed solely
towards the benefit of that portion, Paul ends up with a renewed affirmation
that God desires the salvation of all, and that God's dealings with any portion
of humanity are directed towards the salvation of all.

Yet it is also clear that Paul knows of no form of salvation that is not based
on recognizing, believing in, and confessing Jesus of Nazareth. There is no
hint here that he moves away from that. For him, that is simply what 'salvation' means, and a hope for the salvation of all is a hope that all will be
brought to confess Christ. So, what we find in this passage is a commitment
to these four ideas:

1 God desires to save everyone.
2 God's desires cannot ultimately be outwitted by human actions.
3 Salvation is found only in Christ.
4 Not everyone does find salvation in Christ.

Taken at face value, these four ideas seem to be incompatible. 1 and 2 imply
that God will save everyone. 1, 2 and 3 therefore imply that everyone will find
salvation in Christ. 1, 2 and 3 therefore directly contradict 4. Something has
to give.

Exercise

Look at those four propositions again. Do you agree that they are incompatible? If one of them has to give, which do you think it should be?

Paul begins by deleting 1, and supposing that God does not desire the salvation of all – but he ends up rejecting that position by the end of chapter 11.

He never questions 3. Some argue that he must not mean 2 absolutely – and that it is possible for people to live in such a way as to snatch condemnation from the jaws of salvation, and to condemn themselves even though God desires to save them. They would say that when Paul says 'all Israel', he didn't mean 'all' but, perhaps, 'a sizeable majority of Israel' – or, at least, 'many more Jews than believe in Jesus at the moment'.

Some who follow this line think that 2 is the obvious one of the four to give because they have a strong account of free will. God gave human beings free will, and human beings are able to use that free will to pursue aims that God does not desire – and surely it is simply an extension of that to claim that people can use their free will to thwart God's final desire for their whole lives. God gives people the opportunity to choose salvation or not to choose salvation, but the rest is up to them.

Now, as we have already seen, debates over free will are notoriously complex. It is important to realize, however, that the account of free will just described is a good deal more confident, a good deal stronger, than any with which Paul seems to have been operating. Statement 2 would have looked a whole lot less flexible to him, with his very strong theology of God's sovereignty even over human choices.

Others therefore argue that it is 4 that must give – and that when Paul said 'all' he meant 'all', every last one – and that therefore one must envisage that even those Jews who have already died without recognizing Christ will somehow be brought by God to recognize Jesus as messiah. Everyone recognizes Christ eventually, even if it takes place after death.

All of these solutions, however, are attempts to tie down what Paul leaves enigmatic and pregnant with possibilities. They are entirely speculative solutions, and I don't think that we have any evidence to suggest to us exactly how Paul would have taken further the hints he gives here. I rather suspect that it was not at all clear to him, and that he was willing to leave it in the safe hands of God. Nevertheless, I do think that Paul's logic pushes towards 'all' meaning 'all', and that by the end of chapter 11 he has glimpsed a thoroughly universalist vision, even if he does not know how that squares with other things to which he is committed.

No clear vision

'We should not, then, be more curious than Scripture allows us to be. With Paul, we may say that grace is far more powerful than sin, that all die in Adam, but that all will also be raised to life in Christ, who will lay a perfected creation at the Father's feet (Romans 5.12–21; 1 Corinthians 15.21–2, 28). But we must also stand with Christ himself, and with his gospel, at the edge of eternal destruction and gaze down into it. To want to overcome this final antinomy through a premature "synthesis" is not appropriate for theology in this present age.'

Hans Urs von Balthasar, Cosmic Liturgy[1]

There are a few more points that I want to make before leaving Romans 9–11 behind. We are not, at this point, discussing what 'not being saved' is actually like. That is a separate question, and one that we won't be considering for now. You can ask 'Who will be saved?' and 'How will they be saved?' without deciding on questions about the existence and nature of hell. All that matters for our current purposes is the question of whether there can come a point where a person finally ceases to be drawn deeper into the life of God – where a person drops out of the ongoing process of salvation.

It is also worth noting that the question about whether everyone is saved, or about whether Christ is the only way of salvation, is not a question posed only by modern liberal culture or by political correctness. It is a question that emerges in the Bible itself, and is tussled with there. To think it through, to work hard to understand the question, is not to bow to some anti-Christian agenda, but is to follow in the footsteps of Paul. That doesn't mean that Paul was any kind of modern pluralist; it doesn't mean that he thought 'anything goes'; it doesn't mean he watered down his commitment to the centrality of Christ. It does mean that he found himself caught between an acknowledgement of God's desire to save everyone, his belief that Christ was the only means of salvation, and his recognition that not everyone turned to Christ.

As one ponders this question, it is important to pay serious attention to the anguish with which the passage we have been exploring begins. If one claims that it is possible for God to desire someone's salvation and yet for that person not to be saved, then one must recognize the gravity of what one is saying. One is claiming that God can fail, that God can ultimately be defeated and frustrated by the creation that God has made. One is claiming that human actions can render the life of God, into which God has called all humanity, incomplete. And one is claiming that the rejoicing that Christians picture as the expression of that life must forever be marred by mourning – by anguish like Paul's – over those who have excluded themselves from this life.

Key points

- Romans 9–11 pushes towards universalism – that is, the idea that all people will be saved.
- It suggests that condemnation is subordinated to, and oriented towards, salvation.
- It suggests that the proper response to the idea of some not being saved is anguish.
- At no point does Paul abandon the idea that salvation is found only in Jesus.

Election, rejection and Christ

[47]Again, the kingdom of heaven is like a net that was thrown into the sea and caught fish of every kind; [48]when it was full, they drew it ashore, sat down, and put the good into baskets but threw out the bad. [49]So it will be

at the end of the age. The angels will come out and separate the evil from
the righteous [50]and throw them into the furnace of fire, where there will be
weeping and gnashing of teeth.

Matthew 13.47–50

Exercise

If you take this passage seriously, what will it do to your answer to the previous
exercise – that is, your thoughts about which of the four claims that I enumer-
ated in the previous section has to give?

There is a good deal in the Bible that speaks very firmly of a division between
the saved and the unsaved, the elect and the reprobate, and the final condemnation of the latter – including much on Jesus' own lips. What are we to make
of such passages in the light of what I have been saying? Do they pull us decisively away from any universalist answer to Paul's questions?

I am going to approach that question obliquely, by telling a story.

A man arrived at the gate of heaven one day, to be met with open arms by
Peter. 'Welcome, brother; welcome to your new home. Your name is one of
those written in the book of life, so the gate is open to you.' Peter showed him
through the gate into the green landscape beyond, where he was met by an
angel, dispatched to show him around and explain the workings of the place.
He was shown where he would live; he was shown how to get in touch with
relatives and friends who had died before him. The procedures for booking
a chat with any of the more famous inhabitants of heaven were explained
– and he asked, rather timidly, to be put down for a meeting with Mozart.
He was given his library card, the menu for the nearest eateries, and some
information about flying lessons. And then the angel brought him up short
with a further comment: 'Of course, you'll probably want to visit the Viewing
Platform as well.'

'The viewing platform?'

'Yes, you know: it's where you can look down into hell. You must have heard
about it – it's one of heaven's best-known attractions. Lots of theologians and
preachers have talked about it; ask one of the librarians to show you some
examples, if you like. You can visit the viewing platform and look into hell,
and be filled with joy and amazement at the sure justice of God meted out
against sin.'

The man was taken aback, but so much about this orientation was overwhelming that he said nothing. Yet as soon as he was left alone, he nervously
made his way in the direction that the angel had indicated. He climbed a
gentle slope, fringed at the top with a plain railing, and when he reached
it saw that he was on the rim of a vast crater piercing the green landscape.
Though the sun was shining around him, the inside of the crater was as black
as night, lit only by fitful glimmers of red fire, and shrouded with smoke and
mist. He had been worrying about what he might see, or hear, but at first he
could make out nothing. There were not the hordes of writhing sinners that

he had worried he might see, and no tortured cries reached him. It seemed empty – vast, dark, terrible and empty.

He was about to turn away with a smile, believing he had understood, and quite pleased at the joke that had been played on him (if it could be called a joke) when a cry did reach him: a strangled, pain-filled cry from somewhere in the depths of the crater. He peered into the darkness, but could not see from where in the darkness the voice had come. And then he heard it again, and realized with a jolt that he could understand it – that on arriving in heaven all sorts of unlearned knowledge had blossomed in his head. Yes, he could understand it; it was an old, unfamiliar dialect, but it made perfect sense to him. It was Western Aramaic, he knew, of a form spoken two millennia or so ago. A rural accent, for all that he could tell from this pain-filled cry. And it was saying words he knew from something he had read: *Eloi, eloi, lema sabachthani*. My God, my God, why have you forsaken me?

There is one person (and one person only) that the Christian tradition has confidently and with near consensus placed in hell: Jesus of Nazareth. The Apostles' Creed says that Jesus 'suffered under Pontius Pilate, was crucified, died, and was buried. *He descended into hell.*' It was understood by some in the early Church as the extreme point of the exchange or substitution that I talked about on p. 277. Hilary of Poitiers, a fourth-century theologian, wrote 'Christ, the Son of God, dies; but all flesh is made alive in Christ. The Son of God is in hell; but man is carried back to heaven.'[2]

Drawing on this tradition, the twentieth-century theologian Karl Barth suggested that if we are asking who is elect and who is reprobate, the answer to both questions is first of all 'Jesus'.[3] He is the elect man, the fulfilment of the covenant with Israel who lived in full communion with the Father – and all election is *in Christ*, the election of those who share in his body, and so share in his election, his resurrection life. But, said Barth, Jesus is also the one who suffers the consequences of sin, plumbing the depths of the separation from God that sin creates. He is the rejected one, the condemned one, the one who dies godforsaken and under a curse, and descends to hell. When we think of other men and women being 'rejected', we are thinking of them being rejected with Christ, crucified with Christ, dying with him. So, yes, Barth suggests, the Gospel does describe an absolute separation between election and rejection, between good and evil, between the saved and the unsaved – it is the separation between resurrection and crucifixion. Yet, rather than thinking of this separation dividing people into two distinct categories, one of which will end up in heaven, the other in hell, we should think of it as a sword that cuts across all people: all need to die with Christ and all need to rise with Christ – all need to participate in his rejection, to allow the old self to be crucified with him, and all need to participate in his election.[4]

The question about universalism then ceases to be a question about whether there is any condemnation, any wrath, any judgement – of course those exist! – but becomes instead the question of whether there are any who are so defined and dominated by the 'old self', the self that is to be crucified with Christ, that there will be nothing recognizable left of them to share in his resurrection life. Paul's argument in Romans 9–11 suggests that the answer is 'No', without it being at all clear how that meshes with the other commitments of Christian theology.

Exercise

Is what I have written a plausible way of holding together Romans 9–11 with passages like Matthew 13.47–50?

Key points

- In the Christian tradition, even hell is not seen as being beyond Jesus' reach.
- Election and condemnation might not divide people into two distinct camps, but might divide the 'new' from the 'old' creation in each person.
- The universalism question is whether there are any who are only defined by condemnation.

Salvation and other religions

What, though, of other religions? Where do they fit into the picture that I have been painting? It is popular to suggest that there are three main types of answer to this question. In the first place, there are *exclusivists*, who argue that Christianity truly describes salvation and provides access to its source, Jesus Christ, and that other religions, whatever good there may be in them, are not ways of salvation. In the second place, there are *inclusivists*, who regard Christianity as true no less than do the exclusivists, but who accept that God is saving many beyond the boundaries of the Christian Church, and may be using other religions to do so. Those other religions may, in the terms I used earlier, be 'means of grace', leading people into conformity with the God of Jesus Christ, even if those people do not realize that this is what is happening. In the third place, there are *pluralists*, who argue that Christianity might be a true way of describing and providing access to salvation, but not necessarily any *more* true than other religions. Christianity, says the pluralist, is one way of grasping a truth that can also be grasped quite differently: the different religions are paths up the same mountain. Some may be wider, easier paths than others, and there may even be some religions that finally keep people from the summit, but Christianity cannot lay claim to be an absolute or privileged account of the nature of God or of salvation.[5]

Exercise

To which option are you initially most attracted: exclusivism, inclusivism or pluralism?

The theology that I have been exploring so far in this book does not sit neatly in a single one of these categories. In the first place, it has something of the flavour of 'exclusivism' about it: I explained the doctrine of the Trinity as involving the claim that 'God is the one whom Christians know as they find themselves, in the Spirit, caught up in the Son's love of the Father and the Father's sending of the Son.' And when discussing the doctrine of the Spirit, I said that 'God is Christ-shaped' and that 'To get into this space, you must become Christ-shaped; if you take on a different shape, you arrive somewhere else.' And when discussing Paul's argument in Romans 9–11 above, I suggested that one of his axioms is that salvation is found only in Jesus Christ. Knowledge of Christ, or relation to Christ, is essential in the theology I have been expounding – and, as I have repeatedly explained, 'Christ' does not name a general principle or idea, but a person, so it is attention specifically to Jesus of Nazareth that is essential.

However, some of my discussions have pointed in a more inclusivist direction. I suggested in the chapter on the Spirit that *wherever* Christlike life, Christlike love, is emerging in the world, that is the work of the Spirit conforming people to Christ – and it seems obvious that Christlike life and love emerge in all sorts of places, well beyond the boundaries of the Church, or the spread of explicit knowledge of and response to the gospel. The univeralism to which I pointed earlier in this chapter suggests the same thing – that we should not divide the world up into Christians, who will be saved, and non-Christians, who will not, but should see that the judgement and salvation that Christ brings apply to all people, and that they rest upon an acceptance that God offers to all. To put it another way, the human being Jesus of Nazareth may be the only criterion by which Christians can judge, and he may be an unsubstitutably particular human being rather than an idea or a principle, but that does not mean that condemnation is the only judgement that he will offer of life that has grown up independently of devout attention to him.

This 'inclusivist' strand in what I have been saying does, of course, still claim a privilege for the Christian tradition: it still assumes that it is Jesus who is the criterion for judgement and salvation. It is important to notice, however, that most forms of pluralism claim no less a privilege. If one claims that all religions are really paths up the same mountain, even if one claims that one has no direct way of characterizing that mountain except by the language one happens to have learnt in one's own tradition, one is still making the very strong claim that those aspects of all religions that directly oppose or deny or rule out other religions must be secondary or mistaken, and that in outline one knows the secret of the salvation to which those religious traditions point better than do those adherents who cling to exclusivist or inclusivist accounts.

Nevertheless, the kind of theology I have been presenting does include something like a pluralist moment. I have talked a great deal about the ungraspability of God, and about Christian's ignorance about *how* the claims that they believe they are required to make about God are actually true of God. And I have talked a great deal about openness to discovering that one is wrong, or that one needs to expand or reform one's thinking – and about how the different ways of thinking and acting that Christians find in those around them who differ from them might turn out to be *gifts*, helping drive that process of expansion or reform.

As a convinced Trinitarian Christian, I believe that the Word and the Spirit have truly been sent by God, and truly draw me into the life of God, and that God truly is immanently as God is in this economy – so that God really *is* Christlike, and Christ really *is* God's way of saving the world. But I can also say that I *simply do not know how* this fits in with other claims to know God, or to know the meaning and means of salvation. I believe that I am, say, sent into conversation with my Jewish and Muslim friends with the vocation to witness to Christ – and that I don't go into that conversation regarding this as a negotiable point or a temporary working hypothesis: I go in believing it to be *true*. But I also believe I go in called to listen to my friends and to hear from them things I could not have said to myself, which might cause me to understand my own vocation and witness differently: I go in hoping and expecting to learn something new of Christ, and so of God, in encounter with them. And it may be (though I cannot possibly legislate for this) that they approach the conversation with some analogous conviction: a desire to witness to the revelation of God in Torah or in the Quran, but a willingness to be shown the Torah or the Quran afresh in conversation with me and with each other. Each of us, as it were, might approach the conversation as a different species of inclusivist. It accords with the structure of the theology I have been expounding to say that I do not know where all this will end. I do not know whether I will simply be left with this inclusivism. I do not know whether in some unguessed future we might discover that our inclusivisms converge, and that my Trinitarianism has become thoroughly flavoured by the Torah and the Quran, just as my conversation partners find that their vocations have become thoroughly flavoured by the gospel. I do not know whether we will find that there are aspects, perhaps even central aspects, of our respective vocations that will turn out to be incompatible, so that as a Christian I will only see my Muslim or Jewish friends being drawn into the life of God via the loss or overturning of something they hold dear – or whether I might find that I am led to the abandonment of something that I hold dear, even something that I presently regard as non-negotiable. And I do not know whether it may turn out that the ends that each of us longs for and pursues may simply turn out to be different, too different even to be mutually exclusive (as different as being tall is from liking cheese, rather than as different as being tall is from being short).[6] I have hunches, of course, and I can see all sorts of things in our practices and beliefs that look compatible or analogous, and all sorts of things that I cannot imagine leading to anything but serious disagreement, including quite central things. And if I include Buddhism, Hinduism and other religious traditions in the conversation, the variety increases even more noticeably. But standing where I stand, I do not know what end God has in store for this conversation, and nothing in my theology tells me that I *ought* to know. All that I have is the vocation to enter the conversation seriously, to do so as part of my journey deeper into the triune economy of God, and to do so as a witness to the life of God that I believe has been opened to me in Christ and the Spirit.

Exercise

Am I simply cherry-picking the bits I like out of 'exclusivism', 'inclusivism' and 'pluralism' – or does the position I have just sketched genuinely follow from the theology I have been expounding throughout the book?

Key points

- Trinitarian Christianity claims that God is *truly* known only in Jesus.
- Witnessing to God in Christ is a vocation for Christians in all circumstances and all dialogues.
- Christians, however, need claim no final overview about how this claim connects with other religious ways of identifying God.

Going further

1 The question of universalism is worth exploring in much more depth. Along-side the Ludlow book mentioned in the introduction, I recommend Robin Parry and Christopher Partridge (eds), *Universal Salvation? The Current Debate* (Grand Rapids, MI: Eerdmans, 2004).
2. The questions posed by the plurality of religions are even deeper – and discussed in a very broad swathe of theological literature. One debate that is worth following is that between John Hick and Gavin D'Costa on whether the 'pluralist' position is any less exclusive than the alternatives. See John Hick, *God and the Universe of Faiths* (Oxford: Oneworld, 1993), pp. 133–47; Gavin D'Costa, *The Meeting of Religions and the Trinity* (Maryknoll, NY: Orbis, 2000), pp. 19–52; John Hick 'The Possibility of Religious Pluralism: A Reply to Gavin D'Costa', *Religious Studies* 33 (1997), pp. 161–6; Gavin D'Costa, 'Christ, the Trinity and Religious Plurality' in D'Costa (ed.), *Christian Uniqueness Reconsidered* (Maryknoll, NY: Orbis, 2002), pp. 16–29. For some other perspectives, see Gabriel Fackre, 'Claiming Jesus as Saviour in a Religiously Plural World', *Journal for Christian Theological Research* 8 (2003), pp. 1–17, available online at http://www.luthersem.edu/ctrf/JCTR/Vol08/Fackre.pdf, and Mark Heim, *The Depth of the Riches: A Trinitarian Theology of Religious Ends* (Grand Rapids, MI: Eerdmans, 2001).
3 My own response to the plurality of religions has been much influenced by my involvement in the 'Scriptural Reasoning' movement – a joint initia-tive of Jewish, Christian and Islamic scholars focused on the shared read-ing of scriptural texts. For more information, see *The Journal of Scriptural Reasoning Forum* online at http://etext.lib.virginia.edu/journals/jsrforum/, – particularly the sections 'What is SR?' and 'Who does SR?'

Notes

1 Hans Urs von Balthasar, *Cosmic Liturgy: The Universe according to Maximus the Confessor*, tr. Brian E. Daley (San Francisco: Ignatius, 2003 [German third edn: 1988]), p. 358.

2 Hilary of Poitiers, *On the Trinity* 3.15 in Philip Schaff and Henry Wace (eds) *Nicene and Post-Nicene Fathers*, Series 2, vol. 9 (New York: Christian Literature Company, 1898), p. 66, available online at the Christian Classics Ethereal Library, http://www.ccel.org/ccel/schaff/npnf209.ii.v.ii.iii.html.

3 Karl Barth, *Church Dogmatics II: The Doctrine of God*, Pt 2 (Edinburgh: T. & T. Clark, 1957), pp. 306–409, especially p. 346: 'there is only one Rejected, the Bearer of all man's sin and guilt and their ensuing punishment, and this One is Jesus.'

4 Barth speaks of 'the Rejected on Golgotha, and the rejected in ourselves and in all others', *Church Dogmatics* II/2, p. 458.

5 Alan Race, *Christians and Religious Pluralism: Patterns in the Christian Theology of Religions* (London: SCM Press, 1983), drawing on the work of his teacher, John Hick; see also Gavin D'Costa, *Theology and Religious Pluralism* (Oxford: Blackwell, 1986) and John Hick and Paul Knitter (eds), *The Myth of Christian Uniqueness* (London: SCM Press, 1987). The typology has been criticized in Gavin D'Costa (ed.), *Christian Uniqueness Reconsidered* (Maryknoll, NY: Orbis, 1990).

6 See Mark Heim, *Depth of Riches: A Trinitarian Theology of Religious Ends*, (Grand Rapids, MI: W.B. Eerdmans Publishing Co., 2001) and *Salvations: Truth and Difference in Religion*, (Maryknoll, NY: Orbis Books, 2001).

13

One and Catholic

Back in Chapter 1, I suggested that theology emerged as Christian communities tried to make sense of their lives, but until now I have concentrated on sketching the context or backdrop against which Christians believe that their communities' lives are played out: the nature of the God that these communities worship, the texture of the world within which they live, the shape of the salvation in which they believe themselves caught up. In this chapter, however, I finally turn to those communities themselves, and reach 'ecclesiology', or the doctrine of the Church. What is the Church? Why do Christians gather together? What do they do? What are their communities and meetings and institutions *for*? In the present chapter I will explore two of the central themes of ecclesiology: worship and unity, before turning to two more (apostolicity and holiness) in the next.

I am going to

- argue that worship is a central defining feature of the Church;
- explore what the Church says and does in the Eucharist;
- explore what the Church says and does in baptism;
- ask what the implications are of divisions in the Church.

Preparation

- What is the Church for? What are its core activities or structures? Have a think about these questions, and jot down a couple of sentences about your answers before starting on the chapter.
- If you have access to the internet, and type 'define:church' into Google, you will find all sorts of definitions. Glance through them, and see which ones you find most (and least) helpful.

Additional reading

To accompany this chapter and the next, you might like to try the following:

Avery Dulles, *Models of the Church* (Dublin: Gill and MacMillan, 1988). An accessible survey of different ways of thinking about the Church.
Jürgen Moltmann, *The Church in the Power of the Spirit: A Contribution to Messianic Ecclesiology* (London: SCM Press, 1977). A substantial proposal for thinking about ecclesiology and pneumatology together.
Stanley Hauerwas, *A Community of Character: Toward a Constructive Christian Social Ethic* (Notre Dame: University of Notre Dame Press, 1981). A discussion of the Church as a community that forms Christlike people able to make ethical judgements.

Any given Sunday

Last Sunday morning, I went with my wife and two small children (Bridget aged three and Tom aged one) to a large fifteenth-century granite church that dominates a small village on the edge of Dartmoor. We arrived just as the service was about to begin, were each handed a hymn book and a service sheet at the door, and then sat right at the back so that Bridget and Tom would have easy access to the children's play area (crayons and paper, lots of children's books, some cuddly toys, some Sticklebricks). We took little notice of the familiar surroundings: the stone font standing near us, the nineteenth- and twentieth-century stained-glass windows, the plaque with a memorial to those from the village who died in the World Wars, the grave slabs set into the floor and other monuments round the wall, the pulpit, the wooden screen partially separating the chancel from the nave, the communion table in the chancel with a chalice and candles set on it, the pipe organ on one side of the chancel, the piano, the tower behind us with bell-ropes just visible in the loft, the modern white cross hanging in front of the tower. There were perhaps 25 people in this barn of a building, most of them older than us, many of them retired, all sitting in wooden pews facing the chancel. At the division between chancel and nave, a robed vicar stood to lead the service, except when he climbed up to the pulpit to deliver the sermon. We sang a selection of hymns accompanied by the organ; we heard and said various parts of the Anglican liturgy for Holy Communion; we listened to readings from the Bible and heard a brief sermon from the vicar expounding one of those readings. At least, we tried to do all those things, but were often distracted as we tried to keep Bridget and Tom amused and relatively quiet, making sure that they didn't use the crayons on anything other than the colouring sheets, and administering snacks (rather than smacks) when other amusements ceased to attract. When the liturgy reached the relevant point, the four of us joined the queue of people walking to the altar rail at the front of the church, Tom toddling confidently but unpredictably by my side. We knelt, and the vicar said a prayer of blessing for each child, and gave each of us adults a communion wafer; his assistant gave each of us a sip of red wine. After the service was over, we chatted to friends in the congregation about this and that, the affairs of the week, news from the village; we picked up the scattered books and crayons, and then made our way home.

What has any of that to do with the theology that I have been exploring in this book so far? Or what has that theology to do with any of the very different experiences of Church that countless millions of people around the world had on the same day – from ornate and dramatic celebrations of High Mass to the silence of Quaker meetings, from mega-churches holding tens of thousands to rooms with just two or three, from churches that are part of some ancient denomination to unaffiliated house churches and informal groups, from vast stone cathedrals to tiny tin huts?

Key point

- When one looks at the practical realities of real churches, it may not be obvious what connection they have to the theology I have been presenting.

Marks of the Church

In one part of the liturgy during last Sunday's service, my wife and I joined with the rest of the congregation to say the Nicene Creed. The third main section of that creed runs:

We believe in the Holy Spirit,
the Lord, the giver of life,
who proceeds from the Father and the Son,
who with the Father and the Son is worshipped and glorified,
who has spoken through the prophets.
We believe in one holy catholic and apostolic Church.
We acknowledge one baptism for the forgiveness of sins.
We look for the resurrection of the dead,
and the life of the world to come. Amen.

In other services, we might say the Apostles' Creed, the equivalent part of which says

I believe in the Holy Spirit,
the holy catholic Church,
the communion of saints,
the forgiveness of sins,
the resurrection of the body,
and the life everlasting. Amen.[1]

In both creeds, the clause concerning the Holy Spirit introduces a series of apparently disconnected affirmations, which can nevertheless be argued to concern the way in which the speakers of the creed are caught up into the life of the God whose identity they have been declaring: through baptism, through forgiveness, through resurrection – and through participation in the 'holy catholic Church' or 'one holy catholic and apostolic Church'.

The four epithets given in the Nicene Creed – one, holy, catholic, apostolic – have long been called the four 'Marks of the Church', and they have become a common way for theologians to organize many of the things they want to say about the Church.[2] I am going to be no exception: the bulk of both this chapter and the next will be arranged under those four headings (though not in that order). For reasons that won't necessarily be clear until we get there, I am going to look at the Church's worship under the heading 'One'; at diversity and ecumenism under the heading 'Catholic'; at the church as witness and as tradition under the heading 'Apostolic'; and at the Church as sinful and reformed under the heading 'Holy'.[3]

Exercise

Think of any church of which you have had experience. What about that church would make it strange or difficult to confess in it that 'I believe in one, holy, catholic and apostolic church'? What about that church would connect with and support that confession?

Key point

• Traditionally, the Church has been regarded as one, holy, catholic and apostolic.

Unity and worship

For Christian theology, the Church is one because God is one.[4] The Church comes into existence as the one Spirit draws people into the body of the one Son, on the way to the one Father – and Father, Son and Spirit are one. However diverse may be the ways in which the light of Christ's relationship to the Father is refracted by the Spirit in different people, different places and different times, all those refractions are in principle united because they are refractions of light from a common source.[5] They point back towards that one source, and reflect that source to one another and to the world – or so Christian theology claims.

I will have much more to say about the form that this unity of the Church takes or fails to take when I discuss the Church's 'catholicity' later on. For now, my focus is simply on the claim that the unity of the Church is not found in the Church itself, but in the source to which it all points, and toward which it is all moving. It is like a painting of a landscape, drawn in such a way that the vanishing point, the point where the lines of perspective appear to converge, is outside the frame of the picture.

You may, however, notice a problem with the claim that this unity is a mark of the Church. God, I have repeatedly claimed, is the source and goal of the whole world. *Everything* has its unity in God, for Christian theology – and yet a 'mark' of the Church should be something that helps us distinguish the Church from other realities. It is more accurate, therefore, to say that the unity of the Church, its oneness, is not so much to be found in the claim that it has its source and goal in God, but in the claim that it acknowledges, witnesses to, proclaims and celebrates this source and goal. The unity of the Church is therefore to be found in the Church's *worship*.

Worship is a matter of putting God and the world in their rightful places – of acknowledging that God is the source and goal of all things, and of acknowledging that the world has its source and goal in God. More fully, worship is a matter of *praise* as God is acknowledged as the unencompassable source of all goodness, truth and beauty; it is a matter of *thanks* as the goodness, truth and beauty that people find in their lives and their world, and those lives and that world themselves, are acknowledged as gifts from God.

Worship and belief

In the light of my discussion of the nature of knowledge of God in Chapter 2, one could say that worship *is* belief in God, and belief in God *is* worship. To say 'I believe in God' and yet not to worship is to speak nonsense: God is known only in thanks and praise. Similarly, to acknowledge in thanks and praise that one's life and one's world comes to one as a gift from a source, however little one can see or say of that source, *is* belief in and knowledge of God. To say that *worship* holds the Church together is equivalent to saying that *belief in God* holds the Church together.

It might, therefore, be more direct to say that *worship* is a mark of the Church. Many different activities and programmes and tendencies and events and habits are associated with the Church, but it is worship that is its central distinctive activity. Without worship – without people's coming before God in explicit acknowledgement and celebration of who God is and how they stand with respect to God – there is no Church. Worship is what makes all other activities and practices become activities and practices of the Church. Meeting together, for instance, is transformed by worship from being an activity paralleled in any social club anywhere, to being something done before God, for God's sake. Activities of mission in the world are, similarly, transformed from simply being forms of voluntary social action or propaganda, and become aspects of the mission of God, calling all people deeper into the life of God. Worship makes the Church.[6]

Key points

- The Church is one because God is one.
- The Church is where the one God is acknowledged, witnessed to, proclaimed and celebrated.
- Worship of God is a mark of the Church.
- Worship is what makes an activity or practice into an activity or practice of the Church.

Called out in worship

Worship is, in one sense of the word, marked by *ecstasy* – that is, by *ek-stasis*: by being called out of oneself, focused outside oneself, turned to face away from oneself. Worship involves people acknowledging, *knowing*, that they are not their own source; that the goodness, truth and beauty that they meet is not their creation or possession, that everything they have, everything they *are*, they have received from a loving source. It has to do with acknowledging a source of value and strength and life and support outside oneself, which one does not control; it has to do with finding oneself overwhelmed, bowled over and carried away by something beyond one.

Worship understood in this way is poised between two tempting distortions. Worship can become an expression of anxiety: an activity in which the worshippers seek to persuade themselves and others that God is on their side, or an activity in which worshippers try to win God over, placate or bribe God. Worship can become an activity focused on protecting and advancing the anxious self. Ek-static worship, however, is not a way of getting something done; it is not an achievement. Worship, one might say, is fundamentally not useful, not utilitarian; it is not a *technique*. And therefore to engage in worship – or, better, to be caught up in worship – is, in this understanding, one way in which self-centredness is broken open; one way in which illusions of control and security are torn down. We might say that worship is a matter of being *called out* of those things.

Liturgy as play

'The practice of the liturgy means that by the help of grace, under the guidance of the Church, we grow into living works of art before God, with no other aim or purpose than that of living and existing in his sight; it means fulfilling God's Word and "becoming as little children"; it means foregoing maturity with all its purposefulness, and confining oneself to play, as David did when he danced before the Ark. It may, of course, happen that those extremely clever people, who merely from being grown-up have lost all spiritual youth and spontaneity, will misunderstand this and jibe at it. David probably had to face the derision of Michal.

'It is in this very aspect of the liturgy that its didactic aim is to be found, that of teaching the soul not to see purposes everywhere, not to be too conscious of the end it wishes to attain, not to be desirous of being over-clever and grown-up, but to understand simplicity in life. The soul must learn to abandon, at least in prayer, the restlessness of purposeful activity; it must learn to waste time for the sake of God, and to be prepared for the sacred game with sayings and thoughts and gestures, without always immediately asking "why?" and "wherefore?" It must learn not to be continually yearning to do something, to attack something, to accomplish something useful, but to play the divinely ordained game of the liturgy in liberty and beauty and holy joy before God.'

Romano Guardini, *The Spirit of the Liturgy*[7]

Exercise

If you have experience of corporate Christian worship, what, in that experience, do people hope or expect to get out of that worship? What do they hope
or expect it to *do* for them? Think about this for a while, and then ask yourself
what might be involved in people being weaned off these hopes and expectations, to acknowledge the proper 'uselessness' of worship? What might that
do to the people worshipping, and to the forms of worship in which they are
involved? Do you think this *is* a proper aim?

In the other direction, however, worship can become an activity in which
the worshipping self simply tries to disappear. That is, it can become an
activity in which worshippers abandon any sense of God as a source of life
and love, and of their own lives and world as God's gift. Worship can be an
activity or experience in which worshippers are not simply taken beyond
their self-centredness, but are led to despise themselves, to consider themselves as worms, and to hate the world by contrast with the glories of the
heaven to which they direct their gaze. Yet worship, if it is worship of the God
that I have been discussing in this book, should be an activity in which the
worshipper learns to value himself or herself properly – to recognize himself
or herself as a gift of God.

So worship is, in this view, a matter of response to grace, of hearing and
answering a call. Different forms and styles of worship can be seen as tied
to different assumptions about how that call is mediated to the worshipper.
For some, the call is heard primarily in the spoken word – in the words of
Scripture, and of preaching that expounds Scripture; much of worship might
be orchestrated listening giving way to penitent and thankful response. For
others, the call might be mediated particularly by music, with its capacity
to worm its way into our bodies and minds and set us resonating to its own
rhythm: the dynamic of such worship might be less obviously that of call and
response, and more a matter of being drawn into participation with a movement that takes one out of oneself. For still others, the call might be heard
most clearly in silence – as the worshipping self learns to attend to all the
voices running through it, and to discern where among all the self's selfish or
despairing, distracted or obsessed babbling the call of God is echoing.

In some moments in Christian history, the paradigm of the worshipper has
been the individual alone on a mountainside somewhere, glorying in a golden
sunset, dozens of miles from the nearest distracting voice or face. The worshipper encounters a context that vastly exceeds the self, but of which the self
is a constituent part, and there can be a strong sense not simply of acknowledging creation's beauty, grandeur or breathtaking intricacy, but of being
caught up in the song of praise that creation *is*.[8] Yet it is more consonant with
the theology I have been exploring to suggest that the call of God is mediated
more fully not by sunsets and mountains, but by other people. Worship is inseparable from the process in which a person's limited, cramped and narrow
vision of God is broken open and expanded by encounter with other people

who think and see differently, who *are* different – being surprised by them, surprised by what they convey of God, and surprised by what God speaks through them. If worship involves delighting in the call of God, then the doctrine of the Spirit suggests that other people are the widest doorways into real worship, doorways into what has been called the 'constantly astonished joy' that is the keynote of praise.[9]

Wherever the emphasis falls, however, the basic pattern is the same: worship is fundamentally response to the call of God as it is mediated to the worshipper through some creaturely reality.

Key points

- Worship is response to the call of God.
- That call is always mediated by some creaturely reality: words, music, nature, other people, etc.
- Worship is not an achievement.
- Worship is not a debasement of the self.

Sacraments

We need at this point to talk about some particular forms of worship that have been central to most forms of the Christian tradition: sacraments. In most Protestant circles, baptism and the Eucharist are considered the only or chief sacraments; in Roman Catholicism and Eastern Orthodoxy there are considered to be seven: Eucharist, baptism, confirmation, marriage, ordination, extreme unction (anointing with oil at the time of death) and penance (confession). I will be concentrating on baptism and the Eucharist in what follows.

Theologians have come up with many ways of defining 'sacrament' – including the following:

- Sacraments are 'visible words' or 'visible signs of an invisible grace' (St Augustine).[10]
- Sacraments are 'certain sure witnesses and effectual signs of grace and God's good will towards us, by the which he doth work invisibly in us, and doth not only quicken, but also strengthen and confirm, our faith in him' (Anglican Book of Common Prayer).[11]
- 'A sacrament is an holy ordinance instituted by Christ, wherein, by sensible signs, Christ, and the benefits of the new covenant, are represented, sealed, and applied to believers' (Westminster Shorter Catechism).[12]
- Sacraments are 'outward signs, words, or actions, ordained of God, and appointed for this end, to be the ordinary channels whereby he might convey to men, preventing, justifying, or sanctifying grace' (John Wesley).[13]
- 'The purpose of the sacraments is to sanctify men, to build up the body of Christ, and, finally, to give worship to God; because they are signs they also instruct. They not only presuppose faith, but by words and objects they also nourish, strengthen, and express it; that is why they are called

"sacraments of faith". They do indeed impart grace, but, in addition, the very act of celebrating them most effectively disposes the faithful to receive this grace in a fruitful manner, to worship God duly, and to practice charity' (Vatican II).[14]

We can try to put some of these definitions together into something like a common explanation. In the first place, sacraments are certain activities of the Church: fairly formal, liturgical, ceremonial actions that are repeated time and time again. Those actions are not thought of simply as inventions of the Church, however: they are (in the first place) seen as responses to God's promises in Christ. In fact, traditionally, they were seen as activities that were specifically and deliberately instituted by Christ among the apostles.[15] Nevertheless, the idea that the initiative lies with God, and that the Church's activity is a matter of response and participation in something done for them and with them, is still important in most definitions. So, sacraments are regular activities of the Church understood as *responses* to God. They are also seen as activities that represent, dramatically picture or portray some aspect of God's activity towards the world – they 'act it out' as it were. Lastly (and most controversially, though also most importantly) sacraments have been seen not only as activities of the Church that respond to God's promises and that represent God's action, but as activities that provide the vehicle or the context or the occasion or the opportunity for God's action to work upon the recipients afresh. So as well as responding to God's action, and as well as representing God's action, sacraments have been seen as activities in which the recipients are acted upon by God's grace.

The controversies that surround this last idea are legion. There is, for instance, a spectrum from those who focus most upon the sacraments as a means by which God acts upon the believer, to those who focus upon the sacraments most as a context in which the believer responds to God – 'objective' and 'subjective' understandings of the sacraments, as they are sometimes known. At the objective end of the spectrum are those who believe that in the sacramental activity something *happens* to the believer; he or she is given something or changed in some way – and the sacrament is said to be effective in and of itself (or *ex opere operato*, as the Latin tag goes).[16] At the subjective end of the spectrum are those who believe that the sacraments mediate God's grace only to the extent that they are received in faith – they are vehicles for the awakening and feeding of faith, and it is only when that faithful reception and response is present that the sacraments can be said to be doing anything.[17]

I am going to take a fairly middle-of-the-road route through the debate about the nature of sacraments at this point. That does not mean that it is right (I cannot solve a long-standing and very complex debate as simply as that), but it might mean that readers who lean towards differing ends of the spectrum of possible answers will be able to see something of worth in the route that I take. I am going to ask two questions of each of the sacraments that we look at: How is the Church describing itself here? and What is the Church becoming here?

The first question assumes that sacraments are activities of the Church that *say something* about what the Church is. They are activities that set out in a dramatic way some claim or claims about the nature of the Church. They *witness* to the Church's self-understanding. The second question assumes that sacraments are activities of the Church that don't simply *say* something about what the Church is, but are part of the process by which the Church actually *becomes* what it should be. They shape the Church, or make the Church to *be* the Church. That is, the two questions lean respectively in the direction of the subjective and objective ends of the sacramental spectrum.

Key points

- Sacramental worship has had a key place in the Christian tradition.
- Sacraments are fairly formal, liturgical, ceremonial actions of the Church that are repeated time and time again.
- They are seen as responses to God's promises in Christ.
- They are also seen as activities in which the recipients are acted upon by God's grace.
- Some Christians focus on what objectively happens to the believer in sacramental worship; others focus on the believer's subjective response.

What is the Eucharist?

An ecumenical definition

'The eucharist is essentially the sacrament of the gift which God makes to us in Christ through the power of the Holy Spirit. Every Christian receives this gift of salvation through communion in the body and blood of Christ. In the eucharistic meal, in the eating and drinking of the bread and wine, Christ grants communion with himself. God himself acts, giving life to the body of Christ and renewing each member. In accordance with Christ's promise, each baptized member of the body of Christ receives in the eucharist the assurance of the forgiveness of sins (Matthew 26.28) and the pledge of eternal life (John 6.51–58).'

World Council of Churches, *Baptism, Eucharist and Ministry* (1982)[18]

When people talk about sacraments they are very often talking about the Eucharist, or Holy Communion, or Lord's Supper: that activity in which the members of the Church eat bread and drink wine, connecting those in some way with the last supper that Jesus shared with his disciples, and specifically with his declaration over their bread and wine that 'This is my body' and 'This is my blood' (Mark 14.22–25; Matthew 26.26–29; Luke 22.19–20; 1 Corinthians 11.24–25).

During his ministry, and climactically at the last supper, Jesus used food and drink as a vehicle for creating unexpected fellowship. He ate and drank with others – with sinners, with tax-collectors, even with Pharisees – without setting preconditions.[19] He shared himself with them, welcoming them to share his life. When, at the last supper, Jesus broke and shared bread, and distributed wine, it was the climax of this strand of his ministry. He was once again establishing fellowship with his disciples without setting conditions upon that fellowship, sharing with both the faithful and the faithless; handing himself over to his disciples, rather than holding aloof and protecting himself from them. In the drama of that night he was later to hand himself over more directly, by refusing to defend himself from his faithless disciples, but at the supper he already symbolically put passive bread and wine into their hands and declared that in handling it, the disciples were handling him, that they had power to do as they would with the life that he had gratuitously shared with them. He makes the disciples at table with him (including the ones who are about to betray him) his guests.

Within hours, he has died a bloody death on the cross, and his symbolic handing of his body and blood to the disciples at the supper has taken on a deeper and more terrifying resonance. He did not simply place in their hands a gift of his 'life' in some safe metaphorical sense: it was his physical life – his real body and blood. He was given into their hands for them to do with as they wished, and they betrayed and abandoned him, letting that body be broken and that blood be spilt. The bread and wine of the supper retrospectively become vehicles, not just of the life of fellowship that he has been sharing with others, but of his total, costly self-gift made upon the cross. And the last supper, as it were, reads the cross *as* a gift – not as the unwilling tearing of Jesus' life from him, but as a gift freely made.

When Christians celebrate the Eucharist, after the cross and after the resurrection, they relinquish the bread and wine as their possessions, matter under their control, and receive them back from Jesus' hands. As Christians receive bread and wine from his hands, they are welcomed to his table; they accept the gift of fellowship, the sharing of his life. The gift that he made to his disciples of his body and blood is a gift made for them also – and it is a gift that sets no preconditions. It is given to faithful and faithless alike, and is given again and again despite the deepest failures and betrayals.

So, on the one hand, in the Eucharist we find the Church *describing* itself. It describes itself as the extension of that group of disciples who sat and ate with Jesus, who were given the bread and the wine by him, who betrayed and abandoned him, and who he met and forgave after his resurrection. It describes itself as having been given the body and blood of Christ, the gift Christ made of himself as he shared his life with sinners and made a new life possible for them. It describes itself as a body that goes on being given this life, and needs it in order to live: this life is its food, its medicine. It describes itself being given that life in part by joining in table-fellowship with Jesus: eating and drinking with him. It describes the bread and wine as bread and wine that Jesus has given back to them as he shares his life with them, and so as vehicles of that sharing. It describes itself as a group for whom Christ has died – who have had, as it were, Christ's life handed over to them, and now have it growing within them, and in whose hands it is to betray or glorify it in the world. It says, when it carries out this strange ritual eating and drinking: This is who we are; this is what we are growing into; we are becoming the body of Christ, the community of Christ.

> ## Word and ritual
>
> A ritual is more like a poem than like prose. It cannot be paraphrased, but lends itself to being 'read' in multiple ways. It matters that the Eucharist is not first and foremost a message or form of words handed on in the Church, but a ritual practice (or family of ritual practices). And the words of Christ ('This is my body', 'this is my blood') that Christians remember when they celebrate the Eucharist are not (as Christian history has proved) a commentary that *explains* the ritual: they are part of the ritual's strange script.

The celebration of the Eucharist is not the Church's declaration that it is a perfect community; rather, the Church acknowledges in the Eucharist that it is a community held together despite its failures and betrayals by the capacious, gracious giving of Christ. It is a community given the terrifying privilege of handling this gift, and passing it on, made by this gift into givers. So the Eucharist is an activity of the Church in which the Church tells itself about the nature of its own life. It represents its life to itself: representing its life as a gift, representing itself as frail and fallible recipient of that gift, and representing itself as charged to carry that gift in the world – bearing the question of Christ wherever it might go.

On the other hand, we also find in the Eucharist that the Church is *becoming* itself. The Eucharist is not simply an activity in which the shaping and growth of the community is described, it is an activity in which the community actually grows and is shaped. So, it is an activity in which (during the preparation), however distractedly and dimly, those gathered hear the words of Christ, confess their sins and repent. It is an activity in which the community comes together and eats together – having to face up, however fleetingly and feebly, to the reality of sharing the same table or communion rail or building. In this activity, we could say, Christians come into a context in which they can be challenged, judged, remade. And they do not understand this as primarily their own achievement, but as God shaping them – this sacramental activity of theirs being a space in which they become aware of and open to the divine activity that enfolds them and is drawing them more deeply into God's life.

This is, of course, still a rather idealized description of what happens in actual eucharistic services. What about those times when it is simply routine? What about those times when the recipients don't pay attention? What about those times when they ignore the people around them? What about the times when they are more focused on not letting the toddler by their side trip and bash his head on the hard communion rail? Is anything happening then? It seems to me that even then there *is* something objective about it: even if nothing appears to change, this activity sets the terms by which the recipients are to be judged. It is rather like saying 'I promise' in front of witnesses. (And it is, perhaps, worth noting that in saying this I am following the Swiss Reformer Huldrych Zwingli, who is often taken to mark the most 'subjective' end of sacramental theology.)[20] If you say 'I promise' in front of witnesses, you cannot then wriggle out of the obligation that promising involves by saying 'I wasn't really concentrating; I wasn't being serious; I don't feel like I promised; it wasn't a product of deep conviction'. If you say 'I promise' then you have indeed promised. Imagine being in an army where the general were looking for volunteers for a particular mission, and standing to say 'I'll go'. The standing and speaking would commit you, even if you were not taking it seriously, even if your subsequent behaviour denied it, or showed that you had not realized what you were letting yourself in for. You would be, thanks to that action, a volunteer. In the Eucharist, even if recipients fail to take it seriously, even if they fail to let themselves be practically reshaped, they accept again (verbally and in their actions) that Christ's life has been given to them. They take it in their hands.[21]

Whatever they then do with it, however they react, I think it makes sense to say that the handing over of Christ's life is something that happens to them in the Eucharist. And I think it makes sense to say that it is Christ who hands his life over to the Church in this way – and so to say that while at one level of description this sacramental worship is clearly the activity of the Church, something that believers do, at another level of description it is something that *Christ* is doing. And whilst at one level of description it is clearly ordinary bread and wine that is handled in this sacramental worship, at another level of description it is the life of Jesus of Nazareth. It is the body and blood of Christ. William Temple put it this way:

> 'My body' is that part of the physical world which moves directly in response to my will, and thus the vehicle or the medium whereby I effect my purposes. ... In precisely this sense (I suggest) the Eucharistic Bread is the body of Christ. ... As through the physical organism which was His Body He revealed in agony and death the utter obedience of Humanity in His Person to the Father, which is the atoning sacrifice, so through the broken Bread He shows it still and enables us to become participants therein.[22]

This is to say more than that the bread and wine take on a particular significance for believers; that is, it is to speak about something more than the way that believers happen to place a particular interpretation on the bread and the wine: I think it proper (as perhaps some at the most subjective end of the spectrum do not) to speak of the activity of Christ making himself present, handing himself over, as well as of the activity of the celebrating believers. But equally, this is to say something quite different from any claim (as may be made in some popular piety at the most objective end of the spectrum) that some disguised change – a hidden chemical change, as it were – has taken place in the bread and wine. (This is not, by the way, to reject the Roman Catholic doctrine of 'transubstantiation': Herbert McCabe, while defending precisely that doctrine, explains that it too involves the rejection of the idea that 'in the Eucharist the body of Christ is *disguised* as food and drink, perhaps to make it easier to eat and drink, as a ferro-concrete house can be disguised as half-timbered Tudor'.[23]) In the Eucharist – whatever the appropriate metaphysical distinctions might be by which this could be said with proper clarity and precision – the life of Christ is handed over to the Church, just as he handed it to the first disciples on the night before he died.

Exercise

Use this section as a testing ground on which to try your skill at critical engage-ment with what you read. This is, after all, very controversial territory, and I am well aware that my attempt to occupy middle ground will probably get me fired on by both sides. Think about whether you want to start that process now. Do you think I have claimed too much or too little for the Eucharist? Do you think my proposed way of 'making sense' of it is coherent? Is it plausible?

If you have trouble coming to your own evaluation of what I have said, try redescribing it in your own words, and note the points at which you find it dif-ficult, either because you're not sure you understand, or because you are not sure you can say what I say. Those stumbling points are your clues: the former kind might well be places where the superficial plausibility of my account covers some leap or slip in logic, or some failure to be coherent. The latter might be places where your own explicit or implicit eucharistic theology differs from mine, and is not covered by my apparently eirenic gestures.

Key points

- The celebration of the Eucharist is a continuation and extension of the meal that Jesus shared with his disciples.
- In the Eucharist, the Church describes itself as the recipient of Christ's life.
- In the Eucharist, the Church grows more deeply into Christ's life.
- In the Eucharist, the Church can be said to receive the life of Christ at Christ's own hands.

Baptism

An ecumenical definition

'Baptism is the sign of new life through Jesus Christ. It unites the one baptized with Christ and with his people. The New Testament scriptures and the liturgy of the Church unfold the meaning of baptism in various images which express the riches of Christ and the gifts of his salvation. These images are sometimes linked with the symbolic uses of water in the Old Testament. Baptism is par-ticipation in Christ's death and resurrection (Rom. 6.3–5; Col. 2.12); a wash-ing away of sin (1 Cor. 6.11); a new birth (John 3.5); an enlightenment by Christ (Eph. 5.14); a re-clothing in Christ (Gal. 3.27); a renewal by the Spirit (Titus 3.5); the experience of salvation from the flood (1 Peter 3.20–21); an exodus from bondage (1 Cor. 10.1–2) and a liberation into a new humanity in which barriers of division whether of sex or race or social status are transcended (Gal. 3.27–28; 1 Cor. 12.13). The images are many but the reality is one.'
World Council of Churches, *Baptism, Eucharist and Ministry* (1982)[24]

If the Eucharist is a sacrament in which the sustaining, growth and flourishing of life in God is celebrated regularly throughout a Christian's life, baptism is a sacrament in which *initiation* into that life is celebrated, once for each person. Instead of the eating and drinking of bread and wine, baptism involves immersion in, or sprinkling with water. But just as the interpretation of the Eucharist has been a major source of controversy in Christian history, so baptism is hotly debated, with debate focusing in particular on the appropriateness or inappropriateness of *infant* baptism, as opposed to the baptism of adult believers.

The American theologian Daniel Migliore gives a useful summary of some of the main lines of New Testament interpretation of the act of baptism.[25] He notes that it is presented as dying and rising with Christ, that it is pictured as the washing of a sin-stained life, that it is portrayed as rebirth or new birth, that it is linked to incorporation into Christ (into unity with Christ); and that it is seen as a sign of God's coming reign.

Baptism is seen as portraying or enacting the beginning of the life of faith – the life in which the Spirit draws people alongside Christ, or in unity with Christ, towards the Father. In baptism, people enter upon the path that Christ took – symbolically going down with him into the grave and rising with him to resurrection life, and they do so not because it is something that they have constructed and achieved, but because this is a life into which the Spirit has drawn them.

The baptized person is being redescribed in baptism. Baptism says of the candidate, this person that you see entering the water and emerging from it has died and risen. From now on, all that you see in them that resists the grace of God, that refuses to unlearn idolatry or to learn the truth of God, you must consider as dead, necrotic tissue in this person's life: material that is as good as dead, that is rotting away – material that has nothing to do with this person's true identity. And from now on, whenever you see this person demonstrating God's love, witnessing to God's life, you must consider that as their true, risen identity: that is who this person most truly is, even if that identity is still hidden by much that is dying. And when you see that healthy identity shining through, you are not to think of it as the achievement or success of this individual, but as the work of the Spirit conforming this person to Christ, clothing him or her (to switch metaphors) with Christ's righteousness. This individual has died, and has risen – and all that you see after this is simply the working out of that basic fact.

And so in baptizing new members, the Church describes itself as simultaneously sinful and holy: as filled with people who have died and risen, but in whom the dying flesh still vies with healthy tissue. The Church points to Christ – whose path through crucifixion and resurrection is represented in baptism – as the touchstone of its own life: pointing to him and saying that its own life is only worth something, only interesting, only powerful, to the extent that it reflects his life; that its life is sinful and distorted and failing to the extent that it makes Christ harder to see.

What actually happens in baptism, however? What is the Church or the believer becoming here? What does baptism *change*? I could give an account like the one I gave of the Eucharist above, that sees the sacrament as involving something like promising or volunteering, something that objectively chang-es the situation of the one baptized, without necessarily requiring of them explicitly felt and understood commitment. However, to go down that route would only be to encounter one of the big debates about baptism that has divided Christians for centuries: does it make sense to baptize infants? Those who defend the baptism of infants tend to lean quite strongly towards the 'objective' end of the sacramental spectrum. They see baptism as a celebration and enactment of what the baptized person *receives* from God – the recognition that God's promises apply to this person too, or – more strongly – a rite in which those promises are in fact made afresh for this person. The focus falls on what God has done (promised) and what God will do (fulfil those promises).

Those who attack infant baptism tend to lean more towards the 'subjective' end of the spectrum – to place the focus on baptism as a *response* to God's promises, an act of reception and obedience on the part of the person baptized. Baptism becomes an act of explicit public commitment on the part of the one baptized.

Opposing views

Baptism 'bears first and final testimony to the work of God on which any response of our own must be grounded ... baptism does not arise *out of* any work of ours. It is baptism *into* the work of God on our behalf ... even our own response is the work of God. ... [R]egeneration is not a human possibility. ...

'[I]t does not stand alone but is part of that total renewing in Christ's image which embraces sanctification and glorification as well. ... Even the adult has neither reached that which baptism signifies nor begun to grasp what its consummation will be. By coming to personal repentance and faith he might be a little further on the road of entry into the divine work. But the Spirit who has brought him thus far is the Spirit who works in infants too – and both he and they have a long way to go before they are brought by the Spirit into the fullness of the baptismal work.'

Geoffrey Bromiley, *Children of Promise*[26]

'The New Testament undoubtedly does provide for the singling out of children who are born and brought up in the community of Jesus Christ which is gathered, built up and sent out by the Holy Spirit. Since they live from the very first with parents who are summoned to this people ... their situation is certainly very different from that of children who do not have this privilege. The fact that the promise which is given to this people and the claim to which it is subjected are from the very first (to varying degrees) presented to them and brought to their attention, means that they enjoy a very special *praevenire* of the grace of God. Even for these children, however, it cannot be cheap grace. ... The Christian life cannot be inherited as blood, gifts, characteristics and inclinations are inherited. No Christian environment, however genuine or sincere, can transfer this life to those who are in this environment. For these, too, the Christian life will and can begin only on the basis of their own liberation

> by God, their own decision. Its beginning ... cannot be made for them by others through the fact that, without being asked about their own decision, they received baptism.'
>
> Karl Barth, *Church Dogmatics*[27]

Exercise

Regardless of which side you fall on (if any), try to think how Barth would respond to Bromiley, and how Bromiley would respond to Barth.

So is baptism primarily the free, deliberate response of the believing person? Or is baptism primarily an acknowledgement of or even vehicle for what God has done and is doing for the person being baptized? That seems to be the core of the debate between those who favour infant baptism and those who don't – and as there can be no hope that I will manage here to resolve a question that has divided thoughtful Christians for many generations, I simply want to offer some personal reflections on the answer that has made sense to me and to my wife, as we have had both our children baptized. These reflections that follow are not meant to *settle* anything: they are not meant to *prove* anything one way or another, simply to explain one point of view.

Why did we have Bridget and Tom baptized when each was only three months old? Baptism has – as I have explained – always been understood as a kind of dying and rising: going down into the water to die to one kind of life, and coming up out of the water to rise to another kind of life. In baptizing Bridget and Tom, part of what we were doing was recognizing that they were already caught up in this dying and rising. This may sound like an odd kind of claim to make about tiny babies, but I mean it quite seriously. They had already taken the first small steps along the path towards recognizing that they were persons among other persons, steps towards recognizing that other people have their own continuity and character, steps towards recognizing that other people have their own needs and desires; steps towards the discovery that they were not the centre of the universe (despite what their parents might have thought); steps towards the discovery that they are called out of themselves to be responsive to others. You can think of this process of calling out as, even at this early stage, a process of 'dying to self' – dying to the kind of life entirely centred on and absorbed in one's own needs and desires. You can also think of it as a process of 'rising to life' – of waking up to a life beyond the self, to a life of communion. It is a path that starts with such things as beginning to recognize a mother's face, and playing games in a mirror; it is a path that leads towards love and justice.

So, one part of what we thought we were doing in these baptisms was *recognizing* that Bridget and Tom were dying and rising. And we proclaimed that we believe that it is the Spirit who leads them on this path – that the tiny psychological and social and behavioural developments that they were undergoing have to be understood by Christians as the work of the Spirit, because that is who the Spirit is: the one who leads the world into love and justice.

But we have done more than that, because baptism is baptism into the dying and rising of *Jesus of Nazareth*, specifically – and in baptizing Bridget and Tom, we have accepted that the path on which they are already set is Jesus' path. It is therefore a path that goes higher, deeper and into stranger territory than one might expect. We have proclaimed our conviction that the path on which they are already set is, if its full length is seen, a path that runs towards a love like Jesus' love, which is God's love. The call that Bridget and Tom already hear in other people, which begins to draw them out of themselves, we recognize as the first whispers of the voice of God; the love that Bridget and Tom feel, that enables them to grow towards becoming loving themselves, we recognize as the first felt warmth of God's love towards them. In having them baptized, we have publicly named the path Bridget and Tom are on as the way of Jesus Christ, the way of the cross, the way of God's love and justice – accepting, on their behalf, that the life, death and resurrection of Christ are the criterion by which what is truly lasting and important in their lives should be judged. And so they, even in the tiny steps which they have already taken towards learning to love, have already been placed in a context in which the moral and spiritual developments that shape their lives even now become witnesses to Christ. They have become those who reflect in their own particular, unreproducible way the life of the one under whose sign they now grow.

And lastly, we have made promises: promises to bring Bridget and Tom up in such a way that they learn the name of the path they are on, the name of the one who is calling them, the name of the one who is loving them into love. We have promised to help them learn that they are called to die and rise with Christ, to grow in love for neighbour and for God. Those promises will, if we even begin to be faithful to them, inevitably shape the particular way in which Bridget and Tom grow and develop. They will bed down in them and become part of who they are.

There is, of course, no way away from such shaping. A large part of what we are is always received from those who bring us up. We could not have chosen to bring Bridget and Tom up in neutrality, entirely free to make their own marks on a blank slate: there is no neutrality; there is no blank state. We hope to bring them up in such a way that they will be able to think and question and choose – but we don't think we will do that by trying to bring them up standing in no particular place. Rather, we choose to bring them up in a way which we think leads to greater freedom.

So, when we had Bridget and Tom baptized, we recognized that they were already dying and rising. We set up a public marker, saying that this dying and rising was dying and rising with Christ, and should be understood in that light. And we made promises – promises that will become part of who Bridget and Tom are – to help turn their faces towards that criterion, so that the path they are on leads more firmly in the direction of this kind of love and justice.[28]

Key points

- Baptism is a response to God's grace.
- The baptized person is dying with Christ.
- The baptized person is rising to new life with Christ.

The Church catholic

Of course, everything that I have just said is controversial. This is one of those topics that splinters churches, dividing the one body of Christ into disagreeing and disagreeable factions, each convinced that its way is true. It is, in other words, one of the tears in the Church's *catholicity*. The word 'catholic' in this context means something like 'universal' (it comes from Greek *kath' holou* – 'as a whole, in general'). If the Church is one, it also must be catholic: each part of it should live by relation to all the other parts of it, learning from (and teaching) every other part, so as to help all the parts together see more of the one source and goal of the Church's life. This is something I have already spoken about: the call for each member of the body to become a gift to the whole body, and to receive the other members as gifts. The Church as catholic is meant to be an 'economy of gift': a society defined and held together by this mutual giving of Christ. According to the credal definition, the Church simply is the community of those who give and receive Christ to and from one another.

Distinguishing marks

It is ironic to describe catholicity as a 'mark of the Church'. If you look for popular discussions of the marks, you will often find that they are used as *boundary markers*. Various writers will tell you that they are marks that enable you to locate the *real* Church, and belong to it. For instance, if you look on-line, and do a search for 'marks of the Church', you will find quite a few that come from sites dedicated to Roman Catholic apologetics. The following is a fairly typical example:

> These four marks of the Church – one, holy, catholic, and apostolic – are fully realized in the Catholic Church. While other Christian Churches accept and profess the Creed, and possess elements of truth and sanctification, only the Roman Catholic Church reflects the fullness of these marks.[29]

You can also find Protestant or Orthodox examples. For example,

> The Church is one because God is one, and because Christ and the Holy Spirit are one. There can only be one Church and not many. ... Orthodox Christians believe that in the historical Orthodox Church there exists the full possibility of participating totally in the Church of God, and that only sins and false human choices (heresies) put men outside of this unity. In non-Orthodox Christian groups the Orthodox claim that there are certain formal obstacles, varying in different groups, which, if accepted and followed by men, will prevent their perfect unity with God and will thus destroy the genuine unity of the Church.[30]

Or, from a (rather older) Protestant source:

> it is evident that truth of doctrine or conformity with the word of God is the true and genuine mark of the true church. ... [I]t is not difficult to gather ... what is that true church to which we are bound to join ourselves in order to

> obtain salvation. Whether it is the modern Roman church, which retains so
> many capital errors and idolatries altogether opposed to the word of God
> in faith and worship; or, on the other hand, ours, which is content with the
> word of God alone.[31]

All too obviously, the Church is divided. There are Coptic, Orthodox, Catholic,
Protestant, Pentecostal churches; charismatics, evangelicals, liberals; Trinitar-
ians and Unitarians, Episcopalians and Presbyterians: all sorts of divisions
emerging from a tangled and complex history.[32] And the history of those
divisions is a history bound up with culture, politics and power – with the
interventions of Roman emperors trying by authoritarian means to keep the
Empire unified and running; with the divisions between Greek culture and
Latin culture; with the political and economic changes surrounding the emergence of the modern nation state in Western Europe; with the marital history
of English kings, and so on. Sometimes the splits look tragically unnecessary;
sometimes they seem to rest on deep, irreconcilable differences in theology
and practice. Sometimes one group or side seems to be pretty largely in the
wrong; more often it is hard to find heroes and villains, and all sides seem to
have equal claim to have grasped something important, something that they
were right to seek to protect or preserve.

What does it mean to affirm the catholicity of the Church in this context?
The Church is *one* because Christians are on one journey, caught up together
by one Spirit into conformity to one Christ on the way to one Father. The
Church is *catholic* because Christians are, fundamentally, on that one journey
together – and it is supposed to be a journey in which they travel not only
towards God but closer to one another, until they are close enough to become
gifts to, and recipients of, one another. Without some form of communion with
one another – a situation in which Christians can learn with and from each
other – everyone's faith is impoverished. Fractures in the church are fractures
in the body of Christ, and they correspond directly to breaks in Christians'
knowledge of Christ: gaps where Christians have not learnt as they might
from others, because their communion with those others is impaired.

Ecumenism in some form – the attempt to work towards reunion or communion between the divided branches of Christianity – is therefore a natural
response to division, for anyone who shares a theology similar to the one I
have described. By the same token, however, a search for *uniformity* is not
called for – indeed, is positively ruled out. One does not learn from those one
has turned into clones of oneself.

Key points

- The Church is divided.
- Yet the Church simply is the community of those who give and receive
  Christ to and from one another.
- Ecumenism is therefore the proper response to division.

Ecumenism

Roughly speaking, we can identify two kinds of ecumenism – two kinds of movement towards the overcoming of denominational and other divisions in Christianity. On the one hand, there are official moves, negotiated by Church leaders, sealed in lengthy technical ecumenical documents and constitutional agreements.[33] On the other hand, there are unofficial moves, co-operation and interaction at a 'grass-roots' level, between individuals and congregations who find themselves in proximity, despite the gaps that supposedly separate their churches.[34]

It would be tempting to think that the problems always exist at the official level, and that the grass-roots level – the level of 'ordinary' believers and congregations – is where real unity is to be found. The reality is more complex. Division can be rooted at either level. It can be rooted in the official teachings of a given denomination, and the expert theologians and church leaders who are tasked with preserving the inheritance of their particular tradition – the truths that they believe this denomination has seen more clearly, or practised more faithfully, than others. But it can also be rooted in the mutual suspicion and antagonism of ordinary believers and congregations – congregations that have learnt, perhaps, to define themselves over against other nearby congregations who do things differently, or who have a different kind of person attending, or who simply 'aren't us'.

On the other hand, moves towards co-operation and communion can take place at both levels. At grass roots, you can find that individuals and congregations, sometimes despite the official line of their denominations, discover that they can work together – share services, co-operate in social outreach, use the same buildings, meet together for worship, become friends. At the official level, you can find that theologians and church leaders, sometimes despite the deep-seated mutual antagonism of the actual congregations they represent, can work towards the point where nothing official stands in the way of communion: the point where historic disagreements in theology, historic differences in practice, are put into a new light – a light that shows that those differences can simply be overcome, or a light that shows that they should not be communion-dividing differences, but are acceptable variations, differences of emphasis and interpretation, within a single faith.[35]

It may be a rather bland thing to say, but it seems pretty clear that a deep-seated ecumenism will need both these forms. If one takes seriously the fact that many churches or denominations do have some kind of official teaching or official practice, it seems clear that they cannot move towards fuller communion without considering whether that official teaching and practice gets in the way – and without considering what the consequences are if it *does* get in the way. Moves towards greater communion between, say, Anglicans and Baptists would be avoiding a vital question if at least *some* consideration was not given to the question of whether the Baptists could recognize those Anglicans who had been baptized as infants as indeed being baptized believers; and Anglicans would in turn need to consider what they thought was going on when someone who had been sprinkled as a baby became a Baptist and decided to undergo believer's baptism.

Simply to avoid these questions, to pretend that they do not matter, would be disingenuous.

On the other hand, you can have all the official agreements you like, but if believers 'on the ground' remain antagonistic it is a sham. Two congregations in the same village, for instance, might belong to denominations that have officially entered into some kind of communion and resolved many of their official differences. Decisions may have been taken at an official level that each church should recognize the ministers and ministries of the other church, so that full co-operation becomes possible. But if the members and ministers of one congregation never darken the door of the other, and if there is no co-operation, no shared worship, no shared ministry, no shared mission, if there is not even a growing of friendships between members of the two congregations, it is hard not to think that the official agreements are, in this context at least, so much hot air.

What, however, is the goal of this ecumenism? It need not be the actual reunification of different denominations into a single, undifferentiated new denomination. From the point of view of the theology I have been exploring, the point of ecumenism is the promotion of unimpeded mutual learning. Each church needs to learn from every other church, and each Christian from every other Christian. Ecumenism at its richest is about promoting the possibilities of mutual learning and enrichment at every level: the mutual learning by which the structures, policies and teaching of one church are challenged, deepened, and opened up by encounter with those of another; the mutual learning by which a believer is challenged and called out of her current limited understanding by encounter with another believer. Ecumenism is about increasing and diversifying the ways in which Christians learn: growing the pool of people from whom each Christian can hear God's call, and building connections that enable border-crossing learning to take place.

Called to be one

'The *catholicity* of the Church expresses the fullness, integrity, and totality of its life in Christ through the Holy Spirit in all times and places. This mystery is expressed in each community of baptized believers in which the apostolic faith is confessed and lived, the gospel is proclaimed, and the sacraments are celebrated. Each church is the Church catholic and not simply a part of it. Each church is the Church catholic, but not the whole of it. Each church fulfils its catholicity when it is in communion with the other churches. We affirm that the catholicity of the Church is expressed most visibly in sharing holy communion and in a mutually recognized and reconciled ministry.

'The relationship among churches is dynamically interactive. Each church is called to mutual giving and receiving gifts and to *mutual accountability*. Each church must become aware of all that is provisional in its life and have the courage to acknowledge this to other churches. Even today, when eucharistic sharing is not always possible, divided churches express mutual accountability and aspects of catholicity when they pray for one another, share resources, assist one another in times of need, make decisions together, work together for justice, reconciliation, and peace, hold one another accountable to the discipleship inherent in baptism, and maintain dialogue in the face of differences, refusing to say "I have no need of you" (1 Corinthians 12.21). Apart from one another we are impoverished.'

World Council of Churches, *Called to be the One Church*[36]

Of course, some will say that the idea is all very well, but that in practice ecumenism works by dulling the distinctiveness of those involved in it, weakening individuals' or groups' commitment to the truths they have perceived. Doesn't it work by washing everything down to shades of grey, so that we may say nothing firm, nothing clear, take no stand, in case it offends one of our ecumenical partners? Doesn't ecumenism involve a drastic failure to take our history, our inheritance, our faith *seriously*?

Against ecumenism

A quick search on the web turns up several examples of people expressing this fear. For instance, one site declares:

Ecumenism tries to make one church, but yet it does not truly unite. It turns a blind eye to differences in faith, belief, doctrine, and practice, as if these things do not matter. On the contrary, these things are of the utmost importance! These things are the very basis and foundation of our lives; they are the Church. If we cast these things aside, what is left? All that is left is a shallow, hollow shell of what was formerly the fullness of the Church. If we cast these things aside, we are casting aside our own salvation. It simply does not work to bring everything down to the lowest common denominator and say that the only criteria for being a Christian is that we all believe that Jesus is the Son of God.[37]

And another site puts it succinctly:

'The word of the Lord endureth for ever and this is the word which by the gospel is preached unto you' (1 Peter 1.25) so there is no 'fear' of his words disappearing – except from the homes and churches of today's modern Ecumenical Christian![38]

There is no doubt that ecumenism is not easy – and probably should not be easy. What one sees in the faces of Christians from across some divide will never be entirely unobjectionable, entirely 'nice', entirely acceptable. It will challenge and question and upset and irritate and shock – sometimes because those other Christians have seen aspects of the truth that one has not seen, and that one is perhaps not prepared to allow, sometimes because what one sees in those other Christians is something distorted and broken. Each Christian, in the theology I have been promoting, has in his or her particular place and time the joy (and responsibility) of being able to see Christ from an angle from which no others can see him; he or she has his or her own contribution to make to the body of Christ, which cannot be made by any other person. On the other hand he or she is inevitably fallible and weak, and his or her vision of Christ distorted, and each Christian and each Christian group dims or pollutes the light of Christ as they pass it on. Ecumenism is not about finding easy uniformity. It is not about finding no surprises in the Christian family. It is not about finding everyone in that family easy to get on with. It is about learning from them more about Christ, and it is about learning to love them. Without such ecumenism – that is, without a visible and active commitment to rediscover the lost catholicity of the Church – there *is* no Church.

Going further

1 The debate about the subjectivity or objectivity of the Eucharist has often been a debate about the nature of Christ's presence or involvement or activity in the Eucharist. There are endless varieties of opinion, language and explanation, and endless debates between those who hold and use them: transubstantiation, consubstantiation, real presence, spiritual presence, sacramental presence, receptionism, memorialism and so on. There are plenty of good books that explain some or all of this: John Macquarrie, *Guide to the Sacraments* (London: SCM Press, 1997); Joseph Martos, *Doors to the Sacred: A Historical Introduction to Sacraments in the Catholic Church* (London: SCM Press, 1981); Robert Jenson, 'The Church and the Sacraments' in Colin Gunton (ed.), *The Cambridge Companion to Christian Doctrine* (Cambridge: Cambridge University Press, 1997), pp. 207–25; Victor Codina, 'Sacraments' in Jon Sobrino and Ignacio Ellacuría (eds.) *Systematic Theology: Perspectives from Liberation Theology* (London: SCM Press, 1996), pp. 216–32; and Timothy Gorringe, *The Sign of Love: Reflections on the Eucharist* (London: SPCK, 1997). There is a fascinating debate about transubstantiation between Herbert McCabe and 'G. Egner' (a pseudonym of P. J. Fitzpatrick) in the former's *God Matters* (London: Continuum, 2005 [1987]), pp. 116–81.

2 Roman Catholic ecclesiology argues that the unity of the Church needs a visible and personal focus, provided by the communion of all parts of the Church with the Bishop of Rome, the Pope. For a discussion of this, see Walter Kasper (ed.), *Petrine Ministry: Catholics and Orthodox in Dialogue* (Mahwah, NJ: Newman, 2005); Adriano Garuti, *The Primacy of the Bishop of Rome and the Ecumenical Dialogue*, tr. Michael Miller (San Francisco: Ignatius, 2005 [Italian original: 2000]); Klaus Schatz, *Papal Primacy: From Its Origins to the Present*, tr. John A. Otto and Linda M. Maloney (Collegeville, MN: Michael Glazier, 1996 [German original, 1990]); Pope John Paul II's 1995 encyclical, *Ut unum sint* §§88–97, available online from the Vatican Archive, http://www.vatican.va/holy_father/john_paul_ii/encyclicals/index.htm; International Anglican–Roman Catholic Commission for Unity and Mission, *Growing Together in Unity and Mission* (2006), §§62–76, available online at Anglican Mainstream, http://www.anglican-mainstream.net/downloads/growingtogether.pdf.

3 For some churches, unity is focused on the common commitment to credal statements or bases of faith. For the historical development, see J. N. D. Kelly, *Early Christian Creeds*, 3rd edn (London: Longman, 1980) and Jaroslav Pelikan, *Credo: A Historical and Theological Guide to Creeds and Confessions of Faith in the Christian Tradition* (New Haven: Yale University Press, 2005). For a modern example, see the World Evangelical Alliance's *Statement of Faith* (available online at http://www.worldevangelicalalliance. com/wea/statement.htm).

Notes

1 I am using the 1988 English Language Liturgical Commission texts, which can be found online at http://www.englishtexts.org/survey.html.

2 Hans Küng, *The Church*, tr. Ray and Rosaleen Ockenden (London: Search Press, 1968 [German original: 1967]), pp. 263–359, with some notes on the history of the 'marks' on pp. 266–7. For a modern interpretation, see Rowan Williams, 'One Holy Catholic and Apostolic Church', Address to the 3rd Global South to South Encounter, Ain al Sukhna, Egypt, 28 October 2005, available online at http://www.archbishopof canterbury.org/sermons_speeches/2005/051028.htm.

3 I'll be mixing in another common way of presenting theological ideas on the identity of the Church: the description of a range of 'Models of the Church' – common metaphors used to describe the Church in Scripture and the Christian tradition. Numerous such models are discussed by different theologians, such as institution, mystical communion, sacrament, herald, servant, people of God, body of Christ, building of God, bride of Christ, army of God, sheepfold of Christ, mother and so on. This list is drawn in part from Avery Dulles, *Models of the Church* (Dublin: Gill and MacMillan, 1988), Daniel L. Migliore, *Faith Seeking Understanding: An Introduction to Christian Theology*, 2nd edn (Grand Rapids, MI: Eerdmans, 2004), pp. 254–62, and George H. Tavard, *The Church: Community of Salvation* (Collegeville: Litrugical Press, 1992), ch. 5.

4 See Ephesians 4.4–6: 'There is one body and one Spirit, just as you were called to the one hope of your calling, one Lord, one faith, one baptism, one God and Father of all, who is above all and through all and in all.'

5 See Chapter 6, pp. 160–2.

6 For works that place worship central to the whole enterprise of theology, see Geoffrey Wainwright, *Doxology: A Systematic Theology* (London: Epworth, 1980), and Daniel Hardy and David Ford, *Jubilate: Theology in Praise* (London: DLT, 1984), published in America as *Praising and Knowing God* (Philadelphia: WJKP, 1985).

7 Romano Guardini, *The Spirit of the Liturgy*, tr. Ada Lane (New York: Crossroad, 1998 [German original: 1917]), pp. 71–2; the whole text is available online at the Eternal Word Television Network, http://www.ewtn.com/library/LITURGY/SPRLIT.TXT.

8 The paintings of Caspar David Friedrich capture this well – especially his 1818 *Wanderer über dem Nebelmeer* (The wanderer above a sea of fog). For online copies, see Nicholas Pioch, 'Friedrich, David Caspar' at The Web Museum, Paris, 2002, http:// www.ibiblio.org/wm/paint/auth/friedrich/.

9 Hardy and Ford, *Jubilate*, p. 76.

10 The first is from Augustine, *Tractates on the Gospel of John* 80.3, translated by John Gibb and James Innes in Philip Schaff (eds) *Nicene and Post-Nicene Fathers*, First Series, vol. 7 (New York: Christian Literature Company, 1888), p. 344; available online at the

Christian Classics Ethereal Library, http://www.ccel.org/ccel/schaff/npnf107.iii.lxxxi. html; it was more recently popularized by Robert Jenson, *Visible Words: The Interpretation and Practice of Christian Sacraments* (Philadelphia: Fortress Press, 1978). The second is based on a pair of Augustine texts, *Questions on the Heptateuch* III.84, on Leviticus 21.15 (Migne, *Patrologia Latina* 134.712–13), and Letter 105.3.12: 'the grace is always God's, and the sacrament God's, but the ministry alone belongs to a human being. … God effects the visible form of the sacrament through him, while he himself bestows the invisible grace' – in E. M. Atkins and R. J. Dodaro (eds), *Augustine: Political Writings* (Cambridge: Cambridge University Press, 2001), p. 169. Peter Lombard gives the Latin equivalent of the wording I have given (*sacramentum est invisibilis gratiae visibilis forma*) in *Sentences* 4.1.2 (English Translation by Alexis Bugnolo available online at the Franciscan Archive, http://www.franciscan-archive.org/lombardus/opera/ls4–01.html.

11 Specifically, Article 25 of the 39 'Articles of Religion' agreed by the Church of England in 1563; available online at the Society of Archbishop Justus, http://www.justus.anglican.org/resources/bcp/1662/articles.pdf.

12 *Westminster Shorter Catechism* (London: 1647), Question 92; available online at the Christian Classics Ethereal Library, http://www.ccel.org/ccel/anonymous/westminster1.i.iv.html.

13 John Wesley, *Sermons on Several Occasions*, ed. Thomas Jackson (New York: Calton and Phillips, 1855), Sermon 16, §II.1, p. 136; available online at the Wesley Center Online, http://wesley.nnu.edu/john_wesley/sermons/016.htm. Wesley is actually defining the related term 'means of grace'.

14 *Sacrosanctum Concilium* ch. 3, §59 in *Documents of the II Vatican Council*, available online at the Vatican Archive, http://www.vatican.va/archive/hist_councils/ii_vatican_council/index.htm.

15 So Pius X, in an encyclical of 1907, condemned the opinion that 'The Sacraments have their origin in the fact that the Apostles and their successors, swayed and moved by circumstances and events, interpreted some idea and intention of Christ', i.e. rather than having their origin with Christ himself. Pius X, *Lamentabili Sane*, 40; available online at Papal Encyclicals Online, http://www.papalencyclicals.net/Pius10/p10lamen.htm.

16 See Council of Trent, Session 7, Canon 8 on the Sacraments in General (1547): 'If any one saith, that by the said sacraments of the New Law grace is not conferred through the act performed, but that faith alone in the divine promise suffices for the obtaining of grace; let him be anathema.' Translated by J. Waterworth, in *The Canons and Decrees of the Sacred and Oecumenical Council of Trent* (London: Dolman, 1848), p. 55; available online at the Hanover Historical Texts Project, http://history.hanover.edu/texts/trent/ct07.html.

17 The Swiss Reformer Huldrych (or Ulrich) Zwingli (1484–1531) said 'But of those who publicly partake of the visible sacraments or signs, yet without faith, it cannot properly be said that they eat sacramentally.' *Fidei expositio* (1531), tr. Geoffrey Bromiley in *Zwingli and Bullinger*, Library of Christian Classics (Philadelphia: Westminster, 1953), p. 259.

18 *Baptism, Eucharist and Ministry: The Agreed Text*, Faith and Order Paper 111 (Geneva: World Council of Churches, 1982), Eucharist, para. 2; available online from http://www.oikoumene.org/index.php?id=2139.

19 See, for example, Matthew 9.9–13; 11.19; 26.2–16; Mark 2.13–17; 14.3–11; Luke 5.27–32; 7.34, 36–50; 19.1–10; John 12.1–8.

20 Zwingli claimed in *Fidei expositio* (1536) that the sacraments were like an 'oath of allegiance'. See Bromiley, *Zwingli and Bullinger*, p. 265.

21 'Whoever, therefore, eats the bread or drinks the cup of the Lord in an unworthy manner will be *answerable for the body and blood of the Lord*. Examine yourselves,

and only then eat of the bread and drink of the cup. For all who eat and drink without discerning the body, eat and drink judgement against themselves' (1 Corinthians
11.27–29).

22 William Temple, *Christus Veritas: An Essay* (London: Macmillan, 1962), p. 251.

23 Herbert McCabe, 'Transubstantiation and the Real Presence', in *God Matters*
(London: Geoffrey Chapman, 1987), pp. 116–29: p. 116.

24 *Baptism, Eucharist and Ministry*, Baptism, para. 2.

25 Migliore, *Faith Seeking Understanding*, p. 283.

26 Geoffrey Bromiley, *Children of Promise: The Case for Baptizing Infants* (Grand
Rapids, MI: Eerdmans, 1979), pp. 107–9.

27 Karl Barth, *Church Dogmatics IV: The Doctrine of Reconciliation*, Pt 4 (Edinburgh:
T&T Clark, 1969), pp. 183–4. The use of this text alongside the Bromiley text was sug-
gested to me by George W. Stroup (ed.), *The Reformed Reader: A Sourcebook in Christian
Theology*, vol. 2 (Louisville: WJKP, 1993), pp. 271–3.

28 These reflections are based on a post I wrote for a blog that we kept after our
daughter was born. See http://higton.goringe.net/?p=81.

29 William Saunders, 'The Four Marks of the Church', *The Catholic Herald* (27 May
1999); available online at http://www.catholicherald.com/saunders/99ws/ws990527.
htm.

30 Archdiocese of Canada, Orthodox Church in America, 'What we believe' (no
date), http://www.archdiocese.ca/homeChurch.htm.

31 Francis Turretin, *Institutes of Elenctic Theology* (1679–85), tr. George Mus-
grave Giger (Phillipsburg, NJ: P&R Publishing: 1992–7), III.95, Topic 18, Question
12, para 29; available online at A Puritan's Mind, http://www.apuritansmind.com/
FrancisTurretin/francisturretinmarkstruechurch.htm.

32 See Wikipedia contributors, 'List of Christian denominations', *Wikipedia:
The Free Encyclopedia*, http://en.wikipedia.org/w/index.php?title=List_of_Christian_
denominations.

33 See, for instance, ecumenical documents from the World Council of Churches
at the Ecumenism in Canada website, http://ecumenism.net/docu/ecumenical.htm;
from Anglican–Roman Catholic dialogue at The Highland Shepherd, http://www.
msgr.ca/msgr–3/ecumenical_oo.htm, and from Lutheran–Roman Catholic dialogue
at the Evangelical Lutheran Church in America, http://www.elca.org/ecumenical/
Resources/lurcrsce.html.

34 This is the sort of ecumenism envisaged in the Church of England Council for
Christian Unity's 2006 document, *21 Ideas for a Richer Ecumenical Life*, available online
at http://cofedev.ilrt.org/info/ccu/england/resources/parish_suggestions.rtf.

35 Quite how this is possible has been explored in some depth by George Lindbeck,
The Nature of Doctrine: Religion and Theology in a Postliberal Age (Philadelphia: Westminster, 1984).

36 *Called to be the One Church: The Porto Alegre Ecclesiology Text* (Geneva: World
Council of Churches, 2006); available online from http://www.oikoumene.org/index.
php?id=2139.

37 Christina Holland, 'Against Ecumenism', *Children of the Church: A Traditional
Orthodox Youth's Newsletter* 2.1 (1999), available online at http://www.orthodox.net/
cotc/highlights.html.

38 Mike Paulson, 'A "Greater" Commission for Bible Believers', Living the Risen
Life, http://www.touchet1611.org/GreaterCommission.html.

14

Apostolic and Holy

This chapter will continue my discussion of the nature and purpose of the Church, focusing on the remaining two 'marks': apostolicity and holiness. I will explore the nature of the Church as a *witness to* and *embodiment of* the life of God – and some of the dangers involved in splitting witness from embodiment, or embodiment from witness.

I am going to

- argue that the Church is called into being *by* witness and *for* witness;
- describe some different ways of understanding the boundaries and distinctivenss of the Church;
- examine different ways in which the Church passes on its life and message;
- suggest that the Church is best understood as both holy and on the way to holiness.

Preparation

- What is the mission of the Church? How should it carry that mission out? Should the Church be engaged in evangelism? Think about these questions, and then briefly jot down your answers before beginning on the chapter.
- We are going to be discussing the holiness of the Church. Before doing so, it is worth having some kind of picture of the *history* of the Church – the good, the bad and the ugly. Consider pausing and dipping into an accessible one-volume history, like Stephen Tomkins's brief and witty *Short History of Christianity* (Oxford: Lion Hudson, 2005) or Justo L. Gonzalez's even briefer *Church History: An Essential Guide* (Nashville, TN: Abingdon, 1996).

Additional reading

The suggestions I made for the last chapter still stand, but you could add:

Hans Küng, *The Church*, tr. Ray and Rosaleen Ockenden (London: Search Press, 1968 [German original: 1967]). A weighty and thorough examination of ecclesiology, with a streak of reformist zeal.

Apostolicity

The Church owes its existence to Jesus of Nazareth. It is called into being by the good news of Jesus, and called into being in order to pass that good news on. It is defined both by its relation to the witness that it has received (the witness passed on by the apostles – those whom Christ chose and sent out to proclaim the gospel) and by its duty somehow to perpetuate and spread that witness itself (that is, to undertake an apostolic ministry itself). To think of the Church as catholic is to think of the circulating of the gift of Christ among the members now. To think of the Church as apostolic is to think of the Church as a recipient of a gift that has been passed down in time, and that is to be handed on to the future. The Church simply *is* the community of those who receive the apostolic witness to Christ and who pass it on.

Apostolic succession

The Catholic theologian Hans Küng writes:

> As direct witnesses and messengers of the risen Lord, the apostles can have no successors. No further apostles were called. ... The apostles are dead; there are no new apostles. But the *apostolic mission* remains. ... This apostolic ministry does not depend on further vocations to apostleship in the narrow sense, but depends on obedience to the apostles as the original witnesses and messengers of the Lord. As a result of the continuing apostolic mission there is, in the apostolic ministry, an apostolic succession: an apostolic succession of obedience. *Who* then are the followers of the apostles? ... There can only be one basic answer: the Church. The whole Church, not just a few individuals, is the follower of the Apostles.[1]

Nevertheless, alongside this 'basic answer', some churches and some theologians have argued that this general 'apostolic succession of obedience' is supported by a more specific one: the commissioning by the original apostles of some who would carry the responsibility of holding the Church to its catholic and apostolic mission, who in turn commissioned others to bear that responsibility, who in turn commissioned others, and so on down the ages in what is claimed to be an unbroken succession. The idea is that a continuity of *witness* is supported by a continuity of *people* – by a physical and personal handing on and entrusting across the generations from bishop to bishop and from bishop to priest, symbolized by the laying on of hands at ordination.[2] Others, on the other hand, see little inherent connection between the two forms of apostolic succession – and so doubt the necessity, or historical existence, of the unbroken succession of bishops.[3]

There is a spectrum of possible ways of understanding the apostolic nature of the Church. At one end of the spectrum is the approach that says that the Church is where the reign of God, the kingdom of God, is made real in the present. It is where response to the call of God, and living out of the life of God, takes place. It is, in a sense, an 'embodiment' of the life of God. Of course, it does not *exhaust* God's action: God is active anywhere and everywhere, and might turn out to have been working in all sorts of unexpected ways in unexpected places. But while it might acknowledge that, the Church's main business is to invite people to join it. It is – even when it is marred by divisions and by sin and misunderstanding – the place where true worship takes place, where the gospel is heard and obeyed, where the learning and unlearning of God has its home on earth. The Church, in pointing to God, points to itself; 'Church' is understood to mean 'the community of the true followers of Christ'. Apostolicity will be a matter of the Church preserving its identity as the embodiment of the kingdom: it preserves and passes Christ's call to the world by being the continuation of Christ's life – by being the body of Christ, living the life of Christ in the world.

Embodiment of the kingdom?

'[O]ur Savior shares prerogatives peculiarly his own with the Church in such a way that she may portray, in her whole life, both exterior and interior, a most faithful image of Christ. For in virtue of the juridical mission by which our divine Redeemer sent his apostles into the world, as he had been sent by the Father (John 27.18, 20.21), it is he who through the Church baptizes, teaches, rules, looses, binds, offers, sacrifices.

'Certainly the loving Mother is spotless in the Sacraments by which she gives birth to and nourishes her children; in the faith which she has always preserved inviolate; in her sacred laws imposed on all; in the evangelical counsels which she recommends; in those heavenly gifts and extraordinary grace through which, with inexhaustible fecundity, she generates hosts of martyrs, virgins and confessors. But it cannot be laid to her charge if some members fall, weak or wounded. In their name she prays to God daily: "Forgive us our trespasses"; and with the brave heart of a mother she applies herself at once to the work of nursing them back to spiritual health.'

Pope Pius XII, *Mystici Corporis Christi* (1943)[4]

'While Christ, holy, innocent and undefiled knew nothing of sin, but came to expiate only the sins of the people, the Church, embracing in its bosom sinners, at the same time holy and always in need of being purified, always follows the way of penance and renewal. The Church, like a stranger in a foreign land, presses forward amid the persecutions of the world and the consolations of God, announcing the cross and death of the Lord until he comes. By the power of the risen Lord it is given strength that it might, in patience and in love, overcome its sorrows and its challenges, both within itself and from without, and that it might reveal to the world, faithfully though darkly, the mystery of its Lord until, in the end, it will be manifested in full light.'

Second Vatican Council, *Dogmatic Constitution on the Church*[5]

At the other end of the spectrum is the approach that says that the Church does not point to itself at all, but always points away from itself to the activity and work of God. It does not regard itself as a place where the learning and unlearning of God are necessarily going on any more deeply or any more 'successfully' than anywhere else – but simply as a place where those processes are *named*. The Church is not the kingdom but the *herald* of the kingdom.

Those who hold this model believe that in all sorts of places and in all sorts of ways, God is drawing people to himself by conforming them to the Son by the Spirit – but that it is only in the Church that this process is described in those terms, and only in the Church that the relation of this activity to what took place in Jesus of Nazareth is made clear. Instead of the Church as 'embodiment' of God's activity (in some sense), this would be the Church as 'witness' to God's activity. 'Church' is understood to mean 'the community in which Christ's name is kept alive'. Apostolicity in this view will be more a matter of the handing on of a message, the repetition of a proclamation, the keeping alive of a language, and not so much a matter of what the Church is as of where the Church *points*.[6]

Now the first view, the 'embodiment' view, at least in its pure form, seems to many theologians to risk tying God's action too much to the Church. Its proponents risk saying that because Christ is here in their church, if you want to meet *him* then you are going to have to join *them* – and so they risk appointing themselves Christ's gatekeepers. Yet the Christ of the Gospels was often to be found where people did not expect him: eating and drinking among sinners. And the same Christ indicated that he would be found among the needy.[7] If the Church sees itself as *possessing* Christ, even if it intends bountifully to distribute that possession to the world, it has missed something important: when the Church goes out into the world it will find Christ already there, and will learn more of who Christ is in its encounter with those it meets.

On the other hand, the 'witness' view, at least in its pure form, has its own problems. The core of Christian faith is to 'know nothing but Christ and him crucified' – to bring all one's thoughts and habits, all one knows and does, to the foot of the cross to be judged and remade there. That, if you like, is the one thing Christians know, the one vocation they have. And while Christians can certainly trust that when they bring people and situations to the foot of the cross they will discover that the God of Jesus Christ has been at work in more ways than they could have imagined, drawing people into his Christ-shaped life in times and places far beyond the Church, that does not mean that to bring things to the foot of the cross will leave them unchanged. To name some process of learning that has been going on outside the Church as a process in which the God of Jesus Christ is active is to point to Christ as a criterion by which that learning can be judged and reshaped.

That is not the same as saying that Christians 'have all the answers': the Christians who point others to Christ in the expectation that those others need to be judged and transformed at the foot of the cross also point themselves to the same Christ in the same expectation of judgement. It might be more true to say that Christians are the 'bearers of a question': that their vocation is to point to a reality that puts all people (inside the Church and outside it) to the question.[8] But that also means that the Church is not simply a passive witness, but is (or can be) a means by which God calls the world to ever-deeper conversion, and that there is therefore a sense in which the Church is to call people to join it – at least in the sense that it calls people to look where it is looking.

I should also say one more thing, which muddies the waters between the 'embodiment' model and the 'witness' model. Accept, for a moment, that the church's vocation is to 'bear the question' – to point away from itself to Christ, to call other people to look where it is looking, and so to call all people to ever-deeper conversion at the foot of the cross. It will only do this compellingly, only do it with integrity, if instead of simply *telling* people about Christ, it lives in motion towards him. The only convincing way of proclaiming this message is by *living it out*; the only compelling way of pointing away to Christ is by being a community that is (however fitfully and inadequately) allowing itself to be converted by conscious and constant return to the foot of the cross. To be a witness, such a community must *embody* what it *says*.[9]

Exercise

As in the last chapter, think of any church of which you have had experience. What, if anything, about that church makes it possible to speak of it as an 'embodiment' of God's life, and what, if anything, makes it possible to speak of it as a 'witness' to that life?

Key points

- The church is 'apostolic' because its life and faith has been and is passed down the generations.
- There is a tension between regarding the Church primarily as an *embodiment* of the life of God, and regarding it primarily as a *witness* to that life.
- Embodiment and witness are nevertheless inseparable.

Boundaries

These two different ways of thinking about apostolicity align loosely with different ways of thinking about the nature of the Church's boundaries. Two different ways of thinking about those boundaries are, quite accidentally, suggested by the two main groups or words used for 'church' in European languages. In most European languages, the Church, or churches, are either referred to using words similar to the English word 'Church' (like the Scottish *kirk* or the German *Kirche*), or words similar to the French word *eglise* (like the Welsh *eglwys* or the English word 'ecclesiastical').

The *eglise* words all come from the Greek *ekklesia*, which itself derives from a root meaning 'summons' or 'call'.[10] The original idea behind the word was perhaps that of a gathering of people called together by a particular summons. Of course, arguments based on etymology are always shaky, and there is no reason to think that people had the details of this original meaning of the word in mind by New Testament times, but it does *suggest* one interesting way of thinking about what the definition of 'Church' should be. That is, one can ask whether we should think of 'Church' as meaning the gathering of all those who are called by God deeper into the life of God, by Christ and the Spirit. Of course, if the theology outlined in this book so far is even slightly on the right lines, *everyone* is called by God deeper into the life of God, but the idea of a gathering of those who are called implies not only a call, but some kind of response to the call as well – some kind of actual gathering together. By 'Church', therefore, we might mean 'all those who respond to the call of God' – or, perhaps, 'all those who are shaped by the call of God; all those who are actually being shaped by the Spirit in conformity to Christ'.

The picture of Church which this brief reflection might start pointing us towards is one that has the call of God at the centre, and then gathering towards that centre all those who in whatever way, to whatever degree, in whatever context, respond to that call.

However, as I said, alongside the *ekklesia* words, there are the church, kirk, Kirche words. And the etymology of these words is more obscure. The dominant theory is that it comes from the Greek word *kuriake* or 'Lord's', and is short for *kuriake oikia*, the Lord's house or Lord's household.[11] I don't want to make anything more of this etymology than a fortuitous suggestion for one way of thinking about 'Church', but it does hint at a different picture. Instead of focusing on the universal call of God, one could focus on the defined group (the household) of those who have a particular explicit identity: those who own a specific allegiance. If 'Church' means *kuriake oikia*, then it refers to the family that takes its surname from the Lord: a specific, identifiable group who have a particular name that marks them out from others. Think of Acts 11.20–26:

> Some men of Cyprus and Cyrene, … on coming to Antioch, spoke to the Hellenists … proclaiming the Lord Jesus. The hand of the Lord was with them, and a great number became believers and turned to the Lord … [F]or an entire year [Paul and Barnabas] met with the church and taught a great many people, and it was in Antioch that the disciples were first called 'Christians'.

The 'church' (*ekklesia*) in Antioch is made up of those who 'turn to the Lord' (the *kurios*) in faith; they become known by his name, as *Christ*ians: those who are named for their *pater familias*.

The difference between these two ways of understanding the nature of the Church can perhaps be illustrated in the following way. In England, a farmer might keep sheep together in a sheep pen: an enclosure with a clear boundary, which helps keep a flock together by setting a limit around it, clearly dividing territory up into 'inside' and 'outside'. In a desert, however, a farmer might not need to do this. She might operate instead by having a well, the only source of water for miles around, and assuming that sheep will have to keep coming back to the well if they want to survive. Her sheep will not need a clear boundary, and she will not need to divide territory up firmly into an inside and an outside. Instead, she will provide a centre in the knowledge that wherever they roam sheep will remain connected to it.

Some models of Church suggest that it needs very clear boundaries: a clear inside and a clear outside to the household of faith, with the saved (or the faithful or the believers or the committed membership) on the inside and everybody else on the outside. You are either an insider or an outsider, even if some hover for a while on the boundary.

Other models of Church suggest that boundaries don't matter so much as a clear centre. What you need is a sustained core of practices in which the universal call of God is repeated (perhaps worship, sacraments, preaching). The Church will then be defined by that centre, and might be rather relaxed about boundaries. There will be people in closer orbits and people further out, people who are utterly caught up in this centre and people who relate to it more distantly. There need be no neat division into insider and outsider. You might even say that everyone is to some extent an insider and to some extent an outsider – everyone has aspects of their life that line up with this central call, this central core of practices, and everyone has aspects of their life that fight against it. All that differs is how much of any individual's life is on one side of the divide, how much on the other.

There is one problem, however, with this description. If the clear centre that defines the Church is made up of a certain kind of corporate life – by 'a community that is (however fitfully and inadequately) being converted by conscious and constant return to the foot of the cross', say – then there might well have to be elements that look more like the 'clear boundaries' model (more like an English sheep-pen than the desert well) even in this 'clear centre' model. Once again, we are pushed away from thinking that there could be a straight choice between utterly distinct models of the Church, and towards a messier negotiation in the middle, pulled both ways by competing visions.

Exercise

Consider any churches known to you. Do they work in such a way as to have a recognizable 'membership'? If so, what is it to be a member? How is entry to membership regulated? How does one remain a member in good standing? What role does being a member play in a person's involvement in the various aspects of that church's life? Does having such a sense of membership, mean that the church ends up near the 'sheep pen' end of the spectrum?

Key points

- A church might preserve its continuity by means of clear boundaries, or ...
- A church might preserve its identity by means of a strong centre.
- These two models are not entirely separable.

Embodiment: The Church as mother

One model of the Church that can help us think further about what it means for the Church to be the *embodiment* of God's work is the model that sees the Church as *mother*.[12] To think of the Church as mother is, most obviously, to think of the Church as the bodily context in which Christians grow and are nurtured – the material and bodily mediation of God's life to creatures. This model helps push away from ideas of the Church as a voluntary association, or as having primarily to do with the propagation of *ideas*. Any passing on of ideas from a mother to her children takes place in a context that is much more than intellectual: it has as much to do with emotions and habits and dispositions and desires; it is as much a matter of feeding and hugging and playing and walking and singing and laughing and tickling as it is a matter of telling. The Church as mother is a Church in which explicit instruction is only a small part of the story: it has as much to do with the shaping of patterns of physical, communal and emotional life – a context in which people learn ways of doing things, rhythms of speech, emotional repertoires, gut reactions, *and by so doing* learn to know and love God and to love the world God loves. This is how the Church passes on its life, how it reproduces itself. It might be that the apostolic nature of the Church is displayed in children's groups and Sunday Schools at least as clearly as in the serious business of adult worship.[13]

Of course, this model is not without its dangers, and rightly attracts similar criticisms to those that I levelled against the pure 'embodiment' end of the spectrum on page 337. When combined with some distinctly unhealthy ideologies of motherhood, it can reinforce the idea that the Church is unquestionably pure (and you may have noticed the maternal language in the passage I quoted from Pius XII). It can help powerful church hierarchies (very often *male* hierarchies) disguise and perpetuate their power by allowing them to cloak it under a fluffy blanket of motherly imagery. And it can keep members of the Church seeing themselves as infants, incapable of standing on their own two feet. It can, in other words, help reinforce 'apostolicity' in a form that is all about the policing of boundaries and the preservation of power.

Cyprian's mother

The English theologian Rachel Muers draws attention to the meanings of this maternal language in its most prominent use in the Christian tradition. She writes:

The text that is quoted most often in later appropriations of the mother church image is the treatise of Cyprian on *The Unity of the Church*, written in relation to the Novatian heresy in the third century. ... It's in this text that the much-quoted line 'no-one can have God for his Father who does not have the church as his mother' appears. ...[14] The key emphasis in Cyprian's text is on purity. ... [T]he chastity of the mother matters above all so that the father knows who his children are, and vice versa. That's the context of the claim that 'no-one can have God for his Father who does not have the church as his mother.' Because the church has and maintains certain visible signs of 'chastity' ... divine paternity, here and nowhere else, is not in doubt.[15]

In other words, this maternal imagery is used in Cyprian as part of a boundary-setting discourse – one whose real point is to help you see where the *true* Church is (and, by implication, to see also where it *isn't*). And as Cyprian dwelt in particular on the apostolic succession of bishops as the key proof of 'chastity', his maternal imagery was also to do with making very clear in whose hands the power to define boundaries lay.

The maternal model itself, however, can suggest a rather different way of thinking about apostolicity and power, if one pays attention to the nature of the relationship between real mothers and their children, and specifically to the complexity of the *negotiation* between mother and child that starts when the child is still in the womb. The child may be receiving everything it needs to survive and grow from its mother's womb, and in one sense may appropriately be seen as *part* of the mother – but (as mothers suffering from morning sickness, or bruised ribs, or a squashed bladder, or an anxious day waiting for the next kick might tell you) the child is also something *other* than the mother, because one of the things it has received is its own individuality. It has an ability not simply to receive from, but to respond to and act upon, its mother.

One of the clearest examples of this is the process by which a mother passes on her language to her child (the language that will be the child's 'mother tongue'). Think of all the games and rituals and repetitions involved, the physicality and time-taking and mess of it all. Yet, however much repetition might be involved, the child does not simply learn to parrot the mother. If that is all that the child learns, then the child has not actually learnt to speak. The child who really learns to speak its mother tongue can hold a conversation with its mother; it can answer back; it can say things she has never said. All that nurturing, shaping, correcting, insisting by which the mother trains the child *frees* that child to be a native speaker. Rather than being an image that silently ties down the boundaries of the Church, and keeps power firmly in the hands of the already powerful, this model seems to pull in a quite different direction. What might it suggest about apostolicity, boundaries and power in the Church?

Importantly stupid parents

One of the ways in which babies learn is by being consistently treated as if they were more advanced than they are. So, for instance, the baby whose wind-induced grimaces are taken by doting parents as smiles, and responded to with delighted cooing, tend to learn to produce real smiles more quickly. Similarly, the baby is pushed towards the patterns of speech when his or her random and accidental noises are treated as if they were just on the borders of meaningful communication.

It is not simply a case of praise and disapproval reinforcing or weakening a given behaviour. Parents' responses give a baby's 'actions' meaning by weaving them in to an ongoing conversation (in a broad sense). So babies don't simply discover that smiling (for instance) is a good thing to do, they (slowly but surely) discover what smiling *means*, by learning the range of responses and reactions that it can generate – the appropriate ways in which the conversation can continue.

This means that it is very important for parents to be a bit stupid about their children – a bit too inclined to read significance into things, a bit too inclined to spot patterns, a bit too inclined to attribute intent and skill to their children. And there is something quite simply beautiful about this notion of winning a child into deeper levels of skill and interaction and communication and relationship by treating her (gratuitously) as if she were already there. And I suspect I mean that word 'gratuitously' quite seriously: this is, I think, a matter of grace.[16]

Key points

- The image of the Church as mother can be used to police church purity and reinforce the power of (largely male) church hierarchies.
- The image of the Church as mother can also be used to emphasize all the complex, embodied ways in which the Church passes its faith on.
- It is also an image that enables us to think of this passing on as, potentially, freeing rather than constricting.

Witness: The mission-shaped Church[17]

If we are to think of the Church as *witness*, we will need to move on from thinking of the Church as mother to thinking of the Church as constituted and impelled by *mission*. Mission is fundamental to the identity of the Church. In the first place, it is *God's* mission that is central. Christians believe that God has reached out and called all people into God's life. But this calling is not a call *from* the world – as if individuals who answered the call were plucked from their nasty surroundings and nastier neighbours so as to enjoy a solo voyage into the heart of bliss. The love of God that is expressed in God's mission is a love *for the world*, and a love for all people – a desire to draw all people and all things into unimpeded fellowship. And if the call issued by God is a call for human beings to share in God's love, then it is a call to become filled with the love of God for the world. The life of God is a life of love, and to be drawn into this life is to be drawn in to love – drawn to share the Son's love of the Father and the Father's sending of the Son. God's mission becomes the mission of God's people.

The mission of the Church

'It is God's design to gather all creation under the Lordship of Christ (cf. Ephesians 1.10), and to bring humanity and all creation into communion. As a reflection of the communion in the Triune God, the Church is God's instrument in fulfilling this goal. The Church is called to manifest God's mercy to humanity, and to bring humanity to its purpose – to praise and glorify God together with all the heavenly hosts. The mission of the Church is to serve the purpose of God as a gift given to the world in order that all may believe (cf. John 17.21).

'As persons who acknowledge Jesus Christ as Lord and Saviour, Christians are called to proclaim the Gospel in word and deed. They are to address those who have not heard, as well as those who are no longer living according to the Gospel, the Good News of the reign of God. They are called to live its values and to be a foretaste of that reign in the world. Mission thus belongs to the very being of the Church. This is a central implication of affirming the apostolicity of the Church.'

World Council of Churches, *The Nature and Mission of the Church*[18]

Now, to love another is to seek that other's good, and the highest good that, in Christian theology, can be desired or sought for another person, is that she too be drawn into the life of God, and be made more fully herself in the process. The highest good is that she fully know herself to be loved and become fully loving herself, and reflect back to God in her own particular configuration God's life of love.

Christianity is, therefore, inherently *missionary*, if by 'mission' we mean that activity by which Christians are impelled and enabled by the Spirit to participate with Christ in the Father's love of the world.

The primary form of mission, therefore, is simply to love people. And if we want to know what that means, we can hardly do better than remind ourselves once again of 1 Corinthians 13.

Love is patient and kind; love is not jealous or boastful; it is not arrogant or rude. Love does not insist on its own way; it is not irritable or resentful; it does not rejoice at wrong but rejoices in the right. Love bears all things, believes all things, hopes all things, endures all things. Love never ends. ...

Let me simply draw attention to two words from that definition: patient and kind. First, love is *kind*. If mission is love, then at the heart of mission will be kindness – attentiveness to the needs of the other, concern about their welfare, tenderness towards them. And you cannot be kind if you do not care, and if you do not look and listen. At the heart of mission will be a serious and devoted paying of attention to others.

Second, love is *patient*. It is participation in the patience of God that is shown in God's giving to creation its own time and space in which to be itself, to have its own way of being. If mission is, first and foremost, love, then it will not be an attitude in which the Christian seeks to cram the other into a preconceived space, making clones for Christ; it will be characterized by the desire that the other person should become fully and wholly herself in Christ.

To desire the fulfilment of another person means, from a Christian point of view, seeking for that other person to be drawn fully into love, because it is only in being loved and in becoming loving that a person becomes fully him- or herself. People are diminished and constricted by hatred and disordered desire; wholeness comes through love. And that may well mean that mission will also involve an element of challenge: a challenge to all that holds people (including oneself) back from love: a challenge to selfishness, a challenge to violence, a challenge to division. And so mission may well involve one in passionate outrage at injustice just as much as it involves one in considerate kindness to one's neighbours.

Exercise

Suppose that you were asked to help draft a church's 'mission statement'. How, on the basis of what I have just said, might you start?

Key points

- Christianity is inherently missionary.
- The heart of mission is loving-kindness.
- Mission does not aim at the making of 'clones for Christ'.
- Mission aims at the freeing of all people to be themselves in Christ.

The nature of evangelism

'Love' can mean many things, and can be twisted and distorted and misunder-stood, and used for ulterior motives. So to desire for someone to become full and whole is to desire the *purification* of that person's love. And this is where things can get more difficult.

Let me start with a bad model. This is the model that says there is no prob-lem in desiring the purification of another's love. The model that says, 'I know what love is; it is obvious. It is an attitude I know and understand fully, and so can spread to others. I may not myself be perfectly loving, but I know how love works.' In effect, this model says that to seek for the purification of love – my own and others' – is for me to point to myself, or at least to my ideas; it is for me to establish myself as a criterion. My well-understood ideals are what I am spreading, and 'mission' is in effect the attempt to make other people like me – or at least like what I identify as best in myself. The purification of love is, in this model, something we seek for other people, but not really – at least not *radically* – for myself.

A better model says, 'No, I can't claim to have become fully loving. I can't claim to have understood love properly. I can't claim to have had my love purified. All I can claim, as a Christian, is that I have been loved by one who is teaching me what love is – however painfully slow and often reversed the process of learning might be. If I am seeking the growth and perfecting of love, it will not be by pointing to myself but by pointing to the source from which I receive love and the criterion by which I learn to discern love: the cross of Christ.' Mission will, in this model, involve not the attempt to make other people like me, but simply to direct their gaze where I direct mine, and so to learn alongside me from the same source.

This better model, however, can collapse back into the bad model. Once I have said that it is my task, in Christian mission, to point people to Christ, I can all too easily start claiming that I know exactly who Christ is and what he has to say, and am an expert on what is involved in entering into relationship with him. Once again, this substitutes something within my grasp and control, something that cannot surprise me, for the dangerous freedom of Christ, and makes mission into a process of self-cloning rather than a process in which I direct people away from myself and towards God.

So, to be involved in Christian mission is first of all to love others; second it is to seek for them to grow in love; and third it is to point people away from oneself and to the source and criterion by which their love and one's own can be purified – and it is that pointing away that can be called 'evangelism', the passing on of the *evangel*, the gospel, the good news.

In the sense just described, therefore, mission has fundamentally to do with witnessing to Christ; it has fundamentally to do with pointing away from oneself. True mission, one might say, is as ek-static as worship. In mission, it is vital for Christians not to try to control what happens, not to try to fit the other person into the paradigm of what has happened to them. In mission, too, Christians must be open to discovering something new by seeing how encounter with Christ works out for someone else. Christian mission – whether it be in forms that focus on the explicit proclamation of the Gospel of love, or forms that focus on the living out of that love among others – faces constant temptation to self-centredness, constant temptation to attempt the taming of God in whose mission one is supposedly participating. 'Let God be God' is a cry that needs to challenge Christian mission as well as every other aspect of Christian life.

My claim is that, if one approaches the question theologically, in the light of the kind of claims I have been exploring so far in this book, one will be pushed towards the idea that Christians are called to evangelism without arrogance, evangelism without control. They are called to love and, as part of that love, called to point to the source and criterion of their love – in their speaking and acting reflecting that source and criterion, but always in such a way as to acknowledge their own fallibility and sinfulness, and their own continued need of conversion. Evangelism, if it is to be spreading the good news of God rather than the news about oneself, *must* involve this humility.

Exercise

Ask yourself: what would such evangelism look like in practice? How would it compare to other forms of evangelism? Can you imagine, say, a mission focused on big evangelistic meetings with an altar call at the end that appropriately incorporated this humility? Can you imagine a programme of Christian social involvement and action that appropriately incorporated this pointing?

I don't intend this as a concession to a cultural environment less comfortable with up-front, in-your-face evangelism than it used to be – a watering down of real, robust evangelism into something safer and weaker and lukewarm. You may disagree, and may think I have fallen into precisely this trap, but my intention is to ask how it is that one can speak about God in such a way as genuinely to speak about *God*, rather than about *one's grasp* on God – in other words, how it is that one can speak about God without secretly speaking about oneself all along.

I suppose one might sum this up by saying that the two aspects of Christian mission are love and worship: love that lives out, by the grace of God and to the best of one's broken and finite ability, the life of God in the world, and worship that gives the glory to God and to God only, and points to God alone as the source of all that is true, good and beautiful.

Forms of witness

'Witness' can be understood in very different ways. One could say, for instance, that the only possible 'witness' to God's life is the imperfect, fragmentary living of a life that reflects it, and that the Church is where one finds such new life, or holiness, or love. One could say, in a similar vein, that the only way the Church can be such a witness is by deliberately, visibly and explicitly 'living against the grain' of the surrounding society, trying to live as a beacon of a different form of living in the midst of an antagonistic or indifferent world. One could say that the only possible sign of God's life is the proclamation of its truth, and that the Church is where one finds true preaching, or explicit witness to what has taken place in Christ. Only in this way is the Church's witness to Christ, and to him crucified, kept alive. One could say that the only possible signs of God's life are the ones instituted as sacraments (whether one thinks there are two sacraments, seven, or some other number); the Church is where one finds the proper celebration of baptism and the Eucharist – the proper holding up of these signs. One could say that the only possible sign of God's life is the ongoing practice of worship, and that the Church is where one finds the ongoing celebration of the liturgy (or perhaps the everlasting singing of choruses). One could say that the proper way in which the Church becomes a sign is as it accompanies the activities of the world and does not preach at them but works in and around them to draw them as close to true as possible, explicitly and implicitly – working (one might say) as a chaplain. And, finally, one could even say that the only possible 'sign' of the redeemed life is the creation of lasting monuments to Christ – the art and architecture that outlast us, and achieve a perfection that our messy lives miss, and that the church is the building with the heavenwards-soaring steeple.

Key points

- Evangelism should point people to the God of Jesus Christ.
- Evangelism should point away from those doing the evangelism.

- In pointing others to the God who can judge and transform them, the Church is pointing to its own judge and transformer.
- Because both point to God, worship and evangelism are closely linked.

Holiness

We have yet to consider the remaining traditional mark of the Church. The Church is, the creeds say, *holy*. The root meaning of the word 'holy' is 'set apart': the Church is holy because it is set apart for God – called out of ungodly life and into godly life; earmarked for the kingdom of love and justice. To speak of the Church as holy is to speak of the Church as a community drawn by the Holy Spirit deeper into the perfect life of God. The Church is the community of those who are being killed and made alive, drawn on a journey of learning and unlearning that will transform their ways of living in the world. The Church is the community of those who are dying and rising with Christ.

The difficulty with this claim comes from the patent unholiness of actual churches. One does not have to dig far to find in every congregation, every denomination, every strand of Christianity there is or ever has been, evidence of the failure of love and justice – of failures of nerve, betrayals of conscience, abuses of power, distortions of truth, delinquencies in care, approvals of violence, and blottings of beauty. What does it mean, in churches like these, to recite a creed that proclaims belief in a holy Church?

One might claim that the true Church – the Church confessed in the creeds – is scattered across and beyond the boundaries of the various institutional churches: that within and sometimes beyond these visible institutions there is an invisible community to which the Creed's description does apply – the community of the holy. The work of the Spirit is not to be identified with or confined to the organizations and institutions that we call churches: the Spirit blows invisibly within and beyond them.

Visible and invisible

According to the 1646 Westminster Confession of Faith,

> The catholic or universal church, which is *invisible*, consists of the whole number of the elect, that have been, are, or shall be gathered into one, under Christ the head thereof; and is the spouse, the body, the fullness of Him that filleth all in all. The *visible* Church, which is also catholic or universal under the gospel (not confined to one nation as before under the law), consists of all those throughout the world that profess the true religion, together with their children; and is the Kingdom of the Lord Jesus Christ; the house and family of God, through which men are ordinarily saved and union with which is essential to their best growth and service.

The implication is that the visible Church may contain those who *profess* the faith but are not *elect*, and that there may, extraordinarily, be those who are elect but do not profess. God's real Church, according to the Westminster divines, does not necessarily have the same boundaries as the visible church.[19]

One would need to be careful, however, about pushing this distinction too far. In the first place, this way of talking can easily become arrogant (*'I'm* a member of the true Church, the living Church of the Spirit; most of the people around me in this institutional so-called church are not.') In the second place, this way of thinking can, as it were, let the visible institutions, the actual concretely constituted churches in which Christians worship, off the hook. If holiness is only to be looked for in the secret fellowship of the real saints through whom the Spirit blows, a fellowship scattered through and beyond the walls of visible churches, then holiness is not really something that one will expect of those visible institutions. And in the third place, the kind of holiness that is envisioned can all to easily become a purely private or individual virtue, a quality that one can make sense of only as the work of the Spirit on the individual believer, rather than a holiness that could be displayed in the organized life of an identifiable, visible community.

Some will claim that the true Church – the Church confessed in the creeds – is not the earthly institutions one sees around one today, but is the communion of saints in heaven: those who have been freed from the inadequacies and failures of this-worldly Christianity, and freed to become the kind of Church that the creeds describe.

Of course, if this claim were simply made without qualification or supplement, it could fuel a kind of complacency. By putting off the description that the creeds give until heaven, it makes it harder for Christians to hear it as a challenge to the state of the churches here on earth in the present. One could, however, make the claim a little more subtle by claiming that this true, eschatological Church is a community into which present, worldly churches are being invited and drawn. The Church, one might say, is both holy *now*, and *not yet* holy: whatever holiness it has now it has as a foretaste and a promise of the holiness that it will have. To confess the holiness of the Church in the Creed is, in this perspective, to acknowledge holiness as the identity that God holds out for the whole Church, individually and corporately. The 'not yet' of this holiness is seen both in the sinfulness of individual Christians, and in the sinfulness of the churches to which they belong: in the failures of love and justice in individual lives, but also the failures of love and justice in the organization and arrangement of the churches' institutional lives.

To confess that the Church is holy, then, is not (or should not be) a doorway to complacent satisfaction with the current state of the Church's life: it is the confession that the Church is not yet what it will be and should be. It is a credal confession that therefore coheres with 'confession' in the other sense of the word: with the penitent acknowledgement of failure, and prayer for God's assistance in becoming holy – whether it is practised as spoken confession to a priest, as liturgical prayers of contrition, or as the individual's prayers of penitence. To say that holiness is a mark of the Church is to say that such penitence or confession is a mark of the Church.

Nevertheless, this focus on penitence as a mark of the Church should not let one accept too easily the sinfulness of the Church as an inevitability. The motor that drives this penitence is a recognition that it is proper to the Church to be holy – and therefore that an unholy Church is a contradiction in terms, an offence against nature. The credal confession of the holiness of the Church is a way of saying of the unholiness found in the life of the Church: this should not be, it does not belong, it has no place, it cannot simply be accepted or overlooked. The Church must be marked by holiness – by loving and just action within itself and towards the world. Wherever the Church is not marked by love and justice it is failing to be the Church.

Donatism

The Donatists of fourth-, and fifth-century North Africa believed that only the holy, only the blameless truly belonged in the Church, and specifically that the ministry of bishops and priests who fell from blamelessness became invalid. Donatists would, for instance, rebaptize anyone who had been baptized by someone whose ministry they regarded as invalid. They flourished in times when the persecution of Christians was still a present reality or a vivid memory, and they could identify all too easily in the ranks of the Church some who had buckled under persecution, handing over Christian Scriptures to be burnt.[20]

Their most formidable opponent was Augustine of Hippo. He argued that the Church in the present would always be a mixed reality, and that unholiness is found inside it just as holiness is found outside it.[21] Its holiness does not come from its own absolute purity, but from Christ – and the Church lives not by its own holiness but by his, witnessing to him, passing on his message, and celebrating the sacraments that he instituted.[22]

Key points

- To confess the Church as holy is not to claim that it is perfect as it now stands.
- To confess the Church as holy is not, however, simply to talk about an invisible or eschatological Church rather than the present, visible, institutional churches.
- To confess the Church as holy is to call those present, visible, institutional churches to become properly themselves.
- Nevertheless, wherever the Church is not marked by love and justice it is failing to be the Church.

Institution and fellowship

Another approach to the issues that we have just been exploring can be found by comparing two more 'models of the Church'. The first model is of the Church as *institution*. This is the model that sees the Church fundamentally as an ordered and clearly defined society, in which life is lived in explicit relationship to God. Someone who favoured this way of thinking might say that those who have embarked on the journey deeper into the life of God recognize that they have a fundamental allegiance, a deep orientation, that is at odds with the ways of the world: they find themselves to be citizens of another country, foreigners who don't truly belong in the world as it has come to define itself. And they recognize that citizenship of this 'heavenly country' should define every aspect of their lives – not just their individual habits and affections, but their ways of organizing and regulating social life. And the only way they can be true to that citizenship and the demands that it makes is by building in the midst of the world an alternative society – an outpost of that heavenly country of which they are citizens, an outpost that runs (as far as is possible in this foreign territory) according to the rules of the heavenly country. Of course, because those who know themselves ultimately to be citizens of this heavenly country also remain for now part of the world (and because they are called to minister to the world) they will inevitably also remain part of their worldly countries, of worldly institutions and societies. Their true citizenship will sit rather strangely alongside their worldly citizenship, and, just as with any foreign enclave within a host nation, there will be endless debates about how this dual citizenship is negotiated. But fundamentally the Church will, as far as possible, be an alternative society, with alternative arrangements, an alternative education system, alternative power structures, alternative politics, even an alternative economy – sitting strangely spread out among the various worldly countries in which its members are found.

Critics of this way of speaking suggest that, while it has some important insights, it unconsciously adopts too much language and too many ideas from worldly societies, and so corrupts the gospel. So, critics might say that the kinds of power structure and hierarchical organization, the kinds of discipline, the kinds of boundary-marking and policing that are promoted by proponents of the 'institution' model of the Church are the ways of the world, and are not appropriate ways to respond to the gospel of Jesus Christ. It is a model that (according to its critics) does not – and cannot – recognize the strange ways in which God is working in the world. Once again, we are back to the 'embodiment' model, and its familiar problems.

The second model is of the Church as *spiritual fellowship*. This is more or less the opposite of the institutional model. The core idea is that the Spirit, who draws people to God alongside Christ, cannot be bound by any formal structure or institution. The Church can only be the free association of those who find that the same Spirit is impelling them, the free association of those who recognize one another as fellow travellers. The Spirit is one who breaks through all conventions, all rules, all habits, to breathe new and deeper life – and although people constantly let the life into which the Spirit is leading them atrophy and solidify into structures that have more of the flesh in them than they have of the Spirit, the Spirit retains the power to break through these structures afresh and take people deeper into the life of God.

The dangers with this model are perhaps as obvious as its strengths. It is important for churches to allow for the iconoclastic work of the Spirit showing them that their present understanding, their present way of doing things, their present structures and habits have become idols. Yet there is also a danger of a deep irresponsibility in this model of the Church. Just as Paul took the Corinthians to task for allowing their ecstatic experiences to lead them away from the difficult Gospel of Christ, away from love, so there is a danger that in apparently ceding control to the deep, inward prompting of the Spirit, Christians can actually be ceding control to their own whims. Unless there are ways in which the apparent promptings of the Spirit can be tested and their authenticity discerned, unless there are checks and balances in place, ways of being called to account by the wisdom of others, past and present, those involved risk heading off into the realm of 'each person doing what is right in his or her own eyes'.[23] The potential for power trips of one kind or another is no less present in this model than in the hierarchical institutional model.

Although it is by no means inevitable, this model of the Church has also sometimes led to other forms of irresponsibility. It has sometimes gone hand in hand with a form of escapism, where the Church is taken to be a realm in which Christians leave all the problems and questions of the world behind, and are taken deeper into a realm of powerful personal experiences. The patient working out of what it means to live under the Lordship of Jesus Christ in the midst of the world – the idea that there might be social, political and institutional implications and a calling to costly service in pursuit of these implications – can sometimes be abandoned in favour of a search for the right kind of feeling.

The tension between these two models is one that we have met before. When discussing the Holy Spirit in the Old Testament, I spoke of the Spirit as the source of just and proper order, who enables individuals to contribute to the building of well-ordered life: the Spirit as a Spirit of Wisdom. Set alongside that, however, I set a picture of the Spirit as a disruptive influence, who challenges the unjust order of things, and names idols for what they are: the Spirit as a Spirit of Judgement. This tension cannot be resolved by picking one side over the other: both are the Spirit's sanctifying work, and both models have something important to say about the nature of the Spirit's Church.

Key points

- The Church is an alternative society in the midst of the world.
- The Church is the community of those impelled and enabled by the Spirit of God.
- These two descriptions need to be held together, despite the tension between them.

Any given Sunday, again

What would it mean to confess the ordinary church that I described at the beginning of the previous chapter as one, holy, catholic and apostolic? Well, in the first place, worship stands at the heart of this church's distinctive life: songs and sacraments are the most obvious things that happen when people gather in this building as church. Worship is what makes this a church rather than another village social club. And the words of the liturgy, of the hymns, of the Bible and of the sermons keep the focus of that worship firmly on the God of Jesus Christ. This church is one because it worships one God. Of course, this church's worship is also marked by distraction, by occasional dreariness, by all sorts of imperfections and inadequacies. Worship is, nevertheless, simply what this church does: it is who we are.

This church is also 'now and not yet' holy. It is holy now, in all sorts of rather ordinary ways: it is made up of people who would not otherwise spend time with each other, learning to get along; and the people in it care in various ways and to various degrees about the life of the church and the life of the wider community within which it is set, and they concern themselves with how best to make a difference, how to care and comfort and support and encourage and challenge. There is nothing very dramatic about this holiness, and it is easy to imagine all sorts of ways in which this church could do more, and to identify all sorts of ways in which it fails at holiness – but still, concern with this kind of holiness, care about it, is part of what this group of people does: it is part of what this church is. And it is also a context in which the 'not yet' of holiness is acknowledged: it is a context in which people regularly hear from Bible passages and sermons challenges and calls to holiness, and it is a context in which there are regular liturgical acknowledgements of our failures and inadequacies – regular opportunities for repentance.

To stand in this church on a Sunday morning and confess 'I believe in one, holy ... Church' may be to proclaim belief in an eschatological fulfilment towards which this church points only partially and hesitantly; it is also, however to give a description of the visible life of this church that is partial and ambivalent, but nevertheless *true*.

Exercise

One last time, think of any church of which you have had experience. Ask yourself again, on the basis of what you have now read, what it might mean to confess belief in the Church as holy whilst standing or sitting in that church?

Key point

- The theological descriptions I have been offering are meant to apply to ordinary churches.

Going further

1 I have not, in my discussion of the Church, discussed the role of ordained ministers within it. It would have been possible to treat that role under the heading of 'unity', and seen it as primarily a sacramental role; or under 'holiness', and seen it primarily as the pastoral nurture of godly lives; or under 'catholicity', with the ordained minister as representative of the congregation to the wider Church and the wider Church to the congregation; or under 'apostolicity', and seen it as primarily associated with the transmission of teaching; or in a number of other ways. For further reading, see Susan K. Wood (ed.), *Ordering the Baptismal Priesthood: Theologies of Lay and Ordained Ministry* (Collegeville, MN: Liturgical, 2003); Avery Dulles, *The Priestly Office: A Theological Reflection* (Mahwah, NJ: Paulist, 1997); Thomas F. Torrance, *The Royal Priesthood: A Theology of Ordained Ministry*, revised edn (Edinburgh: T&T Clark, 1993); Robin Greenwood, *Transforming Priesthood: A New Theology of Mission and Ministry* (London: SPCK, 1994); Rosalind Brown and Christopher Cocksworth, *On Being a Priest Today*, new edn, (Norwich: Canterbury, 2006); and, for good measure, an older classic: Richard Baxter, *The Reformed Pastor*, 3rd edn (London: William Collins, 1829 [orginal: 1656]); available online at the Christian Classics Etherial Library, http://www.ccel.org/ccel/baxter/pastor.html.

2 The nature of Christian mission is also worth delving into more deeply. I recommend, as a starting point, David Bosch, *Transforming Mission: Paradigm Shifts in Theology of Mission*, American Society of Missiology Series, 16 (Maryknoll, NY: Orbis, 1991). See also Lesslie Newbigin, *The Open Secret: An Introduction to the Theology of Mission*, revised edn (Grand Rapids, MI: Eerdmans, 1995).

Notes

1 Hans Küng, *The Church*, tr. Ray and Rosaleen Ockenden (London: Search Press, 1968 [German original: 1967]), p. 355.

2 For a typical polemic in favour of this form of succession, see Catholic Answers, 'Apostolic succession' (San Diego: Catholic Answers, 2006), available online at http://www.catholic.com/library/Apostolic_Succession.asp, and Kenneth J. Howell, 'Does Christ's Church have apostolic succession?' (San Diego: Catholic Answers, 2005); available online at http://www.catholic.com/thisrock/2005/0504sbs.asp.

3 For a typical polemic against this form of apostolic succession, see Mark A. Copeland, 'Apostolic Succession', *Executable Outlines*, 2006 http://www.ccel.org/contrib/exec_outlines/top/aposucc.htm.

4 See, for example, Pope Pius XII's encyclical, *Mystici Corporis Christi* (1943), §§56; available online from the Vatican Archive, http://www.vatican.va/holy_father/pius_xii/encyclicals/index.htm.

5 Second Vatican Council, *Dogmatic Constitution on the Church: Lumen Gentium* (21 November 1964), Ch.1, §8; available online at the Vatican Archive, http://www.vatican.va/archive/hist_councils/ii_vatican_council/index.htm.

6 See Hans Frei, *The Identity of Jesus Christ: The Hermeneutical Bases of Dogmatic*

Theology (Philadelphia: Fortress, 1975), p. 157: 'the Church is simply the witness to the fact that it is Jesus Christ and none other who is the ultimate presence in and to the world'.

7 See Chapter 13, note 19.

8 See Rowan Williams, *The Wound of Knowledge: Christian Spirituality from the New Testament to St John of the Cross* (London: DLT, 1979), p. 30.

9 For the Church's life as its witness, see Stanley Hauerwas, *A Community of Character: Toward a Constructive Christian Social Ethic* (Notre Dame, IN: University of Notre Dame, 1981), and George Lindbeck, *The Church in a Postliberal Age* (Grand Rapids, MI: Eerdmans, 2002), pp. 158–9.

10 See *Oxford English Dictionary*, 2nd edn (Oxford: Oxford University Press, 1989), under *'ecclesia'*.

11 See *Oxford English Dictionary*, under 'church, n.'.

12 These reflections on the Church as 'mother' are heavily indebted to my colleague Rachel Muers, and to the paper cited in note 15.

13 Think of the workers in the field in the sun story I told in Chapter 3, and imagine the ways in which their knowledge of the sun might have been passed on from generation to generation.

14 Cyprian, *On the Unity of the Church* 6, in A. Cleveland Coxe (ed.), *Ante-Nicene Fathers*, vol. 5 (New York: Christian Literature Company, 1885); available online at the Christian Classics Ethereal Library, http://www.ccel.org/fathers2/ANF–05/anf05–111. htm.

15 Rachel Muers, 'Mother churches? Thinking the maternal body in theology', paper delivered at the *Emerging Geographies of Belief* conference, University of Exeter, 2006.

16 This passage is based on an entry in a blog that my wife and I kept after the birth of our daughter, Bridget. See http://higton.goringe.net/?p=150.

17 See Church of England Mission and Public Affairs Council, *Mission-Shaped Church: Church Planting and Fresh Expressions of Church in a Changing Context* (London: Church House, 2004); available online at http://www.cofe.anglican.org/info/papers/ mission_shaped_church.pdf.

18 World Council of Churches, Faith and Order Commission, *The Nature and Mission of the Church: A Stage on the Way to a Common Statement*, Faith and Order Paper 198 (Geneva, WCC, 2005), §§34–5; available online at http://www.oikoumene. org/fileadmin/files/wcc-main/documents/p2/FO2005_198_en.pdf.

19 *The Westminster Confession of Faith* (1646), ch. 25 (28) 'Of the Church', §§1–2, available online at the Christian Classics Ethereal Library, http://www.ccel.org/ccel/anonymous/westminster3.i.xxviii.html.

20 For a Donatist text, see Petilian of Cirta's *Encyclical Letter to the Donatists*, tr. J. R. King, available online at the Patristics in English Project, http://www.seanmultimedia. com/Pie_homepage.html.

21 '[B]oth some things are done outside in the name of Christ not against the Church, and some things are done inside on the devil's part which are against the Church.' *On Baptism* 4.10 in Philip Schaff (ed.), *Nicene and Post Nicene Fathers*, First Series, vol. 4 (New York: Christian Literature Company, 1887), p. 454; available online at the Christian Classics Ethereal Library, http://www.ccel.org/ccel/schaff/npnf104. v.iv.vi.x.html.

22 See both the remainder of *On Baptism* and Augustine's reply to Petilian, in the volume cited in the previous note.

23 Cf. Judges 17.6, 21.25.

15

Biblical Settlements

Christians can make sense of themselves, their communities and their world as being drawn into the life of God. That has been my claim throughout this book. But where does this sense come from? What are its sources? What authorizes this particular way of telling the Christian story? The answer suggested in Chapter 14 was that it is the witness of the apostles that provides theology's foundation – the witness that is found (largely or exclusively[1]) in the pages of the Bible. So what role should the Bible play in theology – and, more broadly, in the kind of Christian life I have described in this book? The simplest answer, but one that fits quite well with the themes of this book, might be: 'Jesus loves me, this I know, for the Bible tells me so.'[2] That is, the Bible might be seen as the means (or a means) by which the love of God in Christ is communicated. That simple answer, however, conceals a clutch of complexities, which I will be exploring in this chapter and the next.

In this chapter, I am going to

- ask where Christians' knowledge of Jesus comes from;
- ask what role the Bible plays in forming this knowledge;
- point out that Christians have had rather different ideas about what the Bible teaches about Jesus, and about *how* it teaches;
- introduce the term 'biblical settlement' to refer to the most resilient of these ideas; and
- claim that there is no easy way to choose between such settlements.

In the next chapter, which forms a pair with this one, I will go on to suggest a 'biblical settlement' that coheres with the Trinitarian theology explored so far in this book.

Preparation

- What is the Bible? What is it for? How does it differ from other books? How should Christians treat it? What can it tell them? Jot down now some brief notes on any answers you have to these sorts of questions. And give some time to thinking about whether you have found the kind of uses I've made of the Bible in this book reasonable, legitimate, and convincing. If not, what has been wrong with them?
- If you type 'doctrine of scripture' into an internet search engine like Google, you will find a whole clutch of theological claims about the nature and importance of the Bible. Skim through a few of these now to get a sense of the kind of claims that people make about the Bible. Are there any of these sites that you feel more comfortable with – that seem to you to be heading in the right sort of direction?

Additional readings

For reading to accompany this chapter, try:

Justin Holcomb (ed.), *Christian Theologies of Scripture* (New York: New York University Press, 2006). A good set of chapters introducing highlights from the history of Christian thinking about the Bible.

John Webster, *Holy Scripture: A Dogmatic Sketch*, (Cambridge: Cambridge University Press, 2003). Short, clear and punchy; Webster gives a Reformed theological account that links the doctrine of Scripture well to other doctrines.

Ellen F. Davis and Richard B. Hays (eds), *The Art of Reading Scripture* (Grand Rapids, MI: Eerdmans, 2004). A wide-ranging collection of papers on Scripture by a number of contemporary theologians.

Knowing Jesus: Imagination

If you have ever watched a film adaptation of a favourite book, you will have had the experience of looking at the actor cast in the lead role and thinking, 'That's not how I imagined him looking!' ('No, no, no – his hair should be curlier. And he should be a bit stockier, shouldn't he? And, anyway, shouldn't Frodo be about fifty when he leaves the Shire? What's Elijah Wood, fift*een*?'[3]) Strangely enough, our ability to make these kinds of judgement does not at all depend upon our having a clear, consistent mental picture of the character in question. We will far more likely have a rag-bag of mental odds and ends: a vague image of what his eyes might look like; a remembered verbal description of his hair, with no real mental picture attached to it; a rather nebulous 'feel' for the kinds of clothes he might wear – and so on. A collection of fragments, glimpses, ideas, feelings and constraints, which will almost certainly not be enough to determine exactly what the character *does* look like for us, and which may not even be consistent.

Something like this can be found in some cubist paintings, such as Diego Rivera's 1914 portrait of Jacques Lipchitz (see Plate 7).[4] Rather than trying to paint the coherent original – the actual human face – to which all his fragmentary perceptions of Lipchitz referred, Rivera tried instead to paint those fragments themselves: a feature here, a vague sense of a shape or a bulk there, all the glimpses and glances, hints and suggestions, seen from a variety of perspectives, which are the bits and pieces that actually lodged in his mind as he got to know the face of his sitter. With Rivera's portrait in hand, one could just about imagine sizing up an identity parade of men pretending to be the sitter and saying of each one, 'No, *he*'s not right', without necessarily being able to construct from the painting a single coherent image of what the real Lipchitz *does* look like.

Christian life, I have claimed, has at its heart penitent attention to Jesus of Nazareth as the visibility of the life of God. In other words, Christian life is, or should be, decisively shaped by what people know of Jesus of Nazareth. But what does it mean to 'know Jesus'?

If you ask what kind of mental image any individual Christian has of Jesus of Nazareth, you are unlikely to find a single, clear, coherent portrait and likely to find something more like a cubist painting: a bewildering mosaic of disparate elements. An individual believer might well carry round in his or her mind fragments of narrative, general impressions of character traits, images from paintings and childhood picture books, snatches of songs, a collection of biblical and traditional titles and epithets, a feeling that some things 'just don't fit' with who Jesus was, and a sense that some other things do or should – a shifting collage of bits and pieces culled from years of sermons, Bible readings, hymns, children's books, conversations and meditations. There will also probably be, tied in rather haphazardly with all this, some rather more nebulous ideas about how this Jesus relates to God, and how God relates to this Jesus, perhaps as no more than a kind of halo or gold background to the main mosaic, perhaps as a central and constitutive element.[5]

Exercise

Try to identify as many as you can of the main sources that have shaped your imagination of Jesus, other than the Bible – children's books, sermons, films, pictures or whatever.

Key points

- An individual believer's mental image of Jesus is likely to consist of a bewildering collage of fragments.
- The collage will be shaped by the particular course that the believer's life has taken.

Knowing Jesus: Life

[21]'Not everyone who says to me, "Lord, Lord", will enter the kingdom of heaven, but only one who does the will of my Father in heaven. [22]On that day many will say to me, "Lord, Lord, did we not prophesy in your name, and cast out demons in your name, and do many deeds of power in your name?" [23]Then I will declare to them, "I never knew you; go away from me, you evildoers."'

Matthew 7.21–23

It may be, however, that to ask about the 'mental image' that people have of Jesus is to get off on the wrong foot. Perhaps one could think of the possession of a good mental image of Jesus as being like the knowledge of the name of Jesus claimed by the evildoers in Matthew 7. They know Jesus' name, but they are not obedient to his Father. Jesus tells them that *he* does not know *them*, and we might also deduce that, in some sense, *they* do not really know *him*. Perhaps we should not be asking how Christians imagine Christ, but how they obey him. That is, perhaps we should be asking how Christians reflect him, or are patterned after him, in all that they do.[6]

If the theology presented in this book is correct, however, we cannot simply turn away from Christian imagination to Christian life in this way – or rather, we can't divorce the two. I have argued that, according to the doctrine of the incarnation, it is Jesus himself who is God's address to the world, calling the world to godly life; God's message to the world is not detachable from the human life in which that message is given. To focus on Christians' living reflection of Christ is also to focus on how they respond to, are shaped by, are held in relationship with, this specific human being. I can't see any way of talking about such response, such relationship, without at least *some* reference to Christians' imagination of Jesus and to how that imagination helps shape their lives. Knowledge of Jesus, we might say, is a matter of imagination wrapped up in a way of life, or a way of life wrapped up in imagination.

Jesus laughing

I remember a discussion when I was at college about what it did to one's understanding of the Gospels if, as a thought experiment, one tried to imagine Jesus as a brawny bull of a man, full of loud laughter. A friend of mine suggested the actor Brian Blessed as a model.[7]

The trouble is that as soon as we ask how a Christian's life is shaped in accordance with his or her imagination of Jesus, we get back into muddy water. After all, the processes by which a person's image of Jesus has been learnt and refined are messily mixed in with the processes by which his or her Christian life itself has been learnt and refined. Neither side of the equation can be described simply, and the way in which the two sides have grown together is difficult to tease out.

Of course, there is likely to be some kind of rough and ready coherence between a person's image of Jesus and her life. It is unlikely, for instance, that someone deeply committed to a 'health and wealth' form of Christian life is going to have an image of Jesus in which poverty is a central part of the collage. This rough and ready coherence might well be strong enough for a serious change in the circumstances or direction of a person's life to send shock waves through her image of Jesus, or for a serious challenge to her picture of Jesus to set off repercussions in her life. So, for instance, the health-and-wealth Christian might find that her image of Jesus comes alive in new ways if her material prosperity is suddenly devastated, or she might start to become uncomfortable about her health-and-wealth thinking if she does become convinced, for whatever reason, that poverty *was* a central facet of Christ's life.[8]

It is hard to imagine, however, someone who could confidently declare what the implication of each facet of her image of Jesus was for her life, or how each part of her life was related to her image of Jesus. We could think instead, perhaps, of a Christian's life and imagination as a giant game of spillikins. That is, life and imagination are jumbled together like a pile of sticks, and as one tries to take one stick, thinking that it is relatively independent and can be moved on its own, or thinking that one knows exactly how that stick rests on others and how others rest on it, one suddenly discovers that the situation is more confused than one thought: the slightest movement sets off unexpected tremors through the rest of the pile – and one's turn is over. Christians' imaginations of Jesus and their living responses to him are not two neatly separable realities, linked in simple causal ways. They are, rather, messily mixed together in a pile that may have settled for now into a reasonably stable pattern, but which has all sorts of unexpected interconnections that will only show themselves when one part of the pile is disturbed.

The rough coherence between image and life that there might be – all the spillikins for now settled into a stable arrangement – will have come about under all sorts of influences, over a lifetime. It may well, for instance, have had a good deal to do with participation in communities that have themselves established patterns of coherence between vision and life over long periods of time. However, one of the main ways in which Christians have played spillikins with their lives and imaginations, deliberately disturbing the pile with the hope of tumbling it into better order, is by reading the Bible.

Key points

- A believer's imagination of Jesus is likely to be messily and inextricably linked in with the life of discipleship he or she lives.
- Christian communities can over long periods of time establish patterns in which imagination and life are held together with relative stability and coherence.
- One of the practices that can challenge and disturb such a settlement is the reading of the Bible.

A biblical kaleidoscope

What effect does the Bible have upon Christian lives and imaginations? One might think, after all, that the way past all the messy confusion I have just been describing is to turn to its pages. Don't Christians find there a true image of Jesus, and a true guide to how to live in response to him? Won't a belief in the authority of Scripture allow the unruly spillikins of Christian life and imagination to be properly disciplined?

One difficulty with this idea is that the biblical portrayal of Jesus of Nazareth is itself already diverse, complicated and difficult to synthesize. There are four Gospels, each of which tells the story of Jesus in its own way, and much of each is made up of collections of short narratives and snatches of teaching that don't readily form simple unities. And then there are numerous other New Testament writings, which witness to Christ in varying degrees and in widely differing ways, which may not contain very much by way of extra narratives of Jesus' life but which certainly affect how Jesus' identity and significance are understood. The Bible itself provides something more like a cubist portrait of Jesus than a photograph.[9]

Of course, there are some forms of unity that Christian readers have fairly consistently found in the text, and which do shape much Christian imagination of Christ. Whatever strange and wonderful esoteric or allegorical forms of interpretation they have gone for, Christians have on the whole agreed that these texts tell the story of a man preaching and healing, going to Jerusalem, being captured, being tortured and crucified, and rising again from the dead – even if some Christians have not regarded every element of that story as straightforwardly factually true.[10] In most of the endlessly varied ways in which Christians have worked with the Gospels, the recognition that they tell versions of this core story has been something like a bedrock, even if very different structures have been built upon it. One could say that the vast majority of Christian imaginings of Jesus will have these bare bones of the narrative somewhere within them.

The moment one goes beyond this basic framework of a narrative, however, and asks what people have learnt of Jesus from the Bible that is rich enough to live by, readings begin to diverge. Even if one simply tries to put a bit of flesh on the bones, and fit in more of the detail that the Gospels have to present concerning the course of this man's life, things start to get difficult. It *is* possible to create syntheses that tie the different Gospels into one coherent, graspable story, that might then bid to become *the* image of Jesus burnt onto the reader's retina, but such harmonization has proved to require significant ingenuity, and each person who has done it has produced a synthesis that looks different (in at least some respects) from all the others.[11] And if one goes further and begins to ask how it is that the Jesus whose identity is portrayed here is not simply an interesting character from a bygone era, but is an address from God, a divine call to new life – well, Christian claims and counter-claims become very diverse indeed. What kind of life does the Bible suggest is an appropriate response to Jesus? How should the Bible be used to help form such lives? Christians, even those who share a very high view of the Bible's capacity to give clear and direct answers to these questions, have differed significantly on these matters.

This variety of opinion on what response to Jesus looks like, and how it should be inculcated, can be seen already within the New Testament itself, particularly in the various letters by Paul and other writers placed after the Gospels and Acts. Those letters are all, more or less directly, attempts to explore and spell out the implications of Jesus' life for Christian lives, and the range of ideas and metaphors and models, advice and commands and suggestion that they offer is beyond any simple coherence.[12] Here, too, it is possible to come up with some harmonization of all these ideas, metaphors and models, but it requires a good deal of ingenuity, and different interpreters have done it in very different ways over the years.

In other words, as well as being faced with the strangely diffuse and fractured nature of any person or community's mental image of Jesus, and with the messy and complicated ways in which that image is bound up with the lives Christians live as a response to Jesus, Christians are faced with a bewilderingly complex biblical portrayal of him, and with complex and various biblical accounts of the difference that Jesus should make to human lives. Anyone who claims that there is a simple, graspable answer here, and that the diversity and messiness of Christian imagination of, and response to, Jesus, needs only to turn to the Bible to be made truthful and coherent, has quite a bit of work to do to make that claim convincing.[13]

Differing visions

'The vision of Christ that thou dost see
Is *my* vision's greatest enemy;
Thine has a great hook nose like thine,
Mine has a snub nose like to mine;
Thine is the friend of all mankind,
Mine speaks in parables to the blind;
Thine loves the same world that mine hates;
Thy heaven doors are my hell gates. ...
Both read the Bible day and night –
But thou read'st black where I read white.'

William Blake, 'The Everlasting Gospel' (c.1818)[14]

Perhaps even more important than the variety and complexity of the biblical portraits of Jesus is the fact that reading is not a process in which those portraits are simply downloaded into the reader's brain. The relationship between the Bible and Christian imagination and life is two-way. The lives and imaginations of Christian communities and individuals will be shaped in some ways by their readings of the Bible, but their readings of the Bible will also, however hard they try to be faithful to it, be shaped in some ways by their lives and imaginations. After all, nobody who reads the Bible is an empty and spacious room, simply ready to be filled with ideas and ways of living carried in from the Bible. People always already have plenty of mental furniture (some expectations, some pre-judgements, some prior entanglements with some of the subject matter) cluttering their minds. As they read the Bible, they will be trying to find space in this cluttered room for what they read – and it will only be by some more-or-less awkward process of rearrangement and clearing out that a workable arrangement will be found. They will throw away some of their existing furniture, but keep hold of much of it, even if some of it has to be put in new places or pushed into the background. They will find good, prominent spaces for what they take to be the most important or attractive items they have found in the Bible, but they will cram in a lot of other stuff from the Bible any old how, squeezing it into odd corners, perhaps rather squashed and hidden away; and there will be plenty more for which they simply don't find room. Everyone's arrangement will look different, depending on the furniture they started with. If I may push this metaphor one step further, we might also say that people are in any case living in rooms of very different shapes and sizes. That is, people live in very different contexts, facing very different demands; the space in which one person arranges her mental furniture may be very, very different from the space in which another person arranges his. To put it another way, reading the Bible is not simply the preserve of those who read out of curiosity, interested in the abstract in seeing how their ideas might be rearranged and supplemented by it. The Bible is not simply read by people arranging the furniture in spacious rooms in detached houses far from the bustle of the city. It is done by people embroiled in relationships and institutions and projects and crises and movements and histories: in rooms squeezed in between other rooms in crowded apartment blocks, having to find ways of living in those rooms that will still allow them to get on with their neighbours and keep some kind of workable life in the midst of others' din and bustle. What people take from the Bible, the meaning that they find there, will be subtly or dramatically, explicitly or implicitly affected by all of this.

Even a very biblically minded believer, who may well end up with a very biblically informed image of Christ that has a fair amount of coherence to it, will certainly also find that her image is not simply and straightforwardly *the* undisputed biblical image of Jesus, still less that her understanding of what call this Jesus makes upon her life is *the* undisputed understanding. On the one hand, her working image of Christ will be mixed from biblical and non-biblical sources, shaped by hymns and sermons and picture-books and films and conversations and dreams and meditations that subtly or blatantly, consciously or unconsciously go beyond or even against what is written. And on the other hand, even to the extent that this image *is* biblical, not every element of the biblical portrayal of Jesus will be equally well caught by this believer's imagination: there will be elements of the biblical witness that are emphasized, elements that are downplayed, elements that are ignored or forgotten, and elements that don't really seem to fit, and which continue to act as irritants, calling into question the image that the believer has constructed.

Jesus and alcohol

As one fairly small example, consider the way in which many devoutly Bible-believing Christians are adamant that Jesus never touched a drop of alcohol – and that Christians should forswear it too. They regard the accusation recorded in Luke 7.34 that Jesus was a 'winebibber' to be an entirely groundless slur (rather than an exaggeration) and argue that the 'wine' that he is said to drink in Luke 7.33, or into which he turned the water at Cana, or that was consumed at the Last Supper, must have been *unfermented* grape juice – often getting embroiled in long philological arguments at this point. If you try typing 'Jesus alcohol' into an internet search engine, you will soon find impassioned arguments on both sides of the question.[15] It does not take much examination of the arguments employed to see that a given commentator's position is seldom defined purely by their unbiased reading of the Gospel texts in question: they read the texts in the light of a whole maze of ideas and feelings that subtly or dramatically, consciously or unconsciously shape what meanings they find there.

Exercise

If you have internet access, spend some time hunting out arguments used on both sides. How would you characterize the debate? Is it one that truly focuses on differences about particular matters of fact (the etymology of certain words, the parsing of certain passages), or are those matters proxies for broader, deeper concerns?

Key points

- The Bible contains a variety of differing portraits of Jesus, which cannot be harmonized without effort.
- There is basic agreement among most Christian readers on the bare bones of the story that the Gospels tell about Jesus (though not on the factuality of that story).
- There is wide disagreement on the detail and implications of the Bible's portrayal of Jesus.
- A person's understanding of Jesus will be shaped by his or her reading of the Bible, but not simply dictated by that reading.

Biblical settlements

Despite all this diversity and complexity, Christian individuals and communities do tend in the end to come up with answers. That is, they come up with claims about the meaning of the Bible that seem to them to do justice to all of its diverse materials and that help them make sense of their own lives.

One very resilient example of such a conviction is that held by many evangelical groups, whose reading of the Bible (or at least the New Testament) revolves around a simple narrative that they believe to be the clear message of the New Testament. Human beings were made for eternal glory with God, but all have sinned and fallen short of this glory; the penalty and power of sin is such that no one is capable of saving himself; nevertheless, Christ has died to pay the penalty for this sin, and all you have to do to be saved is acknowledge that you are a sinner and incapable of saving yourself, accept Jesus into your heart as your personal saviour, and confess openly that he is Lord. For the sake of convenience, I'll refer to this as the 'personal saviour settlement'.

Of course, you will not find this precise narrative set out plainly and in full in any one place in the Bible, even though some parts of the book of Romans get close; neither will you find the phrase 'personal saviour'. The proponents of the personal saviour settlement claim, however, that it is a way – or, rather, *the* way – of summarizing the central teachings of the New Testament. This narrative has become, for many evangelical Christians, the lens through which the whole New Testament is read, such that most if not all of the rest of the New Testament is taken to be reinforcing or amplifying aspects of this narrative, or spelling out its implications – even in those books in which this narrative itself does not make any very obvious appearance.

Although in certain circumstances proponents of this narrative will quote individual verses or short passages in order to justify their claim that it is the core meaning of the New Testament, the real support for that claim is more difficult to grasp quickly. Much of the justification for the claim that this narrative does justice to the New Testament lies in its *capaciousness* and its *resilience*. That is, the justification lies on the one hand in the *capacity* of interpretation that takes this narrative as its guide to make good enough sense of very large amounts of the New Testament, and its ability to make sense of otherwise obscure and difficult passages. The justification lies on the other hand in the *resilience* with which interpreters committed to this narrative can respond to challenges from those who claim that particular verses or passages contradict it.

Those who make this kind of claim to have identified the core meaning of the Bible will tend to privilege certain parts of the Bible over others, having what is sometimes called 'a canon within the canon'. The proponents of the personal saviour settlement, for instance, tend to find their core ideas more easily in the Pauline epistles than in the Gospels. That does not mean, of course, that they ignore the Gospels, simply that some interpretative work is needed in order to see how the Gospels, too, proclaim this core narrative. Such interpretative work may involve emphasizing those passages that can more easily be seen to support this narrative, such as Jesus' forgiveness of sins in response to people's faith (for example, Mark 2.1–12); it may involve carefully explaining how other passages really do fit with the personal saviour narrative, even though at first blush they seem to contradict it (such as, the tying of entry into the kingdom to full obedience to the law in Matthew 5.17–20). The Gospels are interpreted so as to fit the personal saviour narrative, even though it might not be all that clear that someone who *only* had the Gospels would necessarily hit upon this narrative as a summary. Other books or passages which sit rather awkwardly with this narrative (the book of James, for instance, with its emphasis on works, or Colossians 1.24, in which Paul says, 'In my flesh I am completing what is lacking in Christ's afflictions for the sake of his body') are argued about and discussed until an interpretation is found that allows them to fit with the narrative.[16]

There is more going on here, however, than a simple claim as to the central meaning of a text. The interpretation offered by proponents of the personal saviour settlement coheres with various convictions about what the Bible is for, and how it should shape Christian life. They are likely to think, for instance, that the Bible's role is at least twofold: that it is there to convict the world of sin, and that it is there to give the good news of what Jesus has done, so that people may explicitly put their trust in it. So, for instance, someone committed to this settlement is liable to look at Matthew's Sermon on the Mount, and in particular at Jesus' claim there that unless your righteousness exceeds that of the scribes and Pharisees, you will never enter the kingdom of heaven (5.20) and that people should 'Be perfect, therefore, as your heavenly Father is perfect' (5.48), and think that the *primary* role of these passages is to convince us how far we have fallen short, how incapable we are of obeying, and how much we must therefore throw ourselves upon the mercy of Christ.[17]

These convictions about what the Bible is for will also shape the interpretation given in more subtle ways, however. They are likely to mean, for instance, that the ability of the Bible to present one accurately with the facts about Jesus and what he has done is highly valued, because knowledge of those facts is necessary if one is to place one's trust in him. And they are likely to mean that passages of the Bible that sound most like direct evangelistic address to non-believers or waverers (or the reminders of such address) are consciously or unconsciously given special weight in determining what the meaning of the whole is.

These convictions about meaning and function also live in complex symbiosis with many other aspects of the life of the Christian communities in which they are found. So, for instance, the personal saviour construal of the meaning of the New Testament coheres with certain kinds of evangelistic preaching, focused on inviting people to an explicit moment of commitment; it coheres with the idea that individual believers will normally be able to give their testimonies, describing how they became Christians (perhaps referring to the verses that convicted and convinced them); it coheres with calling individual members of the Church 'believers' in the first place – and so on. There is a whole weave of practices, of ways of living and talking, that make sense in the light of this way of reading the Bible, and that weave of practices in turn helps reinforce the sense that this is the true and proper way to read the Bible.

This is why I refer to this personal saviour interpretation as a 'settlement'. It is not just a claim to have identified the true meaning of the Bible. It is also a set of ideas about the Bible's nature and function that underpins those claims about its meaning. And those ideas in turn seem convincing in part because of their coherence with the weave of practices that make up the common life of those who hold it. The proponents of this settlement have reached a point where these three things mutually reinforce one another: their convictions as to the proper shape of Christian life, their understanding of what the Bible is for and how it should be read, and their claims about what the Bible actually says. Each confirms and supports the others.

Think of it this way. Imagine a tribe living in a clearing in the rainforest. They devote a good deal of their energy to coppicing the trees around the clearing's edge in a particular way. When tended in that way, the trees yield strong, straight, flexible timbers that the tribe are able to use in their lives. They use them to build their huts in the middle of the clearing, for instance, and as fishing rods and as weapons. They also use them, however, to provide the very tools that they need to do the coppicing on the trees around the edge of the clearing. They have reached a 'settlement': their ways of using the trees yield material that supports their whole way of life, and the production of that material justifies and enables their ways of using the trees. Just so, proponents of a biblical settlement like the personal saviour settlement have found ways of approaching and using the Bible that yields materials that support and enable their whole way of life, and that includes supporting and enabling their ways of approaching and using the Bible.

Key points

- Mainstream evangelical Christianity's 'personal saviour' is one example of a Biblical settlement.
- It is both drawn from the Bible and provides the lens through which the Bible is seen.
- It can be judged according to its capaciousness and resilience.
- It involves privileging a canon within the canon.
- It coheres with, and is supported by, appropriate practices.

The multiplicity of settlements

There is more than one robust biblical settlement in existence. The personal saviour settlement that I described in the last section is not the only possibility. There are other contenders, whose adherents claim that they are just as capacious, just as resilient, just as habitable as the personal saviour settlement.

Settlements can differ in multiple ways. They may have different focal meanings – so they may, for instance, not agree that 'accept Jesus as your personal saviour' is a good summary of the New Testament. They may even have no focal meaning at all: some settlements don't like the assumption that there is one central meaning to the diverse New Testament texts.

Settlements may involve different assumptions about how the Bible functions. So while the personal saviour settlement might involve regarding the Bible as convicting of sin and telling readers enough about Jesus that they can put their trust in him, in other settlements the Bible may be construed more as a connected narrative of salvation-history that tells the story of which one has now become a part, or as a manual of moral and spiritual teaching that one is to follow, or as a source of metaphors and symbols by which one may imagine God more truly, or as the historical record of the early years of the faith, or as something else again.

Settlements may also differ in the practices that surround and support, and are in turn supported by, the practices of biblical reading: where one settlement has evangelistic proclamation, the other may have meditative homilies; where one has the giving of personal testimonies of conversion, the other may have stories of the lives of saints; and so on. Settlements have differing weaves of practices roughly cohering with different emphases and tendencies in biblical reading – and those practices are both supported by the settlement's way reading of the Bible, and help make that way of reading the Bible seem natural and appropriate.

Settlements may also differ in the social organization of biblical reading. In some settlements, a minister's sermon will be the primary location in which the meaning of the Bible is expounded, in others it will be Bible-study notes and popular books, in others small-group Bible study, in others the teaching office of the Roman Catholic Church.

Of course, for someone firmly socialized into a particular settlement, the idea that there could be multiple working settlements might seem absurd. Within a settlement, the preferred interpretation of the Bible might seem so natural, so unforced, so attentive and honest that talk of an alternative settlement is likely to be seen simply as a fancy way of covering up the fact that some churches and Christian groups are just plain unbiblical.

One of the things that can help overcome this sense of the inevitability of any one settlement is a sense of history. All settlements evolve over time, getting shaken by changes in circumstances, challenged by new currents of theological thinking, fragmenting over controversial issues or simply breaking up because different groups have drifted off in their own directions. But this means that settlements have a *history*; it is possible to tell the history of the personal saviour settlement, for instance, and see that, far from being a clear ongoing consensus among honest Bible-believing Christians as to the obvious way of reading the Bible, that settlement has changed and evolved over time, and now exists in multiple differing forms. The version of the settlement to be found among eighteenth-century Prussian brethren looks different from the version to be found among nineteenth-century English Methodists, or among twentieth-century American Baptists, or among twenty-first century Nigerian Anglicans. Emphases change; the way the focal meaning of the New Testament is expressed changes; the passages that are regarded as central change; the explanation of problem passages change; the implications for Christian life change; the reading practices of those involved change; and all the surrounding and supporting ways of life of the communities involved change.[18]

Ecumenical reading

The best way to convince yourself of the existence of multiple settlements, each with its own internal plausibility, is to read widely. One could, for instance, read evangelical Protestant and Roman Catholic texts alongside one another, and try to see whether and how authors on both sides regard themselves as inhabiting settlements that are true to the Bible.

Key points

- There are multiple settlements that are capacious, resilient and habitable.
- Such settlements may be very different from one another.
- From within one's own settlement, it can be difficult to believe that other settlements have any integrity.
- Settlements evolve; they have a history.

Deciding between settlements

To acknowledge this diversity and evolution of biblical settlements does not mean opting for a simple relativism. That is, it does not mean that one can only say, 'Each group to its own interpretation; who are we to judge?' It does not mean that one has to abandon the idea of conversation, challenge, argument or agreement between people from different settlements. It does not mean one has to abandon the idea of *responsible* interpretation.

I explained above that a settlement can be judged, in part, by its capaciousness (its ability to make sense of as wide a range of biblical texts as possible) and by its resilience (its ability to respond to difficult questions and problem passages). We might add that a settlement can also be judged by its habitability – that is, by the extent to which it makes for a context in which human lives can be lived, and be sustained across the generations, and provide its inhabitants with resources to meet the challenges of a changing and crisis-ridden world.

In other words, any given settlement is open to genuine critique. Faced with a working settlement, one does not simply have to accept it wholesale or reject it outright. One can ask whether it really does justice to the full range of Scripture; one can press its available interpretations of crucial passages; one can ask whether, in the end, people are truly able to live under its branches. Real criticism, real argument is possible. And while it is extraordinarily unlikely that one critique is going to deflate an entire settlement, these kinds of challenges are one of the motors by which settlements evolve – and one of the pressures that lead some settlements over time to collapse.

So settlements are not take-it-or-leave-it supermarket options: they can be the subjects of real discussion, real debate. Nevertheless, it is seldom possible to find any simple, knock-down argument that tells you which settlement is the right one, which has got the best reading of the Bible. Arguments *between* settlements (rather than arguments that seek to test the limits of a settlement in its own terms) are notoriously unproductive, because so often what seems to be a crucial point or a key verse to one group will seem secondary or irrelevant to another, and because any settlement worth the name has over time developed a whole host of strategies for seeing off challenges and difficult questions, and because arguments that look simple on the surface are often plugged in underneath to large complexes of practices, tendencies and attitudes buried deep in the settlement's heart. Arguments between settlements – at least, any which look for a quick victory for one side or the other – very often sound like dialogues of the deaf.

Exercise

Using the suggestions for reading given at the end of Chapter 11, look at the debate about penal substitution. Defenders of penal substitution are, in fact, defending an entire biblical settlement: look at the arguments used against them, and their responses and defences. Do they have the character of debate between settlements that I have described above?

Key points

- Settlements can be critiqued as to their capaciousness, resilience and habitability.

- Such criticism is one of the motors by which settlements evolve or crumble.
- Nevertheless, any decent settlement will possess strategies for seeing off most kinds of criticism.
- Dialogue between settlements is notoriously difficult.

A Trinitarian settlement

Rather than spend time arguing against other settlements, therefore, I am going to devote it to exploring my own settlement in some detail – looking particularly at the way in which the meanings championed by this settlement affect the way its proponents think it appropriate to use the Bible, indeed their understanding of what the Bible *is*.

Most of that exploration has, of course, already been put before you. The whole of this book could be thought of as an outline sketch of a biblical settlement that differs from the personal saviour settlement. Instead of the personal saviour narrative described above, I have been arguing that a certain kind of Trinitarian picture – one whose core narrative has to do with a journey into the triune life of God – can provide an organizing framework for making good sense of the Bible, and I have been suggesting some of the ways of life that might cohere with, and help make sense of, this Trinitarian picture.

You may already have noticed that I have worked with biblical materials in a variety of ways. And some of you may well have found my biblical forays rather inconclusive or unconvincing. If, for instance, you come from a biblical settlement that tries to back up every theological claim with lists of verses in which the principle at stake is clearly stated and defended, my uses of the Bible may well have seemed eccentric and inadequate.

I am sure that there is some truth in that, and that some of the attempts I have made to expound biblical passages will have been failures. Nevertheless, another factor is also in play. I have taken myself to be introducing readers to a whole settlement, and one that may well be unfamiliar, rather than trying to convince people of particular points of controversy within an already-shared consensus. That is, I am trying to lure people in to a whole way of seeing the Bible's meaning (indeed, as we shall see, a whole way of seeing what the Bible is and what it is for), and that cannot be done simply by the citation of 'proof-texts'.

Proof-texting

The practice of citing individual verses or short passages in order to prove a theological point is sometimes called 'proof-texting'. It sometimes comes in for strident criticism, but there is no doubt that, between people who share a settlement, it can be a very powerful technique. To those who share ground-rules for reading Scripture, and who share assumptions about the big biblical picture within which individual verses sit, the citation of particular verses can be an important argumentative move. For instance, in the debate mentioned earlier, some argue that Jesus can't have drunk alcohol because Proverbs 31.4 says 'It is not for kings to drink wine, or for rulers to desire strong drink.'[19] For this to work as an argument, you must inhabit a settlement that sees Jesus as the fulfilment of Old Testament kingship, that believes that this can only be true if Jesus fulfilled all the righteous demands made of kings in the Old Testament, that regards a text like this from Proverbs as an unambiguous command, and so on. If all that is in place, the proof-text really does work – or at least leaves your opponent with a strong case to answer.

Such proof-texting seldom makes sense when speaking to those outside a settlement or who inhabit a different settlement, however, because they will not necessarily share enough of the surrounding interpretative framework for that verse taken out of context to mean the same to them. So people who inhabit a different kind of biblical settlement may well, when faced with Proverbs 31.4 in an argument about Jesus' attitude to alcohol, simply not see that it is particularly relevant – whether because they see the nature of Proverbs differently, or the nature of Jesus' relationship to the Old Testament, or the nature of moral instruction, or for other reasons.

Exercise

Next time you come across an apparent proof-text (that is, some passage which appears to cite a biblical verse as proof of a theological point) ask what assumptions are in play. What do you have to believe for that citation to *count* as an argument in favour of that point?

In Chapter 2, I made use of material from Exodus and 1 John. I chose passages that have been taken by many Christians (and, in the case of Exodus, many Jews) as keys to understanding the nature of God; these passages have become, as it were, common currency across several very different Christian and Jewish biblical settlements, historical and contemporary. I worked within that broad tradition of reading by taking these texts as guides to the nature of God – but tried to provide a reading of the text (highlighting various features, suggesting ways of 'making sense' of the passages as a whole) that would lead people towards the particular settlement I find most convincing. Of course, my reading of these individual texts could not provide a knock-down proof that my favoured settlement was superior or even simply plausible. Those kinds of conclusion could not rest on the reading of any one passage in Exodus or 1 John or anywhere else; they have to rest on the overall capaciousness, resilience and habitability of the settlement as a whole.

In Chapter 4, I tried to make at least an initial case for the broad plausibility of a Trinitarian construal of the New Testament. I talked about broad narrative patterns in the Gospels (both that which has Jesus and the Spirit pointing to the Father, and that which has the Father and the Spirit pointing to Jesus); I talked about particular narrative incidents in which those patterns receive a crystallized form (Jesus' baptism and transfiguration); I talked about discursive passages in which aspects of those patterns are directly described (particularly in John's Gospel); and I talked about what one could call the distinctive twofold and threefold grammar for talk about God that began to emerge in the early decades of the Christian Church. Just as in the previous chapter, none of this amounted to a direct and deductive proof of the doctrine. It was, rather, a way of saying, 'Do you see how these Trinitarian claims help us to take account of, and make coherent sense of, a wide range of biblical materials? Do you see how this might even be a framework for making sense of all relevant New Testament material?'

Exercise

Look at other uses of the Bible in this book, such as the discussion of multiple passages on the Spirit in Chapter 6, or the discussion of Adam and Eve in Chapter 11. What is plausible and what is implausible about those uses? What kind of assumptions have I been making about the nature of the biblical text? How has my reading of those texts fitted in to my sketching of the whole Trinitarian theological settlement?

In the next chapter, I want to explore this Trinitarian settlement a little further, but from a somewhat different perspective. Most of what I have said in the book so far could be thought of as an attempt to spell out the focal meaning, the core narrative, that this settlement proposes – a story about being drawn by the Spirit into conformity to Christ on the way to the Father. I want now to ask what role, in this settlement, the Bible actually plays. What, in the terms of this settlement, *is* the Bible? What is it *for*? How should it be read, and by whom?

Key points

- In the bulk of this book, I have been outlining the *content* of a Trinitarian biblical settlement.
- In the next chapter, I will examine how the nature of the Bible, and of Bible reading, is understood in that settlement.

Going further

1 The question of the historical factuality of the Bible is a fiercely contested one, and covers everything from debates about creation to debates about what Jesus really said and did. For an understanding of some of the issues involved, it is worth understanding the history of biblical hermeneutics a little better. I recommend Robert M. Grant and David Tracy, *A Short History of the Interpretation of the Bible*, 2nd edn (Minneapolis: Augsburg Fortress, 1984); Hans Frei, *The Eclipse of Biblical Narrative: A Study in Eighteenth and Nineteenth-Century Hermeneutics* (New Haven: Yale University Press,

1974); and Stephen Neill and N. T. Wright, *The Interpretation of the New Testament, 1861–1986*, 2nd edn (Oxford: Oxford University Press, 1988).
2 The formation of the biblical canon – the authorized lists of which books are and are not to be included in the Bible – took place over a long and complicated history. To explore this history – and its implications – further, see Bruce M. Metzger, *The Canon of the New Testament: Its Origin, Development and Significance* (Oxford: Oxford University Press, 1987); and John Barton, *The Spirit and the Letter: Studies in the Biblical Canon* (London: SPCK, 1997), published in the USA as *Holy Writings, Sacred Text: The Canon in Early Christianity* (Louisville, KY: WJKP, 1997).

Notes

1 For some extra-biblical stories and sayings of Jesus that might plausibly have an apostolic origin, and might even go back to Jesus himself, see David Ford and Mike Higton, *Jesus*, Oxford Readers series (Oxford: Oxford University Press, 2002), texts 21 and 22.

2 This is the first line of a hymn written by Anna Bartlett Warner for inclusion in a novel on which she collaborated with her sister Susan: *Say and Seal*, vol. 2 (Philadelphia: J. B. Lippincott, 1860), pp. 115–16, available online at Indiana University, http://www.letrs.indiana.edu/cgi/t/text/text-idx?idno=Wright2–2650v2;view=toc;c=wright 2. It was set to music, and given a chorus, by William Batchelder Bradbury in *Bradbury's Golden Shower of Sunday School Melodies: A New Collection of Hymns and Tunes for the Sabbath School* (New York: Ivison, Phinney and Co., 1862), no. 68, available online at the Shaping the Values of Youth Project, http://digital.lib.msu.edu/projects/ssb/display.cfm?TitleID=605&Format=jpg&PageNum=71.

3 I'm referring, of course, to Peter Jackson, *The Lord of the Rings: The Fellowship of the Ring* (New Line Cinema, 2001); see http://uk.imdb.com/title/tt0120737/. Frodo is 33 when Tolkien's book (London: Allen and Unwin, 1954) opens, but 50 by the time he leaves the Shire; Elijah Wood who played him in the film was 20.

4 For more on Rivera, see National Gallery of Art, *The Cubist Paintings of Diego Rivera: Memory, Politics, Place* (2004) online at the National Gallery of Art, http://www.nga.gov/exhibitions/2004/rivera/intro.shtm. For comparison, a photograph of Lipchitz, albeit one taken some three decades later, can be viewed at Encyclopaedia Britannica Online, http://www.britannica.com/eb/art–12632. One wonders whether Lipchitz liked the portrait. He later wrote 'My cubist friends were all making cubist portraits. I was always against that. I had long discussions about it, especially with my good friend [Juan] Gris. I felt, and still do, that it is not legitimate because a portrait is something absolutely different. It has to do with likeness, with psychology, and at the same time it must be a work of art.' In Bert van Bork, *Jacques Lipchitz, The Artist at Work* (New York: Crown, 1966), p. 115.

5 The collage that any individual carries around will be idiosyncratic, shaped by the particular course that his or her life has taken, but the majority of the elements from which it is made up will be part of the cultural currency of the churches and other contexts through which the believer has passed. See my 'Jesus in Modern English Popular Culture' in Leslie Houlden (ed.) *Jesus in History, Thought and Culture: An Encyclopaedia* (London: ABC Clio, 2003), pp. 240–4, reprinted as *Jesus: The Complete Guide* (London: Continuum, 2005). For histories of representation of Jesus, and collections of relevant

texts, see Jaroslav Pelikan, *Jesus through the Centuries: His Place in the History of Culture*, new edn (New Haven: Yale University Press, 1999) and David Ford and Mike Higton (eds), *Jesus*, Oxford Readers series (Oxford: Oxford University Press, 2002).

6 For some related reflections on this topic, see James Alison, *Knowing Jesus*, 2nd edn (London: SPCK, 1998).

7 See his profile on the Internet Movie Database: http://www.imdb.com/name/nm0000306/.

8 The poverty of Christ was much debated in the medieval Church. See Malcolm Lambert, *Franciscan Poverty: The Doctrine of the Absolute Poverty of Christ and the Apostles in the Franciscan Order, 1210–1323*, revised edn (St Bonaventure, NY: Franciscan Institute, 1998). The debate makes it into Umberto Eco's novel, *The Name of the Rose* (Orlando, FL: Harcourt Brace, 1994 [Original Italian edition, 1980]), p. 340.

9 For standard introductions to Christology in the New Testament, see Christopher M. Tucker, *Christology and the New Testament: Jesus and his Earliest Followers* (Louisville, KY: WJKP, 2001); James D. G. Dunn, *Christology in the Making: A New Testament Inquiry into the Origins of the Doctrine of the Incarnation*, 2nd edn (London: SCM Press, 1989); and Larry W. Hurtado, *Lord Jesus Christ: Devotion to Jesus in Earliest Christianity* (Grand Rapids, MI: Eerdmans, 2003).

10 Hans Frei referred to this consensus as 'ascriptive literalism'; see 'The "Literal Reading" of Biblical Narrative in the Christian Tradition: Does it Stretch or Will it Break?' in Frei, *Theology and Narrative*, ed. George Hunsinger and William C. Placher (New York: Oxford University Press, 1993), p. 122. It may seem an entirely trivial form of agreement, but there have been thinkers who have disagreed. For instance, John M. Allegro, in *The Sacred Mushroom and the Cross* (London: Hodder and Stoughton, 1970) argued that the Gospels are not really stories about a man called Jesus at all; they are coded descriptions of a cult based around hallucinogenic mushrooms, giving instructions for finding and consuming the drugs, and portrayals of the effects; the name 'Jesus', and the stories apparently about him, are ciphers. I'm not making this up.

11 See, for example, Stanley N. Gundry, *The NIV Harmony of the Gospels* (San Francisco: HarperSanFrancisco, 1988) – but there are many others; Amazon.com currently lists several dozen. Roger Forster and Paul Marston, authors with a strong commitment to the detailed historical accuracy of the Gospels, present a harmonization of the resurrection narratives in their *Reason, Science and Faith* (Crowborough: Monarch, 1999), ch. 6, available online at Ivy Cottage, http://www.ivycottage.org/group/group.aspx?id=6826. They demonstrate well the ingenuity involved in such harmonizations.

12 See Richard B. Hays, *The Moral Vision of the New Testament: A Contemporary Introduction to New Testament Ethics* (London: Continuum, 1997).

13 Some readers will think that I am, for my own polemical purposes, exaggerating this diversity and complexity of the biblical witness. Surely, they will say, the Scriptures are coherent enough and clear enough to teach a common message to all those who are truly willing to learn? Well, a famous experiment has been done to explore that claim. It is an experiment that has involved watching what kinds of agreements and disagreements arise when one tracks very large numbers of Christians who are committed to following the Bible as their supreme authority, and to mining the clear, coherent message that it offers. The experiment is called Protestantism, and it has been running for nearly 500 years – and it has turned out to lead to what is, by a very wide margin, the most fissile form of Christianity on the planet. By some counts, there are something like 8,000 Protestant denominations, most of which claim that *their* way is truly biblical, and that their distinction from the 7,999 other forms of Protestantism can be put down to their own more perfect understanding of Scripture.

14 William Blake's 'The Everlasting Gospel' is a collection of fragments published posthumously by Michael Rossetti in *Poetical Works of William Blake* (London: G. Bell,

1874); I have used the text from Nicholson and Lee (eds), *The Oxford Book of English Mystical Verse* (Oxford: Oxford University Press, 1917), no. 58, available online at Bartleby. com http://www.bartleby.com/236/58.html.

15 For a website arguing that Jesus did drink alcohol, see J. Barry O'Connell, Jr., 'Notes on Jesus and Alcohol' (no date), at Barry O'Connell's Notes on the Bible: http:// biblenotes.homestead.com/files/bn9928.htm. For a website arguing that he did not, see 'The Meaning of the Word Wine in the Bible', Marysville Church of Christ, 2003, http://www.msvlcofc.org/Devo/wine.htm.

16 Martin Luther went so far as to argue that the Epistle of James, because it harmonized so little with his 'justification by faith' settlement, should not be numbered among the full books of the Bible and should be relegated to a secondary status. See his 1522 Preface to James in *Luther's Works*, vol.35, ed. E.T. Buchanan (Philadelphia: Muhlenberg Press, 1960), pp. 395–8. Luther says of the epistle that it 'is flatly against St. Paul and all the rest of Scripture in ascribing justification to works'.

17 See, for example, George Zeller, 'The Sermon on the Mount: Is it for the Church Today?' (no date), Middletown Bible Church, http://www.middletownbiblechurch. org/dispen/sermon.htm. He says 'The purpose of the Sermon was not to reveal Church truth but to condemn the Jews and to show them that they were not fit to enter the kingdom' … 'Though the gospel is not revealed in this Sermon, the Lord did make it clear that the solution for those who lack the needed righteousness is found, not in SELF, but in HIS RIGHTEOUSNESS (Matt. 6.33). Thus we have the first beatitude (Matt. 5.3) showing the blessedness of the person who recognizes his own spiritual bankruptcy.'

18 For good general histories of Christian thinking, see Margaret A. Miles, *The Word Made Flesh: A History of Christian Thought* (Oxford: Blackwell, 2004), William Placher, *A History of Christian Theology* (Louisville, KY: WJKP, 1983) and Justo L. Gonzalez, *A History of Christian Thought*, 3 vols (Nashville: Abingdon, 1988).

19 See, as an example of this use of Proverbs 31.4, Ronnie Hoover, 'Drinking' (no date), at Chi Alpha Christian Fellowship, http://xaua.com/xaweb/resources/drinking policy.rtf.

16

Trinitarian Reading

This is the last chapter of the book – and the one in which I finally explain what I have been up to. That is, this chapter is the closest I get to explaining my theological method. In Chapter 15, I introduced the idea of 'biblical settlements', and began to talk about a 'Trinitarian settlement'. The focal meaning or core narrative of that settlement has been the subject matter of this whole book: the story that the world is being drawn by the Spirit into conformity to Christ on the way to the Father. In this chapter, I will suggest how the role and authority of the Bible can be understood in this settlement, and how it relates to tradition, to experience, and to reason as the source and foundation of theology.

I am going to

- suggest that the Bible should be read 'around Jesus', with its primary purpose being to enable the formation of Christlike life in the world;
- suggest that the Bible should be read 'in the Spirit', with its interpretation being the task of the whole body of Christ held together by the Spirit; and
- suggest that the Bible should be read 'on the way to the Father', with its interpretation being a driver of the journey into ever deeper participation in the Father's kingdom of love and justice.

Preparation

- What role do you think the Bible can and should play in enabling the following of Jesus of Nazareth? And what role do you think the Spirit plays – both in the original production of the Bible, and in its interpretation now? And what role should the Christian tradition play, either in guiding one's reading of Scripture, or in providing a source of insights or information alongside it? Take some time now to jot down your initial answers to these questions.
- If you type 'inspiration of scripture' into an internet search engine like Google, you will find a large number of sites that discuss the involvement of the Spirit in the production of the Bible (and sometimes discuss the involvement of the Spirit in its interpretation and use as well). Most of these sites seem to come from a conservative theological stable. It is worth glancing through a few of these now, and then comparing them with what I have to say about the Spirit later in the chapter.

Additional reading

The books that I suggested for Chapter 15 are still relevant, but you could add:

Stephen Fowl, *Engaging Scripture: A Model for Theological Interpretation*, Challenges in Contemporary Theology (Oxford: Blackwell, 1998). A well-rounded theology of Scripture, particularly good on what it means for the Bible to be read in a community.

Gustavo Gutierrez, *A Theology of Liberation: History, Politics, Salvation*, tr. Caridad Inda and John Eaglson, revised edn (London: SCM Press, 2001 [Spanish original, 1971]). A classic text in which the basis of liberation theology is set out.

Reading around Jesus: Witness

Jesus of Nazareth is, according to the doctrine of the incarnation, a word spoken by God to the world, calling the world into communion with God. And the same doctrine claims that the Jesus who is God's word is a fully human being, who lived his life in a particular time and place in history. How is that address, made at one time and place, to be an address to the whole world, unless there is some means by which it can be spread or passed on? The argument of Chapter 6 could be summarized in the claim that it is the Spirit who is the one who is responsible for the spreading or passing on of the divine address to the world in Jesus. It is the Spirit who allows others to hear God's address in Jesus Christ; it is the Spirit who impels response to this address. The Spirit is the one who witnesses to Christ, and the Spirit does so by forming lives that witness to Christ – whether we think of that as the Spirit splitting the white light of Christ into the rainbow of diverse faces in which that light is refracted, or as the Spirit forming a community of givers and receivers whose currency is Christ. The Spirit forms a Church that, as I argued in Chapter 14, is called into being *by* witness, called into being *to* witness, and lives by *being* witness.

In this chapter, I am going to ask what role the Bible, the Christian tradition and experience play in this work of the Spirit. And I will ask how *theology* is formed by engagement with the Bible, with the Christian tradition and with experience. Reflection on the Bible will be the central thread running through the chapter, but I will argue that attention to tradition and to experience, far from being competing sources that need to be balanced with this biblical focus, are essential to making that biblical focus possible.

The simplest way of understanding why the Bible is important in the picture I have just sketched is to focus on one element of that picture. I said that, according to the doctrine of the incarnation, the divine address to the world that is Jesus of Nazareth is an address spoken in a specific time and place in history. If Christians were primarily followers of a philosophy, it would not particularly matter *when* the message that they followed was first spoken. Later restatements of that message might well be clearer, better argued and more accurate. In Christianity, however, the message that constitutes the religion is not a free-floating philosophy but a life lived in history, and so Christians are bound to have a stake in *historical* witness to that life: testimony to the events of Christ's life and to the impact that they had upon those around him. Christianity lives by constant return to this historical witness, because it lives by constant return to the history of Jesus.[1]

Exercise

What kind and quantity of knowledge of the historical Jesus of Nazareth, if any, is *essential* to Christian faith?

As this chapter goes on, it will become apparent that there are several factors that complicate this picture. Where does the Old Testament fit in, for instance? What difference does it make when Christians claim that Jesus is alive, and so not straightforwardly confined to one time and place? Does appeal to the Spirit's role as witness mean that Christians need not rely on the ordinary processes of historical witness in order to know Jesus?

Nevertheless, the central theological claim about the Bible is that it can (in some way, and in the right circumstances) convey the divine address originally spoken in and as Jesus' life to readers who live in times and places far removed from the original utterance; it can (in some way, and in the right circumstances) call believers to, and guide them into, ever fuller participation in the Christlike love and justice that are the life of God. I will be suggesting that the Bible can best be seen as a constant companion and guide for those who are on a journey into knowledge of God.

Key points

- The phrase 'Word of God' refers primarily to Jesus.
- The Church is called into being by witness to Jesus, and it is called into being to witness.
- Christians have traditionally claimed that the Bible can convey to them the divine address originally spoken in Jesus.
- Christians have traditionally claimed that the Bible can guide them into ever fuller participation in Christlike love and justice.

Reading around Jesus: Imagination and life

[14]Continue in what you have learned and firmly believed, knowing from whom you learned it, [15]and how from childhood you have known the sacred writings that are able to instruct you for salvation through faith in Christ Jesus. [16]All scripture is inspired by God and is useful for teaching, for reproof, for correction, and for training in righteousness, [17]so that everyone who belongs to God may be proficient, equipped for every good work.

2 Timothy 3.14–17

Exercise

Read this passage carefully. Pause before reading my comments, and ask what the passage actually claims about the nature and purpose of 'all scripture'.

There are two sides of my claim about the Bible that need to be held together, and this passage can be read as touching on both of them. In the first place, in 2 Timothy 3, 'scripture' is described as useful for 'training in righteousness'. The Bible has been seen in Christian theology as a school for godly life, helping direct the feet of any who desire to walk in the way of love and justice, and indeed awakening and strengthening that desire in the first place. The claim that these 'sacred writings' are 'inspired by God' in 2 Timothy 3 seems to mean no more and no less than this: that these writings are, by the grace of God, in the fullest sense *edifying* for godly life.

In the Trinitarian settlement, however, it would be a serious theological distortion to take the Bible as some kind of moral handbook, or guide to holy living, in a way that is detached from its role as witness to Jesus of Nazareth. As we have seen, Christian theology declares that the Word spoken by God in Jesus Christ is not a message that can be understood without reference to the messenger; he, the human being from Nazareth, *is* the message, and so 2 Timothy speaks not just of training in righteousness, but of 'salvation *through faith in Christ Jesus*'.

In the second place, therefore, the Bible is a witness to Jesus of Nazareth. If the Bible is to convey adequately to its readers the divine address, it can only do so if it is an adequate witness to this particular man. And 'adequate' in this case will mean 'able to convey the way in which this particular man was a word from God'.[2]

In the Trinitarian settlement, however, it would be another serious theological distortion to take the Bible to be an adequate witness to Jesus Christ in a way that is detached from its role as inspired training in godly life. So, although Christian theology also has a considerable stake in the ability of the Bible to teach us about the particular historical individual Jesus of Nazareth, it should be no surprise that we run into problems if we try to think of it simply as a means to an exact and comprehensive factual reconstruction of what Jesus did and said. Its purpose, according to the Trinitarian settlement, is neither to satisfy curiosity, nor to provide accurate reportage of the life of Christ – it is to witness to the way in which Jesus is God's compelling, captivating, life-transforming address. Its purpose, according to this settlement, is to enable the believer to be caught up in the movement of God's life that took place in history in Jesus of Nazareth, and which began catching up those around him who became his witnesses.[3]

Probably the most controversial aspect of what I have just said is that line about 'an exact and comprehensive factual reconstruction of what Jesus did and said'. Some readers will probably be thinking that I have just opened a doorway to the downplaying or dismissing of the Bible's historical accuracy. These are very controversial waters, as this is a topic that has been, and will no doubt continue to be, very hotly debated. My point is, however, that Christian theology does not need to have much of a stake one way or the other in claiming that the Bible provides 'an exact and comprehensive factual reconstruction of what Jesus did and said'. Its claim, after all, is somewhat different: it claims that these writings are, by the grace of God, edifying for Christian life, and that they are so by being adequate witnesses to the man Jesus of Nazareth, able to convey the way in which this man was a word from

God. The New Testament authors were not reporters or historians, trying to set down a neutrally accurate account of Jesus' doings; they were those who believed they had been addressed by God in and through Jesus' life, death and resurrection, and they were witnessing to that address so that others could also hear it and be bowled over by it.

Witness not replacement

My words could also be taken in a milder sense, simply as claiming that the biblical text is not and cannot be *identical* to the human being Jesus of Nazareth, whatever one might think of its historical accuracy. The Bible is, after all, a text, and so cannot provide more than a pen-portrait of a human being. John 21.24–25 acknowledges this:

> This [i.e. the disciple who reclined next to Jesus at the supper] is the disciple who is testifying to these things and has written them, and we know that his testimony is true. But there are also many other things that Jesus did; if every one of them were written down, I suppose that the world itself could not contain the books that would be written.

A book, even one with such a multifaceted, diverse and complex portrait of Jesus as the Bible, is not and cannot be a substitute for the person himself. It is a witness to Jesus, not a replacement for him.

Of course that witness crucially involves narratives and anecdotes about Jesus, and theology will clearly have some kind of stake in the broad accuracy of those stories; but the witness that the Bible offers is far more than a set of accurate narratives: all sorts of other forms of writing are used to convey the impact that Jesus had upon his followers, and to help catch them up into the movement into new life that he initiated among those followers. The New Testament records, as it were, the captivating music that is made when human lives are taken hold of by God's hand in Jesus Christ, and lifted up to new life.

We should also note that the New Testament authors wrote under the conviction that Jesus was still alive and, by the Spirit, still present and active in their midst. They were not writing memorials to one long gone, they were engaged in an ongoing relationship with one still living, and their witness was therefore intended to introduce people into that living relationship, rather than simply to provide information about past events. The Bible is written from within that ongoing relationship, as an invitation or guide to it.

A secondary matter

All this, of course, leaves plenty of room to debate exactly what level of factual accuracy can be attributed to the Gospel accounts. What I have just been saying does not force the issue one way or the other – it would be compatible with a maximalist account that claimed a very high level of historical accuracy, and it would be compatible with a more minimalist account that claimed that the bones of a 'historical' account had been fleshed out with all sorts of other materials that a modern mind would not think of as straightforwardly historical. The debate between those positions, and all shades of opinion in between, is one that will run and run. The only point I wish to insist upon is that this debate is, theologically speaking, a secondary matter. That is, it is an argument about the precise nature of the underpinnings of what is theologically primary, rather than itself being a debate about what is primary. The primary thing, from a Christian theological perspective, is the ability of the New Testament writings to convey to people the address of God in Jesus of Nazareth, who is not dead but alive.

Exercise

Whether or not you agree with me, spend some time thinking about how you would construct an argument against my position. First, spend some time thinking about how you could argue for a maximalist account, arguing for a very high level of factual accuracy in the New Testament accounts, on grounds that you think ought to convince me. How, on the basis of what I have written, do you think I might respond? Second, spend some time thinking about how you could argue for an even more minimalist account, one that did not require that the New Testament texts be taken as referring to real events at all. Once again, try to argue on grounds that mesh with the theology I have been expounding, and try to work out how I might respond.

Key points

- Christian theology claims that the Scriptures are, by the grace of God, edifying for godly life.
- Christian theology claims that the Scriptures are able to convey the way in which Jesus is God's compelling, captivating, life-transforming address.
- The biblical witness was intended to introduce people into a living relationship with Jesus, rather than simply to provide information about past events.

Jesus in the Hebrew Scriptures?

I have been talking primarily about the New Testament so far, but the New Testament writings are relative latecomers on the scene. For the vast majority of the time in which the New Testament writings were being produced, the only Scriptures that Christians had were those Hebrew Scriptures that we now call the Old Testament. It is, for instance, primarily Hebrew Scriptures that are being discussed in 2 Timothy 3.[4]

Marcion

The acknowledgement of the importance of the Hebrew Scriptures has not always been made in Christian theology. Most famously, it was denied by a second-century theologian who established a popular and resilient Christian network as an alternative to the more established networks with which he had come into conflict: Marcion. He seems to have regarded the God of the Hebrew Bible as a malevolent and arbitrary tyrant, and contrasted him with the God revealed as the Father of Jesus Christ, who he regarded as entirely unknown before Christ's coming. This Marcionite rejection of the Hebrew Scriptures was itself rejected by more mainstream Christians, and mainstream Christianity eventually ended up with Hebrew Scriptures firmly part of its canon. Nevertheless, 'Marcionite' rejections of the Hebrew Bible have cropped up again and again in Christian history.[5]

Exercise

It is sometimes claimed that most modern churches are functionally Marcionite – in other words, that the Old Testament barely features in their lives. Is this true in blatant or subtle ways in churches that you know of?

Most importantly for theological purposes, the Hebrew Scriptures were *Jesus'* Scriptures. I have already said, in Chapter 5, that Jesus' identity was

> a thoroughly and ineradicably Jewish identity, formed by Jewish practices, Jewish Scriptures, Jewish ideas, Jewish people. ... [T]o deny that it is constitutive of his identity is to deny his full humanity: Judaism provided the womb from which the baby Jesus emerged, the swaddling bands that surrounded him from the moment that he appeared, and the nurture that allowed him to grow towards maturity.

The Hebrew Scriptures were central to that Jewish context. Jesus drew upon those Scriptures in order to make sense of himself and his ministry, and they provide the essential backdrop against which his life, death and resurrection make sense. In fact, one can properly think of Jesus Christ as himself a living commentary upon the Hebrew Bible: he lives in response to it, and his life gives Christians new ways of reading it.

In fact, the New Testament as a whole, precisely because it can and should be read by Christians as witness to this Jesus, can and should be read by them as a commentary upon the Hebrew Scriptures. It is a commentary written with a conviction that the story told in the Hebrew Bible continued in a startlingly unexpected way – but it is told with the conviction that this startling continuation enables a new kind of sense to be made of the story so far. It is a commentary that has led to the 'Hebrew Scriptures' being renamed 'Old Testament', indicative of the fact that these are now seen as the early episodes of a story that has continued in this new way. But 'Old' does not mean 'dispensable', nor does it mean 'secondary': Christian theology cannot survive without the Hebrew Scriptures that are its bedrock, even if it is committed to reading them only in the light of the divine commentary that it believes has been spoken in Christ.

Paul's reading

In a recent book, Francis Watson has made this argument very strongly about the writings of Paul. He argues *against* those who think that

> Paul's disagreement with Judaism derives from a christological conviction that is self-grounded and self-sufficient, and that the pervasive appeal to scripture is merely a secondary consequence of that primary conviction. In this account, the relationship between christology and scripture is a unilateral one: christology determines how scripture is read, but christology itself is not itself determined by the reading of scripture. In the last resort, that would mean that scripture is dispensable to Paul.

Instead, he argues

> Scripture is not a secondary confirmation of a Christ-event entire and complete in itself; for scripture is not external to the Christ-event but is constitutive of it, the matrix within which it takes shape and comes to be what it is. Paul proclaims not a pure, unmediated experience of Christ, but rather a Christ whose death and resurrection occur 'according to the scriptures' (1 Corinthians 15.3–4). Without scripture, there is no gospel; apart from the scriptural matrix, there is no Christ. The Christ who sheds light on scripture is also and above all the Christ on whom scripture simultaneously sheds its own light. ...
>   [S]cripture is not overwhelmed by the light of an autonomous Christ-event needing no scriptural mediation. It is scripture that shapes the contours of the Christ-event, and to discern how it does so is to uncover the true meaning of scripture itself.
>
> Francis Watson, *Paul and the Hermeneutics of Faith*[6]

The Hebrew Scriptures are, however, texts that have another major body of religious readers, who do not read with the same New Testament commentary that Christians use. If they have any commitment to taking these texts of the Hebrew Bible seriously, and any commitment to being challenged by them, Christian readers can and should be challenged by reading in dialogue with Jews who, simply because they read the same texts differently, can help Christians see where they have relied more upon their assumptions about what the texts *should* say than on what they do *in fact* say. Reading alongside Jewish readers can help Christian readers become more attentive to the difficulty and strangeness of the texts, and to see ways in which they have misread them or read them inadequately – just as there may be ways in which the dialogue with Christians can recall Jewish readers to see their Scriptures differently, and notice things about them that they have underplayed. Of course, there is not likely to be any easy resolution to such a debate – Jews and Christians do read these texts differently, and the differences are far from trivial – but that does not mean that commitment to such dialogue, even if it simply means getting hold of some Jewish commentaries, cannot become a challenging and enlivening part of Christian practice.

Key points

- The Hebrew Scriptures provide the essential backdrop against which Jesus' life, death and resurrection make sense.
- Jesus can be thought of as a living commentary on the Hebrew Bible.
- The New Testament as a whole can be thought of as a commentary upon the Hebrew Bible.
- Christian readings of the Hebrew Bible can be challenged and deepened by Jewish readings.

Reading around Jesus: Unity and diversity

What I have said so far points us toward a way of thinking about the diversity of the biblical text. Think, for instance, of the strange fact that the New Testament preserves four Gospels. The reader concerned to rush to a harmonious or unified reading will need to explain away the differences, the particularities, of each Gospel – or at least reduce them to minor and clearly harmonious variations. The reader who resists too-easy harmony, on the other hand, will spend time with each Gospel, registering the differences between the portraits that each paints: the differences of style, of emphasis, of purpose, of interpretation. Rather than producing a harmony in which all differences are quickly resolved, the reader will know that these differing texts need to be read in constant counterpoint with one another, and that rather than finding *the* answer to the riddle posed by these differences, the reader is called to live a life in which these distinct voices become constant companions. The unity does not need to be provided by reconstruction of the one factual story to which the differing Gospels are witnesses: it is provided by the unity of a life that is being moulded into conformity to Christ by the buffeting of these differing texts.

Accompanying voices

I have been very aware, as I have written this book, that I have internalized a set of different critical voices. That is, as I write I have found myself asking, 'What would x have thought of this bit?' – and thinking I could guess what they would say. It is almost as if I hear their different voices, making their very different criticisms, and redirect my writing so as to head these criticisms off at the pass. Those very disparate voices are not in harmony with one another, but they have become constant companions to my writing. What I am suggesting about the role of the Bible's multiple voices is not entirely dissimilar.

Christians do not need to be embarrassed, therefore, that the Bible was not produced by a single author setting down in one go a coherent vision, but by individuals and communities stretched over time, struggling to come to terms with the reality that they had encountered – and struggling to come to terms with one another. The Bible was not, after all, dropped fully formed from heaven. It was written by human beings – precarious, finite, weak and mortal people – who witness to God's address precisely as they are caught up and shaped by it, and drawn by it into the life of God. To believe in the inspiration of the Bible is not, in this settlement, to believe that the humanity of the Bible's authors (or of the communities that collected, reworked and preserved these texts) was somehow overcome or rendered irrelevant. It is, rather, to believe that these human beings, as human beings, were truly being caught by the one Spirit into conformity to the one Christ, on the way to the one Father, and that the Bible was written from within the journey to that one goal that the various authors took in their very different contexts.

How far can this diversity stretch? If Christians believe that Jesus of Nazareth is the one wholly given over to the life of God, then he can and should be the criterion for Christians' judgements concerning all other claims about where godly life is to be found – and that includes being the criterion for claims about the godliness of the life portrayed and expressed in the Bible. Jesus is the touchstone for the movement in which biblical readers *and* biblical authors are caught up. A Christian reading of Scripture – a reading that looks to the Bible as revelation inspired by the Spirit of Christ – will therefore be a reading in which Christian readers bring all the meaning that they think they are finding to Jesus, to be judged and sifted by him. After all, it is Jesus who is God's Word; it is Jesus who is God's life lived fully in the world. All other voices – including the voices of his followers and witnesses – lisp and stutter as they try to repeat that Word.

And that means that the Trinitarian settlement can cope with (though it need not insist upon) the claim that there might be portions of Scripture in which the witness given to this movement towards God is, shall we say, oblique. Take Psalm 137, for instance, in which one of the exiles in Babylon calls down curses upon his captors: 'Happy shall they be who take your little ones and dash them against the rock.' Christian readers cannot simply cut this verse out of the Bible, but that does not necessarily mean that they have to find some sense in which this sentiment is *acceptable*. If Christians allow their reading of this verse to be questioned and judged at the foot of the cross, they will have to refuse the violent fantasy that it offers to them. They still need to take this verse seriously, however, and that might mean taking seriously what it reveals about the cycle of violence and counter-violence in which those being drawn by the Spirit deeper into God are nevertheless still caught, and about the dangerous liaisons into which faith can enter with that violence. In other words, Christian readers may find that, read in the stark light of Christ, this text offers an uncomfortable insight into their own violence, and that it too can become a part of God's address to them, even while they deny that it is a direct description of God's will. We might say that such a text becomes Scripture precisely as it is allowed to give this witness in Jesus' light.[7]

Key points

- The Bible was written by many different authors, from very different perspectives.
- Christians claim that the authors were being drawn by the Spirit into the life of God, and wrote as witnesses to that movement.
- Jesus is, for Christians, the criterion by which they judge what belongs to the life of God, and so is the criterion for Scripture.
- Judged by that criterion, the witness to God's life that some texts give might be oblique.

Reading around Jesus: An example

[1]Blessed is the man
   who has not walked in the council of the ungodly,
nor followed the way of sinners,
   nor taken his seat among the scornful.
[2]But his delight is in the law of the Lord,
   and on that law will he ponder day and night.
[3]He is like a tree planted beside streams of water,
   that yields its fruit in due season.
Its leaves also shall not wither
   and look, whatever he does, it shall prosper.
[4]As for the ungodly, it is not so with them:
   they are like the chaff which the wind scatters.
[5]Therefore the ungodly shall not stand up at the judgement,
   nor sinners in the congregation of the righteous.
[6]For the Lord cares for the way of the righteous,
   but the way of the ungodly shall perish.

Psalm 1 (ASB Liturgical Psalter)[8]

Exercise

Ask yourself: What would it mean for a Christian to claim that this Psalm was 'about Jesus'? Would that claim be plausible? What objections might be raised to it?

Working within this Trinitarian biblical settlement, a Christian reader is bound to ask how Psalm 1 relates to Jesus. In what way might Jesus of Nazareth be seen as a commentary upon this Jewish expression of delight in God's life-giving law?

The Psalm sets out a contrast between the ungodly and the godly. The ungodly are those who, superficially, seem to have a stable and attractive life: a person might be tempted to walk with them, stand with them, sit with them;

they have a way of thinking (the counsel of the ungodly) and of acting (the way of sinners), and a position from which to inspect the rest of the world (the seat of the scornful). Despite this apparent stability, however, they are ultimately insubstantial: they blow away like chaff, their path leads nowhere, and they have nowhere to stand when faced with God's judgement. Their lives are founded on nothing and lead to nothing.

The righteous, on the other hand, may at first sight seem insecure: they are defined negatively as those who do not take part in the stability of the wicked. Yet they know where true stability lies: they hold fast to God's word, the law, and meditate upon it, allowing themselves to be shaped by it. They have *true* stability, like well-rooted trees; their way does not lead to nothing, but to prosperity. God cares for their way, and they will stand firm in the face of his judgement.

When placed in the wider canon of the Hebrew Bible, the Psalm could itself be seen as a commentary upon the kind of theology expressed in Deuteronomy 11.26–28:

> See, I am setting before you today a blessing and a curse: the blessing, if you obey the commandments of the Lord your God that I am commanding you today; and the curse, if you do not obey the commandments of the Lord your God, but turn from the way that I am commanding you today, to follow other gods that you have not known.

Like Deuteronomy, the Psalm sets out two ways to live, the way of blessing and the way of the curse, and as in Deuteronomy it is the delectable law of God that marks the boundary between them.

The wider canon of the Hebrew Bible raises an important question about this Psalm, however. The equation between obedience and prosperity promised in verse 3 is called into question in the book of Job, which makes it clear that obedience can – indeed, that obedience *must* – be capable of surviving the end of prosperity, and that obedience that is tied too closely to the promise of prosperity might be no obedience at all. The queasiness we might feel over the Psalm's promise that the righteous will prosper in all that they do is therefore itself biblically warranted. (Note that it is *not*, therefore, a Christian queasiness with a Jewish doctrine, but a queasiness internal to the Hebrew canon.)[9]

What happens, then, when this Psalm is read by Christians? Older Christian interpretations would have said pretty straightforwardly that the Psalm was *about* Jesus, with Jesus being 'the man who has not walked in the counsel of the ungodly'.[10] Either the authors knew that they were being inspired by God to speak of the coming messiah, or God in some sense caused these words to be written as a messianic prophecy without the apparent authors' knowledge.

Many Christian readers now would probably reject the idea that this Psalm should in any sense be seen as a direct prophecy of Christ, or that it could in any straightforward sense be seen as being 'about' Christ. They are more likely to begin with a reading of the Psalm in its own terms, as a Jewish depiction of righteousness. Yet readers who follow the Trinitarian approach to

Scripture that I am outlining might well ask what happens when, with playful seriousness, they ask what it would mean to take this description of godliness and apply it to Jesus. Jesus is, I have repeatedly said, the one who shows what godly life looks like for Christian theology, and it would be thoroughly Marcionite to think that the righteousness he displays could be anything other than a commentary upon the righteousness of the Hebrew Bible. To take this Psalm to be about Jesus is playful, because it does not involve one in the claim that the Psalm was somehow written *so as* to be about him; but it is serious because it is a playfulness that is unavoidable once one has recognized the nature of the Psalm and of Christian claims about Jesus.

In the first place, one might find the rejection of the attractive stability of the ungodly sharpened. To the progression of metaphors from walking to standing to sitting we could add lying down, and note that Jesus was said to be one who had no place to lay his head. In Jesus' case, the way of righteousness leads to the cross – a leafless, unwatered tree. His way looks like the way that leads to destruction, to the curse, to the end of prosperity. And yet Christians claim that this way of the cross is the way of life, that it is watched over by God, and is the only way that stands on the day of judgement.

Once one has got that far, however, the Psalm asks us whether Jesus' righteousness, the way of the cross, can be understood as 'delight ... in the law of the Lord'. We might find ourselves led to think of Jesus' claim that not one stroke of a letter will pass from the law until it is all accomplished, and that no one whose righteousness does not exceed that of the scribes and the Pharisees can enter the kingdom of heaven; we might also think of Jesus' claim that the whole of the law and the prophets hangs on the command to love God and to love neighbour. The commentary upon this Psalm that Jesus' life offers is not a commentary that rejects its focus on the law (it does not see delight in the law as a Jewish doctrine that needs to be rejected or overcome); it accepts it and provides a particular interpretation of what delight in the law means. The way of righteousness is the way of the cross; the way of the cross is the way of love and justice; the way of love and justice is the way of obedience to and delight in the law.

A Christian meditation on the Psalm, therefore, might take the already-existing question mark about the link between prosperity and obedience, connect it to the Psalm's own rejection of the attractive stability of the ungodly, and be led into serious questions about what, in the light of Christ, true stability and true prosperity look like – and one's understanding of the Psalm's subject-matter, true righteousness, might begin to develop. And a Christian meditation might take the Psalm's focus on the law, connect it to New Testament materials about Jesus and the law, and be led into serious questions about what, in the light of the Psalm, Christ's righteousness looks like – and one's understanding of the Gospels' subject matter, Jesus of Nazareth, might similarly begin to develop.

The Psalm can send one deeper into the gospel; the gospel can send one deeper into the Psalm. It is not, though, that there is a straightforward sense in which these meditations are *the* meaning of the Psalm, if by that we are claiming that they were intended by the original author or understood by the original audience. They are, nevertheless, meditations that are made possible by, prompted by, even made unavoidable by this Psalm when read in the context of the wider Hebrew canon and the Christian canon that holds together both Old and New Testaments. This kind of reading is not an attempt to discover the one, plain meaning of the Psalm, but to be led by the Psalm into deeper thinking.

This process of being led into deeper thinking does not end there, however. Were a Christian to read this Psalm alongside a Jewish reader, the Christian might have her attention drawn to one of the elements that my exposition so far has ignored: the reference to the 'congregation of the righteous'. What this Psalm opposes to the way of the ungodly, the Jewish reader might say, is obedience to God's law in the context of the people of Israel. It is a different kind of continuity and stability: the continuity and stability of people and observance. Holiness and blessing, in the Psalm's terms, can't be detached from these things. And yes, these contrast with the stability of the ungodly (the history of the Jewish people over the last 2,500 years is enough to show us that), but one should not overdraw that contrast until it becomes a contrast between the purely material stability and prosperity of the ungodly and the purely spiritual stability and prosperity of the godly. In a Jewish reader's hands, therefore, the Psalm might become a challenge to think about the material conditions of holiness in the Hebrew Bible: law, people, land. Isn't that what it really means, the Jewish reader might say, to be in the congregation of the faithful, planted, watered and in the deepest sense prosperous? To put it another way, hasn't the Christian reading too easily airbrushed out the full meaning of 'law'?

In other words, when this text from the Hebrew Bible is read in discussion with a Jewish reader, a Christian's reflections might be pushed still deeper, and he might have some aspects of his Christian reading challenged.

I don't mean to bring this discussion to any kind of closure. Attention to the text in this light both of the Christian canon and of Jewish respondents does not lead to a decision about the one thing that this text really says: it does not close down one's options in that way. Rather, it opens up a field for discussion and enquiry, for argument and exploration. This is not the Bible providing the answers with which thought can stop; this is the Bible as constant companion on a journey that never ends.

Key points

- This text from the Hebrew Bible makes sense in its original historical and canonical context.
- Christian readers will ask what sense Jesus makes of it, and what sense it helps them make of him.
- The attempt to answer those questions will not necessarily lead to any easy answers.
- The attempt to answer those questions may bring Christian readers into dialogue with those who read differently.

Reading in the Spirit

I said in Chapter 6 that

> The Spirit is, for Christian theology, that power of God that lures and woos
> and impels and drives and enables and drags and excites people on jour-
> neys deeper into the God of Jesus Christ.

If the Bible is a constant companion on those journeys deeper into the God of
Jesus Christ, then it is embroiled somehow in the agency of the Spirit.

That does not necessarily mean that the Spirit acts as the guarantor of any
supernatural accuracy in the Bible's texts. Nor does it necessarily mean that
the Spirit gives readers of the Bible any supernatural ability to arrive at the
right interpretation of Biblical passages. Some will want to make those claims,
of course, but I am not sure that they follow all that neatly from what I have
been saying. I think there are more important ways in which the Spirit and
the Bible relate.

In the first place, the kind of use of the Bible that I have been discussing
involves trust that the Spirit was at work conforming the biblical authors to
the God of Jesus Christ. That is, it involves the trust that these texts really are
words spoken from within the movement of their authors into the life of God.
And that movement is one that is drawing them into conformity to Christ.
That is, I think, an assumption that lies behind the willingness to trust the
witness of these texts, whether it is a positive or negative one, to the nature of
that journey – and so lies behind much that I have said already.

In the second place, the kind of use of the Bible that I have been discussing suggests that it is most appropriately read by people who are themselves
being led by the Spirit into conformity with Christ on the way to the Father.
That is, the vantage point from which the Bible can be seen properly as Holy
Scripture is the vantage point of those who are being drawn into Christlike
love and justice, and so into knowledge of God. This will lie behind much of
what I will say in the final two sections of this chapter.

Lastly, the kind of use of the Bible that I have been discussing is part of the
process by which not just individuals but the whole body of Christ is drawn
into closer conformity with Christ on the way to the Father. And that means
that one reads in ways that are open to the Spirit when we read in ways that
are open to the whole body of Christ. I said in Chapter 6 that 'The Spirit's
work is to allow each person to give such a gift – a gift that contributes some
aspect, some part of Christ to the whole body of Christ.' Reading 'in the Spirit'
is reading that can receive as a gift the reading of the Bible by other members
of the Body. That is the main point that I want to examine in this section, and
as we will see, I take it to mean that reading the Bible in the Spirit will involve
reading that is ecumenical, traditional, inclusive and eschatological.

First, reading in the Spirit is ecumenical reading. Different Christians read
differently, and the ways in which they read differently are closely bound up
with the ways in which they live the Christian life differently. That was one
of the main claims of Chapter 15 – and, given all that we said about the Spirit

and the body of Christ in Chapter 6 and about the unity and catholicity of the Church in Chapter 13, its implication is obvious. Christians should be open to the possibility that the reading of those Christians who read differently can be a gift to them, calling them back to the biblical text, teaching them to see more there, or to see what is there differently. Of course one does not want to be uncritical; of course one does not simply want to say that anything goes. Nevertheless, to read in the Spirit of the body of Christ is to approach the reading of Christians from different communities, different settlements, with humility, openness and charity. It is also to trust that one's own reading can be a gift to others. To read in the Spirit is to read ecumenically – that is, it is to read in pursuit of fuller communion with those Christians with whom one differs.

Second, reading in the Spirit is traditional reading. The Christian tradition is nothing other than the communion of Christians extended through time as well as space. That earlier generations are now dead does not mean that their ways of being Christian, of knowing Christ, of reading the Bible, cannot be gifts to present-day Christians just as surely as current generations of Christians can be gifts to one another. Attending to the Christian tradition is, one might say, a form of ecumenism in time. The Christian tradition is not a deposit of correct readings that today's Christians must adopt at all costs, but an unruly and argumentative community of those who see the same things differently. To read in the Spirit is to read in the company of those who read long before, seeking and expecting a gift in what they said and did.

Living tradition

'[T]he theology of past periods, classical and less classical, also plays a part and demands a hearing. It demands a hearing as surely as it occupies a place with us in the context of the Church. ... We have to remember the communion of saints, bearing and being borne by each other, asking and being asked, having to take mutual responsibility for and among the sinners gathered together in Christ. As regards theology also, we cannot be in the Church without taking as much responsibility for the theology of the past, as for the theology of our present. Augustine, Thomas Aquinas, Luther, Schleiermacher, and all the rest are not dead but living. They still speak and demand a hearing as living voices, as surely as we know that they and we belong together in the Church. They made in their time the same contribution to the task of the Church that is required of us today. As we make our contribution, they join in with theirs, and we cannot play our part today without allowing them to play theirs. Our responsibility is not only to God, to ourselves, to the men of today, to other living theologians, but to them. There is no past in the Church, so there is no past in theology.'

Karl Barth, *Protestant Theology in the Nineteenth Century*[11]

Third, reading in the Spirit is inclusive reading. The Spirit is the Spirit of Christ, and like Christ is to be found where respectable people don't go, among the marginalized, the dispossessed, and the weak. To read in the Spirit will be to listen particularly for the gift that one might receive from those readers whose voices have been marginalized or hidden in the tradition of the Church: the voices of women, of the laity, of the poor, of non-whites, of non-Westerners, of gays, of the disabled. Precisely because they have not been prominent voices in Christianity's ongoing conversations, these marginalized Christians may have the most exciting gifts to give: ways of recalling one to the Bible to see differently what one thought one knew. To read in the Spirit is to seek to widen the interpretive conversation until it becomes more fully inclusive.

Fourth, reading in the Spirit is eschatological reading. In all the ways I have just described – ecumenical, traditional and inclusive – all Christians' present readings are incomplete. Christians do not yet read in a fully united body of Christ; they do not yet read in a body of Christ that remembers and holds fast to its earlier generations, and they do not yet read in a body of Christ that has overcome the exclusions that keep some categories of members marginalized. Reading in the Spirit can only be reading in hope and anticipation; reading in hope of a perfected body of Christ that will have been lifted by God's redemptive action beyond all these forms of disunity, and shaping one's readings now as much as possible in the light of that vision.

Key points

- The vantage point from which the Bible can be seen properly as Holy Scripture is the vantage point of those who are being drawn into Christlike love and justice, and so into knowledge of God.
- To read in the Spirit is to read ecumenically.
- To read in the Spirit is to read in conversation with the Christian tradition.
- To read in the Spirit is to read with openness to previously excluded voices.
- To read in the Spirit is to read in hope.

What is tradition?

The Christian tradition is, I have just said, the extension of the Church in time – and attention to the tradition is simply the temporal form of ecumenism: holding on to other, differing Christian communities and individuals in the trust that one will receive a blessing from their difference. There are other ways of thinking about the theological necessity of attending to tradition, however.

Attention to the tradition – to the voices of the Christian past – can also be a matter of understanding more clearly the etymology or genealogy of one's current beliefs and practices. Some configuration of ideas and practices may seem inviolable, an eternal and inherent part of Christianity – until a genealogical investigation shows the specific circumstances in which it arose, the specific purposes it fulfilled, and reveals its contingency and malleability. So, for instance, careful investigation of the history of the 'personal saviour' settlement is likely to suggest that it is just that: a particular, evolving settlement. Other ideas or practices may seem thoroughly dispensable, until a genealogical investigation shows the deep questions that were at issue when those ideas or practices were formed – and so make one realize more clearly what would be involved in abandoning or altering them. So, for instance, one could imagine investigating the history of the idea of creation *ex nihilo*, having started with the assumption that it is an irrelevant bit of speculative metaphyics that has little to do with biblical theology – only to discover (as I suggested in Chapter 7) the deeper theological and pastoral roots of the idea. Attending to the Christian tradition is an important part of making enough sense of current practice and belief to know how to go on.

Attention to tradition can also be a matter of *apprenticeship*. After all, listening at the feet of old hands is one of the ways of learning the Christian language well. If one learns only from those who speak the language in one's own present context, however, one's ability to speak that language in new contexts may be limited. To learn that language at the feet of those who spoke it in contexts far removed from one's own may give one's own speech the resilience and flexibility to survive.

Attention to tradition can also be a matter of looking at a vast collection of experiments in Christian life and thought. There is nothing new under the sun, and what seem to people now to be bold new moves in Christian life and thought have probably been tried before. On the other hand, one can never step into the same river twice,[12] so one cannot deduce that today's development will simply follow the course of its well- or ill-fated precursors – but some of the possibilities and pitfalls inherent in the development might become clearer. Take, for instance, the emerging church movement's experiments in the form of church life. There are, it turns out, all sorts of historical parallels and echoes to those experiments, and recognizing those parallels and echoes informs both support and criticism of the movement.[13]

One question remains, though. Is there any specific content that can be regarded as firmly established by the Christian tradition? Are the creeds, for instance, to be regarded as fixed points that it is now incumbent upon all future generations to accept? Christians differ on this point. Some will argue that the guidance of the Church by the Spirit is such that, from time to time, a hard-won consensus or near consensus emerges, which is then recognized by the Church at large as an authoritative clarification of the faith – and becomes a fixed point of dogma. For the Orthodox Church and some others, the Ecumenical Councils of the Church were (and, in principle, could be again) the bodies capable of recognizing and defining such moments of dogmatic consensus, and the key examples are the Nicene Creed and the Chalcedonian Definition.[14] For the Roman Catholic Church, the Pope is regarded as having the authority to recognize and define such decisive points in the mind of the Church that lives in communion with him – and so (and only so) to define doctrine infallibly.[15]

Infallibility

'That apostolic primacy which the Roman pontiff possesses as successor of Peter, the prince of the apostles, includes also the supreme power of teaching. ... For the holy Spirit was promised to the successors of Peter not so that they might, by his revelation, make known some new doctrine, but that, by his assistance, they might religiously guard and faithfully expound the revelation or deposit of faith transmitted by the apostles. ...

Therefore, faithfully adhering to the tradition received from the beginning of the Christian faith, to the glory of God our saviour, for the exaltation of the catholic religion and for the salvation of the Christian people, with the approval of the sacred council, we teach and define as a divinely revealed dogma that when the Roman pontiff speaks *ex cathedra*, that is, when, in the exercise of his office as shepherd and teacher of all Christians, in virtue of his supreme apostolic authority, he defines a doctrine concerning faith or morals to be held by the whole church, he possesses, by the divine assistance promised to him in blessed Peter, that infallibility which the divine Redeemer willed his church to enjoy in defining doctrine concerning faith or morals. Therefore, such definitions of the Roman pontiff are of themselves, and not by the consent of the church, irreformable.'

First Vatican Council, *First Dogmatic Constitution on the Church*[16]

'The greatest theological problem with infallibility is that it makes it very difficult for the church to admit it was wrong. I have considered making a T-shirt to wear to Catholic meetings with the slogan: "Infallibility means never having to say you're sorry." But being unable to say you're sorry is to be unable to repent. Not to be able to repent means not being able to be open to divine grace. Thus infallibility is the sin of sins: a sin against the Holy Spirit. All areas where the church's teachings are inadequate, distorted or erroneous are blocked from corrective development by the assumption of infallibility. One cannot change previous mistaken teachings, such as the ban on contraception – even if the worldwide church has come to a consensus that it needs to change – if you can't admit that you have been wrong.'

Rosemary Radford Ruether, 'Infallibility: Untenable on Every Ground'[17]

Others believe that while there might be some aspects of the Christian tradition that, because of the weight of deliberation that lies behind them, the breadth of the consensus they demanded, and the pervasiveness of their subsequent influence, have an especially strong authority for subsequent generations, they are not in themselves 'irreformable': it could in principle be shown that they distort or misdirect the apostolic witness to Christ, and need to be abandoned or reformed. For them, tradition cannot be seen as a deposit of authoritative dogmas, even if it is a deposit of much that the contemporary theologian cannot simply ignore, but must work through.

> ### Exercise
>
> Based on your reading of this book, or any other theological explorations you have undertaken, can you identify any examples of your theological under- standing being deepened or expanded by contact with a voice from the Christian tradition? In what way did that voice help? Can you identify any ex- amples where learning about the tradition has been disturbing or confusing?

Key points

- The Christian tradition is simply the extension in time of the one, catholic Church.
- Attention to the Christian tradition can help Christians make sense of their present beliefs and practices.
- Attention to the Christian tradition can provide an apprenticeship in speak- ing the Christian language.
- Christians differ over whether the tradition is a repository of assured truths.

Reading on the way to the Father: Experience

The Trinitarian settlement that I have been exploring calls for reading around Jesus, reading in the Spirit – and reading on the way to the Father. As I said above, the vantage point from which the Bible can be seen properly as Holy Scripture is the vantage point of those who are being drawn into that Christ- like love and justice on the way to the Father. To read on the way to the Father is to read in pursuit of the Father's kingdom of love and justice.

This insight is one that has been renewed in recent decades by proponents of liberation theology. Liberation theology began when various Latin Ameri- can theologians, driven by their understanding of the implications of the Gos- pel, committed themselves to working with the Latin American poor as they struggled for social and political liberation. They understood this as a way to pursue the love and justice of the Father's kingdom. Once they were involved with the poor, however, they found that their understanding of theology and of the Bible in particular got shaken up. Things that had once seemed impor- tant receded into the background; things that had once seemed trivial as- sumed renewed urgency and importance. Interpretations of the Bible that had once seemed natural and helpful now began to seem stilted and irrelevant. Involvement in the practical struggle for liberation, alongside those whose struggle it was, led to new theological and biblical insights. But the process did not stop there. The liberation theologians had got involved in the struggle for liberation thanks to their existing theology and interpretation of the Bible, so it was inevitable that their new theological and biblical insights in turn changed the ways that they thought about and practised their participation in that struggle. In other words, a spiral of change emerged: participation led to new insights and changed theology, which in turn led to changed participation, which in turn led to new insights and changed theology, and so on. Throwing themselves into the pursuit of the Father's kingdom of love and justice set these theologians on an ongoing journey of transformation that was a journey of ever-deeper participation in the struggle for love and justice in the world.

> [20]Blessed are you who are poor,
> For yours is the kingdom of God.
> [21]Blessed are you who are hungry now,
> for you will be filled.
> Blessed are you who weep now,
> for you will laugh. ...
> [24]But woe to you who are rich,
> for you have received your consolation.
> [25]Woe to you who are full now,
> for you will be hungry.
> Woe to you who are laughing now,
> for you will mourn and weep.

Luke 6.20–21, 24–25

To see how this hermeneutical and participatory spiral might work, think of the beatitudes as they appear in Luke's Gospel. Traditionally, Christian readers have tended to 'spiritualize' these blessings and woes – to assume that Jesus was talking about those who are *spiritually* rather than literally poor, hungry and tearful.[18] Now imagine a Christian who had understood the blessing on those who are poor to be a blessing on those who were 'poor in spirit', and so a blessing on those who were humble, and who sought nothing for themselves. He might, on the basis of his existing understanding, think that it was a mark of being 'poor in spirit' not to seek prominent and powerful forms of Christian work, but to seek quiet service in little-regarded places – and so he might, say, get involved in running a shelter for the homeless.

As his involvement brought him into contact with the homeless people, hearing their stories, he might find that his compassion for them, and his desire to be with them and work for them, was awoken in new ways – ways that went beyond the desire for selfless service that had been his original motivation. With this new feeling in mind, he might find on returning to this passage that it made more sense to him now to read it as speaking primarily of literal, material poverty, hunger and mourning – of God's real compassion for these people. His theology might begin to shift until he saw that God was not simply on the side of those who humbly and kindly give to the poor, but on the side of the poor themselves.[19] He might begin to see from this passage – and then from others elsewhere in the Bible, as this realization set off a chain reaction of rethinking and rereading – that the anger he was beginning to feel at the forces that kept these people in poverty was a reflection of God's own anger. His participation in the homeless shelter might subtly shift from being his good work on behalf of the poor to his sharing of their life and their struggle, working with and alongside them in their struggle against poverty, hunger and distress.

The transformation might not stop there. As he spends more time trying to work properly alongside the people in the shelter, he might begin to see that alongside the social and political forces that create the poverty traps into which these people have fallen, there are some traps of a more inward nature: ways in which, for some of them, their poverty, hunger and distress are bound up with such deep hurts as a blighted imagination, chronic hopelessness, an inability to value oneself, and so on. His participation in the shelter might begin to teach him that his earlier rejection of a spiritual interpretation of Luke's blessings and woes in favour of a material interpretation was too simplistic, and that the links between material poverty and some forms of spiritual poverty are, at least some of the time, crucial even if complicated. He might return to the passage, and to other passages in the Bible, and try to understand more of what a spiritual interpretation of these blessings and woes might have to contribute to the material interpretation to which he had been won over. And so the cycle might go on, with his changed insights into the biblical passages once again changing the nature of his participation.

That something like this would happen should be no surprise. I know, for instance, that when writing this book, I often feel that I don't really know what I think on some point until I write about it; then, when I have written something, I can see it clearly enough to see that it is wrong. And so I revise – only to discover that although what I have written is better, it now helps me see the issues more clearly, which helps me in turn to see that I am still wrong. This cycle can go on many times – so there are parts of this book that, in one form or another, I have written ten or eleven times.

The same happens in Christian life more generally. It is only when one seeks to put into practice one's present theological understanding, and one's present understanding of the Bible, that one discovers what one's present understanding really is – and perhaps discovers some of its limitations and inadequacies. That can drive one back to look again at one's interpretation of the Bible and at one's ideas, and to revise them. It is not primarily in classrooms and academic studies that theology, and Christian interpretation of the Bible, is truly tested and refined, but in practice, in real-life pursuit of that Christlike love and justice that constitute the kingdom of the Father.

'Experience' in theology is not the name of some faculty that delivers theological information independent of the Bible or the tradition. Rather, it is a name for what people discover, and go on discovering, as they live with faith in the world.

Natural theology

I have not, in this book, talked about one major area of theological discussion that relates to this question about the role of experience. That is, I have not discussed whether it is possible for people to attain any kind of theological truth prior to, or in the absence of, or logically independent from, their encounter with revelation – that is, their encounter with what God has done in Jesus Christ and witnessed to in the Scriptures. Does a person's general experience of the world before or apart from their experience of God's address in Christ, allow any knowledge of God? To put this into traditional terminology: is a 'natural theology' possible as well as a 'revealed' or 'positive theology'?

I am limiting myself to two comments, here. In the first place, if my account of 'knowledge of God' back in Chapter 2 is correct, then the question is not whether unaided human reason can form proper *concepts* of God; it is whether human beings can, without the explicit help of revelation, learn to *live in the world* in certain ways – receiving their existence as a gift, recognizing themselves as loved, learning to become loving, and so on. And in the second place, if my account of knowledge of God is correct, then we are not asking about whether human beings without the explicit help of revelation can arrive at truth, since truth is not a matter of arrival but of constant journeying. The question is, rather, whether human beings can find themselves, without the explicit aid of revelation, travelling in the right direction – or being drawn out of themselves, beyond reliance upon their own resources, in the right ways.

So, for me, to ask the question of natural theology is to ask whether, when people turn to Christ to be drawn by him into the life of God, they might discover that Christ says yes to much in the existing shape and direction of their lives, including the ways of seeing the world that inform their living. That, it seems to me, is a question that can't be given a generalized, theoretical answer: it can only be answered by seeing what, in fact, happens in life after life.[20]

Key points

- According to Christian theology, the Bible is most truly read when its readers are growing in godly life.
- One's experience deeply affects one's interpretation of the Bible.
- The experience gained when trying to live a godly life, shaped by the Bible, might change one's understanding of the Bible.
- Reading and experience can affect each other in an ongoing spiral of interpretation.

Reading on the way to the Father: Vulnerability

Scripture, tradition, reason, experience

You will sometimes come across reference to 'Scripture, tradition and reason' or 'Scripture, tradition, reason and experience' as the three or four sources or authorities for theology. The threefold form seems to be Anglican in origin and gets attributed to the sixteenth-century divine Richard Hooker; the fourfold form is Methodist and gets attributed to John Wesley – though in both cases the neat formulation is a twentieth-century summary.[21] In some discussions, the impression can be given that there are here four distinct *sources* from which theological claims can be generated, and that the theologian's job is to know how to balance, integrate or prioritize the claims. So we might have the Bible telling us that God is the God of Abraham, Isaac and Jacob; tradition telling us that God is Triune; reason telling us that God is omnipotent, omniscient and omnipresent; and experience telling us that God is intimately present to us – and the theologian's job would be to work out how all those go together.

In effect, this chapter has led to a rather different way of seeing the relationship between Scripture, tradition, reason and experience. We have been focused on Scripture, but I have argued that Scripture is properly read in conversation with tradition ('ecumenism in time', I called it), that it is properly read in the midst of the experience of pursuing love and justice in the world, and in general that it is properly read with attentiveness and readiness to have our ways of making sense disrupted and remade – that is, with what I called 'rationality' in Chapter 1, and can call 'reason' now. In other words, I don't think that one should imagine Scripture, tradition, reason and experience as four coordinate sources of theological truth, but as four different aspects of the one journey into the knowledge of God that Trinitarian theology describes.[22]

To read on the way to the Father is to read not simply for *in*formation, but rather trusting that the Bible, when read around Christ and in the Spirit, can be an engine of ongoing *trans*formation, individual and corporate. This ongoing biblical challenging and transformation of Christian life and vision is, Christian theologians claim, a central process by which Christians are brought closer to the truth of things: closer to the truth of Jesus of Nazareth, and closer to the truth of the divine life into which God invites the world in Jesus.

In Chapter 1, I wrote that Paul called the Corinthian community to take stock of themselves in the light of God's address to them in Christ; in Chapter 2, I suggested that to have knowledge of God 'consists in the ongoing process by which the believer's love is actively shaped into ever deeper conformity to God', and in Chapters 4, 5 and 6, I wrote of the Trinitarian belief that one is led deeper and deeper into true love and true justice as the Spirit enables one to hear ever more clearly the address of the Father spoken to the world in Jesus Christ.

The reading of the Bible can be understood as part of this process of learning, part of the attempt to listen carefully to the address of God, and to allow one's current ideas, expectations and habits of thought to be challenged and remade by it. Christian theology involves allowing oneself, one's community, one's world to be 'put to the question' by God's address. And just as I have suggested that Christian life as a whole cannot be understood as static, or as involving the arrival at some plateau on which believers can expect no further challenge and no further learning, so too with the interpretation of the Bible. If the interpretation of the Bible is understood as an aspect of the kind of Christian life that I have been discussing, it will not be understood as involving the secure adoption of a set of final explanations and fixed ideas. It will not be understood as a talisman that will protect the theologian from all further questioning. In fact, quite the opposite: the proper pursuit of biblical interpretation will expose the theologian more and more thoroughly to searching questions.

One could say that having the questioning address of God in Christ at the heart of Christian interpretation of the Bible will mean that Christian reading of the Bible will be characterized by both trust and suspicion. On the one hand, Christian readers will take their stand on a trust in what they have learnt above all from the Bible: that in Jesus Christ the world is truly being addressed by God. Christian theology will involve trusting that the Bible is a trustworthy witness to this, and that to order one's life by the light of what one learns from the Bible is not an arbitrary or foolish thing to do. But alongside this trust Christian interpretation also involves suspicion: suspicion of one's current understanding. Christian theologians may trust that God has spoken in Christ, and that the Bible witnesses to this truly, but that doesn't mean they trust that *their present interpretation* of the Bible is perfect and complete, and does not need itself to be challenged, deepened and reformed.

Christian ideas – even when they are the schemes that Christians believe they have derived from the Bible – are not invulnerable. Christian theologians have to keep on listening, keep on looking again, in all the ways that I have discussed in earlier sections of this chapter. And they will keep on looking with the knowledge that they might find that they have been mistaken, that they have got things wrong, that they have oversimplified, that they have deceived themselves yet again.

Think again of the structure of Paul's argument in his first letter to the Corinthians. Yes, he returns to the faith that the Corinthians were taught in the beginning; yes, he refers them back to a gospel that they already know. He does so, however, in such a way as to show that they have been misconstruing that gospel. He demonstrates that their use of gospel language to divide and exclude each other follows from their failure to understand what that language means – and then he takes them back to the sources of their faith and helps them reconstruct their theology on new lines. Christian theology is not and never can be immune from the need for such reconstruction, any more than any believer can claim that she has no more need of spiritual growth, nor a community claim that it has no more need of reformation.

This means that one of the fundamental characteristics of Christian theology should be *vulnerability*, in the sense of openness to challenge, willingness to discover that what one had taken to be right, what one had taken to be invulnerable, needs to be unsettled, overthrown and remade. To read the Bible on the way to the Father is to read with such vulnerability.

You may be mistaken

In 1650, Oliver Cromwell led an English army into Scotland, where he believed that Scottish forces were assisting Charles Stuart, son of Charles I, in a bid for the English crown. In the bad weather of early August 1650 the conflict looked like a stalemate, with Cromwell failing to draw the Scottish forces out to fight while he still had supplies and men. The two sides seem to have been engaged in a propaganda war, with attempts being made to distribute leaflets among the opposing armies. One Scottish leaflet argued that God would 'arise to execute judgement' against the English if they persisted in their attack upon 'those who in the integrity of their hearts have been following Jesus Christ'. One part of Cromwell's reply to the Scots has become famous. You have sought to establish yourselves, he said 'upon the Word of God. Is it therefore infallibly agreeable to the Word of God, all that *you* say? *I beseech you, in the bowels of Christ, think it possible you may be mistaken.*'[23] However incongruous the context in which it was first written, that last sentence could be a slogan for all Christian theology.

Key point

- One of the fundamental characteristics of Christian reading of the Bible should be openness to challenge, willingness to discover that what one has taken to be right needs to be unsettled, overthrown and remade.

Going further

1 Debates about homosexuality in various churches, particularly in the Anglican Church, highlight the extremely controversial nature of the area I have been exploring in this chapter. What are the authoritative sources for Christian life and Christian moral vision? How should the Bible's injunctions be interpreted? What do we do when Christians disagree in their interpretations? These are not matters of idle speculation: they are the root issues in debates that affect the lives of very large numbers of people. In so much of the debate, however, there is more heat than light, and it is difficult to get a clear view of the issues involved. If you are interested in taking this further, however, you could begin with Timothy Bradshaw (ed.), *The Way Forward: Christian Voices on Homosexuality and the Church*, 2nd edn (Grand Rapids: Eerdmans, 2003), which contains chapters from people with very different theological starting-points, but strives for an eirenic and serious conversation.

Notes

1 See Herbert Butterfield, *Christianity and History* (London: G. Bell, 1949) for an argument about the ineradicable reference to history at the heart of Christianity.

2 One might say that the Bible is an adequate witness only if it is an adequate witness to the divinity of this fully human character.

3 Martin Kähler, *The So-Called Historical Jesus and the Historic–Biblical Christ*, tr. Carl E. Braaten, revised edn (Philadelphia: Fortress Press, 1988 [German original: 1892]) argues something similar: that the Bible allows us to reconstruct not the bare, uninterpreted historical facts of Jesus' life, but the historic impact that he had upon his disciples.

4 This statement should be qualified of course. In the first place, the early Christians might well have known these Hebrew Scriptures primarily in Aramaic and Greek translations; in the second place, there was not yet a clear and rigid 'canon' of Hebrew Scripture stating exactly which writings counted as sacred – nor, necessarily, any very clear idea that there could or should be such a canon, rather than an informal, rough-edged consensus in practice.

5 See E. C. Blackman, *Marcion and His Influence* (London: SPCK, 1948) and (with a pinch of salt) R. Joseph Hoffmann's *Marcion: On the Restitution of Christianity* (Chico, CA: Scholar's Press, 1984). The classic account is Adolf von Harnack, *Marcion: The Gospel of the Alien God*, tr. J. E. Steely and L. D. Bierma (Durham, NC: Labyrinth, 1990 [German original 1924]).

6 Francis Watson, *Paul and the Hermeneutics of Faith* (London: Continuum, 2004), Introduction – available online at http://www.abdn.ac.uk/divinity/documents/Paul-and-the-hermeneutics-of-faith.doc.

7 I do not mean to suggest that it is *only* the Christian gospel that might lead to a questioning reading of Psalm 137. Specifically, I do not mean to set up any opposition between Jewish and Christian readings: Jewish readings can be just as complex, just as deeply challenged by strands of the Hebrew Bible which oppose the violence of this text.

8 David L. Frost, John A. Emerton and Andrew A. Macintosh, *The Psalms: a New Translation for Worship* (London: William Collins, 1977); reproduced in the Church of England *Alternative Service Book 1980* (Newgate: William Clowes, 1980), pp. 1095–1289.

9 See Susannah Ticciati, *Job and the Disruption of Identity: Reading Beyond Barth* (London: Continuum, 2005) for a discussion of Job's critique of Deuteronomistic theology.

10 For example: '"Blessed is the man that hath not gone away in the counsel of the ungodly". This is to be understood of our Lord Jesus Christ.' Augustine, *Expositions on the Book of Psalms* in Philip Schaff (ed.), *Nicene and Post-Nicene Fathers*, First Series, vol. 8 (New York: Christian Literature Company, 1888), p. 1; available online at the Christian Classics Ethereal Library, http://www.ccel.org/ccel/schaff/npnf108.I_1.html.

11 Karl Barth, *Protestant Theology in the Nineteenth Century: Its Background and History* (London: SCM Press, 1972), p. 17. Cf. Stephen R. Holmes, *Listening to the Past: The Place of Tradition in Theology* (Carlisle: Paternoster, 2002), esp. chapters 1 and 2; Rowan Williams, *Why Study the Past? The Quest for the Historical Church*, Sarum Theological Lectures (London: DLT, 2005); and John Webster, '"There is No Past in the Church, so There is No Past in Theology": Barth on the History of Modern Protestant Theology' in John C. McDowell and Mike Higton (eds), *Conversing with Barth*, Barth Studies (Aldershot: Ashgate, 2004), pp. 14–39.

12 You cannot step twice into the same river according to Heraclitus, as quoted in Plutarch, *On the 'E' at Delphi*, §18 (392b), tr. A. O. Prickard (Oxford: Clarendon, 1918); available online at James Eason's Thomas Browne site, http://penelope.uchicago.edu/misctracts/plutarchE.html.

13 See Wikipedia Contributors, 'Emerging church movement', *Wikipedia: The Free Encyclopedia*, http://en.wikipedia.org/wiki/Emerging_church_movement – which includes a good, and constantly evolving, set of links to online critiques and defences of the movement.

14 The ecumenical councils in question are Nicaea I (325), Constantinople I (381), Ephesus (431), Chalcedon (451), Constantinople II (553), Constantinople III (680–1) and Nicaea II (787); some Orthodox also recognize Constantinople IV (879–80) and Constantinople V (1341–51). For the first seven, see Leo Donald Davis, *The First Seven Ecumenical Councils (325–787): Their History and Theology* (Wilmington, DE: Michael Glazier, 1983); the primary texts are available in Philip Schaff and Henry Wace (eds), *Nicene and Post-Nicene Fathers*, Second Series, vol. 14 (New York: Charles Scribner's, 1900),

available online at the Christian Classics Ethereal Library, http://www.ccel.org/ccel/ schaff/npnf214.html. On the question of the recognition of the eighth and ninth, some useful resources are gathered by Thomas Ross Valentine, 'The Eighth and Ninth Ecumenical Synods', 2003 http://www.geocities.com/trvalentine/orthodox/8–9synods. html.

15 See John Kirvan (ed.), *The Infallibility Debate* (New York: Paulist, 1971); George Lindbeck, *Infallibility* (Milwaukee, WI: Marquette University Press, 1972); and Hans Küng, *Infallibility? An Inquiry* (Garden City, NY: Doubleday, 1972).

16 First Vatican Council, Session 4, 1870, the First Dogmatic Constitution on the Church; see Norman A. Tanner (ed.), *Decrees of the Ecumenical Councils: From Nicaea I to Vatican II* (Georgetown University Press, 1990); available online at http://www.piar. hu/councils/ecum20.htm.

17 Rosemary Radford Ruether, 'Infallibility: Untenable on Every Ground', *National Catholic Reporter* (29 Dec 1995); available online at HighBeam Encyclopedia, http:// www.encyclopedia.com/doc/1G1–17968570.html.

18 For a contemporary restatement of this position, see Gary T. Meadors, 'The "Poor" in the Beatitudes of Matthew and Luke', *Grace Theological Journal* 6.2 (1985), pp. 305–31; available online at http://faculty.gordon.edu/hu/bi/ted_hildebrandt/NTeSources/ NTArticles/GTJ-NT/Meadors-LukePoor-GTJ–85.pdf.

19 'The entire Bible, beginning with the story of Cain and Abel, mirrors God's predilection for the weak and abused of human history. This preference brings out the gratuitous or unmerited character of God's love. The same revelation is given in the evangelical Beatitudes, for they tell us with utmost simplicity that God's predilection for the poor, the hungry and the suffering is based on God's unmerited goodness to us.' Gustavo Gutierrez, *A Theology of Liberation* (Maryknoll, NY: Orbis, 1988), p. xxvii.

20 For the debate about natural theology, see Karl Barth and Emil Brunner, *Natural Theology: Comprising "Nature and Grace" by Emil Brunner and the Reply "No!" by Karl Barth*, tr. Peter Fraenkel (London: Geoffrey Bles, 1946); Eugene Rogers, *Thomas Aquinas and Karl Barth: Sacred Doctrine and the Natural Knowledge of God*, Revisions Series, new edn (Notre Dame, IN: University of Notre Dame Press, 1999); and Denys Turner, *Faith, Reason and the Existence of God* (Cambridge: Cambridge University Press, 2004).

21 For Hooker, see Peter Toon, 'Scripture, Tradition and Reason : Hooker's Supposed Three-legged Stool' (no date), The Prayer Book Society of the USA; available online at http://pbsusa.org/Articles/Hooker%27s%20stool.htm. For Wesley, see Albert C. Outler, 'The Wesleyan Quadrilateral – in John Wesley', *Wesleyan Theological Journal* 20.1 (1985), pp. 7–18; available online at Wesley Center Online: http://wesley.nnu. edu/wesleyan_theology/theojrnl/16–20/20–01.htm.

22 For differing reflections on these matters, see Richard Bauckham and Benjamin Drewery (eds), *Scripture, Tradition and Reason: A Study in the Criteria of Christian Doctrine: Essays in Honour of Richard P. C. Hanson* (Edinburgh: T&T Clark, 1988), and Don Thorsen, *The Wesleyan Quadrilateral: A Model of Evangelical Theology*, revised edn (Lexington, KY: Emeth, 2005).

23 'Bowels' in this context means 'mercy'. Oliver Cromwell, letter to the General Assembly of the Kirk of Scotland, 3 August 1650: Letter 136 in Thomas Carlyle (ed.), *Oliver Cromwell's Letters and Speeches*, vol. III (New York: Scribner, Welford and Co., 1871), p. 18, second emphasis mine. The text is available online at Gesellschaft der Arno-Schmidt-Leser, http://www.gasl.org/refbib/ Carlyle__Cromwell.pdf. Cromwell was replying to the leaflet 'For the Under-Officers and Souldiers of the English Army from the people of Scotland', July 1650.

Sources and Acknowledgements for the Plate Section

1 'Cross'. A photo by Szczepan1990 (szczepan1990@gmail.com) of a crucifix by an unknown artist. Placed on Wikimedia Commons under a Creative Commons Attribution ShareAlike 2.5 license at http://commons.wikimedia.org/wiki/Image: Cross.jpg; high resolution version at http://upload.wikimedia.org/wikipedia/ commons/e/e3/Cross.jpg. File modified by Mike Higton.

2 Anonymous, *Mandylion of Edessa*, tempura on linen, stretched over wood; (?3rd–5th Century); now held in the Papal chapel in the Vatican. Photograph by M. Wolfgang. Placed on Wikimedia Commons under a GNU Free Documentation License version 1.2 at http://commons.wikimedia.org/wiki/Image:39bMandylion.jpg; high resolution version at http://upload.wikimedia.org/wikipedia/commons/a/a8/ 39bMandylion.jpg.

3 Georges de la Tour, *Le Nouveau-Né* (*The Newborn Child*), oil on canvas (c.1645); Rennes Musée des Beaux-Arts. Public domain image available on Wikimedia Commons at http://commons.wikimedia.org/wiki/Image:Georges_de_La_Tour_020.jpg; high resolution version at http://upload.wikimedia.org/wikipedia/commons/4/4d/ Georges_de_La_Tour_020.jpg.

4 A mathematical analysis of Piero's *Baptism*, by Mike Higton.

5 Matthias Grünewald, *Crucifixion* (Eisenheim Altarpiece), oil on wood (1510); Colmar, Musée d'Unterlinden. Public domain image available on Wikimedia Commons at http://commons.wikimedia.org/wiki/Image:Mathis_Gothart_Grünewald_022.jpg; high resolution version at http://upload.wikimedia.org/wikipedia/commons/4/ 4f/Mathis_Gothart_Grünewald_022.jpg. File modified by Mike Higton.

6 Matthias Grünewald, *Resurrection* (Eisenheim Altarpiece), oil on wood (1510); Colmar, Musée d'Unterlinden. Public domain image available on Wikimedia Commons at http://commons.wikimedia.org/wiki/Image:Mathis_Gothart_Grünewald_044.jpg; high resolution version at http://upload.wikimedia.org/wikipedia/commons/b/ b4/Mathis_Gothart_Grünewald_044.jpg. File modified by Mike Higton.

7 Diego Rivera, *Jacques Lipchitz* (*Portrait of a Young Man*), oil on canvas (1914); Museum of Modern Art, New York © 2007. Digital image, The Museum of Modern Art, New York/Scala, Florence.

Index of Names and Subjects

Index of Bible References